Parliament and
Politics in
Late Medieval England

Parliament and Politics in Late Medieval England

VOLUME III

J. S. Roskell

THE HAMBLEDON
PRESS

The Hambledon Press 1983
35 Gloucester Avenue
London NW1 7AX

History Series 20

ISBN 0 907628 30 3

(*Parliament and Politics in Late Medieval England*, Vol. I
ISBN 0 9506882 8 2
Parliament and Politics in Late Medieval England, Vol. II
ISBN 0 9506882 9 0
Set of Vols. I & II ISBN 0 9506882 7 4
Set of Vols. I, II & III ISBN 0 907628 14 1

J. S. Roskell 1983

British Library Cataloguing in Publication Data

Roskell, John S.
    Parliament and Politics in late medieval England.
    – (History series; 20)
    Vol. 3
    1. Great Britain – Politics and government – 1154-1399
    2. Great Britain – Politics and government – 1399-1485
    I. Title   II. Series
    328. 42'09   JN515

Printed and Bound in Great Britain by
Robert Hartnoll Ltd., Bodmin, Cornwall

CONTENTS

CONTENTS

ACKNOWLEDGMENTS

The articles collected here, with the exception of Chapters 7, 8 and 14 which are previously unpublished, first appeared in the following periodicals and are reprinted by the kind permission of the original publishers.

1   *Transactions of the Cumberland and Westmorland Antiquarian and Archaeological Society*, new series LXI (1961), 79-103.

2   *Proceedings of the Suffolk Institute of Archaeology*, XXVII (1957), part 3, 154-75.

3   *Essex Archaeology and History*, VIII (1978 for 1976), 209-23.

4   *Archaeologia Cantiana*, LXX (1956), 68-83.

5   *Lincolnshire Architectural and Archaeological Society, Reports and Papers*, new series, VII, part 2 (1957-8), 117-25.

6   *Transactions of the Devonshire Association for the Advancement of Science, Literature and Art*, LXXXIX (1957), 78-92.

9   *Proceedings of the Dorset Natural History and Archaeological Society*, LXXXII (1960), 155-66.

10   *Transactions of the Cumberland and Westmorland Antiquarian and Archaeological Society*, new series, LXII (1962), 113-44.

11   *The Wiltshire Archaeological and Natural History Magazine*, LVI (1956), 342-58.

12   *Transactions of the Leicestershire Archaeological and Historical Society*, XXXIII (1957), 36-44.

13   *Derbyshire Archaeological Journal*, LXXXII (1962), 43-54.

15   *Proceedings of the Cambridge Antiquarian Society*, LII (1959), 30-42.

16   *Transactions of the Thoroton Society of Nottinghamshire*, LX (1956), 8-19.

17   *Transactions of the Shropshire Archaeological Society*, LVI (1960), 263-72.

18   *Proceedings of the Hampshire Field Club and Archaeological Society*, LII (1959), 43-55.

19   *Proceedings of the Cambridge Antiquarian Society*, LII (1959), 43-55.

20   *The Surrey Archaeological Collections*, LVI (1959), 15-28.

PREFACE

In the preface to Volume II of this work, a volume comprising biographies of thirteen Commons' Speakers drawn from the period 1376-1484, the hope was expressed that another, similar volume might be forthcoming. The hope is realized in this present volume, which contains the seventeen biographies listed in that preface, all of them previously published by local historical societies which have been kind enough to allow their reproduction here (with, in a few instances, a little fresh material in *addenda*). To those seventeen have been added another three biographies, not previously published: Sir John Tiptoft (only once Speaker, but the first to be ennobled), Thomas Chaucer (five times Speaker under Henry IV and Henry V), and Sir John Tyrell (three times Speaker during the minority of Henry VI). Biographies of the seven other Speakers of the medieval period — Sir John Gildsburgh (twice Speaker in 1380), Roger Hunt (1420 and 1433), Richard Baynard (1421), John Russell (1423 and 1432), Sir Thomas Waweton (1425), Sir Thomas Charlton (1454), and John Green (1460) — still remain unpublished in the form adopted here. However, the student of the medieval parliament interested in this aspect of its history, will, should he so desire, find the most significant features of the careers of the seven fairly adequately dealt with in Part II and the Appendix of my book, *The Commons and their Speakers in English Parliaments, 1376-1523* (Manchester University Press, 1965).

J.S. ROSKELL

1

SIR JAMES DE PICKERING OF KILLINGTON

IT was in 1265 that elected representatives of shires and towns were first summoned together to attend a general parliament. But it was not until about the beginning of Edward III's reign (in 1327) that their presence in parliaments came to be regarded as essential. Roughly half a century later still (in 1376), the Commons, as they had now long been called, began the practice of electing a spokesman or speaker from among their own number and for the duration of a parliament, to represent them when they had matters to declare to the King and Lords. In the medieval period the Commons invariably elected their Speaker from among the county representatives, the knights of the shire (as they were called), who in this period, mainly for social reasons, carried most weight in the lower house of parliament.

The origins of the Speaker's office present a number of problems. What influences are likely to have been brought to bear upon his election? When, and to what extent, did he become the agent of the King in the Commons as well as their representative vis-à-vis him and the Lords? These two are perhaps the most important. In the absence of any Commons' Journals in the medieval period to help us with such questions, to investigate the careers and public character of individual Speakers is surely to follow an obvious way of approach.

An inquiry into the lives of Sir James de Pickering of Killington, Speaker at Gloucester in 1378, when knight of the shire for Westmorland, and in 1383 at Westminster, when knight of the shire for Yorkshire, and of Sir Richard

Redman or Redmayne of Levens and Harewood, Speaker in 1415, when knight of the shire for Yorkshire, does not by itself take us far towards a solution of these problems. But it has its value. Pickering's Speakerships fell in a time of weak royal authority, when Richard II was in his minority. It was also a period of disillusionment with a stale and discredited policy of war against France, of uncertainty and friction among men of wealth and ambition doubtless made nervous by unrest in countryside and town (attested by the Peasants' Revolt of 1381), of heavy taxation, and therefore of a constant and testy dissatisfaction on the part of the Commons in parliament. It is of some significance that Pickering was not a royal retainer when he was Speaker, although he became one later in Richard II's reign.

Redmayne's Speakership occurred in a very different situation. Henry V was an experienced and authoritarian monarch, and the parliament of 1415 met immediately after his victory at Agincourt offered the prospect of a successful military *détente* in France on a larger scale, which itself guaranteed national unity and a greater measure of genuine parliamentary understanding and compliance than had been achieved for over half a century. In such circumstances the Commons were ready to choose as Speaker one acceptable on personal grounds to the ruler, and certainly in Redmayne they found such a one. A former, close supporter of Richard II, he had lost nothing by the latter's deposition and the accession of Henry IV in 1399: since then he had ever been an actively faithful retainer of the Lancastrian dynasty. He was, moreover, attached to Henry V's younger brother, John, duke of Bedford, who held the parliament of 1415 as Guardian of the Kingdom (*Custos Anglie*) in the King's absence overseas; and he was a kinsman by marriage of Lord FitzHugh, then Henry V's Chamberlain.

There is no doubt of the importance of the local and even regional standing of both Pickering and Redmayne.

Each had his connexions with a number of peers who had considerable influence in the north of England. Pickering had close relations as retainer with Sir William de Windsor of Grayrigg (husband of Edward III's mistress, Alice Perrers), who was in and out of office as Edward III's Lieutenant of Ireland in the last decade of his reign. He was also connected with the Cliffords and, if more obscurely and tenuously, with John of Gaunt, duke of Lancaster, the eldest of Edward III's sons to survive him, and probably also with Richard Lord Scrope of Bolton, Steward of the Royal Household in 1377/8 and Chancellor of England in 1378/80. Redmayne enjoyed the benefit of family ties with the baronial houses of FitzHugh and Greystoke, and he himself profitably married a Yorkshire peer's daughter, a young widow who soon became one of her brother's two co-heiresses, adding to Redmayne's own modest Westmorland properties valuable estates in the West Riding.

Both Pickering and Redmayne were important notables in Yorkshire as well as in the north-west, and each eventually seems to have moved the centre of his interests over to the eastern and richer side of the Pennines. There is some indication of this tendency in their promotion to local offices of royal appointment. Pickering was acting sheriff of Westmorland (under the Cliffords, the hereditary sheriffs) for all but four of the last twelve years of Edward III's reign, but under Richard II he was three times escheator and three times sheriff of Yorkshire. His activity as parliamentary representative suggests the same sort of shift of influence: knight of the shire for Westmorland in 1362 and 1365, for Cumberland in 1368, and again for Westmorland in 1377 (October), 1378, 1379, and 1382 (October), his last five elections to parliament were for Yorkshire, in 1383 (February), 1384 (November), 1388 (September), 1390 (November), and 1397 (September).[1]

---

[1] *The Official Return of Members of Parliament*, vol. I, 171, 176, 179, 198, 201, 203, 213, 216, 224, 236, 240, 257.

The fact that Redmayne sat in parliament for Yorkshire alone — he was shire-knight in 1406, 1414 (November), 1415, 1420, and 1421 (December)[2] — and that he was twice sheriff and once escheator in Yorkshire, would make it appear that he had switched the centre of his activities to his wife's county. But his interests west of the Pennines clearly still remained powerful: he was entitled to a royal annuity charged on the Crown revenues from Cumberland, and he was sheriff of this county five times in all, for the last time as late as 1412.

Sir James de Pickering has a special interest to the local historian of Westmorland. He is the only parliamentary representative for the county ever to have been Speaker. Incidentally he was the first knight of the shire for Yorkshire to hold the office, Sir Richard Redmayne being the second.

A knight by the time of his first election to parliament, Sir James de Pickering was probably the son of the Thomas de Pickering who, in 1336, was confirmed by royal licence in possession of the manor of Killington, a parcel of a moiety of the barony of Kendal, originally granted to Thomas's father (William) by Peter de Brus in 1259 as a twentieth of a knight's fee. (The family arms were probably derived from those of De Brus.) Killington, some seven miles up the valley of the Lune from (but still in the parish of) Kirkby Lonsdale in south-east Westmorland, was in easy reach of Kendal, where apparently Sir James had a town-house. (He is at any rate occasionally referred to as being "of Kendal".) The family also had holdings at Firbank (near Killington), Millehope, Siggiswick, and at Heversham in the narrow strip of coastal plain that lies between Lancaster and Kendal.[3] At Killington and Millehope, from the time of

---

[2] *Ibid.*, 270, 285, 286, 296, 301.
[3] *CPR, 1334-8,* 280; N. & B. i 261; AA3 iii 272; CW2 xxx 91. I have not been able to discover any connexion between the Pickerings of Killington and Ellerton and the family of the same name who were tenants of the Barons Roos in the North Riding of Yorkshire at Oswaldkirk and Ampleforth (*CFR, 1347-56,* 161; *VCH, Yorkshire, North Riding,* i 549). Of this

Edward II, the family enjoyed rights of warren by royal charter. Sir James also had (or came to have) estates in the West Riding of Yorkshire, in the Humber basin in the vicinity of Selby: at Thorganby and also at Aughton in Spalding Moor, rents from some of which latter (to the amount of one mark a year) he conveyed in 1385 to the nearby Gilbertine priory of Ellerton, for the maintenance of one of their canons who was to be his chantry-priest at a parochial altar in the priory church.[4] Evidently Pickering had a place at Ellerton, too.

It is possible that the James de Pickering who was among those who entered the free chases of John de Mowbray at Kirby Malzeard and Burton-in-Lonsdale and hunted down some of his deer and committed assaults there, so that Mowbray complained and secured the appointment on 20 October 1354 of a special royal commission of *oyer and terminer* to deal with these trespasses, was James de Pickering of Killington; chief among the marauders were a group of knights from south Westmorland.[5]

These included Sir John de Haryngton of Farleton, a near neighbour of Pickering's and a knight of the shire for Lancashire in 1343, 1352, and 1357, who died in August 1359. After the death of Sir John's eldest son (Robert) in January 1361, and following the death of the overlord, Henry, duke of Lancaster, in March 1361, Pickering (by this time himself a knight) came into possession, evidently by right to wardship, of certain of his estates. These comprised tenements in Burton-in-Kendal and nearby Bolton, and at Farleton and Whittington in the Lonsdale hundred of Lancashire, together with a fourth part of the bailiwick of the serjeanty of the Lancashire hundred of Leylandshire, all held of the

family was Sir Richard Pickering, knight of the shire for Yorkshire in 1429, sheriff in 1431-2, J.P. in the North Riding in 1432-3, who died in 1441.

[4] *CPR, 1381-5*, 179; *ibid., 1385-9*, 7.

[5] *Ibid., 1354-8*, 130.

duchy of Lancaster. When Robert died the next heir
was his brother, Sir Thomas de Haryngton, who himself
died overseas in the following August (1361), another
younger brother, Nicholas, then succeeding as heir.

The Haryngton lands held of the duchy of Lancaster
were granted on 30 December 1361 to Pickering to hold
in wardship together with the marriage of Nicholas, who
was still some five years under age. And on 7 November
1362, for 100 marks (to be paid in the following year)
a royal grant secured to Pickering the custody of other
of the Haryngton lands in Winmarleigh (near Lancaster),
then held of the king as of the manor of Wyresdale. When
this particular grant was made, Pickering was himself
at Westminster sitting in the autumn parliament for the
first time as knight of the shire; his fellow-knight, John
de Preston of Kendal, was one of his two sureties in the
royal Chancery. The Winmarleigh estate was granted to
Pickering expressly as lately held by Sir Thomas de
Haryngton who, it appeared, had never actually been
seised, the last tenant being the father, Sir John. Pickering, unable to exercise his right of wardship there, later
drew attention to his difficulty, and to the fact that he
was getting nothing for his 100 marks, and on 4 November 1364 he sued out a writ of *certiorari* from the royal
Chancery to the escheator in Lancashire. His statement
was verified at an inquest held at Preston (Lancs.) on
16 November, and on 26 November the grant of two years
before was renewed with the necessary corrections. The
recognisance, entered into by Pickering on 14 November
1362 and by which he undertook to pay £200 to the
executors of Duke Henry of Lancaster, was doubtless in
respect of the wardship of those Haryngton estates lately
held of the duke.

Apart from his difficulties at Winmarleigh, it would
appear that Pickering had run into other trouble over his
Haryngton wardship. In July 1360, probably at Pickering's instigation, a servant of his had abducted Sir Thomas

de Haryngton's wife at Sedbergh in Lonsdale, taken her
to Bubwith near Selby, and been subsequently indicted
of the felony and outlawed. On 9 January 1364 the
servant received a royal pardon, following good service
in Ireland with Sir William de Windsor and at the latter's
request.[6]

This is the first suggestion of that connexion between
Sir James de Pickering and Sir William de Windsor which
was to be the most important single attachment of the
Speaker's career. Holding the manors of Heversham and
Grayrigg, Windsor was Pickering's near neighbour.
During the Lieutenancy in Ireland of Edward III's second
son, Lionel, duke of Clarence, which began in 1361,
Windsor held a command there, and it is probable that
even before January 1364 Pickering was himself a member of Windsor's retinue in Ireland. If that was the case,
his service there was clearly not continuous. After sitting
in the Westminster parliament of January 1365, again
as knight of the shire for Westmorland, in the autumn
of that year he was appointed under-sheriff of Westmorland under Roger Lord Clifford, who held the shrievalty
in fee. He held this office for two years, until October
1367. Only a year went by and then (after serving as
knight of the shire for Cumberland in the parliament
of May 1368) he was reappointed on 25 October 1368.
Three days before this, a royal licence was issued (for
£5, paid by Pickering) enabling Lord Clifford to grant
him for life an annuity of 10 marks charged on the rents
of his manor of Langton-in-Bongate (Westmorland)
which was held in chief. Pickering held the under-
shrievalty of Westmorland until October 1369.[7] His year
of office saw Sir William de Windsor, after the duke of

---

[6] *DKR* xxxii 342; *Cal. of Inqs. postmortem* xi 204-205, 449; *CFR, 1356-68*,
234; *CPR, 1364-7,* 50; *ibid.,* 1361-4, 439. For Sir William de Windsor, see
D.N.B. xxi 648-650; G. F. Duckett, *Duchetiana*, 285-290.

[7] P.R.O., *Lists and Indexes*, vol. IX, *List of Sheriffs* 150. On 12 February 1367 Pickering in the meantime was appointed to serve on a royal
commission of *oyer and terminer* following a complaint by Sir Hugh de
Lowther of a breach of his close and park at Wythop Hall in Cumberland
(*CPR, 1364-7,* 427). *CPR, 1367-70,* 160.

Clarence's death, himself appointed as King's Lieutenant in Ireland.[8]

The English government, having determined upon a policy of renewal of war against the Irish septs, undertook to furnish the new Lieutenant with £20,000 in instalments, and Windsor crossed in June 1369. On 20 December 1368 commissions had been issued for the furnishing of archers to go in his retinue from Westmorland, Lancashire, Yorkshire, and Nottinghamshire. With Windsor himself, Windsor's nephew, John, and others, Sir James de Pickering was appointed a member of the commission for Westmorland. And on 1 April 1369 Pickering sued out royal "letters of protection" for one year as a member of Windsor's company. His former ward, Sir Nicholas de Haryngton, did the same; the heir of Lord Clifford had done so over a month before.

Pickering in all probability actually crossed to Ireland with the Lieutenant, for he was with him there as a member of his council by 10 July 1369. It is likely that he was away from England more or less continuously for the best part of the next two years. On 24 February 1370 his royal "letters of protection" were renewed for another year, and on 28 March 1370 the sheriff of Westmorland was ordered (in a letter close issued by the Chancery) to allow him a respite until the following Michaelmas regarding the payment at the Exchequer of a fine of £20, imposed by the Treasurer and Barons because he had not appeared to render his account as undersheriff at the end of his term of office. Pickering was stated in the writ to be on royal service in Ireland.[9]

We know all of what we do know of Pickering's activities in Ireland from the series of charges against Sir William de Windsor's first administration (which ended with his recall in the spring of 1372), preferred in an Irish parliament which met in January 1373 (when Sir

[8] For Windsor's Lieutenancies in Ireland, see H. G. Richardson and G. O. Sayles, *The Irish Parliament in the Middle Ages*, especially pp. 80-85.
[9] *CPR, 1367-70*, 185, 238, 385; *CCR, 1369-74*, 178.

Robert Ashton was sent out from England as Justiciar
of Ireland to investigate grievances there), and from some
immediately subsequent inquiries. Carrying on the war
to reduce the clans bordering on the Dublin pale, Windsor
had found himself unable to keep his military expenses
within bounds and had adopted the natural policy of
putting the screw on the Irish themselves when he had
run through his English allowances.

We need only to inspect those of the charges in which
Sir James de Pickering was mentioned to appreciate the
import of the whole schedule, which comprised no fewer
than 87 articles of offence. Pickering was alleged to have
been among those who counselled the Lieutenant to compel the civic authorities in Dublin on 10 July 1369 to
maintain a force of 24 men for three weeks at their own
cost; to have assisted in counselling Windsor in the Dublin parliament of 30 July 1369 to impose certain customs
on foodstuffs and 6d. poundage on all exports, against
the will of the Commons and merchants; to have advised
the imposition on the commons of Meath of a tallage of
half a mark on every ploughland, without the assent of
the county, on 10 December 1369; to have taken a bribe
of 10 marks for a charter exempting from knighthood,
this when holding pleas at Trim on 18 March 1370; to
have been party, three days later at Dublin, to a decision
resulting in the unjust arrest of a chamberlain of the Irish
Exchequer, who was then imprisoned in Dublin castle
until his death, although he had paid 100 marks of the
fine of 500 marks, at which he was assessed, and given
10 marks and a silver bowl to Pickering.

Further charges against him were that on 20 May 1370,
after the knights for the town of Drogheda attending
parliament at Dublin had refused to grant a subsidy and
the Lieutenant, after summoning the mayor, steward, and
bailiffs with 12 burgesses, had compelled these men to
pay £40, they also paid £2 to Pickering for his assistance;
that, only a fortnight earlier, when four Drogheda mer-

chants bought the cargo of two Breton salt-ships, Pickering seized the ships and the salt, which was later sold to the Lieutenant's use (a manoeuvre that was repeated a year later); and that in January 1371, during the Kilkenny parliament, he was in agreement with the counsel which Windsor followed when he coerced the two knights for Meath into granting a tax of 6d. poundage as part of a levy of £3,000. Pickering's importance in this short Irish period of his career was not simply that of an intimate member of the Lieutenant's household and no more. A charge that on 23 May 1370 he received a bribe of 10 marks, prior to the Lieutenant's granting a charter of pardon to a clerk convicted of a murder, described him as then being "Chief Justice of the pleas following the Lieutenant and the principal person of the Lieutenant's *secretum consilium*". This is the only evidence of a direct kind suggesting that Pickering was a lawyer; holding this office, it is almost inconceivable that he was not.[10]

In the summer (of 1372) before these charges were made, Windsor was recalled to England, but he returned to Ireland in April 1374 after his reappointment as Lieutenant in September 1373. He made little headway in face of all the opposition that his first Lieutenancy had aroused. The attack on his administration, developed during his absence in England, was not suspended after his return; it was, in fact, encouraged by Sir Nicholas Dagworth's mission in the autumn of 1375 and once more came to a head in February 1376, when Windsor and other Irish officials were summoned to England. At the same time, so also were summoned representatives of the Irish commons, elected as for a parliament, to come before the English Council on 16 February 1376, two days after the date originally fixed for the meeting of the English parliament. Windsor crossed in June and on 24 July was superseded as Lieutenant of Ireland by the Earl of Ormond. The Irish business was by this time very

[10] M. V. Clarke, *Fourteenth Century Studies*, 186, 206, 220-229.

much intricated with the circumstances behind the general attack that had been launched against the Court party during the "Good Parliament" of this year. The reformers in parliament included in their programme a virulent attack on Edward III's mistress, Alice Perrers, whom by this time (but only recently) Windsor had married. The revival of the Court party, with the duke of Lancaster at its head, saved Alice Perrers, who had been banished from Court and subjected to forfeiture. It also saved her new husband: by her influence a new commission to Sir Nicholas Dagworth, to take back to Ireland the original schedule of charges against Windsor for further action there, was revoked in November 1376, and another commission to Dagworth and others was suppressed on 4 December. But Windsor never returned to Ireland. With these later developments regarding Ireland, Sir James de Pickering had nothing to do, so far as can be ascertained. He had not, in fact, been involved in Windsor's second administration in Ireland of 1374/6, although he retained his connexion with Windsor throughout, until the latter's death in 1384, for after this he acted as his executor.

It is just possible that Pickering was back in England at the time of his appointment on 28 March 1371 to serve on the royal commission authorized by the Council to assess each of the parishes of Westmorland, to the subsidy of £50,000 voted (in the recent parliament) on the basis of an average contribution of 22s. 3d. from each parish in the kingdom. This original assessment, when the number of parishes was found to have been miscalculated, was raised to 116 shillings per parish in a Great Council, which met at Winchester on 8 June 1371 mainly to remedy the error. Fresh commissions to assess and collect were then re-issued, Pickering being again appointed for Westmorland, which contributed least of all the counties.[11] On 10 (or 17) October following,

---

[11] *CFR, 1369-77,* 112, 127.

Pickering entered upon what proved to be a five years continuous occupation of the under-shrievalty of Westmorland; not until October 1376 was he displaced.[12] At the very time of his appointment he was granted at the Exchequer (for £40) the marriage of a royal ward, the son and heir of the Christopher de Moresby who had been a knight of the shire for Cumberland in 1360, 1363, and 1366; Roger Lord Clifford was his only surety. While still under-sheriff of Westmorland, he was appointed to the commission of the peace in Cumberland by patent of 20 January 1373 and eight days later in Westmorland itself. He did not, however, act as J.P. in Cumberland. On 12 June 1376 he was a member of a special royal commission of oyer and terminer following a complaint by Sir John de Derwentwater, the neighbouring sheriff of Cumberland, of assaults on him and his men for refusal to release a prisoner in the gaol of Carlisle castle who had been indicted of felony at the sheriff's tourn in the city.[13]

Pickering may very well have been up at Westminster at this time, when the "Good Parliament" was still in session. In all probability the roll of charges, framed in Ireland against Windsor and himself and others three years before, was being considered by the Council newly appointed in the parliament. Certainly at this time, he and Derwentwater, together with the Lords Scrope of Masham and Bolton, stood bail for Sir Hugh de Dacre who was held in the Tower on suspicion of having murdered his elder brother, Randolf, in his bed at Halton (Lancs.) in August 1375; released from the Tower on 2 July 1376, Sir Hugh was remanded until required to appear to stand trial before the Lords in parliament, or elsewhere if the King pleased.[14] In October, following

---

[12] *List of Sheriffs, loc. cit.* On 25 May 1375 he was ordered as sheriff to make certain arrests (*CPR, 1374-7, 150*).

[13] *CPR, 1370-4, 139, 244, 304; ibid., 1374-7, 325.*

[14] *CCR, 1374-7, 433* (Randolf de Dacre, personally summoned to parliament from 1362 to his death, was a priest, and sentence of the greater excommunication was pronounced against his murderers by the Bishop of

the "Good Parliament", Pickering relinquished his office as under-sheriff of Westmorland. But there seems to have been no particular significance in this. The Court party, with which his friend, Windsor, was now closely involved as the husband of the declining king's mistress, had already recovered from the storm of the recent parliament. And on 6 November 1376 Pickering found himself for the first time appointed as a J.P. in the West Riding of Yorkshire. A week or so after Richard II's accession he was made a commissioner of array in the West Riding (on 1 July 1377, when there was an invasion scare) and, later, a commissioner (by letter close of 30 August 1377) to seize certain lands in Yorkshire and Westmorland forfeited by Edward III's son-in-law, Enguerrand de Coucy, earl of Bedford, when this French nobleman renounced all his English honours, preferring his allegiance to the French Crown. Representing Westmorland once more in the first parliament of the new reign, Pickering was reappointed during the session (on 6 November 1377) to the West Riding commission of the peace.[15]

To the second parliament of Richard II's reign, which met at Gloucester on 20 October 1378 and sat for four weeks until 16 November, Pickering was re-elected knight of the shire for Westmorland. During the somewhat disturbed session he acted as the Commons' elected Speaker. John of Gaunt's recent military failure in Brittany, the need to get financial relief once more from parliament so soon after the grant of a double subsidy less than a year before, the scandal of the recent breach of sanctuary in the abbey at Westminster (with which rumour was associating the duke himself), the very fact of parliament's being summoned to meet for the first time for forty years away from Westminster (perhaps because of a renewal of the bitterness of the previous

Carlisle; Hugh granted livery of his inheritance on 10 July 1376, was thenceforward summoned to parliament as Lord Dacre until his death in December 1383).
[15] *CPR, 1374-7,* 314; *ibid., 1377-81,* 39, 47; *CCR, 1377-83,* 11.

year between Lancaster and Bishop Courtenay of London and the prospect of a recurrence of trouble with the Londoners), made the situation one of considerable difficulty for the administration of the day.

The Commons refused to make a grant of direct taxation, although Lord Scrope of Bolton, who passed during the session from the Stewardship of the royal Household to the office of Chancellor of England, did his best to secure one by tactfully handling the Commons when they insisted on a view of the accounts of the previous subsidy. The session was also marked by a certain irritation between Lords and Commons: when the latter asked for the now usual liaison-committee of lords to confer with them, the Upper House objected but eventually gave in on this point.

It is possible that the Commons' Speaker was himself much interested in the important proposals that were made during the session for the relief of local disorder. To some time in 1378 is to be attributed an undated petition which Pickering addressed to the King's Council. It stated that on 5 December last past when he was acting at Westminster as one of the knights of the shire for Westmorland — 5 December 1377 was actually the last day of Richard II's first parliament — Sir Thomas de Roos of Kendal and his four sons with 300 armed men laid two ambushes for Pickering's men and tenants on the highway at Helsington (a village to the south of Kendal) and assaulted them, killing a servant and another man of his and wounding six others. It may be that Pickering preferred the petition during the Gloucester parliament, but it is more than likely that he submitted it much earlier in the year. In fact, it may very well be that a royal commission, appointed by patent on 7 April 1378 to make inquiry in Westmorland about unlawful assemblies meeting there for the purpose of killing Pickering and his men and tenantry, was the official reaction to his petition. The same day saw the issue of a patent

setting up a commission for the same purpose in Yorkshire. To membership of the Westmorland commission
were appointed Lord Clifford and Pickering's own former
ward, Sir Nicholas de Haryngton, who had been knight
of the shire for Lancashire in the parliament of October
1377.[16]

Not long after the parliament of his first Speakership,
Pickering was appointed to serve in Westmorland on one
of a number of commissions of array (by patent of
18 February 1379). Only the northern shires were so
affected, and the motive for the commission was clearly
need for defence against the Scots. For a second time
Pickering was re-elected knight of the shire for Westmorland in the spring parliament which sat at Westminster
from 25 April to 27 May 1379, his third parliament
running. It is not improbable that he was re-elected
Speaker in this parliament (from which no Speaker's
name has come down to us), but this is no more than a
conjecture. The session had not long been over when,
on 14 June, he and an old servant of his (John of York,
perhaps the brother of his servant, Thomas of York,
killed in the fraças at Helsington) were granted for the
next three years pontage on merchandise carried from
the priory of Hornby to the bridge over the Lune at
Tebay in aid of repairs to another local bridge at Stranger-
wath. On 8 August he was made a member of the Westmorland commission charged with the re-assessment in
the county of the graduated poll-tax voted in the last
parliament. Three months later, on 5 November 1379,
he was appointed to the office of royal escheator in Yorkshire, a post he was to hold until February 1381.[17] He

[16] Ancient Petitions, P.R.O., S.C. 8, file 67, no. 3308. The date of the
ambushes at Helsington is given in the petition as the Saturday before
St. Nicholas. In 1377 this day fell on 5 December. The only other autumn
parliaments attended by Pickering as knight for Westmorland were those
of October 1362 and November 1382, of which the former ended in November, the latter in October. The incident, it seems, could only have occurred
in 1377 (*CPR*, *1377-81*, 204).

[17] *CPR*, *1377-81*, 359, 354; *CFR*, *1377-83*, 164; P.R.O., *List of Escheators*,
187.

was dropped from the West Riding commission of the peace in May 1380, but there now began for him a period of much greater official activity, so far as local royal administration was concerned, in Yorkshire, a fact which had a considerable bearing on his later parliamentary career.

Pickering was not to be again elected as knight of the shire to any of the next four parliaments, not, in fact, until the autumn of 1382. In the meantime, on 20 March 1380 he was appointed to a commission of array in the West Riding; on 5 December in the same year to a commission of inquiry into the circumstances behind a petition (preferred at the Northampton parliament) against the ejection of the mayor of York and the irregular and tumultuous election of a successor; and two days later to a commission to control the assessment of the recently voted triple poll-tax in Westmorland.[18] It was this poll-tax which "triggered off" the Peasants' Revolt of the following year. It is unlikely that the rising affected Pickering in any direct way although, in Yorkshire, Scarborough and Beverley were centres of disturbance. When the revolt broke out in May 1381 he had already relinquished his office of escheator. In what way he was connected with John of Gaunt at this time of savage popular hostility to the duke is not known; but it is of some significance that, after the rising was spent but before he was able to return from taking refuge in Scotland, the duke wrote from Edinburgh on 25 June to his local receiver in Lancashire instructing him to send all his available cash and as much as he could raise by loan to Carlisle, where it was to be handed over to Sir James de Pickering and presumably taken, either personally or by an agent of Pickering's, to the duke himself.[19]

[18] *CPR, 1377-81*, 472 (on 6 August 1380 Pickering was a mainpernor for a King's clerk, Thomas de Broughton, when granted the custody of a small estate in Ribblesdale forfeited for felony, *CFR, 1377-83*, 213), 580; *CFR, 1377-83*, 230.
[19] Royal Historical Society, Camden Third Series, vol. LVI, *John of Gaunt's Register, 1379-83*, ed. E. C. Lodge and R. Somerville, i 184.

Pickering served on no royal commissions in 1381 after the expiry of his escheatorship, but on 8 March 1382 he was appointed to a commission in Westmorland of a type issued for the whole country, to keep the peace, arrest rebels, suppress sedition, call out the *posse comitatus* if need be, and act with judicial powers of oyer and terminer. This commission and Pickering's membership of it were renewed on 21 December following. He was still, as he was to remain, a J.P. in Westmorland. This was after his service in the parliament of October 1382 when he sat for the sixth and last time for Westmorland, a session which saw the failure of Lancaster's first bid for parliament's financial support for his proposed crusade in Spain. Pickering had seemingly used his visit to the south to petition the king for a grant which, in fact, passed the great seal a week after the parliament was dissolved: on 1 November 1382, allegedly in consideration of his long but unrewarded services in Scotland and elsewhere in Edward III's reign, he was allowed the custody of some lands at Thorganby (near Selby), which were then in the king's hand because acquired by the overlord in fee simple without royal licence; farmed at 30s. a year, they were assigned to Pickering rent-free. The grant was warranted by the privy seal, but the original petition is endorsed to the effect that Richard II, after granting the petition, on 1 November himself delivered the bill by his own hands to the Chancellor ordering him to have a patent drawn up in due form.[20] Five days later, on 6 November 1382, Pickering was appointed once more escheator in Yorkshire, on 20 December was reappointed J.P. in Westmorland, and on 3 February 1383 was made a commissioner for preserving salmon in the main rivers of Cumberland, Westmorland, and Northumberland.[21]

[20] *CPR, 1381-5*, 140, 245, 179; Ancient Petitions, P.R.O., S.C. 8, file 252, no. 12565.
[21] *List of Escheators, loc. cit.*; *CPR, 1381-5*, 253-254, 256 (in February 1390 he had to procure a surcease of distress to which he was then being

Early in his year of office as escheator in Yorkshire, Pickering was for the first time elected as knight of the shire for that county, and in the short parliament which sat from 23 February to 10 March he acted for a second time as Speaker for the Commons. Again, as in 1378, the session was very troubled, this time because the knights of the shire carried the day against the Upper House and secured the adoption of the policy of a crusade in Flanders rather than in Spain, where John of Gaunt's own ambitions were involved. One of the Commons' arguments, that the truce with Scotland was due to expire and that this made it inadvisable for Lancaster and his brothers to be out of the kingdom, may very well have appealed to Pickering, as a north countryman himself.

Little is recorded of any official activity on Pickering's part for the next two years. His Yorkshire escheatorship came to an end early in November 1383. The autumn parliament of October 1383 and the Salisbury session of the spring of 1384 went their way without Pickering being again elected as knight of the shire, but to the November-December parliament of 1384 he was once more returned for Yorkshire.

About this time he was extremely busy over the very complicated affairs of his old colleague, Sir William de Windsor, who in 1381 had become a member of the Upper House of parliament. Sir William had died at Heversham on 15 September 1383. Sir James de Pickering, along with Sir William de Melton, Sir Walter de Strickland (who was elected for Westmorland to the next parliament of November 1383 along with Windsor's nephew, Robert), and Windsor's nephew and heir, John de Windsor, was appointed on the day of Sir William's death as executor of his nuncupative will. Probate was granted at York on 19 September 1383, letters of administration being issued to Melton and Pickering by

subjected by the Exchequer, on the ground that the commission to preserve these rivers never came into his hands and that he had not meddled in the business [*CCR, 1389-92* 153]).

the archbishop's vicar-general; at London in the prerogative court of Canterbury on 12 October. Pickering was
one of the witnesses to two deeds, dated 24 October and
1 November respectively, conveying to the heir practically
all the estates of Sir William de Windsor in England, the
second of the two being a quitclaim of Egremont castle
and lordship (Cumberland).

In Hilary term 1385 Pickering and his fellow-executors
were embroiled at the Exchequer over the accounts of
Sir William de Windsor, which, difficult though in themselves they must have been to unravel, were further
tangled by the forfeiture to which his wife, Alice Perrers,
had been subjected by her condemnation in the Good
Parliament and its confirmation by Richard II's first
parliament. Dame Alice petitioned in the November
parliament of 1384 against the awards of 1376 and 1377,
and they were now quashed, but only as regards the
future. All grants of her enfeoffed estates already made
were to stand, including those to her late husband who
had disposed of them in ways far from her liking, and she
subsequently engaged in law-suits with his nephew and
heir, John. Some considerable relaxation of the forfeiture
had been obtained when Windsor undertook to serve at
his own costs in Thomas of Woodstock's expedition to
Brittany in 1380. There were also to be taken into
account the debts due to Windsor from the Crown, dating
from the days of his Irish administration and from the
time of his appointment as keeper of the town and castle
of Cherbourg in Normandy in October 1379.

On 8 May 1385, the executors, principally John de
Windsor, were pardoned all claims against the late Sir
William's lands, excepting accounts proved of record in
the Lower Exchequer regarding advances made to him
there at various times and in his various capacities; this
pardon was backed up on 19 May by a letter under the
great seal to the Upper Exchequer, itself warranted by
a royal signet letter, to allow the pardon to take effect,

and by a further writ of surcease, issued on 22 June,
ordering John de Windsor's account to be received. On
7 March Pickering himself had taken out a pardon,
warranted by the signet, for all felonies, trespasses,
extortions and other offences in England and abroad
(presumably in Ireland), of any consequent outlawries,
and of debts due from him to the Crown. He was still
not clear of the encumbrances of the administration of
Windsor's concerns as late as 12 October 1387, when he
secured "letters of protection" for a year enabling him to
go to Ireland in his capacity as Windsor's executor; he
did not, however, go, and the letters were revoked on
26 November 1388.[22]

For a few years after 1384 Pickering was not to be
elected to parliament, and between his sitting in November 1384 and his next return for Yorkshire to the
Cambridge parliament of September 1388 very little can
be learned of what he was doing apart from his pre-
occupations with the Windsor executorship. In 1386,
however, he was certainly much involved in the dispute
between Richard Lord Scrope of Bolton and Sir Robert
Grosvenor, arising out of the former's eventually successful plea in the Court of the Constable and Marshal against
the latter's usurpation (during the Scottish expedition of
1385) of his exclusive right to bear the arms of "azure
with a bend d'or". In February 1386 royal authority was
given for the appointment of commissioners, nominated
by the parties, to examine witnesses and receive evidence,
and on 26 May following names were tendered to the
Constable, the Duke of Gloucester, at Westminster.

Pickering was among the nine lords and forty knights
nominated by Scrope on 28 May, and on 10 August he
was appointed by the Constable, under seal of his office,
as a commissioner to take depositions and produce them
in sealed certificates on 21 January 1387. The connexion

---

[22] G. F. Duckett, *Ducheliana,* 285-290; *CCR, 1381-5,* 580; 548; *ibid.,*
1385-9, 84; *CPR, 1381-5,* 566, 537, 561; *ibid., 1385-9,* 356, 410.

with Lord Scrope conceivably might have disposed Pickering to the baronial, anti-royalist viewpoint in the October 1386 parliament. This session of parliament saw the impeachment of the Duke of Suffolk, the ex-Chancellor, and the setting up of the parliamentary commission whose appointment Richard II, as he was soon to show, regarded as an act of treason. Scrope was a member of this commission. But Pickering was not a knight of the shire on that occasion. In fact, on 1 October 1386, when the parliament first met, he and his colleague in the business of the plea of arms, the abbot of St. Mary of York, were holding sessions at Nottingham for the taking of attestations in favour of Lord Scrope, first in the parish church of St. Mary and then in the frater of the Franciscan priory there, and on the following day, when they first met in the conventual church, Scrope himself was present, being presumably on his way up to the parliament. In the afternoon of the same day and on 3 and 4 October Pickering held further sessions in the Franciscan priory church at Leicester and then sent on his enrolment of the proceedings under seal to the Constable. Whether he himself moved up to Westminster, where the preparations for the case went on throughout the parliamentary session, is not known.[23]

Of Pickering's activities during the troubled years of 1387 and 1388, nothing is known beyond the little that has already been told. But after the violent storm of the "Merciless Parliament" had blown up and subsided he was again elected for Yorkshire to the parliament which met at Cambridge from 10 September to 17 October 1388. This was at a time when the Lords Appellant were in the saddle, Lord Scrope being then one of those members of the parliamentary commission who were continually attending upon and controlling the King.

In the spring of 1389 Richard II recovered some of the political initiative that had been lost in the débâcles

[23] N. H. Nicolas, *The Scrope and Grosvenor Controversy*, i 49, 148-156.

of the previous two and a half years, and Westminster became again a more comfortable place for those whom the King favoured and upon whom he relied. Personal kingship was once more a force to be reckoned with, all the stronger and the more seasoned for what had recently transpired. The Westminster Abbey Chronicle, written at the heart of things, credits Richard with such a recovery of authority as enabled him in the autumn of 1389 to appoint the next batch of sheriffs of his own personal motion ''cum consilio suo privato'', and to extract from them a special oath of fidelity to himself. Whether or not Pickering needed to trim his sails to new winds, it is just not possible to say, but the next ten years were years of greater employment for him in local royal administrative work than the last decade had been.

On 15 November 1389 he was appointed sheriff of Yorkshire for the first time, his first appointment as a sheriff by direct royal authority. He held the post until 7 November 1390, in the course of his year of office (on 24 February 1390) being granted by royal patent (issued by privy seal warrant) an annuity for life of 40 marks charged on the revenues of his present bailiwick; described as ''king's knight'', he was retained to serve the king in time of war with a company of twenty men-at-arms and a hundred archers. To the second of the two parliaments summoned during Pickering's year of office as sheriff he was himself returned, almost certainly a case (by no means unique in this period) of a sheriff allowing himself to be elected against the tenor of the writ of summons. The parliament met on 12 November and came to an end on 3 December 1390. On 12 December, within little more than a month of his relinquishing the shrievalty of Yorkshire, Pickering was appointed escheator in the selfsame county. Twelve days later still, he was confirmed in his office as J.P. in Westmorland. His year of office as escheator ended on 28 December 1391.[24]

[24] *List of Sheriffs*, 162; *List of Escheators*, 187. It is possible, but I think

Although he was not re-elected as shire-knight, it is probable that Pickering was up at Westminster when the next parliament, that of 3 November—2 December 1391, was in session, being perhaps concerned *inter alia* with the audit of his escheator's accounts in the Exchequer. However that may be, on 27 November 1391 he was granted in the Exchequer — Sir Peter Tilliol, then knight of the shire for Cumberland, was one of his mainpernors — the wardship and marriage of the son and heir of the late Sir Christopher Moresby who had been shire-knight in the last previous parliament for Westmorland. The wardship comprised estates in Cumberland, Westmorland, and Yorkshire. For their custody Pickering was to render the "extent"; for the marriage, what should be agreed between him and the Council. By a later arrangement — the letters patent were drawn up by the new Chancellor, Archbishop Arundel, at York on 24 October 1392 — Pickering undertook to pay £16 a year for the wardship, £40 down for the marriage; Ralph Lord Greystoke was one of his two sureties on this occasion. His continued connexion at this time with Lord Scrope of Bolton is suggested by his appointment in the meantime, on 4 February 1392, as a commissioner of inquiry into the abduction of the heir of a tenant of the honour of Richmond whose marriage Richard II's Queen had granted to Scrope.[25] Whether in this period Pickering was also still in touch with the Duke of Lancaster is not known, although on 28 August 1393 he attested a grant of a rent of 20 marks made by a great Lancastrian retainer, Sir Walter Urswick, to a kinsman, Sir Robert

unlikely (in view of Sir James's appointment as escheator during the parliament), that the "James de Pickering" elected to this parliament was the esquire of that name granted an annuity of £10, charged on the Yorkshire royal revenues in November 1401. *CPR, 1388-92*, 200, 346, 437. (A commission of inquiry, on which Pickering served as escheator, into the local forfeitures of John de Lokton, the serjeant-at-law implicated in the famous declaration of the judges at Nottingham in August 1387; in the previous year when sheriff, Pickering had served on an inquiry into a petition, for certain estates probably involved in the forfeiture, submitted by Lokton's stepdaughter and ward, who had married his son, *ibid.*, 273).

[25] *CFR, 1391-9*, 21, 60; *CCR, 1392-6*, 26; *CPR, 1391-6*, 82.

Urswick, who was another important supporter of the duke.[26]

To none of the five parliaments that sat between the winter of 1390 and the spring of 1397 was Sir James de Pickering elected, but during this time he was sheriff of Yorkshire once more in the year November 1393/4. By then he may well have been in the neighbourhood of seventy years of age and his appointments to serve on royal commissions had now become few and far between. On 4 August 1397 he was, however, put on a commission of oyer and terminer following a complaint, made by the abbot of St. Mary of York, of trespasses on his various properties. During the first session of the parliament of 1397/8, in which Pickering served (for Yorkshire) for the last time as knight of the shire, this commission of oyer and terminer was renewed (on 25 September).[27]

This parliament, which was to prove Richard II's last, in its two short sessions, from 17 to 30 September 1397 at Westminster and from 28 to 31 January 1398 at Shrewsbury, saw the King triumph over his enemies of ten years before. In considering Pickering's likely attitude to these fresh and sinister developments, it is just as well to bear in mind his position as a retainer of the King since 1390, and the fact that during the parliamentary recess (on 3 November 1397) he was appointed as sheriff of Yorkshire for the third time within the last eight years, despite his having procured on 5 April 1396 a patent of exemption for life from the office as well as from being put on assizes, juries, commissions to collect parliamentary tenths and fifteenths, and from being made escheator or coroner, against his will. On 12 November 1397 he was also made once more a J.P. in the West Riding of Yorkshire.

At the end of June 1398 he was put on a commission to

---

[26] *Yorkshire Archaeological and Topographical Journal* xvii 103. (For the Urswicks, see Chetham Society, vol. 96, N.S., J.S. Roskell, *Knights of the Shire for the County Palatine of Lancaster, 1377-1460.*)
[27] *List of Sheriffs*, 162; CPR, *1396-9*, 241, 243; *ibid.*, 236.

make certain arrests in Westmorland, and on 22 January 1399 a servant of his was given a royal pardon for having caused the death of a weaver early in June 1394 (when Pickering had previously been sheriff of Yorkshire).[28] Beyond that nothing further is known of Sir James. It is even very doubtful whether by this latter date (January 1399) he was still alive. It is Sir John Depeden who appears in the *adventus* of the *Memoranda Rolls* of the Exchequer as sheriff of Yorkshire in Richard II's last year, not Pickering.[29] Almost certainly, Pickering did not live to see the revolution of 1399, when Richard II was deposed in favour of Henry IV. But the date of his death, because he held no lands in chief of the King, is not known. It is fairly safe to assume that the Thomas de Pickering who died in 1406, while in office as escheator of Yorkshire and holding the manor of Killington, was his son and heir.[30]

[28] *List of Sheriffs, loc. cit.; CPR, 1391-6,* 691; *ibid., 1396-9,* 236, 434, 479.
[29] K.R. Memoranda Roll, P.R.O. E 159/175; the *List of Sheriffs,* in stating that he held office until Richard II's deposition, is clearly at fault.
[30] *List of Escheators,* 187; *CFR, 1405-13,* 57; G. F. Duckett, *Duchetiana,* 161. It was Thomas Pickering's son and heir, the Speaker's grandson, John, who married Eleanor, daughter of Sir Richard Haryngton, and who died in 1420, and not the Speaker's father, as C. L. Kingsford states in the short biography of the Speaker in *D.N.B.* xv 1129. Cf. Surtees Society, vol. 144 (*Visitations of the North*), 131; *CPR 1416-22,* 298; J. C. Wedgwood, *History of Parliament, Biographies,* 682. The Pickering pedigree in Nicolson & Burn, *Westmorland and Cumberland* (i 261) is completely at sea. Whoever the Speaker married. it was certainly not (as his first wife) Mary, daughter of Sir Robert Lowther, or (as his second) Margaret, daughter and heiress of Sir John Norwood. The Sir James de Pickering of Killington who married Mary Lowther (*ibid.,* 429-431) was probably the Speaker's great-grandson, the same who was knight of the shire for Yorkshire in 1447, November 1449, and 1455, and who, attainted in 1459, was killed, fighting on the Yorkist side, at Wakefield in 1460. C. L. Kingsford (in *D.N.B., loc. cit.*) follows N. & B. into error as to the Speaker's marriages.

2

SIR RICHARD DE WALDEGRAVE
OF BURES ST. MARY

Not until 1376, so far as we know, did the Commons elect one of their own number to act as their spokesman before the King and Lords for the duration of a parliament. The early history of the Speaker's office belongs to a time when the royal authority was accidentally somewhat weak in its exercise—in 1377 old Edward III died to be succeeded by his grandson, Richard II, a mere boy—and when the Commons were rapidly gaining ground as a political force to be reckoned with.

We know next to nothing of what managerial functions were discharged in the Lower House by the Speaker at this date, or how influential was his position there. But clearly his functions were at least potentially important, and are likely to have been so in fact. The Speaker's own attitude to the political problems of the day may have been, in certain circumstances, of considerable significance for the Commons' deliberations. Or, at any rate, his political affiliations and connexions may have had their effect, however indirectly. So very many of the knights of the shire (or representatives of counties as distinct from boroughs), from among whom the medieval Speakers were invariably elected, were closely connected with the Court or with some great magnate (or even more than one) that an inquiry into their careers becomes advisable if we are to try to understand the atmosphere in which parliament met and did its business in this period. One of the main points of significance attaching to Sir Richard de Waldegrave's Speakership in the first parliament after the Peasants' Revolt of 1381 is that, fifth on the list of the Speakers, he is the first one of them to be a proper royal retainer.

Waldegrave's career is of interest, however, on other grounds. Between 1376 and 1390 he partly monopolized one of the two seats for his county of Suffolk: he was elected to the parliaments of 1376, October 1377, 1378, 1381, May and October 1382, February and October 1383, 1386, February and September 1388, and January 1390, that is, to twelve out of the twenty parliaments which met in this period.[1] His earlier military career, as a young

---

[1] *Official Return of Members of Parliament 1*, 194, 198, 200, 209, 211, 213, 215, 218, 229, 233, 235, 238.

man in the service of two heads of the great comital house of
Bohun had been an exciting one; it may even have caught the
attention of the poet, Chaucer, so remarkable are the resemblances
between it and that of the knight of his *Canterbury Tales*. After
being retained by Richard II, Waldegrave became steward of
the lands of Queen Anne (of Bohemia), who came to England in
the course of his Speakership. In the later years of the reign, he
became a member of the royal Council. Too old at Richard II's
deposition and Henry IV's accession in 1399 to accommodate
himself to changed conditions at Court, Waldegrave then went
into retirement, although he survived until 1410. Incidentally,
he was the only knight of the shire for Suffolk ever to be elected
to the Speakership in pre-Tudor times.

Sir Richard de Waldegrave was descended from a family which
took its name from Walgrave in Northamptonshire where the
Speaker himself still held lands. He was, in fact, a tenant here
and at Batsaddle of a knight's fee, the seignory of which, in January
1376, was allocated (as part of her dower estates) to Anne, daughter
of Sir Walter Manny, K.G. (by Margaret Marshall, countess of
Norfolk) and widow of John de Hastings, earl of Pembroke, who
had died in April 1375. Whether he inherited land in the vill
of Hannington (close by Walgrave) and added by purchase to
what he had, or whether he bought *all* his holding there, is not
clear. He also had property in Northamptonshire at Twywell.
He maintained his connexions with that county, although from
early in his career his main territorial interests lay in the valley
of the Stour, especially in and near Bures St. Mary, where he held
the manor of Smallbridge. Since 1363 he had held a knight's fee in
Wickhambrook in west Suffolk. In 1377 he purchased the nearby
manor of Ousden; in 1393 he came (by reversion) into a manor
called 'Merkys' in Raydon St. Mary, near Hadleigh in south
Suffolk, within easy reach of Bures; and in 1405, in this county
again, he secured a group of manors, all near to Bures, those
of Polstead (with the advowson of the church there), Newland-
hall in Polstead, and Leavenheath, as well as property in London,
partly perhaps in exchange for his Lincolnshire manor of Brant
Boughton. Just over the Stour from Bures, on the Essex side of
the river, he also held Wormingford.[2]

---

[2] *DNB*, xx. 477; *CCR, 1374-7*, 190; *ibid, 1381-5*, 92; *ibid, 1377-81*, 93-4;
ibid, 1392-6, 69; *ibid, 1405-9*, 72, 75.
(The following abbreviations have been used in the footnotes:—
  DNB—Dictionary of National Biography; *CPR*—Calendar of Patent Rolls;
  CCR—Calendar of Close Rolls; *CFR*—Calendar of Fine Rolls; *CChR*—
  Calendar of Charter Rolls; *Rot.Parl.*—Rotuli Parliamentorum; *PPC*—
  Proceedings and Ordinances of the Privy Council, ed N. H. Nicolas; *PRO*—
  Public Record Office).

The location of Sir Richard's chief estates at roughly the time of his Speakership is clear from the list of towns where, in his demesne lands, he secured a grant of free warren by royal charter on 10 May 1384: Walgrave, Hannington, and Twywell (Northants), Wormingford (Essex), and Ousden and Bures St. Mary (Suffolk).[3] It was apparently this last place that saw most of Waldegrave: it was his manor house of Smallbridge here that he received royal licence to crenellate, also on 10 May 1384, and it was in the parish church of Bures that he was buried in 1410, in accordance with his will.[4] Bures and others of his holdings in that vicinity came to Waldegrave through his marriage with Joan, daughter and heir of Robert Silvester of Bures and widow of Robert de Bures, whom he had married by 1363.[5]

The son of Sir Richard de Waldegrave of Walgrave (Northants) by his wife Agnes Daubeney, Sir Richard the Speaker was born in or about 1338—in 1386, in the deposition which he made in the famous heraldic suit of Scrope *v.* Grosvenor, he said that he was then 48 years old. In 1329 his father had crossed to France with Edward III and in 1337, as a member of the retinue of Bishop Henry Burghersh of Lincoln, accompanied him to Flanders where the bishop (an ex-treasurer) was in charge of the royal wool-selling operations. Sir Richard the father had been knight of the shire for Lincolnshire at the York parliament of 1335. (A John de Waldegrave, perhaps the Speaker's uncle, had sat for Northants in six parliaments between 1327 and 1341, probably the same who was Queen Philippa's 'serjeant and minister' of Rockingham forest and a justice of the peace in Northants in 1331.)[6] In his testimony in the Scrope *v.* Grosvenor plea of 1386 the Speaker refers to himself as having then been 'armed' for 25 years, that is, since about 1361. But he states that he had heard of the long-established right of the Scropes to the arms in question during the life-time of the earl of Northampton. This was clearly William de Bohun, created earl of Northampton in 1337 and Constable of England in the following year, who saw much foreign service in Edward III's wars with France. Young Waldegrave had been a beneficiary under the terms of the will of Elizabeth, countess of Northampton, in the spring of 1356. Almost certainly he was even then a member of their household, and it was doubtless as a Bohun retainer that (according to his deposition for Scrope) he was

[3] *CChR*, v. 293.
[4] *CPR, 1381-85*, 410; Lambeth Palace Library, Arundel Register, pars. II, fo. 49.
[5] *D.NB, loc. cit.*; F. Blomefield, *Norfolk*, v. 1378; P. Morant, *Essex*, I. 182a; *Harleian Society*, XIII. 119; *ibid*, XXXII. 295; *Feudal Aids*, v. 99. (In 1363 Sir Richard and Joan his wife had paid a relief for their knight's fee in the manor of Wickhambrook, held of the King as of the honour of Montgomery).
[6] *CPR, 1330-34*, 144, 186; *ibid, 1334-8*, 418, 531.

with the army before Paris in April 1360 during what proved to
be the earl's last expedition. After the earl of Northampton's
death in September 1360, Waldegrave stayed on in the service of
the family. The earl's son and heir was Humphrey, a minor, who
in October 1361 also became heir to his uncle, Humphrey, earl of
Hereford and Essex. In early January 1363 the young Humphrey
de Bohun (now earl of Northampton, Hereford and Essex) was at
Thorn on the Vistula, presumably with the object of assisting the
Teutonic Knights in their perennial warfare with the heathen
Letts, and Waldegrave was one of his company: the earl and he,
together with three other knights, borrowed 2600 French *écus* from
local merchants, undertaking repayment at Bruges in the quindene
of Easter following. In the previous year Cypriot and Armenian
knights had been to London seeking Edward III's assistance
against the Turks, and in 1363 the King of Cyprus, Peter de
Lusignan, was himself in England for the same purpose, returning
home to win (in 1364) the victory that resulted in the treaty of
which Waldegrave was to speak in his testimony in 1386. Sir
Richard also stated that he had seen the disputed arms (properly
differenced) being borne by a member of the Scrope family who
was in the company of the earl of Hereford in the eastern Mediterranean (*outre la graunde mere*) at 'Satillie' (Attalia) in 'Turkye',
where took place an important treaty to which the King of Cyprus
was party. Doubtless Waldegrave was also a member of Hereford's retinue there and, with almost equal certainty, at the taking
of Alexandria in 1365, when Hereford was again with the King
of Cyprus.[7]

Waldegrave had surely some of the qualifications possessed
by the 'veray parfit gentil knight' of the prologue of Geoffrey
Chaucer's *Canterbury Tales*: the pilgrim knight had also ridden far
'in his lordes werre . . . as wel in Cristendom as in Hethenesse'; had
been 'at Alisandre . . . whan it was wonne'; 'in Lettowe [Lithuania]
hadde he reysed'; had been at the victory of 'Satalie'; and 'in
the Grete see at many a noble armee hadde he be'. Did, by any
chance, Waldegrave's experiences, as but partly narrated in the
deposition which he made on behalf of Sir Richard Scrope in the
refectory of the abbey at Westminster on 15 October 1386, contribute anything to Chaucer's composite portrait of his ideal knight?

---

[7] N. H. Nicolas, *The Scrope v. Grosvenor Controversy*, i. 165-6; N. H. Nicolas,
Testamenta Vetusta, i. 61; T. Walsingham, *Historia Anglicana* (Rolls Series), ed.
T. H. Riley, i. 296, 299, 301; The *Anonimalle Chronicle*, ed. V. H. Galbraith,
51, 170; *Archaeologia*, LXXIV. 115. (The design of the seals of the two bonds
made at Thorn at Epiphany 1363 suggests that the seals of the earl and three
of the four knights contracting the loan were specially made on the spot and
by the same workman, they having seemingly left their seals in England).

The question is perhaps not without some piquancy. Among the eighteen other deponents, besides Waldegrave, on that very same autumn day of 1386, was Geoffrey Chaucer himself, then sitting for Kent, on the one and only occasion of his return as a knight of the shire, in the parliament which had been opened a fortnight before.

On 29 July 1366 Waldegrave took out royal letters patent authorising his appointment of attorneys to act for him in England while he was overseas. Why he was leaving home on this occasion is not clear, but it is almost certain that he left with the earl of Hereford who was again going overseas at the same time. According to further details that Waldegrave gave in 1386 of his familiarity with the arms of the Scrope family, it is clear that he was at Balyngham Hill (the 'mountayn de Baligate' of the *Anonimalle Chronicle*) and on the 'voyage de Caux' by which are meant respectively the expedition led by Lancaster into the Pas-de-Calais in 1369 (when the duke was accompanied by the earl of Hereford) and the immediately subsequent plundering expedition, led by the earl of Warwick into Lower Normandy and the 'insula de Caws', to which both the St. Albans chronicle of Thomas Walsingham and the *Anonimalle Chronicle* refer. Less than two years later seemingly Waldegrave was again serving as a member of the military retinue of the earl of Hereford. The earl's wife's brother-in-law, Thomas Holland, step-son of the Black Prince, at the jousts in Plymouth on 24 July 1371 granted Waldegrave and his heirs male leave to bear his helm—'party per pale argent and gules, crowned or'. Waldegrave was Holland's companion-in-arms. The jousts took place at an assembly of an English fleet that was to take the earl of Hereford to Brittany on a diplomatic mission, and Hereford was a witness to Holland's grant to Waldegrave.[8] Certainly, in the following summer, Waldegrave was a member of the Bohun retinue once more, when the earl joined the expedition which Edward III himself intended to lead to the relief of La Rochelle; one among the fifty-one knights of Hereford's company, Waldegrave came to the muster on 8 August 1372, over three weeks after the earliest arrivals. The expedition was prevented by adverse winds from reaching Brittany, but it was not until 6 October that Hereford's retinue returned to England with the royal forces and eventually landed at Sandwich.[9]

[8] *CPR, 1364-7*, 303; *Scrope v. Grosvenor Controversy, loc. cit.*; *Historia Anglicana*, I. 307-8; *The Anonimalle Chronicle*, 59-62, 177; *The Complete Peerage*, VII. 154; G. F. Beltz, *Memorials of the Order of the Garter*, 221n.

[9] Exchequer, Queen's Remembrancer, Ancient Miscellanea, PRO., E101/xxxii/20.

Earl Humphrey died on 16 January following (1373), leaving as his heirs two daughters, the elder of whom was soon contracted in marriage (in 1374) to the youngest of Edward III's sons, Thomas of Woodstock, and the other (in 1380) to the heir of Lancaster, Henry of Bolingbroke. There is no sign of Waldegrave's being drawn into the circle of Woodstock, which happened to a number of the members of the Bohun affinity. Hereford's premature death—he was only thirty years old—was doubtless a tragedy from the point of view of Waldegrave's career. He did, however, retain a connexion with his late lord's widow, the dowager countess of Hereford (Joan, daughter of Richard, second earl of Arundel), who lived on till 1419, and in the 1380's, and later, he is to be found acting as a feoffee in certain of the Bohun estates in Essex in her interest and in the interest of his late lord, Earl Humphrey.[10]

These connexions maintained Waldegrave's ties with some of the members of the late earl's entourage. One of these was Sir John de Burgh of Burgh Green (Cambs) and Kirklington (Notts), who early in 1377 made Waldegrave one of the grantees of annual rents amounting to £300 from his Nottinghamshire and Yorkshire estates.[11] A more influential link that the old Bohun attachment supplied was with Sir Guy de Brian, who was summoned to parliament among the knights banneret for the last forty years of his life, from 1350 to 1390. Under-chamberlain to Edward III in 1348, from August 1359 to May 1361 Sir Guy had been steward of the royal household. He was made a knight of the Order of the Garter in 1369. He was a member of the liaison committee of Lords requested by the Commons in the parliament of 1373 and in the Good Parliament of 1376, and in the latter session was one of the nine lords specially chosen to afforce the royal Council. At the beginning of Richard II's reign, from 4 August 1377 to 16 March 1378, Guy was acting chief chamberlain to the young king, and he was one of only three lords who served on each of the parliamentary commissions of reform appointed during the sessions of 1379, 1380 and 1381. He was one of the feoffees and executors of Humphrey de Bohun, late earl of Hereford, and when, in May 1387, he was the surviving Bohun feoffee in the manor of Roding Margaret (Essex), the re-feoffment which he then made appointed Waldegrave as a feoffee along with Thomas Arundel, bishop of Ely and chancellor of England, and another old Bohun retainer and executor to the late earl, Sir John de Gildesburgh (Speaker in both the parliaments of 1380). Waldegrave's own daughter, Alice, married into the Brian family, being very probably the wife of Sir Guy's son and heir, another Guy, who died, some four years

[10] *CCR, 1385-9*, 116, 425-6; *CPR, 1401-5*, 377; *ibid., 1405-8*, 386.
[11] *CCR, 1374-7*, 229, 537-9.

before his father, in 1386. The connexion between Waldegrave and the elder Sir Guy had clearly at times been on a closely personal level and of some considerable importance to them both: on 1 June 1375 Sir Guy entered into two recognisances, undertaking in one to pay Waldegrave 500 marks, and in the second to pay £2000 at Michaelmas 1376.[12]

When this second Brian bond fell due, Sir Richard de Waldegrave had just served for the first time as knight of the shire for Suffolk in the Good Parliament of April—July 1376. He was then about thirty-eight years old. His fellow-knight was Sir William Wingfield, who, although fifty years of age, was also acting in this capacity for the first time. The daughter of the cousin of Sir William Wingfield (Katherine) had married Sir Michael de la Pole, chancellor of England from 1383 to 1386 and created earl of Suffolk in 1385, and Sir William was certainly later on closely connected with the De la Pole family.[13] He may very well have represented the De la Pole interest in Suffolk, for which he was to be returned to half of the parliaments sitting between 1376 and 1390. However this may be, Waldegrave and Wingfield were elected together in that period to no fewer than nine parliaments, Waldegrave serving in those fourteen years on three other occasions with a different partner, Wingfield once only. Four times, in 1382 and 1383, they were re-elected together.

When first returned to Suffolk in 1376 Waldegrave, with his estates in the west of the county and in the Stour valley and with his Bohun connexions, was probably well known in the region. But his interest in local administration, especially so far as the Crown was concerned, had been negligible, and not until the end of 1382 was he to be made a justice of the peace in Suffolk. Before 1376, in fact, Waldegrave had served on only two royal commissions: one by patent of 16 May 1371, when with a group of Lincolnshire notables, headed by the bishop of Lincoln, he was appointed to value the property of the nuns of the Gilbertine house of Sempringham, whose rights were being disregarded by the master, prior and canons, and to provide for the nuns' proper maintenance; the other, by patent of 18 March 1375, when he was associated with

---

[12] T. F. Tout, *Chapters in Medieval Administrative History*, vols. III and IV, *passim*; *CPR, 1401-5*, 377 (In 1404, of these feoffees in Roding Margaret only Arundel, the dowager countess's younger brother, now archbishop of Canterbury, and Waldegrave were still alive); *CCR, 1422-9*, 126 (Guy son and heir of Sir Guy de Brian, certainly married an Alice who was executrix to her father-in-law, see *The Complete Peerage*, II. 362); *CCR, 1374-7*, 229.

[13] In 1392 he witnessed deeds of the earl of Suffolk's heir, in April 1396 was his feoffee, and in October 1396 was godfather to his younger son, William, who was to become earl in 1415 and duke of Suffolk in 1448 (*Complete Peerage*, XII, part 1, p. 443).

Chief Justice Cavendish and William Wingfield in an oyer and terminer following some assaults in his own neighbourhood at Polstead. After his election to the Good Parliament of 1376 Waldegrave began to find employment on short-term, royal commissions in East Anglia.   On 29 April and again on 1 July 1377 he was made a commissioner of array in Suffolk to help meet the threat of French invasion, and in the meantime (on 16 June) was appointed to act on an oyer and terminer after complaints by Bishop Despenser of Norwich of attacks on him and his men in his own borough of Bishop's Lynn.[14]

Waldegrave sat in Richard II's first parliament of October 1377, to which a remarkable number (one out of every three) of the knights of the shire of the Good Parliament were once again returned.   He took the opportunity of the visit to London to get a royal patent on the day before the dissolution of the parliament (4 December 1377), which exempted him for life from serving on juries or in the offices of mayor, sheriff, escheator, coroner, collector of parliamentary subsidies, and so on, against his will.   He seems to have managed to do much more, for it was now that he became attached to the Ricardian court.   If he needed influence to get himself placed in the royal household, other than his own, it is likely that he could call on the new chief chamberlain, Sir Guy de Brian, and perhaps on Warin de Waldegrave, an esquire who steadily served the young king's half-brother (John Holland, later earl of Huntingdon) and who was almost certainly a kinsman of Sir Richard's.   Conjectures on one side, by the time the parliament was over Waldegrave had been retained as a 'King's knight', and on 6 December 1377 (the day after the dissolution), as staying with the king with the approval of the royal council, he was granted for life the custody of the castle and lands of Moresende (Northants), recently enjoyed by Alice Perrers, Edward III's mistress, whose condemnation to forfeiture in the Good Parliament had been renewed during the recent parliamentary session.[15]

---

[14] *CPR, 1370-4*, 110; *ibid., 1374-7*, 144, 497, 502; *ibid., 1377-81*, 38.

[15] *ibid., 1377-81*, 73-4.   In June 1386 the Speaker was a feoffee of Waryn de Walgrave in John Holland's Yorkshire manor of Langton.   In February 1391 he shared with John Holland, Warin Waldegrave and others, a grant of the manor of Milton by Gravesend (Kent), forfeited by Sir Simon Burley in 1388 (*CPR, 1388-92*, 418).   Warin was an unusual name, but it was current in Sir Richard's family.   I have not been able to establish the precise nature of the kinship between this Warin and the Speaker.   Warin was an esquire of John Holland as early as March 1378, when a *donum* was paid at the Lower Exchequer to Holland 'per manus Warini Waldegrave armigeri sui' (Issue Rolls, *PRO*, E 403/465, mem. 17, cf. E 403/499, mem. 17).   In 1385 Warin was Holland's feoffee in Westmorland and Yorkshire (*CCR, 1392-6*, 224), and in 1394 in Holland's manor of Great Gaddesden (Herts) when it was being granted to the nunnery of Dartford (Kent) (*CPR, 1391-6*, 373).   In February 1392,

This custody or stewardship of Moresende castle and manor was confirmed to Waldegrave on 1 February 1378, but then for only nine years and in return for a rent (equivalent to its 'extended' value) payable in the Exchequer. This rent was altered to (or defined as) 40 marks a year in December 1380. Parliament was then meeting at Northampton, and the writ was dated there. Presumably Waldegrave was in the town, but he was not a knight of the shire. His occupation of Moresende at one point, in August 1378 (following a commission of inquiry as to what was included in his grant and its value), had been actually threatened by a resumption, but clearly he had come to terms.[16] Shortly afterwards he was re-elected to parliament and was over at Gloucester on this account for the autumn parliament of 1378.

Waldegrave was not returned to any of the three parliaments of the next two years (1379-80), but he served in the meantime on quite a number of local commissions by royal appointment. On 8 August 1379 he was made an investigator of under-assessments to the poll-tax and evasions of it in Suffolk. He was one of those ordered, on 14 October following, to arrest and bring before the royal Council Edmund Bromfield and those who had abetted him in his installation as abbot of Bury St. Edmunds; Bromfield had secured his provision to the abbacy by Pope Urban VI contrary to the result of a capitular election (which had been confirmed by the King) and in contempt of the statute of Provisors and the royal authority.[17]

In February 1380 Sir Richard was present at the Blackfriars in London when (by order of the parliament then sitting) an examination of the facts at issue in the case of Thomas, son of Sir Robert Roos, *versus* John earl of Pembroke and William lord Zouche of Haringworth took place before the King's justices. Pembroke and Zouche had petitioned in parliament as the heirs of Sir William de Cantilupe, after being impleaded by Roos regarding certain lands in Yorkshire alleged to have been granted him by Cantilupe by means of an enfeoffment; the examination revealed that the enfeoffment was conditional on Cantilupe's not returning from one of John of Gaunt's military expeditions and that, because he did

---

Footnote 15 continued

  described as of Northants, Warin was Holland's mainpernor in a grant of wardship (*ibid.*, 20). Further, it was as Holland's servant and at his request that Warin was exempted for life from jury service, etc., in January 1394 (*ibid.*, 361).

[16] *CFR, 1377-83*, 50, 68, 222; *CCR, 1377-81*, 152; *CPR, 1377-81*, 250.

[17] *CFR, 1377-83*, 163; *CPR, 1377-81*, 420. (For the subsequent long dispute with the papacy over the abbacy which only ended in 1385, unsuccessfully for Bromfield, see Dugdale, *Monasticon Anglicanum*, III., 110).

return, the enfeoffment was annulled and surrendered. Waldegrave was one of Pembroke's tenants in Northants and it is possible
that he was present at the inquiry as counsel to the young earl
and even to Lord Zouche as well, for he was well known to the
latter; but he was more probably there as a king's knight, perhaps
in support of Sir Guy de Brian who was also present with the
Chief Baron of the Exchequer and some royal sergeants-at-law.[18]

Not long after this incident, on 20 March 1380, Waldegrave
was included on a commission of array in Suffolk, against the
contingency of a French invasion, and on 15 April on a commission
to inquire into the alleged extortion of fines from the men of Sudbury
(Essex) at an unlicensed weekly market set up at Colchester by
the town bailiffs. He had not been elected to the parliament of
January 1380. Nor was he elected to the second parliament of
the year which met at Northampton from 5 November to 6 December; it is, however, very likely that he was in attendance here as
a member of the royal court, especially because of his interests in
the county—a licence to elect an abbot of St. John's, Colchester,
was authorised by a patent dated at Moresende on 27 November
and warranted by a signet letter, and it looks as though either
the keeper of the signet (Robert Braybrooke) or Archbishop
Sudbury, the chancellor, stayed with Waldegrave there, for
accommodation in Northampton itself is known to have been
difficult to get during the parliament.[19]

On 16 March 1381 Waldegrave was appointed to serve on
the commission set up to investigate instances in Essex of under-
assessment to (and evasion of) the triple poll-tax voted in the
Northampton parliament, as he had been in Suffolk nearly two
years earlier. He does not appear to have suffered to any remarkable extent in the Peasants' Revolt, which this poll-tax and these
inspectoral commissions especially did so much to foment, although
south Suffolk was thrown into turmoil in the late spring of 1381
and Bures St. Mary itself was in some measure affected by the
rising. The crisis of the rebellion was virtually over when on
24 June Waldegrave was appointed with others to inquire into and
restore the losses in Norfolk suffered by John Helyng, who had been
an usher of the King's chamber for nearly forty years, had only
recently vacated the office of steward of the liberty of the abbey of
Bury St. Edmunds, and was still bailiff-itinerant of Norwich.
The princess of Wales, the King's mother, Joan of Kent, had
certain of her Essex manors ransacked and destroyed, and on

---

[18] *Rot. Parl.*, iii. 79b. (On 21 October 1382 he attested an important deed of
Lord Zouche, *CCR, 1381-5*, 220).
[19] *CPR, 1377-81*, 472, 475, 560.

14 September 1381 Waldegrave was accordingly put on an inquiry into this damage with authority to imprison offenders.[20]

To the first parliament to meet after the rising, summoned eventually for 3 November 1381, Waldegrave was elected as knight of the shire for Suffolk for the fourth time. The Commons chose him to be their Speaker. This may not have been at the very outset of the session. On 18 November he asked to be excused of the office, the first of the Speakers to do what soon became common form, but he was charged by the King to continue and so made his 'protestation'. At that point of the session the Commons were 'en partie de variance', regarding what they had been ordered to offer advice about, and Sir Richard Scrope, the new Chancellor, recapitulated the Commons' 'charge', especially on the subject of the repeal of Richard II's letters of manumission to the peasants. The result was a mass parliamentary declaration in favour of their annulment. The session was otherwise noteworthy for the Commons' resumption of the practice (in abeyance since 1378) of seeking a liaison committee from the Lords; for the rejected claim of the Commons to receive a report of the Lords' advice to the King before they put forward their own; for the refusal of the Commons to make any grant of direct taxation; and for the difficulties which they testily raised over the renewal of the wool subsidies and on the subject of the King's pardon for those involved in the Peasants' Revolt. During the session, on 16 November, William Lord Zouche was one of the witnesses to a grant to Waldegrave of certain lands and rents in Hannington (Northants).[21]

After the King's wedding to Anne of Bohemia and her coronation in January 1382, parliament reassembled for another session—after the first parliamentary adjournment of the reign—and this second session lasted from 27 January to 25 February, when the wool subsidy was renewed until mid-summer 1386. Again, however, economy was the keynote of suggestions for governmental reform. In the meantime, on the day after the close of the first session, on 14 December 1381, Waldegrave had been appointed to a commission to keep the peace and suppress, with armed force if necessary, any rebels in Suffolk. This commission was renewed after the second parliamentary session, by patent of 8 March 1382, and once again on 21 December 1382, at these times with larger powers, including the authority to call out the *posse comitatus* and punish those failing to assist.[22]

[20] *CFR, 1377-83*, 249; A. Réville, *Le Soulèvement des travailleurs en Angleterre en 1381*, 60; *CPR, 1381-85*, 76, 78.
[21] *CCR, 1381-5*, 92.
[22] *CPR, 1381-5*, 86, 141, 247.

Waldegrave and his fellow shire-knight in the previous parliament, Sir William Wingfield, were both re-elected to the Westminster parliament of May 1382. The two men were apparently on very good terms and at least on this occasion lodged together in Fleet Street at the 'Swerd of the Hoope'. Here on 8 May, the second day of the parliamentary session, two 'trussyng cofres' of Waldegrave's, containing jewels worth 40 marks and his seal, were stolen; a couple of days later Waldegrave informed the Chancellor in case his seal should be misused, and his fellow shire-knight attested the truth of the matter. The name of the Speaker in this parliament has not come down to us; and there is no knowing whether or not Waldegrave was re-elected to the office, as Sir John Gildesburgh had been in 1380. How closely Waldegrave had become attached by this time to the developing court party, is made clear by the fact that sometime before November 1382 he was appointed as steward of the lands of Richard II's Queen, Anne of Bohemia. Just when the appointment was made is not known. But it was in this capacity that, on 1 November 1382, he and John Bacon, chamberlain of the Exchequer (and also keeper of the King's signet), were authorised by the Exchequer to have oversight of the prior of Eye as farmer of the priory, a dependency of the Norman abbey of Bernai. Queen Anne was patron of this alien priory, having been granted in May 1382 (as part of her dower) the honour of Eye. Incidentally, she had also then been granted the castle and manor of Moresende (Northants) of which Waldegrave was the lessee. Hence, perhaps, his inclusion amongst her officials.[23]

To the short parliament of 6-24 October 1382 Waldegrave and Wingfield had been (for a second time) re-elected for Suffolk. During the session Waldegrave was witness to charters of grants or enfeoffments respectively made by William Lord Zouche of Haringworth and Sir Simon Burley, the King's under-chamberlain and close friend.[24] On 20 December following, for the first time he was included in the commission of the peace for Suffolk. Then, for the third time running, he and Wingfield were re-elected to parliament in February 1383. Just before and during the session he stood surety in Chancery for a Northamptonshire man, Andrew Brown of Glapthorn, who was being sued for debt by three of his creditors, two of them local men, one a London goldsmith.[25] On 15 March, within a week of the end of the parliament, Waldegrave was put on a royal commission of inquiry into a complaint of a daughter and coheir of Sir John d'Argenten and her husband,

[23] *CCR, 1381-5*, 130; *CFR, 1377-83*, 330.
[24] *CCR, 1381-5*, 220, 620.
[25] *CPR, 1381-5*, 254; *CCR, 1381-5*, 283.

Sir Ivo FitzWaryn, of an assault made by her bastard half-brother, William d'Argenten, on them and their friends at the burial of Sir John at Halesworth (Suffolk) in the previous November, and of the seizure of the prior of the Austin canons of Wymondley (Herts) at Newmarket Heath, when on his way to the funeral, so that he was forced to send for and surrender certain deeds entrusted to his custody at the priory by the late Sir John who was patron of the house.[26] A fortnight or so later, Sir Richard was appointed to an inquiry into certain concealments and withdrawals of rents and services pertaining to the two Suffolk hundreds of Blything and Wangford, both held by royal grant by a former yeoman of the household of the Black Prince and a servant of Richard II before and since the beginning of his reign (William Joce).

It was in the next year, on 10 May 1384, that, directly warranted by a letter under the royal signet, Waldegrave's grant by special grace of the right of free warren in the demesnes of his principal manors in Northants, Suffolk and Essex, passed the great seal (Sir Michael de la Pole had been chancellor since 13 March 1383). On the very same day, again solely by signet warrant, Waldegrave secured a licence under the great seal to crenellate his manor-house of Smallbridge at Bures St. Mary.[27] These grants were made at Clarendon in the middle of the Salisbury parliament, the first parliament for two and a half years to which Waldegrave had not been returned. (For the fourth successive time, he and Wingfield had been together re-elected to the autumn parliament of 1383.)

In view of the support which Richard II had every reason in these years to hope for and encourage in the City of London, it is interesting to note that when, on 7 February 1384, John Northampton (the duke of Lancaster's man in city politics) had led a great number of the London gildsmen through Cheapside intending to overturn his successor in the mayoralty, Nicholas Brembre, news of the riot was brought to the latter when he was at dinner with Sir William Walworth, Sir John Philipot, and other aldermen, at Sir Richard Waldegrave's house in St. Michael Hoggenlane.[28] Brembre was, of course, to identify himself completely three years later with the party of the prerogative and, in 1388, to suffer condemnation for treason because of his support for the King. Incidentally, it looks as though Waldegrave had bought himself a town-house in the City since the 'accident' of May 1382.

---

[26] *CPR, 1381-5*, 260.
[27] *ibid.*, 261, 410; *CChR*, V. 293.
[28] Ruth Bird, *The Turbulent London of Richard II*, 83.

Waldegrave's local interests in East Anglia were, however, now being considerably stimulated and extended by his court connexions. In the middle of September 1384 he was included in a commission to inquire into rebellions and attacks on royal officials at Lowestoft and to bring before Chancery all those indicted. He was associated on 10 February 1385 in an investigation regarding the King's rights over certain sands in Mersea Island in Essex, with a view to exploiting the fishing there. (The commission was later postponed until Easter.) On 14 April following he was put on a commission of oyer and terminer following an appeal in a ransom case pending before the Court of the Constable and Marshal. Five days later, he was appointed to take the musters of the forces under the command of the two admirals, the prior of St. John of Jerusalem and Sir Thomas Percy, brother of the earl of Northumberland. A week later still, on 26 April, he was made a commissioner of array in Suffolk, part of the general measures to meet a threatened French invasion; strict orders to proceed with the array were sent out in the middle of June.[29] Serious though the French threat was, Richard II led a short campaign into Scotland in the late summer. Waldegrave went on the expedition in the King's own company with a retinue of 7 men-at-arms and 18 archers.[30]

For the greater part of this year Sir Richard was a member of a small syndicate of four, of whom he was the most important, granted the custody of the temporalities of the bishop of Norwich, Henry Despenser, who had been sentenced in the parliament of 1383 to undergo this form of forfeiture for his failure to perform his military contracts with the King in his unsuccessful Flemish crusade of that year. Farmed for over a year by the escheators of Norfolk, Suffolk, Essex and Hertfordshire, the temporalities of the see were on 22 February 1385 granted by the Council to Waldegrave, Sir Edmund de Thorpe, William Winter, and Richard Wayte, to be held at farm for a yearly rent of 500 marks payable in the Exchequer, for as long as they should be in the King's hands. Early in the next parliament, on 24 October 1385, at the request of the neighbouring bishop of Ely (Thomas Arundel), Despenser's temporalities were restored, not (if we may believe the St. Albans chronicler) without opposition or ill-will from the Chancellor, De la Pole, now recently created earl of Suffolk; Waldegrave and his fellow-lessees were given orders for their livery.[31]

---

[29] *CPR, 1381-5*, 503, 587 (cf. *CCR, 1381-5*, 613), 596, 589 (cf. *CCR. 1381-5*, 556); T. Carte, *Catalogue des Rolles Gascons, Normans et François*, II. 149.

[30] Issue Rolls, *PRO*, E 403/508, mem. 21. (On 19 August 1385 he was advanced £40 'in partibus borealibus' by two tellers of the Exchequer).

[31] *CCR, 1385-9*, 4; *CFR, 1383-91*, 86; *CPR, 1385-9*, 34.

During the session—Waldegrave was for a third time running not elected—he was on 26 November included in an oyer and terminer commission with powers of imprisonment, appointed following a report that the bond tenants of Little Haugh (Suffolk) claimed to be free and had formed a sworn league to refuse their customary services. As a result of a petition in the parliament, to which the King and Lords assented, an assize of novel disseisin against the abbot of Bury St. Edmunds was superseded; Waldegrave was one of the justices taking the assize.[32] On 6 June 1386 he was on a commission to arrest the archdeacon of Sudbury and bring him before the Council (the order being, however, cancelled three weeks later). He was put on a commission of array for Suffolk on 18 June against the possible event of a French invasion.

No more than five days before the only parliament of this year met on 1 October, and when Waldegrave and Wingfield were almost certainly already knights of the shire-elect for Suffolk once more, the Suffolk commissioners of array were told of the special danger from the French invasion forces to the port of Orwell, and were ordered to follow the instructions of two knights of the Chamber purposely sent down to inspect that port and neighbouring harbours.[33] The threat perhaps, the panic in England certainly, was real enough, and this helps us to an understanding of the crisis out of which arose a threat to depose the King and the successful impeachment of the Chancellor, De la Pole.

In the increasing political bitterness of the next two years there is no cause to think that Waldegrave, despite his close associations with the Court and the curialist party, needed to plot and steer any difficult course. He had many links with both sides in the big constitutional and political crisis that was blowing up. On 15 October 1386 he was prepared to back with his testimony Richard Lord Scrope's claim in the heraldic plea which had been raised in the Scottish campaign of 1385 between this magnate and a Cheshire knight, Sir Robert Grosvenor—he had been, in fact, one of the commissioners to take evidence nominated by Scrope to the Constable on 28 May 1386.[34] Lord Scrope, it is true, was brother-in-law of the impeached Chancellor and spoke in his defence in the Lords, but he was also to be a member of the parliamentary commission which this 1386 session produced, and to which the King was to take such strong exception on the ground that its appointment was even an act of treason. Waldegrave soon became, moreover, indirectly connected with the new (and

[32] *CPR, 1385-9*, 88; *CCR, 1385-9*, 106.
[33] *CPR, 1385-9*, 179, 256; 176, 214.
[34] N. H. Nicolas, *The Scrope v. Grosvenor Controversy*, I. 49, 165-6.

to the King unwelcome) Chancellor, Thomas Arundel, bishop of Ely, when on 15 May 1387 he and the bishop were made co-feoffees in the manor of Roding Margaret and other Bohun property in Essex. Another of the co-feoffees was the former Speaker of 1380, Sir John Gildesburgh of Essex, an old Bohun retainer (like Waldegrave himself) who had joined the affinity of Thomas of Woodstock, the foremost of the opposition magnates; by April 1388 Waldegrave was one of Gildesburgh's own feoffees.[35] He was also feoffee to Joan, dowager countess of Hereford, the widow of Humphrey de Bohun (who had died in 1373) and sister of Richard, earl of Arundel, and of the new Chancellor.[36] In November 1387 the earl was to join Woodstock as an Appellant against the chief members of the royalist party. Before the appeal was brought before the Merciless Parliament in February 1388, Woodstock, Arundel and Warwick had been joined as Appellants by the earl of Derby (Henry of Bolingbroke, Lancaster's heir) and Thomas Mowbray, earl of Nottingham. When, on 9 December 1386, a commision of oyer and terminer was appointed, following a complaint by Mowbray of assaults on his men at Witchingham in Norfolk, Waldegrave was a member of the commission, quite possibly by Mowbray's nomination. Whether Waldegrave was still the Queen's steward of estates is not known, but his connexions with the Court were, of course, of long standing by this time. He certainly knew well, as we have seen, at least one of the appellees of 1387-8, the ex-mayor of London, Sir Nicholas Brembre, to whom he was also feoffee-to-uses at Northholt and Down (Middlesex), estates which were forfeited by Brembre's conviction in the Merciless Parliament but restored to the feoffees in March 1396.[37]

What Waldegrave's attitude was to the events of 1386-8, it is not possible to say with any certainty. But judging from the commissions he was appointed to serve while the parliamentary commission was in control of the royal authority he was not regarded as 'unsafe' from its own point of view. On 28 April and again on 24 July 1387 he was appointed justice of the peace in Suffolk, and on 23 and 30 May he was made by the Council a member of inquiries into the smuggling of wine to Flanders from Orwell and from other east coast ports, from the Thames northwards.[38] Moreover, ten years or so later, in November 1397, he saw fit to take out a general pardon for all past treasons (and other offences) which it is difficult to imagine him having committed in other

[35] *CPR, 1401-5,* 377; *CCR, 1392-6,* 442; *ibid., 1385-9,* 623, 632, 638, 645; *ibid., 1389-92,* 71; *ibid., 1392-6,* 253.
[36] *CCR, 1385-9,* 116, 425-6.
[37] *CPR, 1385-9,* 264; *ibid., 1391-6,* 690.
[38] *ibid., 1385-9,* 254, 324-5, 385.

circumstances than those of 1387-8.[39]   He was, besides, re-elected
knight of the shire for Suffolk to both the Merciless Parliament of
February 1388 and to the Cambridge parliament of the following
September.   Nevertheless, it was not until after Richard II had
re-asserted himself against the Appellants in May 1389 that Waldegrave derived any direct profit from the forfeitures resulting from
the condemnations of the Merciless Parliament.   This was by no
means considerable: on 10 July 1389, by assent of the Great Council
and for 700 marks paid to the King's use, he was one of a syndicate
of sixteen (almost all Essex notables) who received an out-and-out
grant of the manor of Sacombe (Herts), forfeited by Sir John Holt,
Justice of Common Pleas, as a result of the judgement against him
in the Merciless Parliament; not until May 1398, after the annulment of the acts of this parliament, was Holt restored against the
grantees of 1389 (of whom only half were now alive).   On 16
February 1391 Waldegrave shared with the King's half-brother and
son-in-law of the duke of Lancaster, John Holland (since 1388 earl
of Huntingdon), his own presumed kinsman, Warin de Waldegrave
(an old servant of Holland's), and a few others, a grant of the manor
of Milton by Gravesend, which had been forfeited by Sir Simon
de Burley after his condemnation in the Merciless Parliament
nearly three years before.[40]   On 15 July 1389 Waldegrave had
been made for the first and only time a justice of the peace for
Essex.   He was not re-appointed when the commission was re-
constituted on 10 November following, but he was then again
appointed a justice for Suffolk and in this capacity he was to act
until the end of the reign, being re-appointed in June 1390,
December 1391, February 1392, January 1393, June 1394, December 1396, and July 1397.[41]

Waldegrave never again served as knight of the shire after
his third re-election running to the first parliament of Richard
II's majority, that of January 1390; this was the twelfth parliament
that he had attended in fourteen years, and the eighth time that
he had been re-elected.   Apart from his regular activity as J.P.
in Suffolk, he served on a number of local commissions in the next
few years.   He was a member of a commission of oyer and terminer
set up on 11 October 1390 to inquire into a complaint of the grandmother of the earl of Nottingham, Margaret, dowager countess of
Norfolk, of breach of her closes and park and theft of chattels
worth £700 at Chesterford (on the border of Essex and Cambridgeshire).   On 8 February following he was put on another inquiry

[39] Ancient Petitions, PRO, SC8, file 252, no. 12555; *CPR, 1396-9*, 184.
[40] *CPR, 1388-92*, 80; *CCR, 1396-9*, 276; *CPR, 1388-92*, 380.
[41] *CPR, 1388-92*, 135, 139, 342, 525-6; *ibid., 1391-6*, 292, 439; *ibid., 1396-9*,
96, 229.

into close-breaking in Suffolk, and on 24 November 1391 he was told by the Council to make certain arrests. In March 1392 he was included in a commission of array in Suffolk, and in July following in an abortive commission (it was enrolled in Chancery but not delivered) to investigate in Suffolk the export trade in English gold coins which was yielding those exploiting it a 20% profit (according to Chancery information). In January 1393 he served on an inquiry into a petition of Aubrey, uncle and heir of the recently deceased Robert de Vere, duke of Ireland, Richard II's former favourite, who had fled to Flanders at the end of 1387 rather than face the Appellants in the Merciless Parliament, where he had nevertheless been sentenced to forfeiture for treason; Aubrey claimed certain of the forfeitures in Cambridgeshire, Middlesex and Essex, as automatically exempt under an entail of 1341.[42].

In February 1391, as co-grantee of Sir Simon de Burley's manor of Milton by Gravesend, Sir Richard de Waldegrave was referred to as 'senior', and henceforward a number of private deeds to which they were party differentiate between a Richard 'senior' and a Richard 'junior', a Richard 'the father' and a Richard 'the son'. (Over a century four successive heads of the family were, in fact, all called Richard and were all knights.) The grant of Milton by Gravesend apart, no other official record of Sir Richard the Speaker's activities during the last 20 years of his life, whether in letters patent, letters close, or in notices in Council memoranda, etc., draw any distinction between him and his son, who was also a knight. Not all of the references made simply to a plain Sir Richard de Waldegrave can be, therefore, safely taken to allude to the Speaker. It is reasonably certain, however, that the Sir Richard who on 2 November 1393, as a King's knight, was appointed by the King to be attendant on the Council (that is, to be a member of it) with a fee of 100 marks a year, and who on the same day was retained for life to stay with the King with another additional annuity of £40, was the erstwhile Speaker; warranted by letters of privy seal and with the assent of the Council, both grants passed the great seal as letters patent on 22 May 1394. Both annuities were quite certainly granted to one and the same man: half-yearly instalments of both were regularly paid simultaneously to the one Sir Richard at the Lower Exchequer.[43]

Still a member of the Council certainly as late as the end of the year of 1397, Waldegrave was one of that group of knights and esquires (especially conspicuous among whom later on were the

[42] *CPR, 1388-92*, 349, 437, 527; *ibid., 1391-6*, 88, 166 (cf. *CCR, 1392-6*, 287), 236.
[43] *CPR, 1391-6*, 414, 415; Issue Rolls, PRO., E 403/548, mem. 9; *ibid.*, 549, mem. 7; *ibid.*, 551, mem. 8; *ibid.*, 554, mem. 9.

notorious triumvirate, Sir John Bussy, Sir Henry Green, and Sir William Bagot) who were being introduced into Richard II's Council from the middle of the last decade of the reign onwards and who came to be much relied upon by the King in his bid for autocratic power, men of considerable efficiency, expertise, and technical endowment. It was upon such men that the extensive judicial functions being assumed at this time by the Council mainly depended. In this connexion it is interesting to note that, sometime between March 1395 and the end of the year 1397, there was pending before Waldegrave and Lawrence Dru esquire (who by the later date was a member of the royal Council 'en cas coursables de la ley et non pas autrement') the appeal of treason originally laid before the Council by Richard Piryman against John Cavendish, a fishmonger of London, both of whom were in the prison of the King's Bench; late in 1397 Cavendish petitioned that the process should be transferred for determination to the Court of the Constable and Marshal, but the King merely turned the matter over to the Council.[44] Occasionally in 1396 and 1397 Waldegrave was put on commissions to hear appeals against judgements given in those now very rapidly expanding prerogative courts, the Court of the Constable and Marshal (*alias* the Court of Chivalry) and the Court of Admiralty.[45]

In these years of his membership of the King's Council, apart from his being a justice of the peace for Suffolk, Waldegrave was very much more free (than had formerly been the case) from royal commissions of local significance. In fact, the only local commissions of a casual sort of which he was a member after he joined the Council were a commission set up in August 1395 to inquire (in two Suffolk hundreds) into cases of concealment of rents and services and one appointed some two months or so later to investigate a case of treasure trove at Stowmarket. In the meantime, local ties were doubtless the cause of his being chosen by his neighbour, Sir John Howard, in August 1394 to be one of his attorneys in England during his absence with Richard II's first expedition to Ireland. In July 1397 Waldegrave was to act in a similar capacity for Roger Mortimer, earl of March, who was about to proceed to Ireland as the King's lieutenant.[46]

[44] *PPC*, i. 77-8; J. F. Baldwin, *The King's Council during the Middle Ages*, 142, 504 (Not until 1397 did Sir Henry Grene become the King's retainer, but as a Northants man he was already known to Waldegrave who, in February 1394, was one of his mainpernors in Chancery when Grene undertook not to 'maintain' his young nephew, Thomas, in a legal suit pending in the Common Bench, *CCR, 1392-6*, 260.)
[45] *CPR, 1396-9*, 23, 58, 83, 89, 165.
[46] *ibid., 1391-6*, 650, 652, 507; *ibid., 1396-9*, 186.

Between the sessions of Richard II's last parliament, in which the King took his revenge on his opponents of 1387-8 and established his absolute rule, Waldegrave, despite his membership of the Council, saw fit to re-insure himself personally against all eventualities by petitioning for and securing on 14 November 1397 a patent granting him a general pardon for all past treasons, insurrections against his allegiance, felonies, champerties, maintenances, procurements of false indictments, etc., of which he could ever be indicted, appealed, or impeached. On the very same day he also secured a patent of exemption for life from service on certain types of royal commission and in certain royal offices, an exemption drawn in larger terms than the one he had taken out in 1378; he was now, for example, freed from the liability to service as a justice of the peace, justice of labourers, and commissioner of array.[47] On 3 April 1398 he was one of 28 persons, for particular causes moving the King and Council, separately ordered (under penalty of £200) to lay aside all excuse and appear before the Council at Westminster on 21 April to declare what the Council should lay before them at their coming. It is, of course, possible that in the troubles of 1387-8 Waldegrave had acted with a degree of circumspection which now exposed him again, in spite of the general pardon he had obtained in November 1397, to some form of recrimination. But it is more likely that he and the others summoned to appear before the Council were among these 'certaines sufficiantz gentz' of London and sixteen counties of S.E. and S. England (Suffolk and Essex among them) required to swear oaths to maintain the acts of the parliament of 1397-8 and, again acting as the proctors of their shires, to submit the people thereof to the King as having behaved like traitors (*tanquam proditores*), in order to afford the King a pretext for extorting great fines to buy back his goodwill. The resulting fines or 'plesaunces' are said to have been either £1000 or 1000 marks for each shire.[48] Whether Waldegrave continued to be a member of the Council in this time of mounting dissatisfaction with Richard II's autocratic tendencies is not known, but it is perhaps significant that he now falls out of sight until after the revolution of 1399, when Richard II was deposed in favour of Henry of Bolingbroke.

By this time turned sixty years of age, Waldegrave seems to have virtually abandoned political life. He was never again to occupy a position on the Suffolk bench of justices and neither was his son, Sir Richard. Whether it was the father or the son who was appointed to an oyer and terminer commission following a

[47] *CPR, 1396-9*, 184, 262; Ancient Petitions, PRO., SC 8, file 252, no. 12555; *ibid.*, file 221, no. 11004.
[48] *CCR, 1396-9*, 277; M. V. Clarke, *Fourteenth Century Studies*, 105-6, 112-4.

breach of close at the priory of Earl's Colne in November 1400, who served on a commission of array for the defence of the Suffolk coast in the summer of 1402, or who attended a Great Council along with 13 other knights from East Anglia, is not clear.[49] The father was in November 1403 the only one of the feoffees (by deed of 15 May 1387) of the Bohun manor of Roding Margaret (Essex) to have survived, apart from Thomas Arundel, archbishop of Canterbury, and these two remaining feoffees then granted the manor to Henry IV who granted it in mortmain to the Great Hall in the University of Oxford. On 16 October 1404, during the Coventry parliament, Sir Richard saw fit to secure an *inspeximus* and confirmation of the patent (taken out nearly seven years before) exempting him for life from being made to serve on royal commissions against his will.[50]

The upsets, domestic, political and military, of Henry IV's reign did not touch the old Sir Richard nor, for that matter, his son, who did, however, take part in 1402 in the capture of Couquet and the isle of Rhé in Brittany. In November 1405 both father and son, formerly bound with others in £2000 to Sir Thomas Rempston, K.G. (an east Midlands magnate, who had been a member of Bolingbroke's retinue before his accession and, since then, constable of the Tower and a member of the Council), had a release of all actions following their quitclaim to Rempston of the Lincolnshire manor of Brant Boughton, seemingly in exchange for certain manors (near Bures St. Mary) in Polstead and Leavenheath and certain property in London. On 28 June 1406 a Sir Richard de Waldegrave was made a commissioner of inquiry in East Anglia into concealments of profits and extortions by all local royal officials who rendered accounts in the Exchequer, into the value of all royal sources of income demised at farm, and into annuities and other charges on these sources, and on the same date was made a commissioner for raising Crown loans; whether this was the father or the son it is again not possible to say. It is, however, almost certain that it was the former Speaker who on 22 January 1408 was one of the grantees of a royal licence to found a chantry in Foulness in Essex and to endow it with a small amortized estate belonging to the Bohun family; among Waldegrave's

---

[49] *CPR, 1399-1401*, 414; *ibid., 1401-5*, 114; *PPC*, ii. 86.

[50] *CPR, 1401-5*, 377, 482. In 1405, according to the St. Albans chronicler who was suitably impressed by the event, a dragon appeared near Sudbury, hard by the vill of Buryra (probably Bures), and the serfs of Sir Richard de Waldegrave, on whose demesne it was found, shot at it with arrows, but with no effect. After the whole *patria* had been summoned, it made off into a marsh and was not seen again. (*Annales Johannes de Trokelowe*, etc. (Rolls Series), ed. H. T. Riley, 402).

co-licensees were Archbishop Arundel and the dowager countess of Hereford, Joan de Bohun, the mother of Henry IV's first wife.[51]

Sir Richard did not long survive this last transaction. On 22 April 1410, as 'Richard de Waldegrave, knight, senior', he made his will at Smallbridge (Suffolk), providing for his burial on the north side of the parish church of Bures next his wife, Joan, who had predeceased him in 1406. He made certain bequests of money and vestments to the church and its clergy, of vestments to the church of Walgrave (Northants), of a missal (recently bought in London) to the chapel of St. Stephen at Bures, and of a vestment to his chantry at Polstead. He gave £5 to the nearby Dominican priory at Sudbury; 5 marks to the Franciscans of Colchester and the same amount to the Augustinians of Clare; and 2½ marks each to the Carmelite and Franciscan houses at Ipswich. Separate bequests went to individual friars, including one of an annuity for life of £4. To his son, Richard, he left a missal, a chalice, and a vestment of white and red, perhaps a cloth of Richard II's livery whose colours these were. His executors, who were to have the rest of his personalty to dispose of, were rectors of parishes in the two dioceses where lay the bulk of his estates (London and Norwich): the rectors of Bulmer, Hetlingswell and Coney Weston. Walde-grave died on 2 May, and probate was granted by Archbishop Arundel, in virtue of his prerogative jurisdiction, at Ford near Canterbury on 28 May 1410.[52]

[51] *CCR, 1405-9*, 72-5; *CPR, 1405-8*, 154, 200, 386; *CCR, 1385-9*, 116.
[52] Lambeth Palace Library, Arundel Register, pars. II, fo. 49a. Blomefield (*History of Norfolk*, v. 1378) says that he died on 2 May 1400; a Harleian Society note of the epitaph on his tomb at Bures, that it was in 1400 (*Harleian Society*, XXXII, 295); Morant (*Essex*, I, 182a), that it was on 2 May 1401; N. H. Nicolas (*Testamenta Vetusta*, I, 158), that his will is dated 22 April 1401 and that he died 2 May 1401; and the *DNB* (XX, 477) that he died on 2 May 1402. The dates of the will and probate in Archbishop Arundel's Register are, however, conclusive evidence that it was in 1410 that Sir Richard the Speaker died.

3

SIR JOHN DOREWARD OF BOCKING:
SPEAKER IN 1399 AND 1413

In the medieval period, when the Speaker for the Commons in Parliament was invariably a representative of some county and not of a city or borough, Essex happened to elect more 'knights of the shire' who became Speakers than did any other county. There are six of them in all: Sir John de Gildesburgh of Wennington, Speaker in the two parliaments of 1380; John Doreward of Bocking, in 1399 and 1413; Richard Baynard of Messing, in 1421; Sir John Tyrell of East Horndon, in 1431 and 1437; Thomas Thorpe of Great Ilford, in 1453; and John Green of Widdington, in 1460.[1] Of these, John Doreward had not the most exciting career. Nevertheless, he was of some considerable importance in Essex in the late fourteenth and early fifteenth centuries, and far from being an insignificant figure at the centre of royal government at Westminster.

That Doreward was of some standing in Essex might be supposed from a mere catalogue of his estates in the county. The conjecture is confirmed by his election to represent Essex six times in less than twenty years: he was one of the two knights of the shire in the parliaments of January 1395, January 1397, October 1399, January 1404, May 1413, and April 1414.[2] Within the limits of this period only his friend, Sir William Coggeshall, sat for the county on so many occasions. Doreward was never sheriff in Essex, except for a few weeks before Richard II's deposition in 1399. Nor was he ever the king's escheator in the county. But he was a J.P. there, save for a year or two now and then, between 1386 and his death in 1420. Moreover, being also perhaps a lawyer, he was greatly in demand with a number of the noble families and local gentlemen of Essex as a feoffee-to-uses and in such-like capacities.

In the fourteenth century, whenever there was enmity between England and France (which was oftener the case than not), the Crown sequestrated the estates of those English monastic establishments that were dependent upon French abbeys, an action which was felt to be additionally justified at the end of the century, when there was a schism in the Papacy and England and France each obeyed a different pope. The treatment suffered by these 'alien priories' was a source of concern to the English clergy. This was at least partly because Wyclifite criticisms of the value of the monastic life were being used by some of the gentry to support a more general policy of ecclesiastical disendowment, a policy which was ostensibly designed to profit the Crown but which might be turned to their own private financial advantage. It was evidently fear of the effects of this development which resulted in Doreward being elected as Speaker in 1399, that is, during the parliament which met immediately after Richard II's deposition and Henry IV's accession. For then the clergy, prompted by Archbishop Arundel, found Sir John Cheyne, who was the Commons' first choice for the Speakership, objectionable as a Lollard and anti-clerical. Doreward himself was not above profiting from the royal sequestration of alien priory lands, as is shown by his acceptance of the estates of Mersea priory (by a grant for life) immediately after his first Speakership. But otherwise he was entirely 'reliable' from the ecclesiastical point of view. He had already been Steward of the great franchise of the abbey of Bury St. Edmunds in the early 1390s, was a founder of several chantries (to the benefit of more than one Essex monastery), and he had connections with Canterbury, with Christchurch priory as well as with Archbishop Arundel himself. He was also *persona grata* with the new King. Indeed, for the first half of Henry IV's reign (down to 1406), Doreward was a member of the Royal Council, one of a small group of commoners who in this capacity were acceptable to king and parliament alike. He was evidently a man of considerable ability. So far as we know (for there are gaps in the list of the early Speakers), he was the first Commons' Speaker who was not a knight by rank at the time of his election to the office.

Doreward, now no longer a royal councillor, was again made Speaker in Henry V's first parliament in 1413. But he was once more the Commons' second choice and only acted for the last week of a single session. This was after the Commons had expressed dissatisfaction at the attitude of William Stourton, their first Speaker in this parliament, which had been one of subservience to the king.

To the parliamentary historian, it is the contrast between the circumstances which brought about Doreward's two elections to the Speakership which make him chiefly memorable. In 1399 the Commons gave in to pressure from outside when objection was taken to the person of their Speaker; whereas in 1413 it was the Commons themselves who took exception to their Speaker, because in the conduct of his office he had given way to pressure from above. Doreward's election in Henry IV's first parliament suggests a rather subservient attitude on the part of the Commons; his election in Henry V's first parliament suggests that, in the meantime, the Commons had acquired some measure of independence.

By the end of the fourteenth century, the family of Doreward of Bocking, mainly as the result of a succession of suitable marriages, had come into possession of a considerable number of estates in Essex and East Anglia. These were for the most part situated in the eastern districts of Essex. John Doreward's lands, as inherited from his father (William Doreward) and augmented as a result of his own two marriages as well as by purchase, were comprised of the manors of Southall (in Great Dunmow) and Leaden Roding in west Essex; Rawreth in the south-east of the county; then, within easy reach of Doreward's Hall at Bocking and in a rough circle round Colchester, the lands which had come into possession of the family through the Speaker's mother (Joan, daughter and heir of John Oliver), namely, the manors of Olivers in Stanway and Trumpingtons in Great Tey, *plus* Stanway itself; the manors of Park Hall and Morells in Gosfield, and estates in Stisted, Braintree, Fordham, Copford, Bergholt, and Tendring; and, up in the north of the county, the manor of Great Yeldham (held of the honour of Clare and comprising three knights' fees) and the manors of Oldhall and Grapnels (in Great Yeldham). In 1410 Doreward and his son came to hold the manor of Wickhambrook in west Suffolk, where Doreward already had an estate at Haverhill, and in 1412 he and his second wife (Isabel), as a result of a quitclaim by a son of hers by her first marriage, entered into possession of the manor of Alfreston in Great Dunmow (Essex) and of the manors of Old Hall in West Tofts (for Isabel's life only) and Old Hall in Marham (Norfolk).[3] What Doreward's estates were worth is not known. But in 1436 (sixteen years after his death) his son and heir's estates were assessed at £255 a year. Doreward senior's holdings were probably worth more than this, including, as they did for the last twenty years of his life, the estates of West Mersea priory. In 1436 Doreward junior stood as high as fifth among Essex proprietors below baronial rank.[4]

John Doreward's first wife, and the mother of his son John, was Katherine, daughter of Sir William Walcot. She was still alive in March 1397.[5] His second wife (to whom he was married by 1399) was Isabel, daughter of John Baynard of Messing, widow of Walter Bygod (by whom she had had three daughters and at least one son, William Bygod); she was a kinswoman (almost certainly aunt) of Richard Baynard of Messing, knight of the shire for Essex in 1406, 1414, 1421 (when he was Speaker), 1423, 1427, and 1433.[6]

Although John Doreward had interests outside of Essex and wider vistas still were opened up in his career when he was a member of the King's Council in the first half of Henry IV's reign, his main concerns were as an influential member of the land-owning society of the county in which was concentrated the bulk of his numerous landed estates. How considerable was his local standing is sufficiently well attested not only by his election to parliament for Essex on altogether six occasions but also by the way in which his services as a feoffee-to-uses were so very much sought after by members of both the local nobility and the squirearchy of Essex. As early as June 1384 he was a feoffee of Sir William Coggeshall at Great Sampford. In May 1394 he was one of Coggeshall's attorneys-general who were ordered to appear (in Coggeshall's absence overseas) before arbiters appointed to deal with a complaint that Coggeshall had profited by the Earl of Oxford's 'maintenance' in a suit at common law. Two years later (in June 1396) Doreward was again acting for Coggeshall, this time as his agent in a conveyance of the manor of East Tilbury to John, Lord Cobham. The association of the two men continued when Doreward's son John married Coggeshall's eldest daughter, Blanche. The connection was an important one for Doreward: on two occasions (in 1397 and 1414) he was shire-knight with Sir William; on two more (in 1395 and 1399) with Coggeshall's uncle, Thomas Coggeshall; and at another time (in 1413) with Coggeshall's son-in-law, John Tyrell of Herons.[7]

Another important local attachment of Doreward's was to the FitzWalter family of Woodham Walter. He was their tenant in his manor of Stanways, and from this tie probably arose his connection with Baroness Joan de Mohun of Dunster, for her daughter Philippa had married the Walter Lord FitzWalter who died in Spain in 1386 while serving with John of Gaunt. In November and December 1389 Doreward was party to certain of Joan's transactions, presumably occasioned by Philippa's second marriage, her marriage to Sir John Golafre of Oxfordshire, a knight of Richard II's Chamber of the Household. And Doreward stood surety for the Baroness Joan on 30 January 1391 when she was granted (at the Exchequer) exercise of the royal rights of wardship in certain Devon and Somerset estates. Sometime between 1406 and 1409 he was also one of the feoffees of the widow of the Walter Lord FitzWalter who was summoned to parliament between 1390 and his death in 1406: Joan, the only daughter of John, Lord Devereux, and a granddaughter of John de Vere, Earl of Oxford, who now became the wife of Hugh, Lord Burnell, and died in May 1409.[8]

The evidence for John Doreward's connection with Thomas of Woodstock, Duke of Gloucester, Edward III's youngest son, whose lands in Essex in right of his wife (Eleanor de Bohun) gave him a great interest in the county, is not abundant. But some sort of bond between the two men there certainly was: on 4 February 1395, when Doreward was for the first time representing Essex in parliament, he was made one of the Duke's attorneys when Gloucester went to rejoin Richard II's army in Ireland. And when, on 27 July 1397, less than two months before the Duke was, on the King's orders, murdered at Calais, he and his Duchess conveyed the manor of South Fambridge to the support of the new collegiate chapel in their castle of Pleshy, Doreward was a witness to the deed. He continued to have relations with the family after the Duke's death. In August 1400 he stood surety for the late Duke's mother-in-law (who was also mother-in-law to Henry IV), namely Joan, the dowager Countess of Hereford, when she acquired the custody and marriage of a royal ward (the heir of Sir Ingelram Bruyn), and he was still one of her feoffees not long before she died in 1419. Doreward had also been feoffee to her daughter, Eleanor, the Duke of Gloucester's widow, at the time of her death in 1399; in October 1400 he was still one of her feoffees in a moiety of the manor of Wethersfield (Essex) and in two-thirds of the manor of Arnold (Notts.), both of them De Bohun manors, and he remained a feoffee of Wethersfield and Arnold until their incorporation in the Duchy of Lancaster in 1417. This connection with the De Bohun family probably accounts for Doreward's membership, early in 1410, of the committee of feoffees of Sir William Bourchier (later Count of Eu), the second husband of Anne, the eldest daughter and eventual heir of Thomas of Woodstock, in the manors of Little Easton near Great Dunmow (Essex) and Bildeston (Suffolk) during the formulation of a settlement of these estates. In 1416 Bourchier was one of Doreward's own feoffees in the manor of Park Hall in Gosfield.[9]

In the meantime, in February 1395, Doreward had figured among the feoffees of John de la Mare, a Londoner, in a group of Essex manors which had descended to de la Mare as heir-general to his family's share of the Orreby inheritance which had formerly been in the possession of Mary, the widow of John, Lord Roos of Helmsley, and a half-sister of the Earl of Northumberland, who had died childless in 1394.[10] In 1404, Doreward was also a feoffee, in Little Hockley (Essex), to Sir John Wroth, knight of the shire for Middlesex in 1397, 1401, 1404, and 1406.[11] Lastly, in the closing stages of his career, from June 1415 onwards, he was a feoffee of Henry IV's youngest son, Humphrey, Duke of Gloucester, in favour of whom nearly eleven years earlier (during the Coventry parliament of October 1404) he had surrendered his royal grant of income from the fee-farm of Colchester.[12]

In the early years of Richard II's reign there was a John Doreward of Rivenhall (Essex), who, though probably a member of the same family, is not to be identified with John Doreward of Bocking, the son of William Doreward.[13] There must be some doubt, therefore, whether it was Doreward of Rivenhall or Doreward of Bocking who stood surety in Chancery for the Master and Scholars of Corpus Christi College, Cambridge, when, in August 1380 and pending a dispute with the Crown, they received a temporary royal grant of some tenements in the town.[14] But it was certainly John Doreward of Bocking who, on 23 February 1381, was one of a group of feoffees who received a royal licence to grant in mortmain certain small properties in Burnham and Great Dunmow to the house of Austin canons in Great Dunmow. The FitzWalters were patrons of this monastery, and Doreward was probably then acting as a feoffee of the Lord FitzWalter who died in Spain in 1386.[15]

For the early years of Richard II's reign not a great deal remains to be told of John Doreward. There are certainly no signs that he made much advance politically: he was without doubt of mature age before, in 1395, he was first elected to parliament for his county, but such references to his early career as survive are mainly of a local character. What, however, they suggest is a steady accumulation of landed property and the pursuit of 'acquaintance' and reputation in Essex among the county's leading families, especially among the gentry of which he himself was to become a very prominent member.

Essex was profoundly disturbed in the spring of 1381 by the great social upheaval contained in the Peasants' Revolt. It is not known how far, if at all, Doreward and his estates were affected by the rising. But on 5 July 1381, when the young king was himself at Chelmsford, Doreward was included in a royal commission authorised to find recompense for the damage done by the rebels at Cressing Temple and Witham. In January 1383, when an Essex man (of Kirby-le-Soken), imprisoned in the Fleet prison in London as a rebel and for refusing to pay taxes, was set free, Doreward stood surety for his future good behaviour. He was also appointed on 6 December 1384 as a member of a royal commission set up to inquire into the situation in the manor of Langdon Hall (Essex) which, previously, had been seized for the Crown by John Ewell, the royal escheator for Essex; Ewell's execution by the rebels in 1381 had been procured by one Richard Palmer, who had then forcibly put himself in possession.[16]

It was not until 18 February 1386 that Doreward was included for the first time in the Essex commission of the peace.[17] He may very well at that time have had close connections with Richard II's personal friend and supporter, Robert de Vere, Earl of Essex and recently created Marquess of Dublin, who was among the foremost of Essex landowners. He was a tenant of De Vere and his co-feoffee in the Coggeshall lands, and it was expressly on De Vere's recommendation that, on 8 May 1386, Doreward's interest in fee-tail in the manor of Rawreth (Essex) was ratified under the Great Seal. But after the appointment, in November following, of the parliamentary commission which virtually took the royal administration out of the hands of the king and his party, Doreward was confirmed by it, in July 1387, in his office of J.P. in Essex.[18]

Of Doreward's reactions to the political upsets of the next two critical years, we have no notice. Robert de Vere suffered forfeiture for treason during 'the Merciless Parliament' of 1388, but Doreward was perhaps already also connected with the Duke of Gloucester, the chief of the

Lords Appellant who brought De Vere down. All we learn of Doreward at this time, in fact, is of his standing surety in Chancery in November 1387 for Thomas Swinbourne, keeper of Roxburgh Castle in the East March towards Scotland, when the latter shipped cloth for his retainers' liveries to Newcastle upon Tyne without paying customs; of his participation in some private business of his friend, Sir William Coggeshall; and of his again standing surety in Chancery on 20 November 1388, this time for a former Speaker, Sir John Gildesburgh (an Essex notable who had ties with the Duke of Gloucester), when Gildesburgh and a London rector acquired, at the Exchequer, the custody of the rectory of Hornchurch (Essex) and all else that belonged, in Essex, Kent and London, to the hospital of Montjeux in Savoy, which, because of its adherence to the anti-pope (Clement VII), had incurred sequestration of its English possessions.

It was just after Richard II's recovery of personal control of government that, on 18 May 1389, Doreward shared (with Robert Newport of Hertfordshire) a grant of the custody of two Essex manors (Barnston and Beaumont) forfeited by Sir James Berners, one of the knights of the King's Chamber, who had been successfully impeached for treason and executed during 'the Merciless Parliament' of 1388. (The rent fixed by the Exchequer for this property was £34-odd a year.[19]) Then, on 10 July following, Doreward and Newport, having formed a syndicate with fourteen other men of Essex and Herts. and obtained the assent of the Council, paid 700 marks for the manor of Sacombe (Herts.), an estate forfeited by Sir John Holt, a Justice of the Court of Common Pleas, in pursuance of another adverse judgement of 'the Merciless Parliament'. After the reversal of the acts of this parliament in the Shrewsbury parliament of January 1398, Holt was given back his estates, restitution of Sacombe being specifically ordered on 22 May 1398. Clearly, however, the grantees had enjoyed an undisturbed possession for some nine years.[20]

No particular political significance need be attached to the grant of Justice Holt's forfeited manor of Sacombe in 1389. Certainly, it would be unwise to assume from it that Doreward was then personally in favour with the newly re-established royalist party. That the reverse was the case is, indeed, quite likely: at any rate, Doreward was not among the Essex J.P.s appointed on 15 July 1389; nor was he included in the next Commission of the Peace appointed on 10 November following. He did, however, find a place on the Essex bench when fresh commissions were next issued on 28 June 1390, and this appointment was confirmed on 24 December later that year. Doreward was, in fact, to remain a J.P. until the summer of 1397 when, perhaps more significantly, he was once again dropped from the commission.[21]

In the meantime, however, Doreward had not been without his connections at Court, even among Richard II's personal friends: we have already noticed his connection in December 1389 and January 1391 with Baroness De Mohun who had been among the ladies banished from the Royal Household early in 1388, just before the proscriptions of 'the Merciless Parliament'.[22] Certainly, Doreward had some considerable influence outside the limits of his own county. How long he had occupied the office is not known, but already by November 1390 he was acting as steward of the great franchise of the abbey of Bury St. Edmunds. He was still holding that office in July 1393 and perhaps even as late as April 1396, at which time he entered into a recognisance with the man who had been his deputy at Bury in 1393, Edmund Lakingheath.[23] However, none other than Sir John Bushy, one of the most important of Richard II's supporters, had replaced him by November 1397.

Although a J.P. in Essex continuously from June 1390 until July 1397 and knight of the shire in the consecutive parliaments of January 1395 and January 1397, Doreward served on very few local commissions of royal appointment in that period: in July 1391, however, he was a member of an inquiry into the effects of the construction of some fishing weirs on a sandbank on Mersea Island; in June 1394, he was made one of a commission of oyer and terminer appointed when the constable of Colchester Castle complained of the result of the escape of an ex-receiver of the Duke of Gloucester, a misfortune which had involved the constable in paying off his prisoner's arrears (amounting to 400 marks); and on 9 April 1397 he was appointed a justice of gaol delivery at Colchester with authority to enquire into escapes of felons in Essex generally.[24] It may have been his connection with the Duke of Gloucester, who, never forgiven by Richard II for his share in the proceedings of 'the Merciless Parliament', was murdered on his orders at Calais in September 1397, which had been behind Doreward's dismissal as J.P. in July 1397. Nor was he reappointed when new commissions were issued on 12 November 1397, despite the fact that on 28 August he had lent the king 100 marks (in return for a royal letter patent promising repayment shortly after Easter 1398). But he was still in circulation. On 22 November 1397, he was made a royal commissioner of oyer and terminer following a complaint by a probable kinsman (Walter Doreward) of trouble with his bondsmen at Great Bromley over their refusal to perform customary services. A month later, on 20 December, he had been put on the large Essex commission (to which were appointed most of the important local magnates and gentry) ordered to secure the consent of the county, along with Hertfordshire, to a joint communal fine of £2000 which was to be paid to the king in return for a remission of the ancient farm of the two shires and a pardon for all their people's treasons and risings before 1 October 1397. The Essex commissioners had also been ordered to assess and levy the fine in their county, and the then two knights of the shire were to take to Shrewsbury (where parliament was due to meet at the end of January 1398) their personal report to the king and an authority to consent to his orders regarding the payment of the fine.[25]

Doreward's participation in negotiating his county's share in this famous 'crooked pardon' of Richard II's period of absolute rule, a pardon to which seventeen counties of southern England in all were subjected, not to mention his ties with Thomas of Woodstock and the De Bohun family in these years, is likely to have predisposed him to welcome the outcome of the events of 1399 when Richard II was deposed in favour of Henry IV. This seems the more probable when it is realised that he had already formed an additional connection with another important victim of Richard II's tyranny, Thomas Arundel, archbishop of Canterbury, whose banishment and deprivation the king had procured in the purge of September 1397.

John Doreward was of the type of pious layman particularly acceptable to the prelates of the English Church at a time when the Lollard heresy was seeking to popularise its appeal to the gentry by the promotion of political schemes for ecclesiastical disendowment, especially at the expense of the 'possessioners' among the monastic clergy. In July 1392 he had been party to a royally licensed grant in mortmain of a small estate at Little Maldon to the Premonstratensian abbey of Beeleigh. This was by no means important or unusual in itself: in fact, Doreward may only have been acting with his two cograntors on behalf of someone else. But this was not all. He had his own close association (as we have seen) with one of the greatest of English monasteries, the Benedictine abbey of Bury St. Edmunds. He had links also with the monks of Christchurch, Canterbury, into whose confraternity he was to be received in 1401.

Moreover, Doreward's home village of Bocking was the centre of a deanery comprising seven parishes in Essex and Suffolk in which the Archbishop of Canterbury (because of his landed possessions in the area) exercised extensive powers of direct ecclesiastical jurisdiction.[26] In 1362 Doreward's father had founded a chantry in Bocking parish church, and in June 1393 Doreward himself began a series of transactions the aim of which was to found there a chantry of his own. The prior and monks of Christchurch, Canterbury, held a manor in Bocking out of which (by royal licence purchased by Doreward on 20 June 1393) they granted him 100 acres and £3 in rents (held of the Crown in chief) in exchange for a messuage, 112 acres, and a shilling rent in Bocking and at Stisted (not held in chief); in addition, however, the priory was to grant Doreward a garden and £7 in rents at Bocking in exchange for £9 in rents from his manor of Leaden Roding, and it was Doreward's intention, assisted by a second royal licence, to amortise this last acquisition at Bocking to the support of the chaplain who was to serve in his chantry (dedicated to the Blessed Virgin) in Bocking church. These two royal licences together cost Doreward £20 at the Hanaper (fee-office) of the Chancery. Later, between November 1393 and February 1394, by a series of fines in the Court of Common Pleas and other contingent conveyances relating to Doreward's interest in the manor of Leaden Roding, the foundation of the chantry moved a stage nearer its completion. Party to some of these deeds were, of course, Doreward's feoffees in the manor of Leaden Roding: they included Bishop Braybroke of London, Aubrey (de Vere), Earl of Oxford, and Sir Thomas Erpingham, Henry IV's future chamberlain. There may have been difficulties, and it looks as though the plan to exchange Doreward's rents from Leaden Roding for the priory's garden and rent at Bocking broke down, and that, sometime between May 1394 and May 1395, Doreward purchased the Bocking rent outright for the large sum of 650 marks (£433 6s. 8d.), the cost of the priory's recent separate acquisition in the city of London, 'The Crown' in Eastcheap. However this may be, it was not until Lady Day 1397 that the deed for the foundation of the chantry (a tripartite indenture) was executed at Bocking and the chantry properly established. Those specifically for whom prayers were to be offered by the chantry-chaplain included, in addition to members of Doreward's own family, Richard II, Archbishop Arundel of Canterbury, the prior and chapter of Christchurch, Canterbury, and Baroness FitzWalter (the dowager who was soon to become the wife of Edward, the elder son of Edmund, Duke of York, and a cousin of the king). In view of the rapid rise of Doreward's fortunes under Henry IV, with whom Arundel had returned from exile and whose accession he did so much to accomplish, the archbishop's inclusion in the bede-roll of the chantry is perhaps the most noteworthy feature of the deed.[27]

The chantry at Bocking was not the only foundation of this kind for which Doreward was personally responsible. On 13 November 1400 the prior of the Augustinian house of the canons of St. Botolph at Colchester secured a royal licence enabling Doreward to grant it in mortmain some lands and rents there and at Great Tey for the maintenance of a chantry-chaplain in the priory church. On 2 June 1407, in exchange for a release of 200 marks due to him for his previous services on the King's Council, Doreward secured a royal licence to found in the parish church at Stanway, by the grant of a house on the glebe near the graveyard and £7 rent from the manor and his other lands in the place, another chantry of one chaplain. At the same time he received a licence to augment the income of the chaplain of a chantry at Bergholt Sackville by amortising £2 in rents from some of his lands in Colchester, Stanway, Fordham, and Bergholt, as well as to convey his manor of Tendring (although not its advowson) as a gift to the Benedictine abbey of St. John in Colchester. This last grant did not, however, take effect, Doreward's son eventually (in 1440) using the manor of Tendring to endow a maisondieu (or hospital) at Bocking instead.[28] Doreward's good works of this kind were conventional enough, but the number of his endowments for pious uses is unusual, and he himself can only have been regarded as entirely 'reliable' in matters of religious faith and practice at a time when, under the impulse of Wyclifism, many well-to-do laymen were actively critical of Church life and doctrine.

That Doreward was thought to be in sympathy with the Revolution of 1399 (whereby Richard II was succeeded by Henry IV) would appear to be indicated by the fact that on 22 August 1399 (shortly after Richard had surrendered to Henry and the royal administration was functioning under the latter's orders) he was appointed as sheriff of Essex and Herts.[29] Moreover, on 15 September, he was made deputy at Colchester to the Chief Butler of England.[30] These, of course, were interim appointments, only two among many used to keep the royal administration running until the political situation had become stabilised. And, in fact, Doreward's term as sheriff ended on 30 September[31] (the date of Richard's deposition), and his deputy-butlership only lasted until 14 October following (the morrow of Henry's coronation).

In the meantime, in response to writs issued at Chester on 19 August summoning in Richard II's name the parliament which, meeting as an assembly of the estates of the realm, was to witness his deposition and Henry IV's accession, the elections to parliament had been held country-wide, by the sheriffs of course. Evidently, Doreward had used his own appointment as sheriff to his personal advantage in at least one respect, for he was one of the two knights of the shire elected for Essex. Such action was illegal, sheriffs in office being prohibited by statute (and, indeed, by the terms of the writs of summons) from being elected to parliament. But the times were out of joint, and it was only to be expected that normal practice would here and there be in abeyance. After the prelates and lords personally summoned and those elected to parliament had assisted at Richard's deposition and recognised his successor on 30 September 1399, they met again on 6 October, and then what was now the first parliament of Henry IV was prorogued to the day after his coronation, which took place on 13 October. Already the Commons had elected Sir John Cheyne, knight of the shire for Gloucestershire, as their Speaker, and on parliament's reassembly on 14 October he was presented to the king and accepted. On the very next day, however, he sought to be discharged on the grounds of ill-health. This reason was most probably a formal one merely, for already Archbishop Arundel had openly expressed in Convocation his objection to Sir John Cheyne as a renegade clerk and enemy of the Church; and it was probably pressure from the primate (and not ill-health at all) which resulted in Cheyne's exoneration from the Speakership. The Commons' second choice for the office—John Doreward himself, who was then presented and accepted as Speaker forthwith—can only have been agreeable to Arundel personally and, as one whose opinions were orthodox and 'safe', to the lords spiritual in general.[32] Whatever the effect of Doreward's substitution for Cheyne, the threatened attack on ecclesiastical privileges which was evidently dreaded by the clergy, came to nothing. It may also be noted that this parliament of 1399 resulted in the annulment of the measures of Richard II's last parliament (1397–8) and consequently in a restoration of the estates forfeited at that time, a special concession being made in the case of Archbishop Arundel in that he was allowed damages from his supplanter in the primacy (Roger Walden). What particular part in the session was played by Doreward is not known.

A short time before Henry IV's first parliament ended on 19 November 1399, something was done to alleviate the effects of the long sequestration, on account of Anglo-French hostility and the Great Schism, of the property of the alien priories (the English dependencies of French monasteries), a policy which had inevitably resulted in the impoverishment of many of them, especially those whose temporalities had been farmed out by the Exchequer to lay lessees. Sir John Cheyne, whom Doreward had replaced as Speaker, had been a profiteer on a considerable scale from such seizures of alien priory lands. But Doreward himself, whatever his reputation as an endower of chantries and despite links with the 'possessioners', was not above receiving rewards for his services to the Crown in the form of custody of alien priory estates, a practice against which Archbishop Arundel was to make bitter complaint later on, at the Coventry parliament of 1404. In fact, on 24 November 1399, only five days after Doreward's Speakership ended with the dissolution of Henry IV's first parliament, he was granted the custody of the alien priory of Mersea in Essex, a dependency of the Norman abbey of St. Ouen at Rouen, the estates of which priory he was to rent from the Exchequer for 140 marks (£93 6s. 8d.) per annum as from the previous Michaelmas and for as long as the war with France lasted. (His recent fellow-knight of the shire, Thomas Coggeshall, and Thomas Godstone, who had been serving as a parliamentary burgess for Colchester, stood surety for him in this transaction.) Doreward had not long to wait before he secured a firmer hold of these estates: on 14 May 1400 he procured a royal patent licensing the abbey of St. Ouen to grant the priory and manor of Mersea to him and his second wife (Isabel), the grant, which was made for Doreward's life, being shared with Henry Twilloe who, the non-resident bishop of the Irish diocese of Enachdune, was to discharge the customary spiritual obligations of the priory. And, on 29 May, the transfer of the priory and its property, including livestock, was sanctioned. Only another three weeks had gone by when, on 20 June, the abbey of St. Ouen accepted an indenture of conveyance in return for a promise on the part of the lessees to maintain the fabric, divine services and customs of the priory, and to draw up before three years had elapsed a new roll of its tenants recording their names, rents, and duties, a copy of which (in Latin) was to be sent to St. Ouen before a further two years had passed. A royal confirmation of these arrangements was procured on 27 June 1400. However, short of a year later, namely on 28 March 1401, this royal confirmation was itself ratified with an additional and an important concession: the yearly farm of 140 marks referred to in Doreward's original grant of 24 November 1399 was now entirely waived, as was also the ancient *apport* (or rent) customarily due from the priory to the Crown in peace-time, so 'ironing out' the effects of any accidental failure to mention, in the grants and licences made up-to-date, Doreward's first grant, the value of the priory, the abbey of St. Ouen's tenure of the priory by ancient royal grant (Edward the Confessor's), and the abbey's adherence to the anti-Pope (Benedict XIII). Doreward had no difficulty in retaining possession of the priory of Mersea when, in the parliament of 1402, Henry IV approved a petition from the Commons asking that the estates of the non-conventual alien priories should all be made subject to an Act of Resumption, except (the petition itself provided) those of which grants or leases had been made by the Crown (or of which releases had been made by the parent-houses) to laymen during the last three reigns. Henry IV had agreed to consult his Council on this matter, and in the middle of January 1403 certain alien priors and lay *occupatores* were summoned to negotiate either with the Treasurer of the Exchequer or the Council. By this time Bishop Twilloe had dropped out of the reckoning so far as Mersea priory was concerned and, in the list of those required to treat, Doreward and his wife alone figure as occupiers. On 25 January 1403 Doreward duly appeared before a select group of the Council (the Chancellor, the Treasurer, and John Scarle). However, bringing acceptable evidences of his *purchasing* with the abbey of St. Ouen, he was dismissed without more ado. In fact, Doreward had no difficulty in retaining control of Mersea priory until his death; and his widow then continued to hold the lease until, on Easter Monday 1423, she surrendered it in favour of Archbishop Chichele and his nephew, William Chichele, Archdeacon of Canterbury, who together granted it (in free alms) to their new collegiate foundation at Higham Ferrers (Northants.), the archbishop's birthplace.[33]

When, on 24 November 1399, John Doreward had been first given the right to farm the priory of Mersea, he was already a member of Henry IV's Council. He had been appointed, in fact, on 1 November 1399, that is, while he was still Speaker, and he is known to have been present at Council meetings as early as on 4 and 8 December following. Hardly surprisingly, he profited from this promotion by much more than simply his acquisition of Mersea priory and its estates. Indeed, from the beginning of his tenure of office as councillor, he received the large annual fee of 100 marks. But every now and then, he obtained additional grants intended to cover special expenses incurred in his work as a member of the Council: for example, on 9 November 1401, he was awarded £40 for all his travel and costs when sent at different times to the king on important business on the Council's behalf. He was a continual member of the Council until the important change in its composition which occurred on 22 May 1406, during the long parliament of that year. In the meantime, he was among those councillors (including seven commoners) nominated by Henry IV in the parliament of January 1404, to which Doreward himself was once more elected for Essex; and, certainly, he was still *consiliarius regis* on 27 October 1405, when the Exchequer was authorised to pay him £40 in part-payment of a reward for his attendance as such. He did not serve again in this capacity following his dismissal in 1406.[34]

Not long after his first appointment as a member of the Council at the beginning of the reign, namely on 10 December 1399, Doreward (described as 'king's esquire') was granted an annuity of £35 payable from the fee-farm of the borough of Colchester as from 13 September 1399; the grant was made for life or else until some other provision was made for 'his estate'. This sum of £35 a year was, in fact, the whole fee-farm for which the borough was then liable in the Exchequer (that is, the old farm of £42 minus the £7 of which the town was currently acquitted by the Treasurer and Barons). Doreward already had interests of his own in Colchester, and they were to multiply as time went on: he had tenements in the borough; on 11 November 1400 the Royal Council agreed that he should be granted the advowson and patronage of the hospital of St. Cross there (not worth more than £5 a year), which had formerly been dependent upon his manor of Stanway; two days later, on 13 November, he received the royal licence to found his chantry in the priory of St. Botolph; and he and his son very probably were the John Doreward senior and John Doreward junior who, described as of Stisted (where John senior had an estate), were admitted to the freedom of the borough, as members of the weavers' guild.[35] Doreward retained the £35 fee-farm of Colchester until, on 22 October 1404 (during the Coventry parliament and in anticipation of its Act of Resumption), he surrendered it in favour of Humphrey, the youngest of the king's sons, in exchange for a patent exempting him for life from jury service, from appointment as sheriff, justice of the peace, commissioner of array and collector of parliamentary subsidies, from even election as knight of the shire, and from service in other royal offices, against his will. (The grant of the fee-farm was made to Humphrey in tail male, and he was given the castle of Colchester and the hundred of Tendring as well.[36])

Since the beginning of Henry IV's reign, Doreward's services to the Crown in local administration had been of no special importance, although this was presumably because he had been kept busy as a member of the Royal Council. He was not appointed to the first commission of the peace for Essex issued in Henry IV's name (dated 24 October 1399), but after his Speakership he was made a J.P. once more on 28 November 1399, and his commission was subsequently renewed on several occasions, so that he acted in this office continuously (notwithstanding his exemption of October 1404) until December 1411.[37] He was often made a commissioner of array in the county in the early years of the reign: on 18 December 1399, on 14 July 1402, on 28 August, 8 September, 5 November, and 25 November 1403 and on 2 July 1405.[38] Meanwhile, on 11 May 1402, he had been appointed to the Essex commission in a nationwide investigation into unrest, with authority to arrest those who were spreading false rumours about Henry IV's constitutional and political intentions, and on 5 August 1404 he had been put on a royal commission of inquiry into treasons and felonies committed since the middle of the previous January in Essex and Herts.

This last commission was presumably intended to deal with those conspiracies which had been disturbing the region during the previous twelve months. The object of the plots had been the restoration (with French help) of the former king, Richard of Bordeaux, who had been dead for four years but was believed in some quarters to be still alive in Scotland. Essex, clearly, had been the centre of this unrest: privy to it had been the dowager Countess of Oxford (the mother of Robert de Vere, Richard's close personal friend who had died in exile in 1392), Bishop Despenser of Norwich, and the abbots of St. John's at Colchester, St. Osyth's at Chiche, and Byleigh; and it was said that a monk of Colchester had, at one of the many secret interviews afterwards confessed to have taken place, threatened the life of Henry IV and the lives of some Essex notables conspicuously faithful to him, including John Doreward. The plot had collapsed by mid-summer 1404, and the investigation was opened at Colchester on 25 August. Doreward, although appointed one of the commissioners of inquiry, was not present, however.[39] Presumably he was at Court.

Doreward's membership of the Royal Council inevitably involved him in business which frequently kept him away from Essex. It was doubtless on the same account that, on 25 February 1400, he had been included in a commission of inquiry into encroachments on royal rights in Gloucestershire by the abbots of Cirencester. From time to time during his membership of the Council he also acted on commissions appointed to hear and determine appeals against judgements given in the Court of the Constable and Marshal and the Court of Admiralty, courts which were tribunals exercising, in a sense, a conciliar jurisdiction.[40] It was probably as a member of the Royal Council, too, that he acted as one of the arbiters in a dispute over the facilities for trading in fish and with foreigners at Great Yarmouth claimed by the men of Lowestoft, the final agreement concerning which dispute was confirmed (after consultation with the Council) in February 1401. It was soon after this, namely on 5 March, that Doreward played a prominent part in the presentation to Henry IV of an 'advice' from his councillors regarding a petition made by the Commons in the parliament that was then in session, a petition which, as it raised the question of the manner, terms and duration of their appointment, they were suspicious of. Doreward was, in fact, acting as his fellow-councillors' messenger, and they asked the king to accept his explanation of their 'advice'. Doreward's services as an intermediary between Henry IV and his Council were employed on other occasions, for example, when the king's personal leadership of military campaigns against the Welsh (under Owen Glendower) and other rebels separated them. And it is interesting to note too that, on 20 July 1401, Henry IV sent him from the priory of Selbourne (Hants) with a letter under the signet, along with other confidential instructions, regarding the summoning of a Great Council for mid-August, a meeting to which between four and eight knights from every county were to be summoned. Doreward was himself one of those to be summoned from Essex. (This was not the only Great Council to which he was specially summoned in the first half of the reign.[41]) On 4 April 1402 he was also one of twelve members of the Council who were party to an undertaking for the repayment (before Easter) of a loan of £2,500 made to the Crown by John Hende (a London draper), it being understood that the loan would be met by preferential assignments on the London customs. Doreward himself occasionally became a royal creditor, for example, in June 1401 in the sum of £100; and in October 1402 he was one of four notables living in Essex and Herts. who were then asked for a loan for the support of the royal garrisons in south Wales.[42]

Again, it was probably as a member of the Royal Council that during the parliament of September–November 1402, Doreward was put on a committee appointed to investigate certain allegations which had been made against the civic authorities of London by one of their fellow citizens, one John Cavendish. (The committee, which included the two Chief Justices and other royal councillors, was to certify the Chancellor of the outcome of the enquiry.) Doreward was not himself a knight of the shire in that parliament. In fact, after the first parliament of the reign he did not serve again in that capacity during the rest of the reign, except in January 1404, when Henry IV nominated him in parliament as a member of his Council, which was then charged with remedying all complaints made during the session.[43] Another commission to come his way, once more probably by reason of his membership of the Council, was that of 23 August 1405, when, together with his fellow-councillor, Sir John Cheyne (the man whom he had replaced as Speaker in 1399), he was appointed at Worcester to negotiate for the submission of the inhabitants of Usk and Caerleon and other Welsh border lordships who had been an embarrassment to the government during the Glendower rebellion, provide for the administration of those areas, and report personally to the king.[44] This was one of his last commissions as a royal councillor, because in May 1406, when the Council was reconstituted during parliament, he was not reappointed.

Doreward's nearly seven years' membership of the Council had stood him well, personally. For one thing, it can only have made his employment as a feoffee-to-uses even more attractive than before to members of the local nobility in Essex. It also brought him into touch with some of the circle of Henry IV's close friends and supporters: for example, at the end of February 1400 Doreward was one of the sureties for Sir Thomas Erpingham, an old retainer of the king and now his Chamberlain and the Warden of the Cinque Ports, when Erpingham was granted the farm of Framlingham Castle and other estates in East Anglia during the minority of Thomas Mowbray, the Earl Marshal; and he was again Erpingham's surety when, on 12 November 1403, Erpingham was given the right to farm (at 370 marks a year) the castle and lordship of Clare and all the other Mortimer estates in Norfolk, Suffolk, and Essex, during the minority of Edmund, Earl of March. We have already seen something of Doreward's connection with Henry IV's mother-in-law, Joan, dowager Countess of Hereford, and of his continuance in service as one of the feoffees of the king's first wife's sister, Eleanor, Duchess of Gloucester, who had died in 1399, shortly before his accession. In June 1402 he had been a mainpernor for the 'king's knight' and recently appointed chief usher of the hall of the Royal Household, Sir John de Strange, when the latter was granted a royal wardship in Suffolk.

Doreward's royal councillorship had been, of course, more directly profitable in simple financial terms, at any rate at first. His grant of an annual fee of 100 marks (£66 13s. 4d.), expressly for his services in the Council, was a handsome salary, especially as augmented by occasional *regarda* and the £35 a year from the Colchester fee-farm which he enjoyed from 1399 to October 1404. Moreover, his allowance to retain the alien priory of Mersea early in 1404, when the whole question of such grants was under review, proved a source of no great embarrassment to his fellow-councillors, with whom the matter rested, and could only have been gratifying to him personally. Such gains were, however, needed to offset those inevitable postponements of payment of official stipends which arose out of the system of reimbursement by Exchequer assignments on future royal revenues, and most of Doreward's payments as councillor were of that sort. In May 1405, for example, he was restoring to the Exchequer bad tallies, meaning assignments of money he had been unable to collect. Admittedly, the tallies were worth no more than £18-odd, and here he was perhaps quite content to have nothing better than fresh assignments. But, over a year after his dismissal from the Council, namely on 2 June 1407, he was still owed 200 marks (two years' salary) for his services as councillor, and then he was compelled (as we have seen) to forego payment of this considerable sum merely in return for a free licence to found his chantry at Stanway. And a very hard bargain it was at that![45]

After Doreward's failure to be reappointed to the Council in May 1406, he virtually drops out of sight for the rest of Henry IV's reign, save for occasional local transactions of a private character to which he was party, and apart from his membership of the Commission of the Peace in Essex, to which he continued to be appointed (by patents of 3 March 1406, 13 February 1407 and 16 June 1410) until he was retired on the reconstitution of the bench in December 1411. And this was so despite the fact that Archbishop Arundel was Chancellor for three years from January 1407 and then again from January 1412 until the end of the reign in March 1413. It is conceivable (though unlikely) that Doreward represented Essex in the parliament of January 1410, for which the Essex returns are lost. Otherwise, he did not act as knight of the shire in any parliament of Henry IV after January 1404. When, on 22 October 1404, he surrendered his grant of the fee-farm of Colchester, he had in fact secured an exemption for life from appointment to royal commissions and offices against his will and from service in parliament as a knight of the shire. And, not long before he was left out of the Commission of the Peace for Essex in December 1411, namely on 11 November, he renewed his patent of exemption from royal service, the scope of the grant, moreover, being now extended to exclude him for life not only from election as a knight of the shire for any county, but also from summonses to great councils and other council meetings, from service as justice of the peace and commissioner of array, from service in arms, and from distraint to knighthood. It was also on the very same day that he took out yet another patent, one allowing his manors in Essex and Norfolk, and his houses there and in London and elsewhere, for a period of seven years, freedom from billeting and the exemption of his livestock and produce from seizure by royal purveyors.[46] Whether there was any special point in this concession is not known.

At the beginning of Henry V's reign in March 1413, when new commissions of the peace were issued, Doreward was not reappointed to the local bench. But, in spite of his exemption by patent, he was again elected to sit as knight of the shire for Essex in the first parliament of the new reign. This parliament met on 15 May 1413, and three days later the Commons' Speaker, William Stourton, was presented to the king who accepted him. On 22 May, when next Stourton appeared before the king in the Upper House it was to make certain verbal requests which, however, at the king's instance but without the Commons' necessary approval, he there and then agreed to put into writing. On 25 May the Commons objected, and it was now Doreward whom they chose to act as their spokesman in this regard. In that complaint the Commons were successful, but they evidently carried their dissatisfaction with Stourton's conduct still further, for on 3 June, saying that Stourton was ill in bed and unable to continue, they presented Doreward as their proper Speaker with the intention that he should take Stourton's place, and the king accepted the fresh election. Thus was repeated the circumstance of 1399, but with an important difference, meaning that Doreward became Speaker by a substitution, only now the initiative had lain with the Commons. As it fell out, this parliament lasted for only another six days after Doreward's election, being dissolved on 9 June. It may be, as J. H. Round once suggested, that Doreward was chosen because, at a time when the Lollards were once more bestirring themselves politically, he was acceptable on personal grounds to Archbishop Arundel.[47] But this reason seems very doubtful, if only because of the primate's long hostility to Henry V (when the latter was Prince of Wales) and his dismissal from the Chancellorship immediately after Henry IV's death. Perhaps, after registering their objection to Stourton's subservience, the Commons simply wished to stabilise their position by appointing a tried man of affairs who had been free from embroilment in recent upsets on the political stage, from which he had been virtually absent for the last seven years. However this may be, Doreward ended Henry V's first parliament as he had ended Henry IV's first parliament, occupying the office of Speaker.

A year later, Doreward was re-elected as knight of the shire for Essex (possibly, although the returns to the three parliaments of 1415–16 have been lost, for the last time). He was now returned to the parliament which met at Leicester on 30 April 1414, being on this occasion accompanied by his old friend, Sir William Coggeshall. He was not, however, to be re-elected Speaker.

In the meantime, Doreward had been moved to renew his interest in local government in Essex, being appointed on 24 September 1413 to inquire into allegations of wastes committed during the last two reigns in the alien priory of Benstede and, on 16 November 1413, once again included in the local Commission of the Peace. He was, in fact, to be reappointed a J.P. for Essex down to his death seven years later (by patents of 12 December 1414, 3 February 1416, 12 December 1417, and 21 April 1419). On 29 May 1415, with Henry V's resumption of the French war in prospect, he was made a commissioner of array in the county.[48] Then, in the following month, when the king's youngest brother, Humphrey, who was now Duke of Gloucester, was making his preparations for the impending campaign in Normandy, Doreward was made one of his feoffees in an important group of his lands.

A year or so later, Doreward was at variance with Bishop Beaufort of Winchester, who had been Chancellor of England ever since the beginning of Henry V's reign. The bishop, in his capacity as executor to his elder brother John, the late Earl of Somerset, enjoyed the wardship of the FitzWalter estates, the manor of Lexden (Essex) among them. Between Lexden and Doreward's manor of Stanway was a clearing in the woods to which Doreward laid claim, only for Beaufort to dispute his title. It was on 14 May 1416 that Doreward entered into a recognisance in Chancery in a sum of £200, undertaking to abide by the award of the bishop and his counsel, and later in the year (on 22 October) he renewed the undertaking in spite of the appointment on 28 July of a royal commission of inquiry into the claims of the parties, the terms of which indicate that rights of common of pasture were also in dispute.[49] There is little more to relate of Doreward's career. Sometime before his death in 1420, however, he lent £100 to Henry V on the security of certain jewels, a loan for the repayment of only half of which his widow (as executrix) was forced to compound with the Treasurer of the Exchequer, and after almost another six years had passed (payment being made on this basis on 17 July 1426).

Doreward had made his will on 1 February 1418. Its contents, which suggest a moderate affluence, demonstrate a considerable interest on Doreward's part in local churches, especially churches in places where he had property of his own and, even more especially, in the churches where he had already founded chantries. To the fabric fund of the church at Bocking he left £20; and he made small gifts to the churches at Goldham, Gosfield, Stanway, Rothing, and Rawreth. Bequests of 5 marks each he left to the Franciscan friaries at Ipswich and Colchester, the Dominican houses at Sudbury and Chelmsford, the Augustinians of Clare, the Carmelites of Maldon, and the nunneries of Hengham and Wykes. To the nuns of Stratford-at-Bower went 10 marks. A sum of £50 he left to be divided among the prisoners in the gaols at Colchester, Hertford, and Stortford, the prisons in London (namely Newgate, Fleet and Ludgate) and the prisons of the King's Bench and Marshalsea, and among the poor and sick in Essex, especially those living in the vills where he himself had lands. £40 he bequeathed for the repair of roads between Coggeshall and Colchester. The same amount was to be distributed among such of his servants as did not enjoy a retaining-fee given them for life. His three daughters, including Joan,

Lady Waldegrave, received bequests amounting in value to nearly £100. To his son and heir, John, went all his armour, the stock at Bocking (worth £100), and jewels worth £100. £120 was to be equally divided among the six executors whom he had appointed along with his wife, Isabel; and, together, they were to have the disposal of the remainder of his personalty. The will also made elaborate provision for the succession to his estates, with special safeguards for the entails, his wife's life-interests, and his chantries.[50]

Doreward died on 12 November 1420 and was buried at Bocking. Only ten days later, writs were sued out from the Chancery, authorising enquiries about his lands and addressed to the royal escheators in Essex, Norfolk, Middlesex, and London. On 26 December following, the escheator for Essex was ordered to give livery of seisin to John, his son and heir, of all save the dower estates of the widow, orders to assign which were issued on 10 March 1421. An agreement between the heir and the widow (the heir's stepmother), regarding the manor of Leaden Roding, suggests that the testamentary grant of it in tail male to his daughter, Lady Waldegrave, was in process of being defeated.[51] Doreward's widow, Isabel, died shortly before 20 October 1426. John, the heir, was never a knight of the shire, but he was the Duchy of Lancaster steward for the honour of Clare in 1417–18, the sheriff of Essex and Hertfordshire in 1425–6 and 1432–3, and a J.P. in Essex from 1429 to 1435. It was *his* son John, the Speaker's grandson, a member of Lincoln's Inn, who was knight of the shire for Essex in 1453–4.[52]

NOTES

The following abbreviations have been used: *CCR, Calendar of Close Rolls; CFR, Calendar of Fine Rolls; CPR, Calendar of Patent Rolls; PPC, Proceedings and Ordinances of the Privy Council*, ed. N. H. Nicolas; PRO, Public Record Office; *Rot. Parl., Rotuli Parliamentorum;* R.S., Rolls Series.

1. For a detailed discussion of the early development of the office of Speaker and brief accounts of all of those knights of the shire for Essex who became Speakers in the medieval period, see J. S. Roskell, *The Commons and their Speakers in English Parliaments, 1376–1523* (Manchester, 1965).
2. *Official Return of Members of Parliament.* i. 249, 252, 258, 265, 278, 281.
3. *CCR, 1422–9,* 159; Somerset House, Register Marche, fo. 50; *CPR, 1385–9,* 111 (Southall); ibid., *1391–6,* 285; *CCR, 1392–6,* 238, 254, 258; ibid., *1419–22,* 137; Philip Morant, *The History and Antiquities of the County of Essex* (London, 1768), ii. 472 (Leaden Roding); *CPR, 1385–9,* 150; Morant, op. cit., i. 284 (Rawreth); *CPR, 1391–6,* 285; Morant, op. cit., ii. 384; *Essex Arch. Soc. Trans.*, XIII. 73 (Bocking); Morant, op. cit., ii. 192 (Olivers); ibid., 207 (Trumpingtons); ibid., 190; *Collectanea Topographica et Genealogica*, vii. 274 (Stanway); Morant, op. cit., ii. 379 (Park Hall in Gosfield); ibid., 380 (Morells in Gosfield); ibid., 299; *CCR, 1402–5,* 145 (Great Yeldham); *CCR, 1392–6,* 489; ibid., *1402–5,* 145 (Old Hall and Grapnels in Great Yeldham); ibid., *1409–13,* 115 (Wickhambrook); ibid., 335; ibid., *1422–9,* 294; Morant, op. cit., ii. 425 (Alfreston in Great Dunmow, Old Hall in West Tofts, and Old Hall in Marham [in Norfolk]). John Doreward's maternal grandfather, John Oliver, had been M.P. for Essex in 1368 and sheriff of Essex and Herts. in 1366–8.
4. *English Historical Review*, xlix. 533.
5. British Museum, Harleian MS. no. 1408, fo. 177; *CPR, 1385–9,* 150; *Coll. Topogr. et Geneal.*, vii. 277.
6. *CPR, 1422–9,* 399; Morant, op. cit., ii. 384–5, 425; *CCR, 1409–13,* 335–6.
7. *CPR, 1381–5,* 433; *CCR, 1392–6,* 212; ibid., 515; ibid., *1405–9,* 500; ibid., *1419–22,* 137; Morant, op cit., ii. 384–5 (Morant was wrong to make the son of John Doreward Speaker in 1413). For Sir William Coggeshall, see J. S. Roskell, *The Commons in the Parliament of 1422,* 169–70. Sir William Coggeshall was M.P. for Essex in no fewer than ten parliaments between 1391 and 1422, and he was sheriff of Essex and Herts. in 1391–2, 1404–5, and 1411–12.
8. *CCR, 1389–92,* 83, 97; *CPR, 1383–91,* 348; *CCR, 1405–9,* 446. Between Golafre's death in 1396 and October 1404, Philippa de Mohun married (as her third husband) Edward, Duke of York, who was killed at Agincourt in 1415.
9. *CPR, 1391–6,* 533; R. Gough, *The History and Antiquities of Pleshy,* App., 80; *CFR, 1399–1405,* 74; *Catalogue of Ancient Deeds*, iii. C.3007; *CPR, 1399–1401,* 366; ibid., *1416–22,* 105; *CCR, 1419–22,* 75, 202; *CPR, 1408–13,* 158; Morant, op. cit., ii, 379.
10. *CCR, 1392–6,* 398.
11. ibid., *1402–5,* 510.
12. *CPR, 1413–16,* 338.
13. It was John Doreward of Rivenhall (with which place the Speaker never had any connection) who was party to a conveyance of a messuage in Coggeshall to the abbey of Coggeshall in April 1380. A Robert Doreward of Rivenhall attested one of John Doreward the Speaker's deeds in 1412. (*CPR, 1377–81,* 482; *CCR, 1409–13,* 417).
14. *CFR, 1377–82,* 213.
15. *CPR, 1377–81,* 601. (Certainly one of Doreward's co-feoffees, Richard Upston, was then parson of Shimpling [Suffolk], a benefice in FitzWalter patronage.)
16. *CPR, 1381–5,* 76, 507; *CCR, 1381–5,* 248.
17. *CPR, 1385–9,* 82.
18. ibid., 150 (cf. Morant. *Essex*, i. 284); 385.

19. *CFR, 1383–91*, 261, 285.
20. *CPR, 1388–92*, 80; *CCR, 1396–9*, 276.
21. *CPR, 1388–92*, 341, 344.
22. Thomas Walsingham, *Historia Anglicana*, ed. T. H. Riley (R.S.), ii. 173.
23. *CCR. 1388–92*, 268, 374; ibid., *1392–6*, 507; *CPR, 1388–92*, 485; ibid., *1391–6*, 305.
24. *CPR, 1388–92*, 517; ibid., *1391–6*, 433; ibid., *1396–9*, 157.
25. ibid., *1396–9*, 179, 309, 311.
26. ibid., *1391–6*, 129; British Museum, Arundel MS. no. 68, fo. 57. I. D. Churchill, *Canterbury Administration* i. 64n.
27. *CPR, 1391–6*, 285; *CCR, 1392–6*, 238, 254, 258; *Literae Cantuarienses*, ed. J. B. Sheppard (R.S.), iii, 52; *The Register of Henry Chichele*, ed. E. F. Jacob, i. 162; *Archaeologia Cantiana*, xxxix. 68.
28. *CPR, 1399–1401*, 378; ibid., *1405–8*, 330, 331; ibid., *1436–41*, 446; Morant, op. cit., i. 470.
29. PRO, Lists and Indexes, IX, *List of Sheriffs*, 44.
30. *CPR, 1396–99*, 590.
31. In Michaelmas term 1399, Doreward duly made appearance in the Exchequer as ex-sheriff, but (understandably) *nihil tulit*. (K.R. Memoranda Rolls, Exchequer, PRO, E. 159/176).
32. *Rot. Parl.* iii. 424b.
33. *CFR, 1399–1405*, 28; *CPR, 1399–1401*, 284, 293, 308 480; *PPC.* i. 194, 199 (*Rot. Parl.*, iii. 491, 499); *CPR 1416–22*, 441; *CCR, 1422–29*, 300 et seq.; Dugdale, *Monasticon*, viii. 1425; *Rot. Parl.*, iv. 319a.
34. *PPC*, i. 100–1, 144, 146, 155, 168, 222; F. Baldwin, *The King's Council in the Middle Ages*, 150, 154, 399, 413; *Rot. Parl.*, iii. 530a; *Privy Seal* warrants for issue. PRO, E 404/16/72; 17/280; Exchequer, Issue Rolls, PRO, E 403/569, mems. 2, 21; ibid., E 403/571, mem. 8; E 403/573, mems. 9, 13; E 403/576. mem. 13; E 403/585, mem. 2.
35. *CPR, 1399–1401*, 154, 372, 378; *The Oath Book or Red Parchment Book of Colchester*, ed. W. G. Benham 21–2, 92.
36. *CPR, 1401–5*, 467; *The Oath Book of Colchester*, op. cit., 21–2.
37. *CPR, 1399–1401*, 559; ibid., *1401–5*, 517; ibid., *1405–8*, 491; ibid., *1408–13*, 481.
38. ibid., *1399–1401*, 212; ibid., *1401–5*, 114, 288, 290, 358; ibid., *1405–8*, 62.
39. ibid., *1401–5*. 129, 436; J. H. Wylie, *The Reign of Henry IV*, i. 427. Doreward was again being threatened by one Thomas Tailor of Colchester in December 1404, and the latter had then to find sureties undertaking to appear before the Royal Council when required. (*CCR, 1402–5*, 476.)
40. *CPR, 1399–1401*, 218; ibid., 416, 438, 502, 519; ibid., *1401–5*, 118, 190, 315; ibid., *1405–8*, 95; ibid., *1408–13*, 34.
41. ibid., *1399–1401*, 428; *English Historical Review*, lxxix (1964), A. L. Brown, *The Commons and the Council in the Reign of Henry IV*, 2–5, 29; *PPC*, i. 155; ii. 86, 99. (On 17 November 1401 Doreward was granted a *regardum* of £40 over and above his councillor's fees, as a recompense for his costs when sent to the king at different times in this year on the Council's behalf [PRO, E 403/571, mem. 8]).
42. *CCR, 1399–1402*, 563; Issue Roll, PRO, E 403/569, mem. 21; *PPC*, ii. 74.
43. *Rot. Parl.*, iii, 519b, 530a.
44. *CPR, 1405–8*, 64.
45. *CFR, 1399–1405*, 47, 233; *CPR, 1401–5*, 104; ibid., *1405–8*, 330.
46. *CPR, 1405–8*, 491; ibid., *1408–13*, 481, 346, 348.
47. *Rot. Parl.*, iv. 4–5; J. H. Round (in *E.H.R.*, xxix, 717 et seq.) did not make it clear that Doreward was not the Commons' first choice as Speaker, and that he was only Speaker for the last of the nearly four weeks of session.
48. *CPR, 1413–6*, 118, 409, 418; ibid., *1416–22*, 452.
49. ibid., *1413–16*, 338; ibid., *1416–22*, 78; *CCR, 1413–9*, 351, 366.
50. Issue Roll, PRO, E 403/675, mem. 10; Somerset House, *Register Marche*, fo. 50.
51. Morant, op. cit., i. 284; ii. 384; *CFR, 1413–22*, 335; *CCR, 1419–22*, 104, 137.
52. *CFR, 1422–30*, 136; *Reports of the Deputy Keeper of the Public Records*, xliii, 316; Lincoln's Inn, *Black Book*.

4

SIR ARNALD SAVAGE OF BOBBING

The following abbreviations have been used in the footnotes:

D.N.B.   = *Dictionary of National Biography.*
C.P.R.   = *Calendar of Patent Rolls.*
C.C.R.   = *Calendar of Close Rolls.*
C.F.R.   = *Calendar of Fine Rolls.*
C.Ch.R. = *Calendar of Charter Rolls.*
P.R.O.   = *Public Record Office.*
Rot. Parl. = *Rotuli Parliamentorum.*
D.K.R.   = *Deputy Keeper's Reports.*
P.P.C.   = *Proceedings and Ordinances of the Privy Council,* ed. N. H.
          Nicolas.
R.S.   = *Rolls Series.*

NOT until 1376, seemingly, did the medieval Commons elect a Speaker from among their own number and for the duration of a parliament. This constitutional invention is one of the signs of a development towards a greater political maturity on the part of the lower house of parliament at this time, a development that was assisted by the general weakness of the royal authority under Richard II and Henry IV. It was under these two kings that Sir Arnald Savage lived his eventful and significant career: a knight of the King's Chamber under Richard II, after the Lancastrian usurpation in 1399 he became steward of the Household of the future Henry V and then member of Henry IV's Council. He was one of the two knights of the shire for Kent on six occasions, in the parliaments of January and November, 1390, November, 1391, January, 1401, September, 1402, and January, 1404.[1] But he is chiefly memorable for his two occupations of the office of Commons' Speaker at the outset of the Lancastrian period: here he has a distinctive place in parliamentary history. His biography has a special appeal for the local historian, in that he was the first representative in parliament for the county of Kent to be Speaker, the only one in pre-Tudor times.

The family of Savage of Bobbing near Sittingbourne in Kent by the end of the fourteenth century had long been established in that county, almost certainly for over two hundred years. It was well connected locally by marriage. The first wife of Sir Arnald Savage's father, Sir Arnald, was Margery, a daughter of Michael Lord Poynings. The father's second wife who survived him by only a few months—they

[1] *The Official Return of Members of Parliament,* 1, 238, 240, 242, 261, 263, 265.

both died in 1375—was, however, called Eleanor and it is very likely she who was the mother of the Speaker. The Speaker himself married but once, his wife being Joan, daughter of Sir William Eckingham of Eckingham, who survived him by over two years—he died on 29th November, 1410, she in April or early May, 1413. Their only daughter, Elizabeth, was married firstly (some time before Michaelmas, 1395) to Sir Reynold, son and heir of Sir Thomas Cobham of Rundale and Allington Castle, a member of the junior branch of the family of Cobham of Cobham and Cooling (Kent), and then on Cobham's death in October, 1405, to William Clifford, the nephew and heir of Sir Lewis Clifford, K.G. Like the Speaker's father and mother, Sir Lewis had been a member of the closely knit household circle of the Black Prince, to whose widow, the Princess Joan, the mother of Richard II, he was an executor. The Speaker's only son and heir, another Arnald (the third in succession) married Catherine, a daughter of Roger Lord Scales (a parliamentary peer between 1376 and 1385).

This latter alliance was contracted apparently not long before St. George's Day, 1399, when Sir Arnald received a royal licence enabling him to entail upon his heir and Catherine Scales the manor of Tracies in Newington by Sittingbourne and a future interest for life in the manor of Shorne between Rochester and Gravesend. This settlement represents the Speaker as having himself no more than a reversionary interest in Shorne. Although nearly ten years before, on 15th November, 1389, he had been pardoned by the King (with the assent of the Council) for having acquired this manor in fee without licence (it being held in chief of the Crown) from Sir Roger Northwood, it is clear that his interest was actually only in the reversion, because not until it fell in (in July, 1405) did he get full possession. The Speaker's elder sister, Eleanor, had married this Sir Roger Northwood. The explanation of this seeming discrepancy in the record of possession at Shorne seems to be that before 1405 Sir Arnald enjoyed from early in 1388 a tenancy of the manor under the Northwood family, as he certainly did from about the same time in certain other of their estates in Iwade, Halstow, and Milton (all in the vicinity of Bobbing), for which he paid a small rent and performed suit in the manor court of Norwood. He was certainly lord of the manor of Shorne in January, 1407, and he died seised in November, 1410. He also died seised of the manor of Bobbing Court, held in gavelkind along with two water-mills there as of the manor of Milton (which properties then went to his son and heir), and also of the manors of Holmes and Funton (both in Iwade) and of Kemsley (in Milton), all three held in gavelkind and of the manor of Milton, which Sir Arnald's widow then entered as her jointure. Although he had parted with the manor of Tracies in Newington by Sittingbourne in favour of his son and Catherine Scales in 1399,

Sir Arnald had apparently retained some landed estate in that vill, because he left directions in his will for the foundation of a chantry at Chesley (in Newington) as well as at Bobbing, where he was buried.[1] With the exception of Shorne, which lay a dozen miles or so to the west of Bobbing Court between the Medway and the Thames, all his estates were in the immediate neighbourhood of Bobbing, that is, in the thick neck of land connecting the Isle of Sheppey with north Kent proper. What was the value of these lands is not known, but it is unlikely that it was very substantial.

The Speaker's father, Sir Arnald Savage, had been a closely attached member of the household of the Black Prince for a quarter of a century and more, down to the very time of his death in July, 1375. He had served in Edward III's French wars, in the Crécy campaign of 1346 in the retinue of his father-in-law, Michael Lord Poynings. But by 1349 his main connection was with the Prince of Wales: he was then acting as a feoffee in the Prince's interest in two manors of the honour of Wallingford. He was at that time both sheriff and escheator in Kent and he was to be knight of the shire in 1352. In 1359, 1360, 1365 and 1366 there is evidence of his being in Gascony with the Prince. On 12th March, 1359, the office of Mayor of Bordeaux was committed to him and he retained the post until 1363. His connection with the Black Prince involved him in much diplomatic business. In 1363 he was a party to the negotiations with Pedro the Cruel of Castile. In May, 1366, Pope Urban V was using his good offices in his attempts to restore peace in Aquitaine between the Black Prince and Gaston, Count of Foix, and Gregory XI did the same in 1371, in which year and again in 1372, 1373, and 1375, Savage was a commissioner to treat with France, in the last of these instances (in February and April, 1375) as a member of the English diplomatic corps accompanying John of Gaunt to Flanders. In 1372-4 he was acting as one of two proctors for Cardinal William Indicis, one of the Limousin group in the Sacred College and a nephew of Clement VI, in the archdeaconry of Canterbury, for the fruits of which they answered to the cardinal who was, of course, non-resident. How intimately the Speaker's father was still attached to the Black Prince, who now for some time had been in failing health, is suggested by his appearance among the witnesses of the Prince's charter to the mayor and corporation of Coventry at Candlemas, 1375, a document attested by members of the Prince's council, his chamberlain, his land-steward, his receiver-general, his steward of household, and his secretary, and it was at Wallingford, the centre of one of the

[1] *D.N.B.*, XVII, 824-5. *The Genealogist*, *N.S.* XXI, 245; XXII, 229; XXIX, 201-8; *Archæologia Cantiana*, XXIX, 157, 164; N. H. Nicolas, *Testamenta Vetusta*, i, 93; *C.P.R.*, *1396-9*, 571; *ibid.*, *1388-92*, 152; *C.C.R.*, *1385-9*, 475; *ibid.*, *1402-5*, 462; *ibid.*, *1405-9*, 380; *ibid.*, *1409-13*, 165; *C.F.R.*, *1405-13*, 210; *ibid.*, *1413-22*, 323; *The Register of Archbishop Chichele*, ed. E. F. Jacob, ii, 205.

Prince's most important honours, that soon after his return from Bruges, Savage died (intestate) on 22nd July, 1375.[1] It was in the Benedictine priory at Wallingford that he was buried, and so later in the same year was his widow, Eleanor, to whom her son, the later Speaker, acted as principal executor. She left him the wainage of the manors of Bobbing and Tracies. How closely the Speaker's mother had been involved with her husband in the affairs of the Black Prince's household is clear from the fact that it was in consideration of her services as the nurse of the Prince's heir, Richard of Bordeaux, that on 13th March, 1380, there was remitted the fine of £40 which her son Arnald had originally been required to pay for a royal licence to marry at will.[2]

Born in 1358, Arnald Savage (the later Speaker) was at the time of his father's and mother's death still in his minority and was presumably a royal ward; certainly in July, 1376, the manor of Tracies in Newington was in the King's hands as held in chief of the Crown. He was presumably of age when on 28th October, 1379, by a bill of the Treasurer, he received the royal licence to marry whom he wished for a fine of £40 payable in the Exchequer; his sureties were one of his mother's executors and Thomas St. Leger, a near neighbour, in whose manor of East Hall near Sittingbourne young Savage was already a feoffee. As we have seen, the fine was remitted in March following by royal letters patent under the great seal.[3] By October, 1380, Savage had offered proof of age, although livery of seisin of his father's estates was deferred until 9th May, 1382.[4] In the meantime, he already had begun to act as a member of occasional royal commissions in Kent. On 23rd August, 1380, when there was a scare of French invasion he was made a commissioner for the arming of all the landholders of the Isle of Sheppey and the hundred of Milton. A year later, after Kent had undergone all the distress and dislocation of the Peasants' Revolt, Savage was put on a very large commission appointed to keep the peace in the county, with powers of arrest and imprisonment against any who stirred up insurrection and with authority to suppress unlawful assemblies. This commission, issued on 2nd September, 1381, was

[1] *The Genealogist, op. cit.,* XXIX, 202; *Calendar of Inquisitions post mortem Edward III,* IX, 237; T. Carte, *Catalogue des Rolles Gascons,* i, 145, 147, 153; *Cal. of Papal Registers, Papal Letters, III,* 577; IV, 22, 98; *D.N.B., loc. cit.;* *Exchequer, Accounts Various, Q.R., P.R.O.* E.101/316/no. 9; *Foreign Accounts,* E.364/8, file H; *C.P.R., 1422-9,* 187; *C.Ch.R.,* V, 241; *Historical Manuscripts Commission, 5th Report, MSS. of Dean and Chapter of Canterbury,* 427 b (cf. Le Neve, *Fasti,* i, 41).

[2] Nicolas, *Testamenta Vetusta,* i, 93; *Archæologia Cantiana,* XXIX, 164; *C.P.R., 1377-81,* 450.

[3] *The Genealogist,* XXIX, 202-8; *C.P.R., 1374-7,* 294; *ibid., 1377-81,* 313, 396, 450.

[4] *C.C.R., 1381-5,* 70.

renewed on 14th December following and on 8th March, 1382, with enlarged powers. By this date Savage was acting as sheriff of Kent; appointed on 23rd November, 1381, he served for exactly a year. It was only during his term of office that he procured livery of seisin of his father's estates. In June in the same year he was included in a commission for sewers in the hundred of Milton.[1]

It is very likely that already he was attached as an esquire to the household of Richard II. Certainly in the Exchequer year 30th September, 1383-4, he was in receipt of an allowance of £2 a year, for winter and summer liveries, from the treasurer of the Royal Household. (He was to remain a retainer in the Household until the end of Richard's reign.)[2] In this same year, on 29th February, 1384, he was appointed for the first time as a justice of the peace in Kent, a commission to which he was re-appointed in February, 1385 and May, 1386; on 28th June, 1386, however, he was dropped from it. In the meantime, he had served on a variety of casual local commissions of royal appointment: by patent of 6th March, 1384, he was authorized to inquire into the tenure of certain estates acquired by Edward III in Kent, including the castle and lordship of Leybourne, the castle and town of Queenborough, and the manor of Gravesend; on 24th January, 1385, he was appointed a commissioner of array against the eventuality of a French invasion (the commission being re-constituted, with Savage remaining a member, on 15th April following); on 7th March, 1385, he was commissioned to investigate unlicensed hunting in the king's free warren in the Isle of Sheppey.[3] Despite the close threat of French invasion in the summer of this year, Richard II personally led an expedition into Scotland. On 29th June, 1385, as an esquire Savage was advanced £3 at the Lower Exchequer for his own wages in the expedition and for the single archer he retained to serve with him. Whether he performed the service of carrying a white banner on the expedition at his own costs, as his tenancy of the manor of Shorne obliged him to do, is not known. One thing is quite certain: that he was knighted during the expedition; it was as a knight of the Royal Household that, on 7th August, 1385, after the death of the King's mother, the Princess Joan of Kent, he was issued with a black mourning gown by the keeper of the Great Wardrobe.[4] On 20th October following he was again appointed sheriff in Kent and served until 18th October, 1386, again acting in the meantime in the spring of 1386 as a commissioner of array. Earlier in this same year of his shrievalty, on 12th March, 1386, he had

---

[1] *C.P.R.*, *1377-81*, 574; *ibid.*, *1381-5*, 77, 84, 135, 138; *P.R.O.*, *Lists and Indexes*, ix, *List of Sheriffs*, 68.

[2] *Exchequer, Accounts Various*, *P.R.O.*, E.101/401/2, 42.

[3] *C.P.R.*, *1381-5*, 423, 588-9, 594.

[4] *Exchequer, Issue Rolls*, *P.R.O.*, E.403/508, mem. 16; *Exchequer, Accounts Various*, *P.R.O.*, E.101/401/16.

taken out royal letters of protection as intending to go on John of Gaunt's expedition to Spain, but, although Lancaster's plans in this direction matured, Savage's did not, and the letters were revoked on 28th July following, on the grounds that he was not making preparations to accompany the duke.[1] It is certain that he did not go: after the parliamentary commission took charge of the administration in November, 1386, and reversed the Lancastrian policy of appeasement with France, Savage, in spite of his connection with the King, joined the maritime force put under the direction of Richard, Earl of Arundel, to prosecute the war more vigorously in the Channel. Savage's recent enhancement of status is exemplified in the size of his retinue, which mustered on 13th March, 1387; it included another knight besides himself, 28 esquires, and 36 archers.[2]

Sir Arnald Savage's reaction to the political events of 1387-8 is not known. Although he was closely connected with the Court, nothing of ill befell him. Perhaps his joining Arundel's expedition did him no harm. Nothing is known of his doings in 1388 except that he was appointed on 15th March to serve on an enquiry into a complaint of the barons of Faversham that certain presents of fish they had been making to the constable of Dover Castle and warden of the Cinque Ports to secure his good offices with their lord, the Abbot of Faversham, had come to be claimed by him as perquisites of the wardenship; the Faversham barons were evidently turning to their own profit the impeachment (during the Merciless Parliament) of Sir Simon Burley, the late warden, who had also abused his position in other directions. Later in the year, on 22nd October, 1388, Savage was included in a commission of sewers in the Isle of Thanet and between Reculver and St. Mary Cliffe. After the fall of the government of the Appellants in May, 1389, Savage was not restored to the Kentish commission of the peace, but he continued to act on occasional local commissions of royal appointment. On 6th October, 1389, and again on 24th November following, he was appointed to enquire into the previous year's revenues of eleven manors in Kent which, forfeited by the late Sir Simon Burley, had been granted to the prior of Chiltern Langley, who had never received them.

Savage was still retained as a King's knight by Richard II when in January, 1390, he was called upon to act for the first time as knight of the shire for Kent. Re-elected to the second parliament of the year which met in November, 1390, he was shortly afterwards (on 29th December) commissioned to investigate the maladministration of the late escheator for Kent and Middlesex who, first appointed in February, 1388, had been responsible for arranging the seizure of the Kentish

---

[1] *Lists of Sheriffs, loc. cit.; C.P.R., 1385-9*, 176, 198.
[2] *Exchequer, Foreign Accounts, P.R.O.*, E.101/40/33.

estates of some of Richard II's friends who had suffered death and forfeiture during the Merciless Parliament of 1388. Only two days later (on 31st December), retained as a King's knight, Sir Arnald was granted for life or until further order an annuity of 40 marks charged on the issues of the county of Kent, in consideration of his father's good service to the Black Prince and his own to the King.[1] Whether Savage was already one of the knights of the King's Chamber is not known, but he was certainly one of the eight Chamber knights in the financial year 30th September, 1392-3, during which he received 10 marks as his fee and 8 marks allowance for his winter and summer robes from the keeper of the Wardrobe. He was still one of the " milites camere et aule regis " in the year September 1395-6 and probably remained so until the end of the reign.[2] It was with the controller of the Household, Sir Baldwin de Raddington, and two other members of the Household, that on 24th July, 1392, a month after the mayor of London, John Hende, and other prominent citizens had been sentenced to imprisonment for contempt by a Great Council at Nottingham (following the King's quarrel with the City over the raising of a royal loan), Savage went bail in £2,000 for the late mayor; some two months later Hende and his fellow citizens were pardoned and the mainprises annulled. On 4th January following (1393) Savage was granted for life the constableship and custody of the royal castle of Queenborough in the Isle of Sheppey, and five weeks later (by patent of 8th February, 1393) he was given an annuity of 20 marks charged on the fee-farm of Canterbury to offset his own charges while holding this office.[3] In addition, he was advanced during the next three years by the Exchequer various sums amounting to over £220 for his repairs, alterations and improvements to the structure of the castle. He surrendered the constableship on 5th June, 1396, when to compensate him for the loss of the annuity and also for the surrender of the annuity granted him in December, 1390 (together worth £40 a year) Richard II granted him a fresh annuity of £50 for life charged (as from the previous Easter) on the petty customs of the port of London.[4] This annuity he held for the rest of the reign, and Henry IV was later to confirm it.

In the meanwhile, in November, 1391, Savage had been for the second time running re-elected as knight of the shire of Kent. Not for over nine years, however, was he to sit among the Commons again. In the previous February he had been appointed by the Council to act on a general royal enquiry into cases of slackness of administration in the

[1] *C.P.R.*, *1385-9*, 465, 551: *ibid.*, *1388-92*, 131, 142, 152, 358, 435; *C.C.R.*, *1389-92*, 387.

[2] *Exchequer, P.R.O.*, E.101/403/22; *ibid.*, E.101/403/10.

[3] *C.C.R.*, *1392-6*, 78; *C.P.R.*, *1391-6*, 206, 216.

[4] *Exchequer, Issue Rolls*, E.403/541-554, *passim; C.P.R.*, *1391-6*, 286, 719.

seven hundreds of Kent.   On 12th February, 1392, he was put on an
oyer and terminer following reports of the neglect of walls, causeways,
and dykes, and the resulting depopulation of the Isle of Thanet.   At the
end of the same month he was included in an enquiry into merchandise
thrown ashore at Northbourne as wreck of sea, and a day later was
appointed a commissioner of array for Kent in event of a renewal of war
with France if the existing truce was not renewed.   On 18th September,
1393, he was put on a commission to examine the old bridge over the
Medway at Rochester, falling material from which was causing the
tide-race to endanger the new bridge erected there by Lord Cobham
and Sir Robert Knolles, which the commissioners were also authorized
to have repaired.   Earlier in this year, on two occasions (in February
and May) proceedings in the Exchequer against Savage as a royal
commissioner in Kent had been stopped because the commissions had
not come into his hands; one was a commission appointing him a
justice of oyer and terminer; the other, one appointing him to enquire
in Thanet into the liability to find a ferry service over the river Sarre
and to repair causeways on its banks.[1]   For the first time for ten years
he was again made a J.P. in Kent on 1st May, 1396; he apparently
served uninterruptedly on this commission of the peace until the end
of Richard II's reign.   It was five weeks after this that his annuity of
£40 as a knight of the King's Chamber was raised to £50.

What Savage was doing during the last three years of Richard II's
reign can only be the subject of conjecture.   On 3rd April, 1398,
however, he was ordered on pain of £200 to appear personally before
the Council " to declare what shall there be laid before him".   It is
possible that his actions in 1387-8 had been equivocal in the King's
view.   It is also possible that he had had relations at that time with
John Lord Cobham of Cooling, his neighbour, who, as a prime mover
and member of the parliamentary commission of 1386, which Richard
II's judges had declared in 1387 to be a treasonable undertaking, had
recently been condemned to banishment and forfeiture for his offence;
certainly by October, 1395, Savage was one of Lord Cobham's feoffees
in his most important estates in Kent, Surrey, Wiltshire, and in London.[2]
However this may be, on 29th April, 1398, within little more than a
week of his appearance before the Council, Savage was able to secure
repayment of a loan he had made to the King to the amount of £100.[3]
He does not appear to have accompanied Richard II to Ireland in May,
1399.   After Henry of Bolingbroke's landing in July following, he very
probably lay low until Henry's accession was assured.   Perhaps as
something of a precaution in event of trouble, on St. George's Day, 1399,

[1] *C.P.R.*, *1388-92*, 439; *ibid.*, *1391-6*, 85, 85, 357-8; *C.C.R.*, *1392-6*, 120, 142.
[2] *C.P.R.*, *1391-6*, 728; *C.C.R.*, *1396-99*, 277; *ibid.*, *1392-6*, 498.
[3] *Exchequer, Issue Roll, P.R.O.*, E. 403/559, mem. 2.

he had conveyed his manor of Tracies to his son and heir and his young wife (Catherine Scales).

It is reasonably clear, especially from what followed in the reign of Henry IV, that Sir Arnald Savage was not long in giving his adherence to Richard II's supplanter. On 10th September, 1399, some three weeks before Richard was deposed, he was commissioned by the Council to enquire into the removal of the goods and chattels of Roger Walden, who had secured the see of Canterbury following Archbishop Arundel's banishment in 1397 and who was now thrust out to allow Arundel to be restored to the primacy; Walden's property undoubtedly included much of Arundel's own furniture and other household goods which, after their confiscation, Richard II had given to him; the commissioners were to deliver Walden's goods to the prior of Christchurch, Canterbury, and William Makenade.[1] Savage was not elected to the parliament summoned to witness Richard's deposition and Henry IV's accession. But on 28th November, 1399, he was confirmed in his office of justice of the peace in Kent, which he was to continue to hold until his death exactly eleven years later. And on 18th December he was put on a commission of array in the county, which was renewed on 23rd January, 1400.[2]

Nothing further is known of Savage until his election as senior knight of the shire for Kent to the second parliament of the new reign, first summoned to meet at York in October, 1400, and then prorogued to meet at Westminster on 20th January, 1401. On the third day of the session Savage was presented by the Commons " pur lour Parlour et Procuratour en Parlement." The King agreed to his election. Sir Arnald made his official " protestation," then went on to rehearse briefly the declaration of the causes of summons as made by Chief Justice Thirning, and subsequently requested that the Commons should not be hurried into making their answers regarding the most important issues, which was likely if such were only brought to their notice at the end of the parliament. The King, through the Earl of Worcester, disclaimed any such intention. Three days later the Commons asked the King to give no hearing to tale-bearers from among their own number which might excite his displeasure against some of their fellows; the King's answer was that their proposals should be agreed to by all of them before he gave credence to any such bearer of news. The mind of the Speaker can be detected in the Commons' definition on the same day of the three pre-requisites of good government: " seen (sense), humanite et richesse "; and in their statement that they abstained from dilating on the merits of the King, to avoid

[1] *C.P.R.*, *1396-9*, 597; *Chronicon Adae de Usk*, ed. E. Maunde Thompson, 2nd ed., 37.

[2] *C.P.R.*, *1399-1401*, 209, 211, 560.

being accounted " flaterers et glosers."[1] The King's financial requirements were to the tune of £130,000, although no figures were laid
before the Commons. But the smoothness with which, according to the
roll of the parliament, its business was conducted is deceptive and
conceals an uneasy atmosphere. The Commons pressed their advantage
to push forward their claims. At the end of the fifth week the Commons asked that the business of the parliament should be enacted and
engrossed by the clerk of the parliament before the justices left, so that
their memory should still be fresh, and on the same day backed up this
demand with a request to know the King's answers to their petitions
before they made a financial grant. The first of these requests was
favourably answered; the King at first temporized regarding the
second, saying that he would consult the Lords, but on the last day of
the session turned it down as uncustomary. On a later occasion,
when deploring the existence of discord between some of the Lords,
the Commons emphasized the need for unity between the estates, which
could be likened to a Trinity: the King, the Lords Spiritual and Temporal, and the Commons. Here is surely to be discerned the authentic
voice of their Speaker. So, too, in their ingenious demonstration on
10th March, the last day of the session, that a parliament was like the
mass, the archbishop beginning the office, the King in the middle at the
offertory undertaking to uphold the faith of the Church (a reference
perhaps to the statute *De haeretico comburendo* passed during the
session) and to ensure the maintenance of just law to poor and rich
alike, and then finally the coming of the Commons to say *Ite missa est*
and *Deo gratias* for three reasons, namely, that God had granted them
a just, knowledgeable and humane King, that the King had taken steps
to meet the threat of subversive doctrine, and that there was amity
between him and themselves and the Lords. The King had already
pardoned the Commons for any offence they had unwittingly given to
cause displeasure on his part. The Commons granted a tenth and
fifteenth and renewed the subsidies of tunnage and poundage. Savage
had no cause for dissatisfaction with the session. Nor had the Commons with him: the St. Albans chronicler heard and stated that " tam
diserte, tam eloquenter, tam gratiose declaravit communitatis negotia,
praecipue ne de cetero taxis gravarentur, aut talliagiis, quod laudem
ab universis promeruit ea die". Nor apparently had Henry IV much
cause for complaint: three days after the dissolution, on 13th March,
1401, the patent of June, 1396, granting Savage £50 a year for life on
the London petty customs, was confirmed.[2]

When the recent parliament had been in session for a month, on

---

[1] *Rot. Parl.*, iii, 455-6.
[2] *Annales Henrici Quarti*, (R.S.) ed. H. T. Riley, p. 335; *C.P.R.*, *1399-1401*,
444.

21st February, the Commons asked for an examination to be made by the Council of any Welsh-born officials of the Crown. The King, by way of answer, ordered his Council and the Council of the Prince of Wales to scrutinize the relevant statutes of Edward I, which had prohibited the employment of Welshmen in royal administration, and to reform them with the advice of Lords and Commons. In the previous autumn Owen Glendower had developed his quarrel with Lord Grey of Ruthin into a full-scale Welsh national rising, which had already required the King's personal intervention (although to little purpose). The primary responsibility for the suppression of the Welsh revolt rested with the Prince of Wales and Henry Hotspur, justice of Chester and North Wales. At the end of November, 1400, all Welsh rebels had been summoned to present themselves at Chester for submission to the Prince. On 21st March, 1401, the Council authorized him to discharge any unsatisfactory constables of castles. In April he moved with Hotspur into Wales and before the end of May had recovered Conway Castle, which the rebels had taken through the negligence of the constable. Before this surrender took place, the terms of the settlement had been already arranged as between Hotspur on the one hand and, on the other, Sir Arnald Savage and the latter's fellow members of the Prince's Council. How long Savage had been a member of Henry of Monmouth's Council is not known, but it is almost certain that he had joined it before the recent January-March 1401 parliament in which he acted as Speaker. He was personally summoned to a Great Council convened at Westminster in the middle of August following. On 7th October he attested the surrender to the Prince of the Anglesey and other Welsh lands of two Welsh rebel landowners. Some two months later together with the Prince's chancellor and chamberlain and on the Prince's behalf, Savage had requested the constable of Chester Castle to take three Welsh hostages into his custody there. Savage is described in the memorandum of 13th December, 1401, relating to their reception as then being the Prince of Wales's steward of Household. How long he had occupied this important office in the Household of the heir-apparent is again not known, but it is highly probable that he was holding it when one of the chief members of the prince's Council in the previous spring, and very likely that he had been doing so when Speaker. Precisely when he relinquished the post is once more a matter for conjecture. By 2nd April, 1403, he had been replaced in it by Sir John Stanley (a Lancashire and Cheshire knight, whose ties with Richard II, like Savage's, had been very close).[1] But it is almost certain that

[1] *Royal and Historical Letters during the reign of Henry IV*, (R.S.), ed. F. C. Hingeston, i, 69; *P.P.C.*, i, 161; *D.K.R.*, XXXVI, 207, 482; *ibid.*, 380; J. S. Roskell, *The Knights of the Shire for the County Palatine of Lancaster, 1377-1460* (Chetham Soc. N.S. vol. 95), 123.

Savage was compelled to give up the office when he became a member of the royal Council; this appointment had taken place at the latest by Michaelmas, 1402.

Whether Savage was re-elected as knight of the shire for Kent to the parliament which met at Westminster in January, 1402, is not known, because all the returns of knights and burgesses alike have been lost, but he was certainly once more elected for Kent to the second parliament of the year which met on 30th September and sat until 25th November following. In July, 1402, he had acted on a commission of array in Kent,[1] but of much greater interest is his appointment at (or shortly before) Michaelmas, 1402, to be a member of the King's Council with a fee of £100 a year. He was destined still to be a member of the Council at the end of 1406.[2] In the course of the parliament of the autumn of 1402 he was one of a number of recipients of royal letters of privy seal requesting benevolences for the payment of garrisons in S. Wales,[3] but two days after the end of the parliament his new office stood him in good stead when (on 27th November, 1402) he was granted the custody of the manor of Milsted (near Sittingbourne, Kent) during the minority of the heir, a royal ward, at a farm of £4 a year payable in the Exchequer; Savage's son Arnald was one of his sureties.[4] On 4th June, 1403, he was present at a meeting of the King's Council where a petition of his own was favourably considered: he asked that his existing grant of £50 a year for life, charged on the London petty customs, should be raised by 25 marks in view of the additional expenses he would be bound to incur since his appointment (with the assent of a recent Great Council) to be a royal councillor attendant on the King's person; the grant passed the great seal on the same day and, whether or not he was still a councillor at this later date, he was still enjoying the additional annuity along with the old one in October, 1409.[5] In August and September, 1403, he was again a commissioner of array in Kent. On the day after Christmas following he attended a meeting of the Council, when the King was present and expressed his intention of moving out to Sutton, where some of the councillors (including Savage) were to follow for further discussions.[6]

The first parliament to meet after the Percy revolt ended at Shrewsbury in July, 1403, had already been prorogued to meet at Westminster on 14th January, 1404, having first been summoned to Coventry for

---

[1] *C.P.R., 1401-5*, 115.

[2] *Privy seal warrants for issue*, P.R.O., E.404/21/270; *Exchequer, Issue Rolls*, P.R.O., E.403/580, mem. 2; 585, mem. 1; 587, mem. 14; 589, mem. 12; 657, mem. 1; *P.P.C.*, i, 222, 238, 244, 246, 295; ii, 83, 87, 89.

[3] *P.P.C.*, ii, 74-5.

[4] *C.F.R., 1399-1405*, 180.

[5] *Ancient Petitions*, P.R.O., S.C., 8, file 186, no. 9256; *C.P.R., 1401-5*, 236; *C.C.R., 1402-5*, 192, 444; *ibid., 1409-13*, 6.

[6] *C.P.R., 1401-5*, 290; *P.P.C.*, ii, 83.

3rd December, and Sir Arnald Savage had been re-elected knight of the shire for Kent. On the second day of the session the Commons presented him once more as their Speaker. His otherwise normal " protestation " was extended to include a request that the Commons should not incur the King's displeasure (as a result of unauthorized reports) if they complained of his conduct of affairs. The Commons were not long before they expressed (on 25th January) their concern about the dangerous state of the North after the Percy rising and the abuses of the practice of giving liveries, complained of excessive royal expenditure, and attacked the Royal Household as extravagantly organized and as overrun with aliens, the Breton entourage of the Queen included. A two years' appropriation of income from certain specified sources of revenue, amounting to over £12,000, was agreed upon, together with the appointment of special treasurers of the yield from whatever taxes parliament would be prepared to grant. The King's Council Henry IV was prevailed upon to nominate at the Commons' special and insistent request, in order to ensure the remedying of all the complaints and grievances disclosed during the session, and twenty-two lords, knights and esquires were appointed in parliament to act until it should meet again: among the seven commoners were three knights of the shire in the parliament, John Doreward (for Essex), John Curson (for Derbyshire), and the Speaker himself who was continued in office.[1] The parliament ended (after nearly ten weeks of session) on 20th March, 1404, with a provisional grant of a novel tax of five per cent on landed income which, as further concessions of taxes in the Coventry parliament of the following October suggest, proved quite inadequate to the King's needs. The rôle played by Savage suggests one of two things, or perhaps both: that being a royal Councillor did not prevent a supporter of the King from offering loyal criticism as a member of the Commons, or that the Speaker for the Commons could in that capacity only speak and act as the Commons required him to do. It had been a very unsatisfactory session from Henry IV's point of view. And it proved to be Savage's last; he never again sat as knight of the shire.

In the course of his Speakership Savage had been re-appointed a justice of the peace in Kent (on 10th February, 1404) and he was re-appointed again two years later when the next commissions were issued. He continued in the meantime to act as a member of the King's Council, perhaps in this capacity taking the musters of the retinues of the admirals for the North and West respectively at Sandwich and Southampton, along with one of the receivers of the parliamentary subsidies, in accordance with writs of 11th June, 1404. Although his re-appointment as King's Councillor in the January, 1404, parliament was

[1] *Rot. Parl.*, iii, 530a.

expressly made (according to the terms of a special grant of 50 marks as a reward for his attendances made to him on 2nd December, 1404) until parliament should reassemble, Savage evidently continued in office after the Coventry Parliament of the autumn of 1404. By the middle of August, 1406, some £208 was owing to him for his fees during the previous four years, of which he then managed to secure a cash payment of little more than a third at the Lower Exchequer. During the second session of the long parliament of this year, on 22nd May, 1406, he had been again personally nominated in parliament by Henry IV as one of his Council, and two days later the reconstructed Council undertook office provided that funds were made available for its proper functioning.[1] Governmental and administrative inefficiency and the character of Household rule were again the burden of the Commons' complaints, but finance was the root of the trouble. After the second parliamentary session, on 28th June Savage was made a commissioner for the raising of Crown loans in Sussex and Kent, and on the same day he was included in another commission for the same counties and for the Cinque Ports authorized to inquire into malversation on the part of the sheriffs and other accountable officials, into the state of Crown leases and fee-farms, and into annuities charged on such sources of royal revenue. About this time he was also serving on a commission of array in Kent against the possibility of French invasion and, as a councillor, on commissions set up to investigate specific appeals against judgments given in the Court of the Constable and Marshal.[2] He was in active attendance on the Council during the final and extremely critical session (13th October-22nd December) of the Long Parliament of 1406. Savage was not, however, present at an important meeting of the Council on 8th December, when a group of the most important officials of State and Household foregathered with the Prince of Wales to discuss reforms in the Household, especially the appointment of a good Controller; perhaps because his name was then put forward for this office as an alternative to that of Sir Thomas Brownflete, a Yorkshire knight. Brownflete was preferred, and when Sir John Tiptoft, Speaker in the Long Parliament, who was now appointed Treasurer of the Household, resigned this office in July, 1408, it was to be Brownflete who then moved up into his place.[3]

Savage continued as a royal councillor and it is possible that he acted as such until the Council was re-shaped early in 1410. Certainly as late as October, 1409, he was receiving the 100 marks a year from the petty customs of London, to which figure his old Ricardian annuity

[1] *C.P.R., 1401-5*, 517; *ibid.*, 432; *Exchequer, Issue Rolls, P.R.O.*, E.403/580, mem. 2; *ibid.*, E.403/585, mem. 1; *Rot. Parl.*, iii, 572b.
[2] *C.P.R., 1405-8*, 61, 155, 198-9, 231-2, 269.
[3] *P.P.C.*, i, 295-6; J. H. Wylie, *The Reign of Henry IV*, ii, 475n.

of £50 had been raised in June, 1403, in consideration of his expenses and work as a member of the Council. In the meantime, he had served on a number of royal commissions, local and otherwise. In February, 1407, he was re-appointed J.P. in Kent. In March and April following he was again made a member of commissions of oyer and terminer after appeals had been made against certain judgments in the Court of the Constable and Marshal. In May he was put on an oyer and terminer touching escapes of felons in Kent, and in June was included in a commission of array in the county and in one of sewers from West Greenwich round the Thames estuary to within a short distance of Dover.[1] In October, 1408, he was appointed to serve on a royal embassy to France along with the ex-chancellor, Bishop Langley of Durham; in May and September, 1409, he was one of the further embassies sent to France to treat for reformation of breaches of truce and for a perpetual peace. These were his last important appointments, for the commissioner of array for the Isle of Thanet appointed in March, 1410, was probably his son.[2]

In the meantime, Sir Arnald had acted as a trustee to Sir Nicholas Hawberk, who on the eve of his death on 9th October, 1407, made over to him and a few others all his goods and chattels. These they subsequently transferred to his widow, Joan Baroness Cobham of Cooling (Kent). Sir Nicholas, who was this lady's third husband, had served as sheriff and raglor of Flintshire and as constable of Flint Castle from 1396 to 1406, had fought at the battle of Shrewsbury in 1403 as a member of the Prince of Wales's retinue, and had been one of the knights of the King's Chamber and Hall; within a year of his death his widow married the notorious Lollard knight, Sir John Oldcastle, who was summoned to parliament for the first time in 1410 as Lord Cobham.[3] In the year after Hawberk's death, another friend of Sir Arnald Savage died: John Gower, the " moral " poet, who on 15th August, 1408, made Savage one of his executors.[4]

Little more than two years passed after this before Sir Arnald's own life ended: aged about fifty-two, he died on 29th November, 1410, and was buried at Bobbing. His son and heir was another Arnald, then aged about twenty-eight years; he secured the family estates in July, 1411, was knight of the shire for Kent in November, 1414, went overseas with Henry V's first expedition to Normandy (in the retinue of his wife's step-father, the lieutenant of Thomas Beaufort, Earl of Dorset, Admiral of England) and died childless in 1420. His father's will was

---

[1] *C.C.R.*, *1409-13*, 6; *C.P.R.*, *1405-8*, 493, 303, 326, 350-1, 353, 357.
[2] *Exchequer*, *Issue Roll*, E.403/598, mem. 3; T. Rymer, *Foedera*, VIII, 585-6, 599; *C.P.R.*, *1408-13*, 223.
[3] *Archœologia Cantiana*, XI, 91; *Coll. Topogr. et Geneal.*, VII, 336; Wylie, *Henry IV*, iii, 290-1.
[4] *D.N.B.*, VIII, 300.

then still not fully executed, for provision had not yet been made for the establishment of his chantries at Bobbing and Chesley. The tomb of the former Speaker and his wife was not yet completed either, for Sir Arnald the son left 20 marks for a brass for them both; his mother had not long survived her husband, dying in the spring of 1413.[1] The younger Arnald's wish to have his parents commemorated in this way was evidently fulfilled, for a brass, representing the Speaker as an armoured knight and his wife as a widow in weeds, still survives in Bobbing Church.

[1] *Hasted, Kent*, ii, 635; *The Genealogist*, XXIX, 202-8; *C.C.R., 1409-13*, 165; *C.F.R., 1405-13*, 190, 210; *Chichele Register*, ii, 205.

5

SIR HENRY DE RETFORD

Sir Henry de Retford[1] was a member of a well-established north Lincolnshire land-owning family, being perhaps the son of Ralph de Retford who served on various commissions for sewers and dykes in that region between 1349 and 1374. He possessed the manor of Castlethorpe in Broughton (near Brigg), the manors of Irby-on-Humber and Rothwell (held as of the Neville fee), and the manor of Carleton Paynell (held as of the fee of the Bishop of Lincoln) ; and it is likely that he owned all the lands in Broughton, Killingholme, Worlaby-by-Saxby, Carlton Kyme, and Burton-by-Lincoln which, along with the other estates already mentioned, his son, another Sir Henry, forfeited as a Yorkist in 1459, following the Rout of Ludford. This property was in the parts of Lindsey.[2] The main residences of the Retfords were at Castlethorpe and Carleton Paynell. What lands Sir Henry's two marriages brought under his control is not known, for neither the family of his first wife, Katherine, who was alive in 1397, nor that of his second, Mary, who survived him and married (as his third wife) William Lord Clinton of Maxstoke and later Sir John Heron of Northumberland, has been traced.

When Henry de Retford was born is not known for certain, but it is probable that it was in or about 1354. For in 1386, when he made a deposition in the famous Scrope v. Grosvenor heraldic case, he stated that he was 32 years of age. He was not, therefore, of full age when on 4th November, 1371, at the request of Edward St. John, a Sussex knight and retainer of the Black Prince, he procured a royal pardon (under the great seal) of the King's suit against him for the death of one Thomas Breton of Wrawby, of which he he had been both indicted and appealed, and of any consequent outlawry ; the letter patent described him as being of Worlaby (near Castlethorpe). Nothing further is known of him until, in February 1376, mainprise in £20 was found for him and three other local men, following a Chancery order to the sheriff of Lincolnshire to compel them to enter into sureties not to do hurt to one Ralph de Thirsk, failing which they were to be committed to gaol.[3] More evidence of unruliness in these early years of Retford's career comes in the next year when, on 16th October, 1377, soon after Richard II's accession, he was granted another royal pardon, this time at the petition of the young King's mother, Joan of Kent, and for the death of William Clarell esquire of Yorkshire.[4]

It was not until some seven years after Richard II's accession that Retford began to be appointed to royal commissions in Lincoln-

(1) The Surname is variously spelt as Retford, Ratford, Reddeford, Rydford, or Ryddeford.
(2) *Feudal Aids*, iii. 255, 261, 264, 345, 362, 364 ; *CPR*, 1452–61, 551.
(3) *CPR*, 1370–4, 150 ; *CCR*, 1374–7, 327.
(4) *CRP*, 1377–81, 35.

shire, and even then they were of a transitory sort.   On 1st July, 1384 (by which time he had been knighted), he was included in a commission of oyer and terminer following complaints by the prior of the Gilbertines of Newstead-on-Ancholme of a league among his bondsmen at Cadney to withdraw their customary services.   Later in the same month he was put on another oyer and terminer after Sir Michael de la Pole, the then Chancellor, had complained of a breach of his close and other trespasses at Blyborough, and on 5th December in the same year he was again made a commissioner of oyer and terminer, following a complaint of John of Gaunt that he had been forcibly put out of his wardship rights in the estate of one of his tenants at Fillingham, ten miles or so down Ermine Street from Retford's place at Castlethorpe.   These last two commissions suggest the existence of a connexion on Retford's part with the Lancastrian circle, which his membership of John of Gaunt's expedition to Spain two years later does something to confirm.   In the meantime, on 26th April, 1385, Sir Henry was appointed to act as a commissioner of array in Lindsey, and a few days later he was authorised in a Chancery patent to investigate wastes by the farmers of the estates of the non-conventual dependency of the abbey of St. Sever of Coutances, at Haugham near Louth (Lincs).[5]   He accompanied Richard II's first military expedition to Scotland in July 1385.   In the following September he was acting as one of several justices appointed *ad hoc* to take a local assize of novel disseisin, and on 14th November, later still in the same year, he was put on an oyer and terminer commission following a complaint by John de Ferriby, a neighbour of Retford's, that his close at Bonby had been trespassed upon and that his administration of his offices of escheator and justice of the peace in Lincolnshire had been impeded.

In the following year (1386) occurred an event of considerable national importance, especially in view of its immediate effects on the internal political situation : John of Gaunt's expedition to Spain to prosecute his claim (*jure uxoris*) to the throne of Castile and Leon. This undertaking left Richard II and his curialist party bereft of the duke's support, and so face to face with the aristocratic opposition party led by Thomas of Woodstock and the Arundels.   When John of Gaunt returned to England after an absence of nearly three and a half years, it was to a kingdom still suffering from political tension heightened by the memories of the rising of Harringay Park, of the battle of Radcotbridge, and of the circumstances in which the King's most important friends had been executed, sentenced to forfeiture, or otherwise proscribed, at the instance of the Lords Appellant, during the Merciless Parliament of 1388.   On 12th April, 1386, Sir Henry de Retford was one of 32 knights and esquires who then obtained letters of general attorney as being about to proceed to Spain as members of the duke of Lancaster's army.   There can be

(5)   *ibid.*, 1381-5, 494, 496, 507, 589, 598.

little doubt but that Retford went overseas with the Lancastrian expedition, because it was at its port of departure, Plymouth, and not very long before it sailed, that on 16th June following he made a deposition on behalf of Richard Lord Scrope of Bolton in his armorial suit with the Cheshire knight, Sir Robert Grosvenor : Retford stated that he had not seen or even heard of Grosvenor bearing the heraldic arms in question until the last expedition to Scotland.[6]

Although it is most likely that Retford accompanied Lancaster to Spain, there is no doubt that he did not stay with the duke until the conclusion of his enterprise. When precisely he returned to England is not known, but leaving it in July, 1386, he was back in this country in time to be one of the 21 knights who, along with nearly 400 more notables in Lincolnshire, took an oath (as did the Lords and Commons) to keep the peace and to stand with the Lords Appellant to the end of the Merciless Parliament, in accordance with writs issued to the shires generally on 20th March, 1388 (the last day of its first session), following its adjournment until after Easter. What attitude during this critical time Retford adopted is beyond discovery, but it is perhaps significant that at the next appointments to the shrievalties after Richard II's declaration in May, 1389, that, being of age, he meant to rule his inheritance for himself, and soon after Lancaster's return from Spain, Retford was appointed for the first time as sheriff of Lincolnshire. Appointed on 15th November, 1389, he relinquished the office, however, four weeks later and did not account in the Exchequer. And three years passed before he was again made sheriff. This time, however, he held the office for the customary term : appointed on 18th October, 1392, he was sheriff until 7th November, 1393. In the meantime, by patents of 10th July, 6th August, and 2nd December, 1391, he had been appointed as a commissioner of sewers for the rivers Humber and Ancholme, and on 1st March, 1392, he was made a commissioner of array in Lindsey. It was during his year of office as sheriff that, on 27th July, 1393, he was put by the Council on the Lincolnshire commission for investigating breaches by merchants of the statutes relating to weights used in the buying of wool. Within a week of the end of his first proper term of office as sheriff, namely, on 13th November, 1393, he was granted an annuity of 40 marks, chargeable on the Exchequer, in view of his being retained for life by the King ; paid in half-yearly instalments, he regularly received this annuity throughout the rest of the reign, generally through the hands of a Chancery clerk, John Barnaldby. Between September, 1394, and April, 1395, he was with Richard II in the King's first expedition to Ireland, with a retinue of one esquire and three mounted archers. At Lammastide following, he was witness to a charter relating to the

(6) *CCR*, 1385–9, 20 ; *CPR*, 1385–9, 87 ; T. Rymer, *Foedera*, VII. 508 ; N. H. Nicolas, *The Scrope-Grosvenor Controversy*, i. 54 ; ii. 179.

Lincolnshire manor of Melton Ross, made by some of the feoffees of John, brother of William Lord Roos of Hemsley.[7]

Following the conclusion in the previous year of a long-lasting truce between England and France, cemented by the marriage of Richard II with Isabel, daughter of Charles VI, the *rapprochement* between the Courts of Westminster and Paris was further demonstrated in 1397 by their efforts to bring to an end the Papal Schism, which by this time for nearly twenty years had bedevilled the government of the Western Church. The French and English kings, in association with the King of Castile, had decided to send a joint embassy, first to Avignon, then to Rome, demanding that both contending Popes, Benedict XIII and Boniface IX, follow the procedure of " double cession " and resign before the end of September 1397, failing which reprisals were to be instituted by the kingdoms concerned.

Considerably behind schedule, the English delegation was appointed before the end of February 1397, but it did not leave for Paris, on the first stage of its journey, much before the middle of April. The members of it were Sir Henry de Retford, Sir William Sturmy (a Wiltshire knight who had recently successively represented Hampshire, Wiltshire and Devon in the Commons, and who, like Retford, was a royal retainer and at the same fee), Doctor Thomas Crawley, a theologian, and Richard Holme, a canon of York. On 3rd April, 1397, Retford was the first to proceed, followed by Sturmy and Holme. On 11th April royal letters of protection were issued for Retford and Sturmy, each being described as ' in obsequium regis versus curiam Romanam, Avinionem, et alibi de mandato regis profecturus . . . pro certis negociis regem et regnum tangentibus moraturus.' The triple embassy reached Avignon on 13th June and Rome early in September, when the English delegates took the initiative with Boniface IX, to whose obedience England belonged. Here they met with no more success than had attended the representations made by the French at Avignon. In an atmosphere of frustration the embassy returned, the English delegation being back in England by early November. On 4th December, Retford received £43 15s. at the Exchequer in settlement of what was outstanding from his account.[8]

In the previous January, Retford and his wife had secured a papal indult permitting them to have a portable altar. Two further indults, which were issued at Rome on his behalf on 4th and 5th September, 1397, he was doubtless able to procure for himself directly. The first of these bulls gave to him (and his heirs) the right to have a chapel in his houses, where his own priest might celebrate

(7) *Rot. Parl.*, iii. 401 ; *List of Sheriffs*, 79 ; *CPR*, 1388–92, 516 ; *ibid.*, 1391–6, 89, 356 ; 339 ; Exchequer, Issue Rolls, PRO, E 403/548, 551, 554, 556, 559 ; Exchequer, Accounts Various, Wardrobe, particule compoti, Vadia Guerre, PRO, E 101/402/20, p. 69 ; *CCR*, 1396–9, 401.
(8) T. Carte, *Rolles Gascons, etc.*, ii. 173 ; Exchequer, Issue Rolls, PRO, E 403/556, mem. 17 ; E. Perroy, *L'Angleterre et le Grand Schisme d'Occident* (Paris, 1933), pp. 379–382.

solemn mass ' alta voce ' and administer the sacraments to him and his household, including the baptism of his children; the second indult permitted Retford and his wife (Katherine) to receive plenary remissions from their own confessor.[9]

Just before, or immediately after, his return from this seven-months tour in France and Italy, Retford was again made sheriff of Lincolnshire. His appointment is dated 3rd November, 1397, and he held office until 17th November, 1398. His first appointment to the commission of the peace for the parts of Lindsey in Lincolnshire came along only a few days later : on 12th November, 1397. And during his year of office as sheriff he was made, on 20th June, 1398, a commissioner in Lincolnshire charged with the enforcement of the statutes (of 1351 and 1371) relating to the survey of river-weirs.

In the same period, on 1st May, 1398, Retford had witnessed a deed of Michael de la Pole, recently restored to his father's title of earl of Suffolk, regarding a small estate in Barton-on-Humber and Barrow-on-Humber.[10] Nearly a year later, on 16th April, 1399, Philip Lord Darcy, who had followed his father as a peer of parliament at the beginning of Richard II's reign, appointed Retford as one of the two overseers of his will.[11] Darcy died on 24th April and was buried at Henes priory in Lincolnshire ; his will was proved at York on 3rd May ; his son and heir (John) was summoned to Henry IV's first parliament in the following autumn.

Sir Henry de Retford's employment as a royal diplomatic agent in 1397 and his appointment as sheriff of Lincolnshire in November of that year, when Richard II was doubtless taking steps to consolidate the political gains of his recent parliamentary triumph of the previous September, would suggest that, as a royal retainer, he might look forward with some confidence to furthering his own prospects under Richard's absolutist system. What were his immediate reactions to the revolution of 1399 is not known. His former connexion with John of Gaunt may very well have predisposed him in good time to fall in with the Lancastrian heir who now contrived to depose and succeed Richard II. Certainly, Henry of Bolingbroke's accession put no halt to Retford's career, although it resulted in no spectacular developments so far as he was concerned. On 28th November, 1399, he was confirmed by Henry IV in his commission of the peace in Lindsey, and on 18th December he was made a commissioner of array in the same region. He served on Henry IV's expedition into Scotland in August 1400, following which a truce was made. He was for the first time elected as knight of the shire for Lincolnshire to the second parliament of the new reign, which met in January, 1401, along with the previous sheriff, Sir John Copledyke. During the session, on 25th February, in consideration of his expenses on the Scottish expedition of the previous year, his 40

(9) *Cal. of Papal Registers, Papal Letters,* v. 45, 54, 66.
(10) *List of Sheriffs, loc. cit.* ; *CPR,* 1396–9, 234, 370 ; *CCR,* 1396–9, 301.
(11) Surtees Society, *Testamenta Eboracensia,* i. 255.

marks annuity of 1393 was confirmed to him for life (but not increased in amount), being now made chargeable on the Crown
revenues from his own county of Lincolnshire instead of being
payable at the Exchequer.   Two days after the end of the parliament, on 12th March, 1401, he was involved in finding mainprises
for a knight of the King's Chamber, Sir Nicholas Hawberk, and for
John Kynaston, the two men being in some way at variance.   On
15th May following he was confirmed as a J.P. in Lindsey.[12]

With Scotland unappeased and the Welsh borders in a state of
grave unrest since Owen Glendower's rising in the autumn of 1400,
Henry IV was reluctant to call a second parliament in 1401, but he
summoned a Great Council to meet at Westminster on 15th August,
including a considerable number of knights and esquires from the
different counties.   Sir Henry de Retford was one of four knights
individually summoned from Lincolnshire.   War with both France
and Scotland was accepted by the meeting as feasible.   The outlook, foreign and domestic, continued threatening.   Glendower continued to attract success, and rumours arose of Richard II's being
still alive.   On 11th May, 1402, commissions were generally set up
to arrest those who impugned the King's good intentions and to
send information to the royal Council from time to time ;   Retford
served on the Lincolnshire commission.   When, in August following,
Henry IV began preparations for an all-out effort to suppress the
Welsh rebellion, Retford was one of the two Lincolnshire commissioners appointed to try and supervise the fencibles of the
county and to make provision for their meeting the King at Shrewsbury.   Here they were to certify the King himself of what they had
done.   Retford's colleague in this business was John Rochford,
constable of the Bishop of Ely's castle of Wisbeach.[13]

It was to the parliament which met on 30th September, after the
failure of this Welsh campaign, that Retford was re-elected as
knight of the shire for Lincolnshire, his fellow shire-knight being Sir
Gerard Sothill, who had been in 1399 his co-overseer of Lord Darcy's
will.   It was on 3rd October, after an adjournment over the week-
end, that the Commons presented Sir Henry de Retford as their
Speaker.   A week later the Commons' request to have a Lords'
liaison-committee was granted, but with a protest from the King
(communicated by a deputation which included the Steward of his
Household and his Secretary) that such a committee for " inter-
commoning " between the two Houses was conceded as of the King's
grace only.   It was evidently a device unwelcome to the King.   On
16th October, the Commons commended the King, his two eldest
sons, and also the earl of Northumberland.   The contrast between
the success of the Percies against the Scots at Humbledon Hill (a
fortnight before the session opened) and the King's own failure to

(12)   *CPR*, 1399–1401, 561 : 210 ; 437 : *CCR*, 1399–1402, 320.
(13)   *PPC*, i. 157 ; *CPR*, 1401–5, 129, 138.

resolve the Welsh problem by force of arms was emphasized by the reception, in full parliament on 20th October, of the son of the duke of Albany (the Regent of Scotland) and other captives from the recent battle on the northern border. In spite of the fact that petitions were presented during the session requesting reductions of fee-farms or remissions of parliamentary taxation on behalf of the towns of Lincoln, Newcastle-on-Tyne, Cambridge, Lyme Regis, and Truro, and the marcher shires of Northumberland and Cumberland, the session ended on 25th November with a fairly liberal, if somewhat grudgingly conceded, grant of a subsidy of a tenth and fifteenth and a continuation of the wool subsidy and of tunnage and poundage until Michaelmas 1405.

Retford's choice as Speaker had evidently been satisfactory from the royal viewpoint. But the reason behind his election may well have been his knowledge of the ecclesiastical situation in Europe, because at the opening of the session the Chancellor (Bishop Stafford of Exeter) had drawn attention to the good chances of restoring unity to the Church, and at the end oi the parliament Henry IV was asked to do his best to heal the Schism. Retford was, of course, fully conversant with Henry IV's military and, consequently, his financial difficulties, which was probably an additional factor in moving the Commons to have him as their Speaker on this occasion. So far as he personally was concerned, this point of financial stress was apparently driven home during the parliamentary session : on 21st October he was made the addressee of a privy seal writ requesting a loan for the payment of the garrisons of South Wales.[14]

After his Speakership Retford drops out of sight for a time. In September, 1403 (after the defeat of a revolt of the Percies at the battle of Shrewsbury), he was appointed to serve once more as a local commissioner of array. He was not even re-elected to parliament in January 1404, but, summoned to a Great Council in this year and re-appointed (in March and May) as a J.P. in Lindsey, he was for the third and what proved to be the last time returned as shire-knight to the Unlearned Parliament which met at Coventry in October 1404.[15] The Speaker on this occasion was his former diplomatic colleague on the mission to the rival Popes in 1397, Sir William Sturmy.

Although Retford secured no influential position at Court and never even had his modest annuity as a royal retainer increased or supplemented in any way, he seems to have been ever ready to assist Henry IV in his military necessities. It is possible that Retford, like his sheriff, was with Henry in the Welsh March when, in May 1405, news reached the King of the rising in Yorkshire headed by the northern primate, Archbishop Scrope, and the Earl Marshal. However this may be, when the King moved up into the

(14) *Rot. Parl.*, iii. 485 *et seq.*; *PPC*, ii. 75.
(15) *CPR*, 1401–5, 289, 518.

affected county itself, after the rebel forces had been dispersed by the trickery of the Earl of Westmoreland at Shipton Moor, Retford was evidently in the royal entourage. On 6th June he was one of the commission of oyer and terminer, composed of lords and knights, appointed at Bishopthorpe (the archiepiscopal manor outside York) to try those implicated in the recent treasons. After Chief Justice Gascoigne had refused to act against the Archbishop, it is almost certain that Retford was party to the judgement pronounced on 8th June by his fellow commissioner, Sir William Fulthorpe. In accordance with it the Archbishop and the Earl Marshal were immediately executed. The commissioners, among whom were the Earl of Arundel and Sir Thomas Beaufort (the temporarily appointed Vice-Constable and Vice-Marshal respectively), seem to have acted as a court-martial whose powers of summary jurisdiction were justifiable because of the recent levying of war against the King.

Nothing further is recorded of Retford until, in February 1406, he was re-appointed as a J.P. in Lindsey. He was confirmed in the commission of the peace in August following, then on 5th November, 1406, he was made sheriff of Lincolnshire for the first time under Henry IV, and (consequently, perhaps) was dropped from the Lindsey commission of the peace when its composition was next revised in February, 1407. He was sheriff until 23rd November, 1407. Early in his term of office, by patent of 8th January, 1407, he was again associated with Sir William Fulthorpe and Sir Ralph Evers, another fellow-member of the commission of 6th June, 1405, in a commission authorising them to inquire into the landed possessions and interests of Henry Percy, Earl of Northumberland, in Lincolnshire, Yorkshire and Northumberland, which the earl had forfeited in May, 1405. At this time Northumberland was probably taking refuge in France ; in the summer of 1407 he was in Scotland ; crossing the Border in February 1408, he met his death at the battle of Bramham Moor.[16] Shortly before that event took place, on 28th January, 1408, Retford was party to a recognizance for £200 made in the royal Chancery for the safeguarding of the prior of the Augustinian house of canons at Thornholme (Lincs.).[17]

Nothing further is known of Sir Henry de Retford, except that by midsummer of the following year he was dead. For on 16th June, 1409, the wardship and marriage of his son and heir, another Henry, still under age, was granted for £200 to one John Davys. The profits from Sir Henry's estates were appropriated two days later to repair-work at Nottingham castle. Evidently these arrangements fell through, because by May, 1410, it had been disclosed that the late Sir Henry had not been a tenant-in-chief in any of his lands, so that the Crown had no rights of wardship.[18]

(16) *CPR*, 1405–8, 65, 307, 494 ; *List of Sheriffs, loc. cit.*
(17) *CCR*, 1405–9, 355.
(18) *CPR*, 1408–13, 83, 89, 220.

Retford's son and heir, who became sheriff of Lincolnshire in 1427–8, was subsequently to see service in France and eventually was appointed mayor of Bordeaux in 1452, his wife (whom he had married by June, 1432) being the widow of a former constable of the Gascon capital and treasurer of Harfleur. He returned from France to be again sheriff in his own county in 1454–5, and then, like so many more of the military caste, disillusioned by Lancastrian failures in France, he turned Yorkist, incurring forfeiture by bill of attainder in the 1459 Coventry parliament, after the recent Yorkist setback at the Rout of Ludford.[19] Not until early in this year had died Sir Henry the Speaker's widow, Mary (presumably his second wife). After the Speaker's death, she had apparently remained a widow until, sometime between the death of William Lord Clinton's second wife in October 1420 and 1428, she married this parliamentary peer. Surviving Lord Clinton, who died in 1431, she had married (as her third husband) Sir John Heron of Northumberland. She herself died at Candlemas 1459, some forty years after her first husband.[20]

(19) *DKR*, XLVIII. 268, 270, 281–3, 335 ; Carte, *Rolles Gascons, op. cit.*, i. 237 ; Exchequer, Issue Roll, PRO, E 403/703, mem. 7 ; *Rot. Parl.*, V. 349.
(20) *The Complete Peerage*, iii. 315.

6

SIR WILLIAM STURMY

R OUGHLY half a century after the time when the presence
of the elected Commons came to be regarded as essential
to a normal parliament, they first began to elect a Speaker
who, chosen from among themselves for the duration of a
parliament, would act as their representative before the King
and Lords. This was in 1376, the year of the Good Parliament,
a parliament in which there was much and virulent criticism
of certain aspects of royal government. During the minority
of Richard II (1377-89) the capacity of the Commons for
independent political action grew. In the later phases of
Richard's reign, however, partly because of adroit management by their Speaker, the Commons became more than
complaisant. After Richard's deposition in 1399 the political
difficulties of his supplanter Henry IV, the first of the Lancastrian Kings, provided the Commons with opportunities to
re-assert their proper influence upon affairs of state. That
some of these opportunities were not neglected is certain.
And that some of the early Lancastrian Speakers were required
by the Commons to play an important part in their recovery
of a more significant role in parliamentary affairs, can be
just as confidently asserted, however close the personal association of the Speaker with the King and his administration
may have been on occasion. It was in this period of political
unrest and constitutional movement that the greater part of
Sir William Sturmy's political career was passed, and the
troubles of Henry IV were at their height when, as knight of
the shire for Devon, Sturmy was Speaker in the parliament
which met at Coventry in October 1404.

In the course of his life, Sturmy sat in no fewer than twelve
parliaments over a period of nearly forty years. By 1404, he
had already served seven times as a knight of the shire and,
at different times, for as many as three counties: for Hampshire
in April 1384, for Wiltshire in January 1390, for Hampshire
again in November 1390, for Devon in November 1391, for
Wiltshire once more in January 1393, October 1399, and
January 1401. After 1404 he sat again in parliament in May

1413, November 1414, October 1417, and November 1422, on each occasion for Wiltshire.[1] It is possible that Sturmy was also elected to one or more of the five parliaments of 1410-11 and 1415-16, for which the returns have been lost for one or another of the counties of Devon, Hampshire, and Wiltshire (especially for Wiltshire, namely in 1410, 1411, and 1416). Clearly in these three counties of southern England, particularly in Wiltshire where was the bulk of his landed property, Sturmy wielded great influence and considerable power. Much of this is likely to have been the product of his connections with the Court and centre of royal government at Westminster, under Richard II and each of the three Lancastrian Kings. That these connections were frequently close and not significant for Sturmy's career alone, an investigation of his life makes clear. Incidentally, Sturmy was the only knight of the shire for Devon to act as Speaker in pre-Stewart times.

Sir William Sturmy held lands in the north of Hampshire including the manors of Belney and Polling, and lands in Elvetham and at Hartley Wintney, where he took out a royal licence in 1403 to impark 300 acres. These estates were assessed at the end of Henry IV's reign at £37 a year. He drew £40 a year from lands he held in Devon ' jure uxoris '. His biggest estates, however, lay in east Wiltshire between Marlborough and Ludgershall and were assessed as being worth as much as £91 6s. 8d. in 1412; they comprised the hereditary seat of the family at Wolfhall near Bedwin and the manors of Tidcombe, Axford, Stitchcombe, Burbage, Knowle, Crofton Braybrook, Huish, Standen, Wick Sturmy, and Stapleford. He also had the hereditary forestership of the west bailiwick of the royal forest of Savernake.[2] In this office as well as in the succession to the family estates, William, as representative of his father Geoffrey, had followed his uncle, Henry Sturmy, who died in the late spring of 1381. This uncle, who had had connections with the Court, must not be mistaken, however, for the Sir Henry Sturmy who was admitted three years later to the company of poor knights attached to the college of the royal chapel of St. George in Windsor Castle. (The latter may have been a relative.) By this date William was probably already in possession of the Devon estates of his wife, Joan Crawthorne, the widow of Sir John Beaumont of Sherwell (Devon).[3]

Not long after succeeding to his own family estates in Hampshire and Wiltshire, William Sturmy's position was recognised in his return for the former shire to the parliament which met at Salisbury in the spring of 1384. Later events indicate his close connection with the Court, and certain commissions on which he served in the troubled period of the middle years of Richard II's reign (1386-9) point to the fact that his political sympathies were already with the King. Nearly three weeks before the " Wonderful Parliament " met on 1 October 1386, when Richard II was probably already expecting trouble, Sturmy and the mayor of Marlborough were ordered to make an examination of the castle there, ascertain its equipment, and make an inventory of the armour in it. Again, on 18th June 1387, Sturmy had been put on a select commission ordered ' ex parte Regis ' to arrest and imprison rioters and frequenters of illegal assemblies in Surrey, Hampshire, Wiltshire, and Berkshire. After the " Merciless Parliament " of the following year and its registration of the Appellants' triumph, their party of opposition to the King remained in power for another year.[4]

To the next four parliaments to be summoned after 1388, those of January and November 1390, November 1391, and January 1393, Sir William was elected successively for Wiltshire, Hampshire, Devon, and again for Wiltshire. The royal commissions on which he served in these years similarly reflected his widely scattered territorial interests. Some accession of local influence perhaps came his way when, in November 1389, Sturmy was included in a commission for the conservation of salmon in the rivers Tone in Somerset and Torridge in Devon. In February 1392, he was instructed (with others) to investigate trespass by way of unlicensed hunting on the De Brian property at Lundy Island off the north Devon coast, then being administered by the Crown. During the session of the 1393 parliament he was appointed to act on a committee which included three other West Country knights of the shire, authorised to arbitrate following a petition to the King and Lords in parliament from Nicholas Pontingdon of Bigley (Devon), who had been unjustly ousted from his manor there by Sir Philip Courtenay on the grounds of his illegitimacy. A year later he was put on an inquiry into a case of an intimidated jury at Crediton (Devon), pending a plea in the King's Bench. Meanwhile, during the first parliament of 1390, he had been a member of a commission of inquiry into waste in the sequestrated estates of the alien priory of Stratfield Say, near his own north Hampshire property, in that county and in Berkshire. Three months

later he was again on a commission authorised to examine
the condition of Marlborough castle. In February 1392, and
again a year later, just after the Winchester session of 1393,
Sturmy procured patents of pardon for all indictments of
felony and trespass preferred against him and for any consequent outlawries. That he was on good terms with the government is further evident from his ability to secure an Exchequer
lease of two-thirds of the Fitz Waryn manor of Tawstock
(Devon) in May 1392, and from his being retained for life
in the following October as a royal household knight at an
annual fee of 40 marks, to be paid direct at the Exchequer.
Two years later he was preparing to accompany Richard II
on his first expedition to Ireland. On 10 August 1394 he
took out letters of attorney for a year, and sailed with the
royal forces from Haverfordwest at the end of September,
returning in May 1395, his retinue being an esquire and six
mounted archers.[5]

Between the return of this first of Richard II's two Irish
expeditions and the revolution of 1399, not a great deal is
known of Sir William Sturmy's activities. In July 1395 he
was associated with the Chief Justice of Common Pleas, a
knight of the Chamber, and a Chancery clerk, in a commission
to receive certain recognisances entered into by the burgesses
of Salisbury after the submission of a dispute with their bishop
to the royal Council. This was of no great personal importance.
On 9th April 1397, however, he was granted letters of
protection as a member of a diplomatic mission ' per regna
diversa . . . . . pro negotiis regis expediendis '. This was
very significant of the regard in which Sturmy was now held.
He was, in fact, absent from England from 11th April to
8th November 1397, proceeding by way of Paris and Avignon
to Rome and assisting in negotiations with both the rival
Popes of the day (Boniface IX and Benedict XIII) ' in quibus-
dam arduis negociis et negociis statum pacis et tranquillitatis
universalis sacrosanctae ecclesiae tangentibus contra scismam
in dicta sacrosancta ecclesia pendentem '. He took advantage
of this mission to secure papal indults on 4th September 1397:
that a confessor of his choice might grant him plenary
remission as often as he pleased, and that in his manors he
and his successors might have chapels and baptismal fonts
where fit priests could officiate, celebrate mass (even *alta
voce*), administer the sacraments to them and their children
and household, and baptize their children.

In spite of the close attachment to the Court which this diplomatic employment suggests, Sturmy's career received no set-back from Richard II's deposition. He was one of the Wiltshire representatives in the parliament which acclaimed the new régime, and nine days after the close of the session (on 19th November 1399) he was appointed a justice of the peace in the shire. In the following month he was made a commissioner of array there, and in March 1400 served on an inquiry into the maladministration of the prioress of the Benedictine convent at Amesbury. Sir William was re-elected for Wiltshire to the second parliament of the reign, which sat from 21st January to 10th March 1401. On 20th March following, the annuity of 40 marks granted him by Richard II in 1392 was confirmed. In May he was made a justice of the peace in Hampshire as well as in Wiltshire.[6]

Already, two days after the end of the 1401 parliament, Sturmy had become a member of the royal Council with an annual fee of 100 marks, and he continued to act (and to be paid) in that capacity until July 1402. For the greater part of this time, however, he was absent in Germany on diplomatic missions that were part of a drive to secure foreign recognition for the House of Lancaster. Between 12th May and 9th August 1401, Sturmy was associated in an embassy to the Duke of Guelders with Master John Kington, a canon of Lincoln, and with Robert Waterton (who had accompanied King Henry, then Earl of Derby, on the Prussian 'reys' of 1390 and 1392 and who was still Henry's Master of Horse). The three were to receive the Duke's homage and treat with him for the observance of the conventions agreed on between him and Richard II—the Duke had early recognised the Lancastrian usurpation. It is probable that one of the objects of Sturmy's embassy to the Duke of Guelders was to bring about his recognition of the new Emperor, Rupert III of Bavaria, who had recently been elected King of the Romans in place of Wenzel of Bohemia, brother-in-law of Richard II, who had also been deposed.

In this same year negotiations had been successfully proceeding for the marriage of the new Emperor's eldest son, Lewis, Count Palatine of the Rhine and Duke of Bavaria, to Henry IV's elder daughter, Blanche. Probably it was to help arrange this important alliance that Sturmy was again away in Germany from 12th September to 5th December 1401. Certainly, when on 16th February 1402 Sturmy and Master

Kington once more sailed from London it was to take with them an indenture under the great seal touching the dowry of 40,000 marks. They had conversations with the Bishop of Utrecht and made arrangements for safe-conducts and transportation for the Lady Blanche's company. On 27th April Bishop Clifford of Worcester, John Beaufort, Earl of Somerset, and Lord FitzWalter, who escorted the Princess, were empowered to co-operate with Sturmy and Kington in treating for alliances with both the Emperor and the Duke of Guelders. Nearly a month later, Sturmy and Kington wrote from Dordrecht to a clerk in the Privy Seal office informing the Council of Rupert's return from his expedition against the Visconti in northern Italy. They themselves returned to England with Blanche's escort after her marriage at Heidelberg, and were in London on 23rd July 1402. On 18th November following, they delivered into the treasury certain documents affecting the marriage. Before her marriage took place, Sturmy had been steward of household to the Princess Blanche. He had probably acted in this office from the time of the arrangement of the marriage, when the ten years old princess is likely to have been given a household of her own for the first time. Unfortunately the hopes of a lasting *entente* between the English and the Rhenish courts were to be dashed by the death of Blanche in May 1406.[7]

During his absence in the Rhineland, Sturmy had been included, perhaps as a matter of form, on two Wiltshire commissions, the first issued on 11th May 1402 for the suppression of seditious talk and the other, on 14th July, authorising him to act as a commissioner of array. It is very improbable that he served on either. He had been home for some time, however, when on 21st October 1402 writs were circulated requesting benevolences or loans for the payment of the south Wales royal garrisons, copies of which were sent to him in Devon, Wiltshire, and Hampshire. A month later he was included in an inquiry as to what estates of the hospital of St. Thomas near Marlborough were to revert to the Gilbertine convent there. Sturmy served on no more royal commissions until after the unsuccessful Percy rebellion (defeated at the battle of Shrewsbury) in the summer of 1403, being then appointed a commissioner of array in both Hampshire and Wiltshire by patents of 28th August and 8th September respectively. Four days after the issue of the second letter, he was himself ordered to join the royal forces gathering at Hereford for an incursion into Wales.

English foreign relations, particularly with France and Burgundy, were still in a parlous condition. Piracy among Flemish and English merchant-ships made the Narrow Seas unsafe, and when parliament met at Coventry on 6th October 1404 there was a serious prospect of French invasions from Sluys and Harfleur. In the course of the year Sturmy, who was elected to the parliament as knight of the shire for Devon, had been over in Rotterdam, negotiating with Flemish merchants who were demanding compensation for their shipping losses. Henry IV expressly required the sheriffs not to permit the election of lawyers on this occasion. It is very unlikely that Sturmy was a lawyer in the sense of the writs of summons; but that he was well-versed in law and legal procedure is almost certain. At any rate his diplomatic employment and his occasional inclusion on commissions of oyer and terminer to deal with appeals from judgments on cases brought before the Courts of Chivalry and Admiralty, would suggest a sound working knowledge of the Civil Law. It may well be that on this account and because of his experience in foreign affairs Sturmy was now elected Speaker for the Commons. His wife's son-in-law, Sir Hugh Luttrell, for whose lease of the English estates of the French abbey of St. Nicholas of Angers he had gone surety early in the reign, was one of the knights for Somerset.[8]

This autumn parliament of 1404 was a stormy one. Special Treasurers for War were appointed, and to the emergency measure of a stop on Exchequer payments of Crown annuities (which would directly affect the Speaker) the Commons added a demand for the appropriation of the temporalities of the Church for a year, in order to meet the costs of the war against the Welsh and the prospect of a French invasion. Archbishop Arundel in reply invoked the Great Charter and, turning to the bar of the Upper House where stood the knights of parliament, rated them for their own cupidity, pertinently demanding what had become of the sequestrated alien priories. The session closed on 14th November, three days after Sturmy had been able to announce what proved to be the largest grant of the reign, two whole tenths and fifteenths, payable within the year, and a tax of 5 per cent on landed incomes of over 500 marks.

Bad political relations with France and Burgundy were having an adverse effect on English trade, but it was more purely commercial grievances that lay behind the breach with the Prussian and Baltic towns of the Hanseatic League.

On 31st May 1404, Danzig had prohibited the annual
voyage from the Baltic to England and an embargo had been
placed on imports of English cloth. It looked as if the claim
—which the cloth-exporting east coast towns of England
especially were making—for treatment similar to that meted
out to Hansards in England, was to founder in a storm of
mutual exasperation. That the need for settlement came up
before the Coventry parliament is certain: it was with the
advice of the Parliament that at the end of the session the
Speaker was authorised to accompany his former fellow-
ambassador, Kington, and William Brampton, an alderman
and member of parliament for London, on a diplomatic
mission to Conrad of Jungingen, High Master of the Order
of the Teutonic Knights, still the principal force in
Baltic politics. After allowing time for a compilation of
English counter-claims and for making a settlement of his
own estates, Sturmy received his instructions on 13th May
1405, and the embassy left England on the last day of the
month.

On 8th August 1405, Sir William and his companions were
received by the High Master at Marienburg. The embargo on
trade was removed and then claims and counter-claims were
considered, a period of a year commencing on 1st May
1406 being assigned for the settlement of all differences,
failing which the interdict was to be re-applied. The treaty
between the English envoys and the High Master's commissaries was signed at Marienburg on 8th October 1405.
The London alderman, Brampton, immediately left for
England, but his ship foundered and he and his papers were
lost. Sturmy and Kington, however, made a more leisurely
voyage, calling at the Hanseatic ports of Greifswald, Stral-
sund, Lübeck, Hamburg, and Bremen, and negotiating with
their burgomasters. At Dordrecht, where the Danzigers had
recently established a counter, they met a united gathering
of the Hanse, and on 15th December arranged a truce for
nineteen months, undertaking to rediscuss the question of
damages there on 1st May 1406. Sir William and his fellow-
envoy were back in London on 18th February 1406.[9]
A slight hitch after the passage home from Dordrecht to
Orwell formed the subject of a petition presented by Sturmy
and Kington to the Commons in the parliament which met
on 1st March following. Jan van Covour of Dordrecht, whom
they had engaged to carry them across, had been arrested
when on the point of return and, when brought before the

mayor and sheriffs of London in the Gildhall, had been detained. This not only broke the truce but infringed their letters of protection which extended—as the ambassadors successfully pleaded—to their servants as well as to themselves.

Sturmy did not himself sit in the long-lasting parliament of 1406. The elections in the counties where his interest was strong were probably over by the time of his return from abroad. The results of his recent diplomatic tour formed, however, an important item on the parliament's agenda. On the third day of its first session, the Chancellor advised the Lords to assent to a proclamation and the issue of commissions for the verification of the complaints of foreign merchants and the restitution of German prizes taken at sea; and, three months later, on 4th June, it was agreed that parliamentary authority be given for the setting up of a central commission of oyer and terminer instead of the previous commissions.[10] In the meantime, on 10th March, Sturmy and Kington had written to the Copman at Bruges, the Consuls at Lübeck, and the High Master at Marienburg, suggesting a three months' postponement of the meeting at Dordrecht to 1st August 1406. Further delays occurred until there was danger of the Hanse accepting the Burgundian offer of help in the event of a final break with England. However, on 14th November fresh commissions authorised Sturmy and Kington to arrange another meeting with the High Master and the Members of the League, and on 24th February 1407 Sir William left England with explanatory letters and arrived at Marienburg on 11th April.

Sturmy was out of England for almost the whole of the year, manoeuvring for delay over the question of time and place of the long postponed meeting of representatives. After a visit of three weeks to England in July, he and Kington set out again, this time for Middelburg, and on the last day of August negotiations were begun at the Hague. After referring certain disputed matters to the arbitration of the King of the Romans in a letter of 20th October, the English envoys returned home to appear before parliament, then in session at Gloucester. Negotiations dragged on and, in the changed atmosphere which followed the Polish victory over the Teutonic Knights at Tannenburg in the summer of 1410, were still uncompleted when Henry V was at Southampton waiting to take ship for Harfleur another five years later. After 1407, however, Sturmy seems to have taken little part in these long drawn parleys. Two years after his return to England, he was claiming £108 as compensation for his diplomatic activities and, by patent of 3rd October 1409, he secured that the fee-farm of over £53 a year at which he leased from the Crown two-thirds of the manor of Tawstock (Devon) should be altogether remitted.[11]

Precisely when Sir William Sturmy acquired the office of chief steward of the estates of Henry IV's Queen, Joan of Navarre, is not known; but his appointment must date from sometime before the summer of 1412, when he was put on an inquiry into wastage in her forest of Wichwood (Oxon.). He may have owed the connection to his step-daughter's husband, Sir Hugh Luttrell of Dunster, who was Queen Joan's steward of Household. At the time of his return to the first parliament of Henry V, in May 1413, Sturmy was certainly occupying the position, and it is possible that he was still holding it at the time of the Queen's disgrace in 1419 when he was granted the lease of a parcel of her Wiltshire estates, including the manors of Corsham and Ludgershall and the alien priory of Clatford. His inclusion in June 1414 on an inquiry in Gloucestershire into cases of concealment of feudal incidents due to the Crown may have been owing to the fact that the Queen's estates expressly came within the scope of the commission.

Sir William was not less than twice again returned to parliament for Wiltshire in Henry V's reign, namely, in November 1414 and November 1417. In the meantime, he had his Crown annuity of 40 marks renewed on 5th November 1413. On 10th May 1415, he was associated with Sir John Pelham as the bearer of a proclamation asking for loans in aid of Henry V's first military venture into Normandy, and at the end of the month he was put on a commission of array in Wiltshire[12]. Sturmy was apparently on the best of terms with the King who kept in touch with him after his second French invasion in the summer of 1417.

The letter which Henry V sent Sturmy in October 1417 probably had to do with diplomatic matters, for on 3rd March 1418 he and Master Richard Leyot, LL.D., were appointed ambassadors to treat for the marriage of the King's brother John, the Duke of Bedford, to Jacqueline of Hainault, the daughter and heiress of the late Duke of Bavaria and Count of Holland. They received instructions regarding dower and were informed that Bedford's inheritance amounted to seven or eight thousand marks a year. The two ambassadors actually made the passage to Holland, although nothing came of the proposal.

Sturmy can hardly have been *persona grata* with the prince who was eventually to marry the Lady Jacqueline of Hainault, namely, Humphrey, Duke of Gloucester, the King's youngest brother. Sir William's position as hereditary steward and chief forester of the royal forest of Savernake (Wiltshire) had brought him in 1417 into conflict with Duke Humphrey. The latter, acting presumably in his capacity as Warden of the royal forests south of Trent and on the strength of a grant by Henry IV of the revenues of Savernake forest, dispossessed Sturmy of his stewardship and confined his interest to the occupation of three out of the five bailiwicks of the forest, where, moreover, he was now to act merely as any other forest bailiff. Sturmy petitioned Henry V against Gloucester's action and eventually, in October 1420, he was restored to his wardenship by the Duke's letter patent.

In November 1418, Sir William had been appointed to the shrievalty of Wiltshire and in this capacity he held the shire elections to the parliament of October 1419. In the course of his year of office he was granted, in May 1419, certain lands in Caux and then, in February 1420, he was granted the lease of a portion of the Wiltshire property of Queen Joan, who had been imprisoned at Pevensey after charges of necromancy had been laid against her.[13] Sturmy was at the time serving on a Crown loan-raising commission in Wiltshire. On 18th February 1420 he was one of Sir John Mortimer's guarantors for his safe custody in the Tower. In June 1421, following Henry V's last visit to England, he acted as a commissioner of array in Wiltshire and the Isle of Wight, and in the following month was party to an inquiry into the fall in rent and venison from the parks at Devizes which was laid to the charge of Robert Tyndale (one of the Devizes burgesses in the parliaments of 1417 and 1419). Tyndale had been dismissed by the Duke of Gloucester, acting as Warden of the royal forests south of the Trent, but had been re-instated by the King himself.

On 12th February 1422, Sir William was restored to the Wiltshire commission of the peace from which he had been absent since November 1415, and in the following autumn he was elected for the county to the first parliament of the reign of Henry VI.[14]

Turned sixty years of age at this his last and (at least) twelfth return to parliament, Sir William Sturmy's already wide range of acquaintance in the Commons was re-inforced by the election of his illegitimate son, John Sturmy, and his grandson, John Seymour, as burgesses for Ludgershall (where Sir William was Crown lessee), and of his cousin, Robert Erle, for Bedwin, where Sir William also held considerable inherited property. Erle, who had been present at Sir William's elections in 1413 and November 1414, was one of the feoffees to uses in Sturmy's lands. These also included Chief Justice Sir William Hankford and Justice Robert Hull of the Common Bench and his son, who were his neighbours in Somerset. Robert Erle and Sir William's own son, John, had been his sureties at the shire-elections.[15]

After the parliament of November-December 1422, Sir William entered upon a period of almost complete retirement from public affairs. The Crown annuity he had held for thirty years was confirmed to him ten days after the close of the session, but apart from his office as justice of the peace in Wiltshire, which he held until July 1425, he served on no more royal commissions, and he died at his north Hampshire manor of Elvetham on 22nd March 1427.

From proceedings instituted by a petition preferred in Chancery in 1451 by his grandson and heir, John Seymour, against his feoffees, it appears that Sir William died in the arms of his chaplain, the vicar of Collingbourne Abbot's, in the presence of his bastard son, John, and his kinsman and friend, Robert Erle. The writs of *Diem clausit extremum*, authorising inquiry into his estates (to find out if the Crown had an interest), were issued to the respective royal escheators in Hampshire and Wiltshire, Somerset, and Devon on 1st April 1427, and by the end of the year his widow was in possession of her dower. She was to survive her husband by two years.[16]

Only two days before his death Sir William Sturmy had been at his London inn in the parish of St. Bridget, and there he had made his will. To his servants, the pages of his chamber, and his gardener, went various gifts of his clothing, tapestry, pieces of plate, and sums of money amounting to nearly £50. The fabric fund of the cathedral church of Salisbury benefited by the bequest of a noble (6s. 8d.), and the bells of the parish church at Elvetham were to be repaired at his expense. To the Trinitarian priory at Easton in the forest of Savernake, where he was to be buried, he left fifty ewes, the mass vestments of his chapel, including a chasuble of blue velvet into which had been woven a pattern of falcons and flowers, and also his books. These latter comprised three psalters, a great missal (which the priory already had in keeping), a volume of Decretals, the *Pupilla Oculi* (a devotional book by Joseph de Burgo, Chancellor of the University of Cambridge from 1384 to 1386), and, possibly significant of a flair for historical study, two volumes of Ranulph Higden's *Polychronicon*. Among the more personal of his gifts may be noted a bequest of plate and armour to Sir Robert Shotesbroke, who had been knight of parliament for Berkshire in 1423 and for Wiltshire in 1426; one of armour to his wife's son-in-law, Sir Hugh Luttrell of Dunster (Somerset), his feoffee, who had been Seneschal of Normandy during the last two years of Henry V's reign; one of plate to another feoffee, Bishop John Stafford of Bath and Wells, who only a week before had resigned from the office of Treasurer of England; and a similar gift to Bishop Polton of Worcester, who was both Sturmy's feoffee and overseer of his will. Sir William's executors were his son John, Robert Erle, and William Turney. Probate was granted in the Prerogative Court of Canterbury on Lady Day 1427 and on 21st October letters of acquittance were issued to the executors.[17]

Sir William Sturmy's heirs were his daughter, Agnes (once wife to William Ringbourne, a son of a former steward of the lands of the bishopric of Winchester and kinsman of Bishop Wykeham, and now wife of John Holecombe), and John Seymour (the son of his eldest daughter, Maud, wife of Roger Seymour of Hache Beauchamp), through whom Sir William was an ancestor (great, great-grandfather) of Henry VIII's third Queen—the royal marriage took place at Wolfhall—and of her brother, Protector Somerset.[18]

FOOTNOTES

The following abbreviations have been used in the footnotes:—

CPR=Calendar of Patent Rolls.

CCR=Calendar of Close Rolls.

CFR=Calendar of Fine Rolls.

Rot. Parl.=Rotuli Parliamentorum.

Proc. and Ord. P.C.=Proceedings and Ordinances of the Privy Council, ed. N. H. Nicholas.

D.K.R.=Deputy Keeper's Reports.

H.M.C.=Historical Manuscripts Commission.

P.R.O.=Public Record Office.

R.S.=Rolls Series.

The name Sturmy is variously spelt in the records as Sturmy, Esturmy, Lesturmy. Sir William Sturmy is not to be confused with the William Sturmy, wool-buyer, who lived at Alton in east Hampshire and was appointed in 1395 to the royal office of alnager of cloth in the county.

Official Return of Members of Parliament, i. 221, 239-41, 246, 259, 261, 266, 280, 285, 290, 304.

[2] *CFR, 1391-99*, 165; *CPR, 1392-96*, 628; *ibid., 1446-52*, 555-6; *ibid., 1401-5*, 220; *CCR, 1402-5*, 498, 511; *ibid., 1413-19*, 457; *Feudal Aids*, VI, 416, 450, 530.

[3] *CFR, 1377-83*, 257, 266; *Records and Transactions of the Devon Association*, 1913, 265.

[4] *CPR, 1385-89*, 260, 323; *CCR, 1385-89*, 617.

[5] *CPR, 1388-92*, 208, 217, 272; *ibid., 1391-96*, 82, 430, 39, 220, 186, 487; *Rot. Parl.*, iii, 302; *CFR, 1391-99*, 45.

[6] *CPR, 1392-96*, 651; *ibid., 1399-1401*, 269, 453, 564, 566; T. Carte, *Catalogue des Rolles Gascons, Francais, et Normans*, ii, 173; Enrolled Foreign Accounts, Exchequer, L.T.R, PRO, E 364/36, mem.A; *Cal. of Papal Registers, Papal Letters*, V. 45, 68; *Proc. & Ord. P.C.*, i, 126; J. H. Wylie, *The Reign of Henry IV*, ii, 70n.

[7] Carte, *op. cit.*, ii, 181, 183; F. C. Hingeston, *Royal & Historical Letters of Henry IV* (R.S.), i, 99; F. Palgrave, *Ancient Calendars & Inventories of the Treasury of the Exchequer*, ii, 68; Wylie, *Henry IV*, i, 166, 253; *CCR, 1399-1402*, 463; Enrolled Foreign Accounts, *loc. cit.*

[8] *CPR, 1401-5*, 115, 127, 200, 289, 290, 295; *Proc. & Ord. P.C.* ii, 73, 75; *Literae Cantuarienses* (R.S.), iii, 78; *Rot. Parl.*, iii, 546; *CFR, 1399-1405*, 54.

[9] Wylie, *op. cit.*, ii, 71-78; F. C. Hingeston, *Royal & Historical Letters of Henry IV* (R.S.), ii, lii; *H.M.C., 5th Report* (*Mss of Dean & Chapter of Canterbury*), 443; *Literae Cantuarienses, op. cit.*, ii, 90, 94.

[10] *Ancient Petitions*, P.R.O., S.C.8, file 109, no 5406; *Rot. Parl.*, iii, 568, 574.

[11] Wylie, *op. cit.*, IV, 1-7; *Literae Cantuarienses, op. cit.* iii, 101, 104; F. C. Hingeston, *Royal Letters* (Cancelled), *op. cit.*; *CPR, 1408-13*, 113.

[12] *CPR, 1408-13*, 373; *ibid., 1413-16*, 160, 262, 408, 425; H. C. Maxwell Lyte, *History of Dunster*, i, 104; J. H. Glover, *Kingsthorpiana*, 15; *CFR, 1413-22*, 321-2; T. Rymer, *Foedera*, IX, 241.

[13] J. H. Wylie, *The Reign of Henry V*, i, 468n; *Proc. & Ord. P.C.*, ii, 241, 343; *DKR*, XLIV, 599; *ibid.*, XLI, 783; British Museum, Galba B 1, article 168; *Wiltshire Archaeological and Natural History Society Magazine*, li. 271 *et seq*; *List of Sheriffs*, (P.R.O., Lists and Indexes, IX), 153; P.R.O., C219, bundle 12, no. 3.

[14] *CPR, 1416-22*, 251, 323-4, 389, 461; *CCR, 1419-22*, 63.

[15] *CCR, 1402-5*, 498, 511; *ibid., 1413-19*, 457-8; I. H. Jeayes, *Catalogue of Muniments at Berkeley Castle*, 181; P.R.O., C219, bundle 11, nos. 1, 5; *ibid.*, bundle 13, no. 1.

[16] *CPR, 1422-29*, 35, 449-50, 571; *ibid., 1446-52*, 555-6; *CCR, 1422-29*, 349, 355, 362, 414; *CFR, 1422-30*, 137, 177, 237.

[17] Somerset House, Wills, Register Luffenham, fo. 7. (The illegitimacy of Sturmy's son John is deduced from the fact that Sir Williams's heirs were John Seymour, son of his daughter Maud, and her sister Agnes.)

[18] *Wilts. Arch. & Nat. Hist. Soc. Mag., loc. cit.*, 271 *et seq.*, 500 *et seq.*; *Herald and Genealogist*, V. 200.

POSTSCRIPT

Sturmy sat most often for Wiltshire. But occasionally he was elected for Hampshire or Devon. In view of the fact that before 1407 the records do not even afford information regarding the chronological order in which parliamentary elections took place in the different counties, one is not entitled to conjecture that Sturmy's election in either Hampshire or Devon was a consequence of a failure to be elected for Wiltshire. In this period, owing mainly to the frequent meeting of parliaments, re-election for one county to successive parliaments was very much more unusual than usual, and cases where one man was allowed to monopolize a county seat are exceptional. The inference is that in most counties election as knight of the shire was regarded as something desirable which, within certain limits, ought to go the rounds of the gentry of the county. And so, an individual, after representing one shire in one parliament might very well regard it as advisable, if he wished to sit in the next parliament, to seek election in another county where he had estates and interests and could command support. An interesting case in point is that of Sir Thomas Hungerford who between 1380 and 1393 sat in nine parliaments, alternately in a regular fashion, for Wiltshire and Somerset.

7

SIR JOHN TIPTOFT
COMMONS' SPEAKER IN 1406

A detailed biography of Sir John Tiptoft's only son, John (born c. 1427, created earl of Worcester in 1449, and executed as a Yorkist during the Lancastrian Readeption of 1470-1), has long been available in R.J. Mitchell, *John Tiptoft 1427-1470* (1958). Not so of Sir John himself. And yet his career, being over-all one of considerable importance in the context of the greater part of the Lancastrian period, would seem to merit careful enquiry.

Land inherited (mainly on his mother's side), a long succession of lands in wardship acquired by royal grants, and more lands still as brought by the two good marriages Tiptoft made (the second more profitable than the first), provided the material basis for a career in the course of which, in 1426, seventeen years before his death, he was raised to the peerage. What, however, was the chief factor in his rise was, as will be seen, the service, mainly administrative and diplomatic service, which he rendered to each in turn of the three Lancastrian kings. Having joined Henry of Bolingbroke's household two years before his accession in 1399, he now became, as did his father (Sir Payn), one of the select company of knights of the King's Chamber, a place he was still occupying when Speaker for the Commons in the parliament of 1406.[1] (This was not only the longest parliament to sit before 1445, but was a parliament so important for what it both attempted and achieved as to have led William Stubbs to say that it 'seems almost to stand for an exponent of the most advanced principles of medieval constitutional life in England'.) The three years which followed Tiptoft's Speakership were almost equally divided between his tenure, first, of the important office of treasurer of the King's Household (which he was only the second layman ever to hold, the first since 1265) and, second, of the greater office of treasurer of the Exchequer. His dismissal from this post in December 1409 was a facet

1   *Rotuli Parliamentorum*, III. 568.

of the "take-over" of the government at that time by Henry, prince of Wales; and in the last years of Henry IV's reign and the earliest of Henry V's, Tiptoft was among the "outs" rather than the "ins". It was not, in fact, until Henry V's renewal of the war with France immensely extended the range of opportunities for employment in the king's service that he again found a proper outlet for his talents: first, in 1415, as seneschal of the duchy of Guienne; then, in 1416-7, in important diplomatic operations, vis-à-vis the Emperor Sigismund in Germany and at the Council of Constance; next, in 1417-9, in presiding over the financial administration of the English-held parts of the duchy of Normandy; and finally, in 1420-3, as once again active in person as seneschal of Guienne, the office he had always nominally held ever since 1415. What forward strides Tiptoft had made before the end of Henry V's reign is possibly best revealed by his second marriage early in 1422, so important a marriage as to have required the king's express permission. Certainly, it was one which provided him with a superabundance of the highest aristocratic connexions. For the lady in question, Joyce, the younger daughter and co-heir of Edward, lord Charleton of Powys, was uterine (half-) sister to Edmund, earl of March (ob. 1425), and also to Anne, mother of Richard, duke of York; and among Joyce's maternal aunts still living were Margaret, dowager duchess of Clarence, and Joan, dowager duchess of York. Useful though connexions with his wife's kinsfolk sometimes were, witness his appointment by the Crown in 1425 as chief steward of the Mortimer lands in Wales during the minority of the duke of York, who was sole heir, more cogent reasons for Tiptoft's elevation to the peerage in 1426 must be sought elsewhere.

Having been appointed a member of the King's Council at the beginning of Henry VI's reign in 1422, Tiptoft had always assiduously attended its meetings. And before 1426, as after, he had consistently adhered to the principle (defined in the parliament of 1422) that in a time of royal minority the supreme responsibility for the conduct of the king's government rested with the Council, unless a parliament or great council was in session, in which event it would rest with the peers generally; and, this being so, he constantly gave his support to Henry Beaufort, bishop of Winchester, in his opposition to Duke Humphrey of Gloucester who, conceded in 1422 the distinctive rôle of protector and chief councillor, had frequently exceeded the limits of his authority, to the great disquiet of his fellow-councillors. It was doubtless to help strengthen Beaufort's party in the Upper House that, in a time of serious threat to the king's peace and of acute political strain, Tiptoft was first called upon to enter the Lords in the Leicester parliament of 1426; and to strengthen the party's hold on the royal Household that, at the end of the first session of the parliament, he was appointed to its stewardship, the topmost place in its hierarchy of officials. It was in this capacity, and also as one of the king's councillors, that after Henry VI's coronation in England in November 1429 he accompanied him to France in 1430 for his crowning there too, only to be dismissed his Household office in February 1432 when, on the king's return to England, Duke Humphrey so re-asserted himself as to effect a purge of the highest offices of State and Household alike. Although Tiptoft always was to remain a member of the Council, still continued to attend parliament, occasionally participated in diplomatic business done in England, and was appointed to numerous *ad hoc*, mostly local commissions, his career from 1432 onwards was at a stand, or rather lost its aura. In poor health even by the end of Henry VI's minority in 1437, he died in 1443.

In concluding this introduction it is not without interest to compare with Tiptoft's career in Lancastrian service that of his contemporary and friend, Sir Walter Hungerford, whose emergence into the parliamentary peerage, in 1426, precisely coincided with his own. Hungerford, too, was Commons' Speaker (1414), steward of the King's Household (1417-21, 1424), and treasurer of the Exchequer (1426-32). But then his career more notably benefited from a friendship with Henry V always closer than Tiptoft's, and had a more firmly progressive momentum: his chief stewardship of the estates of the duchy of Lancaster south of Trent and in Wales (1413-37) led to his appointment as one of Henry's executors; and this clear sign of trust was given added emphasis by Henry's choice of him as one of the personal guardians of his heir. The engagement of the two men in Henry V's diplomacy was more nearly comparable. Hungerford, however, greatly involved in Henry V's own campaigns in France, sometimes, as especially at Agincourt, in hazardous situations, had a military career of far higher distinction than Tiptoft's, a difference between them made clear by his election, in 1421, as a knight of the Garter. Both men served each one of the Lancastrian kings well, and, in doing so, themselves also.

John Tiptoft was the only son of Sir Payn Tiptoft, himself a younger son of John, lord Tiptoft (ob. 1367), by his second wife, Elizabeth, daughter of Sir Robert Aspal and widow of Sir Thomas Waweton. John's mother was Agnes, daughter of John Wroth of Enfield (Middlesex) and sister of Sir John Wroth of the same place.

The Tiptoft family had first become important in the reign of Edward I. John's great-great-grandfather, Robert de Tiptoft of Langar (Notts.), had been with Edward on crusade in the Holy Land at the time of his accession to the throne in 1272, and had later served in his Welsh, Scottish and Gascon wars; in 1280 he was justice of South Wales, and in 1291 the king's lieutenant for the whole of Wales; and he sat in parliament by personal summons, certainly in 1276 and 1290. Robert's son, Payn, served in Edward I's later and in Edward II's earlier Scottish campaigns, and was killed in the English defeat at Bannockburn in 1314; justice of the royal forests north of Trent, he had been summoned as a baron to each of Edward II's parliaments meeting before his death. Payn's son and heir, John, the Speaker's grandfather, was summoned to Edward III's parliaments from 1335, soon after his coming of age, until he died in 1367; he served on Edward III's Scottish military expeditions of 1334-5 and on the French expeditions of 1338-41, was keeper of Berwick-on-Tweed in 1346, and campaigned with the Black Prince in Gascony in 1359-60. John, lord Tiptoft's first marriage had put him in the forefront of the lesser baronage: in ward in 1319 to Bartholomew, lord Badlesmere (one of the leaders of the "Middle Party" in the baronage during Edward II's reign, who joined the earl of Lancaster in 1322 and was hanged as a traitor), he married Margaret, one of Badlesmere's four daughters and eventual coheirs. (Her sisters were married, respectively, to the earls of Northampton and Oxford and Lord Roos of Helmsley.) Such of the Badlesmere lands as came into Tiptoft possession went first, of course, to the only son of this marriage, the Speaker's father's half-brother, Robert, lord Tiptoft (who, dying in 1372, had survived his father by only some five years), and then, along with the bulk of the family's own estates, to Robert's three daughters, two of whom married sons of Richard, lord Scrope of Bolton, when the latter, treasurer of England as he was at the time, secured for himself a grant of their wardship. The only Tiptoft estates of any importance to go to Payn, the Speaker's father, were Harston and Burwell in Cambridgeshire and Beeston in Norfolk. Burwell seems to have become the main residence of the cadet branch of the half-blood.[2]

Sir Payn Tiptoft did what he could to remedy the deficiency of landed estate in his own branch of the family by marrying Agnes, sister

2   Sir William Dugdale, *The Baronage of England*, ii 38-40; G. E. Cockayne, *The Complete Peerage*, xii, part 1, 746; T. Blore, *History of Rutland*, 44; R. Thoroton, *Antiquities of Nottinghamshire*, ed. J. Thoresby (London, 1797), i. 204; *CCR, 1339-41*, 279; *ibid., 1346-9*, 525; *ibid., 1354-60*, 605; *ibid., 1360-4*, 370; *ibid., 1364-9*, 343; *ibid., 1369-74*, 396-7, 445, 565; *ibid., 1385-9*, 27.

and eventual heir of Sir John Wroth of Enfield (Middlesex). But it was not until October 1413 that his son John secured possession of such of the lands of his cousin, Elizabeth Wroth, in Middlesex, Hampshire, and Wiltshire, as were not the subject of dower rights, including, in Middlesex, the manor of Enfield and, in Wiltshire, the manors of Puckshipton, Barford near Downton, and Redlynch.[3] It was left to John himself to do most towards building up a large fund of landed property. Some of this came into his possession only temporarily as a result of grants of royal wardships or forfeitures; at times, however, these can only have amounted to a considerable holding. Early in Henry IV's reign (in 1403), although apparently not without some difficulty, he procured the wardship and marriage of the son and heir of a Suffolk knight, Sir Robert Shardelow. In November 1403 he and another prominent Lancastrian retainer, Sir John Pelham, shared a grant of a rent worth £4 a year in Broughton-by-Aylesbury (Bucks), as well as a bond for 40 marks, forfeited by Sir Thomas Shelley for treasonable participation in the rising of Richard II's supporters in January 1400.[4] In February 1404, during Tiptoft's first parliament, he and Pelham again shared a grant, that of the right to farm the Suffolk manor of Stansfield. In August 1405 the forfeited Leicestershire manors of Sir Ralph Hastings in Kirby and Branston were granted to Tiptoft for life, together with the prospect of the dower lands of Ralph's mother. At the beginning of the following year (1406) the wardship (worth 20 marks a year) and the marriage of another Suffolk heir (the son of John de Tuddenham) came his way. At the end of 1406, the year of his Speakership, he secured a grant of the estates of a Welshman (Rhys ap Griffith) in Carmarthenshire, Cardiganshire and elsewhere in South Wales, forfeited by reason of their owner's support for the rebellion of Owen Glendower, together with the forestership of Waybridge and Sapley in Huntingdonshire.[5] Early in 1408, following his appointment as treasurer of Henry IV's Household, he obtained the custody of his mother's family's manor of Enfield (Middlesex); the wardship and marriage of the heir of Sir Roger Heron; and the wardship and marriage of the grandson and heir of one of the greatest of non-noble West Country proprietors, Sir William Bonville of Shute (Devon). This last grant, however, he was immediately constrained to surrender to Edward, duke of York.[6]

John Tiptoft's interest in the south-west undoubtedly resulted from

3   *CFR, 1413-22*, 43; *ibid, 1422-30*, 37; Hoare, *Wiltshire*, vol. iii, part II, p. 44. The Wroth lands now still subject to rights of dower were to come to Tiptoft in 1423.

4   *CPR, 1401-5*, 170-1, 260; 329.

5   *CFR, 1399-1405*, 240; *CPR, 1405-8*, 39, 54; 109, 145; 318.

6   *CFR, 1405-13*, 97, 98, 101; *CPR, 1405-8*, 393.

another sort of speculation, one which made financially feasible these recent ventures of his in the market for royal wardships. Sometime after the death, in September 1406, of her husband, Sir Matthew de Gournay (an old campaigner in the French and Spanish wars of Edward III's reign and a West Country landowner), but before January 1408, Tiptoft married Philippa, daughter and eventually coheir of Sir John Talbot of Richard's Castle (Herefordshire). Philippa, evidently from the first, had been a tempting prospect as heiress: before, when still a young woman, she married the aged Gournay, she had been the wife of Edward III's last chief chamberlain, Sir Robert Ashton, who had died in 1384; and when she married Tiptoft she herself brought him an interest in property in no fewer than ten counties of the south and west, including three English counties bordering Wales. However, it was doubtless the prospect of getting hold of the Gournay estates, at least during Philippa's lifetime, which especially attracted Tiptoft, for Sir Matthew had died without heirs. Those Gournay estates were considerable enough to warrant Henry IV's youngest son Humphrey being prepared in 1407 to pay 5,000 marks for the reversion alone; and when, in May 1417, Philippa died, Henry V himself was ready to pay even as much as £4,000 (6,000 marks) to have the lands after Tiptoft's death. Indeed, within a year of Philippa's death, Tiptoft had actually received, for the reversion, an advance of £1,220, paid through the King's Chamber. During the parliament of May 1421, it was arranged that the Gournay estates were to go (when they reverted) into the duchy of Cornwall, in exchange for the duchy manor of Isleworth (Middlesex), which had been given up by Henry V to his Bridgettine nunnery at Sheen; comprising, as those estates then did, the Somerset manors of Curry Mallet, Stoke-under-Hamden, Milton-Falconbridge, Stratton-on-the-Foss, Inglishcombe, Midsummer Norton, Welton, Widecombe, Farington Gurney and Laverton, and a moiety of the manors of West Harptree and Shepton Mallet, the Dorset manor of Ryme, a moiety of Maidencote in Berkshire, a quarter of Sellinge in Kent, and Magor in Wales, their value in 1421 surpassed that of the manor of Isleworth by £200 a year. In January 1408, through this first marriage of his with the relict of Sir Matthew Gournay, Tiptoft also obtained possession of an important collection of estates and rights in the Bordelais in the duchy of Guienne, property which perhaps had much to do with his subsequent appointment as seneschal of Landes (in February 1408), and as seneschal of Guienne (in April 1415). All of the English and French estates of Sir Matthew Gournay, Tiptoft retained until he died.[7] In the meantime, in addition to the Gournay estates in England and the estates of his father's and mother's families already listed, John Tiptoft had come into possession of the following manors:

Chadworth, Badlingham, Fordham, Soham, Eversden, and Bassingbourne, in Cambridgeshire; Wooley, in Huntingdonshire; Fastolf, Mulford and a third of Layham, in Suffolk; Woodham Mortimer, in Essex; Shepperton, in Middlesex; Brockley, Over and Nether Wallop, Broughton, and a moiety of Alton, in Hampshire; Langton Herring (with lands in Long Budy, East Baglake and Sturminster Newton), in Dorset; Woverton, Linlegh, Inglestone, Stowell, Tellisford-near-Frome and (for his first wife's life only) Pitney, in Somerset.[8] Certain of these estates, however, came into Tiptoft's control, as a result of his second marriage, shortly after 28 February 1422, when (following a contract between the parties dated sometime between May 1417 and July 1421) Henry V allowed to Tiptoft and Joyce, daughter and coheir of Edward, lord Charleton of Powys, his royal licence to marry.

This second marriage of his brought Tiptoft into family connection with some of the most important noble houses of the time. Joyce's mother, Eleanor Holland, a niece of Richard II, had died in 1405, and her uncle, Edmund Holland, earl of Kent, in 1408. Of that same generation of the Holland family there still survived, however, Margaret, dowager duchess of Clarence, Joan, dowager duchess of York (widow of Edmund of Langley), and Elizabeth, widow of the eldest son of Ralph Neville, first earl of Westmorland. Joyce's mother, by her first marriage with Roger Mortimer, earl of March (ob.1398), was mother of Edmund, earl of March (ob.1425), and of Anne, widow of Richard, earl of Cambridge (who had been executed for his share in the Southampton plot of 1415). This Anne Mortimer was the mother of Richard, duke of York, who at the time of Tiptoft's marriage with Joyce Charleton was a boy of about ten years old. By her second marriage with Lord Charleton of Powys, Eleanor Holland was mother of Joyce, and of her elder sister Joan, who married Sir John Grey K.G., count of Tancarville (who was killed at the battle of Baugé in 1421). When Joyce's half-brother Edmund, earl of March, died without issue in Ireland in January 1425, she did not of course became a coheir of the Mortimer inheritance − her half-sister Anne Mortimer's son Richard, duke of York, was sole heir to the earls of March − but she did become one of Earl Edmund's coheirs in that share of the Holland estates to

7   *Complete Peerage, loc. cit; CPR, 1405-8,* 297, 412; *Rot. Parl.,* IV 140-1, 373; Exchequer, Issue Roll, P. R. O., E403/636 mem. 3; Somerset Record Society, vol. XXII (*Feet of Fines, Henry IV-Henry VI,* ed. E. Green), p. 171. For the exercise of his rights of advowson, see *ibid,* vol. XXIX (*Register of Nicholas Bubwith, Bishop of Bath and Wells*), vol. 1, p. 63; *ibid.,* xxx, vol. 2, 392, 395, 403; *ibid.,* vol. XXXI (*Register of Bishop John Stafford*), vol. 1, 44; *ibid.,* vol. XXXII, vol. 2, 164, 196, 198, 230, 273.

8   *Feudal Aids,* i. 63, 178, 184, 188, 190; ii. 75, 105, 373, 474; iii. 78, 615; iv. 371, 373, 374, 377-8, 386-7, 426; v. 232; Dugdale, *Baronage,* ii. 40; *H. M. C. Reports, MSS. of the Duke of Rutland,* IV. 86-7; *MSS. of R. R. Hastings,* i. 252; T. Blore, *Rutland,* 44; J. Collinson, *History and Antiquities of Somerset,* ii. 118, 139; iii. 66-7, 130; J. Hutchins, *History of Dorset* (3rd ed.) ii. 188; P. Morant, *History of Essex,* i. 341.

which their mother had been coheir, Joyce's fellow coheirs to these lands being Richard, duke of York, and her elder sister Joan's son, Henry Grey, count of Tancarville, both of whom were still under age.[9] Joyce was also, of course, her sister Joan's coheir in the estates of their father Edward, lord Charleton of Powys, who had died without male issue in March 1421. Joyce had received her purparty of her father's lands in Shropshire in the summer after his death, perhaps just about the time when it was first agreed that she should marry Tiptoft. But Joan, as the elder sister, took the feudal lordship of Powys, and though Tiptoft called himself (after his first summons as a peer of parliament in 1426) Lord Tiptoft and of Powys, he was never summoned to parliament by that title, and the latter designation descended to his wife's sister's representatives.[10] In view of the various accretions of territory Tiptoft enjoyed, especially by means of his two marriages, it is not surprising that when, in 1436, a parliamentary tax was levied on annual incomes, Tiptoft was assessed (and the assessment is hardly likely to have been too strict) as worth very nearly £1,100 per annum.[11]

Between 1408, i.e. soon after his first marriage to Philippa, the relict of Sir Matthew Gournay, and her death in 1417, Tiptoft seems to have been content, so far as lands were concerned, to manage what he already had secured. During that time, at any rate, he acquired no further rights of wardship as a result of royal grants. However, in July 1419 he obtained the wardship and marriage of the son and heir of Thomas House esquire who had lands in Essex and Suffolk, for £300 payable in the Exchequer. This was the beginning of a resumption of Tiptoft's interest in this sort of investment, promoted perhaps by an enlargement of horizons offered him by his second marriage. In February 1422 he paid 400 marks to the Exchequer for the wardship and marriage of the son and heir of Sir Thomas de la Pole. In May 1423, now himself a member of the King's Council (the disposing body), he also secured the wardship and marriage of Edmund, the infant grandson and heir of Sir John Ingoldsthorpe, which (apart from certain reserved estates) were confirmed to him in July 1428 for a payment of 500 marks to the Exchequer. Tiptoft married Edmund off to his own second daughter, Joan, the marriage being made all the more acceptable by the fact that young Ingoldsthorpe was, on his mother's side, the grandson and heir of Sir Walter de la Pole (a member of a cadet branch of the family of the De la Poles, earls of Suffolk, who died

9   *CPR, 1416-22*, 415; *Complete Peerage*, vii. 156; *CCR, 1422-9*, 223.
10   *Complete Peerage*, iii. 161-2; *ibid*, xii, part 1, 748.
11   *E. H. R.*, XLIX. 615 (H. L. Gray, 'Incomes from Land in England in 1436').

in July 1434) and of his wife Elizabeth de Breadstone, from whom Edmund also inherited the estates of Thomas, lord Breadstone, who had died in 1360.[12] Then, in July 1431, Tiptoft was ready to put down £800 for a grant of the wardship and marriage of the three-years-old Thomas, son and heir of Thomas, lord Roos of Helmsley, and a grandson (through his mother, Eleanor) of Richard Beauchamp, earl of Warwick. Tiptoft married off this young heir to his eldest daughter, Philippa. Young Roos's mother, Eleanor Beauchamp, subsequently (but before 1438) procured for her son a very eligible step-father in Edmund Beaufort, nephew of Cardinal Beaufort, who in 1442 was created earl of Dorset, in 1443 marquess of Dorset, and in 1448 duke of Somerset, and who became the leader of the Lancastrian party from the retirement of his uncle, Cardinal Beaufort, down to his death in the first battle of St. Albans (1455). Lord Roos was still in Tiptoft's wardship at the time of the latter's death in January 1443.[13] The Roos wardship was not the last which Tiptoft secured. In November 1431 he was granted the custody of the estates of Sir Richard Hankford (elder son of Henry V's chief justice of the King's Bench, William Hankford) in Staffordshire and Gloucestershire, having already acquired the custody of the Hankford family's lands in Shropshire and Herefordshire during the previous summer. Some four years later, on 15 November 1435, in company with John Merbury, he farmed the lordship of Abergavenny after the death of Joan, widow of William Beauchamp, lord Abergavenny. Then, in July 1437, he secured control of the estates of the alien priory of Linton (Cambs.), for ten years as from the death of the previous grantee, Henry IV's queen, Joan of Navarre. (He held this property, however, no longer than July 1439, having failed to reach agreement with the Exchequer over the rent.)[14] The wardships of Roos and Inglesthorpe were quite probably secured by Tiptoft with a view to the marriages of his daughters, but both those and the other royal wardships and leases which he secured at the Exchequer were doubtless part of his general policy of establishing his influence and wealth by the acquisition, however temporary, of more and more landed estate. In half a century, in one way and another, his branch of the Tiptoft family made up for what, by want of male heirs, had been lost by the main line of the family to the Scropes of Bolton.

There is no evidence to suggest that the marriages of John Tiptoft's half-cousins of the family of Tiptoft of Langar (Notts.), contracted

12   *CPR, 1416-22*, 218, 412; *ibid., 1422-9*, 520; *ibid., 1441-6*, 176; *CFR, 1422-30*, 39, 73. 233, 277; *CCR, 1429-35*, 341; *Complete Peerage*, II. 273.

13   *Complete Peerage*, XI. 104-6; *CPR, 1429-36*, 145; *ibid., 1441-6*, 171; *ibid., 1461-7*, 87.

14   *CFR 1430-7*, 43, 59, 254, 344. 15

when they were under the guardianship of Richard, lord Scrope of Bolton, had any influence on the careers of either John Tiptoft or his father, Sir Payn. The latter evidently attached himself to the service of Richard, earl of Arundel, one of the Lords Appellant of 1387-8, who appointed him as one of his feoffees and executors and gave him the manor of Beeston-on-Sea in Norfolk for life; it was probably his association with Arundel which lay behind Sir Payn's arrest and appearance before Richard II's Council shortly before the earl's condemnation for treason in the parliament of September 1397, and again in April 1398.[15] After the accession of Henry IV in 1399, Sir Payn was to become one of the twelve knights of the King's Chamber. His son John was another to do so.

So far as John was concerned, the way was already well prepared for this new departure by the circumstances of his short career down to this time. By the spring of 1397, as a young esquire, he had joined the household of Henry of Bolingbroke, son and heir of John of Gaunt and (as he then was) earl of Derby; and between April and September 1397 he spent most of his time (125 days) serving *infra curia* at a wage of 7½d. a day. In the parliament which met that September, Bolingbroke, for his complacency towards the establishment of Richard II's 'tyranny' (remarkable in one who, as one of the Lords Appellant, had been so hostile to the king in 1387-8), was promoted to be duke of Hereford. In September 1398, however, the duke had been condemned to a ten years' exile which, soon after the death of his father in February following, was changed into banishment for life and attended by the loss of his Lancastrian inheritance. In July 1399 Bolingbroke returned from exile in France, avowedly only to recover the duchy of Lancaster. In three months he had deprived Richard II of his crown and taken it for himself.

In the year previous to Bolingbroke's being sentenced to exile (October 1397-September 1398) John Tiptoft had continued to serve him, being actually present in his household for altogether 138 days.[16] It is unlikely that he accompanied his lord into exile, but highly probable that both he and his father rallied to Henry's banner soon after his landing in Yorkshire. However this may be, the father, Sir Payn, was elected as a knight of the shire for Cambridgeshire to the 'convention' assembly which, having witnessed, all on the same day (30 September 1399), Richard II's deposition and Henry's accession,

15   *CPR, 1385-9*, 440; *ibid., 1391-6*, 598; *ibid., 1396-9*, 242; *ibid, 1399-1401*, 557; *CCR, 1396-9*, 72, 84, 277; *ibid, 1422-9*, 221; N. H. Nicolas, *Testamenta Vetusta*, i. 133.

16   Duchy of Lancaster, Accounts Various, Account Books of the Treasurer of Household to Henry, earl of Derby (later duke of Hereford), P. R. O., D. L. 28/1/9; D. L. 28/1/10.

continued in being as the new king's first parliament. John Tiptoft was among the 46 esquires who were knighted by Henry on the eve of his coronation on 13 October, in honour of the occasion.[17] During the single session of the parliament, Sir Payn became for the first time a justice of the peace in Cambridgeshire, an office which he was to retain until his death, and, on 13 November, John Tiptoft himself was retained for life as a 'king's knight', with a large annuity of 100 marks charged on the royal revenues from Cambridgeshire.[18] (This annuity was to be confirmed to him at the accessions of Henry V and Henry VI.) In May 1400 he secured (as we have seen) the Shardelowe wardship. In November 1401 his father was appointed sheriff of Cambridgeshire and Huntingdonshire, but for some reason did not act or render account. On 7 August 1402 Sir John and another commissioner were appointed to supervise and try the fencibles of Huntingdonshire who were to meet with the king at Shrewsbury in order, if possible, to help suppress the Welsh rebellion led by Owen Glendower; Sir Payn was to do the same in Cambridgeshire; they were both to certify the king in person when they and their contingents arrived.

By this time both father and son were among the twelve *milites camere et aule Regis*.[19] It was with a fellow Chamber-knight, Sir John Pelham, that at the end of November 1403 Sir John was granted a £4 rent in Broughton-by-Aylesbury (Bucks.) during the minority of the heir (both knights having been willing to sue for the recovery of the rent by the Crown at their own costs)., *plus* a bond for £40 forfeited for treason (in January 1400) by Sir Thomas Shelley (the bond having been similarly concealed). To the parliament which met in January 1404 both Tiptofts were elected as knights of the shire, the father for Cambridgeshire again, Sir John for Huntingdonshire. Two others of the twelve Chamber-knights at this time, Sir John Strange and Sir John Pelham, represented, respectively, Suffolk and Sussex. The Commons on this occasion, under the Speakership of Sir Arnold Savage, were outspoken in their criticisms of extravagance at Court, especially of the profiteering of its officials and knights, and parliament only made its grant of a 5% tax on land-rents conditional upon the appointment of four special treasurers who were to control expenditure under the direct oversight of the Council and be answerable to parliament. The king's shortage of money, so acute as to warrant a stoppage of all royal

17   *The Great Chronicle of London*, ed. A. H. Thomas and I. D. Thornley (London, 1938), p. 73.

18   *CPR, 1399-1401*, 98; *CCR, 1399-1402*, 338.

19   *CPR, 1401-5*, 138; Exchequer, Accounts Various, Wardrobe Accounts, Account of the Treasurer of the Household, September 1402-3, P. R. O., E101/404/21, fo. 44v.

annuities on 5 July, necessitated another meeting of parliament in the following autumn, this time at Coventry. Negatively, according to the writs of summons, no lawyers were to be elected; positively, Henry IV used his influence with the sheriffs to secure a Lower House more attentive to his needs. In the meantime, on 18 February 1404 (during the first parliament of the year), Tiptoft had shared (again with Pelham) a grant of the custody of the Suffolk manor of Stansfield, at a farm of 16 marks a year; on 6 July (the day after the Exchequer's suspension of payment of annuities) he secured appointment for life as steward of the duchy of Lancaster manor of Soham (Cambs.); and, on 30 September (a week before the autumn parliament met), the king, then at Maxstoke castle, on his own authority granted him corn belonging to the alien priory of Swavesey (Cambs.), up to the value of 50 marks.[20] He and his fellow shire-knight in the January parliament had been re-elected to the Coventry parliament; so had his fellow knights of the King's Chamber, Strange in Suffolk, Pelham in Sussex, and, with the latter, came along a fourth of their number, Sir John Dallingridge. During the session, John's father, Sir Payn, who had not been re-elected, was appointed sheriff of Cambridgeshire and Huntingdonshire.

The Coventry parliament of 1404 was a stormy affair. The Commons brought forward sweeping proposals for financial reform, and there was an attack on the *possessionati* of the Church (the monks). But this anti-clericalism was quashed by Archbishop Arundel, and the king secured considerable subsidies, the control of which was now given to two of his supporters, Thomas, lord Furnival, and Sir John Pelham, the Chamber-knight, who were appointed as special treasurers-for-the-wars. The following year was, however, one of excessive expenditure, mainly the result of domestic unrest which culminated in fresh treasons on the part of the earl of Northumberland, and in the great rising in northern England of May 1405, the leaders of which, Archbishop Scrope and Thomas Mowbray, the earl marshal, were executed outside York on 8 June. Before the end of the year it was decided to summon parliament again, first to Coventry, then to Gloucester, but finally to Westminster. By this time opposition to Henry IV's methods was growing within the Council itself, his half-brothers, the Beauforts, at its centre. When parliament came together on 1 March 1406 the political situation was in an uneasy state of flux.

---

20   *CPR, 1401-5*, 329, 451; *CPR, 1399-1405*, 240; R. Somerville, *History of the Duchy of Lancaster*, i. 601.

In the meantime, since the 'Unlearned Parliament' of Coventry, Sir John Tiptoft, as one of the knights of the Chamber, had had a busy but, on the whole, personally profitable year. Glendower's rebellion in Wales was doubtless behind the business he was required to do in Yorkshire when, in the middle of March 1405, he was given permission for two months to commandeer horses for the purpose. On 22 May, a week before the earl of Westmorland inveigled Archbishop Scrope and the earl marshal into surrendering at Shipton Moor, Tiptoft and his father were commissioned by the king (then at Hereford) to raise forces in Cambridgeshire and Huntingdonshire (where Sir Payn was sheriff) to join him for the suppression of that northern revolt. Presumably, Sir John went up into Percy country, stamping out rebellion with the royal army, after the executions at York. On 28 June he and the sheriff of Lincolnshire, Sir Ralph de Rochford, who had just been given the office of chief steward of the Mowbray lordship of Axholme, shared a grant of the late earl marshal's clothes, armour, and saddles; and on 3 August Tiptoft secured for life two Leicestershire manors forfeited by a Yorkshire knight, Sir Ralph Hastings, who had been executed at Durham for his part in the recent rising. At first this grant was limited to £10 a year, but on the very next day a fresh patent was issued allowing him 20 marks instead, together with the reversion of the dower of Sir Ralph's mother up to the value of another 8 marks a year. Sir John now probably moved with the king down through the Midlands into the south parts of the Welsh border, to resist a French incursion and retaliate once more against Glendower's partizans. At Worcester on 5 October, when the king was on his way back into England, he received the gift of a ship then lying in the East Anglian port of Orwell; and two days later he was granted for life an annuity of £20 from the fee-farm of Norwich and a tun of Gascon wine a year out of the prisage at Ipswich. (This latter grant was to be confirmed at the accessions of Henry V and Henry VI.) It was at Kenilworth less than a month later (1 November) that he was given the stewardship of the Mortimer lordship of Bottisham (Cambs.), with a fee of £5 a year, this lordship having come into the king's hands with the death of Eleanor, countess of March (the mother of the girl who was later to be Tiptoft's second wife), pending the minority of the heir, Edmund, the young earl of March. And on 1 January 1406 Tiptoft added to these recent acquisitions the Tuddenham wardship, worth 20 marks a year.

If Sir John Tiptoft's two returns to parliament in 1404 were not sufficient evidence of his growing local importance in the fenland shires, his inclusion on 27 January 1406 in the commission of the peace in Cambridgeshire (alongside of his father) and only four days later in that of Huntingdonshire also, would confirm it.[21] (He was to continue in both appointments until foreign military service caused his temporary withdrawal in 1417.) Possibly already, he had been re-elected, for the second time running, as knight of the shire for Huntingdonshire. Having first been summoned to meet at Coventry on 15 February and then at Gloucester on the same date, parliament finally met at Westminster on 1 March.

This parliament of 1406 was destined to last for longer than any previous parliament. It underwent two adjournments (3-25 April, 19 June-13 October), but by 22 December, when it was dissolved, its three sessions had together taken up 23 weeks. (And no parliament was to sit over a longer period, for more sessions, or for more weeks in all, until 1445-6.) On the second day of the parliament, Tiptoft was elected by the Commons as their Speaker and, although he protested his youth and want of sense and discretion, he was accepted by the king. The latter can have had no qualms in confirming the election of one who was a knight of his Chamber. And Tiptoft himself no doubt found comfort in the knowledge that he had friends in the Lower House: his fellow Chamber-knights, Sir John Dallingridge and Sir John Pelham, had been re-elected for Sussex, and Sir John Strange, a former Chamber-knight now promoted as controller of the Household, for Suffolk; and his uncle, Sir John Wroth of Enfield, was knight of the shire for Middlesex. For Tiptoft, the whole period of roughly ten months covered by the parliament can only have been extremely busy and at times one of great difficulty. The best documented of his activities probably caused him least anxiety: on 3 April, the day of the parliament's first adjournment (for Easter), he was appointed, virtually *ex officio*, one of the Commons' committee of six knights who were to confer with the Council on the subject of the safe-keeping of English coastal waters by the merchants, to whom the subsidy of tunnage and poundage was to be diverted for the purpose; on 7 June (in the middle of the second session) it fell to him as Speaker to seal, with the seal of his arms, the enactment which, sealed also with the Great Seal and the seals of the individual peers present, declared the royal succession to be restricted to the king's male heirs, the effect of which was to be undone on 22 December (the last day of the parliament) when another statute, again sealed by Tiptoft as Speaker, re-settled the succession on the heirs of the king's body. Meanwhile, on 28 June, early in the second recess of the parliament, Tiptoft had been made one of five commissioners appointed for Cambridgeshire and Huntingdonshire, authorized to

21   *CPR, 1401-5*, 513; *ibid., 1405-8*, 66; 31, 54, 80, 81, 101, 109, 145, 490, 492.

inquire into malpractices and acts of deceit on the part of local royal officials, and also to raise Crown loans in the two counties and notify the outcome to the king in person with all despatch. And, again at the end of the parliament, once more *ex officio*, he was one of the Commons chosen to be present when the roll of the parliament was finally engrossed.[22] Important though were the above-recorded activities in which Tiptoft took part, what must have given him far greater anxiety as Speaker was the Commons' obstinacy regarding a variety of problems facing the parliament, it being his official duty to convey to the king and lords the criticisms of the Lower House and its demands for 'good and abundant governance', requirements which inevitably included economies in the Household as elsewhere. Especially unpalatable to the king was the Commons' insistence that taxation and redress of their grievances were related questions (interdependent questions, indeed); and it was only reluctantly that, having conceded an audit of the accounts of the treasurers-for-war appointed in the Coventry parliament of 1404, he also accepted a long series of articles imposing a variety of constraints upon the operations of the departments of State and Household and a severe restriction of his own freedom of prerogatival action, the latter to be controlled by a partially reconstituted Council whose members, nominated in parliament, were to swear oaths to implement the whole scheme of reform, at least until the next parliament. Even so, the Commons, especially the knights of the shire, continued to make difficulties over taxation. Indeed, if we may believe Thomas Walsingham, the St. Albans chronicler, it was only when, in the darkness of the night of 22 December, the king flew into a passion and threatened armed violence against the recalcitrants, that the knights, partly to pacify the king, partly in hope of reaching home for Christmas, granted a subsidy of a fifteenth. Whether Tiptoft had had his fill of the Commons' carping and intransigence, he never again served as Speaker; in fact, seven years and four parliaments were to pass before even he was next elected as a knight of the shire. It is, however, likely that, in so far as his office of Commons' Speaker had allowed, he had done his duty by the king, with whom, as events of the rest of Henry's reign were to reveal, he remained *persona grata*.

Certainly, there is no reason to believe that, however personally

22   *Rot. Parl.*, iii. 568, 569, 574, 576, 581, 585; *CPR, 1405-8*, 154, 200. For the significance of the enactments declaratory of the royal succession, see P. McNiven, 'Legitimacy and Consent: Henry IV and the Lancastrian Title, 1399-1406' in Pontifical Institute of Mediaeval Studies, Toronto, *Mediaeval Studies*, vol. XLIV (1982) especially pp. 484-8.

distasteful must at times have been the discharge of his responsibilities as Speaker, Tiptoft's tenure of the office did his reputation any immediate harm. Quite the contrary, indeed. The remodelled Council thought well enough of him to entrust him with such a post as could only involve him in playing an important part in the execution of the plan to reform the royal Household. On 8 December, whilst this long parliament of 1406 was still sitting, but when the dissolution was doubtless felt to be imminent, the Council met to appoint new officials in the Household, to ensure its 'moderate governance'. Regarding the office of controller, the names of Sir Arnold Savage, one of the three commoners on the Council, and Sir Thomas Bromflete were then proposed. Tiptoft alone was nominated for the treasurership of the Household, taking the place of Richard Kingston, clerk, a tried servant of the king's who had been his treasurer when on expedition to the Barbary Coast and in Prussia as long ago as 1390.[23] Then, on the very same day, with the Council's assent, Tiptoft was granted a forfeiture of £150 and also (to him and his heirs and assigns) the forfeited estates of Rhys ap Griffith (an adherent of Owen Glendower) in Carmarthenshire and Cardiganshire and elsewhere in South Wales, together with the custody of the royal forests of Waybridge and Sapley (Huntingdonshire). Both these concessions were warranted by King and Council in Parliament, and the grant of the Welsh forfeiture was made notwithstanding Tiptoft's current enjoyment of annuities and grants worth £150 a year. An exception was, moreover, made in his favour to that one of those articles (which members of the new Council were to swear to keep) which provided for the annulment of any royal grants of feudal casualties and forfeitures made between the beginning of this 1406 parliament and the end of the next parliament, such casualties and forfeitures having now been generally assigned to the Household account.[24]

In the course of the following year, on 13 May 1407, Tiptoft was also appointed (during royal pleasure) as chief butler of England. This was an office whose occupant, acting through deputies in the ports, was responsible for supervising the administration of the royal right of prisage of imported wines, an element of Household management which could usefully be combined with the duties of the treasurership. Since November 1402 the office had been held (under a grant for life) by

23   J. H. Wylie, *History of England under Henry IV*, ii. 475-6 (Tiptoft's account as treasurer of the Household covers the period from 8 December 1406 to 17 July 1408; the first reference to him acting in that capacity on the Exchequer Issue Rolls is dated 13 December 1406. P. R. O., E. 403/589, mem. 11.).

24   *CPR, 1405-8*, 313, 318; *Rot. Parl.*, iii. 586, 591.

Thomas Chaucer, cousin of Henry Beaufort, bishop of Winchester, and perhaps the idea behind Tiptoft's appointment, involving Chaucer's dismissal as it did, was to effect an economy. However, on 3 December that same year (1407), the day after the dissolution of the Gloucester parliament in which Chaucer had been the Commons' Speaker, he was re-appointed chief butler. Tiptoft remained treasurer of the Household, and only ceased to fill that post when, on 14 July 1408, he was promoted treasurer of the Exchequer.[25] In the meantime, on 8 February 1408, as a consequence of his marriage with the widow of Sir Matthew de Gournay, which brought him possession of a number of important lordships in the Bordelais, he had been given the office of seneschal of the Landes in Gascony (an office formerly held by Gournay), together with the custodianship of the castle of Dax and, seven months later (8 September), the office of *prévôt* of D'Entre-deux-Mers between the rivers Garonne and Dordogne. (He was still in retention of the castellanship and *prévôté* in 1423 and of the seneschalship of the Landes in 1441.)[26] He remained, however, in England, administering the office of treasurer of the Exchequer from 14 July 1408 to 11 December 1409, towards the end of his first year of office (on 23 May 1409) receiving a *speciale regardum* of 200 marks, in addition to the ancient fee of 100 marks a year and the annual incremental fee of £300.[27]

It was only to be expected that Tiptoft, who while treasurer of the Household had picked up one or two useful wardships as well as the Gascon appointments, would add to his normal emoluments as head of the Exchequer. In fact, during his year and a half as treasurer of England he came to enjoy the following: the issues of the duchy of Lancaster manors of Glatton and Holme (Huntingdonshire) estimated at that time as worth £88.6s.5d a year; an annuity of £5.6s.8d from the farm of the forests of the duchy lordship of Kidwelly in south Wales; the farm of manors in the duchy lordship of Brecon worth £7.6s.8d a year; the fee of £20 a year attached to the stewardship of this lordship, to which he had been appointed; and the farm of the duchy manor of Trowbridge (Wiltshire) estimated in 1408-9 at £73.10s.5d. The Brecon stewardship he was to have relinquished by 1414, after first being re-appointed by Henry V; but he retained his custodies of Glatton and Trowbridge, certainly until 1418-9 when together they were considered to be worth as much as 200 marks annually.[28]

25   *CPR, 1405-8*, 327, 334, 457.
26   T. Carte, *Catalogue des Rolles Gascons*, etc., i. 191-2, 205, 223.
27   Exchequer, Issue Roll, P. R. O., E. 403/599, mem. 7; E. 403/602.
28   Duchy of Lancaster, Accounts Various, P. R. O., D. L. 28/27/8; 27/10.

It was also in the course of his tenure of the highest office in the Exchequer that, presumably in consequence of his possession (*jure uxoris*) of the Gournay lands in Somerset, Tiptoft became a justice of the peace in that county (as well as in Cambridgeshire and Huntingdonshire.) It was, however, strictly in his official capacity as treasurer that, on 21 January 1409, when Henry IV was gravely ill at Greenwich and drew up his last will and testament, Tiptoft was a witness to the instrument; and that, on 25 February following, he and Archbishop Arundel, the chancellor, were assigned by the Council the sum of £1,100 charged on the wool-customs, which had already been appropriated to the upkeep of Calais, the object of the transaction being to indemnify them for a bond to that amount in favour of Richard Whityngton, the London mercer, who had advanced that sum to pay all that was due to the Calais garrison. It was only a fortnight later (10 March) that Tiptoft was present at Greenwich when the chancellor secured a grant of the castle and lordship of Queenborough (Kent), momentarily surrendering the Great Seal, perhaps, lest he should lay himself open to a charge of personal acquisitiveness, out of caution.[29]

The remainder of the year 1409 was a period of increasing political tension. This was mainly because of Henry IV's physical incapacity for continuous administrative work, of the restiveness of his heir-apparent, Henry of Monmouth (now comparatively free of military involvement in Wales), and of the ill-feeling which now arose between the prince's friends and supporters, notably the Beauforts, and the existing administration, now chiefly represented in the person of the primate, Thomas Arundel. And before the end of the year there was a change in the two most important ministries of state: Tiptoft was dismissed from the headship of the Exchequer on 11 December 1409, and Arundel relinquished the Great Seal ten days later. Not until 6 January 1410, however, was Tiptoft succeeded by Henry, lord Scrope of Masham, a close friend of the prince, and it was not even until 31 January that Sir Thomas Beaufort was made chancellor. Perhaps in anticipation of these mutations, on 24 October 1409 Tiptoft had taken out a patent pardoning him all debts, accounts, etc. demanded of him at the Exchequer or elsewhere. During 1410 he was retained on the commission of the peace in Cambridgeshire, Huntingdonshire, and Somerset, but otherwise slips almost completely out of view for the rest of Henry IV's reign. In July 1411, when Prince Henry and his Council were still decidedly in charge of the government, he was put on a

29   N. H. Nicolas, *Testamenta Vetusta*, i. 18; *CPR, 1408-13*, 54; *CCR, 1405-9*, 498.

commission to seize, in the Crown's interest, the Somerset manor of Frome Branche, and perhaps he was down there at the time.

When the Council headed by Prince Henry was discharged during the parliament of November-December 1411, the early return of Archbishop Arundel as chancellor made little or no difference to his former associate in the administration, Tiptoft. And during 1412 Sir John was no more active than of late: his only special royal commissions were one to help determine an appeal against a judgement in the Court of Chivalry in the dreary case of the hostage of the count of Denia (in Aragon) which had been dragging on since the second year of Richard II's reign, and another authorising him, as steward of the duchy of Lancaster lordship of Brecon, to be party to negotiations with Owen Glendower for the ransoming of a son of one of the Brecon tenants, David Gamme esquire. It was on 12 April in this year that he made a pilgrimage to Canterbury, where he was received into the confraternity of Christchurch priory.[30]

For an ex-treasurer of the royal Household and ex-treasurer of England, such as Tiptoft was, all this relative inactivity of his in the last three years of Henry IV's reign and the first two of Henry V's is rather difficult to understand. It may well be that his Speakership and subsequent offices had led him to favour conciliar control of government in ways unacceptable to Henry IV, while his former long and close personal association with the latter led to his being regarded with some suspicion, or at least with no great sympathy, by Henry of Monmouth. Tiptoft, in fact, was to remain in comparative obscurity until 1415. In the meantime, however, in the first fortnight of Henry V's reign (5 April 1413), he was confirmed in his duchy of Lancaster stewardship of Brecon and, on 1 November following, he secured renewal of the various royal patents which had secured him a considerable income as a royal annuitant in the previous reign, on condition that he was retained only by the king, and that his fees did not overstep the sum of £120 a year.[31] Both he and his father were as usual re-commissioned as J.P.s in Cambridgeshire, and Sir John himself in Huntingdonshire as well. His commission of the peace in Somerset was not renewed, although it was here that in January 1414, after the abortive rebellion of the Lollards under Sir John Oldcastle, he was appointed to serve on the general inquiry into malignant heresy on the part of members of this troublesome Wycliffite sect. It was as knight of the shire for Somerset, moreover, that Tiptoft was elected to Henry V's

30   *CPR, 1408-13*, 114, 303, 391, 406; British Library, Arundel Ms. No. 68, fo. 57ᵛ.
31   R. Somerville, op. cit., 646; *CPR, 1413-16*, 127.

second parliament, which met at Leicester on 30 April following. During the month-long session he was appointed to judge and settle a mercantile case arising out of a breach of the truce with Castile (possibly an anticipation of the Statute of Truces and Safeconducts passed in this parliament), and he took personal advantage of his presence at the centre of affairs to obtain, on 28 May, a royal grant of the right to a weekly market and an Ascensiontide fair in his Somerset manor of West Harptree. Then, in the middle of July following, he was appointed to act as a royal commissioner for the investigation of treasons, acts of rebellion, felonies and trespasses in Devon.[32] However, no really important office under the Crown had so far come Tiptoft's way since the change of ruler.

Sir John Tiptoft was, of course, too able a man, and fundamentally too devoted to the Lancastrian dynasty, to remain in a backwater for much longer. His chance came when Henry V decided to renew the French war, with its inevitable calls on soldierly qualities, administrative talent, and diplomatic expertise. That decision, once taken, was almost bound to bring Tiptoft back into the main current of political life. And so it did: on 30 April 1415 he was appointed seneschal of Guienne, in place of Thomas Beaufort, earl of Dorset, who had returned to England in the previous summer; and he was destined to hold that office for eight years (until the appointment of Sir John Radcliffe in May 1423), although he by no means spent all of his time in the province. His personal fee as seneschal was very substantial, in theory at least: £500 (or 4,000 francs) a year.[33] At the time of his appointment, Gascony was especially disturbed by the recent military incursions of the duke of Bourbon, and on that account alone it was necessary that the new seneschal should proceed as soon as possible to exercise his authority in person. But just when Tiptoft was appointed, there were other, and more immediately important, questions at issue.[34] For it looks as if Henry V's first invasion of France might just as well have taken place in Guienne as in Normandy, and, if that had been the case in fact, Tiptoft's responsibility would have been to organize, in advance, Gascon support. Indeed, although, apparently by June 1415, the king had decided to invade in northern, not south-western France, it still remained a possibility that if the king's

---

32   *CPR, 1413-6*, 138, 192, 263; *Cal. Charter Rolls*, v. 467.

33   T. Carte, *Rolles Gascons* etc., i. 199, 205; *Proceedings and Ordinances of the Privy Council (PPC)*, ed. N. H. Nicolas, iii. 62.

34   For an admirably full discussion of Henry V's initially doubtful intentions regarding his first invasion of France, and of Tiptoft's rôle, see M. G. A. Vale, *English Gascony 1399-1453* (Oxford, 1970), pp. 72-7.

army met with a resounding success in Normandy, it would then move overland to Bordeaux and continue its operations in that region after all. If this was to be phase II of Henry's grand strategy, it was entirely vitiated by the heavy casualties suffered at the siege of Harfleur, and by the fact that the long siege lasted into the early autumn when the king decided upon a return to England *via* Calais, in the course of which journey befell, as late as 25 October, the battle of Agincourt (a "crowning mercy"). The abandonment in June 1415 of that one of the two original plans which envisaged the king's descent upon Guienne, accounts for the changes in the terms upon which Tiptoft undertook office as seneschal. When first retained for service at the end of April his retinue was to be 30 men-at-arms and 60 archers in time of truce, 80 and 400 in time of war; the numbers were subsequently raised to 140 and 700, only to be reduced by 3 June to their former level. (Clearly, this final limitation points to a *terminus non post quem* for Henry V's decision to make for Normandy in the first instance, not Guienne.) However, the preparations for Tiptoft's enterprise, now in an advanced state, still went ahead. Already, on 18 May, Roger Hunt, a Huntingdonshire lawyer acting as Tiptoft's financial agent, was paid at the Lower Exchequer £1,883 odd for delivery to Tiptoft at Plymouth, his port of embarkation; on 6 June Tiptoft received this sum with an additional £2,183 odd, again for his own and his retinue's wages; on 10 June the sheriffs of London were ordered to proclaim in the city that all members of the retinue were to be at the coast by the 24th; and the mustering of the force was put in train on the 19th. Precisely when Tiptoft sailed is not known, but he had arrived in Bordeaux sometime before 20 August.[35] Quite probably, having had time to take stock of the local situation, he was the source of a letter which prompted Henry V, then at Harfleur, to write to the mayor and jurats of Bordeaux on 3 September, telling them that he had been informed that the threat posed in Guienne by the French would soon be greatly reduced, at the same time urging them to help the seneschal 'to resist the malice of our enemies on your coasts', meaning, presumably, Castilian threats to shipping. Evidently, 'the problems of the Franco-Castilian alliance, and the naval power thereby given to the French, proved more dangerous in the south-west than the activities of the French on the frontiers [of Guienne]' (M.G.A. Vale). Although Tiptoft was to be empowered on 13 January 1416, along with the constable and the mayor of Bordeaux, to treat for an extension of a truce between England and Castile, he had

35   Exchequer, Issue Roll, P. R. O., E403/621, mem. 5; ibid., 640, mem. 5; Exchequer Accounts Various, P. R. O., E101/48/4; Privy Seal Warrants for Issue, P. R. O., E. 404/31/354; R. R. Sharpe, *Letter Books of the City of London, Letter Book I*, 49.

in fact left Gascony for home on 18 December 1415.[36]

During 1416 Tiptoft was very much involved in activities that were part of Henry V's great "build-up" for his intended conquest of France. Early in May, in London, he and Sir Walter Hungerford were involved in treating with the representatives of Dietrich von Mörs, archbishop of Cologne, for an alliance. This was just after the Emperor Sigismund had arrived in England to mediate between Charles VI of France and Henry V. The chief result of the imperial visit was, however, the treaty of alliance, expressly offensive as well as defensive, concluded at Canterbury on 15 August (the feast of the Assumption of the Blessed Virgin) between Sigismund and Henry, ten days after which the emperor left for Calais where, in order that they might together meet Duke John of Burgundy and convert the dual into a triple alliance, the king soon joined him. Whether Tiptoft had gone on ahead with Sigismund or waited to take passage with the king (which is perhaps the more likely), when he took out royal letters of protection on 1 September it was formally as a member of the imperial retinue that he did so; he was then, in fact, officiating as steward of the emperor's household, whose finances Henry V was subsidising. The king returned to England on 16 October; and Sigismund left Calais on the 24th, en route for Constance where he was bent upon resuming his rôle of protector of the General Council of the Church. Tiptoft, understandably, was one of the English escort which accompanied the emperor on the short passage along the coast to Dordrecht. He possibly quite soon returned to England, only to be appointed, on 2 December, to take part in an important diplomatic mission to Constance – to treat with the Genoese, the princes of the Empire, and representatives of the Hanseatic League, and for an alliance with Alfonso V of Aragon. On this occasion, however, Tiptoft evidently got no further than Luxembourg where, in January 1417, he had conversations with Sigismund regarding the latter's obligations to co-operate in Henry V's renewal of the war in France, and then came home, leaving his fellow-envoy, Philip Morgan, to go on to Constance. It had been on 25 January that Henry V despatched to Tiptoft a letter, written in his own hand and sealed with his signet of the eagle, charging him to reveal to Sigismund the news that the duke of Bourbon, one of the most important of the Agincourt prisoners, had offered personally to carry to France fresh terms for a settlement, failing acceptance of which the

36   It was perhaps now that Tiptoft was defendant in an action brought in the Court of Chivalry by one of his captains in Guienne, Henry Inglose, esq., who had supplied 16 men-at-arms and 80 archers: the latter accused him of failing to honour his contract for wages (British Library, Titus C 1, fo. 229).

duke had promised to do him homage as rightful king of France. In England, the king wrote, only he himself and Bishop Langley of Durham knew about this. Since Sigismund had left Luxembourg on 21 January and was to arrive in Constance on the 27th, it is more than doubtful whether the message ever reached him. However, apart from the significance of its contents, the letter plainly indicates the extent to which Tiptoft enjoyed the king's confidence. And further evidence of this was soon to be afforded. Although not any earlier in the year, Tiptoft did actually make the journey to Constance in the following spring, an advance of £60 being made to him for the purpose on 24 April, through his usual agent, Roger Hunt; and in May he was made personally responsible for paying 500 marks to Dietrich von Mörs, archbishop of Cologne, and, specifically at Constance, and on the king's verbal instructions (*oretenus*), £90 to two knights 'de Ducheland' of the emperor's company. From what follows, it will be apparent that soon he again returned to England.[37]

In the meantime, early in 1417, Henry V had been going ahead with his financial and military preparations for the renewal of the onslaught on northern France. In mid-February Tiptoft had been one of three knights — the other two were Sir Hugh Lutterell and Sir John Blount — nominated by the Council, for the king's consideration, as candidates for the post of *miles constabularius* in the approaching expedition; and in May this matter was further discussed. With Tiptoft abroad at the time, and in any case likely to be too continuously involved in work of diplomacy, he was then passed over. Admittedly, back in England by 21 June, he then took out royal letters of protection as a member of the king's own retinue in anticipation of the re-invasion of France. It is, however, obvious that he himself was in no position to stay with the army which sailed for Normandy at the end of July, for in the following month he was once again at Constance. Here his most pressing duty was, as early in the year, to urge upon Sigismund the prompt performance of his undertakings under the treaty of Canterbury. All he secured, in fact, was a promise to be on the French frontier on 1 May 1418, a promise to afford military help which was not to be fulfilled either then or at any other time.[38]

It is clear that Tiptoft, at Constance in August 1417, was nevertheless in Normandy before the end of the autumn. Much of

37   Carte, *Rolles Gascons*, etc. ii. 226; ibid., 228-9, 232; *Reports of the Deputy Keeper of the Public Records*, (*DKR*), XLIV. 584-5; *Itinerarium Symonis Simeonis et Willelmi de Worcestre*, ed. J. Nasmith, 350; J. H. Wylie & W. T. Waugh, *The Reign of Henry V*, iii. 30-3; Exchequer, Issue Rolls, E. 403/630, mems. 2, 3, 7; T. Rymer, *Foedera*, etc., IX. 427-30.

38   *PPC* ii. 204, 232; *DKR*, XLIV, 599.

Lower Normandy (Normandy west of the Seine) was already under English control when, at Alençon on 1 November, he was appointed as president of the Norman Exchequer, alias *Chambre des comptes*, and other judicial tribunals of the province, and also as treasurer-general. There was much to do beside control the finances of occupied Normandy: he must conduct occasional military musters, receive the fealties of Normans offering surrender and compounding for their estates, and so on. He was only to be replaced in these offices in May 1419, first as treasurer-general on 1 May, then as president shortly afterwards. Meanwhile, on 10 February 1418, he had been given the captaincy of the castle of Essay (near Sées) on the southern frontier of the province (an office which he was not to retain beyond the spring of 1422). Unquestionably, however, Caen, as the financial centre of Henry V's Norman administration even after Rouen fell, was where Tiptoft normally operated; and, in March 1418, he received a grant in entail of a forfeited manor there. A certain amount of diplomatic work, too, now came his way, during, but especially after, his tenure of the presidency of the Norman Exchequer: in April and June 1418, along with the English *bailli* for the Côtentin, he was instructed to redress violations of the truce with Brittany; in May he was engaged on similar tasks with the *bailli* of Alençon, regarding the truce with Yolande, widow of Duke Louis II of Anjou; a year later, in May 1419, he was appointed one of the envoys who were to arrange a meeting at Mantes between Henry V and Charles VI of France; and in November 1419 he assisted in negotiations for a truce with the French, after the murder of John the Fearless, duke of Burgundy, by close supporters of the Dauphin Charles, an act which made an Anglo-Burgundian alliance certain and, therefore, a compromise peace with France feasible.[39]

In view of the date of this latest embassy, it seems certain that Tiptoft, after relinquishing his high office in the Norman Exchequer in May 1419, had remained in northern France. And it was perhaps partly because he himself was overseas that, so far as were concerned the large arrears of payments due to him at the English Exchequer for past services, his agents had enjoyed very meagre success in their efforts to recover them in the spring and summer of 1419. The payments made were not only, in the main, hugely disproportionate to what was owed, but all of them took the form of assignments on the revenues, which was tantamount to indefinite deferment. It was by an Exchequer assignment that on 22 May 1419 payment was made of the £208

---

39   *Rotuli Normannie*, ed. T. D. Hardy, i. 205, 245, 359; *DKR*, XLI. 685, 687-9, 775, 783; Wylie and Waugh, *Henry V*, iii. 250.

Tiptoft was owed for his last embassy to Constance in 1417. On the same day, too, payment of £125 odd was made for his active service as seneschal of Guienne in 1415, and on 8 July following a further such payment was made of £300, both again by assignment. What must be noted of these two 'payments' for Tiptoft's services in Guienne, however, is not simply that they provided him with no immediate satisfaction, but that, together amounting to £425 odd, they represented little more than a sixth of what had been in arrears, viz. £2,535 odd.

Regarding the duchy of Guienne, Henry V had refused to expend his military resources there to the detriment of his campaigns in northern France, and Tiptoft, appointed seneschal in April 1415, had not acted in person since December that same year. Even had he done so, there was perhaps not much he could have accomplished. But then, early in 1419, failing an injection of military support, there was serious danger of Castilian intervention in the province on the side of the Dauphinists. So much so that on 30 March the mayor and jurats of Bordeaux petitioned the king for a seneschal who would be resident. It is possible that when Tiptoft was relieved soon afterwards of his position as treasurer of Normandy, it was so that he might return directly to Gascony, and certainly nobody was appointed to take his place as seneschal. For the rest of the year, however, he remained (as has been seen) pre-occupied in one way and another in northern France, and it was not, in fact, until the spring of 1420 that active steps were taken to bring about his return to the duchy, and not until the late summer that he did actually once more set foot there. It was on 15 April 1420 that his chief agent in England, Roger Hunt, received on his behalf an Exchequer payment of some £80 odd. This payment again took the form of an assignment, but at the same time, at Southampton, Tiptoft also received a payment of £2,541 odd, and this was in cash. Formally made as in aid of his future expenses in Gascony, this payment did more than cover all that had still been left owing to him, for his previous service in the duchy, in May 1419, and, moreover, it was followed by further advances on 10 June, one of 200 marks (appropriated to the repair of the castle of Bayonne) and another for as much as £2,622 odd.[40] Meanwhile, in May, ships had been commandeered and harbourages allocated at Southampton, Poole, Weymouth, Melcombe, Plymouth and Bristol, to help Tiptoft resolve his problems of transport and commissariat. On 3 June his English subordinate in Gascony, Sir John Radcliffe (the constable of

40   Exchequer Issue Roll, E403/640, mems. 5, 10; 403/645, mems. 1, 7.

Bordeaux), and Sir John St. John (the mayor) were ordered to muster his company, which now numbered 60 men-at-arms and 300 archers. Nine days later (12 June), he was given authority as seneschal to pardon rebels in the duchy and make restitution of forfeited estates, and especially to receive oaths to observe the recently concluded treaty of Troyes from John de Grailly, count of Foix, and others. At the same time he was granted the castle and town of Lesparre for the billeting of his forces. He landed at Bordeaux on 23 August.

In view of previous English lack of interest and his own long absence from the duchy, Tiptoft had now much to do. There were disputes between the city and the archbishop of Bordeaux over limits of jurisdiction; and there was considerable military pressure on the part of the French. Tiptoft was far from inactive; and, although military operations were somewhat desultory (being largely based on local supplies of men, if not money), the war went tolerably well for the English. But even two years did not substantially alter the situation. How difficult at times was Tiptoft's position is suggested by the official response to a petition he made to the Council in England in February 1421, asking that corn should be purveyed in Gloucestershire and Somerset and sent out to him via Bristol, without payment of customs; although the Council agreed to most of his requirements, it imposed a condition that part of the wheat should be grown on his own lands (*de sa propre cressance*), and there was to be no question of the export-tax being remitted.[41] It must have been not long after this that Tiptoft came home, doubtless timing his visit to coincide with that of Henry V himself. However, he soon returned to Guienne: on 9 June 1421 at Dover (where, on the following day, the king left for France), his authority to receive homages in Gascony was renewed, and on 18 June certain notables of Devon were instructed to take the muster of his company. Back in Gascony he soon showed himself commendably active; indeed, as soon as August following the jurats of Bordeaux were able to report to the king that, with the 'soldiers, siege engines and artillery' of their commune, Tiptoft had recently besieged and taken Burdos, a place 'which had caused great destruction to your land.'

It was very probably during his recent visit to England in the first half of 1421 that Tiptoft contracted to marry Joyce Charleton, half-sister to Edmund, earl of March; and when, in February 1422, he secured official permission for the marriage to proceed, he was once again back in this country. It was from England that he now visited Henry V in person in France, taking him 1,000 marks from the English

---

41   *CPR, 1416-22*, 278, 319-20; *CCR, 1419-22*, 76; Carte, *Rolles Gascons*, i. 203; Wylie and Waugh, *Henry V*, iii. 368-72; Ancient Petitions, P. R. O., S. C. 8, file 162, no. 8076.

Exchequer as well as with the object of 'declaring certain business and special matters'.[42] His appointment in May 1422 as J.P. in Herefordshire, Worcestershire, and Shropshire suggests that by this time Tiptoft had, in fact, married Joyce Charleton, and that he was again in England. The events of the next few months predetermined the conclusion of his administration in Guienne, an administration spasmodic in terms of personal attendance but at times quite strenuously conducted.

At the end of August 1422 Henry V died, and, in the first parliament of the reign of his infant son, Henry VI, which met on 9 November following, Tiptoft was appointed a member of the newly constituted English Council, whose authority was so defined by parliament as to enable it to hold in check the king's younger uncle, Humphrey, duke of Gloucester, who was to be protector and chief councillor in England in the absence of his brother John, duke of Bedford, now the infant king's regent in France. Tiptoft's salary (as a knight-banneret) was to be £100 a year. Appointed on 9 December, he was to remain, as things turned out, a member of the Council until his death, almost without a break. Soon afterwards, on 21 December, he secured a renewal of all those annuities which Henry V had confirmed to him in 1413.[43] During the early years of the new reign he was to show himself very assiduous in his conciliar attendance. This, of course, was far from being to his personal disadvantage, fees for attendance all on one side. Only three days after the appointment of Sir John Radcliffe to take his place as seneschal of Guienne on 3 March 1423, in a meeting of the Council at which Tiptoft himself was present, it was resolved that the Exchequer should come to a settlement of accounts with him for his own term of office, on the basis of a sworn declaration on his part. Moreover, in July following, he was allowed to remain *prévôt* of D'Entre-deux-Mers and castellan of Dax, in addition to which posts, although not until December 1426, he was to be granted the lordship of Lesparre, near the mouth of the River Garonne.[44]

Meanwhile, in February 1423, Tiptoft had been put on an embassy to the General Council of the Church, which, first meeting at Pavia in April, was soon transferred to Siena where it assembled in July. However, he cannot possibly have visited Italy, for he was attending

42   Carte, *Rolles Gascons*, i. 203; *CPR, 1416-22*, 324; *DKR*, XLIV, 630; M. G. A. Vale, op. cit., 86; Exchequer Issue Roll, E403/652, mem. 16.

43   *Rot. Parl.*, V. 404; *PPC*, iii. 10, 17, *et passim*; but see especially 42, 52, 62, 155, 167, 169, 213, 227, 253, 266, 286, 312, 323; *ibid.*, IV. 82-3, 110, 149, 154, 212, 246, 289, 367; *ibid.*, V. 71-2, 153, 196; *ibid.*, VI. 313, 346-50; *CPR, 1422-29*, 34.

44   *PPC*, iii. 52, 62; Carte, *Rolles Gascons*, i. 205, 209.

meetings of the royal Council regularly through the spring, and in both May and September that year he was one of the commission appointed to arbitrate between Richard Beauchamp, earl of Warwick, and James, lord Berkeley, in their dispute over the succession to the Berkeley inheritance. Moreover, in the second parliament of Henry VI, which sat from October 1423 to February 1424, he was re-appointed a member of the Council. It was in that capacity that he was present in the castle at Hertford when, on 16 July 1424, Bishop Langley of Durham surrendered the Great Seal to the new chancellor, Bishop Beaufort of Winchester.

It was with the latter's cousin, Thomas Chaucer of Ewelme, himself a fellow-member of the Council, that Tiptoft was sent to France early in December of the same year (1424), on an embassy to the duke of Bedford, the regent, 'about certain special matters moving the King and Council'[45] What these 'special matters' were is not known, but it is highly probable that Tiptoft's mission was to communicate his colleagues' views on the duke of Gloucester's activities in the Netherlands, where the duke himself was at this very time. Duke Humphrey had crossed to Calais with his wife Jacqueline in October 1424, bent on conquering her inherited county of Hainault, the estates of which province formally recognised him as regent on 4 December. The whole affair cut clean across the Anglo-Burgundian alliance; and it seriously jeopardised Bedford's policy in France which so much depended on a good understanding with Duke Philip, whose interests in the Low Countries were diametrically opposed to Gloucester's. Gloucester's plans soon failed, and there now ensued a period of uneasy relationship between protector and Council which culminated, during the autumn of 1425, in an open rupture, most notably in a violent quarrel between the duke and his uncle, Henry Beaufort, the chancellor, a quarrel so violent as to threaten to lead to civil war. This was all despite the lenient attitude the Council had adopted to Gloucester's conduct in the course of the past year.

During 1425 some attempt to alleviate Duke Humphrey's financial distress, mainly caused by his private foreign scheme, had been made when, on 22 May, he was granted the keeping of most of the Mortimer estates. These had come into Crown custody consequent upon the death of Edmund Mortimer, earl of March, in Ireland early in the year, and by reason of the minority of the earl's nephew and heir, Richard, duke of York. Tiptoft was present at the meeting of the Council where the relevant decision was made. In view of his own wife (Joyce

45   *PPC*, iii. 42; *CCR, 1422-9*, 62, 154; *Rot. Parl.*, IV. 200; Exchequer, Issue Roll, E403/669, mem. 8.

Charleton) being one of the coheirs of the late earl, her half-brother, in the Holland estates of their mother, Tiptoft's interest in the transaction was, of course, directly personal. Besides, on 24 February 1425, he had himself been appointed by the Council as chief steward of all the late earl's lands in Wales, during York's minority.[46] Evidently at this time Tiptoft was quite immersed in conciliar business, and in a variety of ways. For instance, only two days after this last appointment (26 February), when three of his fellow-councillors — Lords Cromwell and Scrope and Sir Walter Beauchamp — were given custody of the temporalities of the vacant see of York for 2,000 marks a year, he was one of their sureties. Along with other councillors he was making loans to the Crown, and, on 1 March, in return for a personal loan of 250 marks, he was given a share, with four other members of the Council, in the right to dispose of the marriage of the young earl of Oxford, John de Vere. On 14 May, during the parliament of April-July, he was present in parliament as a member of the Council which, in the Upper House, was attending to the dispute over precedence between John Mowbray, earl Marshal, and Richard Beauchamp, earl of Warwick, a dispute resolved by the Lords in favour of the former by his promotion as duke of Norfolk.[47]

The next parliament to meet did so at Leicester on 18 February 1426, in circumstances of considerable anxiety and threat of disorder. Faced with the Londoners' readiness to give armed support to Duke Humphrey in the previous autumn, the chancellor, Bishop Beaufort, had called in the duke of Bedford, whose return from France in December (1425) made him, under the settlement of 1422, protector in Gloucester's stead. Not until 12 March, at Leicester, could a reconciliation between Gloucester and Beaufort be contrived. A compromise of sorts was arrived at: all on the same day, 16 March, Beaufort resigned the Great Seal in favour of John Kemp, archbishop of York; and John Stafford, bishop of Bath and Wells, treasurer of the Exchequer and a supporter of Gloucester, gave way to Tiptoft's friend and colleague on the Council, Walter, lord Hungerford. The latter had been summoned to this parliament for the first time by individual writ, and thus joined the peerage. So had Tiptoft. The facts suggest that both men were in total sympathy with Bedford and Beaufort, who, with the Council, were in control of the administration at the time of the issue of the writs (2 January). Certainly, Tiptoft must have been in high favour with Bedford: on 18 March, two days after being present at the delivery of the Great Seal to the new chancellor in St. Mary's abbey, he

---

46   *PPC*, iii. 169; *CPR, 1422-9*, 266.
47   *CFR, 1422-30*, 101, *CPR, 1422-9*, 271; *PPC*, iii. 167; *Rot. Parl.*, IV. 262.

was appointed steward of the Household, the office vacated by Hungerford on 11 July 1424, and left unfilled since then. Two days later still (20 March), parliament was prorogued to 29 April, from when it sat until 1 June. Incidentally, it had been during the first session that, on 8 March, orders had been issued to the escheators in Suffolk, Kent, Sussex, and Nottinghamshire to put Tiptoft and his wife in possession of her purparty of those Holland family lands that had once been her mother's.[48]

Tiptoft as steward of the Household was occupying the topmost position in its administrative hierarchy. And he was to continue in the office for nearly six years, i.e. until 25 February 1432 when, on that and the next day, Gloucester was to make, in favour of his own friends, an almost clean sweep of the leading officers of State and Household. In the meantime, of course, Tiptoft had remained a member of the Council. Indeed, as steward of the Household he was virtually an *ex officio* member. On 11 July 1426 he was one of the lords of the Council who entered into obligations undertaking the repayment of Bishop Beaufort's loans to the Crown.[49] He was also present at a meeting of the Council at Reading on 24 November following when, faced with the prospect of Bedford's return to France and Gloucester's resumption of the office of protector, it drew up a series of articles confirming its rules for the conduct of state business; and in January 1427 both the royal dukes recognized the Council's powers of governmental control.

Busily involved in routine administration in the Household and as a member of the Council though he was, Tiptoft evidently found time enough to look to his own interests. On 10 December 1426, when he had still not been paid 7,000 marks (roughly only two-fifths) of what remained due to him for his former service as seneschal of Guienne, the Council agreed that he should have the Gascon lordship of Lesparre and the *hospicium* of Castas (worth £375 a year) until that debt had been cleared.[50] And before long, another matter engaged the attention of the Council which can only have personally concerned him, however indirectly: he was present at its meeting on 6 March 1427 when his wife's cousin, John Holland, earl of Huntingdon, was admitted to fine with the Crown for £800 for marrying the widow of the late earl of March, Tiptoft's wife's half-brother.

---

48   *Report touching the Dignity of a Peer of the Realm*, IV. 864; *CCR, 1422-9*, 269; *CFR, 1422-30*, 127.

49   *CPR, 1422-9*, 355, 481; *PPC*, iii. 199.

50   *PPC*, iii. 213, 227; Carte, *Rolles Gascons*, i. 209.

At the end of May 1427, Tiptoft was about to proceed on an embassy with Bishop Alnwick of Norwich, the keeper of the Privy Seal, to the dukes of Bedford and Burgundy, 'for certain special matters moving the King and Council.' Burgundy they visited at Arras, where the business in hand was mainly the *'materia ducisse Hollandie.'* Deserted by Gloucester for the past two years, Jacqueline of Hainault was now in great distress, and in the spring of this year sent fervent appeals to both her husband and the English Council. Gloucester himself now showed keenness to help and, on 9 July, eleven days before a Burgundian embassy was expected to arrive in England bringing an answer to Tiptoft and Alnwick's mission, the duke persuaded the Council to furnish him with a loan of £6,000 merely for the defence of Holland. However, nothing came of the business and, a year later, Jacqueline was to submit to Philip of Burgundy and renounce her marriage with Gloucester.[51]

Perhaps rattled by this recurrence of the crisis in Anglo-Burgundian relations of 1425, the Council re-asserted its dominance over the protector in the parliament of 1427-8. Present in the first session (October-December), witness his appointment as a trier of petitions from Gascony etc., Tiptoft, on 3 March 1428, during the second session, subscribed the important declaration of Gloucester's constitutional position (under the settlement of 1422) made by the Lords.[52] He next appears at Windsor on the eve of St. George's Day (22 April 1428) when, as steward of the Household, he was present at a chapter of the Order of the Garter. He himself was never to be elected K.G. and, although installed on this occasion in the presence of the boy-king, who was attending as sovereign of the Order, it was only as a proxy for Peter, duke of Coimbra, the third son of King John I of Portugal by Philippa of Lancaster, sister of Henry IV, who had been elected in 1427. A year later (April 1429) Tiptoft was involved in a matter which again had to do with the Order of the Garter, only now the incident in question was of immediate political significance, concerning, as it did, Henry Beaufort. Beaufort, now made a cardinal and papal legate in England by Pope Martin V, was being subjected, when recruiting forces for a renewal of a crusade against the Hussites in Bohemia, to attacks on his status and authority: after a protest that he had no right even to retain his see of Winchester now that he was a cardinal, a specially afforced meeting of the Council held on 17 April warned him to abstain from exercising his right, as *ex officio* prelate of

51   *PPC*, iii. 253, 271, 276; Exchequer, Issue Roll, E403/680, mem. 6.
52   *Rot. Parl.*, IV. 316, 327.

the Order, to officiate at the annual Garter feast. It was Tiptoft and three other lords who were charged by the Council to take its demand to the cardinal.[53] The latter made a personal appearance in Council on the following day, only to be asked to withdraw. Nothing, however, came of the larger issue touching the see of Winchester.

Tiptoft, as a matter of course, attended the next parliament, which sat, with nearly a month's break for Christmas, from 22 September 1429 to 23 February 1430, and in which, incidentally, the Speaker for the Commons was Sir William Allington, one of the knights for Tiptoft's own county of Cambridgeshire and, ten years previously, his successor as treasurer-general of Normandy. The chief event of the first session was the king's coronation on 6 November. The main reason for this event occurring just then – for Henry was still a month short of his eighth birthday – was so that he might soon go to France and be crowned there, in order to offset the effects of the French military revival inspired by Joan of Arc and of the recent coronation of the Dauphin Charles (Charles VII). And to finance the expeditionary force that would be essential, parliament voted, in fact, a double tenth and fifteenth for that purpose (the first such subsidy of the reign). The English coronation, however, had immediate constitutional and political consequences for the government at home: it was an event which the Lords decided did away with the Protectorship; and although Gloucester was to remain chief councillor and, in the king's absence abroad, become (as once he had been under Henry V) *custos Anglie*, his formal authority was *pro tanto* reduced. That this was so, was made clearer still when the Upper House agreed to the Council's articles for the conduct of the administration while the king was in France. Tiptoft was one of the councillors who took an oath to abide by the articles.[54] These, supplemented by further regulations drawn up at Canterbury a week before, on St. George's Day (23 April 1430), Henry VI left England, were mainly concerned with the fact that, with the king's departure, the Council would perforce be split up, part being left behind in England, part accompanying the king. Matters of any weight first entertained by the councillors in England were to be agreed, it was decided, by those in France as well, and vice-versa. So, any prospective *coup* of Gloucester's would, it was doubtless hoped, be at least impeded. In any case, no existing councillor or important official was to be dismissed, or any new one appointed, except with the consent of the whole Council. Tiptoft, as steward of the Household, naturally was

---

53   J. Anstis, *The Register of the Most Noble Order of the Garter (Black Book); PPC*, iii. 323.
54   *Rot. Parl.*, IV. 336, 344.

included among those councillors who were to be with the king. By the end of February 1430, at latest, his personal retinue for the expedition was in course of formation; on 6 March, he was a member of a commission for the raising of a special royal loan in Cambridgeshire and Huntingdonshire; on 15 April, he procured royal letters of attorney applicable in his absence; on 24 April, the day after the king had sailed, he was appointed to array forces that were soon to follow; and on 17 May he took out letters of protection as being himself about to proceed.[55] Not until after the capture of Joan of Arc on 24 May was it considered safe for the king to be conducted overland from Calais to Rouen where, on 29 July, he made a state entry, and, although Paris was recovered by the English in August and Bedford entered the capital in January 1431, it was only on 16 December following that the king was crowned there.

In the meantime, Tiptoft had returned to England, and it is significant of his political attachment to Henry Beaufort that he made the journey from Rouen to Westminster in the cardinal's train and kept Christmas (1430) with him in the priory of Christchurch, Canterbury. Both men attended the parliament of January-March 1431, and Tiptoft was again a trier of petitions.[56] But he also had much business to see to there on his own private account. He presented a petition, which the Commons and then the Lords approved, asking for consideration of an agreement he had made with Henry V over the lands of his first wife's former husband, Sir Matthew de Gournay, an agreement under the terms of which the lands were to revert to the Crown when he himself had been paid £4,000 and certain of the manors in question discharged of annual rents; the £4,000, Tiptoft affirmed, had been paid, and some of the relevant conditions met, but his manor of Overton Waterville (Hants.) was still not disencumbered of an annual rent of 10 marks; and so he now asked that this should be done by allowing him an equivalent sum from a rent payable by the prior and canons of Huntingdon to the local sheriff, and that the Exchequer should remit to him the arrears, amounting (since the bargain with Henry V) to £80. Again during this session, he and his second wife (Joyce Charleton) and her fellow-coheirs of the Holland estates (Joyce's aunts, Margaret, widow of Thomas, duke of Clarence, and Joan, widow of Edmund of Langley, duke of York, and her cousins, Richard, duke of York, Ralph, earl of Westmorland, Richard, earl of Salisbury, and his countess, and Henry Grey) jointly petitioned the Commons against Eleanor, wife of James,

55   *DKR*, XLVIII. 269, 275, 283; *CPR, 1429-36*, 51.

56   *Chronica Monasterii Sancti Albani, Chronicon Rerum Gestarum in Monasterio Sancti Albani, 1422-31*, (R. S.), ed. T. H. Riley, i. 56; *Rot. Parl.*, IV 368.

lord Audley, who pretended to be the legitimate daughter of Edmund Holland, earl of Kent (ob.1408) to the exclusion of the rights of the coheirs. The latter requested, successfully in the event, that if, in any English court entertaining their complaint, issue should be joined on a plea of bastardy (a plea only determinable before an ecclesiastical tribunal), the court should not allow a writ of *certificate* to go to the ordinary (normally a bishop) before it had informed the royal Chancery, so that proclamations might be made inviting objections. Incidentally, shortly before the parliamentary session was over, on 12 March at Carisbrooke, Philippa, widow of Edward, duke of York, made Tiptoft overseer of her last will and testament. (He was already one of the dowager's feoffees.)[57]

It had been during the same parliament of 1431 that the Commons had petitioned the king concerning the disputes which had arisen, over the payment of the wages of the knights of the shire for Cambridgeshire, between the inhabitants of the Isle of Ely and the commons of the county outside the liberty. The petition stated that Lord Tiptoft and Philip Morgan, bishop of Ely, who together had recently mediated between the parties, had proposed that the people of the Isle should compound for their liability by paying £200, this sum to be invested in land worth 20 marks a year, so creating a fund from which a third of the expenses of the county's elected representatives in parliament could be met as occasion required. The Commons having requested that the lords of the Council should be permitted to license the arrangement, the petition was granted.[58] (It was evidently expected that if the wages of the shire-knights remained payable at the customary rate of 4 shillings a day each, parliament would not, on average, sit for more than a hundred days a year.)

It was clearly intended that Tiptoft should, as steward of the Household, rejoin the king in France as soon as possible after the parliament of 1431 had ended. Already, on 16 March, four days before the dissolution, he had received at the Exchequer, as an advance for his next half-year of service, £160 for himself and his retinue of 6 men-at-arms and 18 archers, and a further £100 as *regardum* for his attendance as a member of the Council overseas; and on 19 April councillors meeting at the London Blackfriars agreed that he be paid another *regardum* of £200, plus 20 marks for his cross-Channel passage. Tiptoft himself was present at a session of the Council held at Westminster on Sunday, 1 May, when he and those councillors —

57   *Rot. Parl.*, IV. 373, 375; *CPR, 1429-36*, 118; *CCR 1441-7*, 228; *The Register of Henry Chichele*, ed. E. F. Jacob, ii. 459.
58   *Rot. Parl.*, IV. 382.

Cardinal Beaufort, Bishop Alnwick and Lord Cromwell — who were also soon to go to France conferred with Gloucester and others who were to remain in England. The meeting was one of great importance. For, having confirmed the previous year's arrangements for interconciliar communication, those present went on to discuss a wide range of questions concerning the situation in France: would it be possible for the king to be crowned at Rheims? when would he return to England? what form would English rule in France assume thereafter, and who would be in charge? how could the Anglo-Burgundian alliance be made more effective, and on what terms? and how would the continuation of the conquest be financed? Later in the same week (4 May) orders were issued by the Chancery for the muster of Tiptoft's retinue. Presumably, he sailed for France shortly afterwards.[59]

Little is recorded of Tiptoft's activities during the second half of 1431, but it may safely be assumed that, taking up his office of steward of the Household again, he was mostly attendant upon the king. (His appointment as governor of the castle of Marck in the Pas de Calais at the end of September need not have detained him.[60]) And it is highly probable that he was at the king's coronation in Notre Dame in Paris on 16 December, and that he only returned to England when the king did, early in February 1432. Their return found Gloucester staging a *coup* directed mainly against members of Cardinal Beaufort's circle, of whom Tiptoft was one.

There had already been something of a disturbance of the fairly easy relations which, during the king's absence, had prevailed between the *custos* and the other councillors in England. In November 1431 the Council had been sharply divided over a proposal that Gloucester's official salary should be increased, and over the duke's determination to humiliate Cardinal Beaufort by having proceedings begun against him under the Statute of Praemunire. Over the question of Gloucester's salary, Archbishop Kemp, the chancellor, and Lord Hungerford, the treasurer, had opposed the duke's party in the Council, led by John, lord Scrope of Masham, and, within a few days of the king's arrival at Westminster on 21 February, those two major officers of state were deprived, Kemp on the 25th, Hungerford on the 26th. As steward of the Household, Tiptoft attended Kemp's surrender of the great seals and their delivery on the next day to Bishop Stafford of Bath and Wells, a friend of Gloucester's.[61] Lord Scrope was now appointed

59   Exchequer, Issue Roll, E403/696, mems. 19, 20; *PPC*, iv. 82-3; *Rot. Parl.*, V. 415-8; *CPR, 1429-36*, 133; *DKR*, XLVIII. 283.

60   *DKR*, XLVIII. 284; Carte, *Rolles Gascons*, ii. 274.

61   *CCR, 1429-35*, 181.

treasurer *vice* Hungerford; and by 1 March Tiptoft himself had been replaced in office by Sir Robert Babthorpe. Moreover, not only was Bishop Alnwick, who had been keeper of the Privy Seal since the beginning of Henry VI's reign, also replaced, in favour of Dr. William Lyndwood, 'secondary' in that department and another friend of Gloucester's, but Lord Cromwell, too, was dismissed from his office of king's chamberlain, being succeeed by Sir William Phelip, yet another of Gloucester's adherents. Although doubtless assisted by his friends, obviously by those who had themselves profited by these changes, the *coup* must be laid at Duke Humphrey's door. For the time being at any rate, he had disposed of some of the most influential members of the Council who had stood in his way during both his earlier Protectorship and his period of office as *custos* when the king was absent in France. So far as Tiptoft was concerned, he now went into retirement from high politics, certainly for the rest of the year, if not for longer. There is no evidence that he even attended the parliament of May-July 1432, for he was not then appointed as a trier of petitions (as had been the case during the three previous parliaments). Nor until February 1433 is there any record evidence to suggest that he had resumed attendance as a member of the Council; and even when he did so, his appearances at meetings remained infrequent.[62] He did, however, attend the parliament of July-December 1433: at the beginning of the first session he was once more appointed as a trier of Gascon and other overseas petitions, and in November he was one of the Lords who took the oath to abstain from maintenance of any who should break the king's peace.

When this parliament of 1433 met on 8 July, the duke of Bedford, disturbed by the state of Anglo-Burgundian relations and its effect on the military situation in France, had already returned to England. His intention was partly to compose domestic differences, but mainly to obtain a greater measure of co-operation from the English Council. Finance was the stumbling-block, and on 11 August (two days before parliament was adjourned until 13 October) Lord Scrope was replaced at the Exchequer by Lord Cromwell. In the new treasurer's full report on the state of the king's revenues, put before parliament on 18 October, Tiptoft himself figured as receiving an annual fee of £100 as a member of the Council.[63] At the beginning of the parliament it was a long-serving agent of his, Roger Hunt, whom the Commons had elected as their Speaker, and it has also to be pointed out that Tiptoft was to remain an active member of the Council. Even so, he was not now given any other office; and it may be that he was in course of losing, at least

62   *PPC*, iv. 154.
63   *Rot. Parl.*, IV. 420, 422, 436.

for a time, something of his former eminence in the conduct of government. A sign of this might be thought to be his more frequent inclusion in local royal commissions of one sort and another, from which (apart from his commissions of the peace in Cambridgeshire and Huntingdonshire) he had long been generally absent: soon after the end of the 1433 parliament, in December, he was put on the commission to apportion reductions in parliamentary taxation in Huntingdonshire; in February 1434, he served on Crown loan-raising commissions there and in Cambridgeshire (having himself just made such a loan of £200); and at the beginning of May following, he and the bishops of Lincoln and Ely were, along with the respective knights of the shire, authorized to receive oaths to maintain the king's peace from the notables of the two shires.[64]

Lord Cromwell's policy of economy at the Exchequer, in face of a decline in royal credit, militated against a recovery of the initiative in France, and Bedford remained in England, at the head of the Council, until July 1434. In late April and early May a great council had met to consider a plan of Gloucester's for the conduct of the war, a plan involving his own direct participation, and, consequently, Bedford's replacement in command by himself. However, Gloucester's ideas were unacceptable to the lords, and, Tiptoft among them, they rejected the scheme. Its presentation had involved Gloucester in criticism of his brother's policy in France, but the quarrel was patched up and, in July, Bedford returned to Normandy to do the best he could. Only loans from Cardinal Beaufort were available for the payment of his escort. On 20 June Bedford had asked for a grant (to him and his heirs) of the castle and barony of Lesparre and other Gascon estates, but in consideration of the claims of Tiptoft, who enjoyed assignments drawn on their revenues to meet Crown debts still owing to him, the Council persuaded Bedford to refrain from pressing the matter. Tiptoft was himself present at the meeting. His own and the Council's attitude, correct perhaps in itself, may possibly suggest that faith in Bedford's ability to carry on the war, or even to salvage Normandy, was fast waning. More trust was likely now to be put in diplomacy, partly in view of papal efforts to mediate a peace, more especially in view of the doubtful loyalty of Burgundy to the English alliance. In the meantime, at a meeting of the Council held at Cirencester on 12 November 1434, Tiptoft had been party to a protest made to the youthful king criticising his inclination to overlook its advice and his susceptibility to 'sturinges or motions maad to him apart, in thinges of greet weight and

---

64   *CFR, 1430-7*, 186; *CPR, 1429-36*, 354; 375, 385; Exchequer, Issue Roll, E403/717, mem. 11.

substance'. A recurrence of trouble-making by Gloucester is suggested by his absence on this and other recent occasions of the Council's meeting.[65]

The great peace congress at Arras, in which the French significantly reverted to the attitude of their embassy to England of 1414 whereas the English stood by the Treaty of Troyes of 1420, dragged fruitlessly on, for a whole month, until 6 September 1435. The defection of Duke Philip of Burgundy at the congress, followed by Bedford's death, misdirected English military efforts into anti-Burgundian channels for a time. In July 1435 Tiptoft was still an active member of the Council with his fee at £100 a year, the equivalent of which, however, he had recently loaned to the Crown.[66] He attended the parliament of 1435 (October-December), where he acted as a trier of English petitions. And he there agreed with the rest of the Lords to Gloucester's having custody of Calais, for nine years as from July 1436.[67] This was to meet the Burgundian threat to the town. In fact, the main business of the session was to consider how best to offset Burgundy's withdrawal from the English alliance; and, to this end, parliament granted a novel income-tax on freehold land worth over £5 a year, as well as a subsidy of the usual kind (a tenth and fifteenth). Early in the following year, on 29 January 1436, Tiptoft was appointed to serve on the commission set up to assess landed revenues to the income-tax leviable in Cambridgeshire and Huntingdonshire, and before the end of February he was also engaged in once more raising Crown loans in these two counties. His own assessment to the income-tax − his revenues being estimated for the purpose at some £1,100 per annum − would, according to the agreed scale, involve him in no larger a contribution than just over £80, no more than 7½ per cent of his income (even assuming the assessment not to have been in his favour).[68] Incidentally, half-way through the recent parliament he had secured from the Exchequer the right to farm the lordship of Abergavenny which, however, he only retained for three months. Earlier in the same session, along with Lord Cromwell, the treasurer of the Exchequer, and Bishop William Alnwick of Norwich, he had been appointed an executor of the will of Philip Morgan, his own diocesan of Ely and, formerly, another fellow-member of the Council.[69]

Early in June 1436 it was realized by the Council that there was

65   *PPC*, IV. 212, 246, 289.
66   *CPR, 1429-36*, 467; Exchequer, Issue Roll, E403/719, mem. 11.
67   *Rot. Parl.*, IV. 482, 484.
68   *CFR, 1430-7*, 261, 269; *CPR, 1429-36*, 530.
69   *Chichele Register*, ii. 531; *CFR, 1430-7*, 254.

urgent need to prevent Calais from falling into the hands of Philip of Burgundy, who was then bringing up an army to besiege the town. An English expeditionary force, which was to be under Gloucester's command, was soon in preparation. By 2 August, when Gloucester was ready to cross to Calais, the siege had been raised, and on 23rd, after a brief pillaging excursion into Artois, the duke returned to England. It is highly unlikely that Tiptoft accompanied the English army, but certainly he contributed a large retinue of 16 men-at-arms and 69 archers which, mustered at Sandwich in accordance with letters patent of 26 July, probably crossed the Channel with the main body.[70] Whatever the nature of Tiptoft's participation, there is no need to believe that it signified any softening of his attitude to Gloucester. The expedition had attracted warm general approval.

About this time there was also a serious deterioration in the conditions under which English and foreign shipping operated in the Channel. The 1414 Statute of Truces and Safe-conducts had been relaxed in 1435, and attacks on Flemish shipping soon developed into a general dislocation of coastal trading as West Country pirates wrought indiscriminate havoc among the vessels of neutral and enemy merchants alike. It was probably an effort on the part of the Council to curb this licence, by arranging commercial treaties with the Hanseatic League as well as with Flanders, which was behind Tiptoft's employment on a commission, appointed on 6 November 1436, to negotiate with an embassy representing the High Master of Prussia and the most important German coastal communes of the League regarding attacks at sea detrimental to the Anglo-Hanseatic alliance; and Tiptoft was party to the treaty which was arrived at in London on 22 March 1437, five days before the dissolution of the parliament which had met on 21 January.[71]

Tiptoft is known to have attended this parliament, having been a trier of petitions. Not long after, on 16 April 1437, he agreed to lend the Crown 250 marks, on the understanding that he was supplied by the Exchequer with sound assignments upon royal revenue, for all the debts he was owed. A month later he was serving on the commission appointed to apportion tax-reductions in Cambridgeshire, following the recent parliamentary grant of a subsidy. In July, his continuing membership of the Council was evidently sufficient to secure him a ten years' lease at the Exchequer of the alien priory of Linton (Cambs.), following the death of Queen Joan, Henry IV's widow, who had been

---

70   *CPR, 1429-36*, 611 (where the date is wrongly given as 1435); Exchequer, Issue Roll, E403/724.
71   Carte, *Rolles Gascons*, ii. 289; *CPR, 1436-41*, 62.

farming the property of the place, a lease which, however, Tiptoft let go only two years later. Incidentally, it was during August of this year that the new king's lieutenant and regent of France, Henry VI's old tutor, Richard Beauchamp, earl of Warwick, made Tiptoft one of the executors of the will which, before leaving for France, he drew up at Caversham (Oxon.). Associated with Tiptoft in this charge was Lord Cromwell, who was still treasurer of the Exchequer.[72]

By a process not easily discovered, but one in which Henry VI's attainment of his majority and clearer personal emergence into politics were factors of great significance, the conduct of his government passed during the next few years into the grip of a select camarilla, chief of whom was Cardinal Beaufort, now sixty-odd years old. High officials in the Household were an important element in Beaufort's system of control, and so was an influential group in the Council itself. Of this Beaufort faction in the Council, Tiptoft was himself a member. When, on 13 November 1437, the king's minority was deemed to have ended and a reconstituted Council was appointed to advise him, Tiptoft was continued as a member of it, with a fee of 100 marks. This new fee represented a reduction by a third of his former fee of £100. But, then, his present grant was for his lifetime, in case he fell into 'suche unweldenesse or impotence that he shal not nowe entende unto the Kynges saide Counseil'; and, moreover, on the same day it was made (at the hospital of St. John in Clerkenwell), he received royal letters patent entitling him to draw the fee from the issues of the manor of Bassingbourne and the bailiwick of Babraham (Cambs.), on condition that he retained himself with the king alone and took no other's fee. Well could Tiptoft afford the reduction of his conciliar salary by a third, for not only was the annual income assured, as given him for life and deriving from landed estate, but the grant by letters patent was made expressly notwithstanding his continued enjoyment of his old annuity (of 1399) of 100 marks from the issues of Cambridgeshire and Huntingdonshire, his £20 a year from the fee-farm of Norwich, and his annual tun of wine from the royal prisage of wines at Ipswich. The grant was confirmed (at Sheen) on 8 December next.[73]

In the following year, 1438, Tiptoft does not seem to have been especially active outside the Council, to which it may be assumed he gave up some of his time. On 27 May, however, he was appointed to a commission of oyer and terminer regarding disturbances in Kent. And then, late in the year, proceedings were in train in the Exchquer against

72   *Rot. Parl.*, IV. 496; *PPC*, V. 13; *CFR, 1430-7*, 351; 344; *ibid., 1437-43*, 101; W. Dugdale, *Antiquities of Warwickshire*, 329.
73   *PPC*, VI. 313; *CPR, 1436-41*, 120, 193.

him and his wife, Joyce, who, as one of the descendants and coheirs of Edmund, earl of Kent, half-brother of Edward II, was in possession of a fractional part of lands once granted to the earl in return for a rent which had remained unpaid for so long that its arrears now amounted to over £1,200. The other coheirs of the Holland family had obtained pardons of all accounts; but Tiptoft had been reluctant to pursue this course, possibly because for him to have done so would have stood in the way of his recovery of those arrears of wages still owing to him for his service as seneschal of Guienne (the office he had relinquished nearly 16 years ago). If this action in the Exchequer reflected over-zealousness on Lord Cromwell's part, it overreached itself: on 24 November 1438 Tiptoft and his wife were granted a discharge.[74] It is tempting to regard Tiptoft's connection at this time with Dr. Adam Moleyns, who now was 'in all but name the King's principal secretary' (K.B. McFarlane), as likely to have helped ease Tiptoft out of this difficulty. At least it may be noted that, as recently as 19 November, Moleyns had been instituted as rector of Curry Mallet (Somerset), a benefice the patronage of which Tiptoft enjoyed and is known to have exercised on this occasion.[75] Or perhaps Tiptoft's influence in the Council, or with officials in close touch with the king, had been adequate to deal with the trouble.

There can be little doubt, however, that with advancing years and presumably a continuance of ill-health, such influence on affairs as Tiptoft had retained was now diminishing. Admittedly, he was one of a number of commissaries appointed on 4 February 1439 to negotiate with representatives of the archbishop of Cologne for an alliance.[76] But then, in June following, were surrendered and cancelled those letters patent of November 1437 which, whether or not he was ill or unable to act, had guaranteed him for life his councillor's fee of 100 marks, the fee charged on the issues of the manor of Bassingbourne and the bailiwick of Babraham. Possibly Tiptoft attended the parliament which first met at Westminster in November-December 1439 and again at Reading in January-February 1440, but it was in this second session that Sir James Butler, eldest son of the earl of Ormond, was summoned, under pain of £2,000, to answer a charge of harbouring men who, at Cambridge, had been assaulting Tiptoft's servants, and Tiptoft himself was ordered to be present at the enquiry to help decide who were to blame for the affray. Neither the cause or final outcome of this apparent enmity between Butler and Tiptoft is known; but that the incident could even occur hardly suggests that Tiptoft's position was

---

74   *CPR 1436-41*, 200, 235.

75   Somerset Record Society (vol. XXXII), *Register of Bishop John Stafford*, ii. 230.

76   Carte, *Rolles Gascons*, ii. 294, 302; *PPC*, V. 126; *Foedera*, X. 834. Tiptoft was party to the treaty of alliance with the archbishop of Cologne which was ratified at Windsor in December, 1440.

now as strong as formerly. However, still a member of the Council, he continued to serve the Crown, not least on commissions of a local character, including the commission of the peace. In April 1440 he was once again made an apportioner in Cambridgeshire of the county's share of the now usual rebate on the subsidies granted by the recent parliament. At the end of August all the sheriffs (save those of the northern counties) and certain members of the nobility, including Tiptoft, were ordered to put a stop to unlawful assemblies and hasten to join the king in the event of serious disturbances. On 18 February 1441 he was appointed to act as a commissioner in Cambridgeshire for anticipating, by raising loans, collection of part of the parliamentary subsidies granted a year before, the reason for haste being the immediate need to despatch forces to Normandy under the duke of York as the king's lieutenant in France.

The summer and autumn of 1441 saw the trial, for witchcraft, heresy, and treason, of the duke of Gloucester's second wife, Eleanor (*née* Cobham), an event which, despite the fact that the duke was heir-presumptive to the throne, marked the beginning of the end of his political influence. The party of Cardinal Beaufort and his friends was left in command of the situation, and Tiptoft was still a member of the Council. Indeed, on 23 August he was able to obtain an *inspeximus* and confirmation of his patent of November 1437 (cancelled in June 1439), which in effect restored to him the manor of Bassingbourne and the bailiwick of Babraham (Cambs.) as the source of his councillor's fee, together with a pardon of all his arrears and accounts between then and now. According to this same patent of August 1441, he was not in future to be bound to attend the Council.[77] By now he must have been turned sixty, and no doubt was already in very poor health. But though he may not have attended meetings of the Council regularly, he certainly still put in the occasional appearance. For instance, he was present in the Council on 14 October 1441, three days before being appointed to serve on the commision set up to conduct the trial for treason of the necromancers who had accused the duchess of Gloucester of instigating their enquiry (by the black arts) into her husband's prospects of achieving the crown, and also the trial of the duchess herself as an accessory.[78] Whether or not Tiptoft attended the parliament of January-March 1442, he was immediately after its

77   *CCR, 1435-41*, 304; *CFR, 1437-45*, 140; *CPR, 1436-41*, 537, 559.
78   *CPR, 1441-6*, 109; *PPC*, V. 153.

dissolution included as usual on the commission for apportioning the tax-reduction in Cambridgeshire, and also among the commissioners for raising Crown loans in the shire. Apart from his re-appointment as justice of the peace in Cambridgeshire and Huntingdonshire in July following, no more local commissions were to come his way. His last recorded set of daily appearances in the Council falls between 21 and 24 August in the same year, when he came up to Sheen (Surrey) for a discussion of diplomatic exchanges with the Emperor Sigismund and, no doubt of more directly personal interest, to hear a statement by the archbishop of Bordeaux about the situation in Guienne. Consideration of this latter led on to the adoption of financial measures for the equipping of a special expedition, and Tiptoft himself advanced £100 towards it.[79]

By the end of 1442 Tiptoft can only have been very rapidly declining in health. Gloucester was evidently expecting his early demise when, on 4 January 1443, he secured the reversion of the custody of the forests of Waybridge and Sapley (Hunts.) which Tiptoft had acquired when Speaker in 1406. Tiptoft died, in fact, some three weeks later, on either 24 or 27 January.[80]

Gloucester's enemy, Cardinal Beaufort, was to profit to a far greater extent from Tiptoft's death. But before so doing, he was at least content to wait awhile. It was not until 25 May 1443 that he was granted all the issues of Tiptoft's estates (to help him recoup a loan to the Crown of £11,000), during the minority of the son and heir, John, who was now rising sixteen; and it was only by October 1444 that the cardinal's nephew, Edmund, marquess of Dorset, had laid hands on the bulk of the Gournay estates in Dorset and Somerset, following their reversion to the Crown at Tiptoft's death. Moreover, the cardinal did not obtain the wardship and marriage of the heir. Rights over these incidents evidently went to the youth's mother, upon whose death, in September 1446, they were granted to Henry VI's collegiate foundations at Eton and Cambridge. Even so, when in 1447 the cardinal bequeathed 500 marks to the heir, this was to cancel a debt for which the latter was obliged to him 'by his writing'.[81] The Tiptoft-Beaufort connection, soon to end, had at least continued until then.

How far forward in social importance the first Lord Tiptoft had brought his own family was to be demonstrated even early in the career of the second: in the spring of 1449, the heir married Cecily, daughter

79 *CFR*, *1437-45*, 215; *CPR*, *1441-6*, 61, 468, 472; *PPC*, V. 196, 198, 201-2.
80 *CPR*, *1441-6*, 198, 171.
81 *ibid*., 182, 324, 358; N. H. Nicolas, *Testamenta Vetusta*, i. 254.

of Richard Neville, earl of Salisbury, niece of the duke of York's wife, and the widow of Henry Beauchamp, duke of Warwick (ob.1446); and shortly afterwards (July 1449) he was created earl of Worcester. Eventually becoming a devoted Yorkist, he so remained until his execution during the Lancastrian Re-adeption of 1470-1. There is much to suggest that he was a polished humanist and discriminating patron of letters. In this connexion, it is worth noting that his father, the first Lord Tiptoft, had quite likely been a modest practitioner in historical writing, and quite certain that he had given his heir an advanced education, perhaps at Oxford where, as Leland knew, there was a tradition of his membership of Balliol College.[82]

82   *DNB*, xix. 891.

8

THOMAS CHAUCER OF EWELME

Although not all historians of fifteenth century England will know of M.B. Ruud's *Thomas Chaucer* (1932), none will be unaware of K.B. McFarlane's important article entitled 'Henry V, Bishop Beaufort and the Red Hat, 1417-21' (first published in 1945 in *English Historical Review*, vol. LX, re-printed in 1981 in *England in the Fifteenth Century, Collected Essays*, published by the Hambledon Press), an article in which Thomas Chaucer figured so largely as to prompt its author to note the salient points of his career, and to provide, especially regarding his landed interests, a considerable amount of ancillary detail. It seemed to the present writer, however, that to omit a biography of Thomas Chaucer from a collection of papers mostly devoted to biographies of Speakers for the Commons in medieval parliaments, would be something regrettable. For Chaucer, who represented Oxfordshire in fourteen parliaments between 1401 and 1431 (roughly half the parliaments of that time), was elected Speaker on on fewer than five occasions, i.e. in the consecutive parliaments of 1407, 1410 and 1411, and the parliaments of 1414 (November) and 1421 (May). These five parliaments were all of them short, and each ran only to a single session, but Chaucer's record as Speaker, in terms of frequency of election rather than of length of tenure of office, was not to be equalled until the reign of George II (when Arthur Onslow, M.P. for Surrey, was Speaker in all of that king's parliaments, a record number of years of service which, extending from 1728 to 1761, has never been surpassed). Even in Chaucer's lifetime, however, his achievement was to be run pretty close: by Roger Flore of Oakham, who similarly was Speaker in three consecutive parliaments under Henry V (in 1416, 1417 and 1419) and held the office yet again in the first parliament of the reign of Henry VI (in 1422).

Thomas Chaucer had been given a good start in life, chiefly by reason of his parentage.[1] Born probably in 1367, he was the son of Geoffrey Chaucer, poet-laureate in all but name, and his wife, Philippa, daughter and coheir of Sir Paon Roet, a herald from Hainault who, coming to England in the entourage of Edward III's queen, Philippa, had risen to be Guyenne king-of-arms. Both parents had been brought up in court circles, and each remained attached to one or other branch of the royal family. Geoffrey, the son of a London vintner, had been a member, successively, of the households of Elizabeth, countess of Ulster, her husband, Lionel, duke of Clarence, Edward III, and Richard II. By 1371, when he was an esquire of the King's Chamber, he was granted fees amounting to 40 marks a year which, confirmed in 1378 but suspended in 1388, were again renewed in 1394 and then supplemented by another annuity of £20. In the meantime, apart from occasional diplomatic missions abroad (e.g. in 1372-3 to Genoa and Florence, in 1377 to Flanders and France, and in 1378 to Lombardy), he had served the Crown in a variety of ways: as controller of the wool customs in the port of London from June 1374 to December 1386, although not above acting through a deputy; as a J.P. in Kent from October 1385 to July 1389, in which period he was knight of the shire for Kent in the 'Wonderful Parliament' of 1386 (for him a unique experience); and as clerk of the works at Westminster, the Tower of London, etc. from July 1389 to June 1391 and, in his last twelve months in this office, at St. George's Chapel, Windsor, as well. As a career in the public service, all of this was nothing very outstanding; and, moreover, such as it was, it can only have been assisted by his wife's connection with the menage of John of Gaunt, duke of Lancaster, especially on account of the circumstances which had brought that connection into being. Admittedly, Geoffrey Chaucer had long been well-known to John of Gaunt and, indeed, soon after the death of Blanche, John's first wife, in 1369, had composed the *Boke of the Duchesse*, an elegiac in which was related, with great delicacy and charm, John's courtship of her. But, then, Chaucer's wife Philippa, having long served as a lady-in-waiting (damsel) to Queen Philippa, had proceeded, after the queen's death in 1369, to serve as attendant to

---

1   'Fuit idem [Galfridus] Chawserus pater Thome Chawserus armigeri, qui Thomas sepelitur in Nuhelm [Ewelme] juxta Oxoniam.' So was Thomas Chaucer identified as son of Geoffrey Chaucer, by Thomas Gascoigne in his *Theological Dictionary*. The author was chancellor of the University of Oxford in the year before Thomas Chaucer's death and, as resident at Oxford, must have known Chaucer well. K. B. McFarlane, op. cit., pp. 96-9. For particulars relating to Geoffrey's career, see *Chaucer Life-Records*, ed. M. M. Crow & C. C. Olson (Oxford, 1966). For light on the problem of Thomas's parentage, see also *Oxoniensia*, vol. 5, pp. 78, 83; and *Notes and Queries*, vol. 183 (1944), p. 287.

Lancaster's second duchess, Constance of Castile, following their marriage in 1371. There can be little doubt but that this new 'situation' of Philippa's had been directly procured for her by her sister, Katherine, the wife of Sir Hugh Swynford, whose position in the Lancastrian household was by this time become extremely influential. For not only after the death of the Duchess Blanche, in whose service she had been engaged since her youth, did Katherine continue to act as the governess of her children (Henry of Bolingbroke, Philippa, and Elizabeth), but before long, probably in 1371, became the duke's mistress and, after her husband's death in Aquitaine in 1372, his mistress *en titre*. How especially important to Geoffrey Chaucer was his wife Philippa's membership of the ducal household is clear from the fact that when, in June 1374, John of Gaunt granted him £10 a year for life, this was in consideration of her services to the Duchess Constance (and previously to the late Queen Philippa) as well as of his own services to the duke himself. And, of course, the significance of the attachment could only have been enhanced as Philippa's sister Katherine strengthened her hold on the duke's affections by bearing him, all of them during the 'seventies, four children (John, Henry, Thomas, and Joan), who took the name of Beaufort. These children, whose legitimation, following their parents' marriage in January 1396, was obtained later in the same year from Pope Boniface IX, and early in 1397 by authority of parliament, were Thomas Chaucer's cousins-german. Such was the social milieu into which Thomas had been born, and in which he came to maturity.

Soon after Thomas Chaucer had reached his majority, his career was already taking shape, under the patronage of John of Gaunt. It was, in fact, in March 1389 that the duke retained him for life, granting him in aid the modest fee of £10 a year from the issues of the Lancastrian honour of Leicester. However, the ducal letters patent were dated at Bayonne, eight months before John of Gaunt's return to England from his expedition to Castile and after a long sojourn in Gascony, and it is highly probable not only that Thomas was then with the duke, but that he had sailed with the Lancastrian army from Plymouth in July 1386. In January 1394 his fee as one of the duke's esquires was doubled, and at the time of Lancaster's death in February 1399 he was constable of the duchy castle of Knaresborough and chief forester of that Yorkshire lordship. In a few weeks time (18 March) John of Gaunt's son and heir, Henry of Bolingbroke, then in exile in France, was disinherited by Richard II, and the duchy estates were declared forfeit to the Crown. This transaction, however, made no great immediate difference to Chaucer: his grant of the annual fee from the honour of Leicester was soon confirmed by the king, and although he was deprived of his Knaresborough offices, the loss was compensated for by a grant of 20 marks from the fee-farm of the royal borough of Wallingford (Oxon.).[2] All the same, he can hardly have been other than cheered by the replacement of Richard II on the throne by Bolingbroke on 30 September following, an event which, given his Lancastrian background, would be almost bound to lead to his own advancement.

And so it soon proved. For not only were Thomas's former annuities of £20 and 20 marks, charged respectively on the duchy of Lancaster honour of Leicester and the fee-farm of Wallingford, confirmed, but then, by royal letters patent of the 16 October 1399, three days after Henry IV's coronation, he was appointed for life as constable of Wallingford castle and, apparently without delay, took possession. The grant was in itself a sign that the new king regarded him as entirely trustworthy, for Richard II, before leaving for his expedition to Ireland in the previous spring, had established his young queen, Isabel of Valois, in the castle, and she and her household were still there; indeed, one of Chaucer's first actions was to take over supplies of wine, corn, wood and charcoal from her officers. (Isabel was soon, however, to be moved down-river to Sonning.) Moreover, on 23 October orders were given for the deposed king's nephew, Thomas Holland, duke of Surrey, to be transferred from the Tower of London to Wallingford, only for him to be shortly afterwards delivered (with others of doubtful loyalty) into the custody of the abbot of Westminster. Meanwhile, on 26 October, Chaucer had also been appointed, again for life, as steward of the conjoined honours of Wallingford and St. Valery and the four and a half hundreds of Chiltern, with a fee of £40 a year and an allowance of £10 for a deputy. These properties, parcels of the duchy of Cornwall, had been granted on 15 October to Henry, prince of Wales, Chaucer's appointment foreshadowing, therefore, what was to become an important relationship for them both.[3]

Chaucer's grants of the Wallingford offices can only have been made in light of the fact that the nucleus of his own estates was in this area of the middle Thames valley, and that he mainly resided at Ewelme (Oxon.), under the Chiltern scarp, only some four miles from Wallingford. His father was still alive, and when in another year's time (25 October 1400) Geoffrey died, all Thomas inherited was a property in Golding Lane in the city of London (worth £8 a year) and the recent

2   *CPR, 1396-99*, 490, 494.
3   *CPR, 1399-1401*, 15, 33-4; ibid., *1413-16*, 157; *CCR, 1399-1402*, 28; PRO, Duchy of Lancaster, Accounts Various, D. L. 28, bundle 4, no. 3; *Rot. Parl.*, iii. 667; J. H. Wylie, *History of England under Henry the Fourth* (London, 1884-98), iv. 235; ibid., i. 72.

lease of a house in the garden of the Lady Chapel of Westminster Abbey. What Thomas possessed at the beginning of Henry IV's reign had all come to him when, in or shortly before 1395, he married Maud, younger daughter and coheir of the late Sir John Burghersh (ob. 1391) and a great-niece and ward of Joan, lady Mohun of Dunster (one of the 'grandes dames' of Richard II's court until her dismissal by the Lords Appellant in 1387). It was in his wife's right that Thomas held 'Wace's Court' and 'Burghersh manor' in Ewelme, the advowson of its church, the manor and advowson of Swyncombe, and lands in Nuffield. Similarly *jure uxoris*, he held, in Hampshire, the manors of East Worldham and West Worldham; in Essex, the manor of Hatfield Peverel; in Suffolk, a moiety of the manor of Stratford St. Andrew; in Norfolk, two knight's fees in Gresham (which he was to sell to William Paston in 1429); in Cambridgeshire, an estate of 123 acres at Bourne; and in Lincolnshire, a moiety of a third of the manor of Skendleby, with a share of the tolls of the markets and fairs at Partney. Of course, as he grew wealthier, he added, by purchase, lands of his own, and these, understandably, were mostly in the region between the Chilterns and the Cotswolds: in Oxfordshire, he acquired by this means the manors of Hook Norton, Kidlington, Garsington, Hanwell and Thrup, and lands in a number of places including Woodstock, Begbrook, Newnham and Iffley; and in Berkshire, the manors of Buckland and Hatford. In Berkshire also he bought, from Sir Richard Abberbury in 1415, the castle and manor of Donnington and the manors of Peasemore, Penclose and Winterbourne Mayne, but this was only in order to settle them on his daughter Alice following her marriage to Sir John Phelip (probably in the autumn of 1414). Save this last batch, all Thomas's lands so far noted were held on a permanent basis. And so, in a sense, was the lease he acquired in February 1411 at the hands of Henry IV's queen, Joan of Navarre: a lease for life of the royal manors of Woodstock, Handborough, Wootton and Stonesfield, and the hundred of Wootton (all in north Oxfordshire), for possession of which he undertook to pay an annual rent of £127 odd.[4] But at frequent intervals (as will be seen) other lands, mostly in the middle Thames valley, also came Chaucer's way through royal grants of wardships and leases of a temporary nature (some of them long-lasting all the same), in both instances making a considerable addition to the stock of land he had already accumulated, and greatly increasing his income from that most important of many sources. It hardly needs saying that with lands

4   K. B. McFarlane, op. cit., pp. 97-100; *Feudal Aids*, ii, 214, 357, 370; iii. 575; iv. 187; vi. 456, 490; F. Blomefield, *Norfolk*, viii. 127; *CCR, 1429-35*, 335-9; *1435-41*, 2; *1447-54*, 346; *1468-76*, 216; *CPR, 1408-13*, 298-9.

went patronage, and where, as to some extent was the case with Chaucer, a man's lands were geographically concentrated, he normally attained to such great local influence as would of itself command respect on the part of the king's central government.

Chaucer's first election as knight of the shire for Oxfordshire was to the second parliament of Henry IV's reign. Having been originally summoned on 9 September 1400 to meet at York on 27 October, the parliament was prorogued on 3 October to meet instead at Westminster on 20 January 1401. In the meantime, on 24 November 1400, Chaucer had been appointed sheriff of the joint-bailiwick of Oxfordshire and Berkshire. As usual, the writs of summons expressly prohibited the return of sheriffs, but although there was ample time before parliament met for Chaucer as sheriff to have the county court hold a fresh election and replace him as knight of the shire, he evidently chose not to follow this course, and it was therefore while in office as sheriff that he attended the parliament of 1401. (If this was in breach of the intention of the writ of summons, it is only fair to note that the circumstances of this case were always liable to occur, and not infrequently did so with the same result.) Chaucer continued to serve as sheriff for the usual annual term, and his appointment ended in the following autumn. His next Crown appointment was of an even more temporary nature, namely, as a member of the Oxfordshire group of commissioners set up, on 11 May 1402, to combat the spread of seditious lies about the king's governmental intentions. Then, about four weeks later, he sailed from Harwich in the entourage of Henry IV's elder daughter, Blanche, then on her way to Cologne to meet Lewis of Bavaria, the heir of Rupert, the anti-Kaiser, to whom she was married at Heidelberg on 6 July. In aid of his expenses Chaucer received a grant of £4 from Blanche's treasurer. And when all but her close retinue returned to Harwich on 26 July, he was evidently one of those who now came home. He was thus back in time to be included in a commission appointed on 29 July to enquire into reports of treasonable activities in Oxford on the part of Welshmen, presumably students in the University openly sympathetic to the cause of Owen Glendower. When the next parliament was called, eventually for 30 September, he was re-elected as knight of the shire. (Incidentally, his wife's sister Margaret's husband, Sir John Grenville, was returned for Devon.) The session had still three weeks to run when, on 5 November, Chaucer was appointed for life to the important Household office of chief butler of England, with a fee of 20 marks a year payable by the treasurer of the Household, and with the right to appoint deputies in the ports to administer the royal prerogative of prisage of wine. (The chief butler was *ex officio* coroner of the city of London, where also he acted by deputy.) Except for a short period of seven or eight months in 1407, and for a much longer period from March 1418 to May 1421, when he was constantly overseas, Chaucer was to fill the office continuously until his death in 1434.

The office of chief butler, time-consuming though it must have been, did not stand in the way of Chaucer's assumption of other duties, some of which arose quite naturally out of his position as a local landowner of importance. It is rather surprising that it was not until May 1403 that he was made a justice of the peace in Oxfordshire, and the appointment may perhaps be thought of as a consequence of his cousin Henry Beaufort's appointment as chancellor in the preceding February. But once appointed, Chaucer was to remain on the bench for the rest of his career, save only again when he was out of the country during Henry V's campaigns in Normandy. No record survives of any unusual activities in the critical summer that followed, when occurred the first of the rebellions of the Percys which, in July, culminated in the battle of Shrewsbury. But, certainly, at the end of September he was at Carmarthen where the king himself was engaged in helping to contain the spread of Glendower's revolt. And then, early in November, Chaucer was again appointed sheriff of Oxfordshire and Berkshire, and it was now that, exchanging an annuity of £20 deriving from the duchy of Lancaster honour of Tutbury (Staffs.) given him in the previous June, he secured a royal grant of the marriage of Thomas, son and heir of Sir Ralph Stonor, a near neighbour in south Oxfordshire; and to the grant of the marriage was to be added, a year later, the wardship of the heir's estates in Stonor, Bix Gibwen, Bix Brand, and Brownesdon, for the custody of which, together with that of others outside Oxfordshire, he made a down-payment to the Exchequer of £200 (something of a bargain, for the wardship was to last till 1415). Meanwhile, on 20 February 1404, Chaucer had taken out a royal pardon of all debts, accounts and arrears. However, possibly in consequence of a virulent attack on the Household by the Commons in the parliament then sitting, the pardon was not to extend to his occupancy of the office of chief butler, but simply related to fines for escapes of felons from Chaucer's custody in the royal gaols at Oxford, and to his appropriation of the household property of Richard II's queen left behind in Wallingford castle when she had been moved to Sonning in the autumn of 1399. No more of him is heard until, at Leicester on 16 May following, he was ordered to arrest the recorder of Southampton and bring him before the king himself. Then, by royal letters patent of 10 October 1404, he shared with Sir John Pelham, who was sitting as knight of the shire for Sussex in the second parliament of the year which had only just met at Coventry, a grant of the custody of the temporalities of the recently vacated see of Winchester. It looks as if Henry IV, as soon as Bishop William of Wykeham died on 27 September, intended that his half-brother, Henry Beaufort, should if possible be translated from Lincoln. And, indeed, as early as 19 November, Pope Innocent VII (who had succeeded Boniface IX as recently as 17 October) provided Beaufort to Winchester. Both the king and Beaufort were probably sanguine as to this outcome; and Beaufort, as chancellor, might well have proposed his cousin Chaucer's appointment as a custodian of the Winchester temporalities, and the king have readily concurred, in order to safeguard his interests in the see generally, once his translation by the pope had been effected, pending restitution of the temporalities. Not until 14 March 1405 were the custodians ordered to release them, and until then they accounted for the issues in the King's Chamber. Admittedly, Chaucer owned land in Hampshire, and (as may be gathered from other evidence) sometimes resided in the Winchester diocese. Even so, this appointment of his in 1404-5 can safely be attributed to his close kinship with the new bishop.[5]

Save for the continuance until March 1405 of his shared custodianship of the temporalities of the see of Winchester, there is little to note of Chaucer's doings in that year. He was still occupying, of course, the office of chief butler and, an esquire of the Household, was as such receiving robes worth £2.6s.8d a year (according to the 1405-6 account-book of the controller). Whether or not he was with the king at Hereford when news came of the rising of Archbishop Scrope of York, the earl of Northumberland, the earl Marshal and Lord Bardolf, he and the sheriff of Oxfordshire and Berkshire were commissioned, in writs issued on 22 May, to array all local knights, esquires, yeomen and other fencibles, the sheriff in the whole of his bailiwick, Chaucer only in Oxfordshire. This was on the day before the king left Hereford for Yorkshire, where, at Shipton Moor, another three days later, the northern rebels met the forces of the earl of Westmorland, who then deceived them into surrendering. It was towards the end of the year that, on 23 November, Chaucer was appointed by the Crown as farmer of the forests of Neroche, Exmoor and Mendip and keeper of the park at Petherton (all in Somerset) at a rent of £40 a year, the appointment to last for as long as the owner, Edmund Mortimer, the young earl of

5   PRO, *Lists and Indexes*, xi (List of Sheriffs), 108; *CPR, 1401-05*, 128, 133, 170, 324, 335, 356, 432, 473; Wylie, *Henry IV*, iii. 117, 248-51; F. Devon, *Issues of the Exchequer (Henry III-Henry VI)*, 285.

March, was a royal ward. The latter, whose claim to the throne had always been a source of serious concern to Henry IV, was in fact in custody until Henry V's accession when, upon his release and restoration to his estates, he confirmed Chaucer in his lease, only in return, however, for an increase of the farm-rent from £40 to £50. On this basis Chaucer was to retain the farm until his death.

No parliament sat in 1405, but on 21 December the writs of summons were issued for a meeting at Coventry on 15 February 1406; on 1 January the place was changed to Gloucester; and then, with only six days to go (9 February), both time and place were changed yet again, parliament being prorogued to meet on 1 March at Westminster. So began what was to be the longest parliament ever held thus far: its first session lasted from 1 March until 3 April; the second, from 25 April to 19 June; and the third and final session, from 13 October until 22 December. Chaucer had been returned as elected for Oxfordshire. It was in the second session that, on 25 May, following a statement then made before the Lords in parliament by John, lord Lovell (a member of the King's Council), and William Doyle, that they would submit their dispute over the manor and advowson of Hinton near Brackley (Northants.) to a panel of six arbiters chosen by them, Chaucer accepted appointment as one of the six, it being understood that if he and his fellow-arbiters, who were ordered to meet in London on 1 July, had not made their award within a month, Archbishop Arundel and Edward, duke of York, should act as umpires (*nomperes*) and arrive at their decision before Christmas. When Chaucer appeared on 1 August, the final date for the arbiters' award, no such settlement had been reached. In the meantime, on 20 June, the day after the second prorogation of parliament, Bishop Beaufort, then at his inn in Southwark, had appointed Chaucer as constable of the castle of Taunton and overseer of the episcopal estates in Somerset, at an annual fee of £40 (a fee which would nicely offset the farm-rent Chaucer had, in 1405, undertaken to pay for custody of the Mortimer forests in the county); and the patent was confirmed by the cathedral chapter at Winchester on 16 July, and even, although not until 14 February 1408, by royal letters patent issued under the Great Seal. Hardly a week had passed following Chaucer's appointment by his cousin the bishop, when, on 28 June, he was put onto a commission of enquiry in Oxon. and Berks. into financial abuses and extortions on the part of royal officials, the annual value of lordships held of the Crown at farm, and annuities charged to the issues of either shire; and on the same day he was made a commissioner for raising Crown loans from people in the same two counties able to contribute. It was in December of the same year, a fortnight before this long parliament was dissolved, that Chaucer was appointed escheator in Oxon. and Berks. He was still holding this office when re-elected to sit in the parliament summoned to meet at Gloucester on 20 October 1407. However, in the meantime, on 13 May previous, he had been superseded as the king's chief butler by Sir John Tiptoft, Speaker in the 1406 parliament, who, in its last session, had been appointed treasurer of the Household.[6]

Despite Chaucer's demotion, when the next parliament met at Gloucester the Commons elected him as their Speaker (on 25 October 1407). This choice possibly suggests that the political alliance, already formed, between his cousin, Bishop Beaufort, and the prince of Wales was now making some headway, at least in the Lower House. But if as a result of Chaucer's election as Speaker, that party hoped to make more headway still, such hopes proved unfounded. For, certainly, the personnel of the king's government, major officials and members of the Council alike, were to emerge from the parliament intact. Indeed, the only incident that was to disturb the single session occurred early on, and it then affected the Commons' relations with the Lords as well as the king. It was nevertheless a serious matter that was in question. When the Commons were told by the king to send a deputation to the Upper House, there to receive notice of a monetary grant already decided upon by the Lords, and then merely to return, inform their fellow-members, and secure their acquiescence, they strongly objected. What was happening in their view was an infringement of their right to consent to taxation freely, and therefore independently. Even the roll of the parliament records 'altercacion moeve entre les Seigneurs et les Communes'; and, certainly, the dispute was important enough to require a written 'cedule de Indemnite' for the protection of both parties. However, it had been provoked by the king's peremptory demand; and it was he who, finding it prudent to do so, conceded that grants of taxation should be announced to him only when agreed by both Houses, and, moreover, only through the Commons' Speaker. (This would obviously have the effect of leaving the Commons with the last word on such matters.) In this instance, what the Lords had recommended was finally accepted, viz. a grant of one and a half tenths and fifteenths; and, evidently, so relieved was the king at this eventual result that he undertook not to ask again for such taxes between Lady Day (25 March) 1408 and Lady Day 1410. The session can hardly have

6   British Library, Harleian Ms. 319, fo. 46; *CPR, 1405-08*, 66, 153, 199, 406; *Rot. Parl.*, iii. 573; *CPR, 1405-13*, 21; *PRO, List of Escheators*, 119. Regarding Thomas's farm of the Mortimer forests in Somerset, there is no indication in records in the PRO that his father Geoffrey ever preceded him as farmer (see *Chaucer Life-Records*, ed. Crow and Olson, pp. 494-9).

been a pleasant experience for one acting as Speaker for the first time, but the outcome for Chaucer personally was far from unfavourable. It was of no great consequence that, on 15 November, he had been appointed overseer of the administration of pontage-dues at Wallingford (where the levy had been granted to the town-bailiffs for three years); but on 3 December (the day after the parliament's dissolution) he was re-appointed as the king's chief butler, although the appointment was now only 'quamdiu regi placuerit', not for life as in his original patent of 1402. It was doubtless taking advantage of this re-appointment that he petitioned king and Council concerning difficulties over the collection of dues from prisage of wines in the ports of Bristol and Hull; and in March 1408 he was authorized to take securities, for their appearance in Council, from all defaulters wherever they might be.[7]

After the Gloucester parliament, nearly two years passed before the next parliament was even under contemplation. First summoned on 26 October 1409 to meet at Bristol on 27 January 1410, it was re-summoned on 18 December to meet on the same date, but now at Westminster instead. The re-summons was among Archbishop Arundel's last acts in this spell of office as chancellor, for he was dismissed on 21 December, having already been preceded out of office by Sir John Tiptoft, the treasurer of the Exchequer, on the 11th. The treasurership was to be filled three weeks before parliament met (on 6 January 1410) by Henry, Lord Scrope of Masham, a close friend of the prince of Wales. The chancellorship, however, remained vacant until 31 January when Sir Thomas Beaufort, Bishop Henry's younger brother, was appointed. By then parliament was in its fifth day, and not only had the 'pronunciatio' or opening address already been delivered by the bishop, but so had Chaucer, the Beauforts' cousin, been re-elected Commons' Speaker. Given these related appointments, it is reasonable to assume that supreme direction of the royal administration had already been taken over by the party of the prince of Wales who, early in May, during the second session of the parliament, was to be formally recognized as head of the Council, with his friends in a clear majority there. Whether this party had taken steps to influence the elections to the parliament generally, is not known. But Chaucer himself would seem to have done so at Taunton (where he was Bishop Beaufort's steward of the lordship), and with at least some success: one of the two Taunton burgesses originally elected by the town, William Motte, was Chaucer's co-feoffee to Robert James esquire of Boarstall (Bucks.), and when Motte's name was later erased from the electoral return, that of

7   *Rot. Parl.*, iii. 609, 611; *CPR, 1405-08*, 327, 380, 374, 386-7; PRO, Ancient Petitions, S. C. 8, file 173, no. 8635.

Thomas Edward, Chaucer's co-feoffee to John Golafre of Fyfield (Berks.) was substituted for it. James and Golafre, with both of whom Chaucer was intimate, were elected for Berkshire. It may also be noted that Sir Thomas Brooke, Chaucer's wife's uncle by marriage, was returned as knight of the shire for Somerset.[8]

Judging from what Henry IV was to say about it in the next parliament (1411), Chaucer's conduct as Speaker in 1410 obviously offended him. And, even from the point of view of the new ministry headed by the prince of Wales, the demeanour of the Lower House was perhaps not always all it might have been. (Two sessions were required to elicit grants of taxation, and although one and a half tenths and fifteenths were eventually forthcoming, their collection was to be spread over two years.) But no doubt Chaucer did the prince's party good service in the Speaker's rôle. And he himself, too, obtained a modicum of satisfaction from the parliament, if only in respect of his office as chief butler. It was in this capacity that he personally petitioned the Lords, drawing attention to the unacceptable number of exemptions from liability to prisage of wines resulting from the admission of non-residents to the freedom of the city of London (where the royal prerogative of prisage did not apply to citizens who lived there), and requesting that the King's Council send for the mayor and aldermen and the masters of the gilds and command them to desist from the practice, and also to repeal all existing enfranchisements irregularly allowed. The petition was granted, although, judging from Chaucer's procurement, on 20 October 1412, of letters patent of exemplification, the possibility of abuse would require constant vigilance. It can only have been after the dissolution of the parliament of 1410 that Chaucer, along with his fellow-knight of the shire for Oxfordshire and the two Berkshire representatives, was in a position to act, in accordance with his appointment on 20 April, as a commissioner of oyer and terminer, following a complaint from Sir John Drayton of a breach of the latter's close and of assaults at Nuneham (Oxon.), apparently by clerks at the University who had made his servants swear not to implead them in any court save that of the chancellor of the University.

The last parliament of Henry IV's reign to count as a parliament, and have its record preserved, met on 3 November 1411 and sat until 19 December. Earlier that year, Chaucer had strengthened his landed holdings in Oxfordshire by securing a lease, from the queen (Joan of Navarre), of a group of her estates in the north of the county, viz. the

8   *Return of Members of Parliament*, i. 274-5; *Oxford Hist. Soc.* vol. lxxxviii (*The Boarstall Cartulary*), 266; *CCR, 1405-9*, 400.

manors of Woodstock, Handborough, Wootton and Stonesfield, and the hundred of Wootton, for all of which he undertook to pay an annual rent of £127.16s.6d. Granted the lease for life, he was in fact to retain it until he died (which must mean that he had been satisfied with its profitability).[9] Re-elected to parliament for Oxfordshire in the autumn, he was then also re-elected as Commons' Speaker for the second time running. This in itself indicates that the party of the prince of Wales and his friends, including the Beauforts, still commanded some support in the Lower House. However, whether or not it had gone too far in proposing that the king should abdicate in favour of the prince, that party was in disarray by the end of the session: the prince had been deprived of the headship of the Council; and both Sir Thomas Beaufort, the chancellor, and Lord Scrope, the treasurer, were on the point of dismissal. (The latter was replaced by Sir John Pelham on 23 December, the former by Archbishop Arundel on 5 January.) That such a reaction against the domination of the prince's party had been impending may be gathered from an incident which occurred before the session had hardly begun, an incident involving Chaucer in his rôle as Speaker. For the king, ailing though he was, took advantage of Chaucer's official claim to freedom of speech to inform parliament in general that he intended to maintain his own royal prerogatives intact, and to tell Chaucer in particular that he would tolerate no sort of innovation in this parliament ('nulle manere de Novellerie en cest parlement'), and that he might use his Speaker's privilege only as was customary. That, even so, tempers ran high in the parliament, and parliament's dealings with the king were rancorous, as evidently they had been in the parliament of 1410, is revealed by the Lords and Commons' final petition that the king would declare himself satisfied with the loyalty of those who had attended both this parliament and its predecessor.

In what remained of Henry IV's reign, there is little to be recorded of Chaucer's activities. Sometime in 1412 Philip Repingdon, bishop of Lincoln, appointed him for life as constable of the castle and seneschal of the episcopal lordship of Banbury in north Oxfordshire (an office he was to be still holding in September 1415). It must also be noted that, despite the part he had played as Speaker in a succession of troublesome parliaments, he continued to be the king's chief butler. It was, of course, in this latter capacity that he was much occupied in purveying especially large amounts of wine for Household consumption during the parliament which, having met on 3 February 1413, was brought to an end by the king's death on 20 March; and it was early in

9   *Rot. Parl.*, iii, 646; *CPR, 1408-13*, 434, 222, 283, 298.

the session that, along with the Welshman, Lewis John, and John Snypston, leading vintners in the City, he received at the Exchequer, in earnest of a settlement of the large debt of £868 odd incurred, a preferential assignment of nearly £800 from tunnage and poundage leviable in the port of London. In view of the loss of all the electoral returns from the counties, it is not known whether Chaucer himself sat in this last of Henry IV's parliaments.[10]

That, on the accession of Henry V, Chaucer would continue in office as chief butler, was only to be expected. His cousin, Bishop Beaufort, having succeeded Archbishop Arundel as chancellor on the first day of the new reign, Chaucer was soon confirmed in all his offices under the Crown. Indeed, he was re-appointed to the office of chief butler on the following day (22 March 1413), although not on the terms of his initial appointment in 1402, i.e. for life, but on those of his re-appointment in 1407, i.e. at the king's pleasure. This same second day of the reign saw the issue of writs summoning parliament for 14 May, and, now certainly, on the 27 April, Chaucer was once again elected as knight of the shire. For Oxfordshire, of course. The parliamentary elections at Wallingford and Taunton, too, show that his influence in each of those boroughs was no wit abated, for his associate in London, Lewis John, was returned by both. And how closely connected were the two men is additionally confirmed by the fact that when, on 14 April, Lewis John was appointed master of the royal mints in the Tower of London and Calais, Chaucer was the first of his mainpernors (or sureties) before the King's Council. Chaucer's interest in the government's financial affairs of a different sort had, in the meantime, on 1 April, involved him in standing surety also for Henry Somer when the latter, who had been appointed chancellor of the Exchequer in the previous January, was then bound over, with his mainpernors, to answer at the end of the parliamentary session to certain offences of which he stood impeached by the Council. It was later in this same year that, quite apart from his renewed appointment as chief butler, other signs of the king's confidence in Chaucer were forthcoming. First, on 3 September, he was given the keepership of the royal forests of Woolmer and Aliceholt in Hampshire; and in this connexion it is of particular interest that the letters patent embodying the grant were not only warranted 'by the King', but also were dated at Chaucer's own nearby manor of Worldham, a fact which may reasonably be taken to mean that when the patent passed the Great

---

10   *Rot. Parl.*, iii. 648, 658; J. W. F. Hill, *Medieval Lincoln*, 258n; *The Register of Bishop Philip Repyndon. 1405-1419*, vol. 3, *Memoranda 1414-1419*, ed. Margaret Archer, Lincoln Record Society, vol. 74 (1982), pp. 68-9; *CCR, 1409-13*, 377.

Seal, his cousin Henry, the chancellor, was visiting him there. Second, on 6 November, Chaucer was appointed sheriff of Hampshire. Evidently, this appointment did not prevent his inclusion in the commission of enquiry into activities of local Lollards in Oxfordshire and Berkshire set up on 11 January 1414, only a day or two after the Lollard rising in London under Sir John Oldcastle. Nor, far more significantly, was it allowed to stand in the way of his entry, for the first time proper, into the arena of royal diplomacy. For when, on 2 March, he was paid £76.13s.4d at the Lower Exchequer, it was on account of a journey to William, duke of Holland, and other foreign lords which he alone had been called upon to make, the object of the mission being to discuss 'certain secret matters moving the king and specially touching the advantage of the kingdom'.[11]

By this time Henry V was already negotiating for acceptance of his claim to the French crown, although still ready to compromise. But then he was also angling for a renewal of the alliance he had entered into with John, duke of Burgundy, when, in 1410-11, he had been head of the Council, an alliance of which Burgundy, with the Armagnac government in France now up in arms against him (notably in Artois), stood in great need. Indeed, Burgundian as well as French envoys were present at the parliament which met at Leicester between 30 April and 29 May 1414. Chaucer was not re-elected to this parliament, although it is possible that he attended it in his capacity as chief butler. In any case, it was no later than 4 June that he was authorized to serve with Henry, lord Scrope of Masham, and others, on an embassy to Burgundy, in order to negotiate for an alliance and the king's marriage to one of the duke's daughters. According to an entry on the Issue Roll of the Exchequer recording a payment to Chaucer of £60 for his expenses, the embassy was also to go to treat with the duke of Holland again. Its members crossed to Calais on 26 June and, after a series of rather inconclusive interviews with Burgundy, notably at Ypres and St. Omer, during the next three months, were all back in England by the end of October. Their return was in time for Chaucer to hold, on 5 November, the county elections for Hampshire to the parliament summoned to meet at Westminster on the 19th, and to secure from the

---

11   *CCR, 1413-19*, 66, 61; *CPR*, 1413-16, *102, 178; List of Sheriffs*, 55; McFarlane, op. cit., 101 n. 80. Like his father (who was not averse to making pilgrimages), Thomas Chaucer would appear to have been conventional in his attitude to formal religion: in January 1405 he and his wife had procured a papal indult allowing them to choose their own personal confessor with powers of absolution for all but the graver sins (*Papal Letters*, vi. 20); and in September 1429 they were granted letters of confraternity by the prior and convent of Christ Church, Canterbury (*HMC., 9th Report, Mss. of the Dean and Chapter of Canterbury*, 113; *Literae Cantuarienses* (R. S.) iii, 152).

electors the return of his friend, and business-partner, Lewis John, as one of the knights of the shire. Three days later (8 November), he himself was once again elected for Oxfordshire. And then, as soon as parliament met, he was elected as Commons' Speaker, an election very likely to have been officially inspired.[12]

Although this was his fourth election as Speaker, Chaucer was no doubt willing to accept, if only because he had important business of his own to prosecute in the parliament. Along with Lewis John and John Snypston, he himself presented to the Commons a petition which the Lower House adopted and, as one of its own petitions, promoted in the Lords. What the petitioners were requesting was that, by authority of parliament, they should be repaid by Henry IV's executors the whole of the debt of £868 odd they themselves had incurred in purchasing wines for the Household in the last year of the late king's reign, Chaucer's own share of the debt standing at no less than £523 odd. Nothing of the debt, they pointed out, had so far been recovered, despite Exchequer assignments of revenue made early in 1413, not long before Henry IV's death; indeed, tallies of re-payment formerly levied in the Lower Exchequer had been invalidated, partly by the dismissal of the customs officials named, partly by the insufficiency of the customs-revenue itself; and, moreover, the late king's executors had been demanding, as proof of his indebtedness, bills of debenture under the seal of the former treasurer of the Household. Read in parliament, the petition met with only a somewhat dubiously favourable answer: just as the late king's creditors in general were to be treated, so in this case the executors were to make re-payment of what the petitioners were owed, but only, however, on condition that non-payment was confirmed by a scrutiny of the accounts of the customs-officials and others upon whose revenues the Exchequer tallies had been levied, a condition bound to result in delay. Whether Chaucer and his co-petitioners were ever fully satisfied of re-payment has not been ascertained; but considering that less than a quarter of Henry IV's debts had been met by the end of Henry V's reign (6,000 marks paid out of 25,000 due), it is unlikely. But this was not the only petition made on Chaucer's behalf; and the other, understandably (given its simplicity), was more satisfactory in its outcome: the Commons successfully requested the king that, with the Lords' assent, he would grant that all charters and letters patent issued by John of Gaunt, Richard II, Henry IV and himself, by which Chaucer held offices, lands or annuities,

---

12   *DKR*, xliv. 554; J. H. Wylie, *The Reign of Henry V*, i. 414; PRO, Exchequer Issue Rolls, 2 Hen. V, Easter term, E 403, no. 617, mem. 6; PRO, Chancery, C 219, bundle 11, no. 5; *Rot. Parl.*, iv. 35.

should be fully effectual, and that the petition together with the response should be enacted of record on the roll of the parliament. (It is perhaps worth noting that the concessions so confirmed had not been specified in the petition.)[13]

When, after a session of only three weeks, the parliament ended on 7 December, Chaucer no doubt felt that as Speaker he had deserved well of the king. Certainly, the latter had every reason to be satisfied with the behaviour of the Commons, who had agreed upon a grant the like of which had not been made since the Coventry parliament of ten years before, viz. two tenths and fifteenths, the first instalment of this double subsidy, moreover, leviable in two months time (Candlemas 1415), the second a year later. Apparently even before parliament met, it had been decided in principle that the king would, if necessary, go to war for his rights in France; and evidently, although both Lords and Commons were of a mind that negotiations for a peaceful settlement should be continued, parliament had shown, by the size of its financial grant and the timing of collection, that it was ready to back the royal policy. Accordingly, preparations for an invasion of France went ahead, activity to this end being speeded up early in the spring of 1415. Amongst other measures taken, commissions of array were issued on 29 May, and Chaucer was appointed to the commission for Oxfordshire. Of course, the main corps of the army of invasion was to consist of indentured retinues; and four weeks later, Chaucer was party as mortgagee to a deed whereby Edmund Mortimer, earl of March, mortgaged the castle and lordship of Ludlow and over forty of his manors in the Welsh March and southern England, his mortgagees to furnish him with £100,000 with which to meet the costs of his participation in the coming campaign. (The earl's contract was to supply a retinue of 60 men-at-arms and 160 archers.) Chaucer himself undertook to serve with the sizeable retinue of 11 'lances' and 36 archers. The expedition, its final preparations only briefly interrupted by 'the Southampton plot', sailed out of the Solent on 11 August, but Chaucer, who five days before had been granted a pardon, warranted 'by the King', of all debts, arrears, dilapidation of castles, concealments, actions and demands, did not accompany it, having fallen ill. His son-in-law, Sir John Phelip, however, did so, with a retinue of 30 men-at-arms and 90 archers, and he took part in the siege of Harfleur, only to die, either from wounds or, more probably, from dysentery, ten days after the town's surrender on 22 September (so leaving Alice Chaucer, Thomas's daughter, a widow at the age of eleven). Chaucer's

13   *Rot. Parl.*, iv. 37, 39.

own retinue served at the siege (two of its members dying in the course of it) and also fought at Agincourt.[14]

No older now than in his late forties, Chaucer evidently soon recovered from the cause of his indisposition. Indeed he was soon all too ready to add to his numerous commitments, and on 4 December following he assumed responsibility as havener at Plymouth and in Cornwall. This office, with all its appurtenant rights to 'maletolt', prise of wines and import-dues, wreck of sea, etc. he undertook to farm as from the previous Michaelmas at £80 a year, payable at the Exchequer. He must have administered the office by deputy, as no doubt some of his others, if only because of his continued duties in the Household as chief butler. And how burdensome were they, and how chronic the harassment their discharge caused him, may readily be gathered from the fact that in the following summer he was still owed £2,842 for wines purveyed for the expedition of 1415; and when, by a letter patent of 21 July 1416, formal acknowledgement of this debt was made, provision for re-payment took no more satisfactory form than assignments on Lower Exchequer income, the customs and subsidies on wool exported through the ports of Southampton, Hull, Sandwich and Melcombe, and tunnage and poundage collected in London and Bristol, with the dubiously encouraging proviso that if these sources should have proved insufficient by Christmas, the treasurer of the Exchequer would make other, additional assignments. There is little else to report of Chaucer's activities in 1416.

Nor is there much more in 1417, or not at least until in the summer Henry V led his second invasion force to France. It was doubtless by virtue of his office as the bishop of Winchester's steward in Somerset that, in the meantime, in April, Chaucer was made a commissioner for embankments and dikes in the county. And in May he was included in a commission of enquiry into treasons in Berkshire. However, at Worldham (Hants.) early in June, he mustered a retinue of 9 men-at-arms and 30 archers, in anticipation of the impending campaign, and very probably went overseas with the army on 30 July.[15] The king's first object was to conquer Lower Normandy; but after the fall of Caen early in September, Henry was prepared to negotiate if only to

---

14   *CPR, 1413-16*, 408, 360, 259; *Feet of Fines for Essex* (Essex Archaeol. Society), iii. 264-5; PRO, Accounts Various, E101/47/29; *Transactions, Royal Historical Society*, 3rd series, vol. 5, 138-9. Sir John Phelip's brass in Kidderminster Church, where he was buried with his first wife Maud, widow of Walter Cokesay esq., says that he bravely fought at Harfleur and died on 2 October 1415, and that 'Henricus quintus dilexerat hunc ut amicus.' (H. A. Napier, *Historical Notices of Swyncombe and Ewelme*, 33). Phelip's mother was Juliana, a sister of Sir Thomas Erpingham, steward of the King's Household (March 1413 – May 1417).

15   *CFR, 1413-22*, 141; *CPR, 1416-22*, 137, 140, 175 (409).

deceive or confuse the French. And on 1 October ambassadors were appointed to treat for a peace, and their commission was renewed in mid-December. Chaucer was one of their number. Throughout 1418 he remained in France, being present at the siege of Louviers in June and at the siege of Rouen from October until the city fell in January 1419, the men of his retinue having been arrayed there in the meantime. Doubtless because it was expected that his absence from England would be so prolonged, Chaucer had been replaced as chief butler by Nicholas Merbury esquire on 16 March 1418, and it looks as if he did not recover the office before the end of Henry V's reign.[16] However, soon after the fall of Rouen, he returned to England. And he was in this country from March 1419 until the summer of 1420: his name appeared in a commission of array in Oxfordshire issued on 5 March 1419; in April, Sir Lewis Robessart, a Hainaulter by birth, whom in 1420 the king was to appoint as his standard-bearer, and in 1421 (after his recent election as K.G.) as an executor of his will, authorized him to act as one of his attorneys in England; and in May he was put on an enquiry in Oxfordshire and Berkshire into all treasons, escapes of felons, illegal bailments and cases of concealment of royal fiscal rights. Later in the year, on 26 November, he was included in a commission for the raising of loans to the king in Oxfordshire; and perhaps his meeting with the sheriff (John Willicotes) and others at the Crown Inn near St. Michael's in the Cornmarket at Oxford, when wine was provided for their refection by the borough authorities, was an opportunity for deliberation on the question of loans (the mayor of Oxford was one of the commission).[17] On 11 March 1420 Chaucer was at Ewelme, for it was then and from there that he wrote a most secret letter to the king.

This letter[18] is the only one extant of evidently a series of reports Chaucer made on the conduct of his cousin, Henry Beaufort, whose ecclesiastical ambitions had for some time been giving rise to trouble with the king, trouble serious for them both, and also for Chaucer as their intermediary. When Beaufort had resigned as chancellor in July 1417, it had been in order to go to the Council of Constance and help bring about the election of Pope Martin V; and it was while the bishop was still at Constance that, in December 1417, a grateful pope, but with

16   T. D. Hardy, *Rotuli Normanniae*, 167, 169, 205; *DKR*, xli (Norman Rolls), 713, 715, 717-8, 720; *Rotuli Normanniae*, 284.

17   *CPR, 1416-22*, 212, 269, 251; *DKR*, xli. 776; Oxford Hist. Soc.,   vol. lxxi (*Munimenta Civitatis Oxonie*, [Chamberlain's Accounts, Michs. 1419-20]), 281.

18   For the surviving greater part of the text of this letter, see K. B. McFarlane's article 'Henry V, Bishop Beaufort and the Red Hat, 1417-21, referred to above. I have relied heavily upon his illuminating commentary.

his own ends in view, appointed him to the Sacred College and as legate *a latere* in the British Isles and the lands in France subject to Henry V, entitled, moreover, to hold the see of Winchester *in commendam*. However, when in March 1419, following a year spent on pilgrimage to Jerusalem, Beaufort next met the king (at Rouen), the latter would allow none of these appointments, insisting indeed that Beaufort should resign them. But then, upon Beaufort's return to England in the summer, so distrustful was the king of his obedience that he arranged for Chaucer to make confidential reports to him direct concerning Beaufort's actions and plans for the future. What Chaucer's letter of 11 March 1420 revealed was not only that his cousin was now, twelve months after his last meeting with the king, still hoping to retain the legateship (perhaps with reduced powers), but even was in process of compounding his original offence by disobeying the king's summons to attend his marriage to Katherine of Valois at Troyes, an event which would follow closely upon the conclusion there of the great treaty making the king 'regent and heir of France'. Clearly, Chaucer knew of this, and of Beaufort's reason — that, when voyaging to or from the Holy Land in 1418, he had made a vow that once he had returned to England his first journey overseas thereafter would be to the shrine of St. James at Compostella. He was also able to inform the king of Beaufort's intention to follow up this pilgrimage with a second to Jerusalem and then, on his return home, to resign episcopacy, and even, too, of his thoughts of a possible successor to the see of Winchester when once he had vacated it. And, finally, Chaucer offered to go to France, if the king so commanded, to explain to him more fully in person. Evidently, the king gave no such order, for come midsummer Chaucer was still in England. In the meantime, Beaufort himself wrote to the king explaining in humble terms the reasons for his disobedience of the summons to Troyes, but this was not until 6 June, four days after the royal wedding had taken place. The quarrel as to this particular issue had all been to no purpose, for Beaufort never went to Compostella. However much of a strain Chaucer's part in the imbroglio caused him personally, it says much for his intelligence and abilities that, bound as he was to both parties, he had been able satisfactorily to discharge his duty as intermediary to each, without losing the confidence of either (not that he would have dared to cross the king).

Although Henry V did not take up Chaucer's offer to attend upon him at once (as contained in the letter of 11 March 1420), it was not long before Chaucer again crossed the Channel. The letters of attorney he procured before doing so were issued by the Chancery on 26 June, and evidently he had joined the king by 15 July. This was when, at Corbeil (close to Melun, the siege of which had just begun), Chaucer was included in an embassy authorized to negotiate with the vicomte de Rohan, lieutenant of Brittany, and the prelates and barons of the duchy, for their recognition of the treaty of Troyes; and on 1 August the same commissaries, and to the same end, were instructed to contact Duke John V himself. The latter's policy was to remain neutral, and with nothing, therefore, of the main object of the embassy achieved, Chaucer was evidently back in England before the end of the year. Certainly, during the parliament which sat in December he went surety for John Warfeld, parliamentary burgess for Wallingford, when the latter was granted the farm of the royal mills outside the south gate of the town, and on 21 December he himself secured the right to arrange for the marriage of a royal ward, the daughter of the late Sir Richard Arches, a former neighbour of his.[19]

When, on 26 February 1421, the next parliament was summoned, over three weeks had passed since Henry V, accompanied by Queen Katherine, had returned to England after an absence of three and a half years; and another nine weeks were to elapse before parliament assembled (on 2 May). The long interval between summons and meeting was clearly designed to allow for the queen to be crowned and, more importantly, to enable the king to set about revitalizing interest in the war in France in the country at large. Ratification of the treaty of Troyes by parliament (as the treaty itself required) would emphasize the high degree of military and diplomatic success already achieved; but a continuance of effort in France was still urgently needed, and in England, therefore, not only recruitment of fresh forces, but also a large injection of financial support quickly obtained. However, the notion that the French conquest ought to pay for itself was doubtless gaining ground, and, certainly, the last parliament had broken with recent practice and voted no taxation. But if, ideally, none was now to be demanded, money would have to be raised by loans, forced loans if necessary, for repayment of which the Council could be empowered to offer securities on parliament's authority. This, evidently, was the policy the king adopted, and his own cross-country progresses, ranging from Bristol in the south-west to Bridlington in the north-east, taking in most of the important towns of the Welsh March and the Midlands, and then extended to East Anglia, were largely organized to that end. The king's personal exertions were, of course, supplemented by those of local commissioners. And, in the batch of appointments issued on 21

19   *DKR*, xliv. 620; xlii. 375, 379; *CFR, 1413-22*, 363, 371.

April, Chaucer was appointed to serve in Oxfordshire and Berkshire, along with his friends, John Willicotes (the receiver-general of the duchy of Cornwall) and John Golafre (receiver-general of the duchy of Normandy in 1418-9); and, like all such commissioners for raising loans, they were ordered to certify the treasurer of the Exchequer ten days later, the eve of parliament's opening. Chaucer and Willicotes had been elected to parliament for Oxfordshire on 17 April, Golafre for Berkshire a full fortnight before then (2 April). A week or so earlier still (24 March), Chaucer's wife's first-cousin, Sir Thomas Brooke, had been elected for Somerset and, at the same time, William Bord, an Oxfordshire man who was one of Chaucer's feoffees-to-uses and was before long (Dec.1422) to be appointed his deputy-butler at Bridgwater (Somerset) and Topsham (Devon), had been returned as parliamentary burgess for Taunton (where Chaucer's occasional influence on parliamentary elections has already been noticed). And, on 17 March, even a week before the Somerset elections, Cornwall had elected Sir John Arundell, Chaucer's wife's sister Margaret's father-in-law, the duchy of Cornwall steward in the county since 1402. Evidently, Chaucer was not without friends and acquaintances among the Commons, who, when parliament met on 2 May, elected him their Speaker.[20]

Regarding the question of his suitability for the office on this particular occasion, it is worth noting that the only other previous Speaker to have been returned to the parliament was Roger Hunt (M.P. for Huntingdonshire) who had officiated just once, viz. in the last parliament (Dec.1420), after a contested election, whereas Chaucer had already done so four times. The latter had, moreover, other qualifications more impressive than mere past experience. For one thing, it being necessary for parliament to approve of the treaty of Troyes, it would be no disadvantage, however formal the procedure of approval, for the Speaker to be well-informed about the treaty, which, considering Chaucer's diplomatic assignments of the previous year. he unquestionably was. But more important still, especially in view of the circumstances in which this parliament met, was the fact that Chaucer enjoyed the confidence of both the king and his own cousin, Henry Beaufort. Of the difficult part he had played in the long quarrel between the two, all save the parties had been, and still remained, in ignorance. It must, however, have now become common knowledge that the quarrel itself had been resolved. But if the king was prepared to let bygones be bygones, it was only in return for the heavy price

20   *CPR, 1416-22*, 385; *Return of Members of Parliament*, i. 296-8; *Rot. Parl.*, iv. 130.

Beaufort was willing to pay, if on conditions; and if the king did not now, as was the case, ask parliament for a subsidy, it was mainly because the bishop was about to advance him a loan of £17,666 odd, a huge loan far in excess of any other individual loan, and all despite the fact that £8,306 odd was still unpaid of the loan of £14,000 he had made in 1417. Not the least important items of business of the single session of this parliament was to authorize the Council to provide securities for the repayment of *all* loans recently exacted. However, parliamentary confirmation of the royal letters patent embodying the security for Beaufort's loans was made the subject of a special petition emanating from the Commons, and in recommending its approval, they recorded their proper appreciation of the bishop's loans, noting that they would not only greatly assist the prosecution of the war, but also be *pur l'aise de vostre povre Communalte d'Engleterre* (a form of words perhaps hinting that a demand for direct taxation would have been unwelcome). No doubt the successful outcome to the petition owed something to Chaucer's ministrations. What appears to have been an equable session ended sometime before Henry V's departure for France on 10 June. In the meantime, on 30 May, Chaucer and his wife, Maud, had been granted livery of seisin of the manor of Hatfield Peverel (Essex), held in dower until her recent death by Maud's mother. Then, on 8 June, from the Chancery had been issued royal letters patent of *inspeximus* and confirmation ratifying a grant made by Richard Fleming, bishop of Lincoln, as recently as 12 April (and accepted two days later by the dean and chapter), to his predecessor, Philip Repingdon, and the latter's associates, of whom Chaucer was one. The grant, which was to last for Repingdon's life and was presumably in consideration of his resignation of the see in November 1419, was of an annual pension of 500 marks payable from the revenues of the episcopal lordships of Banbury and Dorchester (Oxon.) and Newark (Notts.). Of the lordship of Banbury, Chaucer may well have continued to be steward until Repingdon's resignation, but whether or not he retained the office under Bishop Fleming remains undiscovered. In fact, nothing more of any importance is known of him until after Henry V's death, with which event began the long minority of Henry VI.[21]

In view of the great prospective importance of the first parliament of the new reign, which was summoned at Michaelmas 1422, a month after Henry V's death, and met on 9 November, it was only to be expected that Chaucer, who had not been re-elected to the last parliament of the previous reign (Dec.1421), would now be returned

21   K. B. McFarlane, *England in the Fifteenth Century*, 110; *Rot. Parl.*, iv. 132; *CCR, 1419-22*, 162; *CPR, 1416-22*, 379-80.

once again for Oxfordshire. The parliament was bound to be faced with the task of winding up the late king's affairs, which had weighty financial implications for royal creditors and accountants alike, and also with the even more important business of establishing an acceptable basis for the conduct of royal minority government. With his cousins, Bishop Henry Beaufort and Thomas Beaufort, duke of Exeter, directly involved both as executors with a special responsibility for the administration of Henry V's will and as personal guardians of the infant king, Chaucer can only have had a keen interest in the outcome; and when once the parliament had met, and Humphrey, duke of Gloucester's determined bid for the position of regent had been opposed by the Lords in general, and by Henry Beaufort in particular, that interest doubtless became even more acute. Thanks to that opposition, all Duke Humphrey was able to secure of a distinctive place in the scheme of government now established by parliament was appointment as protector of the realm and chief councillor to the king, offices which, moreover, he was only to occupy in the absence of his elder brother, John, duke of Bedford. Thus was generated a mutual enmity between Gloucester and Henry Beaufort which was to last as long as they lived. There can be no doubt as to which side in the feud Chaucer favoured, either in 1422 or later. But with tempers bound to run high in the parliament of 1422 from the start, it may well have been with a sense of personal relief that Chaucer witnessed the Commons' election of another for the office of Speaker, viz. Roger Flore, a high official of the duchy of Lancaster, who himself had been Speaker previously (three times, indeed). However, as might have been surmised, Chaucer was now no more without friends or acquaintances in the Lower House than in 1421: John Golafre, with whom since May 1420 he had shared an Exchequer lease of the manor of Bradfield (Berks.), had been elected for Berkshire; their co-feoffee of the Stonor family estates, John Warfeld, was again parliamentary burgess for Wallingford; Sir Thomas Brooke, Chaucer's wife's cousin-german was returned for Somerset; and the Cornish knights of the shire were Sir John Arundell of Lanherne and his son and heir, John Arundell esquire of Bideford (Devon), who was Chaucer's wife's brother-in-law.[22]

Doubtless Henry Beaufort's influence was partly involved when, during this parliament of 1422, Chaucer was restored to his former office of chief butler in the Household, and again re-appointed for life. But this renewal was, directly, the result of a petition of the Commons, followed by a special statement of recommendation by the chancellor,

22   *Return of Members of Parliament*, i. 302-3; *CFR, 1413-22*, 338. For Chaucer's wife's kinsmen, see McFarlane, op. cit., 98.

Bishop Langley of Durham, to all the Lords Spiritual and Temporal, and it was therefore 'by authority of parliament' that Chaucer's appointment by Henry IV twenty years before (November 1402) was now ratified, his new letters patent of *Inspeximus* and confirmation first passing the Privy Seal, and then, on 5 December, the Great Seal, in each instance free of payment of any fine. And Chaucer did, in fact, now remain chief butler until his death. He was still, it must be noted, enjoying the custody of the royal manors of Woodstock and Handborough (Oxon.), along with the park at Woodstock; and he also continued to hold the office of havener in Cornwall, soon, early in 1423, paying off arrears of the farm-rent amounting to £240. Nor had he long to wait before, on 3 July following, he was granted the keeping of the manor of Drayton (Hants.) during the minority of the heir, Philip, son of William Pagenham; and, since Philip only obtained livery of his inheritance in 1438, Chaucer's custody lasted, in fact, for the rest of his life.[23]

Although it was not until 16 July 1424 that Henry Beaufort succeeded Bishop Langley as chancellor, it was quite probably due to his powerful influence on affairs that on 25 January previous, during the second parliament of the reign (Oct. 1423 – Feb. 1424), Chaucer had been 'elected' by the lords of the Council, and there and then sworn in, as one of its new members. The fact that the publication of the list of councillors was in response to the final one of a number of requests for information made by the Commons to the Upper House, and that, after a first session of eight weeks, ten days of the second had passed before the few changes made were revealed, rather suggests that the selection of the newcomers had given rise to some difficulty or delay (which is perhaps hardly surprising in view also of the formulation of a fresh set of regulations imposing, by means of more closely defined procedures, a stricter control of the conduct of the Council than had been provided for in 1422). Careful attention was also given to the question of councillors' annual fees, and of deductions for absence, and Chaucer's fee was fixed at £40 a year, reduced by 2 shillings for every day's meeting he missed. It would appear that his conciliar attendances were very infrequent, but evidence ready to hand clearly indicates that he attended the odd meeting in November 1424 and May 1425 (during the first session of the parliament which had met on 30 April), and that he was still a member in March 1427. When, in December 1424, he and Sir John Tiptoft undertook a mission to

23   *Rot. Parl.*, iv. 178; *CPR, 1422-29*, 7; PRO, Accounts Various, E 101/546/6; McFarlane, op. cit., 100; PRO, Exchequer, Receipt Roll, E 703, mem. 14; *PRO, Lists and Indexes*, no. xi. (Foreign Accounts), p. 25.

France, in order to have talks with the duke of Bedford, the regent, and his councillors, it was doubtless in their capacity as members of the English Council, the subject under discussion being 'certain special matters' moving it. In the meantime, in February 1424, shortly after his appointment to the Council, Chaucer had been allowed a royal grant, shared with Thomas Haseley, an Oxfordshire neighbour who was one of the clerks of the Crown in Chancery, of those Burghersh family estates previously held by his wife's late sister Margaret, more recently by her husband, John Arundell of Bideford, who now had also died, the lands to be held in wardship until their son John (Chaucer's wife's nephew) came of age.[24]

Chaucer's appointment to the regency Council apart, it was significant of his still continuing rise in status that Alice, his only child and heir, married, as her second husband, Thomas Montagu, 4th earl of Salisbury, K.G. The date of their marriage is not known. But, unquestionably, they were married by November 1424 when, at a great feast held in Paris to celebrate the wedding of Jean de la Trémouille, Duke Philip of Burgundy is alleged to have insulted the earl by making an attempt upon the virtue of his countess, whom the chronicler writing of the incident described as a very handsome woman, without, however, giving her Christian name. In view of the fact that the earl's first wife, Eleanor (a younger daughter of Thomas Holland, 2nd earl of Kent, a nephew of Richard II), who was still alive in April 1421, had died sometime before June 1424, the countess in Paris in November 1424 can only have been the earl's second wife, Alice Chaucer (now aged twenty).[25] Whenever the marriage occurred, it must surely have taken place in France, for the earl had been engaged in campaigning there since 1417, without ever returning to England in the meantime. (Indeed, it was not until in the first half of 1427 that he did so). A personal triumph for Alice, the marriage may also be considered to have been quite a coup for her father. For the earl of Salisbury had, in the course of the war in France, developed into the most famous and skilful captain on the English side. (Early in 1419 Henry V had made him his lieutenant-general of Lower Normandy, and in 1420 of all Normandy and in Maine.) However, although by the time of his second marriage all had gone well with the earl's military career in France, his ambitions in England had fallen someway short of total success. The elder son of John, the 3rd earl, who, beheaded as a traitor by a mob at Cirencester in January 1400, had then been adjudged in parliament to have

    24   *Rot. Parl.*, iv. 201; *Procs. & Ords. P. C.*, ed. N. H. Nicolas, iii, 155, 157, 163, 169, 266; iv. 263; PRO, Exchequer, Issue Roll, E 403/669/8; *CPR, 1422-29*, 330; *CFR, 1422-30*, 72.
    25   *CCR, 1419-22*, 140; *CFR, 1422-30*, 81.

incurred forfeiture of all save his entailed estates, Thomas had been restored to the comital title and a seat in parliament in 1409, only to have a petition he presented in 1414, for restoration to all his father's lands, met with a refusal, and a similar petition he made in 1421, with the full support of the Commons, granted only in part, he being then recognized as his father's heir, but not heir to the lands his father had held in fee simple (which were still deemed to be forfeit to the Crown). Nor had his first marriage proved to be of much help: in 1400 Eleanor Holland's father had suffered the same fate as her husband's, and when, in 1408, her father's brother and heir, Edmund, 3rd earl of Kent, died without lawful issue, leaving Eleanor and her sisters to succeed him as coheirs, they were so numerous as to make their several purparties of no great value. In contrast, Earl Thomas's marriage to Alice Chaucer, her parents' sole heir to a considerable amount of landed estate, can only have seemed at the time a very profitable step for him to take, at least prospectively. But, then, so it was for Alice too. For with the earl's grants of lands in France, not to mention the spoils of war in ransoms and booty, his overall financial situation had so improved since the time when, in 1417, he had needed to mortgage his estates in order to equip himself for Henry V's second invasion of Normandy, that when he came to make his will, in London on 20 May 1427, he was able to make his wife ample provision for her future: by that testament, of which the Countess Alice was one of the three supervisors, he left her 3,000 marks in gold, 4,000 marks in jewels and other valuables (apart from her trousseau), and, in addition, half of the residue of his moveables once all the other personal and institutional bequests had been met by his executors, *plus*, if possible, an annual income, from the *vicomtés* of Falaise and Exmes (Normandy), of 600 livres tournois (approx. £80-90 sterling). The earl's testament also left a jewel worth 40 marks to his father-in-law, Thomas Chaucer: a modest bequest, but one which suggests that their relationship was at least friendly.[26] There can, of course, hardly be any question but that Chaucer had favoured his daughter's second marriage. It is, however, a not impertinent question to ask, whether his cousin, Henry Beaufort, might not have had something to do with bringing it about. For not only had Beaufort long been (and still was) one of the earl's feoffees, but Alice Montagu, the earl's only child by his first wife had, in or before February 1421, married the bishop's nephew, Richard Neville, first son of Ralph, earl of Westmorland, and his wife Joan Beaufort, the bishop's sister, a marriage perhaps just as likely to have been arranged by the bishop as was to be

26 *DNB*, xiii. 655-8; *Complete Peerage*, xi. 393-5; *The Register of Henry Chichele*, ed. E. F. Jacob, ii. 390-400.

the marriage of his niece Joan (his late brother John's daughter) to James I of Scotland in February 1424 when, whether or not he actually officiated as celebrant in the church of St. Mary Overy in his lordship of Southwark, he entertained the royal couple and guests in the episcopal palace close-by.[27] If Henry Beaufort had arranged these two matches, involving a nephew and a niece, why not a third, involving his cousin Chaucer's daughter? Certainly, Chaucer's connection with Beaufort was still a major factor in his career.

Comparatively little is known of Chaucer's doings in either 1425 or 1426. However, in the circumstances of the bitter quarrel which arose in 1425 between Bishop Beaufort, the chancellor, and his nephew, Duke Humphrey of Gloucester, the protector, a quarrel which, when it flared up that autumn, so endangered the public peace as to cause the chancellor to persuade the duke of Bedford to return from France, it is easy to imagine that the one year ended and the next began with Chaucer (and most other members of the Council) reduced to a state of great perturbation. Only when, before Christmas, Bedford had come home and automatically assumed authority as protector, could steps be taken to reconcile his brother and their uncle. Bedford and Beaufort soon saw eye to eye and, with Gloucester continuing intransigent, then agreed to summon parliament; and, on 7 January 1426, the Chancery issued the writs arranging for parliament to meet on 18 February, not at Westminster (which would be inviting trouble from the Londoners), but at Leicester (in which region pro-Beaufort influences were strong). Two additional peers were summoned, Sir John Tiptoft and Sir Walter Hungerford, both of them friends of Beaufort. Perhaps Gloucester expected support from the Commons who, in the last parliament (April-July 1425), had shown themselves quite disenchanted by the chancellor's mercantile policy. But that support would depend on how the local, principally the county, elections went in the meantime, and doubtless there were some counties where the elections would be to Beaufort's advantage. In the event, this was certainly the case, at least in some measure, in the counties of the middle-Thames valley, Chaucer's own region. He himself, not having sat in the Lower House since 1422, was elected once more for Oxfordshire, and he surely can be regarded as a true friend of the bishop. So may *his* friend, John Golafre, Beaufort's co-feoffee in the Montagu estates, now elected for Berkshire, again for the first time since 1422. And so may, it can reasonably be assumed, Lewis John, another old friend of Chaucer's, elected for Essex, for the first time since 1420; and Richard Wyot, once

27   *CPR, 1416-22*, 108; *Complete Peerage*, xi. 395; L. B. Radford, *Henry Beaufort*, 119-20.

Beaufort's steward, elected for Buckinghamshire, for the first time since 1421. Sir Richard Vernon, who, elected for Derbyshire, again for the first time since 1422, was to be Speaker in the parliament, had close family links with the Beauforts. At Leicester feelings ran so high between the parties that members, ordered not to carry weapons, hid cudgels up their sleeves, hence the sobriquet, the 'parliament of battes'. Beaufort, fulfilling his customary duty as chancellor, opened the parliament, with Bedford acting as the king's commissary (or president). However, when, on 12 March, a specially appointed panel of arbitrators, headed by Archbishop Chichele and Thomas Beaufort, duke of Exeter, at last effected a reconciliation between the protagonists, it was evidently only on the understanding that the chancellor should resign in favour of John Kemp, archbishop of York (who, so far, was on good terms with Gloucester), and that John Stafford, bishop of Bath and Wells (a friend of Gloucester's), treasurer of the Exchequer since 1422, should be replaced by Lord Hungerford, the latter to be succeeded as steward of the Household by Lord Tiptoft. On 20 March, soon after these various arrangements had been perfected, the session ended. Although a second session lasted from 29 April to 1 June, the long discontinuance (since 1421) of grants of direct taxation persisted. Indeed, all that the Commons had done in this connection, apart from renewing the subsidies on trade, was to have agreed that the Council might borrow up to £40,000 before midsummer 1427. So far as Chaucer's activities during the parliament are concerned, all that the records reveal is that on 26 February he had obtained a grant of the marriage of Joan, one of the daughters of the late Sir John Drayton of Nuneham (Oxon.), on payment of 100 marks to the Exchequer, with Thomas Haseley, clerk of the Crown in Chancery, again figuring as a surety. During the following summer, however, by letters patent of 23 July, he was appointed to serve, along with John Golafre, on a commission set up to raise loans, as parliament had authorized, in Oxfordshire and Berkshire.[28]

Although, on 14 May 1426, during the second session of the Leicester parliament, Bishop Beaufort had requested the Council for leave to go on a long-postponed pilgrimage, and ten days later Pope Martin V had promoted him to the Sacred College, it was not until 19 March 1427 that, along with Bedford, Beaufort crossed from Dover to Calais, there to receive investiture in his new dignity within a week of

---

28   *Return of M. P. s*, i. 310-11; *CPR, 1422-9*, 330; 354. Sometime after the death of Sir John Drayton, Chaucer had paid £400 to his widow, Isabel, for the manor of Nuneham (Oxon.), which was in dispute in 1452 between Chaucer's daughter Alice and Drew Barantyn and others (*CCR, 1447-54*, 346).

their arrival (25 March). Thomas Chaucer accompanied them. In view of this intended absence from England, he had procured royal letters of attorney on 14 and 18 February; and, moreover, by letters patent dated at Canterbury on 8 March, he and Richard Wydeville, Bedford's chamberlain, and Richard Bokeland, the treasurer of Calais, were appointed members of the *quorum* of a commission charged with the preparation of a rental of Crown property and rights at Calais.[29] From here, the cardinal, who had been appointed as papal legate in Germany, Hungary and Bohemia, went on to lead a futile crusade against the Bohemian Hussites. Chaucer, however, had returned to England. He was presumably back in time to secure, on 8 July, a share in a lease by the Exchequer of estates at Shutford (Oxon.) which, following the death of Sir William Birmingham, the tenant of the bishop of Lincoln, were in Crown custody because of a vacancy in the see; Chaucer's partners in the lease, which they were to hold until Sir William's son and heir came of age, were John Danvers of Banbury and Robert Danvers, common serjeant of the city of London. He had certainly returned home by 25 September when he was re-elected to the parliament summoned to meet on 13 October, his companion as shire-knight being his former ward, Thomas Stonor. His friend, John Golafre, was re-elected for Berkshire, and his wife's cousins, Sir Thomas Brooke and Richard Cheddar esq., came up from Somerset. For Wallingford, where Chaucer was still constable of the castle and steward of the honour, was returned Stonor's receiver, John Warfeld, along with Chaucer's feoffee and his deputy-butler at Bridgwater, William Bord, who had last sat, for Taunton, in 1421.[30]

In this parliament, which ran to two sessions (13 Oct. − 8 Dec. 1427, 27 Jan. − 25 March 1428), there was no shortage of embarrassments for, and within, the king's government; and, in the first session, the adverse state of its finances was also a major source of difficulty. There is now no evidence to suggest that Chaucer was still a member of the Council. But, certainly, his son-in-law, the earl of Salisbury, had joined it, not long after his return from France early in 1427. And he too, like Chaucer's cousin the cardinal, was now deeply concerned about his position as a royal creditor. So much so, in fact, that he was party to two important petitions for repayment of debts for which the authority of parliament, which required the assent of the Commons, was requested.[31] The first asked that the earl and other creditors should, before Michaelmas 1428, be furnished with adequate

29   *DKR*, xlviii. 247-8; *CPR, 1422-29*, 404.
30   *CFR, 1422-30*, 132; *Return of M. P. s*, i. 312-4.
31   *Rot. Parl.*, iv. 317-8, 320-1.

securities for their repayment of debts amounting to £24,000, and the earl, evidently (as the only creditor actually named in the petition), was the principal creditor involved. But, then, governmental finance was currently bedevilled by the long-deferred administration of Henry V's will, and it was doubtless trouble with the late king's executors as well as in the Exchequer that now led Salisbury to combine also with the duke of Gloucester (with him alone) in presenting to parliament a joint-petition, in which they demanded an equitable settlement of their claims for repayment of what each was owed for his military services to Henry V in 1415 and later. Both petitions met with a favourable response, which was doubtless a matter for Chaucer's satisfaction, at least so far as his son-in-law was concerned. And that, in the second session of the parliament, Beaufort's enemy, Gloucester, was compelled by the Lords to "toe the line" and, contrary to his inclinations, re-affirm his acceptance of the limitations placed on his powers as protector by the parliament of 1422, no doubt left Chaucer equally gratified. (The Lords' demands on Gloucester were subscribed, *inter alios*, by the earl of Salisbury.) The little that is known of Chaucer's doings during the rest of 1428, however, bears no relation to these matters of high importance for his kinsmen: on 13 May he was again made a commissioner for the raising of loans for the Crown in Oxfordshire and Berkshire; then on 8 July, he was appointed to help enquire into cases of insurrection, felony and trespass in the same two counties; and on 3 October he was included in a commission of oyer and terminer following an assault at Taunton by Sir William Haryngton of Orchardleigh (Som.) on Richard Cheddar, Chaucer's wife's cousin, who had sat in the last parliament.[32]

By this time, Chaucer's son-in-law, Salisbury, had returned to France (in July 1428), and his cousin, the cardinal, to England (in the following month). The former's main engagement now became the siege of Orleans, of which he took command on 12 October. But not for long: severely wounded on 27 October, he died at Meung-sur-Loire on 3 November.[33] Beaufort's main object, now that he was back home, was to raise funds and recruit an army with which to renew his crusade against Bohemia, and to exploit his papal legateship to that end. The office of legate itself again landed him in a sea of troubles, and before long it was once more questioned whether he, as now cardinal and legate, should retain the bishopric of Winchester. Regarding the crusade, the Council gave him to understand that he could not have

32   ibid., 326-7; *CPR, 1422-29*, 481, 495, 549. In the spring of 1427 Salisbury had been prepared to assist Gloucester in an expedition to Hainault against Philip of Burgundy, but this was for reasons of personal enmity, and in any case the proposed expedition came to nothing.

33   Salisbury's body was brought back to England and buried in the Augustinian priory

both men and money; and when he had raised his army, its number cut by the Council to roughly half its originally intended size, it was only to be induced on 1 July 1429 to allow the force to be diverted for service in France where, after the raising of the siege of Orleans in May, such further reverses had befallen English arms as to have left the duke of Bedford in urgent need of re-inforcements from home. Early in July the cardinal crossed to Calais, and on the 25th joined the regent in Paris. Only a week or so before (17 July) Charles VII had been crowned at Rheims. When, late in October, Beaufort next returned to England, it was to assist at the coronation of the nearly eight-years-old Henry of Windsor, which took place on 6 November.

What part Chaucer had played in his cousin's activities between the latter's return to England in August 1428 and his departure for France in July 1429 (or, indeed, what else he had done in that time, save as a justice of oyer and terminer in Somerset in the autumn of 1428) is obscure. However, parliament having been summoned on 12 July 1429 to meet on 13 October, and then re-summoned for 22 September, Chaucer and his former ward, Thomas Stonor, were both re-elected for Oxfordshire on 25 August; and on 6 September, Stonor's receiver, John Warfeld, was re-elected for Wallingford, and, next day, Chaucer's friend, John Golafre, for Berkshire.[34] This parliament, too, ran to two sessions (22 Sept. − 20 Dec. 1429, 16 Jan. − 23 Feb. 1430). Highly satisfactory to Beaufort and his supporters must have been the decision that Gloucester's protectorate should automatically end with the king's coronation, likewise the Lords' resolution that Beaufort should actually be encouraged to attend meetings of the Council (unless matters affecting the papacy were to be deliberated); moreover, the Commons, when making the second of their two grants of a tenth and fifteenth in the last fortnight of the first session, specially commended the cardinal, presumably for his loans amounting to £24,000 in the course of the year. Fortified by the first grants of tenths and fifteenths conceded by parliament during his reign thus far, the king was enabled to leave England on 23 April (St. George's Day) 1430, with a retinue of a size calculated to hearten Bedford and his hard-pressed forces in Normandy, and accompanied by councillors and other nobles, Beaufort among

---

at Bisham (Berks.), in a chapel for the building of which (at an anticipated cost of 500 marks) he had provided in his will, and where he wished his wives, Eleanor and Alice (if *she* would have it so), to be buried with him. Probate was granted by Archbishop Chichele on 11 December 1428, and the executors received powers of administration on 7 February 1429 (*Chichele Register*, loc. cit.).

34   *Return of M. P. s*, i. 315-6.

them. Meanwhile, on 25 November 1429, during the first session of the recent parliament, Chaucer had been party, as a feoffee of his daughter Alice's first husband, Sir John Phelip, to a 'final concord' in the Court of Common Pleas at Westminster, by which the reversion of certain of Phelip's estates held by Alice for life was sold to Richard Beauchamp, earl of Warwick (the king's 'magister'), and his feoffees. Then, on 6 February 1430, when parliament was still in session, he was made one of a special panel of justices of oyer and terminer in Berkshire, regarding all treasons and felonies. Parliament had been dissolved only a week when, on 1 March, he was appointed to a similar commission set up to deal with charges of extortion and oppression in Herts. and Bucks. laid against Sir John Cheyne of Drayton Beauchamp (Bucks.), a riotous character and justifiably suspected of Lollardy, whose return to the previous parliament as shire-knight for Bucks. had been so irregular a proceeding on the part of the sheriff as to have been quashed by justices of assize early in the parliament's first session. Whatever difficulties arose, the commission needed to be renewed on 6 July following, when Chaucer was re-appointed.[35]

During Henry VI's absence in France, the Council, headed by Gloucester who had been left behind as *custos regni*, called parliament together only once. Summoned on 27 November 1430, it met on 12 January 1431 and sat until 20 March. The election for Oxfordshire of Chaucer and Stonor (of the former for the fourth time running, of the latter for the third) only took place on the eve of parliament's assembly, and that of Warfeld, Stonor's receiver, at Wallingford, on the opening day itself.[36] Although two more parliaments were to meet before Chaucer's death, this one proved to be his last. (He was now well into his sixties.) The cardinal, too, having been prompted by discussions with Duke Philip of Burgundy (his nephew by marriage) to press for greater English financial assistance for the war or, failing this, to support papal initiatives for a negotiated peace, came from France to attend the parliament. So also, summoned for the first time since his succession to the earldom of Suffolk in 1415, did William de la Pole. Suffolk, having taken part at the siege of Harfleur (but not at Agincourt where his elder brother, Michael, was killed), had been on active service in France continuously from 1417 until now, save for a brief visit to England with Henry V early in 1421 (in the course of which he was elected K.G.). In the meantime, in 1425, he had been appointed

35   *Feet of Fines, Dorset*, 306; *CPR, 1429-36*, 70, 81, 75. For the disputed election in Bucks. in 1427, and for particulars of Sir John Cheyne, see J. S. Roskell, *The Commons in the Parliament of 1422* (Manchester, 1954), 17-9.

36   *Return of M. P. s*, i. 318-9.

lieutenant-general of Lower Normandy and the Côtentin, serving also at that time with the earl of Salisbury as constable of his army; in 1428 he had again been Salisbury's companion-in-arms on the campaign leading up to the siege of Orleans where, immediately after Salisbury's death, he was appointed to the chief command; forced by Joan of Arc to abandon the siege in May 1429, he was himself besieged at Jargeau until, on 12 June, compelled to surrender; then, on 15 March 1430, following his release after payment of a ransom of £20,000, he had been appointed to the command of the English forces at Caen and in the Côtentin, no doubt, however, relinquishing this post for good on his return to England. Quite possibly even now pessimistic as to the eventual outcome of the war, he is likely to have been ready to support the cardinal, in the parliament of 1431, in his policy of peace by negotiation. But, if so, there was now another basis for such support, one in which Chaucer himself can only have been directly involved: Suffolk's marriage to Chaucer's daughter, Alice, the widowed countess of Salisbury. (Alice was now about 26 years old, some eight years younger than the earl.) When precisely the marriage took place is not known, but certainly the betrothal stage had been passed by 11 November 1430 when, presumably before the earl's return from France, Alice was granted a royal licence under the Great Seal to marry him. This marital alliance probably gave additional encouragement to Suffolk to work for peace alongside of the cardinal; and, although the parliament of 1431 voted a series of grants as necessary for the continuance of the war, both Lords and Commons, having considered 'the birden of the werre' and 'howe behoffull therfore the Pees', advised negotiations to that end with France as well as Scotland and Castile, proposing the cardinal as best suited to undertake the necessary diplomacy, along with Bedford and Gloucester. Beaufort now returned to France to witness the end of Joan of Arc's trial at Rouen in May, and eventually, on 16 December, in Notre Dame in Paris, to 'hallow' Henry of Windsor at his crowning. In February 1432 the king was back in England, by which time, on 30 November 1431, Chaucer's son-in-law, Suffolk, had been formally admitted as a member of the Council.[37]

Of what Chaucer himself had been doing in the meantime, throughout the remainder of the year after the parliament of January-March 1431, little is known. On 26 March, within a week of parliament's dissolution, he was appointed, as in the past, to a commission ordered to raise Crown loans in Oxfordshire and Berkshire.

37   *DNB*, xvi. 50-56; *CPR, 1429-36*, 86; *Rot. Parl.* iv. 371.

Otherwise, so far as records reveal, more directly personal concerns occupied his attention. For instance, on 7 November 1431 he secured the wardship and marriage of Eleanor, daughter and heir of Sir William Moleyns who, at the time of her father's death at the siege of Orleans, had herself been with the army, although then only two years old. It was now thought by the Council only right that Chaucer should have the child's wardship, especially because it had been at the request of Lord Hungerford, the treasurer, that in May 1429 he had arranged for her to be escorted back to England from the Loire by 'men of armes, archers and womman'. With the grant came, of course, control, for the duration of the ward's minority, of such of her lands as were not held by dowagers, viz. the whole manors of Henley-on-Thames, Broughton Poggs, and Aston in Bampton (Oxon.), and of Brill, Beachendon in Waddesdon, Stoke Poges, Ilmer, Aston Mullins, Datchet and Great Pollicott (Bucks.). Although said not to exceed £30 a year in value, they must have been worth much more, for Chaucer was ready to pay 500 marks for the grant, 400 marks at once and the rest within a year of the ward's having reached the age of fourteen. Thomas Haseley again, this time with John Fortescue, serjeant-at-law (the future C.J.K.B.), stood surety. In the meantime, ever since 17 July 1431, the date of the death of his wife's kinswoman, Philippa, widow of Edward, duke of York, Chaucer can only have been busily occupied as one of her two most important executors, the other being Sir John Cornwall (Henry VI's great-uncle by marriage, who was to be raised to the peerage as Lord Fanhope in the following year). The dowager duchess's will, dated at the castle of Carisbrooke (Isle of Wight) on 12 March 1431, had appointed John, lord Tiptoft, as overseer, but a special responsibility 'to aid and perform the will of the testament' was laid upon Cornwall and Chaucer, and the latter, in recognition of his involvement, was to receive the handsome bequest of 100 marks. Probate was allowed by Archbishop Chichele at Lambeth on 13 November, and by the end of the month the executors had been discharged.[38]

When, on 25 February 1432, four days after Henry VI's return from France, parliament was next summoned to meet (on 12 May), the country was already entering upon a time of serious political crisis, one in which some of Chaucer's kinsmen and friends were implicated. At Gloucester's instigation, Beaufort was likely to be impeached of

38   *CPR, 1429-36*, 127, 156; *Procs. & Ords. P. C.*, iv. 98; Eleanor Moleyns had been born on 11 June 1426 at Stoke Poges where she was baptized, Alice (Chaucer), countess of Salisbury, being one of her godmothers. By November 1430 Thomas Haseley was Chaucer's deputy butler in the ports of Chichester and Shoreham. K. B. McFarlane, op. cit. 99; *Chichele Register*, ii. 457-8.

treason; moreover, on the day of issue of the parliamentary writs of summons, Lord Tiptoft was dismissed from the office of steward of the Household and Bishop Alnwick of Norwich from the keepership of the Privy Seal, and on the following day (26 Feb.) occurred the dismissal of the chancellor, Archbishop Kemp, and of the treasurer, Lord Hungerford, all by the contrivance of Gloucester who replaced these officials by men who supported him. How tense was the situation is indicated by the fact that when parliament was about to meet, seven lay peers, including the only other duke (Norfolk), five of the six earls, including Chaucer's son-in-law (Suffolk), and Lord Cromwell, who had recently been superseded as king's chamberlain, were ordered not to bring up over-large retinues to Westminster. On the whole, parliament went well for Gloucester, rather unsatisfactorily for his opponents, not least for the cardinal who, although cleared of imputations of malfeasance, owed what influence on affairs he retained to his ability to make fresh loans to the Crown and, temporarily, to forego repayment of previous advances. In view of the circumstances in which parliament had met, it is perhaps surprising that (as noted above) Chaucer was not re-elected as a knight of the shire. Indeed, of all his identifiable friends, only John Warfeld was returned (as usual for Wallingford). In view of the turn of events, however, it is not at all surprising that, during the remainder of the year, the government, as so largely reconstituted, had little recourse to his services locally. The only special royal commission to come his way was a commission of oyer and terminer regarding excessively numerous illegal assemblies in Berkshire, to which he was appointed on 29 August 1432. The commission was headed by Chaucer's son-in-law, Suffolk, who, on the very day of its appointment, as it happened, was given the custody of Charles, duke of Orleans, a charge he was to retain until 11 November 1433.[39]

When the next parliament met in July 1433, it was again in an atmosphere of disquiet, but for other reasons than in 1432. The Anglo-Burgundian alliance, upon which Henry V and, until recently, Bedford had set such store, had begun to open at the seams; and the French, reading the signs aright, were showing themselves reluctant seriously to consider such preliminary moves towards a diplomatic settlement as the English were now ready to make. And not even Bedford's presence in parliament, for the first time for seven years, was able to move the estates to vote supplies sufficient to restore the financial stability of the government, let alone to provide funds with which the deteriorating military situation in France might be redressed.

39   *CPR, 1429-36*, 218; *Complete Peerage*, xi. 395.

So far as political stability at home was concerned, it was something that, two days before the first session of the parliament ended on 13 August, Lord Cromwell was appointed treasurer of the Exchequer, and that, three days before the second session ended with parliament's dissolution on 21 December, Bedford agreed to remain in England as head of the king's government. And doubtless much to Chaucer's personal satisfaction was his son-in-law Suffolk's appointment during the year (certainly by August) to the stewardship of the royal Household, a position of real importance now that Henry of Windsor was fast growing up. But Chaucer's own career was now drawing to a close. In 1433 he was appointed to no local royal commission, save that on 10 December he was authorized, along with Thomas Haseley, who was now his feoffee-to-uses, and John Warfeld, who was again M.P. for Wallingford, as overseer of the bailiffs of the borough in respect of their collection and administration of pontage-dues. (Report had been made that the town's bridge over the Thames was in such a state of disrepair that passengers and horses had been injured, and carts damaged.) Then, on 26 February 1434, he was once more charged (with John Golafre and the sheriff) to raise Crown loans in Oxfordshire and Berkshire. In May following he was one among the many Oxfordshire notables and gentry required, in accordance with a ruling made in the 1433 parliament, to take the oath not to 'maintain' persons who had broken or otherwise put in jeopardy the king's peace, an oath administered, county by county, throughout England. Some two months later, on 6 July, he was included in a commission set up to enquire into cases of concealment of royal fiscal rights, and into financial abuses generally, over the whole region of the west Midlands, as well as in Oxfordshire and Berkshire. If Chaucer acted at all, it was most probably only in the latter area. This commission proved to be his last.[40] And three days after its issue he received his last acquisition by royal grant: on 9 July he obtained, for the duration of the minority of his ward, Eleanor Moleyns, the custody of her manor of Addington (Bucks.) in return for a rent payable to the Exchequer on terms to be agreed with the treasurer of the Exchequer before Easter 1435. However, judging from the fact that he had already, on 18 June previous, surrendered the patents by which he held the offices of constable of the castle of Wallingford and steward of the honours of Wallingford and St. Valery and the Chiltern hundreds, in order that a grant in survivorship might be made to him and his son-in-law, the earl of Suffolk, it would appear that he was now in failing health. And, in fact, five months later to the

40   *CPR, 1429-36*, 330, 354, 395, 426.

day, 18 November 1434, he died. He was buried in the chancel of his manor church at Ewelme.[41]

Chaucer's widow, Maud, survived until 4 May 1437, by when she had arranged for a memorial in the form of a brass of very conventional design, representing Thomas armed in the plate-armour of the day and herself in widow's weeds, to be inlaid on their tomb-chest. In the meantime, on 30 November 1434, no fewer than eight escheators (Oxon. and Berks., Bucks., Hants., Essex, Suffolk, Cambs., Lincs., and London) had been ordered to enquire into the estates Chaucer had held in their respective bailwicks. Not until 12 July 1435, however, were the escheators most heavily burdened (in Oxon. and Bucks.) ordered to give livery of seisin of Chaucer's local lands to his sole heir, the countess of Suffolk, and her husband; who, it was ordered on the following day, were to be present when the same officials made assignment of the widow's dower. Chaucer's executors were to be busy for much longer still, but were evidently not embarrassed for want of funds, being able in the spring of 1436 to provide the king's government, for the furnishing of a fresh expedition to France, with a loan of £200, an individual contribution in answer to a general appeal only exceeded by that of Archbishop Chichele of Canterbury.[42]

As regards Thomas Chaucer's posterity, it is a story of both good and bad fortune. But good fortune at first: for when Thomas's cousin the cardinal, having achieved firm control of the government following Henry VI's attainment of his majority in 1437, virtually retired in 1443 (four years before he died), it was his son-in-law, Suffolk, who took over, certainly *then* becoming 'the priviest of the King's counsel'. As steward of the Household until December 1446, and then as Lord Great Chamberlain of England, Suffolk lorded it over the court. In the country at large, however, he eventually became as unpopular as powerful. This was partly because of his open pursuit of a policy of self-aggrandisement, in the course of which he so exploited the king's characteristic indulgence as to obtain promotion first (in 1444) to the rank of marquess, and then in 1448) to a dukedom; partly because of the failure of the war with France, but especially on account of the sacrifices of French territory which, after his negotiation of Henry VI's marriage to Margaret of Anjou, he was believed to have countenanced in aid of a permanent peace. So futile in the end was his diplomacy that the loss of most of Normandy in 1449 led directly to his impeachment for treason by the Commons in January 1450 and, when the king let

41   *CFR, 1430-37*, 206; *CPR, 1429-36*, 346; H. A. Napier, op. cit., 44.
42   *CPR, 1430-37*, 216, 239-40; *CCR, 1429-35*, 339; *Procs. & Ords*. P. C., iv. 323; Oxford History Society, vol. xxiv (*Three Oxfordshire Parishes*), 27.

him off with banishment, indirectly to his murder off Dover on 2 May following, when on his way into exile. Chaucer's daughter Alice, who had enjoyed great social advantages from her husband's rise to power (she was, for example, the principal lady in the great retinue which escorted Margaret of Anjou to England in 1445), soon felt the repercussions of his disgrace: she was one of those who, within a month of Suffolk's murder, were denounced by the Kentish rebels under Jack Cade, and who then, at their instance, were formally indicted of treason and extortion before a court which met in London Guildhall early in July; and when parliament met in November following, the Commons, not content with petitioning for her late husband's attainder, also demanded her immediate removal from court, along with, *inter alios*, her second-cousin, Edmund Beaufort, duke of Somerset. The Commons' first petition was rejected by the king and, so far as Alice and Somerset were concerned, the second effectively as well. But that, before so long, the dowager's influence was somewhat diminished would appear to be indicated by what befell her eldest son John, whom she had borne to Suffolk in 1442.[43] Suffolk had brought about John's marriage to his ward, Margaret Beaufort, daughter and heir of Somerset's deceased elder brother and, despite the Commons' insinuation in their impeachment of the duke that, in so doing, he was 'presuming' upon Margaret's being 'next enheritable to the Crowne' in the event of 'lakke of issue' to the king, the alliance was confirmed in August 1450 (when a dispensation allowed the couple to remain in marriage). Even so, early in 1453, the marriage was dissolved, and, on 24 March following, Margaret's wardship and marriage were granted to Henry VI's half-brothers, Edmund and Jasper Tudor, the recently created earls of Richmond and Pembroke, respectively, quite possibly, even then, with a view to her marrying one or the other. (She was, in fact, married to Edmund by 1455.) Alice was then given the wardship of her son's inheritance (her own dower apart) as from Easter 1453, together with his marriage. But whether or not this grant succeeded in mollifying any resentment Alice may have felt at the dissolution of John's marriage to Margaret Beaufort, she evidently chose to keep her options open; and it was not until February 1458 that arrangements were made for him to marry Elizabeth, the second daughter of Richard, duke of York. Possibly by then Alice was realizing the necessity of having a foot in both Lancastrian and Yorkist camps. However this may

43   *Complete Peerage*, xii. Pt. 1, 443-8; *DNB*, xvi. 50-6. For the later career of the Dowager Duchess Alice and the life of her son John, duke of Suffolk, see the comprehensive account in the article by J. A. F. Thomson, entitled 'John de la Pole, duke of Suffolk' in *Speculum*, vol. LIV (1979), pp. 528-42.

be, this second marriage of John's was soon to bring advantages for both his mother and himself: as dowager duchess, Alice lived securely until her death in May 1475;[44] and John was brother-in-law to Edward IV and Richard III, and, soon after the accession of Henry VII (John's first wife Margaret's son by Edmund Tudor), uncle by marriage to his queen (Elizabeth of York). How soon the young duke of Suffolk joined the Yorkist side is unclear, but certainly he had done so by the spring of 1461. (There is, indeed, reason to believe that he took part in the battle of St. Albans in February that year and, soon after Edward IV's accession, fought again at Ferrybridge and Towton.) Admittedly, he temporised during the Lancastrian Re-adeption of 1470-1; but he then soon regained Edward IV's trust, witness the assignment of Henry VI's widow, Queen Margaret, to the custody of him and his mother at Wallingford in January 1472, and his election that same year as knight of the Garter. In 1483, following Edward IV's death, Suffolk supported his other brother-in-law, Richard, in his seizure of the throne, and if he himself, with his evidently limited capacities, derived no special benefit from this usurpation, his eldest son John was soon to do so. The latter, Thomas Chaucer's great-grandson, created earl of Lincoln by Edward IV in 1467, was now not only confirmed by Richard III in that title, but soon afterwards, on the decease of the king's son in April 1484, was designated as his heir-presumptive. However, Bosworth Field, where the younger John stood by his royal uncle, put paid to the realization of that ambition, and, having rebelled against Henry VII on the part of Lambert Simnel, he fell at the battle of Stoke in 1487. Suffolk himself, however, retained Henry's trust until his death in the summer of 1492. The second of his sons, Edmund, who succeeded him in the dukedom only to accept demotion to the status of earl in the following year (Feb. 1493), was to be attainted for alleged rebellion in the parliament of 1504 and, after a period of exile followed by imprisonment in the Tower from March 1506, beheaded on Henry VIII's orders in May 1513. Whereupon, his youngest brother, Richard, who, also attainted in

---

44   Alice was buried alone, close to her father and mother, in the chancel of Ewelme church, in a splendid canopied tomb, 'under the finest alabaster effigy of our period' (K. B. McFarlane). Adjacent to the church, she and Suffolk had, in 1437, founded the almshouses, the inmates of which were to attend the services in the church. The royal licence dated 3 July that year, for which the founders paid 250 marks, allowed the almshouses to be endowed with lands etc. worth 100 marks a year (*CPR, 1436-41*, 80). Thomas Chaucer, as lord of the manor of Donnington (Berks.), had been patron of Christ's Hospital in Abingdon, founded there in 1393 by his predecessor in the title, Sir Richard Abberbury, and endowed with the manor of Iffley (Oxon.); and he was a member of the Abingdon gild of St. Cross, which in 1441 was to build the Long Alley Almshouses of the Hospital. Such charitableness ran in the family: the perhaps best known of all English almshouses, that of St. Cross at Winchester, was enlarged and re-endowed by Chaucer's cousin, Bishop Beaufort (*Oxoniensia*, vol. 5, p. 93).

1504, was now in service with Louis XII of France, not only styled himself duke of Suffolk, but claimed the English crown, supported in this by both Louis XII and his successor Francis I, by whose side he died fighting at the battle of Pavia in 1525. These three sons of Thomas Chaucer's grandson John were not the latter's only sons, but not long afterwards, about 1539, the male line of the De la Poles became extinct, and with it Thomas Chaucer's descendants.

NOTE

Regarding Thomas Chaucer's career in the early years of Henry VI's reign, the following additional facts should be noted:

1   Wallingford castle, of which Chaucer had been constable ever since 1399, was, in the 1420s, occasionally used as a residence by the child-king and his mother, Queen Katherine. Indeed, on 8 May 1428, the royal council specified Wallingford and Hertford castles as most suitable for Henry to occupy in the summer months, and Windsor and Berkhamsted castle during the winter (*Procs. and Ords. P.C.,* III. 295).

2   Queen Katherine drew a fraction of her annual income in dower from the honors of Wallingford and St Valery, of which Chaucer was steward, and also received, without prejudice to Chaucer's own grant from this other source, a portion of the fee-farm of the borough of Wallingford (*Rot. Parl.,* IV, 184, 203).

9

WILLIAM STOURTON OF STOURTON

I

THE English parliament began its history as an occasion when the King met the magnates of his realm, prelates and lay barons, for the discussion of royal business which to some extent was also theirs. Parliament only came to include, as a matter of course, elected knights of the shire, citizens and burgesses—the Commons, that is—about the beginning of Edward III's reign (in 1327). It is not easy to punctuate the development by which these representative elements combined to form the Lower House. But a significant point in this amalgamation was reached at the end of this Edward's long reign when, during the "Good Parliament" of 1376, the Commons for the first time chose a continuing Speaker: one of their own number whose duty it was to propose, on behalf of them all, to the King and Lords, their views about taxes, their petitions, and other matters. A royal instruction to the Commons to elect a Speaker and his formal acceptance by the King, once he had been chosen, soon became conventional items on the formal agenda at the opening of every parliament.

Those among the Commons who represented counties were, as individuals, generally much more important socially, and also, collectively, more influential politically in parliament, than those who sat for the towns, although the latter outnumbered them. That this was so is illustrated by the way in which the Commons' choice for the Speaker's office fell upon a knight of the shire and not a burgess. This was invariably the custom down to 1533. It had persisted until then in face of the fifteenth century development whereby so many country gentlemen came to sit in parliament for their local boroughs as to afford an even numerical preponderance among the Commons to members of their class, which in turn had the effect of blurring the line of division between knights and burgesses.

Originally, it had been officially intended that the knights of the shire elected to parliament should be actually knights by rank and even following the profession of arms. Locally, however, this principle was never strictly adhered to. There were many men of substance who did not assume the degree of knight, although able and liable to do so. And among such were those who would willingly sit in parliament for their own county, often quite frequently, or even for another county in which they had lands or other concerns and in which they disposed influence. William Stourton, father of the first Baron Stourton of Stourton and ancestor (in the direct male line) of the present representative of this peer, was one of this sort. He was elected as knight of the shire to certainly no fewer than six early fifteenth century parliaments in the course of a dozen years, and for three counties in all; firstly he sat for Somerset in the parliaments of January 1401, September 1402, and January 1404; then, for Wiltshire in that of October 1407; and, finally, for Dorset in those of January 1410 and May 1413[1]. All of these sessions took place at Westminster, except in 1407 when parliament met at Gloucester, and all, except the latest, during the reign of Henry IV. It was in the parliament of May 1413, the first of Henry V's reign, that Stourton acted as Speaker for the Commons.

To this parliament of May 1413 it came about that as many as three former Speakers were elected, including the Speaker in the last three proper parliaments of

---

The following abbreviations have been used in the footnotes:
  CPR=Calendar of Patent Rolls.
  CCR=Calendar of Close Rolls.
  CFR=Calendar of Fine Rolls.
  Rot. Parl.=Rotuli Parliamentorum (Record Commission).
  P.R.O.=Public Record Office.
  H.M.C.=Historical Manuscripts Commission.
1 *The Official Return of Members of Parliament,* i. 261, 263, 266, 273, 274, 278.

Henry IV (Thomas, the son of Geoffrey Chaucer the poet). It did not often so happen. But, even when it did, it was just as likely as not that the Commons would pass over a former Speaker in favour of a man with no previous experience of the Chair. It was, however, only very rarely that the Commons elected as Speaker one with no previous parliamentary experience. Stourton (as we have seen) certainly had a considerable first-hand knowledge of recent parliaments. Moreover, he had been connected with the King when he was Prince of Wales, very probably in the administration of his Principality and in his Duchy of Cornwall too. And his re-appointment in 1413 as J.P. in Wiltshire, Somerset and Cornwall, suggests that he still enjoyed Henry of Monmouth's confidence now that he was King. In 1413, moreover, he was a man with influential friends at Court: he was well-acquainted with Sir Walter Hungerford, a Wiltshire neighbour of his who, himself now elected to parliament for that county, had lately been appointed by Henry V as Chief Steward of his Duchy of Lancaster south of Trent; and he was also friendly with Sir William Hankford who had been promoted by the new King to be the doyen of the English legal profession as Chief Justice of the King's Bench. Stourton was himself a lawyer, with the status of apprentice-at-law. The day had passed when he was retained as counsel to the Duchy of Lancaster. But it is very likely that in 1413 he was still Recorder of Bristol (as he certainly had been a few years earlier) and also counsel to the Dean and Chapter of Wells and to the civic authorities at Salisbury.

A demand in so many places for his legal and administrative services suggests that Stourton was professionally useful and competent, and that he could be trusted to do what was required of him. But his failure to rise higher as a lawyer or as an administrative official also implies a certain mediocrity. It even seems that his Speakership in 1413 was something of a disappointment. What happened to curtail his occupation of the Chair—for cut short it was—is obscure. Before the end of the brief session Stourton agreed, it seems, to a particular royal demand in a way which aroused doubts among the Commons of his reliability. Whether the illness which (in the record of the parliament) is expressly said to have kept him in bed and occasioned his retirement, was either real or merely convenient, cannot be said; but it is possible that Stourton's infirmity was political (from the Commons' point of view) as well as physical. It is at least worth noting that the man who followed him as Speaker (John Doreward) was he who had led the Commons' protest against Stourton's action which, they alleged, had been done without their authority and assent. The question has surely some general constitutional significance: if the Commons could reject a Speaker, once formally accepted by the King, for having acted *ultra vires* and elect another in his stead, it suggests that the Commons' control of their Speaker in this period was greater than some parliamentary historians have been prepared to admit. And if they could then elect to succeed the first Speaker one who had been party to the objections against him, it suggests that the Commons' right to elect their Speaker was conducted with a greater measure of freedom than, again, some parliamentary historians have been ready to allow. To local historians, however, the main interest attaching to Stourton's Speakership maybe arises out of the fact that he is the only knight of the shire for Dorset (indeed, the only member of parliament for any constituency in this county) ever to have occupied that office.

II

By the time of William de Stourton's generation, his family had been in possession of its main holding at Stourton (in the south-west corner of Wiltshire) for something like two-and-a-half centuries. Almost certainly the Robert de Stourton who in 1166 held 3 knights' fees there (as tenant of the Lovels of Castle Cary) was the direct ancestor of the later Stourtons. William Stourton himself held the manor and advowson of Stourton at his death in 1413 as tenant of the manor of Castle Cary, which was then held by Alice, daughter and heir of Richard Lord St. Maur[1]. The Stourton family had come to have estates in Somerset also, including lands at Preston Plucknett where John Stourton, William's younger brother, lived after their father's death. But otherwise the family holdings do not appear to have been considerable and, although he was his father's heir, most of William Stourton's lands seem to have been held by him in right of his wife (whom he married before 1398): Elizabeth,

---

1 *The Complete Peerage*, XII, part 1, 296 *et seq.*; R. C. Hoare, *The Modern History of South Wiltshire*, i, 49.

daughter and heir of John Moigne of Maddington (Wilts.) and Easton (Essex) and his wife Joan, daughter of John Belvale.

The Moigne property which came by this marriage into the ownership of William Stourton was quite substantial. Within easy reach of Stourton itself, he acquired estates in south-west Wiltshire in Maiden Bradley and Hill Deverill, further to the east property in Maddington and Little Langford, and then a solidly compact group of lands (between Westbury and Devizes) in the townships of West Ashton, Steeple Ashton, Marston, Bulkington, Hinton, Poulshot, Worton, and Potterne. Up in Gloucestershire was Shipton Moyne, while over in east Somerset were estates at Frome Branch, Marston Bigot, and Othery. Also easy of access from Stourton, in the north-west corner of Dorset were lands in Gillingham and Buckham Weston and then, progressively further to the south in Dorset, there were holdings in Tarrant Villiers, Dewlish, and at Broadway (near the coast). In east Devon there was a Moigne estate at Kilmington and, in the valley of the Hampshire Avon (to the west of the New Forest), more properties in Fordingbridge and in nearby Gorley and Ibsley. In north Hampshire William Stourton enjoyed a rent at Litchfield and, far away in Essex, he held the Moigne manor of Great Easton near Dunmow as tenant-in-chief of the Crown.

Besides these places, in his own right Stourton held a knight's fee in Silton by Gillingham (Dorset) and a small estate in Othery (Somerset) as tenant of the Montagues (earls of Salisbury), the manor of Little Marston near Yeovil, purchased in 1403 from Lord Grey of Ruthyn, and a small estate in Lye (Somerset), the manor and advowson of Tarrant Rushton and a moiety of the hundred of Combs Ditch (Dorset), and lands in Fonthill Gifford (Wiltshire). Only a few of the outlying possessions which came to him through his wife were further away than twenty-five miles from William Stourton's own family place at Stourton, which lay roughly at the centre of the greater part of the considerable number of estates under his control[1].

William Stourton's father, John Stourton, was never knight of the shire, but at the beginning of Richard II's reign (in June 1377) he was a justice of the peace in Somerset, and during the first two years of the reign he was the king's escheator in Somerset and Dorset. When he died is not known, but in July 1380 he secured a royal licence to entail upon himself and his second wife (Alice) a small estate at Preston Plucknett, with remainder to his son William[2]. This is the first recorded reference to the later Speaker.

William Stourton was probably already of full age and may even have been launched on his career as an apprentice-at-law. Certainly, on 18 November, 1381 one of the executors of Sir Nicholas Bonde used his services as attorney when required to appear in Chancery to show cause why the Wiltshire manor of Mere (very near Stourton) should not be given in dower to the widow of the Black Prince, who in 1366 had granted it to Bonde; Stourton failed in his plea. On 8 March, 1386 he was himself granted by royal patent the custody of the castle and park of Mere with the office of bailiff of the hundred. This was with the assent of one of the King's porters who, as a retainer of the Black Prince, had been given these offices for life just ten years before; on the same day, by a royal warrant under the signet, Stourton's grant was made one for life[3].

Apparently Stourton was not disturbed in his possession of these local offices during the political troubles of the next three years and, in fact, he retained them without interruption until the end of the reign of Richard II. The crisis of the "Merciless Parliament" of 1388 affected him not at all except that on 2 December, 1388 he shared (with Thomas Street and two others) a grant in fee simple of a messuage and 2 shops in Barnardscastle Ward in London forfeited by the late Steward of the royal Household, John Lord Beauchamp of Holt, following his condemnation in parliament for treason; the Council made the grant in return for 500 marks payable at the Lower Exchequer.

In the previous April Stourton's partner in this enterprise, Thomas Street, had appointed him as one of his attorneys during his absence in the Isle of Man. The island was at this time under the lordship of William Montague, earl of Salisbury.

1 *CCR, 1402-5*, 179; *ibid., 1413-9*, 139, 170; *ibid., 1419-22*, 159, 165; Charles Botolph Joseph, Lord Mowbray, Segrave and Stourton, *History of the Noble House of Stourton* (1899, privately printed), 103-8, 143; *CPR, 1396-9*, 356; *CFR, 1413-22*, 95.
2 *The Complete Peerage, loc. cit.*
3 *CCR 1381-5*, 26; *CPR, 1381-5*, 403; *ibid., 1385-9*, 109.

Street had connexions with this Wiltshire magnate. So, in fact, had Stourton himself. For in June 1384 moneys had been paid to the earl at the Lower Exchequer (in respect of his keepership of Carisbrooke castle in the Isle of Wight)`"by the hands of William Stourton". And so were, a year later, advances up to £243 odd made to the earl at the Exchequer in anticipation of his own and his retinue's services in the impending royal expedition to Scotland of the summer of 1385[1].

In spite of these important local connexions and royal offices, Stourton had served on no local royal commissions since 1382, when in March and December he had been appointed to act as a commissioner in Wiltshire for keeping the peace after the Peasants' Revolt of the previous year, and for suppressing any attempts to resuscitate the rebellion in that county. On 10 November, 1389, however, he was for the first time appointed a justice of the peace proper. This was in Dorset. He continued to be reappointed as a J.P. in Dorset until November 1397, having in the meantime been also appointed, on 1 July, 1394 as a J.P. in Wiltshire. The Wiltshire commission of the peace he was to retain without a break until his death[2].

Considering his membership of these two county commissions of the peace, Stourton was far from overburdened with other royal commissions during the 1390's. On 5 February, 1392 he was put on a commission of inquiry into the title of the widow of Sir Richard de Burley K.G. to the Hampshire manor of Nether Burgate, for restitution of which she had petitioned, on the ground that it was entailed and in any case ought not to have been deemed subject to forfeiture by her late husband's uncle, Sir Simon de Burley, Richard II's under-Chamberlain, who, condemned for treason in the "Merciless Parliament" of 1388, was alleged never to have had any interest in the manor. Over a year later, on 29 March, 1393, Stourton was included in a Chancery inquiry in Somerset (prompted by a bill of the Treasurer) into the lands of a lesser tenant-in-chief, Peter de Bratton. More than four years passed, however, before he was appointed on 12 June, 1397 to a commission set up to ascertain the facts regarding the estates of another minor tenant-in-chief in Somerset, John Payne, a London armourer. The only other royal commissions to come Stourton's way before the end of Richard II's reign were issued in the spring of 1398: on 31 May he was appointed to assist in an examination of the state of the nunnery at Amesbury (Wiltshire), and on 30 June to act as a surveyor of weirs in the rivers of Wiltshire[3].

In the meantime, there is some record of Stourton's participation in private business. At Michaelmas 1390 he had been witness to a demise of a rented tenement at Mere by the Dean of Salisbury[4]. Two years later, his services as legal counsel were being used by the Dean and Chapter of Wells, his retaining fee being £1 a year. In 1400-1 and 1407-8 he was still acting in this capacity for the Wells chapter, of which his brother Richard was, by 1410, one of the prebendaries[5]. By September 1394 he was a feoffee in fourteen manors in Hampshire, Dorset, Wiltshire, and Northants, belonging to John de Lisle of Wootton in the Isle of Wight. In the summer of 1395 he was evidently acting at Westminster as an agent of the abbot of Glastonbury: on 2 July a recent loan to the King by the abbot amounting to 500 marks was repaid at the Lower Exchequer *per manus Willelmi Stourton*, the royal letters of obligation being surrendered to the Chancery[6]. On the 17 February, 1397 he acted as surety for the widow of William Lord Botreaux when she made arrangements with the Exchequer to have the wardship of her son's estates during his minority. It was probably a purely local connexion which promoted the Dean of the King's Chapel, John Boor, when about to go to Ireland on the royal expedition of May 1399, to appoint Stourton (on 16 April, 1399) as one of his attorneys in England; Boor was a

---

1 *CPR, 1385-9*, 441, 534; Exchequer, Issue Roll, P.R.O., E 403/502, mem. 9; *ibid.*, 508, mem. 12.

2 *CPR, 1381-5*, 141, 248; *ibid., 1388-92*, 139, 342; *ibid., 1391-6*, 439, 587; *ibid., 1396-9*, 95-6, 230 (and see below for his commissions of the peace under the Lancastrians).

3 *CPR, 1391-6*, 81, 291; *ibid., 1396-9*, 160, 347, 372.

4 *ibid., 1388-92*, 488.

5 *H.M.C. Report, Mss. of the Dean and Chapter of Wells*, 24, 35; Somerset Record Society, vol. XXX, *The Register of Bishop Nicholas Bubwith*, part ii, 468.

6 *CCR, 1392-6*, 374; Exchequer, Issue Roll, P.R.O., E 403/551, mem. 13.

canon at Salisbury, and Stourton's fellow-attorney was a colleague of his on the Wiltshire bench, Thomas Bonham[1].

Some notice of Stourton's own private interests appears in the records of the last decade of Richard II's reign. He was, of course, still enjoying the royal grant of the custody of the castle and park at Mere and the office of bailiff of the hundred there, made to him in 1386 for life. By a final concord levied in the Court of Common Bench on 5 May, 1391 he purchased (for 100 marks) messuages and lands at Fonthill Giffard (Wilts.) and, a year or so later (on 20 July, 1392), he and his feoffees secured a royal licence to convey this and other Fonthill Giffard property of his, worth altogether £10 a year, to the Carthusian priory of Witham (Somerset), where eventually he was buried; on 16 September next he followed this up by getting a second licence in favour of the same monastery, this time to amortize the reversion of a messuage and shop in Bristol. Some three years later, by a patent of 13 July, 1395, he secured another royal licence, enabling him and his heirs to effect an enclosure of 50 acres of pasture and woodland in the royal forest of Selwood and to cut down (for sale) timber in his wood of 'Bygoteswood', the Deputy-Warden of the royal forests south of Trent having already decided that such action was not detrimental to the King's or other interests[2].

The revolution of 1399—the deposition of Richard II and the accession of Henry IV—proved something of a turning-point in Stourton's own career. Certainly it was so, as far as went his employment on royal business as a member of local commissions and as legal counsel. And all this evidently had its effect on the estimation in which Stourton was locally held: he was to sit as knight of the shire in six of the ten Parliaments which met between the accession of Henry IV and his own death in 1413, representing in succession each of the three counties in which his landed interest was at its strongest, namely, Somerset, Wiltshire, and Dorset.

At first, however, Stourton had some difficulty in retaining his custody of the park at Mere (Wilts.) which on 7 October, 1399 was granted for life to Thomas Bolour who put him out of possession; and, although a month later (on 8 November) Stourton's grant of 1386 was confirmed and on 20 November Stourton indentured with the Prince of Wales (Henry of Monmouth) to have the farm of the lodge and herbage of the park for five years (from Michaelmas 1399) at 5 marks a year (an arrangement which received a royal *inspeximus* and confirmation on 19 November, 1400), it was not until 20 February, 1401 that Bolour's letters were revoked. Stourton had petitioned against his exclusion and, following the appearance of the parties in Chancery, judgment had been given on 9 February, 1401 in his favour. He was then acting for the first time as knight of the shire (for Somerset) in Henry IV's second parliament. It may very well be that Stourton got over his trouble about Mere Park as the result of a closer association with the Prince of Wales. In 1402 he was Steward of the Principality of Wales. In 1405 he also became a J.P. in Cornwall, an appointment which, in view of his having no landed interest in the county, could be taken to imply that he concurrently discharged some other duty in the Prince's administration in Cornwall, which was part of his Duchy of Cornwall. But his connexion with the future Henry V is not otherwise very strongly confirmed[3].

In the meantime, on 28 November, 1399, Stourton had been re-appointed as a justice of the peace in Wiltshire, an office he was to retain until his death. On the following day, he was included in a royal commission to inquire into wastes in the royal castle of Old Sarum; on 13 December, he was one of those appointed to investigate infringements of the royal rights of coinage of tin in Somerset, Devon, and Cornwall, and to look into cases of concealment of the goods of the late King, of those of the late earl of Wiltshire, Sir John Bussy, and Sir Henry Green, Richard II's counsellors, all of whom had been executed at Bristol at the end of the previous July, and of those of others who had returned from service in Richard's Irish expedition through these south-western counties; and on 18 December he was put on a commission of array in Wiltshire[4]. In the following year, he was included (by patents of 4 and 12 May, 1400) in a commission of oyer and terminer regarding cases

1 *CFR, 1391-9*, 207; *CPR, 1396-9*, 520.
2 Hoare, *Wiltshire*, vol. IV, part 1, 230; *CPR, 1391-6*, 124, 158, 726.
3 *CPR, 1399-1401*, 57, 388, 436; A. Collins, *Peerage of England* (ed. Sir E. Brydges, London, 1812) VI, 634 (Unfortunately, Collins gives no reference for Stourton's Welsh Stewardship.)
4 *CPR, 1399-1401*, 566; 125, 209, 211.

of treason and illegal meetings since Candlemas at Bristol (but apparently did not act); and on 8 November, 1400 he was authorized to be party to an inquiry into a case of assault at Kentsford (Somerset) by a gang instigated by the Cistertian abbot of Cleeve[1].

Early in this year, 1400, following the abortive conspiracy of Richard II's supporters led by the earls of Salisbury and Huntingdon which ended in their deaths and probably led to the death of the ex-King himself, Stourton had procured a royal grant to himself of the custody of the manor of Knowle (just over the Somerset border from Stourton), as from the time of the forfeiture of the late earl of Salisbury until the majority of the heir, at a farm of £10 a year to be rendered at the Exchequer; his younger brother, John Stourton, was one of his mainpernors (or sureties). And on 25 May following, when John shared a grant of the late earl of Huntingdon's manor of Fremington (Devon) at a farm of over £130 a year, William stood in turn as one of his sureties[2].

Stourton was elected, for the first time for Somerset, as knight of the shire to the parliament summoned to meet on 20 January, 1401. As has been stated, he took advantage of his being at Westminster to get the dispute over his tenure of the castle and park at Mere (Wilts.) cleared up. And it was apparently during this parliamentary session that he was for the first time retained as one of the apprentices-at-law acting as legal counsel for the administration of Henry IV's private inheritance of the duchy of Lancaster; he was to continue to act in this capacity for the next four years, down to February 1405, after which he was not re-appointed[3]. The parliament ended on 10 March, 1401. On 29 April following, Stourton was put on the royal commission of oyer and terminer appointed to deal with the case of the collector of the royal tax of ulnage of cloth in Somerset who had been murdered when proclaiming his office at the fair of Norton St. Philip (near Bath). Two days later, on 1 May, he secured for himself a royal letter patent of *inspeximus* and confirmation of his previous grant of 1395 allowing him to make enclosures in Selwood forest, on payment of a fine of a noble (6/8d.) in the Hanaper office of the Chancery. On 16 May, already a J.P. in Wiltshire, he was for the first time appointed to the commission of the peace in Somerset as well; here, as in Wiltshire, he continued to be appointed until his death. A month later, on 16 June, in letters patent dated at Bristol, he was appointed to deliver the prison and gaol of this town, and on 7 July to enquire there about all treasons, etc.[4].

Whether Stourton was already the Recorder of Bristol is not known. But it is quite possible. He was certainly holding this office by the middle of March 1407, but that he had connexions with the town earlier than this date is suggested by a reference in the will of John Bount of Bristol, which was drawn up in August 1404, to a book of the Gospels in English then in Stourton's keeping[5]. Meanwhile, on 10 July, 1401 he was included in a royal commission of oyer and terminer appointed for Hampshire, Wiltshire, Dorset, and Somerset. A few days later, on 20 July, Henry IV wrote to his Council ordering provision to be made for a Great Council to meet on 15 August, from four to eight knights being summoned from each shire; on the following day the King decided that a certain number of esquires as well should be called in, and Stourton was among those ordered to be summoned from Wiltshire[6]. Stourton's royal commissions showed no signs of slackening off in number. On 10 November, 1401 he was put on a commission of inquiry into counterfeiting of coin in Somerset, although he later claimed in the Exchequer that he never received his patent, and on 18 November he was appointed to act as a justice of special oyer and terminer following complaint of an ambush at Nailsea (Somerset). He was one of a group of commissioners authorised on 18 February, 1402 to inquire about certain

1 *ibid.*, 272, 313, 413; *CCR, 1399-1401*, 388.
2 *CFR, 1399-1405*, 53, 58.
3 Duchy of Lancaster, Accounts Various, P.R.O., D.L. 28/4/2-4 (Robert Somerville in *Duchy of Lancaster*, i. 452, is in error in terminating his duchy appointment in 1403).
4 *CPR, 1399-1401*, 516; 483; 564, 566; 520, 521.
5 *The Little Red Book of Bristol*, ed. F. B. Bickley, ii, 81; Bristol and Gloucestershire Arch. Soc., *Notes or Abstracts of the wills in the Great Orphan Book and Book of Wills in the Council House at Bristol*, ed. T. P. Whalley (Bristol, 1886), p. 73.
6 *CPR, 1399-1401*, 552; *Proceedings and Ordinances of the Privy Council*, ed. N. H. Nicolas, i. 161.

lands of the late earl of Salisbury in the Isle of Wight which, though forfeited for treason, had been concealed and not surrendered into the King's hand. On 11 May following, he was a commissioner in Wiltshire and Somerset for the arrest of such men as were openly questioning the King's constitutional intentions and indulging in seditious talk, and in the middle of July he was also made a commissioner of array in Wiltshire for coastal defence. Three weeks later, on 5 August, he was appointed to an inquiry into the treasonable activity of certain English and Welshmen living at Bristol, which again may suggest that he was already Recorder there[1] To the parliament which met at Westminster on 30 September, 1402 he was re-elected knight of the shire for Somerset. On 2 December following, a week after the end of the single session, he was made one of a committee set up by the royal Council to supervise repairs and the sale of ancient oak-trees in the forest and park of Gillingham (Dorset), where he himself had some property.

The financial grant of the 1402 parliament did not fall due for collection until Whitsuntide 1403 and, on 1 April, 1403, hard pressed for ready cash with which to meet the threat from Scotland and especially from Wales where Owen Glendower was raising the country in revolt, Henry IV had letters dispatched to prominent churchmen, secular and regular, and other notables requesting specified loans to the Crown to assist the special Treasurers for the Wars; Stourton was written down for a loan of £200, a sum in excess of most anticipated contributions to the fund. In May 1400 and May 1042 the abbot of Glastonbury had advanced loans to the Crown amounting to over £132, and on 28 May, 1403, perhaps by way of indirectly settling an obligation on the part of the abbot to Stourton, although in this transaction it is possible that Stourton was acting (as earlier in 1395) as the abbot's agent, an Exchequer assignment of £66 1s. 3d. was made to the abbot *per manus Willelmi Stourton*[2]. Stourton about this time had other, private relations with the abbey at Glastonbury; only a week or so before this Exchequer assignment was arranged, either (as has been said) through Stourton's mediation or to benefit himself, he had taken out (on 20 May, 1403) a royal licence under the great seal allowing him to alienate in mortmain to the abbey a messuage and two virgates in Marton and Ebbesbourne (Wilts.) for the upkeep of a lamp burning daily in the abbey-church at high mass[3].

Casual royal commissions continued to come Stourton's way in a steady stream. On 10 April, 1403 he was a commissioner for investigating delapidations and wastes in the royal castle and manor of Marlborough (Wilts) and also (somewhat late in the day) the whereabouts of the *personalia* of William Lescrope, late earl of Wiltshire, executed three-and-a-half years before; and on the same day by a different commission, which (he later claimed) came not to hand, he was put on an inquiry into trespasses against the venison in the royal chase of Filwood (Somerset). On 21 May, he was made one of a commission authorized to ascertain the facts following a petition from the King's sister Elizabeth, countess of Huntingdon, and her present husband, Sir John Cornwall, to be reinstated in the manor of Barford St. Martin and the forestership of Grovele (Wilts) from which they had been excluded. Early in July following, Stourton was at Bridgwater acting as arbiter in a dispute over a £5 rent in Little Durnford (Wilts), and then, after the Percy revolt and among continuing threats from Wales and France, he was appointed to serve as a commissioner of array in Somerset by successive patents of 28 August and 8 September, 1403[4].

Stourton was again elected for Somerset to the first of the two parliaments of 1404. It met at Westminster on 14 January. The single session had still some three weeks to run when, on 28 February, Stourton was appointed a justice for the supervision of the river Avon between Bath and Bristol in pursuance of the statutes of 1351, 1371, and 1399 relating to weirs, mills, etc., on river courses. On 16 March he was party as a feoffee to the marriage settlement of his chief lord at Stourton, Richard Lord St. Maur and Lovell of Castle Cary, who had been summoned to (and very likely attended) the parliament[5]. The session ended on 20 March. On 6 July following Stourton was associated with the mayor of Bristol in a royal commission to deliver Bristol gaol of Welshmen and others imprisoned for treason and felony, and this

1 *CPR, 1401-5*, 64, 65, 69, 126, 115, 135.
2 *ibid*., 179-80; *Proceedings, Privy Council, op. cit*., i. 202; Exchequer, Issue Roll, E. 403/576, mem. 6.
3 *CPR, 1401-5*, 229.
4 *ibid*., 275, 276, 282, 288, 290; *Catalogue of Ancient Deeds*, ii, C 1836.
5 *CPR, 1401-5*, 427; *CCR, 1402-5*, 323.

commission was renewed three months later, on 6 October, the day of the opening of a new parliament at Coventry. Recently returned as knight of the shire on three occasions, Stourton was not now re-elected, perhaps because the writs of summons had expressly forbidden the election of lawyers.

During the parliament of January-March, 1404 the Commons had petitioned against any violation of the privilege of protection covering elected members and their servants coming to, attending, or returning from parliaments, had drawn particular attention to the *orrible baterie et malfait* done by one John Savage to Richard Chedder esquire, a menial servant of Stourton's fellow-knight of the shire on that occasion, Sir Thomas Brook, and had asked that murder in such circumstances should be held to be equivalent to treason-felony and that mayhem (as perpetrated in this instance) should involve the felon in the loss of a hand. The official answer to the petition had been that Savage should surrender to the King's Bench within three months of a proclamation *ad hoc* or pay double damages and make fine and ransom to the Crown. Chedder had evidently in the meantime been disposed to take the law into his own hands, and the Coventry parliament had been in session only three weeks when a commission was issued there (on 26 October) appointing Stourton (among others) to inquire into a report that Chedder and some friends had laid in wait at Marshwood (Dorset) to kill Savage in ambush[1].

The parliament of January 1404 proved to be the last to which Stourton was returned for Somerset. He missed the Coventry parliament of October 1404 and the long-lasting Westminster parliament of 1406 altogether, but was elected to the next parliament, which met at Gloucester in October 1407, this time as knight of the shire for Wiltshire, his own county proper. In the meantime, he had almost inevitably continued to serve on a number of sporadic royal local commissions. On 5 February, 1405 the Cistertian abbey of King John's foundation at Beaulieu (in south-west Hampshire), which was undergoing a period of financial stress due to the wasteful policies of recent abbots, had all its estates taken into royal control; and Stourton was one of a committee, which included the earl of Kent and the Cistertian abbot of Quarr (Isle of Wight), appointed to administer the property. As late as May 1407 Stourton was associated with the sheriff of Cornwall in an enquiry into the abbey's Cornish estates, being charged to discover who had occupied them and received the rents since the establishment of the trust of February 1405[2]. Since the end of 1405 Stourton had had a continuing interest in Cornish affairs generally, having been made on 18 December, 1405 a J.P. in the county; apart from a brief interval between March and July 1410 he served on the Cornish commission of the peace, as during these years in Wiltshire and Somerset, until his death[3]. On 8 January, 1406, soon after his appointment to the Cornish bench, he and his fellow J.P's and the sheriff were specially commissioned to enquire about illegal assemblies in the county and bring the leaders before the King's Council, using their discretion whether to imprison or release on bail others whom they arrested. On 28 June following, he was appointed as a commissioner to search out cases of concealment and extortion by royal officials, and also to investigate the annual value of Crown leases and annuities charged on local royal revenues, in Wiltshire and in Dorset and Somerset; this commission and other similar ones issued throughout the kingdom were the result of pressure put upon the administration by the Commons during the long parliament of 1406. On the same day the same commissioners were authorised in separate letters to raise Crown loans in these counties, bringing the results of their importunities with all speed to the King himself. Stourton alone shared with his own diocesan bishop of Salisbury the distinction of serving on these loan commissions in all three counties[4].

Doubtless Stourton was himself expected to contribute to this royal loan of 1406. In view of his attitude just a year earlier to the efforts of Edward of Norwith, the duke of York, to raise loans for the payment of his retinue on royal service in south Wales, he may very well have found resistance difficult: early in 1405 the parliamentary subsidy next leviable in Somerset stood assigned for the payment of the royal forces in Wales, and on 22 June the duke of York, only recently freed by the King from close arrest (for his complicity in the plot to gain possession of the person of the young earl

1 *CPR, 1401-5*, 434, 504; 502.
2 *CPR, 1401-5*, 488; *ibid., 1405-8*, 354.
3 *CPR, 1405-8*, 490, 497, 499; *ibid., 1408-13*, 480, 485, 486; *ibid., 1413-6*, 417, 423, 425.
4 *CPR, 1405-8*, 152, 153, 199.

of March), was at Glastonbury in possession of privy seal letters, despatched to him by the royal Council, authorizing him to borrow from the abbot and other Somerset notables, including William Stourton. Sir William Bonville the duke found ill, and Sir Thomas Brook, conveniently away from home; and, although the duke met the abbot and others, Stourton among them, these assured him that they were unable to subscribe, saying that they had previously made loans to the King without being able to secure repayment; the duke was further annoyed to learn that the local collectors of the subsidy had left for London, and that, in any case, assignments on *their* subsidy (as well as on the levy in Wiltshire and Hampshire) had already been made in favour of Lord Berkeley. In some lowness of spirits, the duke wrote off to the Council that he dared not send word of his ill-success to his retinue, to whom he had already, and only recently, conveyed news of his high hopes of a settlement of their pay by Lammastide[1].

After having served on a commission appointed on 16 February, 1407 to inquire into a report that recent mayors of Malmesbury had been in the habit of selling wines and foodstuffs both wholesale and retail, although their office (which included the administration of the assizes of wines and victuals) forbade this practice, Stourton was for the first and only time in his career elected as knight of the shire for Wiltshire in the autumn parliament of this year which met at Gloucester. During the parliament, in letters dated at Gloucester on 6 November, he was appointed to act on an inquiry into a case of breach of close and arson at Norton-by-Malmesbury[2]. Stourton was certainly by now Recorder of Bristol and, on 17 February, 1408, probably by reason of his office, he was put on a commission set up to investigate reports of wastes in the royal hospital of St. John in Bristol by its wardens. On 28 March following, another commission of inquiry came his way, this time into the concealment of lands in Somerset forfeited in 1400 by the late earl of Salisbury[3].

By this time Stourton's personal connexions with men of influence and substance were showing signs of expansion. In May 1408 Sir John Grey, the son of Lord Grey of Ruthyn, appointed him to be one of his attorneys for a year during absence in Wales. In the summer of this same year he was acting as feoffee to John Arundel, Lord Mautravers, during a settlement of some of his Dorset estates[4]. About this time, too, he became a feoffee in certain Berkshire lands belonging to Sir William Hankford, a Justice of the Court of Common Pleas (since 1398) who was to be promoted to the office of Chief Justice of the King's Bench at Henry V's accession. In 1410 Hankford was to consent to act as one of Stourton's executors and was to share in the wardship of Stourton's lands when the latter died in 1413[5]. In November 1408 Stourton was one of the feoffees, in the manor of Rushall (Wilts), of Sir Walter (later Lord) Hungerford, who had been his fellow-knight of the shire at Gloucester in 1407.

It was to Hungerford and Stourton together that, on 18 May, 1409, was committed the keeping of the temporalities of the then vacant Cluniac priory of Monkton Farleigh (Wilts), a house founded by the family of Henry IV's first wife, Mary de Bohun, and consequently now under the King's patronage. Dispute was pending between Henry IV and the Cluniac prior of Lewes over the latter's right to collate to the Farleigh priorate, and not until 3 September did the King present the prior of Lewes's nominee (in letters under the duchy of Lancaster seal). On 1 February, 1410 Hungerford and Stourton were ordered to meddle no further with the temporalities of Farleigh priory. Process, however, had been begun against them in the Exchequer, requiring them by distraint to account for the custody, despite the fact that, because of the upset over the nomination of the new prior, they had not received any of the issues of the property. The result was that Hungerford and Stourton joined with the new prior of Farleigh in laying a series of protests in Chancery, the two laymen that their custody had been ineffectual, the prior that any such custody of temporalities constituted an interference with the customary privileges of the priory; and, on 12 February, all three complainants were accorded a royal pardon of all demands, and the prior an additional undertaking that the custody should not be held as a precedent. Two days before this pardon was forthcoming, a commission had issued

---

1 *Rot. Parl.*, iii, 565; *Proceedings, Privy Council, op. cit.*, i. 272-3.
2 *CPR, 1405-8*, 308, 415.
3 *The Little Red Book of Bristol, loc. cit.*; *CPR, 1405-8*, 419, 420.
4 *CPR, 1405-8*, 437; *Somerset and Dorset Notes and Queries*, VIII, 283, 286.
5 *CCR, 1422-9*, 110.

requiring an investigation into a report of waste at Farleigh during Hungerford and Stourton's custody of the place. All this business was going on during the parliament summoned to meet (first of all at Bristol and then at Westminster) on 27 January, 1410, to which Hungerford had been elected for Somerset and Stourton (for the first time) for Dorset. During the second session of the parliament Hungerford petitioned the Commons, asking them to request the King that when he traversed the findings of the inquest into his alleged wasting of the Farleigh priory estates, as he proposed to do, the sheriff of Wiltshire should be ordered on parliament's authority not to impanel jurors with less than £20 worth of land in the county. The Commons approved the petition, and so later did the King[1]. Stourton did not apparently take personal action, and it is possible that his interest in the whole matter of the custody had been subordinate to that of Hungerford. However this may be, the whole episode is interesting as showing the closeness of Stourton s connexion with Hungerford who, immediately after Henry V's accession, was to become a figure of some considerable political importance.

In the meantime, during the course of the year 1409, Stourton had continued to act on a number of royal commissions of mainly local interest and minor importance. On 16 May, 1409 he had been commissioned to hold an inquisition post mortem on one William Wroughton, on 26 June to act as a justice of oyer and terminer regarding a case of refusal of services by the bondsmen of the prioress of Amesbury at her manor of Melksham (Wilts), on 28 August to investigate a murder in the New Forest, and on 16 October to inquire into the goods of a Newbury (Berks) man which were to be delivered to the Prince of Wales as forfeit. One of his fellow-commissioners, Thomas Chaucer, acted as Speaker for the Commons in the January 1410 parliament. During its first session, Stourton was appointed, on 25 February, as a justice of oyer and terminer following a complaint of a trespass at Chaffcombe (in S.E. Somerset)[2]. Dropped, a week before the end of the first parliamentary session (on 10 March, 1410), from the commission of the peace for Cornwall, he was reinstated on 12 July following; no interruption had occurred in his justiceships of the peace in either Somerset or Wiltshire.

Whether Stourton was elected as knight of the shire for either Dorset, Somerset, or Wiltshire to the last proper parliament of Henry IV which met in November 1411 is not known, because the electoral return from none of these three counties has survived. But it is possible that he was elected. Certainly, on its third day, 5 November, 1411, he was one of three Wiltshire notables for whose grant in mortmain to the nunnery at Shaftesbury of a small estate at Kelston (Somerset) the abbess procured a royal licence. At the beginning of this year he had figured as one of the feoffees of Thomas, earl of Salisbury, in certain of his estates in the Isle of Wight, Sussex, Hampshire, and Wiltshire, when the earl made a settlement on his mother[3]. Sometime during the year he also acted as legal counsel to the civic authorities of Salisbury in return for a retaining fee of £2 and a livery worth 10s.[4]. Of Stourton's activities in 1412 nothing is known except that, on 22 April, he was made one of a royal commission appointed to hear and determine an appeal against a ruling in the Court of Chivalry in the well-known case of the hostage of the Spanish count of Denia which had been dragging on since the battle of Najera in 1367, and, on 30 November, he and his younger brother shared a royal grant of the right to farm at the Exchequer the wardship of the estates of their sister Edith's late husband, Sir John Beauchamp of Bletsoe. (Sometime shortly after Henry V's accession they agreed with the Exchequer to pay £100 for the wardship and marriage.)[5].

Henry IV died on 20 March, 1413. On the next day the new commissions of the peace were issued in Henry V's name: Stourton was re-appointed a justice in Wiltshire, Somerset, and Cornwall. He served on no occasional commissions down to his death in the late summer, but he was elected as knight of the shire for Dorset to the first parliament of the new reign. As has been already seen, he was friendly with Sir Walter Hungerford, whom Henry V now appointed to be Chief Steward of the duchy of Lancaster south of Trent and who represented Somerset in this parlia-

---

1 *CPR, 1408-13*, 21; 143, 163, 181; *CFR, 1405-13*, 149; *CCR, 1409-13*, 28; *Rot. Parl.*, iii. 632.
2 *CPR, 1408-13*, 109, 110, 111, 180.
3 *ibid.*, 349; 271.
4 R. C. Hoare, *Wiltshire, New and Old Sarum* (ed. Benson and Hatcher), i. 110.
5 *CPR, 1408-13*, 391; *CFR, 1405-13*, 253; *ibid., 1413-22*, 34.

ment[1]. It is very probable that Stourton had long been *persona grata* to the new King. Perhaps, however, the Commons chose Stourton to be their Speaker on this occasion just because he was not a figure of any political importance, or possibly because he had connexions with both of the parties whose bids for the control of the royal authority had made so uneasy the last five years or so of Henry IV's reign, the party of Prince Henry and the Beauforts and the party which drew its motive force from the alliance between Henry IV, his second son (Thomas, duke of Clarence), and Archbishop Arundel of Canterbury. It may be that Stourton had some personal connexion with the primate, because when, on 20 July, 1410, Stourton had drawn up his will he had left to the archbishop (whom he described as 'my reverend lord and father') a drinking cup with a cover of gold[2]. This is as may be, for it is not entirely out of the question that the bequest was simply designed to secure the archbishop's good offices when probate should be required in his Prerogative Court of Canterbury. Whatever the reasons for their choice, the Commons, on 16 May, 1413 (the second day of the session), elected Stourton as their Speaker and presented him for the royal acceptance two days later. At this ceremony Stourton pleaded to be excused, according to the account of the roll of the parliament, 'a cause de son petit estat, noun sufficientie de science, et infirmitee de corps', but Henry V insisted on his assuming office. It was Stourton who, as Speaker, put forward certain complaints on 22 May, but, when the Commons made certain representations three days later, they did so through a delegation led by John Doreward, knight of the shire for Essex; and on 3 June, when the parliament (as it turned out) had less than a week to run before its dissolution, the Commons presented Doreward to act as Speaker instead of Stourton, on the ground that the latter was ill in bed and could not do his duty. It is, however, likely that Stourton's manner of exercising the Speakership had already proved not altogether acceptable to the Commons, and that there was something of a political motive in his withdrawal: after disclosing, on 22 May, the Commons' requests for good governance, Stourton had agreed to the King's demand that their complaints should be put into writing; on 25 May, Doreward and his fellows objected that Stourton had acted *ultra vires* in having conceded this point without the assent of the Lower House, and went on to ask that the King would not press them to do more than put forward a schedule of the articles previously submitted, *briefment appoyntez*; this the King allowed and excused them from Stourton's undertaking[3]. Whether Stourton's alleged illness was real or convenient cannot be said, but it may well have been both. After no longer a session than three-and-a-half weeks in all, the parliament ended on 9 June.

Nothing further is known of William Stourton except the day of his death: 18 September, 1413. On 26 September royal commissions were issued by the Chancery ordering the customary seizure of his lands in Hampshire, Wiltshire, Somerset, Dorset, and in Essex, and the preliminary holding of inquisitions to ascertain formally what these were and who was his heir. On the very same day, the new Chief Justice of the King's Bench, Sir William Hankford, and Stourton's younger brother John (both of them being Stourton's executors) were granted the custody of the estates, to hold until the full age of Stourton's son and heir and to have the latter's marriage, paying the yearly extent (or value) for the lands to the Exchequer and for the marriage as should be agreed with the Treasurer. The wardship was likely to be profitable in view of the age of Stourton's son John, who was only 14 years old, and also because the Dorset, Somerset, and Wiltshire estates were extended at no more than £22 16s. 4d., to which an incremental charge of £3 17s. was added, bringing the amount up to 40 marks, which was certainly a considerable under-assessment. The writs of *diem clausit extremum* had issued from the royal Chancery on 15 November, 1413 to the escheators of Somerset, Dorset, Wiltshire, and Essex[4].

Originally drawn up on 20 July, 1410, William Stourton's will had been already proved in the Prerogative Court of Canterbury on 22 September, 1413, only four days after his death, the administration being granted to his brother and executor, John Stourton of Preston Plucknett. The testator had bequeathed his soul to God by the intercession of the Blessed Virgin, the Archangels Michael and Gabriel, and

---

1 For Sir Walter Hungerford, see *Wiltshire Archaeological and Natural History Magazine*, vol. LVI. *Ante,* Vol. II, pp. 95-135.
2 Somerset House, Register Marche, fo. 216.
3 *Rot. Parl.*, IV, 4-5.
4 *CFR, 1413-22*, 22, 30, 80; 3.

all Holy Angels, his body to be buried in the Carthusian priory at Witham (near Frome in Selwood) with which he had been connected since at least 1392. To John, his heir, William Stourton left two missals (one worth £10, the other £8), a psalter (worth 5 marks), and other books, including a book of physic and a Legend of the Saints (each worth £2). Archbishop Arundel profited (as has been said) to the extent of a cup with a cover of gold. Margaret, Stourton's only daughter, who was eventually to marry William Carent esquire of Toomer (Somerset) (later knight of the shire for Dorset in 1420, 1426, and 1427, and for Somerset in 1423, 1445, and 1450), received under the will £200 for her *maritagium* (marriage portion). The rest of Stourton's personalty was to be at the disposal of his executors: Chief Justice Hankford, his younger brother John, and a man of the name of Gough (the Christian name is indecipherable in the Register of wills), perhaps the John Gough who represented Devizes in the parliament of 1437. The executors moved expeditiously, and on 27 November, 1413 they had their acquittance[1].

William Stourton's career as a lawyer and man of affairs, however disappointingly it had ended during his Speakership, had been one of somewhat more than average scope, and he had certainly brought his family forward into a respectable position. The young son and heir he left behind was to do much better. Unlike his father, John Stourton was to hold the shrievalty and on not a few occasions: he was sheriff of Wiltshire in 1426-7, 1433-4, and 1437-8, of Somerset and Dorset in 1428-9, and of Gloucestershire in 1432-4 and 1439-40. Like his father, he sat in parliament, and for the same counties, if less frequently: he was knight of the shire for Wiltshire in December 1421, for Dorset in 1423, and for Somerset in 1432. But he was evidently more of a courtier and politician: by October 1437 he was closely enough attached to the entourage of the young Henry VI (then emerging from his minority, although still dominated by the family of Cardinal Beaufort) to be made a member of the royal Council and, as such, important enough to have the keeping of the duke of Orleans, a prisoner-of-war since Agincourt (1415), who was now becoming an important factor in Anglo-French diplomacy, at Stourton between July 1438 and May 1439. It is clear that John Stourton was closely connected with the Beauforts, for in 1444 he and his brother-in-law, William Carent of Toomer, were executors to John Beaufort, duke of Somerset, who had married Stourton's cousin (his aunt Edith's daughter), Margaret Beauchamp (the maternal grandmother of Henry VII). By November 1446 John Stourton was Treasurer of the royal Household. He was created Baron Stourton of Stourton in May 1448 and was summoned to parliament as a peer thenceforward until—for he came through the Yorkist triumph in 1461 unscathed—his death in 1462. It is possible that for his only marriage, to a daughter of Sir John Wadham of Merrifield (Somerset), a puisne justice of the Court of Common Pleas (from 1388 to 1397) who died in 1411, he had his father, the apprentice-at-law, to thank, young though he had been at William Stourton's death[2].

NOTE

Since this biography was first written, Stourton's connection with Henry of Monmouth before the latter's accession in 1413 has been found to be closer than then considered (cf. p. 197). In the Assession Roll: Duchy of Cornwall May-June 1406 (P.R.O., E 306/2/7) Stourton is noted as then holding the office of 'the prince's chief steward in the West and South'. Although the dates of his appointment and its termination are not known, that Stourton's commissions in Cornwall long preceded and post-dated the spring of 1406 does perhaps imply that his occupation of the chief stewardship was of extended duration.

1 Somerset House, Register Marche, fo. 216.
2 *The Complete Peerage*, XII, part 1, 301-2; *CPR, 1461-7*, 150; *Collectanea Topographica et Genealogica*, i. 312-3, 409. Sir John Wadham was the direct ancestor of Nicholas Wadham, the founder of Wadham College, Oxford.

10

SIR RICHARD REDMAYNE OF LEVENS

IN the introductory paragraphs of part i (CW2 lxi 79 ff.) of this article, something was said in very general terms about the career of Sir Richard Redmayne who was Speaker in the next parliament after Henry V's first expedition to France in 1415. It is now Redmayne's turn to be discussed in such detail as the available sources for his life allow.

Sir Richard Redmayne was a member of a family which by the end of the 13th century had come to be of some local importance in south Westmorland. Their home was at Levens, in the corner of the county dividing Lancashire proper from Lancashire beyond the sands (or Furness). Levens had been in the family from the time of Henry II. Sir Richard's great-grandfather, Matthew, had been knight of the shire (or M.P.) for Lancashire in 1295 and 1307, and for Westmorland twice in 1313. His grandfather, another Matthew, had also represented Westmorland in two parliaments (in 1357 and 1358) and was sheriff of Cumberland at his death in 1360. Sir Richard's father (the last of three Matthews running), who died soon after 1390, was never a knight of the shire. Nonetheless, he had a career of great military and some administrative activity.

This Sir Matthew had evidently taken part in the last victorious phase of Edward III's war with France, being in 1362 a hostage (in the custody of the Dauphin) whom John II of France then refused to surrender. Eventually, however, he was released and in 1369 accompanied his near neighbour, Sir William de Windsor, to Ireland where

the latter was the King's Lieutenant; in 1370 he fought
with Sir Robert Knolles, one of the greatest of Edward's
captains; and then, in 1373, when the war with France
was going badly, he accompanied John of Gaunt on
the duke's quite ineffectual *chivauchée* from Calais to
Bordeaux. In 1375 he was in Britanny. When the Good
Parliament met in the spring of 1376 he had recently
been a prisoner-of-war and was one of those prisoners,
described as being of greater prowess than wealth, on
whose behalf the Commons petitioned the King for help
with their ransoms. (Edward III granted no less than
1,000 marks towards Sir Matthew's ransom.) By 1379
he was one of the wardens of the Scottish March and in
the following year was serving there with a retinue of
40 men-at-arms and 50 archers. In 1382 he was still one
of the joint-wardens of the March and by this time was
also keeper of the royal castle at Roxburgh. In 1388,
when nearly sixty years old, he was taken prisoner in
the battle of Otterburn, but he was soon freed and became
sheriff of Cumberland late in the next year. Meanwhile,
he had been appointed a justice of the peace in this county
(in 1380) and also in Northumberland (in 1382). Sir
Matthew's standing in the highly militarised society of
the north is suggested by the fact that his second wife
was Joan, a daughter of Henry Lord FitzHugh of Ravensworth and in turn the widow of William Lord Greystoke
(who died in 1359) and of Anthony Lord Lucy (who
died in 1368). Sir Richard Redmayne was thus stepbrother to Ralph Lord Greystoke, a warden of the Marches
between 1377 and 1386 and a peer of parliament from
1376 to 1417. Henry Lord FitzHugh, Henry V's
Chamberlain, Treasurer of England from 1416 to 1421,
a peer of parliament from 1388 until his death in 1425,
was a nephew of Sir Richard's stepmother. Joan survived
her third husband, Sir Richard's father, by at least a
decade, dying in 1403.[1] Some further indication of Sir

Matthew's status is supplied by the marriages made by his two surviving children. (His elder son, Matthew, died during his lifetime.) His daughter, Felicia, was first married to a London mercer, John Wodecock, later, however, to a younger son (but eventually the heir) of Ralph Lord Lumley (who was executed for his treason in the 1400 rising against Henry IV). Sir Matthew's son, Richard, by his marriage, did better still.

It was sometime between 1393 and 1399 that Sir Richard Redmayne married Elizabeth, the elder daughter of Sir William Aldbrough of Aldbrough in Richmondshire, a retainer of Edward Balliol (whose claim to the Scottish throne Edward III had supported against David II). Summoned to parliament as a peer from 1371 to 1386, Aldbrough had died in 1388, leaving a son, Sir William, who died without issue in August 1391. The latter's co-heirs were his two sisters, Elizabeth, the widow of Sir Brian Stapleton of Carlton (Yorks.), and Sybil, the wife of Sir William Ryther of Ryther (Yorks.).[2] Sir Richard's

ABBREVIATIONS IN THE FOOTNOTES.

The following abbreviations have been used in the footnotes:

D.N.B.	— *Dictionary of National Biography*
V.C.H.	— *Victoria County History*
CPR	— *Calendar of Patent Rolls*
CCR	— *Calendar of Close Rolls*
CFR	— *Calendar of Fine Rolls*
C. Ch. R.	— *Calendar of Charter Rolls*
DKR	— *Deputy Keeper's Reports*
PPC	— *Proceedings and Ordinances of the Privy Council,* ed. N. H. Nicolas
Rot. Parl.	— *Rotuli Parliamentorum*
P.R.O.	— Public Record Office
R.S.	— Rolls Series
G.E.C.	— *The Complete Peerage*

[1] *G.E.C.*, vi 194; W. Greenwood, *The Redmans of Levens and Harewood* (Kendal, 1905), p. 1; pp. 57-69. The surname of Sir Matthew's first wife Lucy (the mother of his children, including Sir Richard) is not known.

[2] *G.E.C.*, i 101-102. The families of Aldbrough and Balliol would appear to have been related, *c.f.* the bequests by Margery, widow of the Sir Wlliam Aldbrough who died in 1391, of an *aula* of 6 pieces (of tapestry)

marriage with Elizabeth brought him a half of the estates of the Aldbroughs in the West Riding. Moreover, this interest was uncomplicated by any claims to dower, the wife of the first William having predeceased him, the widow of the second having survived *him* by less than two months. Lord Lisle of Rougemont had conveyed his interest in the castle and manor of Harewood in Wharfedale to Redmayne's wife's father in 1364, and Sir Richard and Elizabeth came into possession of this estate among others, including the nearby manors of Kearby and Kirkby Overblow, their title to these being confirmed by the last of the Lisles of Rougemont in 1410.[3] The acquisition of a moiety of the Aldbrough estates did not only substantially increase Redmayne's land-holdings — among which his own estates seem not to have comprised much beyond the manors of Levens (held of the barony of Kendal as no more than a tenth of a knight's fee) and Lupton-in-Levens, the park of Troutbeck (which he rented), and some property he acquired in nearby Hutton Roof and Heversham[4] — but gave him an obviously firm footing among the gentry of Yorkshire. These interests in the West Riding, as his election to parliament for Yorkshire on as many as five occasions suggests, tended to predominate over the local interests of his own family in Westmorland. His father Sir Matthew's career, however, had already opened up the possibility of wider prospects for the Redmaynes of Levens.

That Richard Redmayne cannot have been born much later than 1355 is suggested by the fact that he was already a knight when on 14 March 1376 he and his father, along with John Shakele, Esquire, undertook that Robert Hawley, Esquire, should perform an agreement

with the arms of Balliol and Aldbrough and of a breastplate that had belonged to Edward Balliol, and also the repetition of the Balliol arms in the chapel of Harewood (Surtees Society, *Testamenta Eboracensia*, i 150).
   [3] *Yorkshire Archaeological and Topographical Journal*, iv 92; xviii 266n; *CCR*, *1409-13*, 83.
   [4] *Cal. Inquests post mortem*, Edward III, ix 457; Greenwood, *op. cit.*, 68, 80; W. Farrer, *Records of Kendal*, ii 44, 126.

then made with Edward III, regarding the ransoming of the Count of Denia, an Aragonese nobleman whom these two esquires had taken prisoner in the battle of Najera (1367). This case, which in Richard II's first year resulted in the imprisonment in the Tower of both Hawley and Shakele for refusing to surrender the count's hostage, gave rise in 1378 to a serious dispute between the Crown and the abbot of Westminster over the violation of the abbey's rights of sanctuary, for when Hawley and Shakele escaped from the Tower and took refuge in the abbey precincts and eventually in the church, the former was killed there and the other abducted, in especially sacrilegious circumstances. There is no evidence that either Sir Richard or his father were involved in the consequences of this affair.

Meanwhile, sometime during Richard II's first regnal year (1377-8), the younger Redmayne had taken out "letters of protection" from the royal Chancery. This he did as being about to serve in a military capacity at sea. Sir Richard may have joined that naval expedition whose first object was to attack a Spanish fleet operating in the French interest, from its base at Sluys, against English shipping in the Channel. (This English squadron left London on 20 October 1377 but, hindered by gales, was able to accomplish little beyond the rescue of Brest before its return to Southampton late in January 1378.) Alternatively, he could have been a member of the naval force which, gathered together by the Duke of Lancaster early in 1378, operated with such lack of success in the Bay of Biscay and at St. Malo.[5] Whichever force Redmayne joined, there is no further reference to his employment in military enterprises in these early years of Richard II's reign, although expeditions, enough and to spare, were being organised against the French. Whether or not Sir Richard was abroad all this time, he was certainly

[5] *CCR*, 1374-7, 338; *The Anonimalle Chronicle*, ed. V. H. Galbraith (Manchester, 1927), 116-117, 188; T. Carte, *Catalogue des Rolles Gascons, Français, et Normands*, i 123.

back in England by 5 February 1382 when his father,
Sir Matthew, as keeper of Roxburgh Castle, was paid at
the Exchequer *per manus Ricardi Redman militis* £10
towards the £100 which (so the King's Council had
agreed) were to be paid him over and above the wages
of his retinue there. It is very probable that Sir Richard
acted along with his father in the Scottish Marches during
the next few years and accompanied him in the royal
expedition to Scotland in 1385.

In the autumn of the following year (1386), when the
aristocratic party led by Thomas of Woodstock was
attacking Richard II's first curialist party, Sir Richard
had formed some sort of connection with the king's
intimate friend, Robert de Vere, hereditary King's
Chamberlain and Earl of Oxford, now promoted as Duke
of Ireland: on 26 October 1386 De Vere was paid at the
Exchequer of Receipt a part of the wages of the retinue
of 600 men whom he had recently brought up to London
to help meet the threat of a French invasion, some £26
of which were paid him by the hands of Sir John Mallory,
Richard FitzNichol, Esquire (the Duke's attorney), and
Sir Richard Redmayne.[6] Whatever the connection, it
must have ended after the battle of Radcot Bridge in
December 1387 when De Vere, after raising forces for
the king in Cheshire and Lancashire and deserting them
in the rout, sought safety abroad. Robert's flight did not
prevent his being condemned on charges of treason,
brought by Thomas of Woodstock and the other Lords
Appellant in the "Merciless Parliament" of 1388.

There is no reason to regard the young knight of Levens
as seriously caught up in these happenings, which were
to affect the political character of the rest of Richard II's
reign. On 30 April 1388, during the second session of
the "Merciless Parliament", along with Sir John de Irby,
then knight of the shire for Cumberland, Redmayne was
bound in a recognisance for £80 to the Duke of Gloucester.

---

[6] Exchequer, Issue Roll, P.R.O., E 403/487, mem. 18; *ibid.*, 516, mem. 7.

Whatever lay behind this transaction, it is unlikely that Sir Richard was regarded as in any way hostile to the party of the Appellants, which was then in control of the royal administration, because it was on the following day, 1 May 1388, that as a "king's knight" he was granted for life all the Crown lands in Blencogo (Cumberland) free of rent up to £10 a year.[7] His father, now governor of Berwick, was taken prisoner at the battle of Otterburn in August following, but was soon freed and, after serving on inquiries into damage done by the Scots in Northumberland, was made sheriff of Cumberland in November 1389.

Sir Richard was also almost certainly quite preoccupied at this time with Border affairs. In October 1389 Henry Hotspur, the Earl of Northumberland's son, was confirmed in his Wardenship of the Marches, and when a year later (on 16 October 1390) he was instructed to repair the castle, gates, and walls of Carlisle, it was decided at Westminster that the work should be under the control of Sir Richard Redmayne. Less than three weeks later, on 5 November, Redmayne was retained for life by the King with a grant, to which the Council assented, of 40 marks a year for life charged on the Crown revenues from Cumberland.[8] By the end of January following (1391), however, he was about to take passage overseas, making provision for a foreign credit of £100 through a regular agent in such transactions, Angelo Christofori of Lucca. It looks as though pilgrimage to Italy was Redmayne's object. How long he was out of the country is not known, but he was certainly home by the beginning of 1393 when, by letters patent dated 26 January, he had a royal licence to enclose 3,000 acres of his estate at Levens for the making of a park there.[9] His continued interest in the Border and its affairs, although there was now a truce between England and Scotland, is suggested by his petitioning

[7] *CCR, 1385-9,* 486; *CPR, 1385-9,* 451.
[8] *CPR, 1388-92,* 305, 322.
[9] *CCR, 1392-6,* 543; *CPR, 1391-6,* 211.

the King for the right to hold jousts (at which he and three others were to take on four Scotsmen) in Carlisle between 21 and 27 June 1393; the royal licence was forthcoming on 27 April, and Hotspur was ordered to deputize for the King.

Although Redmayne had served thus far on no royal commissions, except the one of 1390 to oversee the repairs to the defences of Carlisle, he was appointed as sheriff of Cumberland on 7 November 1393. He was in office until 1 November 1394.[10] Within the next twenty-two years he was to be appointed sheriff on no fewer than six other occasions, four more times in Cumberland, and twice in Yorkshire. It was while serving this first term of office as sheriff that he petitioned for a royal pardon for a man who had been indicted for breaking into the house of the vicar of Crosby Ravensworth (Westmorland) in November 1392; the pardon was issued on 16 February 1394.[11] Before his year's occupation of the shievalty of Cumberland was at an end, Redmayne and a small retinue of two esquires and four mounted archers indentured with Richard II to serve in the king's first Irish expedition. Richard II was out of the country from 30 September 1394 until roughly the middle of May 1395; Redmayne's own and his retinue's wages were paid him by the Treasurer of the Household on the basis of a period of service extending from 7 September 1394 to 21 April 1395.[12] He was evidently still out of the country when, on 27 March 1395, his request for a royal pardon for a servant of his late father's, indicted of murder, had a successful outcome. On 3 October following, the King ordered a fine of £20, payable by Edmund Hampden, a royal esquire, for marrying the widow of Sir Ralph Stonore without royal licence, to be given to Redmayne. On 1 December 1395 he was appointed to serve with Lord

10 T. Rymer, *Foedera*, vii 745; P.R.O., *Lists and Indexes*, ix; *List of Sheriffs*, 27.
11 *CPR, 1391-6*, 373.
12 P.R.O., E 101/402/20, fo. 68.

Greystoke, his stepbrother, on a commission to arrest, and deliver to the sheriff of Westmorland for production before the King's Council, certain men who were at enmity with the house of Premonstratensian canons at Shap, and to have others appear before them to find surety for good behaviour. (The abbey had protested to the Council because their patron, Lord Clifford, was in royal wardship.) The constitution of the commission was enlarged on 16 March 1396 to include the Earl of Northumberland, Lord Beaumont and others, and its powers were expanded to allow it to imprison those who declined to find surety. When a fresh commission about this trouble at Shap was issued on 16 April 1397, Redmayne was once more sheriff of Cumberland — he acted from 1 December 1396 to 3 November 1397 — and he and the sheriff of Westmorland were to arrange for the conveyance to Westminster of a number of delinquents who were to be arrested.[13] His second appointment as sheriff, only two years after the expiry of his first term of office, was against the statute of 1371 which provided for the elapse of three years between such appointments. Such breaches of this statute as Redmayne's premature re-appointment were among the points of Haxey's famous bill in the parliament of January 1397 at which Richard II took grave offence.

That Redmayne's conduct of affairs as sheriff of Cumberland in this year (1396-7), which saw the establishment of Richard II's system of autocratic government, was satisfactory from the king's point of view, is suggested by the fact that on 2 October 1397, before Redmayne's term of office came to an end, he was granted for life an annuity of 40 marks, additional to the one charged on the issues of Cumberland; this second annuity was charged on the exchequer of the royal Earldom of Chester and granted in a patent sealed with the seal of that office.[14]

---

[13] *CPR, 1391-6*, 688; 621, 654, 731; *ibid., 1396-9*, 157; *List of Sheriffs, loc. cit.*
[14] *CPR, 1399-1401*, 47

It may well be that Sir Richard Redmayne had already enhanced his estate by his marriage with the elder daughter and coheir of the late Lord Aldbrough of Harewood, for on 28 November 1397 he was appointed to his first royal commission in Yorkshire: an inquiry into various illegalities — champerty, embracery of quarrels, maintenance, false suits at law, etc. — in the city of York as well as in the county, and on 4 February 1398, just after the closure had been applied at Shrewsbury to what proved to be Richard II's last parliament, the commission was re-constituted by the royal Council, the city of York being now excluded from its competence. During the year Redmayne was appointed to serve on a few other Yorkshire commissions: on 20 June 1398 to survey weirs in the rivers of the West Riding, on 7 August to investigate cases of concealment of royal rights (early in 1400 Redmayne protested that this appointment had never been delivered to him), and on 16 November to act on a commission, which included the Percies (the Earl of Northumberland and his son, Hotspur), the Earl of Westmorland, and the sheriffs of Yorkshire and Westmorland, charged with making arrests to stop illegal meetings organized by the enemies of one John Preston, perhaps the lawyer of that name of Preston Patrick (Westmorland), and with bringing those arrested before the King's Council.[15]

On the day after this last commission passed the Great Seal, namely, on 17 November 1398, Redmayne was appointed sheriff of Cumberland for the third time within five years.[16] As in the case of his second appointment, this third appointment broke the statutory restriction of 1371; only now, no more than a year had elapsed since his last occupation of the office. He remained sheriff for the whole of this last Exchequer year of Richard II's reign, until 30 September 1399, on which day the revolu-

---

[15] *Ibid.*, 1396-9, 310, 313, 370, 438, 503.
[16] *List of Sheriffs, loc. cit.*

tion which saw Richard II's deposition and Henry IV's accession was consummated. Redmayne's appointment as sheriff in November 1398 suggests that he was well trusted by Richard II, who by this time was far gone in his despotic courses. That this was so is more clearly evident from the fact that by 8 January 1399, when he was recompensed at the Exchequer of Receipt for £5 which he had paid to a valet of the Duke of Berry, who had brought a destrier as a present from the duke to the king, he was Master of the King's Horses.[17] Moreover, he accompanied Richard II on his second and, from the point of view of later events in England, disastrous expedition to Ireland in the spring of 1399. On 10 April Redmayne nominated as many as six attorneys to act for him in England during his absence (including his neighbour of Gawthorpe, William Gascoigne, at this time one of the King's Serjeants-at-law), and on 18 May (at Haverford West, when on his way to the port of embarkation) two more, Richard Clifford, Keeper of the Privy Seal, and Thomas Stanley, Keeper of the Rolls of the Chancery. In the meantime, on 17 April, Redmayne had been granted the wardship (and marriage) of the heir of Sir Richard Kirkbred, a Cumberland tenant-in-chief, to the value of £50 a year, although six days later the concession was reduced to 20 marks a year.[18]

Whether or not they were tricked into doing far more towards achieving Henry of Bolingbroke's accession than they intended, the Percies were foremost in supporting him on his return to Yorkshire (from exile in France) early in July 1399. But the northern baronage generally rallied to assist the heir of Lancaster to recover his recently sequestrated inheritance. Perhaps it was the Percies, with whom Sir Richard Redmayne and his father had been long connected in one way and another, who spoke for

[17] Exchequer, Issue Roll, P.R.O., E 403/561, mem. 11.
[18] *CPR, 1396-9,* 519, 553; 532, 560.

him in the new situation which rapidly brought Richard II's reign to an end. His relationship with Lord Greystoke can only have been helpful. Perhaps Redmayne's absence in Ireland, however, saved him (and many others closely connected with Richard II) from adopting an equivocal attitude at the moment of crisis. However this may be, it was soon clear, once the revolution had been effected, that whatever Redmayne stood to lose by the change of sovereign, he did, in fact, lose little. Admittedly, on 8 October 1399 he and his brother, John, were required to undertake in Chancery that they would not harm Master Thomas Dalby, Archdeacon of Richmond, or his servants, on pain of forfeiting £200, and three of their neighbours in Westmorland found mainprise in the same amount on their behalf. But on 26 October Sir Richard's enjoyment of the Kirkbred wardship was confirmed, and on 31 October all the grants made to him by Richard II were made the subject of a royal *inspeximus* and confirmation: the grant of all the royal lands in Blencogo of 1388, the grant for life of the annuity of 40 marks (charged on the issues of Cumberland) of 1390, and the grant for life of 40 marks a year (charged on the Exchequer of Chester) of 1397, a further confirmation of which grants he secured, by letters under the Seal of Chester, from the royal heir-apparent, Henry, Prince of Wales, on 15 May 1400.[19]

Of Sir Richard Redmayne's doings in 1400 nothing is known, although it is likely that he was involved in Henry IV's brief expedition into Scotland in the summer, York being the rendezvous of the royal army. That all was going well with him under the new régime is suggested by the conversion of his grant for life of the Blencogo royal lands into a grant to him and heirs by a patent of 14 April 1401. Six days later he and his wife were allowed a royal licence enabling them to entail their moiety of the manor of Harewood on their heirs male in accordance

---

19 *CCR, 1399-1402*, 88; *CPR, 1399-1401*, 48; 47.

with a fine levied in the Court of Common Pleas in this term — they already had two sons, Matthew and Richard — with a remainder in tail male in favour of Lady Redmayne's son by her first marriage, Brian Stapleton.[20] On 8 July 1401 Sir Richard was appointed for the first time as a justice of the peace in Westmorland.[21] And, soon after 20 July, when Henry IV wrote to his council from the priory at Selbourne, ordering a Great Council to be summoned to Westminster for the middle of August, the council decided that Redmayne should be among the knights to be called up from Yorkshire; in a second list he also appeared as one of the three summoned from Westmorland. It was there decided that a policy of war with both France and Scotland should be accepted. Redmayne seems to have taken the opportunity given him by this visit to London to secure a clarification of the terms on which he held the Kirkbred wardship, for he took out a new patent (on 19 August 1401).

On 8 November 1401 Sir Richard was for the fifth time made sheriff of Cumberland; his re-appointment after the elapse of only two years since the end of his last spell of office was again an infringement of the Statute of Sheriffs of 1371.[22] He held the shrievalty until 29 November 1402, in the meantime serving on the commission (for Westmorland), set up on 11 May 1402, ordering the arrest of malcontents spreading lies about the king's failure to keep his promises of good government.[23] Whether or not Redmayne had any part as sheriff in the manœuvres resulting in the brilliant success of the Percies against the Scots at Humbleton (on 14 September 1402) is not known. But it is very doubtful, because in June a large force of Scots had attacked Cumberland in the region of Carlisle, and, although the next Scottish movement was to be across the Eastern borders, Cumberland is likely to have engaged Redmayne's continuous attention.

[20] *CPR, 1399-1401,* 533; 476; *ibid., 1422-9,* 104; *CFR 1471-85,* 241-244.
[21] *Ibid.,* 565; *ibid., 1401-5,* 520.
[22] *PPC,* i 157, 161; *CPR, 1399-1401,* 545; *List of Sheriffs, loc. cit.*
[23] *CPR. 1401-5,* 129.

While this victory of Humbleton relieved pressure in the North, subsequent trouble with Henry IV over the very important persons taken as prisoners in the engagement fanned the discontent of the Earl of Northumberland and Hotspur. And in the summer of 1403 they revolted. The rising was crushed at Shrewsbury on 21 July. Hotspur and his uncle, the Earl of Worcester, met their deaths, and Henry IV received Northumberland's surrender some three weeks later at York (on 11 August). Redmayne's attitude in this crisis was apparently one of complete loyalty to the king. On 16 July, when, from Burton-on-Trent, Henry IV had called up the Midlands and demanded the arrest of all suspected rebels, he had also appointed commissioners in Yorkshire, including Chief Justice Gascoigne (Redmayne's neighbour) and Redmayne himself, ordering them to arrest some of the Yorkshire gentry who were under suspicion, and, if these proved a nuisance, to execute justice on them as traitors and rebels. On 13 August, by letters issued by the Chancery from York, Redmayne was put on the commission of oyer and terminer for the West Riding set up to deal with cases of trespass against persons and property during the revolt. Two days later, by letters issued at Pontefract, he was included in a commission of array of forces in the Riding, presumably for service with the king on the borders of Wales.

Meanwhile, at York on 9 August, Redmayne had been given the custody of his wife's former husband Sir Brian Stapleton's manors of Carlton (near Otley) and Kentmere (near Kendal), the first at £70 a year, the second without rendering any farm so long as its income did not exceed £46 a year. This latter concession was expressly to recompense him for arrears of royal fees. The grant had been made possible by the recent execution and forfeiture of Thomas Percy, Earl of Worcester, who had had an interest in the whole Stapleton wardship since 1394, when he and Sir William Scrope had paid £400 for it. And then, on 5 November 1403, only a year after ceasing to be sheriff of Cumberland, Redmayne was appointed to the same office in Yorkshire; he held it until 4 December 1404.[24]

It was in his capacity as sheriff that Redmayne was concerned in June 1404 in taking from York to Ponte-fract a former close servant of Richard II, William Serle, who had just been seized on the Border and brought south by the Earl of Northumberland (on the occasion of the earl's visit to Pontefract to meet the king and surrender his castles). Serle, who in 1399 had escaped to France and then returned to Scotland, had helped to foster the notion that Richard II was still alive, which had given the Percies some help in raising revolt in 1403 and always caused the government some embarrassment. Also accused of the murder of the king's uncle, Thomas of Wood-stock, in 1397, Serle could hope for no mercy from Henry IV and at Pontefract he was condemned for treason. On 3 November 1404, at Coventry (during the holding of the autumn parliament there), the Upper Exchequer was ordered, when auditing Redmayne's account as sheriff, to allow him up to £3. 13s. 4d. for the expenses which (as he was to declare on oath) he had incurred regarding Serle, and also for his costs in distributing the head and quarters of another traitor likewise adjudged to death at Pontefract, one Richard Tiler.[25] Shortly after he was rid of Serle but while Henry IV was still at Pontefract, Red-mayne was empowered on 7 July to array men-at-arms and archers from Lonsdale and round Kendal: these were to go with him for the defence of the Marches when required, although only on the previous day a truce to last until Easter 1405 had been arranged at Pontefract with plenipotentiaries from Scotland.[26]

Redmayne's influence at this point was such that, some time before he surrendered the shrievalty of Yorkshire

24 *Ibid.*, 297; 284; 253; *List of Sheriffs*, 162.
25 *CCR, 1402-5*, 391.
26 *Rotuli Scotiae*, ii 167b.

early in December 1404, he had already been appointed
as royal escheator in the county. This appointment, dated
22 October 1404, lasted until 1 December 1405.[27] A
month after his assumption of this new office and over a
week before he gave up to his successor the shrievalty
of Yorkshire, Redmayne was associated with Sir Richard
Arundell in a commission (dated at Westminster on 23
November 1404) ordering them to take the muster of the
force which, under the Prince of Wales and his brother,
Thomas, was to attempt the relief of the castle of Coity
in Glamorgan (Oldcastle Bridgend).[28] This place, which
was then in great danger of having to capitulate to the
Welsh rebels who were besieging it, was so important as
to warrant the immediate diversion of a London loan
of 1,100 marks for its rescue.

Although Redmayne had been re-appointed J.P. in
Westmorland as late as 23 November 1404, early in the
year of his escheatorship in Yorkshire (on 16 February
1405) he dropped out of this commission of the peace,
having meanwhile been appointed for the first time as
J.P. in the West Riding (by patent of 22 January 1405).
He continued to act on this commission without a break
until January 1414.[29]

The year of Redmayne's escheatorship in Yorkshire
(1404-5) saw the North of England once more gravely
disturbed by fresh treasons on the part of the old Earl of
Northumberland, who was now joined by Lord Bardolf;
and the disorder in Yorkshire itself was intensified by the
revolt of Archbishop Scrope and the young Earl Marshal
who, tricked by the Earl of Westmorland into surrendering at Shipton Moor, were shortly put to death on Henry
IV's orders. There is no record of Redmayne's behaviour
during the particularly unquiet time of this year, except
that in June and July he was with the royal army

27 P.R.O., *Typescript List of Escheators*, 187.
28 *CPR, 1401-5*, 475.
29 *CPR, 1401-5*, 521; ibid., *1405-8*, 500; ibid., *1408-13*, 487; ibid., *1413-16*,
426.

which went north to recover Berwick from the Earl of Northumberland's forces and to occupy some of Percy's own strongholds. (On 4 November 1406 the king gave him £20 towards his costs on this expedition.) But by the beginning of August 1405 the work of confiscating the estates of rebels and rewarding royal supporters was proceeding apace, and as escheator Redmayne is bound to have had his hands full. On 5 August he was with the king at Pontefract and acted as surety for the grantee of the Leicestershire estates of one of the foremost of the Cleveland rebels, Sir Ralph Hastings, who had been taken prisoner at Topcliffe (before this force could reach the main rebel body at York) and later executed at Durham (on 20 July). Redmayne himself seems not to have profited from any of the confiscations. But on 9 August, still at Pontefract, the wardship of the Stapleton manor of Carlton, granted him for an annual farm-rent of £70 two years before, was now re-granted to him rent-free, except for a charge of £20 for the upkeep of his stepson, the heir, and a month later the grant was made retrospective to Michaelmas 1404. This was equivalent to an out-and-out yearly gift of £50.[30] On 13 August he was at Wetherby, holding as escheator an inquisition by which Nicholas Tempest was thrust out from the manor of Walton-by-Spofford when it was found that the Earl of Northumberland had given him the manor as late as 24 April in this year in exchange for an annuity of £10. Later in the year, on 4 December 1405, he was put on a commission to produce before the King's Council early in the New Year certain men disturbing the peace.[31]

To what was to become the longest medieval parliament until then, the parliament which met on 1 March and was not dissolved until 22 December 1406, Sir Richard Redmayne was for the first time elected as knight of the shire for Yorkshire, along with Sir Thomas Rokeby

[30] Privy Seal warrants for issue, P.R.O., E 404/22/194; *CFR, 1399-1405,* 316; *CPR. 1405-8,* 53, 54.
[31] *CPR. 1413-16,* 115; *ibid., 1405-8,* 149.

who was then enjoying the custody of some of the estates
of one of the leading Yorkshire rebels of the previous
year, Sir John Colville of the Dale. The three sessions of
this parliament were extremely contentious, the Commons
especially insisting on appropriation of supplies and
conciliar and ministerial accountability to parliament,
which, much against the king's will, the knights of the
shire compelled him to accept. On 19 June, at the end
of the second session, the Commons pressed for an audit
of the accounts of the two Treasurers for the Wars who,
appointed at Coventry in the autumn parliament of 1404,
were now seeking release from office. The king, after first
refusing the audit, had to give way and, in addition, to
allow a request from the Commons that, along with Lord
Roos and the Chief Baron of the Exchequer, there should
be associated as auditors six of their own number, five
knights of the shire and one of the London members.
Redmayne was one of the knights chosen by the Lower
House for this duty, and he and the others were commissioned to execute the audit by royal letters patent
issued at the beginning of what proved to be the last
week of the parliament (on 16 December 1406).[32] It may
well have been the remembrance of this commission, so
formally conceded by letters under the Great Seal, which,
when the knights refused to grant any fresh taxation,
so enraged the king that he decided to continue the parliament until they capitulated. Which they only did on
22 December, too late for most of them to get home for
Christmas.

Redmayne had not been idle during the parliament
in doing a certain amount of business at Westminster
on his own account. On 27 May 1406, during the second
session, he secured a grant of the wardship of the estates
and the marriage of the son and heir of one Richard New-
land, which, by further letters of 3 December (embodying his agreement with the Treasurer), he eventually

[32] *Rot. Parl.*, iii 577b; *CPR, 1405-8*, 351.

secured for 10 marks. The Keeper of the Hanaper of the Chancery, moreover, had already (on 28 November) been instructed to deliver the patent without taking the great fee for the seal.[33] The third session of the parliament had been going on for a fortnight when, on 27 October, the royal Council considered a request submitted by Redmayne along with Sir Robert Lowther and William Stapleton. In it the petitioners asked to be examined on oath by the Chancellor separately, touching their denial that letters patent appointing them as collectors in Cumberland of the aid for the marriage of the king's eldest daughter (Blanche) had ever been served on them. Despite this, process of distraint was now being entered against them in the Exchequer, and so they asked for the inquiry and also for writs of surcease if their excuses were accepted. The petition was successful, the Council allowing a suspension of proceedings and authorising a fresh commission to collect. Redmayne and his co-petitioners had evidently held the Exchequer at bay for nearly five years, for the commissions for the aid had originally left the Chancery in December 1401 when Redmayne was sheriff of Cumberland.[34] This business satisfactorily settled, a week or so later, on 4 November, Sir Richard secured a privy seal warrant authorising the Exchequer to pay him £20, a gift from the king for his services in the North, especially at the siege of Berwick in the summer of 1405; and a week or so later again, on 12 November, he obtained an exemplification under the Great Seal of the terms of an enrolment of a charter of 1209 granting to Warin FitzGerald a warren and the right to hold a three days fair and a market at Harewood, and on 4 December a patent of *inspeximus* and confirmation.[35] Redmayne was not elected to any of Henry IV's later parliaments.

Towards the end of the summer of 1407 the situa-

---

[33] *CFR, 1405-13*, 32; *CPR, 1405-8*, 274; *CCR, 1405-9*, 161.
[34] Ancient Petitions, P.R.O., S.C. 8, file 262, no. 13064; *CCR, 1405-9*, 226.
[35] P.R.O., E 404/22/194; *CPR, 1405-8*, 275, 278; *ibid., 1441-6*, 348.

tion in the northern counties was again deteriorating. Northumberland's lands had been confiscated and his castles surrendered after the failure of his rebellion in 1405. He and Lord Bardolf had fled into Scotland, then to Wales, and afterwards to France (late in 1406), from where they had returned to Scotland (during the summer of 1407). To do something to dispel a threat which had hardly yet materialized, in August 1407 Henry IV himself again went up into Yorkshire *via* the East Midlands. It was while he was at Rothwellhaigh, just south of Leeds, that on 30 August he commissioned his third son, John, who was Constable of England, and the Earl of Westmorland, who had filled the office of Marshal of England since 1405, to investigate and disperse any unlawful gatherings occurring in Yorkshire, Northumberland, Cumberland, and Westmorland. On the same day was set up another commission, one of oyer and terminer relating to cases of treason in these northern areas, in which Chief Justice Gascoigne, Sir Ralph Eure, Sir Thomas Rokeby (Redmayne's fellow-knight of the shire in the previous year), and Redmayne himself were associated with Prince John and Westmorland. Not until January 1408 did Northumberland and Bardolf cross the Border. Not surprisingly, the response of their friends was uncertain and disappointing; and Sir Thomas Rokeby, in charge of the Yorkshire levies as sheriff, had no difficulty in crushing the rebellion at Bramham Moor (near Tadcaster) on 19 February, when Northumberland was killed and Bardolf died of wounds. Within a month the king was again in Yorkshire and spent Easter at Pontefract on his return from York. Just before he left to go south, on 25 April, he commissioned the Earl of Westmorland, Chief Justice Gascoigne, Sir Ralph Eure, Robert Waterton, John Conyers, and Redmayne (only Waterton being of the *quorum*) to accept submissions from rebels and receive fines for the charters of pardon they were empowered to promise, answering at the Exchequer.

Three days later the same commissioners were authorized to inquire into the death of Sir Thomas Colville at Overton, presumably during the recent revolt.[36] Whether Redmayne, whose place at Harewood was no more than five or six miles from Bramham Moor, had taken the field with Rokeby, is not known. Unlike the sheriff, he did not profit from any of the confiscations that followed the battle (not that any clear inference can be drawn from this).

For a year or so after the spring of 1408 Redmayne slips entirely out of view. He remained a J.P. in the West Riding. But he served on no extraordinary or occasional commissions of royal appointment until, in April 1409, he became involved in diplomatic negotiations with Scotland. He was then appointed with three other northern knights to treat in the Marches about special or general truces. It was in the following summer that Jedburgh fell to the Scots, and in the autumn Fastcastle was besieged (but continued to hold out). The movement towards reaching a *modus vivendi* between the two countries was not, however, wanting in support: letters from the Scottish Regent, the Duke of Albany, written at Edinburgh on 2 October 1409, proposed a conference at Haudenstank on 10 February 1410, asking that the English agreement to participate should be presented at Kelloe on 30 November. On 14 November Henry IV replied that he proposed to send Sir Richard Redmayne and Master Richard Holme, LL.D., canon of York, to meet Scottish commissaries of similar rank at Kelloe on 27 January 1410, in order to settle a proper truce, arrange for a further meeting on the March to negotiate a final

[36] *CPR, 1405-8,* 359; 75, 405, 488 (The commission calendared in this volume on p. 75 should be ascribed not to 1405 but to 1408. When it is compared with that on p. 405 the error is evident, especially when consideration is given to the fact that the commission of 26 April on p. 75, again wrongly attributed in the *Calendar* to 1405, was addressed to Bishop Thomas of Durham and Henry, Archbishop of York, because the former only became bishop in 1406 and the latter archbishop in 1407. This clinches the matter. J. H. Wylie, in his *The Reign of Henry IV,* iii 158, spotted the error).

peace or a longer truce, and investigate breaches of the existing truce; and the letter asked for notice of an acceptance of these proposals to be sent before Christmas to the king's son, John, Warden of the East March, at Berwick. On 20 November Redmayne and Dr Holme were empowered to treat.[37] On 19 January 1410 Redmayne left Harewood, and on the next day Holme set out from York, for Kelloe. Their business concluded, both were in London on 13 February to report to the king, and at the same time Redmayne drew £10 of the £23 due to him as wages at the Lower Exchequer. On 1 March he was seemingly making ready to return to the Border on this business, being advanced at the Exchequer a further 20 marks.[38] Not until 4 April, however, were he and Dr Holme (with whom was now associated Lord FitzHugh of Ravensworth) empowered to treat for a peace or prolongation of the truce with Scotland, to make a settlement of claims, and to punish English violations of the existing truce. It was also a part of their duty to demand the return of Archibald, Earl of Douglas, who, taken prisoner first by the Percies in 1402 and then when fighting for them at Shrewsbury in 1403 by the king, had been finally allowed to go back to Scotland in June 1408 to promote an understanding between Henry IV and Albany. (The Scottish Regent's own heir had been taken prisoner with Douglas in 1402 and was still a captive in England.) On 13 April 1410 Redmayne left Harewood for Haudenstank on the Border, where he acted with Lord FitzHugh and Dr Holme and, after pausing on his way back to London at Harewood for four days (*causa recreacionis*), he was at Westminster, all ready to make his report, on 7 May, two days after

[37] Privy Seal warrants for issue, E 404/24/413; *Royal and Historical Letters of Henry IV*, ed. F. C. Hingeston (R.S.), ii 293. (The letters of both Albany and Henry IV are attributed to the year 1410, but they clearly belong to 1409. The meeting at Haudenstank was proposed by Albany for Monday, 10 February; this date fell on a Monday in 1410, in 1411 on a Tuesday.) *Foedera*, VIII 609; *Rot. Scotiae*, ii 192.
[38] Enrolled Foreign Accounts, P.R.O., E 364/43, mem. B; Exchequer, Issue Roll, P.R.O., E 403/602.

Holme's arrival. (At the rate of £1 a day, £20 were due to him, and he was paid this amount on 9 December following.) Negotiations continued on 17 June, this time the work of another party of commissioners drawn from Northumberland, and the truce was continued until 1 November 1410, only to be renewed later still until in autumn 1411 a long truce was finally concluded to last till Easter 1418. Redmayne was not party to these later interviews.[39]

. In the meantime, when, in the early summer of 1410, there was some fear that the Scots were intending to invade, Redmayne was put on a commission of array in the West Riding (on 5 July 1410). Still a member of the West Riding commission of the peace, he was included on 4 December 1411 in a commission of oyer and terminer, following a complaint by a man of York that he had been set upon at Over Ouseburn (between York and Boroughbridge) by men from Coverdale who then held him to ransom. A week later, on 10 December 1411, Redmayne was for the fifth time appointed sheriff of Cumberland and held office until 3 November 1412.[40]

When Henry V succeeded his father on 21 March 1413 Redmayne was not far short of being sixty years of age. But his services in the North had been, and his influence there still was, clearly enough to warrant the second Lancastrian king in continuing to recognise them. His near neighbour of Gawthorpe, the Chief Justice of the King's Bench since 1400, now saw fit to retire (or was removed), but Redmayne on 21 March 1413 was reappointed a J.P. in the West Riding in the first commissions of the peace to be issued in the new reign, and on 14 June following he secured royal letters patent renewing the confirmation of his letters of October 1399 continuing the annuity of 40 marks from the issues of

39 *Foedera*, VIII 630; *Rot. Scotiae*, ii 193; Exchequer, Accounts Various, P.R.O., E 101, bundle 321, no. 7; Issue Roll, E 403/606, mem. 6; Wylie, *Henry IV*, iii 279-81.
40 *CPR, 1408-13*, 224, 375; *List of Sheriffs, loc. cit.*

Cumberland granted him in 1390, although not, apparently, the supplementary annuity of 40 marks, drawn on the Exchequer of the Palatinate of Chester, which he had enjoyed since 1397. This limited grant was made on condition that he did not seek to be retained by anyone but the king (and for 5 marks paid into the Hanaper of the Chancery). This reverse was to some extent offset by his being paid at the Lower Exchequer, on 9 December 1413, £7. 16s. 10d. which Henry V *de gratia sua speciali* now ordered him to be given as a *donum* in recompense for all the arrears of his Cumberland annuity, and on 13 May 1414 he received an advance of half a year's instalment of this annuity, actually at the Exchequer itself.[41] He had lately (on 16 January 1414) been left out of the West Riding commission of the peace for the first time since 1405, but was then included once more in the commission for his own county of Westmorland.

It was, nevertheless, for Yorkshire that he sat as knight of the shire in the November 1414 parliament, the third of the reign. In May 1415 he was a commissioner of array in the West Riding for levies which were to stand by to resist any attempts from Scotland to upset Henry V's rapidly maturing plans to invade France.[42] And then, on 6 July, Redmayne was put on a commission appointed at Winchester to enquire into the forcible seizure of Murdach, Earl of Fife, the long-captive son of the Regent of Scotland, when passing through the West Riding on his way to the Border, where final arrangements for his exchange for Hotspur's son (the heir to the Earldom of Northumberland) were to have taken place. The small party in charge of the Earl of Fife had been attacked near Leeds on 31 May by an armed gang under one of the Talbots of Bowland, possibly acting in the interests of the plot of Richard, Earl of Cambridge, Henry Lord Scrope of Masham, and Sir Thomas Grey of Heton, which ultimately

---

[41] *CPR, 1413-16,* 67; Exchequer, Issue Rolls, P.R.O., E 403/612, mem. 8; *ibid.,* 617, mem. 4.
[42] *CPR, 1413-16,* 424, 426; 407.

came to light at Southampton at the end of July (when
Henry V was making his final preparations for his first
invasion of France). The commission of 6 July was to
arrest and imprison those responsible for Murdach's
abduction.[43] On the same day, Redmayne was re-included
in the West Riding commission of the peace, of which
he was now to remain a member until his death. He
was now J.P., therefore, in both the West Riding and
Westmorland. Despite the commission of 6 July, Sir
Richard took part in the mustering of the retinue of the
king's youngest brother, Humphrey, Duke of Gloucester,
near Romsey on 16 July. His second son, Richard,
crossed with the expeditionary force and fought along
with his stepbrother, Sir Brian Stapleton, during the
Agincourt campaign, when they took prisoner one
Guillaume Quintin, bastard of France, who came over to
England in 1416.[44]

There is no question of Sir Richard, senior, having
himself accompanied the expedition to Normandy: on
21 October, four days before the triumph of Agincourt,
he and Sir John Etton were re-elected as knights of the
shire for Yorkshire to the parliament summoned by the
Duke of Bedford (as *Custos regni*) to meet on 4 November,
and the Commons presented Redmayne to the duke as
Speaker-elect on 6 November, when he was accepted.
A fact of perhaps some significance in explaining Redmayne's election as Speaker on this occasion is that at
Levens he was now a tenant of the duke, to whom had
been granted the lordship of Kendal. The Chancellor,
Bishop Beaufort, had opened the session with a sermon
preached on the theme, *Sicut et ipse fecit nobis, ita et
nos ei faciamus.* This injunction the Commons certainly
obeyed with a promptitude and above all in a manner
well calculated to please the king: within the short space
of a week they advanced by nearly two months the

[43] *Ibid.*, 348; Wylie, *The Reign of Henry V*, i 515-8.
[44] *Transactions of the Royal Historical Society*, 3rd series, vol. 5, p. 124;
DKR, xliv 579; T. Carte, *op. cit.*, i 228.

collection of the subsidy of a tenth and fifteenth voted a
year ago, and on 12 November ended by granting the
wool subsidy and tunnage and poundage to Henry V
for his lifetime as from Michaelmas 1416, when the existing grant would have run its course (a concession with
no precedent except the short-lived grant to Richard II
of January 1398), and at the same time they made a fresh
grant of a tenth and fifteenth leviable at Martinmas 1416.
The Commons had already (on the fifth day of the
session) appeared before the Lords to ask for a ratification
of the judgments against the authors of the Southampton
plot. There was little time for aught else, and the common
petitions numbered no more than four. On 16 November
Henry V crossed from Calais and came ashore at Dover,
and on 23 November he had his reception in London. A
week later (on 1 December) Redmayne was appointed
once more as sheriff of Yorkshire.[45]

During Redmayne's year of office (which ended on
30 November 1416) there were two parliamentary elections which it was his duty to supervise in Yorkshire.
The returns to the parliament of October 1416 have been
lost, but the sheriff's influence is discernible in the elections to the earlier parliament of March: his stepson, Sir
Brian Stapleton, fresh from the Agincourt campaign, was
elected as one knight of the shire, the other being Sir
Robert Plumpton, a retainer of the Duke of Bedford and
steward of the honour of Knaresborough, whose heir
had just been contracted in marriage with Stapleton's
daughter, Elizabeth. (Incidentally, before the end of Sir
Richard's term of office as sheriff, the wife of his elder
son, Matthew, gave birth at Harewood to his grandson,
Richard.)[46] Whether Sir Richard really did incur heavy
losses as a result of his occupying the shrievalty is not
known, but it was on the ground of excessive personal

---

[45] *Rot. Parl.*, iv 63; *List of Sheriffs*, 162.
[46] Yorkshire Archaeological Society, Record Series, xci: A. Gooder,
The Parliamentary Representation of the County of York, 1258-1832, i
175-6; *Yorkshire Archaeological and Topographical Journal*, xxii 154.

expenditure that a grant was made to him on 28 April
1417, by the king and with the assent of the Council,
of letters patent pardoning him £80 of his dues at the
Exchequer, and at Reading on 8 May he secured a further
patent exempting him for life from again being made
either sheriff or escheator.[47]

The extant records of the proceedings of the King's
Council are unfortunately rather sparse for these years
of Henry V's reign, and little is therefore known of its
regular composition. This is especially true from the time
when Henry V took some of its most important members
with him on his second and more serious French
campaign, upon which he embarked in the summer of
1417. On 20 October 1417, however, Redmayne was
present as a member of the Council advising the *Custos,*
the Duke of Bedford, at one of its meetings. Admittedly,
this is the only one of which there is a record of his
attendance. But it is possible that he remained a member
of the Council in England for some time, although for
how long, or how assiduously he acted, there is no knowing.[48] It is not unlikely that for this office he owed
something to Lord FitzHugh who on 8 December 1416
had been appointed Treasurer of England. FitzHugh was
nephew to the lady who had been stepmother to Redmayne
between 1377 and her death in 1403, and Redmayne's
elder son and heir, Matthew, had married Joan Tunstall
(a daughter of Sir Thomas Tunstall of Thurland), whose
brother had married a daughter of Lord FitzHugh. Redmayne, however, was without doubt quite closely connected at this time with the Duke of Bedford himself:
it was in company with the duke that he was received
into the confraternity of the abbey of St. Albans on 4
October 1417. It is also well worth noting that on this
same day, according to the *Liber Niger* of the abbey,
the duke requested the prayers of the monks for Sir Brian

[47] *CPR, 1416-22,* 102
[48] *PPC,* ii 218.

Stapleton, *multum sibi dilectus,* Redmayne's stepson who had just been killed in Normandy.[49]

During the remainder of Henry V's reign Redmayne was a J.P. in both the West Riding of Yorkshire and Westmorland , and he continued to act on local commissions of royal appointment in each of the two counties. These commissions were, however, mainly occasional in type and infrequent. At the end of April 1418, he and the sheriff of Yorkshire were ordered to supervise (at Hull on 31 May) the muster of a military force for eight vessels which were to serve for six months on patrol off the eastern sea-board. On 5 March 1419 he was made a commissioner of array, in both the West Riding and Westmorland, against possible attacks from the sea by the Castilian allies of France, and, later in the same year, by a patent of 24 August, he was appointed as a commissioner of sewers in the districts between the rivers Ouse and Aire.[50] Incidentally, he was by now in receipt of a pension of £20 (additional to his other royal annuity of 40 marks), charged on the revenues of the estates of the Duchy of Lancaster in southern England and payable at the hands of the duchy's receiver-general. About this time Redmayne was evidently still closely connected with the Duke of Bedford (who was continuing to act as *Custos Anglie* in the king's absence), an assignment to the duke for £24 being made through him at the Exchequer on 27 October 1419, along with another assignment for £40 by the hand of Bedford's receiver-general.[51]

It was in December 1420 that Redmayne again sat as knight of the shire for Yorkshire, in a parliament summoned by the Duke of Gloucester, who had now been *Custos* in England for a year, ever since Bedford's departure to Normandy. The king was daily expected to return home, but parliament did not last long. It was

49 British Museum, Nero D VII, fo. 144.
50 *CPR, 1416-22,* 200, 211, 269.
51 Duchy of Lancaster, Accounts Various, Michs. 1418-9, P.R.O., D.L. 28/27/8; Exchequer, Issue Roll, P.R.O., E 403/643, mem. 2.

on the third day of the session, 4 December 1420, that Redmayne took out an *inspeximus* and confirmation of the letters he had procured in 1406, exemplifying his rights of warren, fair, and market at Harewood.[52] On 7 April 1421, by which time Henry V had been back in England for two months, striving to re-excite interest in the completion of his conquests in France, Redmayne was included in a commission for raising royal loans in the West Riding, the commissioners themselves being expected to lend to the king.[53] Redmayne was not re-elected knight of the shire to the important parliament (of May 1421) which was the last of Henry V's reign to be attended by the king in person. But when the need for further supplies brought parliament together in the following December, once again under the presidency of the Duke of Bedford as *Custos Anglie,* he was for the fifth and last time elected as knight of the shire, once more for Yorkshire.

When parliament next met, in November 1422, it was mainly to sanction the form of government during the long minority of Henry V's successor, his infant son, Henry of Windsor. Although Sir Richard Redmayne was not returned as knight of the shire, in all probability he came up to Westminster on business of his own. At least on 15 December, three days before the end of the parliament, he received a writ under the Great Seal confirming the patents of June 1413, October 1399, and November 1390, by which he had held his annuity of 40 marks, chargeable on the royal revenues of Cumberland. On 26 March following (1423) Redmayne improved on this considerably, by getting an exemplification under the Seal of Chester of the late king's ratification (in 1400) of Henry IV's patent of 1399, confirming all the grants he had enjoyed in Richard II's reign; his right to occupy the royal lands in Blencogo (Cumberland) worth £10 a

---

[52] *CPR, 1441-6,* 348.
[53] *Ibid., 1416-22,* 384.

year, the Cumberland annuity of 40 marks, and the
annuity of 40 marks for which the Exchequer of Chester
was responsible; and on 23 April 1423 he did his best
to get even sounder authority for his pensions, by taking
out a patent under the Great Seal corroborating the confirmation under the Seal of Chester. This last comprehensive grant passed the Chancellor by advice of the
Great Council and by a warrant of the Privy Seal.

By this time the sands were beginning to run out, and
in July 1423 Redmayne dropped out of the commission
of the peace for Westmorland, although he stayed on as
a member of the West Riding commission, to which he
was also re-appointed in July 1424.[54] On 29 April 1424
he had witnessed a demise by Thomas Beaufort, Duke
of Exeter, of all his interest in the estates of the late
Sir Robert de Neville of Hornby (Lancs.), to whom the
Duchess of Exeter was granddaughter and heir, in favour
of Sir William Haryington of Hornby who had married
one of Sir Robert's two daughters (the duchess's aunts).[55]
On 5 September following, Redmayne was appointed to
serve on his last occasional royal commission along with
his stepbrother, Lord Greystoke, and his wife's nephew,
Sir William Ryther: a commission of inquiry in Yorkshire regarding cases of concealment of royal rights,
especially of feudal incidents due to the Crown.[56]

On 1 May 1425 Sir Richard drew up his testament,
instructing his feoffees in the manor of Levens and certain
of the Harewood estates how they were to make a settlement on his second but sole surviving son, Richard,
pending the majority of his eight-years-old grandson,
Richard (the son and heir of his elder son, Matthew, who
had died in 1419) and how to treat the interest of his late
wife's heirs by her first husband (the Stapletons). Aged
about seventy, Sir Richard died on 22 May 1426. There
is evidence for believing that he was buried with his wife,

[54] *Ibid.*, *1422-9*, 48, 104, 573.
[55] Catalogue of Ancient Deeds, iii C3563.
[56] *CPR*, *1422-9*, 275.

Elizabeth Aldbrough (who had died in December 1417), in the church of the Blackfriars at York. With this friary the Aldbrough family was obviously closely connected: Redmayne's wife's brother and *his* widow, both of whom had died in 1391, were buried there, and so was her son (by her first husband), Sir Brian de Stapleton, who had died in Normandy in the autumn campaign of 1417. There is, however, a tomb-chest at Harewood with effigies representing both Sir Richard and his wife.[57]

The writ of *Diem clausit extremum* after Sir Richard's death issued as of course from the Chancery to the royal escheator in Yorkshire on 8 September 1426, and on 5 February 1427 the custody of the Redmayne moiety of the manor of Harewood was given (by bill of the Treasurer of England), for the duration of the minority of Sir Richard's grandson, Richard, to Richard Duckett, the boy's uncle by marriage, and Thomas Redmayne. Already, on 7 November 1426, Sir Richard's second son, Richard Redmayne of Bossall, had secured confirmation of his hold on the manor of Blencogo (Cumberland), in the form of a royal pardon for acquiring it from his father without licence.[58] It was apparently this Richard who was father to Richard Redmayne, Abbot of Shap, who became Bishop of St Asaph in 1471, of Exeter in 1495, and of Ely in 1501. Who was Richard of Bossall's wife is not known. One of the Speaker's daughters (Joan) married Sir Thomas Wentworth of Wentworth Wood-house, and another, Richard Duckett of Grayrigg (Westmorland), a nephew of Sir William de Windsor (the Lieutenant of Ireland in the later years of Edward III) and the same who shared in the wardship of Harewood after Sir Richard's death. The Speaker's grandson and heir, Richard, who only proved his coming of age in November 1437, married the granddaughter of Sir Richard's neighbour and colleague in so many royal

---

[57] *Yorks. Arch. and Topogr. Journal*, iv 92; W. Greenwood, *op. cit.*, 88; *Collectania Topographica et Genealogica*, iv 76.
[58] *CFR, 1422-30*, 136, 159; *CPR, 1422-9*, 381.

commissions, Chief Justice Gascoigne of Gawthorpe. The young Richard, like his grandfather, went into the service of the Duke of Bedford, who before his death in 1435 had made him master-forester of Kendal. It was he who was knight of the shire for Westmorland in 1442, and *his* son, William, who was knight of the shire for the same county in 1478. Another, younger son, Edward, lawyer of Lincoln's Inn, sat for Carlisle in the same parliament and for Westmorland in 1495.[59] These were the only members of the Speaker's family to sit after him in parliament during the 15th century.

[59] Greenwood, *op. cit.*, pedigree facing p. 1; G. F. Duckett, *Duchetiana*, 16; N. & B. i 111; British Museum, Harleian MS. 1178, fo. 109v; J. C. Wedgwood, *History of Parliament (Biographies)*, 709-10.

11

SIR WALTER BEAUCHAMP

Sir Walter Beauchamp of Bromham, Speaker in the Parliament of March 1416, when Knight of the Shire for Wiltshire.[1]

Sir Walter Beauchamp was a member of the family of Beauchamp of Powick, a cadet branch of the family of Beauchamp of Elmley, of which the Beauchamp Earls of Warwick became the senior line. His great great-grandfather, Walter Lord Beauchamp of Alcester and Powick, steward of the Household to Edward I from 1290 to his death in 1303, was a younger brother of William de Beauchamp, Earl of Warwick, who died in 1298. Another branch of this family was that of Beauchamp of Holt: Sir Walter's grandfather, Sir John Beauchamp of Powick, a knight of the Chamber at the end of Edward III's reign, who died sometime between March 1386 and May 1389, was second cousin to John Lord Beauchamp of Holt, who was created Baron of Kidderminster by patent in 1387, when he was steward of the Household to Richard II, and who was successfully impeached of treason by the Commons in the Merciless Parliament of 1388 and executed. Sir Walter's grandfather's younger brother was Roger Lord Beauchamp of Bletsoe (Bedfordshire) and Lydiard Tregoze (Wiltshire), who was Chamberlain to Edward III for a time during the last year of his reign and summoned to Parliament from 1363 until his death in 1380. Sir Walter's father was Sir William Beauchamp of Powick, who died sometime between July 1420 and December 1422; his mother, Katherine, a daughter and coheir of Sir Gerard Ufflete, survived both her husband and Sir Walter, her eldest son, and was still alive in 1431.[2] Sir Walter's father followed *his* father in the constableship of Gloucester castle, being granted the office in 1392 at the request of Thomas of Woodstock, Duke of Gloucester, first for the duke's life and then in 1393 for his own life, a grant which was confirmed to him at the accessions of Henry IV and Henry V; and from 1392 he and his wife enjoyed a royal annuity of 40 marks charged on the issues of Gloucestershire which was similarly confirmed in 1399 and 1413 and, after Sir William's death, to his widow in 1422.[3] Sir William was sheriff of Worcestershire in 1401-2 and of Gloucestershire in 1403-4 and 1413-4, and was Knight of the Shire for Worcestershire in 1407, 1413, and in April 1414.

The matrimonial position of the family at the turn of the fourteenth century reinforces this general impression of influence in Court circles. Sir William's sister, Walter's aunt, Alice Beauchamp, after the death of her first husband, Thomas Boteler esquire, in 1398, married Sir John Dallingrigge, a knight of the King's Chamber, early in Henry IV's reign. Walter did well for himself by marrying into the important Wiltshire family of De La Roche of Bromham. By November 1410 at the latest, and probably by November 1403 (when he was first appointed sheriff of Wiltshire), Walter was married to Elizabeth, one of the the two daughters and coheirs of Sir John de la Roche and his wife, Willelma, daughter and heir of Sir Robert de la Mare of Fisherton Delamere (Wiltshire) and Offley (Hertfordshire). Walter's father-in-law, Sir John de la Roche, who died in September 1400, had been appointed in 1373 (like his father before him) overseer of the royal forests of Chippenham, Melksham, and Pewsham, and in April 1377 had begun to enjoy a royal annuity of 100 marks in which he was to be confirmed by Richard II and Henry IV at their accessions; he had been appointed by Richard II as ambassador to Pedro IV of Aragon to present him with news of his coronation and in 1378 had accompanied John Lord Neville, then King's Lieutenant in Aquitaine, on another embassy to Pedro IV, and in 1382 on one to Gaston de Foix; in this year he had been made keeper of Marlborough castle and of Savernake Forest and was admiral of the South and West; in May 1389 he had followed the Earl of Arundel as admiral to the West and North; in 1390–91 he had been sheriff of Wiltshire; and he had sat in Parliament for Wiltshire on eight occasions in and between 1381 and 1399.[4] To the local influence of the De la Roches Walter Beauchamp was in a sense to succeed.

In view of the survival of Walter's father until after his own career had taken shape, it was largely from a moiety of the De la Roche and De la Mare lands which came into his possession *jure uxoris* that his landed income evidently accrued. These were for the most part in Wiltshire and were in all parts of the county, although the main concentration was within easy reach of Devizes, of which lordship the De la Roche residential manor of Steeple Lavington was held. Near here, in the western approach to the Vale of Pewsey, were also estates and rents in Bromham, Calne, Chittoe, and Goatacre, which came to Walter and his wife on the death of her mother (Willelma) in October 1410, the royal escheator in Wiltshire being ordered to give them livery (after taking security for the relief) in February 1411. At the same time livery was authorized of other estates which fell to Elizabeth as her purparty, including lands and rents at Hardenhuish and Draycot Cerne (near Chippenham), at Berwick Bassett (near Malmesbury), and at Winterbourne Bassett, West Chisenbury, and East Winterslow (in the eastern half of Wiltshire). Further afield was the manor of Lower Heyford on the Charwell in N. Oxfordshire, and the manors of Offley and Putteridgebury (in Offley) in Hertfordshire. Rights of ecclesiastical patronage they succeeded to at Tollard Royal in south Wiltshire and Marsh Baldon in Oxfordshire. Steeple Lavington had already been conveyed to them by Elizabeth's mother before her death, for on 29 November 1410 Walter and Elizabeth secured a royal pardon for their trespass in entering without royal licence.[5] Within a week of the royal order for livery of seisin of his wife's purparty of her mother's estates, Beauchamp moreover secured (on 10 February 1411) the wardship of the other purparty belonging to his wife's nephew, John Beynton, the four-year old son and heir of her sister Joan, for which custody he undertook to pay annually into the royal Exchequer a farm of 80 marks until the heir reached his majority. The wardship was, in fact, to endure to within about a year of Walter Beauchamp's death, John Beynton obtaining seisin in December 1428. In February 1412 the whole of the render was ear-marked as the fee of Henry IV's physician, Master David de Nigarelli of Lucca. But after the latter's early death Walter compounded for his obligations past and future, paid to the physician's executors 40 marks and another 260 marks in hand to the Exchequer, and on 16 May 1412 the annual rent of 80 marks was altogether remitted as from the previous Easter. It would appear that for little more than the equivalent of five years' rent Beauchamp secured an occupation of the purparty in wardship for some eighteen years in all.[6] In addition to his wife's and her nephew's lands, Beauchamp also came into occupation (at some other time before his death) of lands in Quobwell (in Malmesbury) and a Duchy of Lancaster estate of the honour of Trowbridge at Whaddon in Wiltshire, lands in east Somerset at Wanstrow and Brewham, and at South Weston and Wheatfield near Thame in Oxfordshire.[7] He held lands in Gloucestershire, too, judging from the fact that at his death the escheator there was ordered to inquire what they were, but in the counties where were the main estates of his own family, Worcestershire and Warwickshire, he apparently held nothing, although he is occasionally described as being ' of Powick '. Two years after Walter's death, his mother, the widow of Sir William Beauchamp of Powick, was still in possession of an estate there and of the manor of Acton Beauchamp, also in Worcestershire.[8]

Walter Beauchamp's family ties were such as to have ensured him an easy entry into Lancastrian court circles whenever he was ready to profit by it. His father was a life retainer of Richard II, but with no more than a very modest fee, and he seems to have owed his grant of the constableship of Gloucester castle in 1392 to a connexion with the chief of Richard's II political enemies, Thomas of Woodstock. Moreover, he was a kinsman, however distant, of another of the Appellants of 1388, Thomas Beauchamp, Earl of Warwick, who felt the bite of Richard's rancour in 1397. The deposition of Richard II Sir William probably regarded with complete indifference; the accession of Henry IV, sympathetically, especially in view of the renewal of all his royal patents on 20 December 1399. For his eldest son, Walter, the crisis and Henry IV's continuing great need of support were doubtless a godsend, as they were to so many other pushing young men of the day. Without any known previous connexion with the new King, Walter Beauchamp ' of Powick '—he had evidently not yet married his Wiltshire heiress, but was almost certainly of age—ten days after Henry IV's coronation secured (on 23 October 1399) a grant of £40 a year from the royal revenues of Gloucestershire, for life or until he should be given equivalent lands: an annuity half as much again as his father enjoyed from the same source. Already he had doubtless joined the royal Household as an esquire. He was appointed one of the escort for Henry IV's elder daughter, Blanche, when she sailed from the Orwell estuary for Dordrecht on 21 June 1402, *en route* for Cologne and Heidelberg, where (on 6 July) she married the son and heir of the anti-Kaiser, Rupert of Bavaria. Her English entourage returned home on 25 July; on 15 July her treasurer had paid Walter Beauchamp £4.[9] During the next financial year (Michaelmas 1402-3) he figures in the royal wardrobe accounts as an esquire of the Household, and during this year he held by royal grant the Duchy of Lancaster manors of Easterton and Berwick St. James (in north Wiltshire), which were assessed by the duchy auditors for the South parts as together worth £40 3s. 6d. He continued to hold them and was still in possession in 1408-9 and in 1418-9, by which time they had been put into the control of the feoffees charged to complete the administration of Henry V's will. It was probably now that he surrendered his annuity of £40 of October 1399.[10]

The details of his service with Henry IV are not known, but it is probable that he was mainly 'in curia' in the early part of the reign. It is very likely that he fought at the battle of Shrewsbury on 21 July 1403, for only four weeks later (on 17 August) he was granted by the King's own warrant a debt of £20 owing to Sir Henry Percy (Hotspur), which the dead rebel leader had forfeited for his treason. On 5 November following he was appointed sheriff of Wiltshire, his father on the same day being appointed sheriff of Gloucestershire. Walter held office until 22 November 1404.[11] It looks as though his marriage to Elizabeth de la Roche had taken place by this date. In the following June (1405) he almost certainly moved northwards with the King when Henry went up to Yorkshire to cope with the rebellion of Archbishop Scrope and the Earl Marshal and then on into Northumberland to crush another Percy revolt. The work of the royalist army was done and Henry IV on his way south again when, by letters patent dated at Newcastle-on-Tyne on 16 July, Walter Beauchamp, King's esquire, was granted the office of keeper of the royal forest of Braden (north Wiltshire), a recent grant (of 14 March 1405) to his uncle by marriage, Sir John Dallingrigge, one of the knights of the King's Chamber, being surrendered, perhaps for the purpose; Walter's grant was made for life, but he evidently did not hold the office after September 1420. In the account book of the controller of the royal Household covering the period 30 September 1405-8 December 1406, Walter Beauchamp is still listed as one of the esquires of the Household in receipt of livery of robes worth £2 a year.[12] From 20 November 1407 to 15 November 1408 he was again sheriff of Wiltshire; during the year the mayor of Salisbury, on the city's behalf, paid 4 marks for a pipe of wine presented to Beauchamp as sheriff " to make him a friend ".[13]

It is just possible that Walter Beauchamp was elected as knight of the shire for Wiltshire to the Parliament of January 1410, for which the county returns have been lost. For it was while this Parliament was sitting that, on 10 February 1410, he was included in a royal commission to investigate a report of wastes committed on the estates of the Cluniac priory of Farleigh (Wiltshire) when the place was in the temporary custody of Sir Walter Hungerford and William Stourton. Only three days after the issue of this commission he was for the first time put on the commission of the peace in Wiltshire.[14] It was in the autumn of this year that Beauchamp's mother-in-law, Dame Willelma de la Roche died (on 31 October 1410). And in the ensuing months, Beauchamp was much involved in getting livery of those of her lands which descended to him and his wife, and in securing the wardship of his wife's sister's share of the estate, to which her infant son, John Beynton, succeeded. He was also concerned at this time with the administration of his mother-in-law's will of which she had appointed him the overseer, probate being allowed in the Prerogative Court of Canterbury on 22 November 1410. A year or so later he was acting in the same capacity in relation to the testament of his paternal grandmother, Elizabeth Beauchamp of Powick, which was proved on 26 September 1411.[15] He was still probably attached to the royal Household. Certainly in April 1412 he was still described as King's esquire. On 11 November 1411 a payment at the Lower Exchequer to the King's Chamber in the form of an assignment on the abbot of St. Augustine's, Canterbury, had been made by Beauchamp's hand.[16] On 2 January 1412 he was appointed as one of the two commissioners for Wiltshire to inquire into the incidence of liability to the recently voted parliamentary subsidy of a sixtieth on landed incomes of over £20 a year, and on 14 February following he was re-appointed justice of the peace in the county. He was confirmed in the commission at Henry V's accession in March 1413, and on 14 June was made a member of a royal commission set up to inquire into the refusal of customary services by a league of bond-tenants of the abbey of Austin canons at Cirencester. In January 1414, however, when fresh commissions of the peace were generally issued after Oldcastle's Rebellion, he was dropped from the Wiltshire bench. And it was not until November 1415 that he was once more made J.P. . In the meantime he served on no royal commissions at all.[17]

In 1415 Walter Beauchamp was caught up in activities preliminary to the first expedition of Henry V to northern France. The army sailed from Portsmouth on 11 August. On 31 June he had taken out royal letters of protection as a member of the King's retinue. He and a small retinue of three archers first mustered as members of the company of the King's youngest brother, Humphrey Duke of Gloucester, at 'Mikelasshe' near Romsey in July, but when the royal forces left England his retinue was composed of 3 men-at-arms and 12 archers, instalments of whose wages he was still being paid early in 1422.[18] It was just before or during the campaign which resulted in the capture of Harfleur and the victory in the field at Agincourt that Beauchamp was knighted. He is referred to as Walter Beauchamp knight when listed as a witness to a deed, dated 22 October 1415, conveying certain reversions in Wiltshire from Thomas Calston esquire to his daughter, the wife of William Darell. There is no reason to suspect that Beauchamp was back in England by that date, which was three days before the Agincourt engagement; the first of the witnesses was Sir Walter Hungerford, who certainly fought in the battle. On 13 December following Beauchamp was a witness to a deed confirming Hungerford's rights of common of pasture in Great Horningsham.[19] But he was back in England before this, probably returning with the King from Calais on 16 November. Already, on 8 November, he had been once more, after an interval of nearly two years, re-included in the Wiltshire commission of the peace (on which he was now to serve continuously until the summer of 1419), and on 25 November as a 'King's knight' he was able to secure for himself a grant of the keeping of the manor and lordship of Somerford Keynes (on the border between Wiltshire and Gloucestershire) during the minority of Richard, the young nephew and heir of the late Duke of York who had been killed in the press at Agincourt; the manor, which was supposed not to be worth more than £20 a year, was given him rent-free, provided that he answered for any surplus beyond that figure.[20]

To the Parliament which met on 16 March 1416 Beauchamp was elected as knight of the shire for Wiltshire along with Robert Andrews, the sheriff responsible for the election being Thomas Calston, whose deed of the previous October Sir Walter had 'witnessed'. On the third day of the session Beauchamp was presented by the Commons to the King as their Speaker and formally accepted. The first session lasted until 8 April when an adjournment was made for Easter, and the second session began on 4 May, a week after the landing of the Emperor Sigismund in England. When the Parliament was dissolved is not known, but the second session is not likely to have been a long one, for the King was preoccupied with diplomacy and with the situation which was formally clarified by the Anglo-Imperial Treaty of Canterbury in August following. Moreover, the parliamentary grant, which was no more than an anticipation by five months of the payment of the tenth and fifteenth voted in the last Parliament of November 1415 and now made due at Whitsuntide 1416, had been apparently made during the first of the two sessions. One of the important topics discussed during the Parliament was the question of payment of military wages. The matter was soon fairly satisfactorily dealt with from the Speaker's own point of view: on 6 June the Lower Exchequer paid him £286 odd on the account of the Treasurer for the Wars, but a certain amount still remained due for his service in the 1415 expedition as late as February 1422.[21] By that time, more again was owing to him for his service overseas in the meanwhile.

Not very long after the spring Parliament of 1416 was over, Beauchamp was put on an inquiry, instituted by royal patent on 15 June, into allegations of waste in the alien priory of Clatford near Marlborough. But a week before this a Bristol man had been granted letters of protection as a member of Sir Walter's retinue, and it is possible that Beauchamp was soon engaged in the military expedition which, under the leadership of the Duke of Bedford, relieved the siege of Harfleur. Whether this was the case or not, Beauchamp evidently joined Henry V's second expedition to France which set out on 23 July 1417 with the conquest of the whole of Normandy as its first objective. Three months before its departure, Beauchamp had taken out (on 27 April 1417) letters of protection and of attorney as a member of the King's retinue.[22] A member of the Duke of Gloucester's retinue in the expedition of 1415, he was in this year (1417) the Duke's steward for the holding of the courts of the forest of Savernake which Gloucester had been granted and where he was evidently using his authority as keeper of the forests south of Trent to make certain disagreeable changes.[23] But there is nothing to suggest that he now went to France in Gloucester's company.

During the first year and a half spent by Henry V on the conquest of Normandy there is no information of Sir Walter Beauchamp's movements, except that in January 1418 he was commissioned to muster men-at-arms and archers garrisoning a number of places held by Thomas Montague, Earl of Salisbury.[24] He was probably present at the long siege of Rouen from the end of July 1418 to 19 January 1419 when the city surrendered. It says much for Henry V's confidence in Beauchamp's ability that he appointed him on the very day of the surrender of the Norman capital as its first English *bailli*. A few days later Sir Walter received a grant of a house in the city forfeited by a 'rebel', and on 21 March following he was granted in tail male the castle of Beausault forfeited by a 'rebel' Norman seigneur, Sir John de Montmorency, in return for his homage and a yearly rent of a sword. During the year he acted on various ex-officio commissions in Rouen: on 5 February he was ordered to receive an oath of fealty from the Abbot of St. Mary de Voeu, and on the next day to inquire into the characters of certain persons who had applied to the King for office; on 23 July the Earl of Warwick, Lord Willoughby, Sir Walter Hungerford, John Feriby (the Treasurer of the royal Household), and Beauchamp were empowered to treat with the clergy and citizens about certain sums to be paid to the King and, at the same time, the Earl, Hungerford, and Beauchamp were instructed to make provision for the security of the city and inquire into any developments likely to be hurtful to the King's majesty; Beauchamp had authority as *bailli* to grant bills of passage to England to merchants and shipmen. On 11

March 1420 he was granted as *bailli* of Rouen the customary allow-ances while farming out the taxes imposed by the King.[25] It was while Henry V was at Rouen in January 1421, prior to his journey to Calais for the crossing to England, that (on 14 January) Beauchamp was re-placed in the *bailliage* of Rouen by Sir John Keighley.

Sir Walter only relinquished his Rouen office for promotion to the very important office of Treasurer of the royal Household, which carried with it the office of Treasurer for the War. He was certainly occupying this dual office by 21 January 1421. His predecessor, Sir John Rothenale, however, had died during the summer of 1420 and his own appointment, which cannot be precisely dated, perhaps took place then.[26]

Beauchamp naturally returned to England when Henry V made an extended visit home for the coronation of his queen, Katherine of Valois, whom he had married in accordance with the Treaty of Troyes on 2 June 1420, and for the purpose of securing a parliamentary rati-fication of the Treaty and further support for his policies in France. The King landed at Dover on 1 February 1421 and on 24 February Katherine was crowned at Westminster. Among the liveries of cloth made from the Great Wardrobe to members of the Household in pre-paration for this event was one to Sir Walter Beauchamp.[27] Towards the end of March the King's eldest brother, Clarence, was killed by the Dauphinists at Baugé, and Henry began to take steps to return to France as soon as was feasible. On 10 June, the day of his departure from Dover to Calais, the King revised the terms of the will he had made in July 1415, and something of the structure of its future administration. He re-appointed the executors of 1415 who were still alive and added others, among whom was Sir Walter Beauchamp. The latter was pro-bably appointed to succeed Rothenale who, as Treasurer of the House-hold, had been appointed executor in 1415; and, like Rothenale in 1415, Beauchamp was appointed to be one of a select committee of eight out of the total of eighteen executors that was specially authorised to administer the will as " working " executors.[28]

Although Beauchamp had taken out letters of protection and of attorney on 28 May 1421 as being about to go abroad once more in the King's retinue, it is most unlikely that he accompanied the King back to France in June 1421. On 6 July he was put on a commission appointed by the Council to inquire into alleged sales of venison and timber in the parks of Devizes by Robert Tyndale, who was parker there for life by grant of Henry IV; Tyndale had been removed from office by the

Duke of Gloucester, acting as keeper of the royal forests south of Trent, on account of his suspected conduct, but the King did not desire his ejection without reasonable cause, and so the Council was authorizing an investigation. As Gloucester's ex-steward for holding forest courts in Wiltshire, Beauchamp's own appointment to the commission was perhaps no mere formality. And it is probable that he was able to act at the time of the appointment. But what makes it much more unlikely that even if he returned to France in 1421 he did not long stay there, is that on 1 October 1421 his place as Treasurer of the Household was taken by Sir William Philip. On 23 February 1422, Beauchamp was certainly at Westminster and able to receive in person a payment at the Lower Exchequer of some £29 due to him in wages for his own and his retinue's service in the Agincourt campaign.[29] On 11 March 1422, moreover, Beauchamp was acting in England as Steward of the Queen's Household for in that capacity he then received at the Lower Exchequer £78 odd, which Henry V had ordered him to be paid for distribution among the clerks of the Queen's 'closseta' and the 'garciones' and 'pagetti' of her Household.[30] It is not improbable that he had occupied this headship of the Queen's Household from the previous autumn. How long he continued to hold this office is not known, but he also acquired the office of chief steward for those estates of the Duchy of Lancaster which went to make up part of Katherine's dower, and he was certainly still occupying this latter office in 1423, although by 1426 John Leventhorpe was acting as steward of all the duchy estates she held.[31] Beauchamp is almost sure to have accompanied the Queen back to France when she left her five months old son, Henry of Windsor, in order to rejoin the King. Her equipage crossed from Southampton to Harfleur in early May 1422. On 26 March Beauchamp had already taken out letters of protection and, on 16 April at Southampton, letters of attorney.[32] He very likely only returned to England after Henry V's death on 31 August following, in the company of the Queen who left Rouen with her husband's body on 5 October and reached London a month later.

The first Parliament of Henry VI's reign met at Westminster on 9 November 1422. Its main task was to sanction the form of government during the King's minority, and the settlement which emerged provided for the establishment of a limited Protectorship, to be enjoyed by the Duke of Bedford (the elder of the young King's uncles) or in his absence by his younger brother, the Duke of Gloucester. By authority of Parliament the effective power in the State was entrusted to a large, mainly aristocratic Council comprising the three greater officials and seventeen others whose conditional terms of acceptance of office Parliament agreed to. The last of the three commoners who were included in the list of councillors was Sir Walter Beauchamp.[33] The other two, Sir Walter Hungerford and Sir John Tiptoft, like himself were both ex-Speakers. But that is by the way. The reasons for his inclusion were without doubt his place among the effective executors of the late King and (perhaps a lesser consideration) his connexion with the Queen-mother.

There is no actual record of Beauchamp's attendance at Council meetings, but as an ex-Treasurer of the Household and *exofficio* Treasurer for the Wars he is likely to have been quite preoccupied with the tangled problems of the administration of Henry V's will. The work, however, proceeded slowly, and even at Beauchamp's death early in 1430 there was a sum of about £2,050 still unpaid to the executors of the £14,000 which it had been agreed (in 1422) they should receive. The whole position had been complicated by the need to fulfil the will of Henry IV concurrently, and not until December 1429 was this done. And even when in 1432 the deficit of the executors' income had been made up, their liabilities to Henry V's creditors and Household servants still amounted to £8,000. So far as winding up the administration of Henry V's Household was concerned, difficulties had in the meantime arisen, because its minor accounting officials claimed that Henry V had been prepared during his last illness to pardon them all their debts, arrears, and accounts in accordance with his usual annual practice every Good Friday, that he died before they could be acquitted by him personally, and that in any case they had had no opportunity of accounting for their receipts because after the death of Sir John Rothenale, Treasurer of the Household, they had entrusted all their memoranda and accounts to his successors in office, Sir Walter Beauchamp and Sir William Philip. Certain of Henry V's ' sergeants ' and other Household officers petitioned in this strain to Parliament in 1427.[33]

Incidentally, Sir Walter Beauchamp's family had had a special interest in the terms of Henry V's will of 10 June 1421, or rather in the terms of a codicil which the King had written in English with his own hand on the day before and sealed with the signet of the eagle. Henry had desired that Sir Walter Beauchamp's sister, Elizabeth, should be granted £200 worth of land for life on condition that she married by the advice of her mother, Thomas Beaufort, Duke of Exeter, Sir Walter Beauchamp (then Treasurer of the royal Household), and Sir Ralph Butler her kinsman, and took a husband within a year of the King's death with their assent.   If she married contrary to the King's intention, she was to forfeit her interest in the feoffees' grant. If she married in accordance with it and had issue, her heirs were to inherit in fee tail half of the lands granted her for life. If there were no children by the marriage and she predeceased her husband, the latter was to enjoy a life interest in half the estates, the other half reverting to the King's feoffees. If she did not marry but lived chaste, she was to have from the feoffees land worth 200 marks a year for life with reversion to them. In point of fact she did marry Thomas Swinford esquire, the son of the half-brother of the Duke of Exeter, by the advice of the Duke, Sir Walter Beauchamp her brother, and Sir Ralph Butler, and the couple were given estates by Henry V's feoffees in November 1425 in accordance with his will. But the marriage had not taken place precisely within a year of Henry V's death, owing to the feoffees' negligence of the terms of his instructions, with the result that after Swinford's death Elizabeth and her second husband, Thomas Rothwell, had to seek in 1440 a ratification of her estate in the manors in which she had a life interest and in those in which she and her issue by Swinford had an interest in tail. [34]

Sir Walter Beauchamp's sister's marriage with the nephew of the Duke of Exeter and of Bishop (later Cardinal) Henry Beaufort of Winchester, especially in view of his participation in its arrangement, may have done much to draw him clear of any sympathy with the Duke of Gloucester (with whom he had been earlier connected) during the troubled period in English domestic politics which followed Henry V's death.   Both the Beauforts were in 1422 against Gloucester being given that control of the government of England which he thought rightfully belonged to him by his birth and Henry V's will. So was the Earl of Warwick, Richard Beauchamp, Sir Walter Beauchamp's distant kinsman. And if more evidence were required to suggest Sir Walter's adherence to the 1422 plan of ' government by Council ' than his membership of the Council as first constituted in 1422, it would have to be looked for in his connexion with the Beauforts from his sister's marriage to one of their family, and in his evident attachment to the Earl of Warwick. In the Parliament of April-July 1425 when there came to a head the dispute over precedence in Parliament between the Earl Marshal and the Earl of Warwick, it was Sir Walter Beauchamp who acted in the case before the Lords as chief of Warwick's counsel and his spokesman. [35]

Despite the important connexions in high circles which these concerns of Sir Walter Beauchamp suggest, and despite his involvement in the active administration of Henry V's will, he did not long remain a member of the regency Council. Appointed in December 1422, he was not re-appointed, as were the great majority of his fellow-councillors, in the second Parliament of the reign which sat from October 1423 to February 1424. [36] He was, however, almost certainly still a member of the Council on 6 November 1423 when he shared with Lord Cromwell, another member of the Council, and others a grant of the custody of the temporalities of the archiepiscopal see of York, vacated on 20 October by the death of Archbishop Bowet. And he retained an interest in this custody until the vacancy was ended and the temporalities restored on the translation of Bishop Kemp of London to the northern province in April 1426, the custodians having in the meantime paid the Exchequer at the rate of 2,000 marks a year (that is, a sum of £3,344 6s. 5d. in all). [37]

Apart from these various transactions, not a great deal is known of Beauchamp in these last few years before his death. In July 1423 he had been once again appointed J.P. in Wiltshire and was regularly re-appointed to the commission of the peace until his death, in July 1424, July 1425, December 1427 and February 1428. He served in the same county on commissions for the raising of Crown loans in July 1426 and May 1428. These were the only casual local commissions on which he served in these years. With a fellow-member of this second loan commission, Robert Long esquire of Wraxall, and a J.P. of the *quorum* in Wiltshire, Beauchamp incidentally had been at enmity nearly two years before: on 26 October 1426 a commission of oyer and terminer had issued from Chancery after Long had complained that Beauchamp, his son William, and others had assaulted him at Beauchamp's place at Bromham. [38]

Although Beauchamp was still certainly connected with the Queen-mother in the first year after Henry V's death, it seems likely that an intimate relationship with her Household did not continue. But it is clear that his earlier connexion with the King's Household was maintained in Henry VI's reign, although it did not now lead to any such important post as he had held under Henry V. When Henry VI was nearly seven and a half years old Sir Walter was one of a group of four knights and four esquires appointed by the Council on 8 May 1428 to wait on the person of the King under the oversight of the Earl of Warwick, who was then appointed ' magister Regis ' and a few weeks later given a commission under the great seal to take charge of the boy King's education. Sir Walter and the other knights and esquires deputed to be about the King were ordered to appear before the Council, presumably to receive their charge, a month later (on 7 June). The Council agreed that each of the four knights was to enjoy the right of boarding in the Household an esquire and two ' valetti ', to have food in his chamber at Household cost, and to have an annuity of 100 marks a year by way of reward so long as he was engaged in these duties. On the same day the castles of Wallingford and Hertford were appropriated for the King's residence in the summer season, and Windsor and Berkhamstead in the winter time. The annual ' regardum ' of each of these knights for the body was fixed at this time at 100 marks. Beauchamp was still one of the four ' milites assignati pro Rege ' at the time of Henry VI's coronation on 5 November 1429, against which ceremony he received a special livery from the Great Wardrobe. Sir Walter's elder son, William, received the order of knighthood of the Bath on the vigil of the coronation. Sir William Beauchamp and his uncle, Sir John Beauchamp, Sir Walter's younger brother, as well, were in October 1432 stated to have been then long in the King's service as ' dapiscissores Regis '. Earlier in the year of the coronation, on 20 April 1429, Sir Walter was appointed to the office of ' magister equorum domini Regis '. He was not to hold this office for very long, however. For either at the very end of 1429 or early in 1430 he died, his place as Master of the King's horses being taken by Sir John Steward, and his position as one of the knights attendant on Henry VI falling to Sir Ralph Butler, Sir Walter's cousin, who rose to be Chamberlain of the royal Household after being chief chamberlain to the Duke of Bedford, was later created Baron Sudeley in 1441, and was Treasurer of England in 1443–46. [39]

Some eight weeks after Henry VI's coronation, on 30 December 1429, Sir Walter Beauchamp made his will. He left his body for burial in the chantry chapel of the parish church of Steeple Lavington (Wiltshire). The sparseness of the terms of the will suggests that his final illness had caught him somewhat unawares. To the church of St. Bridget in Fleet Street in London he alone made specific bequests: £2 to the church, £1 to its rector, a mark (13s. 4d.) to its parish chaplain, a noble (6s. 8d.) to each of its three clerks. The remainder of his goods and chattels he left to his executors : his wife Elizabeth, Sir William Beauchamp, his son and heir, Richard Beauchamp, a younger son, and John Roche, his cousin.   He died sometime between the drawing up of the will and 14 February 1430, when probate was made in the Prerogative Court of Canterbury. To Richard Beauchamp was then committed the admin- istration of the will, and the executors received their acquittance on 12 July following. In the meantime, on 28 May 1430, the writs order- ing inquiries into Sir Walter's tenures had issued from the royal Chan- cery to the escheators in Wiltshire, Oxfordshire, and Gloucestershire.

Seventeen years later his widow, Elizabeth, was to be buried next to his tomb at Steeple Lavington. [40] She had not lived quite long enough to see members of their family climb up into the ranks of the titular nobility. On 2 May following her death in February 1447, Sir Walter's younger brother, John, was created by royal patent Baron Beauchamp of Powick; already a Knight of the Garter (since 1445), he was to be Treasurer of England from 1450 to 1452. At the time of his uncle's ennoblement, Sir Walter's son and heir, Sir William Beauchamp, was still one of the King's carvers and, since 1441, Chamberlain of North Wales. Having married Elizabeth, the daughter of Sir Gerard Bray- broke, grandson and heir of Almaric Lord St. Amand (summoned to Parliament, 1382-1402), William was himself summoned as Lord St. Amand to Parliament on 2 January 1449, and he continued to be sum- moned until his death in 1457. He, too, was interred at Steeple Lav- ington. His son and heir, Sir Walter's grandson, Richard Beauchamp, Lord St. Amand, born in 1454, became a Knight of the Bath in 1475, rebelled against Richard III in 1483 and was attainted, but was restored at the accession of Henry VII, to whom his mother's second husband, Sir Roger Tocotes, was knight of the body and Controller of Household. At Richard's death, in 1508, without surviving legitimate issue, the barony became dormant (according to modern peerage theories) or extinct. Sir Walter Beauchamp's younger son, Richard, who in 1430 had acted as his father's executor, became Bishop of Hereford in 1448 and in 1450 Bishop of Salisbury, which see he retained until his death in 1481; in the meantime he had been made chancellor of the Order of the Garter in 1475 and Dean of Windsor in 1478. He it was who in June 1481, shortly before his death, joined with his nephew, Richard Beauchamp Lord St. Amand, Sir Roger Tocotes (Lord St. Amand's step-father), and Thomas Beauchamp esquire, in paying £300 for a royal licence to grant in mortmain lands worth £50 a year and found a chantry of four chaplains in the cathedral church of Salisbury. The chantry was to be for the good estate of Edward IV and his Queen, and of the founders, and for their souls after death and for the souls of the bishop's parents, Sir Walter Beauchamp and Elizabeth his wife, and the bishop's elder brother, William Lord St. Amand.[41]

---

1 *Rot. Parl.*, IV. 71; *Official Return*, i. App., xx.

2 *The Complete Peerage*, ii. 46-7; vii. 9.

3 *C.P.R.*, *1377-81*, III; *ibid.*, *1385-9*, 151; *ibid.*, *1391-6*, 108, 200, 209; *ibid.*, *1399-1401*, 171, 173; *ibid.*, *1413-16*, 130; *ibid.*, *1422-9*, 53.

4 *Complete Peerage*, VII. 296; *Wiltshire Arch. and Nat. Hist Mag.*, vol. 50, 379; vol. 51. 18, 23, 264; Cussans, *Hertfordshire*, ii, 100.

5 *C.P.R.*, *1408-13*, 265; *C.C.R.*, *1409-13*, 138; Cussans, *Hertfordshire, loc. cit.*

6 *C.F.R.*, *1405-13*, 204; *C.P.R.*, *1408-13*, 363; *C.C.R.*, *1409-13*, 269; *ibid.*, *1422-9*, 421.

7 *Feudal Aids*, IV. 192, 384, 386; V. 235, 238, 241, 244, 247, 265.

8 *ibid.*, V. 327-8.

9 *C.P.R.*, *1399-1401*, 35; Exchequer, Issue Roll, P.R.O., E 403/573, mem. 20.

10 Exchequer, Accounts Various, Q.R., Wardrobe Accounts, E 101/404/21; Duchy of Lancaster, Accounts Various, D.L. 28/27/1, 8, 10.

11 *C.P.R.*, *1401-5*, 255, 354; *List of Sheriffs*, 153, 50.

12 *C.P.R.*, *1405-8*, 73; *ibid.*, *1422-9*, 107; British Museum, Harleian MS. 319, fo. 46.

13 *List of Sheriffs, loc. cit.*; R. C. Hoare, *Wiltshire*, Old and New Sarum (R. Benson and H. Hatcher, London, 1843), vol. 1, p. 110.

14 *C.P.R.*, *1408-13*, 181, 486.

15 See above, pp. 2-3; N. H. Nicolas, *Testamenta Vetusta*, i. 176, 178.

16 Exchequer, Issue Roll, E 403/609, mem. 1.

17 *C.P.R.*, *1408-13*, 380, 486; *ibid.*, *1413-6*, 38, 425.

18 *D.K.R.*, XLIV, 568; Exchequer, Accounts Various, P.R.O., E 101/45/13; Privy Seal warrants for issue, E 404/31/324; Exchequer, Issue Roll, E 403/652, mem. 18; *T.R.H.S.*, 3rd series, vol. 5, 134.

19 *C.C.R.*, *1413-9*, 219, 294.

20 *C.P.R.*, *1413-16*, 380, 425.

21 Exchequer, Issue Roll, E 403/624, mem. 4; E 403/652, mem. 18.

22 *C.P.R.*, *1416-22*, 76; *D.K.R.*, XLIV. 580, 591, 593.

23 *Wiltshire Arch. and Nat. Hist. Mag.*, vol. 51. 333.

24 *Rotuli Normanniae*, ed. T. D. Hardy, 359.

25 *D.K.R.*, XLI. 724, 725; 782; 747, 790; *ibid.*, XLII. 331, 359, 388; T. Carte, *Catalogue des Rolles Gascons, etc.*, i. 343.

26 *C.P.R.*, *1416-22*, 333; *C.F.R.*, *1413-22*, 334; Exchequer, Issue Roll, E 403/646, mem. 12.

27 Exchequer, Accounts Various, Q.R., Account Book of the Great Wardrobe, 8-9 Henry V, E. 101/407/4, fo. 34v.

28 *Rot. Parl.*, IV. 172-3, 393.

29 *C.P.R.*, *1416-22*, 389; Exchequer, Issue Roll, E 403/652, mem. 12 (cf. Wylie and Waugh, *Henry V*, iii. 258); *ibid.*, mem. 18.

30 Exchequer, Issue Roll, E 403/652, mem. 19.

31 R. Somerville, *Duchy of Lancaster*, i. 207.

32 *D.K.R.*, XLIV. 637.

33 *Rot. Parl.*, IV. 175.

33 J. S. Roskell, *The Commons in the Parliament of 1422*, 117—9; *Rot. Parl.*, IV. 325; *C.P.R.*, *1422-9*, 64, 136, 176, 181, 188.

34 *C.P.R.*, *1436-41*, 364-6; *ibid.*, *1422-9*, 455. For notes on the Swinford family of Coleby and Ketelthorpe (Lincolnshire) to which Sir Hugh Swinford (the first husband of Katherine Swinford, the mistress and later third duchess of John of Gaunt), Sir Thomas Swinford his son (by Katherine), and the latter's son, Thomas (Elizabeth Beauchamp's husband) belonged, see *D.N.B.*, XIX. 244. The identification of the husband of Elizabeth Beauchamp with the kinsman of the Beauforts is assisted by the fact that in 1452 her second husband, Thomas Rothwell, got a grant of two-thirds of the manor of Colby and other estates of the Lincolnshire Swinfords. (*C.F.R.*, *1445-52*, 254).

35 *Rot. Parl.*, IV. 267. (The dispute was concluded by the Earl Marshal being allowed his father's title of Duke of Norfolk in accordance with the creation of 1397 by Richard II, the King's ' worthi predecessour '.)

36 *ibid.*, 200.

37 *C.F.R.*, *1422-30*, 59, 101, 166.

38 *C.P.R.*, *1422-9*, 571; 354, 481; 402.

39 *P.P.C.*, iii. 294; Privy Seal warrants for issue, E 404/44/315 (warrant to pay at rate of 100 marks a year dated 11 June 1428); Exchequer, Accounts Various, Enrolled account of the keeper of the Great Wardrobe, P.R.O., E 101/408/10; *P.P.C.*, *op. cit.*, iv. 128; E 101/106/29. Sir John Steward was appointed Master of the King's horses on 13 March 1430. A payment made to Sir Ralph Butler at the Exchequer in July 1431 described him as appointed by Henry VI to be attendant on his person *vice* Sir Walter Beauchamp, late deceased (Exchequer,Issue Roll, E 403/698, mem. 11).

40 Somerset House, Register Luffenham, fo. 12; *C.F.R.*, *1422-30*, 276. The will of Sir Walter Beauchamp's widow, Elizabeth, dated 6 February 1447, is to be found in the Stafford Register (Lambeth Palace Library), fo. 145b.

41 *Complete Peerage*, ii. 46-7;
   D.N.B. IV. 31; *C.P.R.*, *1477-85*, 276.

12

ROGER FLORE OF OAKHAM

Even well into the Tudor period it was an unwritten rule for the Speaker of the Commons in Parliament to be a knight of the shire, one of the elected representatives of some county, and not a mere Parliamentary burgess. It frequently also came about that the Commons chose someone who held office in the royal "civil service" or household, or who was otherwise connected with the king and personally acceptable to him. In the fifteenth century, just as later, quite a number of these men were lawyers, professional administrators and agents. And among *them,* some were members of the higher administrative staff of the Duchy of Lancaster which Henry IV decided, at his accession in 1399, should be separately governed from the Crown lands proper.

Such a one was Roger Flore of Oakham. He represented Rutland in the Parliament held by Richard II at Westminster in January 1397, in Henry IV's Westminster Parliaments of 1399 and 1402 and his Coventry Parliament of 1404, in Henry V's Leicester Parliament of April 1414, and his Westminster Parliaments of November 1414, 1415, March and October 1416, 1417 and 1419, in each of which last three consecutive Parliaments he was elected Speaker, and for the twelfth and last time in Henry VI's first Parliament of 1422, also held at Westminster, when, for the fourth time, he was again made Speaker.[1] It is a notable record of Parliamentary service, especially in the Speakership. His uninterrupted tenure of this office in three Parliaments running was not to be repeated until the end of Charles II's reign. Flore's appointment as chief steward of the estates of the Duchy of Lancaster north of Trent and as an *ex-officio* member of the Duchy council came just after his first experience as Speaker: he was occupying these important Duchy offices on each later occasion when he was Speaker, for he held them until his death in 1427. Incidentally, he is the only knight of the shire for Rutland ever to have been elected to the Speakership.

Flore's type of the legally-trained civil servant, busy with his administrative routines (into which his service on behalf of more than one of the great magnates and the pursuit of his own private interests were neatly and profitably dove-tailed) but seriously involved in none of the recurrent shifts of political power of this generally unquiet time of "bastard feudalism", is fairly rare among the medieval Speakers. For those who occupied this office were frequently, even usually, men in the thick of affairs of state when political life was sometimes of great hazard to person as well as to fortune and estate. Flore, of course, was lucky, because the peak of his career was reached at a time when, under Henry V, the royal government of England was at its most stable and self-assured in the period of those two centuries which separated the deaths of Edward I and Henry VII.

★

Roger Flore came of a family which before the end of the fourteenth century was already influential in the county town of Rutland. His father, William Flore, knight of the shire for Rutland in October 1382, had been controller of the works at Oakham castle from 1373 to 1380, deputy-sheriff to Robert de Vere, Earl of Oxford, after Richard II granted this great friend of his in 1385 the lordship of Oakham and the shrievalty of Rutland, and king's receiver at Oakham in 1390. This family association with the centre of the youngest and smallest of English shires had been strengthened by Roger's own marriage to Katherine, the daughter and heir of the founder of the hospital of St. John the Evangelist and St. Anne in Oakham, William Dalby of Exton, a Calais stapler. (In 1394 Flore himself had been a partner in an export of wool lost in transit from Lynn to Calais.) After his father-in-law's death in 1404, Flore, as his principal executor, was constantly in touch with the former patron of the hospital, the Carthusian prior of St. Anne near Coventry, until by the end of 1406 the gift of the wardenship had been transferred to him and his heirs and an annual rent of £20 settled on the hospital by the prior, in return for 550 marks (£366 13s. 4d.); in October 1420 Roger procured royal letters patent implementing those statutes of the hospital relating to its patronage. The outward and still visible signs of Flore's close connexion with Oakham are the fine tower and spire of its parish church, which in part owed their building to Roger Flore's munificence, and his town-house.[2]

Following Robert de Vere's flight to the Netherlands, after his failure at Radcot Bridge in December 1387 to suppress the Lords Appellants' opposition to Richard II, the king gave the lordship of Oakham and the shrievalty of Rutland early in 1390 to his cousin, Edward of Norwich, son of Edmund of Langley, Duke of York, together with the title of Earl of Rutland. Later on Edward's feoffee and executor, Roger Flore was already connected with this powerful local aristocratic interest at the time of the revolution of 1399. He doubtless owed his position as verderer in Rockingham Forest to the Earl of Rutland, whom Richard II in 1397 had also made warden of the royal forests south of Trent. A week after Henry IV's coronation, Edward, now Duke of Aumâle, by letters dated at London on 20 October 1399, granted to Flore for life the keeping of his park at Flitteris in the royal forest of Leighfield and the custody of the warren of his lordship of Oakham, and two days later he converted Flore's tenancy of a messuage and three roods of land in Oakham from copyhold to freehold. Flore was at the time sitting for Rutland in Henry IV's first Parliament. He had already sat as shire-knight in January 1397, and from November 1397 to the end of Richard's reign he had served as a justice of the peace in Rutland.

Although he was not re-appointed to the commission of the peace until January 1406, after which he served as a justice continuously until his death in 1427, Roger Flore was appointed to an appreciable number of royal commissions in his county. In April 1401 he was authorised to act as one of the guardians of Sir Robert Plesyngton of Burley (Rutland), with whom he had sat in Parliament four years earlier and who was now *non compos mentis* and (as such) in the Crown's wardship. In December following he acted with the sheriff and escheator in levying and collecting in Rutland the customary aid in anticipation of the marriage of Henry IV's elder daughter, Blanche. On 11 May 1402 he was appointed a member of the Rutland commission for the suppression of seditious talk, and he sat again as knight of the shire in the following autumn. Flore was a commissioner of array in the county when in September 1403, after the defeat of the Percies at the battle of Shrewsbury, Henry IV was resuming operations against rebels in Wales. On 24 March 1404 he was put on the Rutland inquiry as to who were affected by the recent provisional Parliamentary grant of a novel tax on land and chattels, and he was appointed one of the two collectors for Rutland. In the second Parliament of the year, which met at Coventry in October, Flore was again one of the county representatives. He had recently been party to a loan of £100, for the Welsh war, secured on wool exports.[3] Nearly ten weeks before there fell due one of the moieties of the two tenths and fifteenths, voted during the session and leviable at Martinmas 1405, a commission of three was appointed to anticipate its collection in Rutland by negotiating loans equal to the assessment, being ordered to deliver the outcome of their activities to the royal Treasurers for the Wars at London on 26 September 1405; Flore was one of the commission. He was again made a commissioner for the raising of a royal loan in Rutland and Northamptonshire by letters patent of 28 June 1406, and on the same day he was authorised to act in the same area on an inquiry into cases of concealment of Crown rights, extortions on the part of local royal officials, the value of Crown lordships, and regarding annuities charged on the royal revenues there. Flore was at this time escheator in Rutland; he served in this office from 1 December 1405 to 9 November 1406. Nearly a year later he was appointed sheriff of Rutland and acted for a year as from Michaelmas 1407. On the day of his appointment he had been the first to attest the indenture, drawn up between his predecessor and the electors, certifying the validity of the election of the Rutland representatives to the Gloucester Parliament of October 1407, in accordance with a statute of the Parliament of the previous year. He was again serving as sheriff at the end of Henry IV's reign and when Henry V came to the throne, his year of office dating from 3 November 1412.[4] From February 1412 until Henry V's accession in March 1413 he also administered, but doubtless by deputy, the minor position of searcher of ships at Plymouth and Fowey, for which he was answerable to the royal Exchequer.

As sheriff of Rutland, Flore held the shire elections to the first Parliament of Henry V's reign which met in May 1413. He was himself to be elected to each of the next six Parliaments. The first of these was the Parliament summoned to meet at nearby Leicester on 30 April 1414. A justice of the peace in Rutland, Flore had in the meantime served on the inquiry into Lollardy in that county and Northamptonshire, following Sir John Oldcastle's abortive rebellion in January 1414. (This whole region, in the diocese of Lincoln, especially Leicestershire, was much inclined to Wyclifite heresy.) In the summer following the short Leicester session, perhaps by virtue of his office as verderer, Flore was included in an inquiry (authorised by a royal patent of 12 July 1414) into a claim to common of pasture in certain bailiwicks in the forest of Rockingham made by the townsmen and tenants of Benyfield (Northants.). On 12 October he was put on an inquiry into the abduction of a sister from the nunnery at Heynings (Lincs.). Just over a month later, he was re-elected knight of the shire to the second (the November) Parliament of the year. Three days before the elections and a week before the session opened, Flore was appointed escheator in both Rutland and Northamptonshire.[5] At the end of his year of office he was again re-elected to Parliament, the November 1415 Parliament which met at Westminster ten days after Henry V's great military victory in France at the battle of Agincourt. Meanwhile, in the course of the year, he had served on a commission of oyer and terminer, appointed on 14 May 1415, following cases of trespass upon and damage to property belonging to the abbey of Croyland (Lincs.). Much more important had been his appointment as one of the feoffees of Edward of Norwich, by this time Duke of York, whose expenditure, swollen by the charges of his great collegiate church of Fotheringhay and by those which he was incurring in joining Henry V's first proposed expedition into Normandy, was being met by loans secured on his future revenues. The royal letters patent licensing the enfeoffment were dated at Southampton on 5 August 1415. Twelve days later when the expedition had sailed and the Duke was with the forces besieging Harfleur, Flore was appointed one of the overseers of York's will. The Duke met his death in the press of battle at Agincourt some two months later, and the feoffees administered the ducal estates, during the long minority of the heir, until nearly six years after Flore's death.[6] Another aristocratic connexion of Flore's at this time resulted in his acting as feoffee in Northamptonshire, Warwickshire, Bedfordshire, and London (in accordance with charters of 10 July 1415) to William Lord Zouche of Haringworth, who died before the expiry of Flore's year of office as escheator in Northamptonshire on 14 December 1415; the rights of advowson in one of the enfeoffed manors, that of Bulwick (Northants.), were exercised by Flore and Thomas Wydeville, one of his co-feoffees, in 1418 and 1422.[7] Flore was also at this time active as the chief of the feoffees of the late Dame Alice Basset of Bytham (Lincs.), the dowager of Ralph Lord Basset (he died in 1378), in her Leicestershire manor of Breedon, held as of the Lancastrian Duchy honour of Tutbury.[8]

Already employed as one of Henry V's trustees in the estates endowed to the use of his recent religious foundation, the Bridgettine nunnery of St. Saviour at Syon in the royal manor of Isleworth in Twickenham, Roger Flore entered upon a regular career as a royally-employed lawyer on 1 December 1416, when he was appointed (during royal pleasure) chief steward of the Duchy of Lancaster estates north of Trent, that is, in Northamptonshire, Rutland, Leicestershire, Warwickshire, Staffordshire, Derbyshire, Nottinghamshire, Lincolnshire, Yorkshire, Westmorland, and Northumberland. He became an *ex-officio* member of the council of the Duchy in succession to the recent chief steward, Sir Roger Leche of Chatsworth, with an annual fee of £40 and an allowance of 5s. for every day he spent in administering his office, and in accordance with an Act of the Parliament of March 1416 he automatically became a justice of the peace in each of the counties in his bailiwick. He continued to occupy this highly influential Duchy office until December 1427. He was to be separately appointed chief steward for the Duchy in Lancashire and Cheshire in February 1417; but this office he relinquished in July 1425. Re-elected to both the Parliaments of 1416, summoned respectively for 16 March and 19 October, in the latter Flore had been for the first time elected Speaker for the Commons. After producing a lucrative grant of two tenths and fifteenths the session had ended on 20 November, little more than a week before his Duchy appointment.[9]

By May 1417 Roger Flore had been appointed by Henry V as a feoffee in the Bohun manor of Wethersfield (Essex), after its incorporation in the estates of the Lancastrian inheritance, along with others who included three fellow-members of the Duchy council, Sir Walter Hungerford (the chief steward of the Duchy estates south of Trent), John Wodehouse (the Duchy chancellor), and John Leventhorpe (the Duchy receiver-general). And on the day of Henry V's departure on his second and more systematic military expedition into France, 23 July 1417, Flore was one of the twelve nominees of the King upon whom his feoffees in the Duchy estates were to draw in the event of the death of any of their own number. Nearly four months later, on 18 November, re-elected knight of the shire for Rutland, Flore was again chosen Speaker for the Commons in the Parliament which met John, Duke of Bedford (left by his royal brother as *Custos Anglie*), which voted two tenths and fifteenths, and which saw Sir John Oldcastle, *Lollardus Lollardorum,* meet his death for heresy and treason. Bedford again met Parliament in October 1419, and Roger Flore, for the third session running, acted as Speaker for the Commons. The latter dutifully granted a whole tenth and fifteenth and a supplementary third of such a subsidy, on the basis of which securities could be given to those willing to make anticipatory loans to the Crown. A fortnight after the close of the session on 13 November 1419, the Speaker was himself included in the loan-raising commission appointed for his own county of Rutland.[10]

Flore did not sit in any of Henry V's last three Parliaments but his personal presence and influence made themselves felt at the shire elections in Rutland to the Parliaments of December 1420 and May 1421, to the first of which his son-in-law, Sir Henry Plesyngton, was returned, and his kinsman and friend, John Pensax, to the second. In February 1421 Flore was present at the coronation of the new queen of England, Katherine of Valois, and, at the time of the elections to the last Parliament which Henry V opened in person, he was acting as a member of a Crown loan-raising commission in Rutland and Northamptonshire, authorised to summon all lay and spiritual folk before them and contract for the payment of loans so that the proceeds might be delivered to the treasurer of England at the Exchequer on the eve of Parliament.[11]

At this time, in addition to public business and occupation with his Duchy office, Flore's private interests were multifarious. He was made (by a deed of 10 April 1419) a feoffee in ten East Anglian manors belonging to Sir Simon Felbrigge, who twenty years earlier had been Richard II's standard-bearer. During his Speakership in October 1419 he was appointed by Richard Beauchamp, Lord Abergavenny, to act with Richard Whityngton, the foremost mercer in London, as his attorney during his absence on military service in France. And, a year later, at the time of the 1420 elections, he was acting as executor to Robert Wintryngham, a canon of Lincoln.[12] On 12 April 1421 he was appointed, along with the treasurer of England, the chief baron of the Exchequer, and Thomas Chaucer, who was to be Speaker in the Parliament of the following month, as trustee to Bishop Philip Repingdon, who had recently resigned the see of Lincoln. This was in a grant for life of a yearly sum of 500 marks, presumably a retirement-pension, from the revenues of the episcopal lordships of Newark (Notts.), Banbury, and Dorchester (Oxon.). Letters confirmatory of the dean and chapter of Lincoln were issued two days later, and on 8 June following the grant was covered by royal letters patent of *inspeximus* and confirmation which were renewed after two years. It was some time in the year, Michaelmas 1420-21, that Richard Beauchamp, Earl of Warwick, sought Flore's goodwill (*amicitia*) with a present of £2, but for what reason is not known.[13]

His position as a Crown lawyer made Flore a useful addition to any committee of feoffees, and his private connexions with members of the Parliament of 1422, the last and twelfth Parliament he attended as knight of the shire for Rutland, were many and influential. He was a feoffee to Edmund Wynter (one of the Norfolk representatives), to John Harpour (who sat as burgess for Stafford), and to the father of Sir William Eure (one of the Yorkshire knights), Sir Ralph Eure of Witton-on-Wear in Durham, in some estates that were in trust for a younger son. With Bartholomew Brokesby, who was returned from Leicestershire, he had acted at the beginning of the year as an overseer of the will of James Bellers esquire of Somerby who had himself sat for Leicestershire in the Parliaments of 1413 and 1420.[14] One of the Herefordshire knights was the apprentice-at-law, John Russell, Flore's co-feoffee and overseer to the late Duke of York. His own fellow-knight of the shire for Rutland was his son-in-law, Sir Henry Plesyngton, in whose Southampton property he was again a feoffee. Apart from such an "acquaintance" among the Commons, his office as one of the two chief stewards of the Duchy of Lancaster and his connexion with Wodehouse and Leventhorpe, respectively returned on this occasion for Suffolk and Hertfordshire, both of whom were executors to the late King, make Flore's election as Speaker in Henry VI's first Parliament understandable: he must have been quite familiar with much of the business with which this Parliament of 1422 was to be called upon to deal.

The Parliamentary session, which lasted from 9 November to 18 December 1422, produced only a grant of the wool subsidy and tunnage and poundage by way of taxation, its main job being to provide for the winding-up of the business of the late reign, in particular the satisfaction of Henry V's debts and the administration of his will. The latter held an immediate interest for the Speaker as an official and member of the council of the Duchy of Lancaster. Incidentally, a week before the close of the session, Flore completed his purchase of the Leicestershire manor of Leesthorpe; among his feoffees it is interesting to note John Frank, the clerk of the Parliament, and, at the head of the witnesses to the deed of quitclaim, his son-in-law and fellow-knight of the shire, Plesyngton.[15]

After 1422 Roger Flore was not again returned to Parliament, but he continued to act as chief steward in the northern half of the Lancastrian estates down to the autumn of 1427 (very likely until his death), having been re-appointed by a patent issuing from the Duchy chancery on 1 October 1422. He was one of the Syon priory feoffees who on 3 March 1425, by authority of the previous Parliament, were granted the reversion of the English estates formerly belonging to the Norman abbey of Fécamp. (The committee included the Dukes of Bedford and Exeter and the Bishops of Durham and Exeter.) He was present at the Rutland Parliamentary elections in October 1423, April 1425, and February 1426; at the second of these he was the first to attest the indenture of return when his son-in-law, Plesyngton, was again elected. It is interesting to note that the Abbot of Croyland appointed Flore to be one of his Parliamentary proxies at Westminster in April 1425 and again, but then at Leicester, in February 1426. Following this Leicester Parliament Flore was put on a Crown loan-raising commission in Rutland by patent of 23 July 1426. Roger Flore was dead by 12 November 1427 when orders were issued for the election of another verderer in the forest of Rockingham in his stead; on 19 December following John Tyrell, then Speaker for the Commons, succeeded him as chief steward of the Duchy of Lancaster north of Trent.[16]

Nothing better than his carefully prepared *testamentum* and *ultima voluntas* illustrates Flore's successful career and local connexions. The former was drafted in Latin on 15 April 1424 and implemented by a codicil in English added three days later; the *ultima voluntas* relating to his feoffments of land, written in his own hand and under his seal of arms, was dated at Oakham on 26 October 1425. Together they show his possession of property scattered over the eastern Midlands, the estates of a successful lawyer who had clearly invested much of his surplus wealth in land. These comprised the Lincolnshire manors of Stenby and Braceby and an estate in Bramtoft and Halton in Lindsey—in April 1418 Flore had been appointed a commissioner *De walliis et fossatis* (that is, of sewers) in the parts of Lindsey—his purchase at Leesthorpe, and property in Leicester, Whitwell and Little Hambledon in Rutland, his estates in Masthorpe, and his lands and burgages in the town of Oakham; out of them he provided for his second wife, Cecily, his heir, Thomas, and four younger sons, advising the retention of "a wel lerned man of the lawe" and, "for more suerte," the settlement of the grants of land by final concords in the Court of Common Pleas.

Flore's bequests of piety suggest an entirely orthodox religious life and outlook. The friars and nuns of Stamford, the Carthusians of Coventry, the abbey of Westminster, the priories of London, Newstead by Stamford, and Brooke, and the nunneries of Langley and Huntingdon, benefited, in return for celebrations of mass for himself, his first wife, his parents, his parents-in-law, those of his children who had predeceased him, and his old patron, Edward of Norwich, late Duke of York. He left a sum of £40 as provision for a chantry chaplain who was to celebrate mass with prayers for the same persons and for Henry V also. Each priested monk and canon of Westminster was to receive respectively 20d. and 8d. for a Placebo and Dirige and mass of Requiem, and gifts were made to the guild-priests of Coventry and to the parish and other chaplains of Oakham in return for their prayers. Personal legacies in money, in the main to members of the family, amounted in all to over £550. Flore's local interests in Oakham are illustrated by his bequests to his father-in-law's almshouse and bedesmen in the town, the provision of cloaks of "Covyntree frees" and new smocks to a score of needy parishioners, the allocation of fifty shillings to the mending of common roads, bridges, and causeways in Oakham, and by his orders for the payment of 5 marks (£3 6s. 8d.) to the mason, a noble (6s. 8d.) of which had already been paid as earnest-money, if the contract between them for the building of the vault of the steeple of the parish church of All Saints, Oakham, was not fulfilled before his death. (Flore left his breviary to the mason for life.) Forgotten tithes, the fabric of Oakham parish church, where he was to be buried, and three guilds of Oakham were all remembered in the will. There is perhaps something more than conventional devotion in the prayer with which Flore ended the codicil to his *testamentum*: "And I pray to the blessid Trinitye that of his endles mercye and goodnesse he sende my children grace to be gode men and women and to yelde him gode soules thorough the help and praier of oure lady seint Marye and of all the seyntes of hevin. Amen".

Flore appointed to act as his executors John Clerk of Whissendine, Ralph Humberstone of Leicester (one of the town's Parliamentary burgesses in 1411), Richard Hawey (master of the chantry of Manton), to whom he left his rosary with the request that he "have mynde of me sumtime when he seith oure lady sawter on him", and William Baxter, warden of the hospital in Oakham. Flore left them each £20 and a pipe of wine. As overseer of his will he appointed his son-in-law, Sir Henry Plesyngton. The will was proved in the Prerogative Court of Canterbury in its London office in Ivy Lane on 20 June 1428.[17]

Of Roger Flore's own family only his eldest son, Thomas, ever sat in Parliament, and that was no more than twice, in 1432 and 1445 when on each occasion he represented Rutland. It is a rather surprising fact that, despite Thomas's being a lawyer and a sometime bencher of Lincoln's Inn, his father did not find him a place in the administration of the Duchy of Lancaster. But the family's standing in Rutland and Thomas's own credit with the governments of Henry VI and Edward IV were such that he was sheriff of the county no fewer than six times, in 1430-1, 1441-2, 1450-1, 1456-7, 1464-5, and 1469-70, and he was a J.P. in Rutland from 1446 to 1471. His last appointment to the commission of the peace came during the time of the brief restoration of Henry VI in 1470-1, and on Edward IV's restoration he was not re-included. Judging from the issue of a royal commission in July 1471 to arrest and produce him before the king and council, it would seem that Thomas had favoured and assisted the government of the "Re-adeption", and, since he seems to have died shortly afterwards, it would appear that his life ended under something of a cloud. He had never, of course, occupied the same sort of position or exercised the same sort of influence that his father, Roger, had done. In other words, the family had not managed to sustain its early fifteenth-century promise.[18]

NOTES

The following abbreviations have been used:

CPR = *Calendar of Patent Rolls*   Rot. Parl. = *Rotuli Parliamentorum*
CCR = *Calendar of Close Rolls*   V.C.H. = *Victoria County History*
CFR = *Calendar of Fine Rolls*   P.R.O. = Public Record Office

1. *Official Return of Members of Parliament*, Vol. 1, 253-303; App., XX, XXI; 213; Prynne, *Brevia*.

2. *V.C.H., Rutland*, i. 162; ibid., ii. 5; CCR, *1392-96*, 199; CPR, *1405-08*, 265; ibid., *1416-22*, 30, 381; CCR, *1402-05*, 472; A. Gibbons, *Early Lincoln Wills*, 116. On 1 Sept. 1398 Roger and his wife, Katherine, procured a papal indult permitting them a portable altar (*Cal. of Papal Letters*, v. 143).

3. CPR, *1396-99*, 235; ibid., *1399-1401*, 76, 473; ibid., *1401-5*, 128, 287, 417; CFR, *1399-1405*, 258, 148; CCR, *1399-1402*, 368.

4. CFR, *1399-1405*, 319; CPR, *1405-8*, 154, 200; P.R.O., typescript List of Escheators, 95; P.R.O., Lists and Indexes, ix. List of Sheriffs, 112; P.R.O., C 219, bundle 10, No. 4.

5. CFR, *1405-13*, 225; CPR, *1413-16*, 177, 262, 265; List of Escheators, *loc. cit.* For the prevalence of Lollardy in this region, see K. B. McFarlane, *John Wycliffe and the Beginnings of English Non-conformity* (1952).

6. CPR, *1413-16*, 406, 350; A. Gibbons, *op. cit.*, 146; CCR, *1413-19*, 294.

7. CPR, *1413-16*, 395; CCR, *1413-19*, 260, 262. Bridges, *Northants.*, ii. 289.

8. CPR, *1408-13*, 475; CCR, *1413-19*, 247; Nichols, *Hist. Leics.*, iii. 685.

9. CCR, *1413-19*, 402; ibid., *1435-41*, 308; CPR, *1422-29*, 205; *Duchy of Lancaster, Accounts Various*, DL 28, bundle 4, No. 9; Robert Somerville, *History of the Duchy of Lancaster*, i. 420; CPR, *1416-22*, 454-9, 461-3; Rot. Parl., iv. 95.

10. *CPR, 1416-22*, 106, 118, 252; *Rot. Parl.*, iv. 107, 117.

11. P.R.O., C 219, bundle 12, Nos. 4, 5; *Wardrobe Accts.* 9 H V, Easter Term; *CPR, 1416-22*, 386.

12. *CCR, 1419-22*, 41; *Reports of the Deputy-Keeper of the Public Records*, xli. 803; A. Gibbons, *op. cit.*, 155.

13. *CPR, 1416-22*, 379; *ibid., 1422-29*, iii; Longleat MS. 6410, mem. 2 v (I owe this reference to Mr. K. B. McFarlane).

14. J. Gage, *History of Thingoe Hundred, Suffolk*, 174; *CCR, 1429-35*, 359; R. Surtees, *History of North Durham*, ii. 375; A. Gibbons, *op. cit.*, 147.

15. *Rot. Parl.*, iv. 170; *CCR, 1422-29*, 47, 454.

16. *Ancient Deeds*, ii. B 3819; P.R.O., C 219, bundle 13, Nos. 2, 3, 4; *CPR, 1422-29*, 355; *CCR, 1422-29*, 355; P.R.O., S.C. 10, Nos. 2383, 2390.

17. Early English Text Society, *Fifty Earliest English Wills*, ed. F. J. Furnivall, 55-64; Lincoln's Inn Record Society, *Admission Register*, 6.

18. J. C. Wedgwood, *History of Parliament, Biographies of Members of the Commons House, 1439-1509* (1936), 339.

13

SIR RICHARD VERNON OF HADDON,
SPEAKER IN THE PARLIAMENT OF LEICESTER, 1426

B Y the end of the 14th century the family of Vernon had already been in possession of Haddon in the High Peak of Derbyshire for about two hundred years. Lead was mined on the estate, and income from this source, as well as from their other lands in the neighbourhood and elsewhere, probably explains the family's steady growth in prosperity. Their wealth is amply demonstrated by the early building developments at Haddon alone: when the Sir Richard Vernon who is the subject of this paper was born under Richard II, the area covered by Haddon Hall was as extensive as it is now; and it is doubtful whether he himself did much more than improve the chapel by adding a chancel, where in the east window he and his wife are commemorated. This was in 1427, the year after he acted as Speaker for the Commons in the fourth parliament of Henry VI which met, some fifty miles to the south, at Leicester.[1] Tenant and official of the Duchy of Lancaster (the private inheritance of the Lancastrian kings) in his own country of the Peak, and connected with some of the most influential of the titular nobility of the north midlands, Sir Richard Vernon was one of the most important of the lesser magnates of this region. His Speakership is likely to have confirmed the respect in which he was held there. He subsequently rose higher still in the royal service under Henry VI, but it is on account of his occupation of that office that he has a special claim to the attention of the local historian: he is the only member of parliament for Derbyshire ever to have been Speaker.

Richard Vernon was born in 1390. He was the son of Sir Richard Vernon and his wife Jane, daughter of Rhys ap Griffith of Wichnor. Wichnor, which came into Vernon's possession by this marriage, was a feudal member of the great Duchy of Lancaster honour of Tutbury. So were the manors of Nether Haddon (Derbyshire) and Harlaston (Staffs.) where the family resided, and also the manor of Appleby Parva (Leics.). The main concentration of the estates of the Vernons was in the valleys of the Derwent and its tributaries. These, besides Haddon itself, comprised the manors of Baslow, Bubnell, and Rowsley, together with lands in Curbar, One Ash Grange, Over Haddon, Bakewell, Alport and Stanton. In Staffordshire, besides Harlaston, lay their manors of Bridgeford, Pipe Ridware, and Draycott, along with lands in

---

[1] *Rotuli Parliamentorum*, IV, 296.

Edingale and Haselour. These last two estates were close to Harlaston and Appleby Parva, and also to another Vernon manor at Netherseal (Derbyshire) and some property at Seckington (Warwicks.). Just south of the borough of Leicester the family held the manor of Aylestone. The manors of Marple and Wibersley in Cheshire were also in their possession, and here the Vernons occupied the office of forester of the royal forest of Macclesfield. Far to the north, in Westmorland, lay their manors of Meaburn and Newby. Far to the south, in Buckinghamshire, were Adstock and Pitchcott. Pitchcott had been in Vernon possession from no later than the early 13th century, and here Sir Richard (the Speaker) was a tenant of the Earl of Stafford. Certainly by the end of his life he also held the manors of Stackpole Elidor, Bosheston, and Rudbaxton in Pembrokeshire, and of Pendine and Cantrewyn in Carmarthenshire. Whether these lordships in south-west Wales came by inheritance, marriage, or purchase by the Speaker himself, is not known.

Sir Richard, the Speaker's father (not to be confused with the Sir Richard Vernon of Shipbrook, Cheshire, who was executed in 1403 after the battle of Shrewsbury), had enjoyed a small annuity of £5 granted him by Richard II in 1397, had been one of a commission appointed in 1398 to array Cheshire archers for royal service in Ireland, and had himself accompanied the king there in the expedition of May 1399. He died in 1401, Richard his heir being then only ten years old. The latter's marriage and the wardship of such of his lands as were held of the Duchy of Lancaster were granted to Roger Leche of Chatsworth, who paid 200 marks for this privilege to the Receiver-General of the Duchy. Leche was also given custody of the Vernon estates in Cheshire by additional grants of October 1408 and March 1409. By this time young Vernon's guardian was well-established in a career that was soon to lead him to distinguished office under the Crown. He was already Steward of the Household of Henry of Monmouth, Prince of Wales, who came to the throne in 1413. In his first regnal year Henry V made Roger Leche both Treasurer of his Household and Chief Steward of the Duchy of Lancaster estates north of the Trent, subsequently, in April 1416, appointing him Treasurer of the Exchequer and, a month later, Chamberlain of the Duchy of Lancaster. And Leche held these last two offices until his death at the end of that year. Precisely what effect his guardianship had on young Vernon's early career is not known, but very likely it contained advantages. The custody had come to an end, however, late in 1411, when Vernon proved his coming of age and sued out livery of his inheritance.

Following the death of his great-uncle, Sir Fulk de Pembridge, in 1409, Richard Vernon also came into possession of estates in Tong (Salop), Sheriff Hales, and Kibbleston (Staffs.). The Staffordshire lands which had come to Pembridge by virtue of his first marriage with Margaret, the heiress of William Trussell, were later to give rise to keen litigation between Richard Vernon and Margaret's heir-general, Sir William Trussell.[2] In the November

---

[2] Belvoir Castle Archives, MSS. 4027, 5922-3, 7629; *Feudal Aids*, VI, 592-4; *Victoria County History of Buckinghamshire*, IV, 90; *Papal Letters* X, 16; *CPR, 1396-99*, 524; *DKR*, XXXVI, 499; *HMC, Rutland MSS.*, IV, 28; *William Salt Arch. Soc., Parliamentary History of Staffs.*, I, 191; J. P. Earwaker, *E. Cheshire*, II, 50-1; *Accounts Various*, PRO, D.L.28/4/2.

of 1410 a royal licence under the Great Seal was granted to Sir Fulk's widow enabling her to acquire the advowson of the parish church of Tong from the abbey of Shrewsbury and to found a college of five secular priests, one of whom was to be warden. Pembridge himself seems to have been intimately connected with Henry IV's half-brother, Thomas Beaufort, sometime Earl of Dorset and Duke of Exeter, and the latter was included in the charter of foundation among those for whose good estate prayers were to be said by the chaplains of the college. Beaufort, himself then Chancellor of England, had been warden of the castle and town of Ludlow since 1402, an office which may have provided opportunity for contact between him and Pembridge. By 14 June 1414, when another royal licence was granted, this time for the annexation of the alien priory of Lapley to the college, Thomas Beaufort's brother Henry, Bishop of Winchester, had been added to the list of those for whom prayers were said at Tong. Meanwhile, by the deed of 1410, the patronage of the collegiate church of Tong had been conveyed to Richard Vernon and his wife. She was Benedicta, daughter of Sir John de Ludlow of Stokesay and Hodnet (Salop). Richard's sister Isabel was married to a member of the same family.[3]

No further direct notice of Vernon himself occurs before 1 July 1416, when the royal Chancery gave him "letters of protection" as retained by Henry V for military service in France. He actually went overseas but, in view of his appointment as sheriff of Staffordshire at the end of the following November, did not perhaps stay abroad for long. He held the office of sheriff for the usual term of a year (until November 1417). Less than a month later he was made a justice of the peace in the same county, a position in which he served until February 1422. In May 1418 (by which date he had been knighted), and again in March 1419, he was a commissioner of array in Staffordshire.[4] Early in October 1419 he was for the first time elected to parliament as knight of the shire (county M.P.), being returned for Staffordshire. His fellow-knight was Sir Thomas Gresley who, on the same day as the county court was held at Stafford, conducted the Derbyshire elections, being at the time sheriff in that county and Nottinghamshire. On 15 November, two days after the Commons had made their grant of supplies, Vernon was associated with Sir Thomas Erpingham and others, who included Sir John Cokayne (knight of the shire for Derbyshire) and John Mynors, Esquire (parliamentary burgess for Newcastle-under-Lyme), in going bail in Chancery under pain of £20 for the behaviour of Dame Eleanor Dagworth, a Norfolk widow. Eleven days later he was made a commissioner for the raising of a Crown loan in Staffordshire with others who included Sir Thomas Gresley and Hugh Erdeswyk (knight of the shire for Derbyshire during the recent session). Two months were allowed the commissioners in which to negotiate the loan on the security of the third of the subsidy of a tenth and fifteenth leviable at Martinmas 1420. In June 1420 Vernon shared with Sir William Coggeshall and Richard Baynard, two Essex notables, in raising a loan to

---

[3] Dugdale, *Monasticon*, VI (part III), 1402 *et seq*.
[4] *CCR, 1409-13*, 407; *DKR*. XLIV, 581; PRO, *Lists and Indexes*, IX, *List of Sheriffs*, 127; *CPR, 1416-22*, 459, 198, 212.

the Crown of £52. 10s., for which they received tallies of assignment at the Lower Exchequer in the following month.[5]

At the elections in both Staffordshire and Derbyshire to the parliament of May 1421 Sir Richard Vernon was the first to attest the indenture of return, but his own next election was not until the end of October 1422 when he was returned for Derbyshire, with Sir John Cokayne of Ashbourne, to the first parliament of Henry VI's reign. Both knights were included in a commission appointed during the session to inquire into breaches of the statutes governing the netting of salmon and lampreys in the Trent. In the following summer, on 7 July 1423, Vernon was for the first time put on the commission of the peace in Derbyshire. (Apart from a gap between 1432 and 1437, he was to be a justice there until his death in 1451.) On 30 September 1423 he was again first to attest the indenture certifying the election of the Derbyshire parliamentary knights. One of them, Henry Bothe of Finderne, was Vernon's mainpernor (or surety) when, during the first session of this parliament, he was granted on 14 November 1423, with the assent and advice of the royal Council, the custody at farm of the Neville manor of Ashford-in-Bakewell, where he himself already had lands.[6] It was on 3 March 1424 that Vernon was appointed, *quamdiu placuerit*, steward of the Duchy of Lancaster lordship, and also constable of the castle, of the High Peak. This appointment was to be renewed in his favour (during good behaviour) on 10 August 1437 and then, on 5 April 1438, was given to him and his son Fulk for life. The Vernons, after some trouble in their administration, were, however, superseded by Henry, Earl of Warwick, in October 1444. At the time of the original grant of these offices, Sir Richard was also made master forester of the High Peak, and, although he was soon (by June 1425) replaced in this position, he later recovered it and was still holding it in 1445. These various duchy offices in his own locality were together worth £31. 11s. 8d. in annual fees. In the meantime, on 6 November 1424, Sir Richard had been appointed sheriff of Nottinghamshire and Derbyshire.[7] Less than a month after his surrender of the joint bailiwick, he was elected on 13 February 1426 as knight of the shire to the critical parliament which had been summoned to meet at Leicester only five days later.

The previous autumn had witnessed a climax in the dispute between Bishop Beaufort, the then Chancellor, and Henry VI's uncle, Humphrey, Duke of Gloucester, the Protector, both members of the royal family of Lancaster, which almost led to armed conflict between their supporters. A peace, which owed much to the intervention of Gloucester's elder brother, the Duke of Bedford, was still being negotiated when the significantly nicknamed "parliament of battes" met on 18 February at Leicester, following meetings of the Council at St. Albans on 29 January and at Northampton on 13 February. At these meetings attempts had been made to induce Gloucester to meet the Chancellor in the Council, but without success. As its members had feared,

---

[5] *CCR, 1419-22*, 65; *CPR, 1416-22*, 251; *CFR, 1413-22*, 315-7; Issue Roll of the Exchequer, PRO. E403/645, mem. 11.

[6] PRO, C219/12/5; *CPR, 1422-29*, 35, 561; PRO, C219/13/2; *CFR, 1422-30*, 56; R. Somerville, *History of the Duchy of Lancaster*, I, 551-2.

[7] *List of Sheriffs*, 103.

the deadlock affected the normal conduct of the business of the parliamentary session which Beaufort (acting as Chancellor) opened in the great hall of Leicester castle. The Commons were assigned *quaedam bassa camera* for their deliberations, whilst the two committees of triers of petitions were respectively allocated the chapter-house and north chapel in the collegiate church of Our Lady founded by John of Gaunt. The sentimental associations of the place of assembly possibly reacted in the Chancellor's favour, although the honour of Leicester and its tenantry were not a part of those Duchy of Lancaster estates falling under the administration of Henry V's feoffees, of whom Beaufort was the most influential. The Commons were authorized as usual to proceed to the immediate election of a Speaker, but it was not until after ten days that they presented Sir Richard Vernon; only on 28 February was he accepted and able to make the customary Speaker's "protestation". In the meantime, the Commons had signalled their embarrassment at the disharmony among the Lords by the mouth of Roger Hunt, M.P. for Huntingdonshire. The royal charter collegiating Tong church in 1410 and the additional grant of 1414 point to connections between the Beauforts and the Vernon family which may have made Sir Richard acceptable as Speaker to the Chancellor. Be that as it may, Beaufort was worsted during the session and on 13 March, the day after a formal reconciliation was arranged between him and the Duke of Gloucester, he resigned the Great Seal. A week later parliament was adjourned to meet on 29 April. The second session lasted till 1 June when, through Speaker Vernon, the Commons declared before Bedford and the other Lords that with their assent they had granted a subsidy on wool-exports, payable by both aliens and denizens, for two years as from 12 November 1429, and tunnage and poundage, payable by aliens, for the same period; these last subsidies, payable by native merchants, were granted for merely a year, as from 12 November 1426. The grant had apparently not been reached without difficulty: *diverse oppiniones* had been expressed in the Commons as to the grant of tunnage and poundage in the previous parliament of 1425, but the Lords, after taking judicial advice, had declared that the levy must be paid. The grant of 1425 had itself been made only after *moche altercacyon bytwyne the lordys and the comyns* and with the provisos that alien merchants should be put to host (made to live in licensed lodgings) and required to sell their merchandise within forty days of its being imported, and that when English exports, on which tunnage and poundage had been already paid, were lost at sea, the merchants involved should be allowed to export an equivalent amount without further payment of the subsidy. In spite of the Lords' opposition, Vernon, in declaring the Commons' vote, was now in 1426 bound to announce that certain conditions were attached to the present grant, namely, that it should be spent solely on military defence and that there should be a remission of the subsidy on lost merchandise.[8] There can be little doubt that Beaufort had been at a disadvantage in the Lower House from the start, in view of the fact that its mercantile elements had associated him as Chancellor with the failure to fulfil the conditions under which the previous grant of 1425 had been made.

[8] *Rotuli Parliamentorum* IV. 296 *et seq.*, 302.

It is interesting to note that during the Leicester parliament a petition had been preferred by the grandson and heir of the late Earl of Westmorland asking the Council to grant him, towards his keep as a royal ward, some £60 a year from the fee-farm of Newcastle-on-Tyne and £42 from the issues of the Neville manor of Ashford-in-the-Peak. It was asked that this second payment be made by the hands of the then Speaker, who had enjoyed the lease of it since the autumn of 1423. A royal letter patent was issued granting the substance of the petition on 16 March, four days before the adjournment of the first session.

Sir Richard Vernon's next election to parliament was not until the summer of 1433. The seven years' interval was anything but a period of inactive retirement. In March 1427 Vernon was appointed to serve on a commission of array in Derbyshire and in the following November was made sheriff of Staffordshire. It was during this year that he and his wife had seen to the provision of a new east window for the chapel of their Derbyshire home at Haddon.[9] His tenure of the shrievalty in Staffordshire terminated in November 1428. Since the beginning of the reign a justice of the peace in Derbyshire, Vernon was in March 1430 appointed to the same office in Staffordshire as well and served on this commission until 1432.[10] About this time he had close relations with Humphrey, Earl of Stafford, who in April 1430 made him, along with Thomas Arblaster, Esquire (M.P. for Staffordshire in 1426, 1432, 1433, and 1435) and John Harpour (M.P. for Stafford 1419-29, and for Staffordshire in 1431), his feoffee in the lordship of Tonbridge and four other manors in Kent. Less than two months before this transaction, Sir Richard had been appointed to serve on a royal loan-raising commission in Derbyshire and Nottinghamshire. He served on another commission of this sort a year later, at the end of March 1431. On 12 April 1431 he was appointed one of a committee charged with the assessment in Derbyshire of the tax, voted in the previous parliament, on knights' fees and landed income. At the end of the same month Vernon was appointed to be a royal justice in South Wales along with Sir Edmund Stradlyng, chamberlain and receiver of South Wales, Sir John Skidmore, constable of Carmarthen and steward of the commotes in the shire, and two lawyers who were to be of the *quorum*. The commission was issued provisionally, during the absence in France of James Lord Audley, chief justice in South Wales, and in view of Audley's close connections with Staffordshire, it is possible that Vernon was acting as his deputy. To the next parliament, which met in May 1432, William Lee of Aston, one of the *quorum* in the South Wales judicial commission and a feoffee of Lord Audley's estates in Staffordshire, was returned for that county along with one of Vernon's co-feoffees in the Stafford manors in Kent, Thomas Arblaster. Vernon's eldest son, Richard Vernon, Esquire, was elected to the parliament in the shire-court held at Derby on 20 March 1432, Sir Richard being the first to attest the indenture of return.[11]

Sir Richard himself was returned for Derbyshire to the next parliament,

9 *CPR, 1422-29*, 334, 405; *List of Sheriffs*, 127; *D.A.J.*, XIV (1892), 117.
10 *CPR, 1429-36*, 624.
11 *CCR, 1429-35*, 357; *CPR, 1429-36*, 50, 126, 136, 116; PRO, C219/14/3.

which met at Westminster in July 1433, along with his fellow-knight in the first parliament of the reign, Sir John Cokayne. Early in the following year and after parliament's dissolution, the two men were associated in drawing up a list of notables in the shire considered by them important enough to take the oath, against the abuse of maintenance, sworn during the last session by both Lords and Commons alike. A list of 329 names was sent into Chancery, and on 1 May 1434, by royal letters patent, the sheriff was ordered to publish it in the next county court, so that the oath might be taken before the commissioners appointed; these were the diocesan, Bishop Heyworth of Coventry and Lichfield, Lord Grey of Codnor, together with Vernon and Cokayne.[12]

Sir Richard Vernon's election to parliament in 1433 was his last return as a knight of the shire. The remaining eighteen years of his life are, however, richer in recorded incident than is the first half of his career. His local influence in the shires where lay the bulk of his estates is attested by a closely crowded succession of royal commissions. He was involved in no less than five royal loan-raising commissions between 1436 and 1442, the first in Staffordshire, the rest in Derbyshire. (Regarding the Crown loan of 1436, in aid of an expedition to northern France led by the Duke of York, he was himself served with a royal writ of Privy Seal asking for a contributory loan of as much as 100 marks.) Until his death Vernon continuously served the office of the justice of the peace in Derbyshire. In November 1439 he was a member of a commission appointed to deliver Stafford gaol. He was associated, moreover, with several commissions caused by various eruptions of local disorder. In November 1436, for example, he was included with the Bishop of Lichfield, the Earls of Warwick and Stafford, Lord Audley, and three royal justices, in a commission of oyer and terminer set up to investigate a complaint of the Dean and Chapter of Lichfield, that assaults on certain of the cathedral clergy and attempts to break into the cathedral close had been made by the townspeople of Lichfield.[13]

Sir Richard Vernon himself was not free from charges of highhanded action likely to create unrest and disorder. To about the year 1440 must be assigned a series of petitions, either to the council of the Duchy of Lancaster or to the Earl of Suffolk, then chief steward of the duchy north of Trent, demanding redress for injuries done by Sir Richard in his capacity as duchy steward of the High Peak and farmer of the forest of Campana. The alleged offences included distraints for rent on pastures held at farm (under the receiver of Tutbury) by Sir Thomas Stanley, then Controller of the King's Household, and Sir Edmund Trafford, and also illegal imprisonments and amercements contravening the rights to agistment held by foresters of the ward of Campana. (Vernon had been occupying the duchy bailiwick of the Peak since 1424, after 1438 in partnership with his son Fulk.)[14] In July 1441 separate royal letters close were sent to Lord Ferrers of Groby, Sir Richard Vernon, William Newport, and the Stanleys of Elford, ordering them, on their allegiance and

[12] *CCR, 1429-35,* 271; *CPR, 1429-36,* 410.
[13] *CPR. 1420-36,* 529, 527; *1436-41,* 249, 505, 536, 370, 84; *PPC,* IV, 323.
[14] *HMC, 12th Report,* part IV, *Rutland MSS.,* I, 1; *Accounts Various,* PRO, D.L.28/5/2.

on pain of forfeiture, to cease from causing riots and unlawful assemblies in Staffordshire and the neighbouring counties. In November 1443 Sir Richard and his sons, Fulk and John, were required to bind themselves in Chancery by recognizances totalling £280 that John would appear at Westminster on 25 January following. Although John did not in fact appear, the amounts thus forfeited were pardoned by letters patent of 26 May 1444. Between Trinity term 1442 and this date Sir Richard himself had been engaged in a law-suit in the Court of Common Pleas with Sir William Trussell touching the manors of Shotsbrook and Eton Hastings in Berkshire, which Vernon claimed as heir of Sir Fulk of Pembridge. In Easter term 1443 a judgment was given for Trussell who was to recover seisin and 120 marks damages. On 4 June following Vernon sued out a writ of error, and the case was transferred to be heard in the Court of King's Bench. Probably the writ of Privy Seal served on Sir Richard at Haddon on 20 June by one of the criers of the Court of Common Pleas was in connection with this process.[15]

In this middle period of the reign of Henry VI, Sir Richard Vernon seems to have attached himself to the Lancastrian court party, more particularly to the clique in which Suffolk was pre-eminent. In the spring of 1443 his son Fulk was in sufficient favour at court to be entrusted with the purchase and cartage of lead, almost certainly from Derbyshire mines, to be used in the building of the new royal college at Eton. About this time, Fulk was also appointed for life as the Duchy of Lancaster steward of the lands of the honour of Tutbury in Derbyshire and Staffordshire. Sir Richard's own influence seems to have increased in the course of the reign. His appointment on 17 May 1445 as treasurer of Calais and in September 1446 as joint-warden of the Calais mint, he probably owed to Humphrey, Earl of Stafford and recently created Duke of Buckingham, whose feoffee he had been since 1430, and who was captain of Calais and royal lieutenant in the marches there. It will be remembered that the duke was Vernon's feudal overlord of his Buckinghamshire manor of Pitchcott. To the same connection may have been due his appointment in December 1439 to be steward of the Duke of Norfolk's estates in Derbyshire and his probable four years' term of office, ending in November 1448, as knight-constable in the Constable and Marshal's Court, the Court of Chivalry. (The Duke of Norfolk was married to Buckingham's stepsister, Eleanor Bourchier.) Already, on 6 April 1448, a royal Privy Seal warrant had authorized the Lower Exchequer to pay him 200 marks in ready money on the grounds that, "to his great hurt", he had no fee or reward for this office, with the result that this sum was paid to him in Michaelmas term following. The King had been informed by Vernon in a petition (so the warrant ran) that "he hath kept oure Connestable Court as knyght Connestable by the space of three yere and more for diverse greet matiers concernyng the wele of our persone as of this oure Reume of Englande" including the dispute between the Prior of Kilmainan (Thomas FitzGerald) and the Earl of Ormond, and how he had also had men harnessed and arrayed to keep Smithfield (in London), for battles joined between parties to be deter-

15 *CCR, 1435-41*, 422; *CPR, 1441-46*, 268; *William Salt Arch. Soc.*, N.S., III, 161; *PPC*, V, 295.

mined there, to the number of sixty men-at-arms and more, all at his own cost.[16]

Meanwhile, at the end of 1440, Sir Richard had figured as one of the feoffees of Ralph Lord Cromwell, who was then Treasurer of England, in the Nottinghamshire manors of Gunnolston and Widmerpole, an assize of novel disseisin being brought against them at that time by Sir Henry Pierpoint. And in March 1445 he had shared a grant of a royal wardship with the Chamberlain of the Duchy of Lancaster, Sir Edmund Hungerford, Walter Lord Hungerford's second son.

Sir Richard Vernon's tenure of the treasurership of Calais lasted from May 1445 to May 1451, that is, until soon after the Duke of Buckingham resigned his captaincy of Calais to Edmund Beaufort, Duke of Somerset. Vernon seems only intermittently to have given his personal attention to the administrative work involved in the post, although in the summer following his appointment he served *ex officio* on certain royal commissions, in the autumn of 1449 was granted royal "letters of protection" during his absence at Calais, and in the following January sat on a commission of oyer and terminer in a case involving a merchant stapler's failure to recover payment of £525 for wool sold to merchants of Milan and Como.[17]

The chief benefit Sir Richard Vernon derived from his Calais office seems to have been the ready access it gave him to royal "letters of protection" which were useful in holding up the legal proceedings taken against him when, between June 1448 and his death in 1451, the Trussell *v* Vernon litigation over the Pembridge estates came to be renewed. In an assize of novel disseisin taken at Tutbury in September 1448 relating to estates in Kibbleston, Acton, and Hales (Staffs.), the jury had found for Vernon and awarded him damages of £2,080 against Sir William Trussell. In Easter term 1450 the latter appealed against the verdict on a writ of error, returnable in the Court of King's Bench, alleging that the jurors in the Tutbury assize had at Lichfield accepted £5 for food and 13s. 4d. in money (besides other gifts). Two Staffordshire lawyers were also attached to answer for fabrication of deeds. On 6 August following, Vernon, *vi et armis*, ejected Trussell's lessees in the manor of Kibbleston. These were no less than the Shropshire lawyer, William Burley, who had been Speaker for the Commons in 1437 and 1445, and his son-in-law, the historically famous common lawyer, Thomas Littleton, then Recorder of Coventry, who procured a writ of attachment returnable in the Court of Common Pleas in Hilary term 1451.[18] Meanwhile, on 25 October, Vernon had procured royal "letters of protection" for a year as staying in Picardy on the King's service in his capacity as treasurer of Calais. On 11 February 1451, however, these were revoked on the grounds that the sheriffs of London had certified that he was still staying in their bailiwick. Thus instrumental in causing much local unrest on the confines

---

[16] *CPR, 1441-46,* 162; *DKR.* XLVIII, 365, 371; *HMC, Rutland MSS.,* IV, 20; F. Devon, *Issues of the Exchequer,* 463; *Privy Seal Warrants for Issue,* PRO, E404/64/158; *Exchequer, Issue Roll,* PRO, E403/773, mem. 6.
[17] Thoroton. *Notts.* (ed. Throsby), III, 51; *CPR 1441-46,* 326; *1446-52.* 460; *DKR.* XLVIII, 365, 388.
[18] *DKR,* XLVIII, 366, 381; *CPR, 1446-52,* 309; *William Salt Arch. Soc.,* N.S., III, 188 *et seq.,* 200.

of Staffordshire and Shropshire, where the disputed Pembridge estates lay, Sir Richard was himself employed during the course of this litigation on royal commissions appointed in March and July 1449 to arrest certain members of the Gresley family of Drakelow (Derbys.) for offences against the abbot of Burton-on-Trent.

In the meantime, before all the litigation over the Pembridge estates had come to a head, on 6 June 1448, by the King's special grace, Vernon had secured a charter conferring upon himself and his heirs and the collegiate establishment at Tong (Salop) certain rights making the lordship of Tong a franchise: they were granted rights of waif and stray and treasure trove there, the forfeitures of the goods and chattels of felons, the return of writs to the exclusion of the sheriff, escheator and coroner, and the right to appoint justices of the peace and justices of labourers so long as they did not attempt to determine felonies without royal licence.

Sir Richard Vernon did not long survive his resignation of the treasurership of Calais in May 1451. It was only a month later that his son John was granted the offices in South Wales which Sir Richard himself had been granted for life by royal letters patent in June 1450, namely, the shrievalty of Pembroke, the constableship of the castles of Pembroke and Tenby, the master-forestership of Coydrath, and the stewardship of certain appurtenant lordships. Sir Richard was still alive early in August. He had certainly died, however, by 10 September 1451, for it was then that writs of *diem clausit extremum* issued from the Chancery ordering inquiries to be made by the appropriate escheators regarding his lands in Staffordshire, Leicestershire, Derbyshire, Shropshire, Herefordshire, Buckinghamshire and Westmorland. He was buried in the collegiate church of Tong where his effigy in Derbyshire alabaster represents him as a knight in plate-armour wearing round his neck the SS collar of the Lancastrian livery. His wife, Benedicta, had died in the spring of 1444.[19]

If, during the last eighteen years of his life, Sir Richard Vernon did not again serve in parliament, the numerous elections of members of his family suggest that he had firmly established its local power and prestige. His eldest son, Richard, was returned for Derbyshire in 1432. Another son, Fulk, was elected in 1439. His second surviving son, William, who after the younger Richard's death became his father's heir, sat in parliament in 1442, 1449-50, and 1450-1 for Derbyshire, in 1455-6 for Staffordshire, and again for Derbyshire in 1467, the year of his death. This William held his father's office of treasurer of Calais and was the last to hold for life the position of Constable of England. He seems to have remained Lancastrian in political sympathies, and his son, Henry Vernon, the Speaker's grandson and son-in-law to the Earl of Shrewsbury, eventually became governor and treasurer to the elder son of Henry VII, Prince Arthur, and, when the latter was created Prince of Wales in 1489, was made a Knight of the Bath.[20] Sir Richard Vernon's daughter, called Benedicta after her mother, had been married in 1442 to

[19] *CPR, 1446-52,* 411, 285-6, 337, 463; *CChR,* VI, 100-1; *Trans. Shropshire A. & N.H.S.,* V, 329; *CFR, 1437-45,* 276; *1445-54,* 171.
[20] *D.A.J.,* XXII (1900), 11.

Thomas Charlton of Edmonton (Middlesex), who was then an esquire in Henry VI's household, although later on he became a Yorkist. Like his father-in-law, Charlton was also Speaker for the Commons, being their second Speaker in the parliament of 1453-4.

FOOTNOTES

The following abbreviations have been used in the footnotes:

CCR	—	*Calendar of Close Rolls*
CChR	—	*Calendar of Charter Rolls*
CFR	—	*Calendar of Fine Rolls*
CPR	—	*Calendar of Patent Rolls*
DKR	—	*Reports of the Deputy-Keeper of the Public Records*
HMC	—	*Historical Manuscripts Commission*
PPC	—	*Proceedings and Ordinances of the Privy Council,* ed. N. H. Nicolas.
PRO	—	Public Record Office

14

SIR JOHN TYRELL

That the career of John Tyrell of Herons in East Horndon (Essex) is likely to have been one of some distinction is partly suggested by his election as a knight of the shire to twelve of the twenty-four parliaments which met between his first return in 1411 and his last in 1437, but more especially by the fact that he was Speaker for the Commons in three of them (in 1427-8, 1431 and 1437),[1] a record seldom surpassed even in the medieval period when parliaments, generally short, were also frequent. Like many men of affairs of the middling sort, he first acquired experience and won esteem as a retainer and servant of a particular lord, in his case Humphrey, duke of Gloucester. This connection brought him others, but it was doubtless his attachment to Gloucester that secured him appointment to the royal offices which made him somebody to be reckoned with. Of these offices, the most important were the chief stewardship of the duchy of Lancaster north of Trent, which he held for the last nine years of his life, and the treasurership of the King's Household, which he held for the last six. He was occupying the first when made Speaker in 1431 and, obviously, both of them when Speaker in 1437. It can hardly be doubted but that some time before his death, his connection with Gloucester was, if not weakened, far less exclusive than formerly. His two most important offices had brought him into direct contact with, and open to the influence of other magnates, secular and ecclesiastical, whose policies were by no means identical with Gloucester's. Indeed, it is not inconceivable that at the end of his career (and he barely survived his last Speakership), it was Tyrell's close additional connection with Richard, duke of York, which mainly determined his outlook on the political scene. In any case, his own official responsibilities, too, can only have had their effect.

John Tyrell came of a well-established Essex family, the most notable recent member of which had been his grandfather, Sir Thomas Tyrell. The latter had not only represented their county in five of the

---

1   *Official Return of M. P. s. I.* 276, 278, 289, 291, 297, 302, 308, 313, 316, 318, 324, 329; *Rot. Parl., IV.* 317, 368, 496.

seven parliaments meeting between 1365 and 1373, but had then been steward-general of the lands and a feofee-to-uses of Isabel, second daughter of Edward III, and her husband, Enguerran de Coucy, K.G., earl of Bedford, and went on to hold at farm the lands of their son-in-law, Robert de Vere, 9th earl of Oxford, during his minority.[2] John's father, Walter, cut less of a figure and never even served the shire in parliament. But he did at least arrange a satisfactory marriage for his heir: John's first wife was Alice, a daughter and coheir of Sir William Coggeshall, who, on her mother's side, was a granddaughter of Sir John Hawkwood, the most sought-after of all Italian condottieri of the second half of the fourteenth century (who himself came of a family long settled at Hedingham Sible in Essex). Coggeshall, who had served with Hawkwood in Italy, had had important friends, too, at the court of Richard II (pre-eminent among them, the king's chief 'favourite', Robert de Vere, and, later on, the king's half-brother, John Holland, duke of Exeter). But then, following his return from service with Richard II in Ireland in 1399, Coggeshall soon demonstrated his firm acceptance of Henry IV, to whom he gave faithful service, mostly on a local basis: notably as sheriff of Essex and Herts. in 1404-5 (when, as in the previous year, he was active in suppressing treasonable unrest in Essex) and in 1411-2. And, moreover, Sir William represented his county in four of Henry IV's parliaments (in 1401, 1402, 1404 and 1411) and indeed, before his death in 1426, in four more under Henry V and Henry VI (in 1414, 1420, 1421 and 1422). The other of his two daughters, Blanche, married John Doreward, the son of the Speaker of that name in Henry IV's first parliament (1399) and in Henry V's first parliament (1413) also. It was with his father-in-law that John Tyrell was first elected to parliament in 1411, i.e. to the last proper parliament of Henry IV's reign, and the two men were again to be elected together to the first parliament of Henry VI's reign in 1422, during which year had died Coggeshall's daughter Alice, Tyrell's wife.[3]

Doubtless when Sir William Coggeshall died in 1426, Tyrell came, 'by the courtesy', into a half-share of the Coggeshall lands, which in Essex and Cambridgeshire had been taxed in 1412 as worth £126 a year. But even as it was, his marriage to Alice had brought him the manor of North Benfleet and the estate called 'Jervais' in South Benfleet (Essex). And when, in the year after Alice's death (1422-3),

---

2   *CPR, 1377-81*, 143, 174, 260; *1381-5*, 190; *Catalogue of Ancient Deeds*, II. C 2529.

3   *The Register of Henry Chichele*, ed. E. F. Jacob, II. 631; *CFR, 1413-22*, 434; *Trans. Essex Archaeological Society*, vol. 3, 79; *CPR, 1452-61*, 503. For Sir William Coggeshall, see J. S. Roskell, *The Commons in the Parliament of 1422*, pp. 169-70.

Tyrell married again, taking as his second wife Katherine, the widow of John Spenser, keeper of the Great Wardrobe of the Household under Henry V, he acquired by this means the manor of Banham (Suffolk). By 1428, he had come into more real estate still: lands in Northavon and Middleton (Hants.), Hunsdon, Bradfield and Standon (Herts.) and Wendy (Cambs.). So much so that in 1436, when a graduated income-tax was levied on lands, rents and royal annuities granted in lieu of land, his annual income was reckoned at £396, the highest assessment in Essex of anyone below baronial rank. In considering the hold on Essex his family was then enjoying, it has also to be borne in mind that his eldest son, Thomas, had lands estimated as worth £40 a year, and his brother, Edward, lands worth £135.[4]

When John Tyrell was first elected to parliament in 1411, it was doubtless in the shadow of his father-in-law, Coggeshall. For otherwise he had so far made little impression, not yet having served on any even minor royal commissions either locally or elsewhere. It was only after the accession of Henry V that his career really got under way. No great significance need attach to the fact that on 14 April 1413 he was one of five sureties in the Chancery for the newly appointed master of the Royal Mint, namely, Lewis John esq., the London vintner of Welsh parentage who lived at Thorndon (Essex), who in the previous reign had sometimes been the convivial host in the city to the young heir-apparent and his brothers, and who was a close business-associate of Thomas Chaucer, Bishop Beaufort's cousin.[5] It was, however, important to him to be elected again as knight of the shire to the first parliament of the new reign, perhaps no less so in view of the identity of his fellow-representative, namely, his brother-in-law's father, John Doreward, who was to fill the office of Speaker in the last week of the session. Of greater importance still, both for his standing locally as well as with the king, was his appointment on 6 November following as sheriff over the joint-bailiwick of Essex and Hertfordshire, a position he held for the usual term of a year, until 10 November 1414.[6] And, of course, it fell to him to hold the elections for both counties to the two parliaments summoned in his year of office — the parliament which began at Leicester in April, and the parliament which met in November-December. (To the spring parliament was elected Tyrell's father-in-law, Coggeshall, along with, as re-elected, John Doreward.) Moreover, it was while or soon after Tyrell was sheriff in his region

---

4   *Feudal Aids*, I. 190; II. 216, 350, 373, 451; III. 588; VI. 445, 523; *E. H. R.*, XLIX, H. L. Gray, 'Incomes from land in England in 1436', p. 633.

5   *CCR, 1413-9*, 66. For further particulars of Lewis John, see pp. 164, 166.

6   *P. R. O., Lists and Indexes, IX (List of Sheriffs)*, 44.

that, both there and elsewhere, he first (as recorded) began those activities, especially as a trustee and feoffee-to-uses, which were to prove a socially, and no doubt sometimes financially, profitable adjunct to his political career. That, in January 1414, he was a co-feoffee of lands given to help found a chantry in the parish church of Wivenhoe (Essex), was of no great moment. But in December following it was as a feoffee of the lordship of Oakham (Rutland) that he assisted in a conveyance by which Anne, daughter and sole heir of Thomas of Woodstock, duke of Gloucester (ob. 1397), and dowager countess of Stafford, along with her second husband, Sir William Bourchier, transferred her interest in the lordship to Edward, duke of York, for his lifetime. (Less than a year later, Edward was killed at Agincourt.) Then, on 8 May 1415 he was party to a recognizance in which Sir John Tiptoft acknowledged an obligation to pay 500 marks to Thomas Langley, bishop of Durham, and Ralph Neville, earl of Westmorland, both of whom were members of Henry V's Council. Tiptoft, appointed a week before as seneschal of Guienne, had clearly begun his preparations for departure.[7]

By this time a whole host of people were similarly engaged, preparing for the king's invasion of either Normandy or Guienne, but then, as finally decided, Normandy; and, in due course, on 11 August, Henry's great fleet sailed from the Solent for the estuary of the Seine. When, meanwhile, on 25 July, Tyrell, as about to take part in the expedition, had obtained royal letters of protection, it was as a member of Sir Walter Hungerford's company. He had, in fact, however, entered into a contract to serve with Humphrey, duke of Gloucester, and the actual mustering of his retinue of 5 'lances' and 18 archers took place, near Romsey, along with that of others of the duke's contingent.[8] It was presumably with Gloucester that Tyrell served out the campaign that followed.

It is unlikely that Tyrell's connection with Gloucester, which was to prove a dominant feature of his later career, only began in this fashion, although it is the first recorded instance of it. For the duke already, of his father's granting, held important estates and other sources of income in Essex, and certainly in 1416 Tyrell was acting as his steward in the county.[9] Clearly no later than the summer of 1418 he had attained to a position of far greater trust, being then numbered among the duke's feoffees, or rather mortgagees. It was, in fact, on 1 July that year that Humphrey, who was then busy besieging Cherbourg, having

---

7   *CPR, 1413-6*, 151, 270; *CCR, 1413-9*, 274.
8   *DKR, XLIV* (French Rolls). 573; Exchequer, Foreign Accounts, P. R. O., E101/45/13.
9   *Colchester Oath Book*, ed. W. Gurney Benham, p. 24.

requested and obtained Henry V's licence, secured royal letters patent issued in England by the Chancery, enabling him to mortgage various sources of income, mostly in land, granted him by the king in tail-male: in Essex, the castle of Hadleigh, the hundred of Tendring, the constableship of Colchester castle, and £35 a year from the fee-farm of the borough of Colchester (effectively the whole fee-farm); in Worcestershire, the manor and forest of Feckenham; in Gloucestershire, the manor and hundred of Barton-by-Bristol; in Carmarthenshire, the castle and lordship of Llanstephan, the manor of Traian, and a third of the manor of St Clear; in Pembrokeshire, the castles, towns and lordships of Pembroke and Kilgerran, the castle and town of Tenby, the manor and hundred of Castlemartin, and the manor of Oysterlowe; and (to return from Wales) the reversion of the lordship of the Isle of Wight, including the castle and lordship of Carisbrooke, then held for life by Philippa, dowager duchess of York. Gloucester's mortgagees were now granted these estates on the understanding that they should continue in legal possession 'until they had levied the sums in which he is at present indebted and will be for life'; and the king had also empowered the chancellor to reform and renew the letters patent, if necessary. Apart from such men in high office at the time as Bishop Langley of Durham (chancellor of England), Henry, lord FitzHugh (the king's chamberlain and treasurer of the Exchequer), and Sir John Tiptoft (treasurer-general of Normandy), Tyrell's associates in this transaction were Geoffrey Lowther (the duke's deputy-warden of the Cinque Ports), Nicholas Thorley (his receiver-general), and Walter Sherington (a clerk in his service). Incidentally, it had been with Tiptoft (and the latter's agent in England, Roger Hunt, a lawyer of note) that, precisely a year earlier (1 July 1417), Tyrell had been party to a recognizance guaranteeing repayment of a loan of £2,000 made to the king by six London aldermen, of whom the most important was the great mercer-financier, Richard Whittington.[10]

Again in the meantime, following his return from France in the autumn of 1415, Tyrell had been elected as knight of the shire for Essex to either the parliament which met in March 1416 or the one which assembled in October that same year. He was also elected to the parliament of November 1417, and was re-elected when, after nearly two years, parliament met again in October 1419. By now (since 21 April 1419) a justice of the peace in Essex, he was appointed, by the King's Council in England on 26 November (roughly a fortnight after the dissolution of the 1419 parliament), as a member of a commission charged with the raising of royal loans in the county. (It was on the

10   *CPR, 1416-22*, 129; *CCR, 1413-9*, 435.

next day that Tyrell became one of the feoffees, in a moiety of the manor and advowson of Bromford, of John Sumpter, parliamentary burgess for Colchester in the recent session.)[11]

Ever since Henry V's second departure for France at the end of July 1417, affairs at home had been looked after by a Council headed by John, duke of Bedford, in his capacity as *custos Anglie*. However, presumably to give Bedford an opportunity to undertake his first active service on the French mainland, the king decided in November 1419 that he should be replaced by their youngest brother, Humphrey, who certainly had earned a respite from campaigning. Gloucester, returning from France about the end of the month, was formally appointed *custos* on 30 December, his commission making it clear that he was only ever to act 'in matters of governance' with the assent of his fellow-councillors and after due deliberation. So far as Tyrell was concerned, the presence of his lord in England, occupying such a station, seems hardly to have affected him, at least in the sense that no Crown appointment, or even commission originating with the Council, now came his way. And, moreover, it was not he but his father-in-law, Coggeshall, who, with Lewis John, was elected for Essex to the only parliament over which Gloucester presided at this time, the parliament which, meeting on 2 December 1420, anticipated by precisely two months the return of the king to England with his queen, Katherine of Valois. Shortly before that parliament met, however, Tyrell had been closely involved in a very shady transaction to which Gloucester was a ready party. What the duke had done was to have interfered in the dispute over possession of the castle and barony of Berkeley (Glos.) between, on the one hand, the heir-general, viz. Elizabeth, daughter and sole heir of Thomas, 5th Lord Berkeley (ob. 13 July 1417), and her husband, Richard Beauchamp, earl of Warwick, and, on the other hand, the heir male viz. Lord Thomas's nephew James (the son of his deceased younger brother, Sir James Berkeley). In *The Lives of the Berkeleys*, the valuable work written by John Smyth of Nibley (ob. 1640),[12] who was steward of the Berkeley family at Netley and had

11   *CPR, 1416-22*, 250, 452 ;*CCR, 1419-22*, 57.

12   J. Smyth, *Lives of the Berkeleys*, ed. J. Maclean (Gloucester, 1883), vol. 2. pp. 40 et seq. On 10 September 1422 the earl of Warwick and Lord James entered into recognizances, in each case for 10,000 marks, undertaking to abide by the arbitration of Philip Morgan, bishop of Worcester, Sir John Tiptoft, and William Babington and William Cheyne, king's justices (with Justice Juyn as reserve), concerning all articles in their indentures needing clarification, and to stand to their award touching all suits involving their servants, except those arising out of an exchange of blows at Hammersmith (Surrey) which had been submitted for settlement to the duke of Gloucester. For the later 'tangled history' of the conflict between the descendants of Elizabeth, countess of Warwick (ob. Dec. 1422) and James, lord Berkeley (ob. Nov. 1463), see R. A. Griffiths, *The Reign of Henry VI* (1982), espec. pp. 572-4. See also *DNB*, II. 341-2.

access to muniments in Berkeley Castle (now no longer extant), it is said that, to defeat Warwick's obstruction of Lord James's suit of livery of seisin of the castle and barony, Lord James 'wisely winneth with his purse the assistance of Humphrey, duke of Gloucester', meaning (as Smyth goes on to relate) that, at London on 1 November 1420, he 'bound himself to [John] Tyrell and [Walter] Sheryngton, men whom the duke much trusted', in a recognizance for 10,000 marks; by which he undertook to pay them (in the duke's interest) 1,000 marks within a year and a half of his having obtained seisin, and to grant to the duke the reversion in fee simple of all the lands in Wales and elsewhere he had inherited from his mother, to the annual value of 400 marks, saving his own estate for life after their recovery. With a metaphor appropriate to the locality, Smyth of Nibley described the immediate, successful outcome of this example of champerty, saying that Lord James 'who before was as a weak hopp, havinge now got a strong pole fastly to wind about, grew up and bore the fruite of his own desires'; and, in fact, not only did he, in Michaelmas term 1421, on a petition supported by Gloucester, obtain a royal licence to sue out livery and pay his baronial relief, but then also received his first individual writ of summons to parliament. Gloucester's part in the dispute over the Berkeley inheritance, although the dispute was of a quasi-private nature, can hardly not have redounded to his public discredit and ultimately, in view of the permanent importance of the earl of Warwick, to his political disadvantage.

Meanwhile, Tyrell had again been elected for Essex to the parliament which, meeting on 2 May 1421, proved to be the last which Henry V attended in person. On 20 June following, shortly after the king, accompanied by Gloucester, returned to France, he was appointed as a commissioner of array in his county, in view of rumours that a Castilian fleet was being organized for an invasion of England. His membership of the commission of the peace in Essex was renewed on 12 February 1422, and a month later (11 March) he was appointed by the Council, along with Richard Baynard (Commons' Speaker in December 1421), John Doreward, and the sheriff, to enquire in the county into cases of concealment of royal rights to wardships and marriages of tenants-in-chief under age, and of other trespasses and deceptions.[13] In undertaking such a commission as this, Tyrell can only have been greatly assisted by the fact that he was now becoming quite immersed in the affairs of local families and other sorts of business of a private or merely semi-public character. Indeed, available notices of his activities in the few remaining months of Henry V's reign mostly relate

13   *CPR, 1416-22*, 452; 422.

to matters of that kind. On the other hand, they were frequently significant as involving him in contacts with persons of some importance, sometimes persons with considerable influence on matters of general governmental concern. Tyrell is mentioned on 14 February 1422 as one of the feoffees of the manors of Messing and Birch Hall and other estates in Essex belonging to Richard Baynard, the purpose of the enfeoffment being to perform, in due course, Baynard's last will and testament.[14] When, four days later, Sir John Tiptoft, who was still seneschal of Guienne, received a grant of the wardship and marriage of the heir of Sir Thomas de la Pole (and a nephew of William, earl of Suffolk), on payment of 400 marks to the Exchequer, Tyrell stood surety (along with the lawyer, Roger Hunt, Tiptoft's financial agent, who had been Speaker for the Commons in 1420). Then, on 27 May, he did a like service for William Yerd, receiver-general to John Holland, earl of Huntingdon, who, in March 1421, had been taken prisoner at the battle of Baugé, a notable Dauphinist victory in which the king's eldest brother, the duke of Clarence, had been killed; Yerd's sureties, who also included Sir John Cornwall, the earl's step-father, undertook in Chancery under pain of £100, and he himself under pain of £500, to appear before the Council within a fortnight of warning received; and, less than two months later (20 July), Yerd offered a further personal guarantee, now in a bond for £1,000, to answer, before auditors appointed by the Council, for all his accounts up to October 1420. (Although it would appear that the Council was already doing what it could towards the ransoming of the earl, it was not until 1425 that his liberation was to be achieved). Meanwhile, on the eve of the first of these mainprises (26 May), Tyrell had been party to the demise of an annual rent of 10 marks charged on the manor of West Thurrock in Essex (which, in certain circumstances, was to be doubled); the recipients for life, Nicholas Rickhill of Hatfield Peverel and his wife, were people of no great account, but most of Tyrell's co-feoffees in the manor were men of importance, namely Nicholas Bubwith (bishop of Bath and Wells), William Kinwolmarsh (treasurer of the Exchequer), Sir Hugh Luttrell (ex-seneschal of Normandy), Sir John Pelham (a wealthy survivor of the retinues of John of Gaunt and Henry IV, and one of the latter's executors), John Leventhorpe (receiver- and attorney-general of the duchy of Lancaster), and John Barton junior (steward of the abbey of St Albans).[15] The three last-named were to be knights of the shire in the first parliament of Henry VI's reign, and Tyrell was to join them there, along with, re-elected as his fellow representative for Essex, his father-in-law, Sir William Coggeshall. (The death, in the course of 1422,

14   *CCR, 1419-22*, 223.
15   *CPR, 1416-22*, 412; *CCR, 1419-22*, 259, 261.

of Alice, Tyrell's first wife, Coggeshall's daughter, had doubtless brought them much together in any case). They were elected less than a week before the parliament met at Westminster on 9 November 1422, two days after the burial, in the Abbey, of the late king.

What this parliament would do towards furnishing a proper constitutional basis for government during an inevitably long royal minority (Henry VI being not yet a year old) was of crucial importance to Tyrell's lord, Humphrey of Gloucester. The duke had ended the previous reign as Henry V's lieutenant in England (May-August 1422); and Henry's will (of June 1421), as amplified by the codicils he had added when on his death-bed at Bois-de-Vincennes, had provided for his appointment as regent in England, as of the elder surviving brother, Bedford, as regent of France. So far as Gloucester's own claim went, he did all possible to get parliament to accept it. However, the Lords refused, and all that Gloucester obtained was a compromise which left him dissatisfied: recognition, in Bedford's absence, as 'protector and defender of the realm of England and the English church, and the king's chief councillor', but with supreme control of affairs assigned to the Lords in parliament or great council, otherwise left to the continual council. So many more members of the Lower House had links with the Lords than with Gloucester that parliament as a whole can hardly have been deeply divided over the problem posed by Gloucester's ambitions, or over their rejection.[16]

In view of Tyrell's strong personal commitment to Gloucester, there can be little if any doubt as to which side he had taken in the dispute. Even so, either this was not held against him, or else because Gloucester was able to impose his authority as head of the Council, it was not long before, on 14 February 1423, he was made sheriff of Essex and Hertfordshire (the appointment to be as from the preceding Michaelmas), and he held the office until 13 November following.[17] Soon after Tyrell took up office he was also appointed (on 4 March) to serve on a commission of enquiry into an appeal against a judgment made by Henry Percy, earl of Northumberland, in his capacity as warden of the East March towards Scotland, in a case arising out of the alleged despoiling of a Scottish prisoner. (His fellow-commissioners, civil lawyers apart, included Lords FitzHugh and Cromwell, both of

16   Regarding this problem, see *ante* vol. I, VII 198-224, 234.
17   *List of Sheriffs*, 44. Other shire-knights elected to the 1422 parliament who were appointed sheriffs at the same time were: Sir John Bertram (Northumberland), Sir William Bonville (Devon), Sir John Cockayne (Derbyshire and Notts.), and Sir Thomas Waweton (Beds. and Bucks.).

them members of the Council, and Geoffrey Lowther, who had not only continued to be Gloucester's deputy-warden of the Cinque Ports, but was now also receiver-general for those parts of the duchy of Lancaster was not enfeoffed by Henry V for the fulfilment of his will.) During his year of office as sheriff, too, Tyrell was party to a final concord (legal settlement) in the court of Common Pleas, regarding title to a moiety of third parts of the manors of West Tilbury (Essex), Henshirst (Kent) and Pontefract (Middlesex), he then acting as a feoffee of John Harpour who, with another of the feoffees, Robert Whitgreve, a teller of the Exchequer, had sat in the previous parliament as burgess for Stafford.[18] And when, on 1 September 1423, the second parliament of the reign was summoned to meet on 20 October, and it became Tyrell's duty as sheriff to hold the county elections in his bailiwick, he accordingly did so, for Hertfordshire on 23 September, and for Essex (at Stratford Langthorne) on 5 October, when were elected the two lawyers, Richard Baynard and Robert Darcy (the clerk of the Court of Common Pleas, who eventually became father-in-law of Tyrell's second son, William Tyrell the elder). When, on 22 November, in the middle of the first of the two sessions of the parliament, Ralph, lord Cromwell, took out a ten years' lease of the castle and manor of Somerton and a moiety of the manor of Carlton-le-Moorland (properties in Kesteven, Lincs., both previously held by the late duke of Clarence), Tyrell was one of the two men Cromwell found ready to stand surety for him before the barons of the Exchequer, the grant having had the approval of his fellow-members of the Council. Before long, Tyrell was himself to have direct dealings with the Council.

It was on the third day of the second session of the same parliament, i.e. on 16 January 1424, that the Council was induced to come to a decision over a matter of considerable financial importance for Tyrell, or rather for him and the lady whom, following the death of his first wife in 1422, he had married before the end of July 1423.[19] This second wife of his was Katherine, widow and executrix of John Spenser who, when Henry V was prince of Wales, had been controller of his household and, during his reign, keeper of the Great Wardrobe of the Household. Spenser, at his death, had been owed on account of his office a debt of no less than £2,700, and when Tyrell and Katherine together put in a petition for repayment, what the Council did was to authorize the issue of a warrant under the Privy Seal instructing Henry

---

18   *CPR, 1422-9*, 78; *Feet of Fines for Middlesex*, (London, 1892-3), ed. W. J. Hardy and W. Page.

19   *The Archaeological Journal, XXVIII*. 33 (Tyrell pedigree); *CFR, 1422-30*, 63.

V's executors to give them preference.[20] This, indeed the whole affair, proved far from simple. In the course of the year the executors, who, in accordance with the relevant act of the 1422 parliament, had been assigned £14,000 for the satisfaction of Henry's creditors, allowed Tyrell and his wife various tallies amounting to some 1,000 marks (£666 odd) as a charge on a particular sum of £3,000 appropriated to their (the executors') use, this £3,000 being part of a debt owed to the late king by Henry Percy, earl of Northumberland, on a recognizance. But then, only not until 18 December 1424, Tyrell was pressed by the Council into accepting a fresh arrangement: he agreed with Northumberland that 1,000 marks (and no more) should be paid him, not by Henry V's executors, but by the Lower Exchequer, the payment to count as a discharge of certain tallies originally levied there in the earl's favour as security for arrears owed him as warden of the East March, and to be made by instalments of 100 marks payable at half-yearly intervals. Thus, satisfaction of even less than a quarter of the whole debt owing to Tyrell and his wife Katherine was to be spread over five years, and all that the king's councillors could now offer them, should this arrangement fail (which, clearly, was thought possible), was that it would be open to them to have recourse once more to the Council and the late king's executors. It can have been little comfort to Tyrell and his wife that the new arrangement took shape in letters patent under the Great Seal.[21] How the matter ended is not known.

In the meantime, following a temporary omission from the commission of the peace for Essex in the year of his shrievalty, Tyrell had been re-appointed to it on 20 July 1424.[22] Otherwise, nothing further of note is known of him until, along with Robert Darcy (for the fourth time), he was elected to the parliament which met on 30 April 1425 and, after a week's break at the end of May (for Whitsuntide), sat until 14 July. So far as Tyrell's patron, Gloucester, was concerned it looked as if the parliament would again be one critical for his reputation and position. For despite the continuing legal dubiety attaching to his marriage to Jacqueline of Hainault (which, previously encouraged by Henry V, had most probably taken place in January 1423), he had led an army to the Low Countries in October 1424 in order to recover her county of Hainault and, if possible, Holland and

---

20   *Proceedings and Ordinances of the Privy Council (PPC)*, ed. N. H. Nicolas, III. 131; *Cal. of Papal Registers, Papal Letters*, VII. 318. (On 31 July 1423 Tyrell and his wife, Katherine, of the diocese of London, were granted papal indults, (a) to choose their own confessors, and (b) to have a portable altar.

21   *CPR, 1422-9*, 267.

22   ibid. 563.

Zeeland as well; and this expedition,[23] from which Gloucester did not return until 12 April 1425, had proved an expensive failure. The people of Hainault were alienated by the invasion, and although the Estates of the county had accepted Jacqueline as countess in December 1424, they had allowed Gloucester only the title of regent, refusing to recognize him as count *jure uxoris*. Meanwhile, Holland and Zeeland held to their allegiance to Jacqueline's rejected husband, Duke John of Brabant, cousin of Duke Philip of Burgundy. Philip, outraged by Gloucester's armed intervention, sent his forces in March 1425 to help get the English out, and, within three months, Hainault had been overrun and Jacqueline put under arrest. It was the bitterly hostile reaction of Burgundy to Jacqueline's marriage to Gloucester and its consequences which, of course, made Gloucester's personal "foreign policy" so objectionable; for upon the Anglo-Burgundian alliance, to which Henry V had attached great importance, and which Bedford's recent marriage to Burgundy's sister (Anne) was designed to strengthen, depended all real hope of retaining the English conquests in France, let alone of their extension. Considering the total failure of Gloucester's expedition, coupled with his desertion of his wife (a desertion all the more dishonourable in that Eleanor Cobham, her lady-in-waiting, had already become his lady-love), it is something remarkable that the parliament which met less than three weeks after his return to England should eventually have turned out so well for him. Admittedly, the duke did not on this occasion act as commissary of the king who, although only three years old, was brought into parliament to witness its opening. But, then, if Henry Beaufort may be thought to have been, in his preliminary address as chancellor, critical of Gloucester's conduct, his remarks (as recorded) were so subtly veiled as to suggest fear of giving offence. Doubtless more to the point, parliament extricated Gloucester from the inconvenience of the duel to which Burgundy had challenged him early in March, it being decided that the Council should send an embassy to Philip to propose the submission of the quarrel to the arbitrament of the king's grandmother (Isabel of France), his mother (Queen Katherine), and Bedford (his regent in France), and also from the embarrassment caused by his treatment of Jacqueline by requiring the same embassy to arrange for her release 'into indifferent handes'.[24] Meanwhile, on 22 May, shortly before the end of the first session of the parliament, the Council had given Gloucester custody of the bulk of the lands of Edmund Mortimer, earl

23   For this expedition, its antecedents and consequences, see R. Vaughan, *Philip the Good* (London, 1970), pp. 32-50.
24   *Rot. Parl.*, IV. 277.

of March (ob. 18 Jan. 1425), a wardship all the more profitable in view of the fact that the sole heir, Richard, duke of York, would not be entitled to sue out livery until attaining his majority in 1432. Then, on the last day of the parliament (14 July), the Commons successfully proposed that the king's 'bele Oncle of Gloucestre' should receive a government loan of 20,000 marks, payable by instalments over the next four years.[25] (It was ironic that, on 6 June, Beaufort had added to his loans to the Crown by one of over £11,000, a sum not far short of what Gloucester was soon to be promised.) And some of Gloucester's friends, too, prospered: a dispute over precedence between the earl of Warwick and John Mowbray, earl marshal, occupied both sessions, but when it was settled, again on the day parliament was dissolved, the decision not only went in favour of Mowbray, who had been in command of Gloucester's army in Hainault, but was achieved by his restoration, at the Commons' request, to his father's title of duke of Norfolk. Such proceedings of the parliament as directly profited Gloucester were no doubt also welcomed by his retainer, John Tyrell. Whatever Tyrell himself might have done to promote such developments is totally obscure, although it may be assumed that he had neglected no opportunity to be helpful. Certainly, he was able to assist another friend of Gloucester's: Walter, 5th lord FitzWalter, whom, early in January 1426, Gloucester was to send out, as his lieutenant in Holland and Zeeland, to rescue Jacqueline's forces there. It had been on 12 July, two days before the parliament of 1425 ended, that Lord FitzWalter had procured royal letters of attorney authorizing him to settle nine of his Essex manors and property in four others in Lincolnshire upon feoffees-to-uses, among whom, along with Robert Darcy, Tyrell was included. Another feoffee was Lewis John of Thorndon (Essex), now receiver-general of the duchy of Cornwall, whom, on 31 January 1426, Tyrell was to appoint as one of his own feoffees in his manor of Bradfield (Herts.), along with Humphrey, earl of Stafford, John Hotoft, treasurer of the King's Household, and John Fray, a baron of the Exchequer.[26]

In view of the difficult political situation at the time of this private transaction of Tyrell's, it may possibly be regarded as a precautionary measure on his part, even though it affected only a single one of his estates. The inclusion of the earl of Stafford is particularly noteworthy. For only two days before the enfeoffment, Stafford, whose countess was Henry Beaufort's niece (Anne, *née* Neville), had been sent by his fellow-members of the Council, along with Archbishop Chichele, to ask Duke Humphrey to join them on their way to the

25   ibid. 289.
26   *CCR, 1422-9*, 260, 341.

parliament which had been summoned to meet at Leicester on 18 February, and to attend the parliament as usual, promising that he and his household would be safe to do so. The fact was that since the parliament of 1425, both official and personal relations between Gloucester (the protector) and Beaufort (the chancellor) had so deteriorated as to have posed a threat to the public peace, especially in London, a threat so serious as eventually to have prompted Beaufort to request the duke of Bedford to return from France and help bring his brother to order. Bedford, who obeyed the recall shortly before Christmas, then automatically (under the 1422 settlement) replaced Gloucester as protector and chief councillor. However, by the time parliament met at Leicester, all efforts to bring about a reconciliation between the opposed parties had clearly failed, and so highly tense was now the atmosphere that it was necessary to order those attending the parliament not to carry weapons (an injunction much honoured in the breach). It was not until 12 March (three weeks into the session) that Gloucester and Beaufort could be induced to shake hands. Whereupon, on the next day, Beaufort resigned the Great Seal in favour of Archbishop Kemp of York, and Lord Hungerford succeeded Bishop Stafford of Bath and Wells as treasurer of the Exchequer: effectively a political compromise with which, a week later (20 March), the first session ended.

Although, to that Leicester parliament of 1426, Robert Darcy of Maldon had been re-elected as shire-knight for Essex, Tyrell had not. (He had been replaced by Lewis John, one of his feoffees at Bradfield, Herts.) Whether he attended the first session, or even the second and final session which ended on 1 June, is not known. It is not until 27 June that he is next recorded, as then standing surety for both Lewis John and Sir John Montgomery, each of whom, on his own account and under pain of £40, undertook not to do harm to Robert Lowth esq. (M.P. for Herts. in 1421). Then, on 23 July, he was again associated with Lewis John, only this time along with Bishop William Grey of London, Sir Lewis Robsart (a Hainaulter by birth who, in June 1421, had been appointed as one of Henry V's executors), and Robert Darcy, all five receiving a commission to raise Crown loans in Essex. (The Leicester parliament had empowered the Council to raise £40,000 in this manner before midsummer 1427.) Then, on 12 December following, Tyrell was made sheriff of Norfolk and Suffolk; and he held office until 7 November 1427.[27] Whatever influences had been brought

27   ibid. 277; *CPR, 1422-9*, 353; *List of Sheriffs*.

to bear upon such appointments, it was doubtless at Gloucester's prompting that, on 13 February 1427, royal letters patent were issued under the Great Seal appointing Tyrell as steward of the Mortimer lordships of Clare (Suffolk) and Thaxstead (Essex), the appointment to apply as from 1 January, the day after the death of Thomas Beaufort, duke of Exeter, who had had custody. Tyrell's appointment on this occasion was only *quamdiu regi placuerit*. But it was not long before, on 1 June, he was granted fresh letters patent giving him the stewardship of the lordships on a more secure basis: his tenure of office was to last until Richard, duke of York, the now 15-years-old heir to the Mortimer estates (most of which, as noted above, were under Gloucester's control), came of age. Meanwhile, on 16 February, Tyrell had joined Lord Tiptoft, the recently appointed steward of the King's Household, in standing surety for the latter's fellow-councillors, Ralph, lord Cromwell, and John, lord Scrope of Masham, and also Sir Walter Beauchamp (one of Henry V's executors), when, in association with the two collectors of the income, they received a grant of all the issues from the temporalities of the see of York since 20 October 1423 (the date of the death of Archbishop Bowet), the grant to last until the temporalities were restored to Archbishop Kemp (the chancellor). The grantees had undertaken to satisfy the Exchequer of £3,344 odd (a little over 5,000 marks), paying off what they still owed at a rate of 2,000 marks a year.[28]

Busy though the year 1427 was already turning out to be, Tyrell was very soon to become much more active still, i.e. in discharging what was for him a responsibility of a novel kind. On 20 March he received at the Exchequer a grant of £60.13s.4d towards the expenses he would incur in accompanying the eminent canon lawyer, Dr. William Lyndwood (then dean of the Arches), on an embassy to Holland, the formal purpose of which was 'to expedite certain royal business and particular matters moving the King's Council on that behalf.' In view of the fact that a year or so later (on 9 July 1428) the Council was to give Tyrell a special *regardum* of £40, payable at the Exchequer, for his labour and costs on the embassy, and because it had impeded his collection of the profits of the shrievalty of Norfolk and Suffolk, there can be no question but that the mission was fulfilled.[29] What was involved was, of course, the problem posed by the situation in which Gloucester's wife, Jacqueline, now found herself. Having escaped from

28   *CPR, 1422-9*, 395, 401; *CFR, 1422-30*, 166. The order to restore the temporalities to Kemp was to be issued on 22 April 1426. (He had been translated from London by Pope Martin V on 20 July 1425.)

29   Exchequer, Issue Roll, P. R. O., E 403/677/mem. 18; E 403/686/9.

Burgundian custody at Ghent in September 1425, when she fled to Gouda in Holland, she had, in the meantime, been concentrating her efforts to retain at least this one of her three Netherlandish provinces, and she and her partisans had gained ground at the duke of Burgundy's expense, especially in the spring and summer of 1426; but now, in the spring of 1427, her forces were under severe pressure, and Duke Philip was clearly bent upon making an end. The beleaguered Jacqueline's first known letter of appeal for help to the English Council was not written until 8 April,[30] nearly three weeks after Lyndwood and Tyrell's embassy had been finally decided upon. If, however, as is quite possible, that letter was not the first of its kind, it is more than likely that the object of the embassy was merely to enquire how matters stood in Holland, not necessarily to deliberate with Jacqueline concerning ways and means whereby military help from England might be furnished. After all, Tyrell's Exchequer advance on 20 March was made only the day after Bedford, accompanied by Bishop Beaufort, had returned to France, and it is hardly conceivable that the duke, who later this year was to protest in the strongest terms to the Council in general and Gloucester in particular against any anti-Burgundian move in the Low Countries, would recently have agreed to the envoys going to Holland to negotiate anything so positive as a renewal of English military aggression there. However, with Bedford out of the way, it looks as if, before long, Gloucester pressed the Council to re-adopt his earlier policy of active intervention, and did so successfully, at least up to a point: on 9 July, perhaps acting on reports from the envoys, Duke Humphrey obtained a Council grant of 9,000 marks, of which 4,000 marks was to count as half his annual salary as protector, the other 5,000 marks being earmarked for Jacqueline's support.[31] An expedition was, in fact, arranged for by Gloucester, and Thomas Montague, earl of Salisbury, then in England, agreed, out of personal animosity towards the duke of Burgundy, to join it. The Council, however, did not intend to promote Gloucester's earlier ambition to occupy his wife's domains as virtually his own, but rather to extricate Jacqueline from a personally dangerous situation; part of the force was to escort her to England, part merely to garrison those castles and towns of hers that could be relieved but, in any event, to abstain from offensive action unless consent was given in parliament. Whether

30   K. H. Vickers, *Humphrey, Duke of Gloucester* (London, 1907), p. 197. Jacqueline was also to write on 6 June, and did so yet again towards the end of the same month. It is possible that these letters and their predecessor of 8 April were members of a series going further back still (Vickers, 198).

31   *PPC*, III. 271-4.

parliament would go further remained to be seen, but on 15 July it was summoned to meet on 13 October. Nothing was more certain than that Gloucester, as arrogant and overbearing as ever, would spare no effort to secure his own ends, including exploitation of what support he could command in the Lower House. And that he enjoyed some support there is evident from the fact that the Commons on this occasion chose John Tyrell as their Speaker.

Tyrell, who, in his capacity as sheriff, had already held the elections for Norfolk and Suffolk, was himself elected, contrary to the normal prohibition of the election of any sheriff made explicit in the writs, to represent Hertfordshire (the only occasion of his so doing). His brother Edward, then royal escheator in Essex and Hertfordshire, was elected for the first time for Essex, and the other knight of the shire was Richard Baynard, a servant and feoffee of Gloucester's adherent, Lord FitzWalter, John Tyrell being one of his co-feoffees. It was Baynard, himself a former Speaker (in the last parliament of Henry V's reign), who headed the deputation from the Commons which, on the second day of the session (14 October), announced to Gloucester and the Lords Spiritual and Temporal their *unanimous* election of John Tyrell as Speaker.[32]

Concerning the Commons' own proper business — petitioning and voting taxes — both sessions of the parliament (13 October — 8 December 1427, 27 January — 25 March 1428) can only have been arduous, not least for their Speaker. No less so for the latter, either, because of the ups-and-downs evidently affecting the position of his lord, Duke Humphrey. It was very probably in the first session that Gloucester, jointly with Thomas Montague, earl of Salisbury, presented a petition which met with a favourable response: that, in view of non-payment of excessive arrears for their past military services in France, they should be exonerated from all charges arising from 'gains of war', and should be allowed to retain royal jewels pledged for their retinues' wages unless, within three years of the end of the parliament, they had been satisfied of the value of the jewels, in which case they were to restore them. However, before the end of the second session, Gloucester's fortunes had taken a downward turn: on 3 March 1428 he rashly challenged the Lords with a demand for a re-definition in his favour of his authority as protector, whereupon they reminded him of the limitations imposed on that office in 1422 and insisted that he

---

32   *Rot. Parl.*, IV. 317. It is interesting that — Tyrell (no first name given) was admitted to Lincoln's Inn on the eve of John Tyrell's Speakership in 1427 (*Admission Register of Lincoln's Inn*, p. 5). The entrant was probably John's eldest son, Thomas, whose son was accorded special admission in 1457.

observe them (as Bedford had promised to do).[33] No doubt the peers were confirmed in their resolve by Gloucester's current unpopularity in London (of all places) arising from his desertion of his wife and his open preference for his mistress, Eleanor Cobham, a commotion sufficient to prompt the women from the city stocks-market to come to parliment to protest and, on 8 March, to cause the mayor and aldermen, doing likewise, to insist that Jacqueline be rescued. Influenced by these expressions of public opinion, the Lower House, when communicating its grant of an ill-sorted tax levied on both parishes and knights' fees, stipulated that 'my Lady of Gloucestre, that lyveth in so greet dolour and hevynesse', should be so provided for by the Council 'that her persone, and the alliance betwene this noble Royaume and her landes had and continued, be put in salvetee and sykernes [security], in singuler comforte of the .... Commens, and of all thoos that they been comyn fore'. This particular appropriation of supply may have done something to salve the conscience of parliament, but even as a promise of support for Jacqueline of Hainault, it was too belated: in little more than three months (on 3 July) she concluded the treaty of Delft whereby she not only recognized Burgundy as heir to her possessions, but surrendered virtually all control of them.[34] That meanwhile, on the day of parliament's dissolution (25 March), John Tyrell, as Speaker and expressly in the name of the Commons, had 'recommended' Gloucester,[35] neither they nor the duke can have regarded as much more than a gesture.

It was perhaps just as well for the future development of John Tyrell's career that the important promotion that came his way during the 1427-8 parliament, had done so immediately after its first session when, without a doubt, Gloucester was still wielding considerable influence. The appointment in question, which took place on 10 December 1427 (two days after parliament's prorogation), was to the office of chief steward of the estates of the duchy of Lancaster north of Trent (excluding Lancashire and Cheshire).[36] This appointment not only meant Tyrell's *ex officio* nomination to the commissions of the peace in the several counties of the northern region, but also involved him in membership of the duchy council. This managerial body, presided over, in his capacity as chamberlain of the duchy, by Lord Hungerford, who also held the chief stewardship of the parts south of Trent (and at this time was treasurer of the Exchequer too), already

33   *Rot. Parl.*, IV. 320-1, 326-7.
34   K. H. Vickers, op. cit., 203; *Rot. Parl.*, IV. 318; R. Vaughan, op. cit., 49.
35   *Rot. Parl.*, IV. 318.
36   R. Somerville, *History of the Duchy of Lancaster* (London, 1953) I. 420.

included, as receiver- and attorney-general of the duchy, another friend of Gloucester's, viz. Geoffrey Lowther (who was still his deputy-warden of the Cinque Ports); and in February 1431 Lowther and Tyrell were to be joined, doubtless again at Gloucester's instance, by Walter Sherington, the duke's clerk and feoffee, who was then appointed as chancellor of the duchy.[37] Serving as a counter-weight in the administration of the duchy of Lancaster to Henry Beaufort and Henry V's other feoffees of duchy estates, all three of these friends of Gloucester's long continued in their duchy offices, Tyrell's own appointment as chief steward lasting until his death in 1437 (when William de la Pole, earl of Suffolk, replaced him). It would, in all probability, have been politically more satisfactory for Gloucester if, instead of complaining of the inadequacy of his powers as protector (as early in 1428 he had done), he had simply been content to take advantage of any opportunity to extend this policy of placing his adherents in influential positions. This was a lesson he had really taken to heart by February 1432 (as will be seen).

Of what befell Tyrell in the interval between the dissolution of the parliament of 1427-8 and 22 September 1429, when parliament next met, not a great deal is recorded. In accordance with royal letters patent of 13 May 1428 he had been appointed, along with the same other commissioners as two years before, to help raise Crown loans in Essex, and in the following summer he was busily engaged as a feoffee in sundry settlements of lands in the county. Of greater interest, both to him and to us, is his involvement, on 26 June 1429, in a transaction providing evidence of a connection with John de Vere, earl of Oxford, who had only just come of age. While still in royal wardship, the earl had not only refused a competent marriage for which the Crown had been offered £1,000, but had recently married, without royal licence, Elizabeth, daughter and sole heir of Sir John Howard the younger (ob. 1410), a lady whose uncle, Robert Howard, was brother-in-law to John Mowbray, duke of Norfolk. Partly in consideration of service rendered by the earl about the person of the boy-king, the Council had allowed a pardon, only in return, however, for a fine of £2,000, half to be paid at the Exchequer in bi-annual instalments of £100 over a period of five years, payment of the remaining £1,000 to be deferred until the king was old enough to decide whether that sum should be paid at all and, if so, how. John Tyrell and his brother Edward were among the earl's ten sureties who, each in a recognizance for £100, guaranteed payment of

---

37   For Hungerford, see *ante*, vol. II, p. 105. Geoffrey Lowther esq. was to hold his duchy offices until December 1437, Sherington his office until his death in 1449.

the £1,000 for which there was to be no possible remission. (Chief to figure among the sureties, who also included friends of John Tyrell like Robert Darcy and Richard Baynard, was John Hotoft esq. of Knebworth, treasurer of the King's Household and, pro. tem., sheriff of Essex and Herts.).[38] It was hardly more than a fortnight after this agreement was formally incorporated in royal letters patent that, on 12 July, parliament was summoned to meet on 13 October.

If this parliament had met as first summoned, over a year and a half would have elapsed since the end of its predecessor. Not for ten years (since 1419) had there been so long an interval. It was doubtless time, therefore, that parliament should meet, whatever the political circumstances. In fact, however, the previous twelve months had been a period of considerable difficulty — thanks mainly, as before, to a clash between Gloucester and Beaufort. The latter, out of the country between March 1427 and August 1428, during which time he had first been invested as a cardinal and then, as papal legate, had led an unsuccessful crusade against the Hussites in Bohemia, had returned to England mainly in order to recruit forces for a fresh crusade. However, he then encountered, first (in November 1428), a protest from the Council against his legateship and, later (in April 1429), misgivings in the same quarter as to his right to retain the see of Winchester. In these attacks on the cardinal, Gloucester was to the forefront, and although they failed of their immediate purpose, they at least had the ultimate effect of compelling Beaufort to accept the Council's decision that he should take the crusading force he had recruited to the help of Bedford in France. Here, there was every need of such a reinforcement. For Joan of Arc's successes in the field (notably her relief of Orleans in May and her victories at Jargeau and Patay in June) had enabled the Dauphin Charles, hitherto 'king of Bourges', to be crowned king of France at Rheims on 17 July. It was this latter event which almost certainly prompted the issue of fresh writs of parliamentary summons on 3 August, Lords and Commons being now ordered to meet on 22 September, three weeks earlier than originally intended. Clearly, it was now necessary that Henry VI should be crowned in France as soon as possible but, if so, imperative that he should be crowned in England first; and time in which both to inform parliament and organize the coronation would be required.

Not until 30 August did the county court meet in Essex to elect its knights of the shire, but then John Tyrell was once again elected for his own proper county. (His brother, Edward, and his son-in-law, William

Skrene, son of a former royal serjeant-at-law, both attested the indenture of return.)[39] However, when parliament met he was not to be re-elected as Commons' Speaker, being replaced by William Allington from Cambridgeshire, who, once (1419-22) treasurer of Normandy and, until recently, a member of the regency Council, had links with the Beaufort family. That Henry Beaufort was even then entitled to hope for better things might, therefore, have been gathered from the Commons' choice; and, in fact, when parliament was prorogued (on 20 December) they were to make a special recommendation in his favour. What was more to the point, the Lords, despite Gloucester's opposition, had recently (on 18 December) resolved upon the cardinal's re-admission to the Council. In the meantime, on 6 November, Henry of Windsor, not yet eight years old, had been crowned, and this event, too, was one which had worked in Beaufort's favour, if only indirectly. For, on 15 November, the Lords had ruled that the office of protector had been terminated by the coronation,[40] a decision which, although Gloucester was to continue to fill the rôle of chief councillor, *ipso facto* reduced his authority, and would be bound, accordingly, to enhance the power of the Council. The Commons were so satisfied with the progress made that, in aid of the king's impending expedition to France, they granted a tenth and fifteenth on 12 December, payable on 14 January 1430, and, a week or so later (on the 20th), a second such subsidy, payable at Christmas 1430, but subsequently, during the final session of the parliament (16 January – 23 February 1430), made payable on 18 November instead; and parliament gave the Council authority to provide security for loans to the Crown up to a sum of £50,000. What had especially worked to the cardinal's advantage had no doubt been the fact that his own personal loans to the Crown in 1429 alone had attained to almost half that amount, viz. £24,000, and the Council would, of course, be counting upon his continued readiness to lend. It was this problem of raising Crown loans which soon, in the aftermath of the parliament, chiefly engaged Tyrell's special attention. On 6 March 1430, within a fortnight of parliament's dissolution, he was called upon to assist in collecting such loans in Essex and Hertfordshire; and he personally was party to a loan of £34 raised in Essex, and shared in other loans of £229 and £41 separately raised in Hertfordshire, the respective royal letters patent promising repayment being issued on 19 May.[41]

In the meantime, on 23 April (St. George's Day), Henry VI had left

39   P. R. O., Chancery, C 219/14/1.
40   *Rot. Parl., IV*. 337.
41   *CPR, 1429-36*, 50, 62; Exchequer, Issue Roll, E 403/694, mem. 2.

for France whence, not having been crowned there until 16 December 1431, he only returned to England on 9 February 1432. Naturally, the king's absence involved the formal appointment of Gloucester, his chief councillor, as *custos Anglie*, Gloucester's authority was strictly limited; and, moreover, now that some important councillors had accompanied the king to join those already in France, so also limited were the powers of the Council left behind in England under Gloucester's presidency, even though this body continued to include, as *ex officio* members, two chief officers of state, viz. the chancellor and the treasurer of the Exchequer. For instance, decisions on matters of importance, e.g. the appointment or dismissal of councillors, were to require the assent of both halves of the divided Council. One royal prerogative, however, was reserved for Gloucester as *custos*, namely, the right to convene parliament. And in the autumn of his first year in office, the duke exercised it, the writs of summons being issued on 27 November, calling parliament together for 12 January 1431.

There can be no doubt but that, although Cardinal Beaufort again returned from France to attend the parliament, Gloucester, whose office required him to to preside over it, meant to be in proper command of the proceedings. It may surely be attributed to the duke's direction that, with the chancellor, Archbishop Kemp of York, out of sorts ('detained by infirmity', as the parliament-roll puts it), the duty of opening parliament with the customary sermon and a declaration of the causes of summons fell upon William Lyndwood LL.D.,[42] who was now 'secondary' in the office of the Privy Seal, and who, in 1427 (it will be recalled), had served the Council (but doubtless more particularly Gloucester) as diplomatic envoy to Holland. And then, when on the following day, Saturday, 13 January, the Commons elected their Speaker, the choice fell upon Lyndwood's fellow-envoy in that mission, viz. John Tyrell, who had been re-elected as knight of the shire for Essex. When, on Monday, the 15th, Tyrell made the customary 'protestation', it was on Gloucester's behalf that John, lord Tiptoft, steward of the Household, accepted it.[43] The session was, on the whole, to go well. Possibly thanks to Beaufort's intervention, both Lords and Commons indicated that a reasonable peace with France and her allies, Castile and Scotland, would be desirable. But, evidently, they were still much concerned with the need to continue to finance the war in France in the interim. And, after a session of ten weeks, Tyrell was empowered to declare what must have seemed at the time a fairly generous series of direct taxes: although the preliminary grant of £1 per

42   *Rot. Parl.*, IV. 367.
43   ibid. 368.

knight's fee or, alternatively, on every £20 worth of annual income from land proved so unworkable as to be rescinded in the next parliament, a tenth and fifteenth, leviable in November 1431, and another third of such a subsidy, due at Easter 1432, had also been granted. It would appear, therefore, that Tyrell had, as Speaker, managed the Commons successfully. Certainly, his conduct did him no harm. Quite the reverse, in fact: by 16 March, four days even before the end of the session, it had been decided that he, along with Lyndwood, should join the king in France as a member of his Council there; and each of them was then, on a Council warrant acted upon at the Lower Exchequer, paid a *regardum* (gift) of £100 in anticipation of six months service as councillors. On the same day, Tyrell received an imprest of £40 for his own wages and those of a personal retinue of 2 men-at-arms and 12 archers, and on 21 April an additional advance of £108 odd. Two days later, however, the Council, while agreeing that Tyrell should have a contract similar to Lord Tiptoft's, reduced the number of his archers from 12 to 9, authorizing payment of his 'gages de guerre' on this new basis, the daily rate of pay to be as before, viz. 4s. for himself, 1s. for each man-at-arms, and 6d for every archer.[44] It was on the self-same day, 23 April, that he was re-appointed as chief steward of the duchy of Lancaster north of Trent and, now that he was going to be out of the country, he was formally given the right to appoint a deputy. (In fact, Tyrell had had recourse to a deputy for the past three years, viz. John Pury, who, first appointed on 1 May 1428, now continued to act.)[45] Over the next week and more, Tyrell must have been busy making final preparations for his journey to France: on 4 May, along with Lords Cromwell and Tiptoft, he was ordered to muster the 570 men of the retinues of William, lord Clinton, and Sir Thomas Tunstall two days later on Portsdown (Hants.), when and where Tiptoft's and Tyrell's musters were also to be taken. (Going over to France at about the same time were their fellow-councillors, Cardinal Beaufort and Bishop Alnwick of Norwich, keeper of the Privy Seal.) It was presumably after joining up with the king that, on 25 May, Tyrell succeeded John Hotoft of Knebworth (Herts.) as treasurer of the King's Household, with which office was co-ordinate that of treasurer for the wars in France. Something of the scale of financial operation involved is attested e.g. by the Exchequer payment of £1,673 odd made to Tyrell at Rouen on 18 July following by Thomas Wytham, secretary to Richard Neville, earl of Salisbury, who had recently arrived from England. And, knighted in the summer (between then and 13 August),

44   *PPC*, IV. 82, 84; Exchequer, Issue Roll, E 403/696, mems. 18, 19.
45   R. Somerville, loc. cit.

Tyrell succeeded, on 25 September, expressly 'for good service to the last and present kings in their French wars', to the same annual grant as his predecessor in office had enjoyed, viz. 100 marks payable as a charge on the fee-farm of the city of Lincoln.[46]

Early in 1432 Tyrell returned to England, presumably when the king did (on 9 February), and to a situation of great political unease for which, once again, Gloucester could be held mainly responsible. In the spring and summer of 1431 the duke's time and interest had been almost entirely occupied in suppressing a Lollard revolt centred on Abingdon (Berks.) and in dealing with other manifestations of social unrest in the Midlands at large. But then, although probably encouraged by these successes, Gloucester can only have been aware that, once the coronation in France had taken place, the king would return home accompanied by at least some of the councillors who had been with him over there. Since these councillors were bound to include men who thought much less of Gloucester than he himself did, the duke, no doubt fearing a loss of influence on the conduct of affairs, took steps to assert himself well in advance. And every success attended his manoeuvres then as well as later on. In a great council held on 6 November (1431), he was behind a renewal of the question of Cardinal Beaufort's retention of the see of Winchester, which resulted in a decision to issue writs of Praemunire (the Council, a fortnight later, doing no more than postpone proceedings until after the king's return).[47] Then, on 28 November, a move in the Council to secure a remarkable increase in Gloucester's annual salary as *custos* (from 4,000 to 6,000 marks) and in the salary he would receive when once again he became simply chief councillor (from 2,000 to 5,000 marks) was also successful in the event.[48] But this monetary settlement, urged on the Council by John, lord Scrope of Masham, a firm supporter of the duke, but only reluctantly accepted by Lord Hungerford, the treasurer, had aroused opposition from other lords present, including Archbishop Kemp, the chancellor. Even so, Gloucester pulled off a far more significant coup when, shortly after the king's return to Westminster on 21 February 1432, he procured the dismissal of each of the three chief ministers of state, replacing them with friends of his own: on 25 February Bishop Alnwick, the keeper of the Privy Seal, gave way to William Lyndwood, and on the 26th Kemp to Bishop Stafford at the

---

46   *CPR, 1429-36*, 133, 155; *Handbook of British Chronology*, ed. Sir F. Maurice Powicke and E. B. Fryde (2nd ed. London 1961), p. 79; Exchequer Issue Roll, E 403/698, mem. 11. John Hotoft had been in office since 1423; in February 1431, having returned from France, he had become a chamberlain of the Exchequer.

47   *PPC*, IV. 100.

48   ibid. 104, 106.

Chancery, and Hungerford to Scrope at the Exchequer. And, regarding the King's Household, on 1 March were dismissed all of the following: Lord Cromwell, as chief chamberlain; Lord Tiptoft, as steward; Robert Gilbert, as dean of the Chapel Royal; William Hayton, king's secretary; John de la Bere, king's almoner. And each of the new Household appointees, it was also agreed by the Council, was to apply to Gloucester for institution into his office.[49] Of the leading officials of the Household, Tyrell alone remained.

On the very day on which Kemp had relinquished the Great Seal, parliament had been summoned to meet, but not until 12 May; and when it met it lasted no longer than 17 July, a session of some nine weeks. Considering the threat to impeach Cardinal Beaufort, who abandoned diplomatic exchanges with the duke of Burgundy in order to face it, and especially in view of the dissatisfactions arising out of the dismissals from high office of one sort and another, the session passed off better than might have been expected. Admittedly, Gloucester refused to treat Cromwell's demand for an enquiry into his dismissal at all seriously; but he let it be seen that he was prepared for the case against Beaufort to be laid aside. Whatever part Tyrell may have played in events leading up to the parliament, he himself did not attend it, or at least he did not do so as a member of the Commons. He had been returned to each of the previous three parliaments, and had served as Speaker in the first and last of them. Perhaps this time he did not seek re-election as a knight of the shire, being possibly content to have his brother Edward returned for Essex along with Robert Darcy, his friend and the father-in-law of his second son (William the elder).

When parliament next met, on 8 July 1433, it was the situation in France which had been causing most concern in the intervening twelve months. Charles VII's armies had continued successful in the field, and the English forces were even more hard-pressed than before. With the Anglo-Burgundian alliance also now in the balance, it is not surprising that the English were paying more attention to the possibility of a settlement by diplomacy, with the French dragging their heels in this respect. Indeed, when, in April and May, Bedford, Gloucester, Beaufort, and Bishop Stafford, the chancellor, all met at Calais to negotiate, no French envoys even appeared. It was immediately on the return to England of Gloucester and Stafford that, as presumably agreed upon at Calais, parliament was summoned; and so serious was the crisis in France felt to be that not only Beaufort, but Bedford, too, came home, the latter, after six years spent continuously overseas, quite

49   *Handbook of British Chronology*, pp. 76, 85, 92, 102; *PPC*, IV. 110.

possibly to encounter complaints of his recent conduct of the war. However, as Gloucester's elder brother (and the king's heir-presumptive), Bedford would automatically replace him as chief councillor; and, with Beaufort at his side, it was possible that a reaction against the dominance of Gloucester and his party would ensue, and perhaps prevail. In fact, the only change in the occupancy of the chief offices of state came with Scrope's dismissal at the Exchequer, there to be replaced by Cromwell, a friend of Beaufort's who enjoyed Bedford's confidence, but no friend of Gloucester's. That appointment, moreover, was not made until 11 August, two days before the end of the first session of the parliament. And so far as the Household was concerned, the only change of any significance in the year was in the stewardship, which had already fallen to William de la Pole, earl of Suffolk, a kinsman of the cardinal by marriage. It was evidently out of the question that Tyrell should be replaced as treasurer of the Household: quite apart from his having been brought into close contact with Bedford, Beaufort, and Cromwell while occupying his office and as a fellow-member of the King's Council in France in 1431-2, and his having most likely served to their satisfaction, it was now essential, if Cromwell was to go on to present the results of a thorough-going enquiry into all the royal finances in the second session of the parliament, that Tyrell should retain his post and be on hand to assist with information as to outstanding Household debts proper and debts owed under the head of 'wages of war'. (Those from Tyrell's own period of office thus far, 1431-3, Cromwell was to state to parliament, amounted, respectively, to £773 and £3,341, those from that of Tyrell's predecessor, John Hotoft, to £3,992 and £2,385.)[50] Tyrell would, of course, be on hand to assist. But then, too, he was himself a member of the Lower House on this occasion, having once again been elected for Essex (along with Richard Baynard).

As it happened, Tyrell was also busy during the parliament in other, different ways. He was concerned, for instance, in a petition presented by the creditors of the late earl of March (ob. 1425) and granted at the end of the second session, a petition in which they asked that, by authority of parliament, he and four others, including a baron and a chamberlain of the Exchequer, should be empowered to act as overseers of the earl's executors until the latter had repaid all the petitioners' debts. In this second session, too, Tyrell headed a deputation of thirty-six members of the Commons when they supported a petition from Roger Hunt, the Speaker, requesting his discharge from the office of sheriff of Cambridgeshire and Huntingdonshire, to which he had

50   *Rot. Parl.*, IV 436.

been appointed on 5 November; and, although this petition failed of its principal object, the chancellor and other members of the Council promised compensation for any losses Hunt incurred. Then, on 18 November, this time in an entirely private matter of his own, and as a tenant *jure uxoris*, he secured, from the heir of the late vicar of East Dereham (Norf.), a quitclaim of three manors in Banham and a moiety of Beckhall to him and his feoffees, viz. Bishop Alnwick of Norwich, Lord Cromwell, Dr. Lyndwood (the keeper of the Privy Seal) and John Fray (a baron of the Exchequer). Moreover, on 8 December, about a fortnight before the end of the parliament, he was included in a royal commission for control of kiddles (weirs and fish-traps) on the River Lea, upstream from the Thames to the bridge at Ware (Herts.), understandably not of the quorum (although his commission was to be renewed in April 1431 and October 1436).[51] But other royal commissions were soon to come Tyrell's way, appointments directly consequent upon decisions taken in the parliament of 1433.

In view of Lord Cromwell's insistence as treasurer of the Exchequer on the need for a substantial grant of taxation to help stabilize the king's finances, parliament's response had been disappointing. It had authorized the Council to raise loans totalling 100,000 marks, nearly the equivalent, that is, of two whole tenths and fifteenths; but, of direct taxation, no more than a single such subsidy was granted, and not only was collection to be made in four instalments spread over two years, but the tax itself was to be cut by £4,000, this reduction to be distributed *pro rata* among the counties, and the share of each county among its poorer parishes. The rebates at county level could readily be calculated by the Exchequer on the basis of the traditional assessments of the counties (which had now been unchanged for precisely a century), but the internal distribution of each county's rebate was obviously a matter for local enquiry and agreement. The Council was at least able to make the necessary arrangements promptly, it being evidently decided that, in each county, its recently serving shire-knights, combining with a peer who was either resident or had local interests, should be entrusted with the enquiry. Commissions issued from the Chancery within a week of parliament's dissolution, i.e. on 27 December, and, in Essex, those responsible were, of course, Tyrell and Baynard, with the young earl of Oxford, John de Vere, as

51   ibid. 470; *CPR, 1441-6*, 150; *CCR, 1429-35*, 291; *CPR, 1429-36*, 350, 356; *1436-41*, 83. Roger Hunt, a friend of Lord Tiptoft, was, in fact, to occupy the joint-shrievalty for even two years (until Nov. 1435); and although his costs then amounted to £200, it was only in February 1443 that the Exchequer allowed him an assignment for that sum on the revenues from tunnage and poundage in the port of London (*CPR, 1441-6*, 6, 150).

partner. Subsequently, on 26 February 1434, Tyrell was one of those charged with the raising of royal loans not only in Essex, but in Norfolk and Suffolk as well.[52]

However important had been Cromwell's statement as revealing the need for financial retrenchment, that problem had by no means monopolized the attention of the parliament of 1433 in its second, longer session. In fact, the most important request then submitted by the Commons was the one they made on 24 November, namely, that Bedford should stay on in England, he being best qualified to ensure 'the welfare of the Kynges noble persone, and also the good and restfull governaille and kepyng, as well of the lande inwarde, as of the Kynges landes outward,' a request which, supported by the Lords, was eventually accepted by the duke on 18 December, three days before parliament was dissolved. The proposal had doubtless been made for reasons of direct political relevancy, in the general belief that Bedford was greatly preferable to Gloucester as head of the Council. Even so, the Commons were seriously concerned over the need for greater social stability generally, being evidently most affected by the prevalence of violence and law-breaking, and especially by acts of maintenance, and other forms of interference with the due processes of law as administered in the courts, on the part of great men on behalf of their servants and retainers. One of the reasons given for the prorogation of parliament after its first session had been that the Commons were without sufficient information about riots, acts of oppression, cases of maintenance, and so on, implying that they would use the recess to obtain it. Then, on 3 November (three weeks into the second session), having first named certain counties notorious for heinous crimes, the Commons not only asked for the renewal of an ordinance of 1315 providing for episcopal sentences of excommunication of offenders, but went on to request that Gloucester and the lords of the Council should renew an oath for the conservation of the peace they had sworn in the parliament of 1429-30, and that Bedford, who had then been absent abroad, and all other lords spiritual and temporal (including any absentees on the day) should take the oath, and similarly, as soon as possible, all knights, esquires and notables everywhere. The request was granted, and at the same time it was agreed that the Commons themselves should be sworn 'in eorum Domo communi'. It was in accordance with such of this ruling as applied to the country at large that, on 20 January 1434, letters close issued from the Chancery ordering all knights of the shire in the recent parliament to draw up and

52   *CCR, 1429-35*, 271; *CPR, 1429-36*, 354.

return lists of the names of those in their own counties who, in their estimation, ought to take the oath. In Essex, however, the responsibility for this preliminary step devolved upon Tyrell alone, his fellow shire-knight, Richard Baynard (for whom, incidentally, he was acting as executor) having died in the meantime. It was on May 1 that royal letters patent appointed the commissioners who, county by county, were to administer the oath; and now associated with Tyrell in Essex were the vicar-general of the bishop of London (Robert FitzHugh being absent at the General Council of Basel), the earl of Oxford, and Sir Henry Bourchier (grandson of Thomas of Woodstock).[53]

The issue of suchlike commissions coincided with a great council convened by writs of Privy Seal, the five recorded meetings of which covered the fortnight between 24 April and 8 May. Most times held in the parliament chamber at Westminster, the meetings were attended by no fewer peers than often attended a parliament proper, and there were also present thirty-eight knights and esquires (roughly half the number of the knights of the shire in a parliament): all told, an impressive gathering. Among the commoners were Sir John Tyrell and five others from Essex. The total attendance is in itself sufficient indication of a crisis, and even the bland record of the proceedings fails to conceal how tense was the atmosphere in which the meetings began and continued. What gave rise to the quarrel between Bedford and Gloucester that clearly erupted in the council was an offer from Gloucester to serve in France. In view of the need for the presence in England of at least one of the king's two uncles, and considering the scale of Gloucester's projected military expedition (reckoned to require £48,000 or £50,000), the proposal can only have meant that Gloucester intended to replace his brother in the over-all command of the king's armies in France. In the event, the offer was rejected by those present, unanimously (as the record says), on the ground that it would be impossible to provide the necessary funds, either by loans or, if Gloucester thought that parliament should be summoned to consider his scheme, by taxation. Regarding loans, it was said that great difficulty had recently been experienced in raising them, as commissioners present could testify. (The sheriffs apart, a majority of Tyrell's fellow-commissioners appointed in the previous January in Essex and E. Anglia were in fact present.) And so, with a reconciliation of the parties, this *affaire* ended.[54] Early in July Bedford left for Normandy, to some extent fortified by loans made personally by Beaufort, and also by a promise from the cardinal and his co-feoffees to

---

53   *Rot. Parl.*, IV. 423-5; 420, 421-2; *CCR, 1429-35*, 271; *CPR, 1429-36*, 400.
54   *PPC*, IV. 212.

divert revenues from their duchy of Lancaster estates to his aid but, otherwise, unhappy at his failure to rouse his fellow-countrymen to the needs of the situation in France. It can hardly be doubted that Tyrell as *ex officio* treasurer for the wars in France shared his unease.

So far as finance went, the situation in England was no more hopeful, even though Cromwell was doing his best to improve it. One feature of the treasurer's drive for a more efficient exploitation of royal rights and entitlements were the commissions appointed on 6 July to enquire into evasions and concealments of one sort and another, and into their causes: cases of non-payment of customs-dues from the beginning of Henry V's reign; non-residence of customs-officers; official ignorance of escheats, and wastes on the Crown lands; neglect of reversions of estates to the Crown; and escapes of felons which ought to have resulted in their gaolers being subjected to fines. And Tyrell was put on the commission of enquiry set up for Essex, Hertfordshire, Surrey, Sussex, and Kent. But Household finances over past years were also under close scrutiny, and one flagrant case of confusion and error on the part of the Exchequer was brought up by Tyrell himself in his official capacity as treasurer of the Household, somewhat belatedly, however (as will appear). What now he was led to demand was, in fact, payment by the Lower Exchequer of 500 marks which, through Thomas Gloucester, cofferer of the Household, he was supposed to have obtained on 16 May 1432, receipt of which he had always denied. The Council evidently decided upon an enquiry and, on 6 July (the day of issue of the commissions of enquiry into concealments), letters of Privy Seal were sent ordering Tyrell's appearance before the Council, and also the appearance of those Exchequer officials who, in office in Easter term 1432, would surely be able to throw further light on the matter, viz. John Darell, who had then been under-treasurer, and four tellers. Lord Scrope, who had been treasurer at the time, but who was now no longer even a member of the Council, was not summoned to appear. The precise date of the hearing itself is not known, but it is unlikely that it was long deferred. At the outset of the proceedings, all the officials in question, Tyrell excepted, were put on oath, and then testified. Darell said that, by Scrope's order, he had delivered to the cofferer a single 'bille' for 500 marks charged upon the London customs. However, not only did the tellers, severally interrogated, deny that they themselves had ever paid the cofferer anything, but so did that one of the two London collectors of customs responsible when, next, he too was called upon to give evidence. What the collector said was that he and his colleague had received tallies of discharge at the Lower Exchequer for two payments *in cash*, together amounting to 500 marks but made there separately on 26 and 27 May 1432. Making full use of all this evidence, Tyrell and the cofferer had no difficulty in justifying their demand for present payment: quite apart from the denials of the tellers and the customer examined that *they* had ever made any payment of the 500 marks to the cofferer, the note on the Exchequer rolls allegedly recording a once-and-for-all payment to the cofferer was entered on 16 May, whereas the record of the tallies discharging the customs-officials, for their two cash payments together amounting to 500 marks, showed that these tallies had been struck on 26 and 27 May, which was ten and eleven days later, a notable discrepancy. Tyrell's case rested at this; the clerk of the Council ended his record of the enquiry, however, with the cryptic, though perhaps pungent, comment that there were 'many moo pregnant causes that at this tyme to reherce or to declare were to[o] longe.' The Council's verdict, although not minuted, presumably went in Tyrell's favour. Certainly, it did not affect his tenure of office. Incidentally, it was not all that long after this affair that he and his wife (Katherine) and their daughter (Joan) went on pilgrimage to Canterbury where, on 28 September, they were together received into the confraternity of the cathedral priory.[55] Thereafter, nothing particularly noteworthy is recorded of him for over a year.

Following the great council of April-May 1434, no parliament was convened that year, and in 1435 none was summoned until 5 July, when writs were issued for a meeting on 10 October. In the meantime, between 5 August and 6 September, there had taken place, at Arras, the great *dieta* of which high hopes of an Anglo-French peace had been entertained. From the English point of view, those hopes had been worse than frustrated, for during the congress Duke Philip of Burgundy had not only defected from his alliance with England, but was persuaded into accepting a 'peace and re-union' with Charles VII of France. To the parliament which, meeting on 10 October, sat until 23 December, Tyrell was not re-elected for Essex; and although, as on recent occasions when this had happened, his place was taken by his brother Edward, his non-election is rather surprising, not least in view of the great excitement generated by Burgundy's perfidy and the close involvement of the duke of Gloucester in that and other consequences of the congress of Arras. Gloucester was certainly now riding high in public esteem: perhaps there would be some who, with long memories, would wonder just how much his persistent hostility to Burgundy in the previous decade had contributed to the latter's recent change of front, but doubtless others would be inclined to see this event as

55   *CPR, 1429-36*, 425; *PPC*, IV. 266-8.

justifying, if only in retrospect, that aspect of Gloucester's policy. That Gloucester would, in any case, have a large part to play in deciding how parliament should react to the new situation was quite inevitable: the death of Bedford on 15 September had left him the king's nearest relative and his heir-presumptive; and Beaufort and his friends, the leaders of the peace-party in recent years, were all too discredited by events at Arras to challenge his authority as head of the Council. And parliament did support the duke, both Lords and Commons showing themselves in favour of a more active continuance of the war in France, but of direct hostilities against Burgundy as well. It was only three weeks after the session began that, on 1 November, Gloucester was appointed to follow Bedford as lieutenant of Calais, with an extended responsibility for offensive measures against Burgundy in Picardy, Artois and Flanders. Parliament also decided to despatch large reinforcements to Normandy under the duke of York, who as the king's lieutenant-general, was to take command. It was, therefore, only to be expected that the following year would see a considerable rise in the scale of military effort. And so it was. By the end of May 1436 York's army of over 5,000 men was ready to proceed to the defence of Rouen (Paris having already been lost). Then, in June, an even larger force was needed to resist an advance by Burgundy into the march of Calais, an advance which soon resolved itself into a siege of the town proper. That the siege which began on 9 July lasted only until the 29th was partly due to the unpopularity of the whole campaign with the Flemish communes, partly to news that great preparations for the rescue of the town were in train in England. Not, however, until 26 July were orders issued by the Council for the mustering of the relieving force which, under Gloucester's personal command, was to include the retinues of the earls of Warwick, Oxford, Huntingdon, and Stafford, and Lords Tiptoft and Fanhope. The responsibility for mustering Warwick's and Oxford's retinues at Sandwich fell chiefly to Tyrell and Geoffrey Lowther (Gloucester's deputy-warden of the Cinque Ports), and they were ordered to execute their commission three days later, on the 29th. This happened to be the day of Burgundy's abandonment of the siege, and when, another four days later, Gloucester's expeditionary force crossed the Narrows, there was nothing left for it to do but launch a punitive raid into Picardy and Artois, after which Gloucester returned home. Incidentally, on 26 July, the date ordered for the muster of the retinue of the earl of Oxford at Sandwich, the Council, meeting at Canterbury, authorized the earl to make a settlement of nine of his manors, chiefly manors in Essex, and Sir John Tyrell and his brother Edward were among those whose services as feoffees were engaged in this transaction.[56] Meanwhile, York had been busy in Normandy and, mostly in the Pays de Caux, achieving some measure of success. But, then, such offensives as had been launched were, in reality, only defensive.

In the course of 1436 it was coming to be a matter for serious debate in government circles (and, witness the *Libelle of Englyshe Polycye*, outside as well) whether royal finances would stretch to both adequate defence of Calais and strenuous resistance to French aggression in Normandy.[57] The taxes voted by the parliament of 1435 had hardly been generous, and that parliament had itself realized this fact was implicit in its authorization of the Council to undertake the raising of Crown loans up to no less than £100,000 (twice the amount of loans required by Gloucester's scheme of April-May 1434 which, for want of their approval, had nevertheless foundered). It was inevitable, therefore, that the claims of Calais and Normandy would be in competition and, with the defence of Normandy given priority by most members of the Council, understandable that there was serious risk of Gloucester being left unsatisfied and discontented, so far as provision of financial support for his command at Calais was concerned. Gloucester, of course, had long been an advocate of the policy of active prosecution of the war in France, retention of as much as possible of Henry V's conquest and, where this had been eroded, recovery of the parts lost; and he had been consistently opposed to all manner of peace-mongering, to which his old enemy, Beaufort, and the latter's friends generally were still prone. This might suggest that Gloucester was hardly likely to enter into a protracted, still less irreconcilable, conflict with those who thought more of the defence of Normandy than of Calais, and who would therefore put York's claims to greater financial consideration before his own. Nevertheless, there was reason for disquiet in many quarters when, on 29 October, parliament was summoned to meet at Cambridge on 21 January 1437; and that disquiet is not likely to have been appeased when fresh writs were issued on 10 December, ordering the meeting to take place at Westminster instead. This change of venue was itself important, for Gloucester's influence on the proceedings could only be enhanced by parliament's proximity to the city of London, which, for economic reasons, shared his attitude to the defence of Calais, and where, at most times, he had enjoyed great popular support.

That, when the parliament of 1437 met, Sir John Tyrell was elected

---

56   *CPR, 1429-36*, 611; 602.
57   For an illuminating discussion of this problem, see *E. H. R.*, LXXVI (1961), pp. 193-216, G. A. Holmes, 'The "Libelle of English Polycye"'.

Speaker for the Commons[58] (the only knight of the shire present to have previously held the office) might seem to suggest that, at least from the Lower House, Gloucester had nothing to fear, rather everything to hope for: that his self-confidence could only have been given a boost thereby. After all, Tyrell's connection with the duke had begun over twenty years before, and certainly had continued long and close enough to have been behind his promotion to high office in more spheres than one.[59] But, then, since his appointment as treasurer of the Household and *ex officio* treasurer for the king's wars, Tyrell had become *au fait* with all aspects of governmental finance devoted to military ends; and, moreover, in 1431-2 he had served as a member of the King's Council in Normandy, in company with the duke of Bedford, Cardinal Beaufort, and Lords Cromwell and Tiptoft, men who had had good reason to be critical of Gloucester's past extravagances and distrustful of his ambitions for the future, and to whose opinions he can hardly have been impervious; and he was still, of administrative necessity, in close touch with all of these men (save Bedford) and other lords of the Council, by no means all of whose views on the conduct of affairs coincided with Gloucester's. These experiences of the past six years cannot have been without their effect on Tyrell's outlook. And as a result of the progressive widening of his political horizons, he may well have now become, if not "his own man", less Duke Humphrey's man than once upon a time. Quite possibly another close personal connection of Tyrell's had had, in the situation facing parliament in January 1437, a bearing upon his election as Speaker: his connection with Richard, duke of York.

Tyrell's connection with York was most probably an outcome of Gloucester's enjoyment of the custody of the bulk of the Mortimer lands, to all of which York at the age of thirteen had become heir, on the death of his uncle, Edmund, earl of March, in 1425. As early as 1427 Tyrell had been made steward of the Mortimer lordships of Clare and Thaxstead, it being intended that he should hold that office until, in 1432, York came of age.[60] But, then, as recently as 20 February

58   *Rot. Parl.*, IV. 496.
59   Regarding Tyrell's status as one of Gloucester's feoffees under the settlement of 1 July 1417, it must be noted that between the death of his co-feoffee, Henry, lord FitzHugh, in 1425 and the death of Philippa, dowager duchess of York, in 1431, the lands in question were released to the duke and settled on fresh feoffees, who then re-granted them to him and his wife Eleanor for life, with remainder to their right heirs. Later, on 3 November 1435, in return for a fine of 2,500 marks payable in the Exchequer, royal licence was given for the lands to be entailed on the duke and duchess, Eleanor to hold for life if she survived the duke, and the king to enjoy the reversion if the duke died leaving no direct heir (*CPR, 1429-36*, 504 *et seq.*). Tyrell no longer figured among the feoffees party to these later transactions.
60   See above, p. 291.

1436, when York was preparing to take up his command in Normandy and making a settlement, in mortgage, of many of his chief estates – in the Welsh Marches, the lordship and town of Radnor and ten other lordships in Radnorshire, and, in England, the castle and lordship of Ludlow, the castle and a third of the lordship of Bridgwater, the towns of Weymouth and Wareham, and thirty-three other lordships or manors –, Tyrell was the most important commoner to have been party to the settlement.[61] This, moreover, was very likely because he was now the duke's receiver-general in England, an office he was certainly holding when Speaker in 1437.[62] How long Tyrell had been York's receiver-general is not known, but that appointment had made him chiefly responsible for the collection of the duke's private income, as his position as *ex officio* treasurer for the king's wars was to make him the paymaster of his army in France. Whether or not Tyrell had now become more devoted to the Yorkist than the Gloucestrian interest, it is impossible to say. (Neither connexion need be considered, at least in personal terms, exclusive of the other.) But whichever way it was, it is not impossible that the Commons, in electing Tyrell as their Speaker, meant to indicate that they preferred for that office one who, by reason of his connections with both Gloucester and York, could be counted upon to help them to promote the *general* aims of the war-party, and who, being aware (as he could only be) that the military commitments of the two dukes were in competition for financial support, might assist parliament to strike a proper balance between the respective claims, perhaps even to reconcile them. When, however, considering what parliament might have done, and what in fact it did, it has to be borne in mind, that whereas York was absent in France, Gloucester was on the spot; and Gloucester, as earlier had sometimes been the case, was able to look after himself.

Whether or not Tyrell used his office as Speaker to assist either Gloucester's cause or York's in the Lower House, Gloucester did not spare himself in the Lords. On 25 February, kneeling before his royal nephew there, he complained that, because in breach of his own indentures of military service, the soldiers of the garrisons at Calais and in other fortresses of the March had not been paid their wages, many of

---

61 *CPR, 1429-36*, 514. When the licence of enfeoffment of 20 February 1436 was confirmed on 4 May following, York was proposing to raise funds by granting the lands enfeoffed for twenty years in return for an annual payment of 2,000 marks (British Library, Harleian Charter 53 Hi 7), and on the same day (4 May) the Crown arranged for all fees etc. accruing to the feoffees to go to the duke as a contribution to his military expenses in France (P. R. O., E28/57). These points derive from Vincent J. Gorman, *The Public Career of Richard, duke of York* (The Catholic University of America, Ph. D. thesis 1981. Washington D. C., 1981), pp. 16-7.

62 British Library, Egerton Roll 8781. (I owe this reference to the late Mr. K. B. McFarlane.)

them were deserting, and went on to request that neither he nor they should be held responsible for any unfortunate consequences.[63] The ultimate outcome of this protest was two-fold. Cardinal Beaufort and Henry V's other surviving feoffees of duchy of Lancaster estates made a loan to the Exchequer of 2,000 marks, the whole of which, parliament agreed, should be for the benefit of the town and march of Calais, £1,000 being earmarked for distribution in soldier's wages by the treasurer of Calais, and the remainder, 500 marks, assigned to the victualler of Calais.[64] And the Commons also proved amenable. To the direct tax they voted — a single tenth and fifteenth, payable in two instalments due in November 1437 and November 1438 — no condition was attached (save that it was to be subject to the now usual rebate of £4,000, so reducing its value by about 11%). But when they extended the wool-subsidy for three years, and now made an appropriation, this was again to be exclusively for the benefit of the Calais garrisons and to maintain the defences of the town, viz. an appropriation of 20s. out of the 33s.4d. per sack levied on English exporters and the same amount out of the 53s.4d. per sack payable by aliens.[65] Moreover, Gloucester, being well aware that, important though this concession was, it would not apply until November following (when the extension took effect), had already petitioned that the treasurer of the Exchequer should be authorized by parliament to make good any deficit on the grant resulting from a continuance of the collapse of wool exports; and, on 25 March, both Lords and Commons agreed, two days before the presentation of the subsidy-bill proper on the day of parliament's dissolution (27 March). Gloucester's petition, to which that agreement was the response,[66] had been addressed by him in the first place 'unto the Speaker and all the wise and discrete Communes assembled'. Just when the Commons received the petition is not known, but if it was something of an afterthought on Gloucester's part, and had only *very* recently therefore come to their attention, Tyrell can hardly have had

63   *Rot. Parl.*, IV. 496.
64   ibid.
65   ibid, 502-4.
66   ibid. 499. The 1437 parliament had gone well for Gloucester in other ways. A petition submitted by him and his wife for a royal licence to empark 200 acres at Greenwich, and to build stone towers there, was read in parliament on 6 March and, having been approved by the Lords and Commons, was granted by the king without payment of a fine. Shortly after the parliament, viz. 9 April, the duke was confirmed in the grant he had been made on 23 November 1436 of the isles of Guernsey and Jersey, which had reverted to the Crown on the death of the duke of Bedford. A month later (11 May) he was given 2,000 marks for his expenses, and although he then agreed to surrender his patent for the 5,000 marks he had been enjoying as chief councillor, he was pardoned an over-payment of that fee amounting to £1,272.

anything to do with it. By 19 March, in the week before the petition received general approval, he had become so ill as to be unable to continue in office, and so was then replaced by William Boerley, knight of the shire for Shropshire, a lawyer well-known, like Tyrell, to both Humphrey of Gloucester and Richard of York.[67] That Tyrell's illness might have been brought on by a stressful session is a matter of pure conjecture. But that it was no feigned, "diplomatic" illness is certain: he died on 2 April,[68] within a week of the end of the parliament. According to Stow, he was buried, with his second wife Katherine, in the church of the Augustinian friars in London.[69] If we may go by the bequest of £40 made in 1445 by Sir William Estfeld, the great merchant-stapler, to be disposed for their souls, Tyrell and his wife had not been without friends in the city.[70] Would that we knew who came to Sir John's funeral, especially from the palace of Westminster!

The usual writs of *diem clausit extremum*, ordering inquests as to the lands and the heir, were not issued by the Chancery until November 1437, first to the escheator of Hampshire on 1 November, and then to the escheator in Essex and Hertfordshire on the 26th.[71] Tyrell's major public offices had, however, been filled long before then. In fact, the office of treasurer of the Household and *ex officio* treasurer for the king's wars was filled in roughly a fortnight after Tyrell's death by the appointment, on 17 April, of Sir John Popham, a veteran of Agincourt, who, between 1425 and Bedford's death in 1435, had been one of his headquarters staff in France, and, since York had taken command, a valued member of *his* council at Rouen. And only a few days later, on 23 April, to Tyrell's office of chief steward of the duchy of Lancaster estates north of Trent (excluding Lancashire) was appointed William de la Pole, earl of Suffolk, an appointment during royal pleasure which, within a month, was converted into one for life.[72] Who succeeded Tyrell as York's receiver-general in England has not been discovered.

Of the five sons left by Tyrell, no fewer than three were to sit in parliament, representing mainly Essex. The eldest, Thomas, who was

67   *Rot. Parl.*, IV. 502.

68   *Handbook of British Chronology*, p. 79. Tyrell is known to have been still officiating as treasurer of the Household on 6 February 1437 (Privy Seal warrants for issue, P. R. O., E 404/53/167).

69   *Trans. Essex Archaeological Society*, vol. 3, p. 79.

70   *Literae Cantuarienses* (R. S. no. 85) ed. J. B. Sheppard, III. 223. Richard Bokeland esq., who, in his will dated 5 August 1436 (proved 15 October), expressed a wish to be buried in Pardon churchyard at St. Paul's, London, appointed Tyrell as an executor (Early English Text Society, vol. LXXVIII, *Fifty Earliest English Wills*, p. 104). Bokeland, fishmonger of London, had been treasurer of Calais from early in Henry VI's reign until replaced on 10 February 1436 (R. A. Griffiths, *The Reign of King Henry VI*, p. 202).

71   *CFR, 1437-45*, 1.

72   *Handbook of British Chronology*, p. 79; R. Somerville, op. cit., I. p. 420.

about twenty-eight years old when his father died, and had served in
France from 1432 to 1437, was sheriff of Essex and Hertfordshire in
1440-1 and 1444-5, and knight of the shire for Essex in 1442, 1447,
1449 and 1459.[73] In the meantime, certainly by 1443, and along with
his brothers, William senior and William junior, he had joined the King's
Household as 'scutifer aule et camere Regis'.[74] Knighted by 1452, he
was a member of the King's Council in 1454, probably through his
connection with Lord Cromwell whom, later that year, he was serving
as a feoffee-to-uses, and, in 1456, as an executor of his will. In Edward
IV's reign he seems to have "kept his head down" and, dying in 1476
when in his middle sixties, he may be said to have lived out his days.
Not so Sir John Tyrell's second son, William senior of Gipping
(Suffolk),[75] formerly duchy of Lancaster steward in Essex, Herts. and
Middlesex (1437-40) and, with his elder brother, Thomas, for life
(1440-61), sheriff of Norfolk and Suffolk (1445-6), and knight of the
shire for Suffolk (1447 and 1459): he was executed on Tower Hill on
23 February 1462, having been arrested for complicity in a failed
Lancastrian rising instigated by John de Vere, earl of Oxford, who
himself went to the scaffold three days later. Another brother, William
junior of Beeches in Rawreth (Essex),[76] Sir John's fifth son, who had
been a parliamentary burgess for Weymouth in 1449, a knight of the
shire for Essex in 1449-50, 1450-1 and 1455-6, and the royal escheator
in Essex and Herts. in 1459-60, was more fortunate than his namesake,
for having been knighted by Henry VI on the morning of the battle of
Northampton on 10 July 1460, he not only survived that Lancastrian
defeat, but received a pardon from Edward IV at the time of his elder
brother William's execution. As between Sir John Tyrell's two most
prominent grandsons, fortunes again varied. Sir Thomas's eldest son,
Thomas,[77] who inherited the family home at Herons in East Thorndon,
did well under Edward IV and Richard III, serving each in turn as
'esquire of the body', and Richard III, additionally, as master of the
King's Horse; and clearly, since he was at the battle of Stoke (Notts.) in
1487 and made banneret after the skirmish with Cornish rebels at
Blackheath (Kent) in 1497, he did even better under Henry VII, whom
he survived, dying in 1510. (He had sat for Essex in the parliaments of
1478 and 1495.) On the other hand, William senior's son and heir,

73   J. C. Wedgwood, *History of Parliament*, *Biographies* (London, 1936), pp. 891-2.
74   Account Book of the Controller of the Household, Michs. 1443-4, P. R. O.,
E101/409/11.
75   J. C. Wedgwood, op. cit. 893.
76   ibid., 893-4.
77   ibid., 892-3.

James Tyrell,[78] after an even more distinguished career than his cousin Thomas, in the course of which he was a knight of the shire for Cornwall (1478), one of the two chamberlains of the Exchequer (1484-5), the steward of the Cornish lands of the duchy of Cornwall (1484-5), and the captain of Guines (1484-1501), died a traitor's death. It was on account of his surrender of Guines to Henry VII's enemy, Edmund de la Pole, earl of Suffolk, that brought back to England following his arrest, he was executed at the Tower on 6 May 1502 (forty years after the same fate, on the same spot, had befallen his father, William Tyrell senior). The surrender of Guines was not the first or most important of Sir James's acts of treachery: it had been he who, in 1483, perpetrated the murder, on Richard III's orders, of the king's nephews, Edward V and his brother, Richard, duke of York, the grandsons of Sir John Tyrell's latter-day patron.

78   ibid., 889-90.

15

WILLIAM ALLINGTON OF HORSEHEATH,
SPEAKER IN THE PARLIAMENT OF 1429-30

IN these papers I propose to deal with two of the fifteenth-century members of the family of Allington of Horseheath and Bottisham: William Allington, Speaker in Henry VI's sixth parliament which met in the autumn and winter of 1429, and his grandson, another William Allington, Speaker under Edward IV in two successive parliaments, the first of which ran for as many as seven sessions in two and a half years, that is between 1472 and 1475, and the other, in 1478, for no more than six weeks. The earlier William Allington was one of the two knights of the shire representing Cambridgeshire when he was Speaker: it was his only return to parliament. The later William, before he sat for Cambridgeshire in the parliaments in which he acted as Speaker, had already served as a parliamentary burgess for the Devonshire borough of Plympton (in 1467–8).[1]

By at least one local authority (Clutterbuck) the Cambridgeshire family of Allington is stated to have had its origin at Allington in Devon. However this may be, the family seems only to have come into Cambridgeshire when it acquired half a knight's fee in Horseheath (in south-east Cambridgeshire) with the marriage of William, the father of the William Allington esquire who was Speaker in 1429, to Dionysia, daughter and heir of William Malet of Horseheath. Before he died, the Speaker's father had also acquired, perhaps by the same marriage, another half-knight's fee in Bottisham, some six miles east of Cambridge. The estates, besides these, of which William Allington was seised in the year before his Speakership, according to an inquiry into liability to a parliamentary subsidy levied on knights' fees in 1428, were all in south Cambridgeshire and within easy reach of Horseheath: one and a half fees in Wickham, one fee in Bergham, and quarter-fees in both Streetly

The following abbreviations have been used in the footnotes:
  C.C.R. = *Calendar of Close Rolls.*
  C.F.R. = *Calendar of Fine Rolls.*
  C.P.R. = *Calendar of Patent Rolls.*
  D.K.R. = *The Reports of the Deputy-Keeper of the Public Records.*
  H.M.C. = Historical Manuscripts Commission.
  P.P.C. = *Proceedings and Ordinances of the Privy Council,* ed. N. H. Nicolas.
  P.R.O. = Public Record Office.
  R.S. = Rolls Series.
  Rot. Parl. = *Rotuli Parliamentorum.*
[1] *Official Return of Members of Parliament,* vol. I, pp. 315, 357, 360, 363; *Rot. Parl.* vol. IV, p. 336; vol. VI, pp. 4, 168.

and Melbourn. He then also held half-knight's fees in Duxford and Linton, two half-knight's fees in Hildersham, and a whole fee in Little Linton.[1] Some at least of his estates are likely to have come into his possession as a result of his own marriage with Joan, daughter and heir of William Burgh of Barningham (Suffolk). The Speaker's wife, who lived to within two years of his death—she died on 27 February 1445—was well connected, and her family relationships may have been as important to her husband as her lands: on her mother's side she was a great-granddaughter of John Stonore, Chief Justice of Common Pleas in the first half of Edward III's reign, a granddaughter of Sir John Berners of West Horsley (Surrey) and Berners Rooding (Essex), and a cousin of the Sir James Berners who, impeached by the Commons in the Merciless Parliament of 1388 as a friend of Richard II, was then executed.

The Speaker in his own lifetime, in fact before his Speakership, saw further and important acquisitions of property come into the possession of his family through the marriages (in the 1420s) of his eldest son, William, and his younger bastard son, Robert, to two sisters, namely Elizabeth and Joan, the granddaughters and co-heirs of Sir William Argentine of Great Wymondley (Herts). These included the manors of Great and Little Wymondley and Weston Argentine and other lands in Hertfordshire, in Graveley, Stevenage, Welwyn, Hitchin, Almesho, and Ippolitts, together with the advowson of the hospital founded by the Argentines at Royston, well-rents in Welwyn, and other estates in Norfolk, Suffolk and Buckinghamshire.

The Allingtons, regarded as a family, were clearly very far from being badly off. In 1436 the Speaker of 1429 and his two sons were together assessed to a parliamentary tax on incomes from land, etc., as being worth £196 a year. Oddly enough, in view of the results of the 1428 inquiry into his holding of knights' fees, William senior's lands in Cambridgeshire and Hertfordshire together were now assessed at no more than £26 a year. One explanation of this strikingly low figure might be that he had settled a considerable part of his property on his sons, William and Robert. In 1436 these two were respectively assessed as worth £110 and £60 a year, and it is their lands which raise the family income to the substantial annual value of nearly £200. Most of this property, however, was outside Cambridgeshire. Both sons held estates in Norfolk, which their father did not. William junior, like his father, had lands in Hertfordshire, but also some in Buckinghamshire, where the father had none. The bulk of these extra-Cambridgeshire accessions evidently came through the sons' marriages. Robert's wife, Joan, died in May 1429, and most of the Argentine estates soon went to William junior in right of his wife, the other sister. It is very probably that which accounts for William junior's estates being greater in 1436 than his father's and brother's together.[2]

---

[1] Sir Henry Chauncy, *The Historical Antiquities of Hertfordshire*, vol. II, p. 114; R. Clutterbuck, *The History and Antiquities of the County of Hertford*, vol. II, p. 542; Catherine E. Parsons, 'Horseheath Hall and its Owners', *Proc. C.A.S.* n.s. vol. XLI, pp. 204 ff.; *Feudal Aids*, vol. I, pp. 179, 181, 182, 190.

[2] Chauncy, *op. cit.* vol. I, p. 317; J. E. Cussans, *History of Hertfordshire*, vol. II, p. 51; 42; G. Lipscomb, *The History and Antiquities of the County of Buckingham*, vol. I, p. 14; E. Hailstone, *History and Antiquities of the parish of Bottisham* (1873), pp. 108 ff.; *Feudal Aids*, vol. II, p. 448; *Collectanea Topographica et Genealogica*, vol. IV, p. 42; *C.F.R. 1422-30*, p. 273; *English Hist. Rev.* vol. XLIX (1934), pp. 631-2.

The considerable increases in estate and reputation made by the family of Allington of Horseheath and Bottisham in the first half of the fifteenth century were very largely due to the successful career and family policy of William Allington, the Commons' Speaker in 1429. Before him little is known of the family, except for Robert Allington, an eminent clerk who had been Chancellor of the University of Oxford in 1394. Robert's kinship with William—perhaps he was his uncle—may be safely presumed: in May 1398 Master Robert was one of William's feoffees in the manor of Horseheath.[1] Possibly he assisted the latter's advancement.

By 1397 William Allington was a King's esquire. Precisely when he joined the royal service is not known. Apparently he was connected with Richard II's court by the beginning of 1394, for in January of that year he successfully petitioned for a royal pardon for a homicide committed in London. But he may as yet have been attached simply to the retinue of John Holland, Earl of Huntingdon, Chamberlain of England, the King's own half-brother and a son-in-law of the Duke of Lancaster, and may have joined the royal household later as a result. Allington was certainly connected with John Holland by 28 January 1395, when 100 marks were paid into his hands at the Lower Exchequer in aid of Holland's passage to Ireland to join the king.[2] The tie became a close one: on 14 April 1399, now promoted Duke of Exeter for his share in the recent proscription of Richard II's enemies in the royal family and among the older aristocracy, John Holland made Allington one of his numerous attorneys when preparing for Richard's second and ill-fated expedition to Ireland; and by 11 July 1399 Allington was Treasurer of Calais, an appointment he almost certainly owed to Holland who was Captain of Calais. (Allington and the Duke's lieutenant were then ordered to leave off harassing the Mayor and other merchants of the Calais staple for payment of some of their fellow-staplers' bonds, which had been delivered to Allington to meet the garrison's wages.)[3] Meanwhile, it was as a King's esquire that, on the eve of Richard II's *coup* in September 1397 and shortly afterwards, Allington shared with Robert Cary (another King's esquire and a retainer, too, of the Earl of Huntingdon) two royal grants: the first, made by a letter patent of 16 September, was a grant for their lives (in survivorship) of the Wiltshire manors of Woodrew and Calne; the second, by a patent of 7 October, gave them the right to hold the estates of the alien priory of Ellingham (Hants), then in the King's hands.

In 1399 Allington's lord, John Holland, after suffering a short imprisonment, found himself degraded to his former rank of Earl in the first parliament which met after the deposition of his half-brother Richard II. Allington had little trouble,

[1] *C.C.R. 1399–1402*, p. 561.

[2] *C.P.R. 1391–6*, p. 363; Exchequer, Issue Roll, P.R.O. E 403/549, mem. 10. It is not inconceivable that William Allington's entry into the household of Richard II was contrived by his wife's cousin, Sir James Berners. If this was so, it must have been before 1388 when Berners was executed. Alternatively, it is just possible that Allington was introduced into Richard's service by the King's friend, Robert de Vere, Earl of Oxford, sometime before 1387 when the Earl had to seek refuge in exile from the Lords Appellant: the De Veres were patrons of the church of Horseheath, where the Allingtons mainly resided. But these are mere, unsupported conjectures.

[3] *C.P.R. 1396–9*, p. 520; *C.C.R. 1396–9*, p. 508.

however, in accommodating himself to the effects of the Revolution, and within little more than a month of Henry IV's accession he was again one of the King's esquires. The new King realized that, to succeed, he must apply a policy of oblivion and indemnity for the members of Richard II's household and retinue. Obviously, this policy involved risks with those who had been attached to and had supported him, and who had hoped to profit from his favour more exclusively than such a policy was likely to allow. But those who had had a stake in the pre-1399 regime must be given one, if possible, in the Lancastrian dynasty. The King needed to buy up loyalties, and it was more of a seller's than a buyer's market. Allington also salvaged his two-year-old interest in the manor of Woodrew (Wilts) with a grant for life (made on 6 November 1399) which he now no longer shared with Robert Cary. (Woodrew was stated to be worth 25 marks a year, and Allington was to have *housbote* and *haybote* in the royal forest of Blackmore besides.) Allington did, however, lose his interest in Calne and in the lands of the alien priory of Ellingham, and by January 1401 he had also lost Woodrew to another former esquire of Richard II's household who, dispossessed by him and Cary in 1397, had now joined the household of Henry IV and recovered his emoluments.[1]

In January 1400 John Holland had been privy to the revolt of Richard II's supporters, had been put to death by a mob at Pleshey in Essex when trying to escape to the continent, and had incurred forfeiture for his treason. If Allington was still connected with the Earl, he managed to evade any personal repercussions from these events. The untimely death of the Earl of Huntingdon was probably very timely for such of his retinue as William Allington, who may well have regarded the demise of his lord with relief. Certainly, its long-term effects were advantageous to him. And for the moment, in 1400, all was well. It is true that, although appointed as royal escheator in Cambridgeshire on 24 November 1400, Allington did not hold this office beyond 3 February 1401 (instead of for the usual term of a year). On 16 May 1401, however, he was for the first time included in the Cambridgeshire commission of the peace. A year later (by patent of 11 May 1402) he was made a commissioner in the county for the arrest of seditious persons who were busy throwing doubt on the King's intention to keep his accession promises, etc.: a proper sign of royal trust. He remained a J.P. until February 1407 without interruption. In January 1403 he and other jurors in a Cambridgeshire assize of novel disseisin were being threatened by John de Windsor esquire, the heir of Sir William de Windsor (Edward III's notorious Lieutenant of Ireland). But before the end of this year Allington had clearly achieved an assured position in the royal service: on 14 July 1403 he was formally appointed (during royal pleasure) as Treasurer of the Exchequer of Ireland, an office which he had already been occupying at the beginning of June.[2]

---

[1] *C.P.R., 1396–9*, pp. 191, 212; *ibid. 1399–1401*, p. 6; *ibid. 1441–6*, p. 262. Robert Cary was the son and heir of Sir John Cary, a former Chief Baron of the Exchequer who had incurred forfeiture for treason and been banished to Ireland during the Merciless Parliament of 1388.

[2] P.R.O. *List of Escheators*, p. 12; *C.P.R. 1399–1401*, p. 557; *ibid. 1401–5*, pp. 128, 234, 272; J. H. Wylie, *The Reign of Henry IV*, vol. III, p. 133 n.

This Irish appointment suggests that Allington had already joined the retinue of the King's second son, Thomas of Lancaster, who had been given the Lieutenancy of Ireland in the summer of 1401. Almost all that is known of Allington for the rest of Henry IV's reign relates to his connection with Thomas of Lancaster and to the latter's spasmodic interest in Ireland. In September 1403, not long after Allington's appointment to the Irish Exchequer, Thomas of Lancaster returned to England and, although confirmed in the Lieutenancy in March 1406 for a period of twelve years (subsequently restricted to a period of three years as from May 1408), did not again personally discharge his duty, except between August 1408 and March 1409. Allington may very well have returned to England with Thomas of Lancaster in the autumn of 1403, because in March 1404 he was called upon to act as a commissioner in Cambridgeshire to inquire into liability to pay the recently voted parliamentary subsidy on landed incomes and personal property and by the following month had been superseded as Treasurer of Ireland. He was confirmed in the Treasurership, however, on 14 July 1406, and from then on he presumably retained the office until June 1413, when Henry V certainly appointed a different Treasurer as well as a new Lieutenant of Ireland. In the first half of 1408, when Thomas of Lancaster was preparing for a visit to Ireland, Allington also made ready to go, and he clearly preceded or accompanied the Lieutenant across the Irish Sea in that year. On 28 January 1408 he took out royal 'letters of protection' for one year as going to Ireland with Thomas of Lancaster, on 18 May nominated four Cambridgeshire men as his attorneys in England, and on 1 June agreed to act himself as attorney in Ireland for John Norbury, Henry IV's first Treasurer of England (1399–1401) and an important supporter of the Lancastrian regime who also had his connections with the King's second son.[1] Allington's interest in the Irish administration was clearly dependent on his connection with Thomas of Lancaster.

How close and constant was this connection of Allington's with the King's second son is clear from the fact that by September 1407 he was one of his feoffees in the lordships of Burstwick and Skipsea and other estates in Holderness (Yorkshire), which had been forfeited first by Thomas of Woodstock in 1397 and then by the next grantee, Edward of Norwich (Duke of Aumâle and later Duke of York), in 1399, at which time they had been conferred on Thomas of Lancaster. When Thomas of Lancaster was killed in France in the battle of Baugé in March 1421, of the original and still continuing feoffees only Bishop Henry Beaufort of Winchester, Thomas Beaufort, Duke of Exeter, and William Allington were then alive; the committee of feoffees had, however, been expanded to include Ralph Lord Cromwell and others, sometime after Thomas of Lancaster's creation as Duke of Clarence in July 1412. In February 1423 the feoffees conveyed their estate for forty years to a syndicate (formed to repay the late duke's debts), with remainder to the Crown. This syndicate included none of the original trust. Nor did it include any of Clarence's executors. The latter, appointed on 10 July 1417, when the duke was about to go to France with Henry V's second great expeditionary force, included three of the original

---

[1] *C.P.R. 1405–8*, pp. 203, 212, 391, 433, 440; *C.F.R. 1399–1405*, p. 254.

feoffees, Henry Merston clerk, Sir John Colville, and William Allington, in addition to Margaret, Duchess of Clarence, and Sir John Pelham.[1]

Sir John Pelham, who was also an executor of Henry IV, had been Treasurer of England at the end of that King's reign when a party, headed by the Duke of Clarence and Archbishop Arundel, had successfully commandeered control of the royal authority. Clarence and his elder brother, the Prince of Wales, did not always see eye to eye. This Clarence group was then in opposition to a political *bloc*, headed by the Prince of Wales and his allies, the two surviving Beaufort brothers (Henry and Thomas), which had previously dominated the royal council from the end of 1408 to the end of 1411. And Clarence's marriage with the widow of John Beaufort, Earl of Somerset, had only helped to widen the breach between himself and the late earl's brothers. What immediate effect, if any, this breach in the solidarity of the royal family had upon Allington's career, it is impossible to determine. He was quite clearly intimately attached to Clarence and a member of his household staff. But nothing is known of him from the time of his proposed visit to Ireland with Clarence in 1408 until 1414, apart from a casual allusion in the *Close Rolls* to his being arbiter in August 1409 in a dispute regarding a house built at Newmarket about which the *headboroughs* of the town were in some way disturbed.[2]

After his accession in March 1413, Henry V's earlier quarrel with his next younger brother, the Duke of Clarence (who from now until his death in 1421 was heir-presumptive to the throne), was overlaid by other considerations regarding which the two brothers were in full agreement. Especially was this so from 1415, when the French war largely absorbed the energies of them both. Meanwhile, Allington acted as a J.P. in the borough of Cambridge from May 1414 until April 1415, as sheriff of Cambridgeshire and Huntingdonshire from Michaelmas 1414 until December 1415, and from then until December 1416 as the royal escheator in the same two shires.[3] Clearly, he was *persona grata* with Henry V's administration.

Appointed executor to the Duke of Clarence on 10 July 1417, a fortnight before Henry V's second expeditionary force embarked for the conquest of Lower Normandy, Allington stayed on in England. And he became, at least for a time, a member of the royal council left behind to guide Henry V's younger brother John, Duke of Bedford (then *Custos Anglie*), in English affairs. Perhaps we may regard him as being in some sense the Duke of Clarence's representative at the council board. There is a record of his attending a council meeting on 20 October 1417.[4] On 28 November following, after an absence of over ten years from the commission, Allington was again appointed as a J.P. for Cambridgeshire; this time his commission lasted until July 1420. It may also be mentioned that in May 1418 he was appointed as a commissioner for sewers eastwards to the sea from a line joining Cambridge

---

[1] *C.P.R. 1405–8*, p. 363; *ibid. 1422–9*, p. 59; *Catalogue of Ancient Deeds*, IV, A 6967; *P.P.C.* vol. III, p. 31; *The Register of Henry Chichele, Archbishop of Canterbury, 1414–1443*, ed. E. F. Jacob, vol. II, pp. 293–6.

[2] *C.C.R. 1409–13*, p. 204.

[3] *C.P.R. 1413–16*, p. 417; P.R.O. *Lists and Indexes*, IX, *List of Sheriffs*, p. 13; *List of Escheators*, p. 13.

[4] *C.P.R. 1416–22*, p. 84; *Chichele Register, loc. cit.*; *P.P.C.* vol. II, p. 218.

and Spalding, and also as a commissioner of array in Cambridgeshire. On 12 July following, however, at the Lower Exchequer he was paid £40 (by assignment) for his expenses and passage-money (*passagium maris*), as being then about to proceed to France, by the King's order, *in presenciam suam*.[1] The moderate amount advanced suggests that his retinue was only a small and personal one, and, therefore, that there was perhaps no intention that he should engage in active service. It is more than likely that he was already earmarked for employment in some administrative capacity in what were soon to become the back-areas of the Conquest.

By this time Henry V's armies had overrun the whole of Lower Normandy, and his main force was threatening Rouen. The siege of the Norman capital began on 30 July 1418 and lasted till 19 January 1419. Certainly by 6 October 1418 William Allington was in France, for he was then appointed to share in the arraying of troops, including those of Thomas Beaufort, Duke of Exeter. On 26 October 1418, and again on 22 January 1419, immediately after the taking of Rouen, he was made a member of an embassy empowered to treat with the French for a final peace and for an interview between the Dauphin and Henry V.[2] And then, in letters dated at Vernon-sur-Seine on 1 May 1419, Allington was appointed Treasurer-General and Receiver-General of Normandy (in succession to John Golafre, esquire). This was a post for which his previous administrative experience at Calais and in Ireland was perhaps thought to qualify him. A fortnight later he indentured to serve with a retinue of six men-at-arms and eighteen archers (later increased to eight and twenty-four). About this time he was made controller of the salt-garner at Vernon and also at Fécamp. What Allington's official salary now was, is not known. But on 12 April 1419, before his appointment, he had been granted certain houses at Harfleur, and on 18 December 1419, after a visit to England which ended with his return overseas in the household-retinue of the Duchess of Clarence, he was given an annual royal pension of £100 sterling. By January 1420 he also had possession of lands and lordships at Iville-sur-Seine and 'La Lounde', in the *vicomté* of Pont Audemer, given him by the Duke of Clarence.

As Treasurer of Normandy, Allington held an office which was exacting in its requirements. In August 1419 he had been authorized, for example, to array the different garrisons in the province every quarter or half-year, and in February 1420 he was ordered to receive homages in the King's name. He was also appointed to hear disputes between the Admiral of Normandy (the Earl of Suffolk) and any sea-captains. He rendered his accounts at the year-end in the Norman *Chambre des Comptes* at Caen, where he himself had his headquarters.[3] In the meantime, more-over, the scope of his administration had been enlarged with the extension of the conquest: on 24 January 1420, in letters dated at Caen, he was formally appointed Treasurer-General not only in the Norman Duchy but also elsewhere in France

[1] *C.P.R. 1416–22*, pp. 450; 200; 198; Exchequer, Issue Roll, P.R.O. E 403/636, mem. 9.
[2] *D.K.R.* vol. XLI, App. 717, 733.
[3] *Ibid.* vol. XLII, App. 318, 320, 325, 339, 344, 356, 372, 400; Exchequer, Accounts Various, P.R.O. E 101/187/14; T. Carte, *Catalogue des Rolles Gascons*, etc. vol. I, pp. 323, 333, 357; J. H. Wylie and W. T. Waugh, *The Reign of Henry V*, vol. III, p. 243 n.

throughout the *pays conquis*. And this office he held until the death of Henry V in August 1422. The importance of Allington's enlarged authority can be gauged from his salary of £4 *tournois*, or roughly 12 shillings sterling, per day (half as much again when riding abroad on duty), and also from the fact that his receipts for his last sixteen months of office amounted to some £58,325 and his expenditure to some £59,537 sterling.[1]

In addition to what Norman estates and property he had already obtained, Allington secured a house at Honfleur in August 1421 (at precisely the same time as he was authorized to negotiate sales of houses there to Englishmen wishing to obtain them), and in February 1422 he had a grant for life of the lands of Warranville in the *vicomté* of Caen.[2] By this latter date he had had for nearly a year an additional interest in Caen, the centre of his administration, having been granted by Henry V the custody of both the castle and town from the time of the death of the previous custodian, Sir Gilbert de Umfraville, who had been killed in the battle of Baugé on 22 March 1421, when the Duke of Clarence also lost his life.[3] As Treasurer-General in Normandy, Allington had also been involved in a certain amount of diplomatic business: on 7 July 1420 he had been made one of the commission appointed to treat for a reconsideration of the conditions of the English truce with the Duke of Brittany; on 10 February 1421, along with the Earl of Suffolk and the English *bailli* of the Cotentin, he had been made one of the conservators of this truce; and on 26 March following, four days after disaster befell Clarence at Baugé, he was appointed a commissioner to redress infractions of the truce.[4]

Under Allington's Treasurership, Normandy at any rate was financially stable and self-supporting, although it was able to make little contribution to the conduct of the war. And Allington remained Treasurer-General of Normandy and the 'Conquest' after the Duke of Clarence's death, sufficient indication that his administration was regarded as adequately efficient. There is, however, no record of Allington retaining his office after the death of Henry V at the end of August 1422, and the likelihood is that he soon returned to England after that event. He was certainly back in England by 13 February 1423, when he entered into recognizances for 1000 marks, the more important one of them being a form of guarantee to the widow of Sir William Argentine, whose two granddaughters Allington's two elder sons were soon to marry. And on the very next day (14 February 1423) he became sheriff of Cambridgeshire and Huntingdonshire and occupied the office until November following.[5] During his term he was also appointed once more as a J.P. in Cambridgeshire (by patent of 7 July 1423), an office he now went on to hold continuously until 1439.[6] The year 1423 must have been one of great business for Allington: in addition to being sheriff, he must have been very preoccupied as a feoffee of the Clarence

---

[1] Exchequer, Foreign Accounts, P.R.O. E 364/61, mem. B; Wylie and Waugh, *op. cit.* vol. III, pp. 254-5.
[2] *D.K.R.* vol. XLII, pp. 416, 431.
[3] Foreign Accounts, *loc. cit.* mem. C.
[4] *D.K.R.* vol. XLII, pp. 375, 401, 412.
[5] *C.C.R. 1422-9*, p. 68; *List of Sheriffs*, p. 13 (but cf. *C.F.R. 1422-30*, p. 12).
[6] *C.P.R. 1422-9*, p. 560; *ibid. 1429-36*, p. 614; *ibid. 1436-41*, p. 579.

estates and as the late Duke's executor. (A royal pardon for Clarence's unlicenced enfeoffments was secured for a fine of 1000 marks on 12 February 1423, but probate of his will was not granted in the Prerogative Court of Canterbury until 23 November 1423.)[1]

If only Clarence had not perished in the foolhardy engagement at Baugé, now, after Henry V's death, and during the minority of Henry VI, as the eldest of the latter's uncles, he would have become either Protector of England or Regent of France. This would have meant an incalculable but potentially substantial advantage to William Allington. For the development of Allington's career, the death of Clarence was sheer tragedy. The great prizes were no longer in prospect. But clearly, even as things were, work as Clarence's feoffee and executor would keep Allington in touch with the government, and his experience might yet be turned to some account. What now were his relations with the Dowager Duchess of Clarence (Margaret) is not known, but her relations with the uncles and natural protectors of her sons by her first marriage (John and Edmund Beaufort), namely with Henry Beaufort, Bishop of Winchester, and Thomas, Duke of Exeter, are likely to have been cordial. And it is possible that Allington's inclusion as a sworn member of the royal council on 25 January 1424, when the council established in 1422 was slightly changed in the second parliament of the reign, was due to Beaufort influence.[2] He had, however, another connection in the council in Ralph Lord Cromwell, whose feoffee in the castle and manor of Tatershall and other Lincolnshire property he had already become by 27 February 1422 when a royal writ licensed the conveyances which brought the trust into being.[3] In July 1424 Allington's fee as a member of the council was fixed at £40 a year (minus 4s. for each day of absence), the normal rate for one of the rank of esquire. There is record of his attendance at council meetings in February and July 1424, in February 1425, and in July 1426, and he was still a member in March 1427.[4]

During this time of his membership of the council William Allington was one of the group of kinsmen and friends of John Holland, Earl of Huntingdon (the son of Allington's first lord of that same name and title, a cousin of the Dowager Duchess of Clarence, and a prisoner in French hands since the battle of Baugé in March 1421), who in July 1425 advanced money for his ransom. Sir John Cornwall, the earl's step-father, had taken prisoner Huntingdon's captor, the Comte de Vendôme, and was prepared to release him on certain conditions to allow the liberation of the earl. Allington's subscription to the ransom-fund was 200 marks. The earl was only one of a number of notables, not all of them Cambridgeshire men, with whom Allington was connected at that time. In December 1425 he appears as a feoffee of the young Walter Lord FitzWalter in respect of an acre of land and the advowson of the church

---

[1] *C.P.R. 1422–9*, p. 59; *P.P.C.* vol. III, p. 31; *Chichele Register, loc. cit.*
[2] *Rot. Parl.* vol. IV, p. 201.
[3] *C.P.R. 1422–9*, p. 212.
[4] *Rot. Parl.* vol. V, p. 404; *P.P.C.* vol. III, pp. 155, 166, 199, 266; vol. VI, p. 312. In the Privy Seal Warrants for Issue there are authorizations dated 25 January 1425 and 25 January 1426 for the payment of Allington's fee as royal councillor at the Receipt of the Exchequer (P.R.O. E 404/41/162; E 404/44/170).

at Great Tey (Essex), and by July 1426 he was one of the feoffees of William Fleet, the tenant of the abbey of St Albans in the manor of Moor Park in Rickmansworth (Herts), who were then licensed to crenellate the manor-house, to empark 600 acres, and to have rights of warren.[1] His interests as feoffee-to-uses were later to include the Cambridgeshire estates belonging to William Fynderne at Weston (by 1431), and also those of Sir Walter de la Pole, a kinsman of the Earl of Suffolk, at Sawston and Darnford, the heir to which was to be (in 1435) De la Pole's grandson, Edmund Ingoldsthorpe, son-in-law of John Lord Tiptoft, a very influential member of the royal council in the first half of Henry VI's reign. (Sir Walter de la Pole had himself been a retainer of the Duke of Clarence in Henry IV's reign.) Allington also became (by 1434) a feoffee at Castle Combe (Wilts) for Sir John Fastolf, K.G., of Caister, a close connection of the Duke of Bedford during the whole of his regency in France, but formerly (in Henry IV's and Henry V's reigns) another member of Clarence's retinue.[2] From how far back these various private connections of Allington's date, it is not possible to say, but he had been connected with Sir Walter de la Pole as early as 1414, and in June 1420 Sir John Ingoldsthorpe (whose son married Sir Walter's daughter) had made him one of his executors. A former Usher of the Chamber to Henry IV and Henry V, Sir William Asenhill, Ingoldsthorpe's brother-in-law, was one of Allington's co-executors of the Ingoldsthorpe will. It was Sir William Asenhill and Sir Walter de la Pole who were chosen as knights of the shire for Cambridgeshire to the parliament of 1423–4, when Allington, as sheriff, conducted the election.[3]

While still a member of the royal council, William Allington was appointed on 23 July 1426 to act as a royal commissioner for the raising of Crown loans in Cambridgeshire, and almost the same commissioners were reappointed for this purpose on 13 May 1428. At the time of this last commission Allington was again sheriff of Cambridgeshire and Huntingdonshire; he acted from 7 November 1427 to 4 November 1428. On 28 April 1429 he was commissioned to inquire into concealment of royal feudal revenues and other sources of income in Cambridgeshire.[4] It was to the next parliament after this that, along with Sir William Asenhill, his former fellow-executor to Sir John Ingoldsthorpe, Allington was himself elected as knight of the shire for Cambridgeshire, the election being held by Sir Walter de la Pole, his successor as sheriff. Rather surprisingly, it is the only occasion on which Allington so served, and he must have been by now at least in his middle-fifties. What is even more surprising is that the Commons elected him as their Speaker,[5] especially because there were as many as four ex-Speakers among them, including the Speaker of the previous parliament. Whether Allington was still even technically a member of the royal council is doubtful. He was certainly no longer an attender of its

---

[1] *C.C.R. 1422–9*, pp. 270; 261; *C.P.R. 1422–9*, p. 351.

[2] *C.C.R. 1429–35*, pp. 185, 340; *C.P.R. 1422–9*, pp. 465; 368.

[3] *C.C.R. 1413–19*, p. 195; W. M. Palmer, 'History of the Parish of Burgh Green', *Camb. Antiq. Soc., 8vo Proc.* vol. LIV, p. 89.

[4] *C.P.R. 1422–9*, pp. 355, 482, 552; *List of Sheriffs, loc. cit.*

[5] *Rot. Parl.* vol. IV, p. 336.

meetings. But his conciliar experience between at any rate 1424 and 1427 is likely to have now stood him in good stead.

The parliament met at Westminster on 22 September 1429, and its first session lasted until 20 December; it was then prorogued to 14 January 1430, from when it sat until 23 February. The outcome of the two sessions was of considerable import-ance. The English conquest in France was imperilled by the French recovery first set in motion by Joan of Arc with her relief of Orleans, and it was thought needful for Henry VI to be crowned as King of France to help balance the effect of this new turn of events and of the coronation of Charles VII. But Henry must first be crowned in England. And so he was, in the middle of the first session of this parlia-ment, on 6 November. By this act the troublesome Protectorship of the Duke of Gloucester came to an end, the actual exercise of the royal authority still remaining vested in the council. An attack that was made at this time on Cardinal Beaufort, one of the several clashes in these years between Gloucester and his uncle, faded out when, near the end of the first parliamentary session (18 December), the Lords resolved that, although a cardinal and legate of the Roman See, Beaufort should not merely be admitted to membership of the royal council but should even be urged to attend its meetings (except when Anglo-papal issues were on hand). The Commons endorsed the Lords' view of the situation on 20 December when, in making their grant of a second tenth and fifteenth (payable at Christmas 1430), additional to one already granted on 12 December (and due on 14 January 1430), they prefaced it with a special recommendation of the Cardinal of England. It was the least they could do: Beaufort's diversion of the English forces from his Crusade in Bohemia in the previous summer to the help of the Duke of Bedford in France, had lost the Cardinal much credit at the Roman Curia. So, in another way, had his loans to the Crown cost him dearly: in the last year or so alone they had run to nearly £24,000. Knowing Allington's background, we may suspect that as Speaker he had had some share in this recom-mendation of the Lower House. The Commons could well afford their own extra-vagance in conceding a double subsidy, for these grants were the first grants of direct taxation of the regular sort to be made in parliament for eight years. Tunnage and poundage were renewed merely until the next parliament. In the second session, however, the wool-subsidy was continued until November 1433, and the time for the payment of the second tenth and fifteenth was advanced to 18 November 1430. In what they probably regarded as an all-out effort to save the situation in France, now so seriously endangered, the Commons had risen to the occasion in their traditional role of grantors of taxes. The young King was at least enabled by their votes to leave England in April 1430, for his crowning in his mother's country, with a company fit to answer the requirements of protocol, and to some extent fit to meet the immediate needs of the military situation.

Allington's former headship of the financial administration of Normandy and the other English conquests in France may well have been his most important single qualification for the Speaker's office. He is also likely to have had a personal know-ledge of the circumstances of the recent disputed parliamentary election in Huntingdonshire, where the sheriff, Sir Walter de la Pole, a friend of his, had been prevailed upon to hold a second election on the grounds that the first had been subjected to undue pressure by intruders from Bedfordshire. This disputed or amended election, together with other disputed elections in Buckinghamshire and Cumberland, may well have been behind one of the most important of the petitions which the Commons put forward in this parliament: that which resulted in the Statute defining for the first time the electorates of the counties as their forty-shilling freeholders, a Statute that was to be in force for the next four centuries.[1] Another successful petition submitted by the Commons in this parliament was one which drew attention to cases of blackmail by threats and deeds of arson in the borough and county of Cambridge and also in Essex, and which requested that such acts be henceforward regarded as treasonable. Another petition put the blame for these occurrences on Irish, Welsh, and Scottish scholars at the University of Cambridge, but this was not approved by the King's Council.

Himself from Cambridgeshire, the Speaker quite possibly had a hand in these complaints. He was a J.P. in the county and, in the second session of the parliament, was made a J.P. in the borough of Cambridge, not for the first time. (He held this additional office from 28 January 1430 to 18 February 1432.) Although he was never again to be knight of the shire, he continued to serve on local commissions. On 6 March 1430 he was once more appointed a commissioner for raising Crown loans, in Huntingdonshire as well as in Cambridgeshire, the creditors' security being the recently voted parliamentary subsidy. A year or so later, on 26 March 1431, he was again appointed a loan-commissioner in both these counties, and a few days afterwards, on 12 April, he was put on the inquiry in Cambridgeshire into liability to contribute to the special aid of £1 per knight's fee (or £20 of annual rent) voted in the parliament of January 1431. In the middle of the following month, on 14 May 1431, he headed the witness-list of an important enfeoffment of Cambridgeshire and Middlesex estates by John Lord Tiptoft.[2]

The information about William Allington, however, now begins to thin out, and it is sometimes difficult to sort what little evidence there is into what relates to him and what relates to his elder son, another William. It is very likely that the five Breton prisoners-of-war from St Malo who on 12 December 1431 were given a safe-conduct to return home to collect their ransoms for payment to William Allington, were the son's and not the father's prisoners. It was certainly the younger William who sat for Cambridgeshire in the 1433 parliament. But it is the father who is likely to have been the Crown-loan commissioner in the county appointed in February 1434. In May following, William senior and his younger son Robert, both described as 'of Horseheath', were among the Cambridgeshire notables sworn to keep the King's peace and not 'maintain' those who infringed it, William junior (as ex-knight of the shire) being a commissioner to receive the oaths (along with the Bishop of Ely and Lord Tiptoft). It was William senior who in January 1436 is likely to have

[1] J. S. Roskell, *The Commons in the Parliament of 1422*, pp. 16–20.
[2] *C.P.R. 1429–36*, pp. 614; 51, 125, 135. H.M.C. *Report, MSS. of the Duke of Rutland*, vol. IV, pp. 86–7.

been both a commissioner of array in Cambridgeshire and a commissioner for the assessment there of a parliamentary tax on landed income, and it was also apparently he who in the following month was the recipient of a privy seal writ from the council asking for a loan of £40 towards the equipment of an army which was to be sent across the Channel under the command of the Duke of York.[1] It was clearly William senior who was still being appointed J.P. in Cambridgeshire in the commissions of March 1437 and of March and July 1439 (for the William Allington who was appointed J.P. in November 1439 is designated 'junior'). On the other hand, it was certainly the Speaker's son who was escheator in Cambridgeshire and Huntingdonshire in 1436–7, sheriff in the next year, and knight of the shire in the parliaments of 1437 and 1439–40. With his exclusion from the commission of the peace in November 1439, William Allington senior drops right out of sight, and all we know of him afterwards is that he died on 19 October 1446 and was buried at Horseheath, where his 'brass' still describes him as having been once Treasurer of Ireland and Treasurer of Normandy.[2]

Members of William Allington's family remained locally influential, although for a time no more than that. His son and heir, William, was sheriff of Cambridgeshire and Huntingdonshire for a second time in 1450–1 and was a J.P. in Cambridgeshire from 1439 continuously until 1458, and from 1455 to his death in 1459 in Suffolk as well. This younger William, however, only survived his father by thirteen years, and his career never came to much. He had probably grown up in his father's shadow. Although he appears to have seen active service in the French war, he achieved no distinction there, not that this was very easy to do when ground in France was being more or less steadily lost. Having a bigger estate and income than his father, he was probably more easy-going. He at least kept safe what he had. But he made little impact. He was content to let his two sons pick up brides in local Cambridgeshire families, respectably well-off but not spectacular in any way. It was William, the younger of these šons, who became Speaker in two of Edward IV's parliaments, nearly half a century after his grandfather's Speakership in 1429.

[1] *C.P.R. 1429–36*, pp. 355, 385, 523; *C.F.R. 1430–7*, p. 261; *P.P.C.* vol. IV, p. 328.
[2] *Proc. C.A.S.* n.s. vol. XLI, pp. 2, 4, 50.

NOTE

Since this biography was first written, the following additional facts have been discovered:

1   Allington's appointment as treasurer of Calais (see p. 319) was made by John Holland, duke of Exeter, at London on 8 February 1398, the salary to be £40 a year (Belvoir Castle Archives, Royal Grants, no. 475).

2   Allington, although replaced as treasurer of Ireland by June 1413 (as noted on p. 321), had been still holding that office on 1 February 1411 (Belvoir Castle Archives, Royal Grants, no. 472).

3   Contrary to the statement (p. 317) that Allington's election for Cambridgeshire to the parliament of 1429-30, in which he served as Speaker, was his only return ever, it must now be said that he had been elected by the same county twice previously, viz. to the parliaments of Jan. 1410 and Oct. 1416 (facts recorded, respectively, in P.R.O., E13/126 mem. 9 and E13/133 mem. 9^v and, following their discovery by Dr. R.W. Dunning, kindly communicated by him to the author).

16

JOHN BOWES OF COSTOCK,
SPEAKER IN THE PARLIAMENT OF 1435

IT was not until about the beginning of the reign of Edward III (in 1327) that elected knights of the shire, citizens and burgesses came to have an essential, if subordinate, place in parliaments. Before then, if only recently, they had been summoned with some frequency, but not regularly. At this time, too, perhaps because they were forming habits of co-operation in the work of making petitions for redress of public grievance and granting taxes, it was possible for them to be officially described together as the commons, that is, by the word, *communitates* or *communes*. In form and reality they represented the local communities of the counties of England and of most of the towns that were of note. Before the end of Edward III's long reign (in 1377) the commons' claims to share in what parliament normally did grew, more rapidly, in fact, than did at first the machinery devised to assist their functions. Not until 1363, so far as we know, did they enjoy the services of a royal clerk specializing in their business, the under-clerk of the parliament. And seemingly not until 1376 did they feel the need to elect, from among their own number and for the duration of a parliament, a common speaker : one who, after his formal acceptance by the king, would declare to him and the lords what the commons allowed him to say on their behalf. The speaker's potential importance as a controller or manager of the business and discussions of the lower house was soon appreciated, not least by the government ; and in the course of Richard II's reign, an order from the king to the commons to elect a speaker and present him for approval became a conventional part of the formal opening ceremonies of a parliament. The function, as functions have a habit of doing, had transformed itself into an office.

Down to 1533 the speakers were chosen from among those who represented counties. The social standing of the medieval knights of the shire was much above that of the rank and file of the parliamentary burgesses : they were members of the landed gentry, locally important for family and other reasons, and influential, too, because most of them and their kind were well aware that one of the best ways of working for themselves was to work in their "country" for the king in some administrative capacity and also, as a general rule, for one or more of the great magnates, whose "good lordship" and fees they coveted in this time of "bastard feudalism". The medieval speakers were, of course, like their fellow knights of the shire in this respect. Most of them, besides, were constantly in the thick of affairs of state, usually connected, the courtiers, administrators and lawyers among them alike, with the king and his central administration or household or with some dominant magnate or faction. The commons would have found it difficult to find eligible for the speakership one of their most influential, knowledgeable and eloquent members who was not so occupied.

In the medieval period many knights of the shire were repeatedly elected for their county. Some of them secured re-election to parliament after parliament, occasionally over many years. Election to the speakership was then, however, a very chancy business. Even if a speaker secured re-election as knight of the shire, which was less likely than not, the odds were against his being re-elected as speaker : only seven cases of a speaker in one parliament being re-elected in the next occurred during the whole of the fifteenth century, in which nearly sixty parliaments met with no very great interval between any of them ; and only two speakers in this period, Thomas Chaucer, son of the poet and cousin of Cardinal Beaufort, and Roger Flore of Oakham, chief steward of the duchy of Lancaster north of Trent, each served the office in three parliaments running. All told the fifteenth-century speakers number thirty-six. The speakership, more by accident than by design, clearly went the rounds. Some measure of the expertise required for the office was likely to be found among more than a few, and there was doubtless much competition.

Whereas it was very rarely that the commons elected as their speaker a knight of the shire who had no previous parliamentary experience at all, they were just as likely as not to pass over a former speaker, or even a number of former speakers, in favour of a man with no previous experience of the Chair. Even so, when in 1435 it happened that no knight of the shire who had before been speaker was returned to parliament, it is rather surprising that the commons chose to be speaker on this occasion John Bowes, knight of the shire for Nottinghamshire. It is true that at this time it was becoming quite normal for the commons to elect a man of law for their speaker, that Bowes was a lawyer, and a good enough lawyer to be appointed within five years time as recorder for the city of London, and that he was not without parliamentary experience, having represented Nottinghamshire in the parliaments of 1429 and 1432.[1] Bowes's career, however, was not remarkable in any other ways than these, and there is little evidence to suggest that he was well-connected, or that he had great influence either locally or in government circles. Elected again for Nottinghamshire in 1439, and for London in 1442,[1] he did not again occupy the Chair. He evidently worked well for the crown in the parliament of 1435, being (as we shall see) specially rewarded with an exchequer cash payment of £13. 13s. 4d. To a historian of parliament it is this payment to Bowes which makes him chiefly memorable, because it is the first instance on record (so far as I am aware) of a money payment made by the crown to the commons' speaker for his services as such. To the local historian, the main interest attaching to Bowes is likely to arise from the fact that he was the only Nottinghamshire knight of the shire who occupied the Chair before John Evelyn Denison, member for North Nottinghamshire, who was speaker, in four parliaments, between 1859 and 1872.

The Bowes family was of no **very** important territorial standing in Nottinghamshire, but the greater part of what estates it held there in the fifteenth century had been in its possession since at least the early thirteenth century and was to remain its own, certainly into the time of Elizabeth I, and

---

In the footnotes the following abbreviations have been used : *C.F.R. = Calendar of Fine Rolls ; C.P.R. = Calendar of Patent Rolls ; C.C.R. = Calendar of Close Rolls ; Rot. Parl. = Rotuli Parliamentorum ; D.N.B. = Dictionary of National Biography ; P.P.C. = Proceedings and Ordinances of the Privy Council*, ed. N. H. Nicolas.

[1]*Official Return of Members of Parliament*, 1. 316, 322, 327, 333 ; *C.F.R.*, 1437-45, 140.

perhaps later. In 1428 John Bowes himself was assessed to a royal tax (of 6s. 8d. on the knight's fee) at 4s. 10d. for various parcels of long-disintegrated fiefs at Costock, which lies some eight miles south of Nottingham near the Nottinghamshire-Leicestershire boundary. There is no mention in this assessment of any estate elsewhere, but the family had held land in Rempstone, the next village, early in Edward I's reign, and certainly in his will of 1442 John Bowes referred to land in his possession here which had been held by his father, John Bowes. No information beyond the references in the speaker's will has been found regarding his father or his brothers, William and Henry, and the name and family of his mother are not known.[1]

Despite its long possession of Costock the Bowes family had made no mark, apparently not even in local affairs. And it was evidently his standing as a lawyer which enabled John Bowes to play for a time a not inconspicuous role in Nottinghamshire life. Nothing, however, is known of him until on 12 February 1422 he was appointed as a member of the *quorum* of the commission of the peace, an office in which, except for the brief interval of a year (from 7 July 1423 to 20 July 1424), he continued to serve until his death in 1444.[2] Despite his being a justice of the peace and of the *quorum*, he seldom acted as a local commissioner by royal authority ; it seems likely, especially in view of his later appointment as recorder of the city of London (in 1442), that his main interests as a lawyer lay in the capital. On 26 January 1424, however, he was appointed as one of a commission, in which Ralph Lord Cromwell, Chief Justice Babington of Chilwell (Notts.), and the then mayor of Nottingham and other local gentry and notables were also included, authorised to inquire by sworn inquest of the county who were responsible for the repair of the bridges over the river Leen at Nottingham which had been damaged by floods and traffic, and to see that repairs were undertaken.

---

[1] *Thoroton's History of Nottinghamshire*, repubd. J. Throsby (London, 1797), vol. 1. pp. 55, 58 ; *Feudal Aids*, iv. 123, 135-6 ; St. Anthony's Hall, York, The Register of Archbishop Kemp of York, 19, fo. 208 ; *Catalogue of Ancient Deeds*, i. C.1212.

[2] *C.P.R., 1416-22*, 457 ; *ibid., 1422-9*, 568 ; *ibid., 1429-36*, 622 ; *ibid., 1436-41*, 588 ; *ibid., 1441-46*, 476.

A year and a half later, by patent of 30 July 1425, Bowes was made one of the *quorum* of a commission set up to investigate allegations of waste in the temporalities of the see of Lincoln ; Bowes, judging from the representative composition of the commission, was evidently intended to be responsible for the inquiry in Nottinghamshire. Provided by Pope Martin V to the vacant see of York in the spring of 1424, Bishop Richard Fleming of Lincoln had soon found himself at odds with the royal council, which supported the capitular election of Bishop Morgan of Worcester and threatened Fleming with the penalties of *Praemunire*. The temporalities of the Lincoln see had been ordered to be seized into the king's hands on 24 May 1424, when news of the papal provision to York enabled the council to presume a state of vacancy at Lincoln. The dispute lasted until 20 July 1426 when Martin V yielded and retranslated Fleming from York to Lincoln ; not until 3 August following were orders given for Fleming to recover his temporalities. The archbishopric of York eventually went to Bishop Kemp of London, the then chancellor of England.

It was while parliament was sitting at Leicester that on 26 February 1426 Bowes was associated with Chief Justice Babington, the mayor of Nottingham, and Sir Thomas Chaworth, in a commission of inquiry (with powers of oyer and terminer) into certain treasons and felonies committed at Nottingham and in the county by three London men and a Ratford ' laborer ' ; the nature of the treasons is not stated.[1]

To one of his fellow commissioners in this last commission, Sir Thomas Chaworth, father-in-law of John Lord Scrope of Masham (a member of the royal council and supporter of the duke of Gloucester) and a former Lollard, Bowes was already a feoffee : by a deed of 16 November 1425 Chaworth had made a settlement of his manors of East Bridgford and Marnham (Notts.), Allington and South Thoresby (Lincs.), and Medbourne (Leics.), and of other less important lands, and Bowes was one of the feoffees, among whom were also Bishop Langley of Durham, Thomas Lord Roos of Helmsley and Belvoir, and Chief Justice Babington.[2] And Bowes was to be

---

[1]*ibid., 1422-9*, 193, 303, 327.
[2]*C.C.R., 1422-9*, 315.

further associated with Chaworth and Babington as feoffees
to Lord Roos when the latter made a settlement of his manors
of Eastbourne (Sussex) and Adderley and Spoonley
(Shropshire) in April 1430, on the eve of his departure in
the royal retinue when the young Henry VI went to his
crowning in France. Lord Roos, who was a son-in-law of the
king's tutor, Richard earl of Warwick, died overseas in
August following, when the wardship of his infant son and
heir went to Lord Tiptoft.[1]

In the meantime, on 29 November 1427, Bowes had shared
with Sir Richard Hastings (then sheriff of Leicestershire
and Warwickshire), Bartholomew Brokesby esquire, and
Gerard Maynell, a royal grant of the right to farm all the
estates in Lincolnshire, Leicestershire, and Hampshire,
recently held in dower by Elizabeth the late widow of Henry
Lord Beaumont, which were of the inheritance of their son,
John Lord Beaumont. The latter, who had been only four
years of age at his father's death in 1413, had two or three
years still to go before he reached his majority. The grantees
were to render the extent of the lands or come to some
alternative agreement with the exchequer before Candlemas
1428. One of their mainpernors or sureties was William
Lord Ferrers of Groby ; the other, William Lord FitzHugh
of Ravensworth, who was uncle of the heir by marriage
(his wife and the late Baroness Beaumont being daughters
of William Lord Willoughby of Eresby). On 16 February
1428 a fresh grant was made to the same farmers on the same
terms, except that the agreement about the alternative to
rendering the extent was postponed until midsummer
following. On the next day—17 February—young Lord
Beaumont and Hastings were given the custody of the estates
recently held in dower by the former's grandmother, Katherine
(widow of John Lord Beaumont), who, dying in 1426, had
survived her husband by thirty years. A final arrangement
was seemingly reached on 8 May 1428 when Bowes and his
fellow grantees received another concession, made by the
royal council's advice, giving them custody of the dower
lands of both the heir's mother and grandmother as from
27 January 1428 at an annual rent (payable in the exchequer)

---

[1]*C.P.R., 1429-36*, 62 ; *C.C.R., 1429-35*, 77.

of £200. The property affected by the transaction comprised
in the main some nine manors in Lincolnshire and Leicestershire. The grantees' mainpernors both on 16 February and
8 May 1428 were Sir William Philip K.G., whose daughter
and sole heiress Lord Beaumont was to marry (or had already
married), and Sir John Radcliffe K.G., seneschal of Aquitaine
at this time.[1]

It was later in this same year in which he shared the
wardship of the Beaumont dower estates that, on 4 November
1428, John Bowes was appointed royal escheator for
Nottinghamshire and Derbyshire.[2] His period of office lasted
until 12 February 1430, so that he was still escheator during
the parliament of September 1429-February 1430, to which
he had been for the first time elected as knight of the shire
for Nottinghamshire. The first of the Nottinghamshire gentry
to seal the indenture of election was Sir Thomas Chaworth,
to whom Bowes was feoffee. His fellow-farmers of the
Beaumont dower lands, Sir Richard Hastings and
Bartholomew Brokesby, were knights of the shire in this
parliament, respectively for Yorkshire and Leicestershire.
Bowes was not re-elected to the parliament of January 1431,
but on the twenty-third of this month he was made a justice
of the peace in Leicestershire and on 12 April following he
was made one of the Leicestershire commissioners appointed
to find out those liable to contribute to the recently granted
tax of 20s. on each knight's fee or on lands worth £20 a year.[3]
He was still a j.p. in Leicestershire, as well as in Nottinghamshire, when he was again returned as knight of the shire
for the latter county to the parliament of May 1432. Following
this session he was re-appointed to the Nottinghamshire
commission of the peace, but on 20 October 1432, when the
Leicestershire commissions were re-issued, he was dropped
and did not again act in that county. On 23 May 1433 Bowes
was one of the *quorum* of a number of commissioners appointed
to act as justices in the surveying and repairing of certain
dikes in the vale of Belvoir which had become choked, and
in the subsequent assessment and apportionment of the costs
of the new drainage. A year or so later, on 6 July 1434, he

---

[1]*C.F.R., 1422-30*, 203, 208, 211, 228.
[2]*ibid.*, 244, 305.
[3]*C.P.R., 1429-36*, 619, 137.

was put on a commission of general inquiry into concealments
of royal feudal and judicial rights and perquisites in Lincolnshire, Derbyshire, Nottinghamshire, Leicestershire, Warwickshire, Rutland, and Northants, and five days later (on 11
July) he was made a member of a local Nottinghamshire
commission headed by Ralph Lord Cromwell, then treasurer
of England, charged with the same sort of inquiry.[1]

It was over a year later that Bowes was once again (for
the third time) elected to represent Nottinghamshire in
parliament. The session began on 10 October 1435 in especially
depressing circumstances for the country at large : the peace
conference of Arras had failed ; the duke of Bedford, the
English regent in France, was dead ; and the Anglo-
Burgundian alliance was broken. As Stubbs put it, " Peace
with France would be welcome ; it would be intolerable not
to go to war with Burgundy ". Why the commons chose
to elect John Bowes as their speaker on this occasion is
not easy even to conjecture. But elect him they did.[2] Apart
from his feoffeeship for Lord Roos of Helmsley, who in any
case had been dead five years, his aristocratic connexions
were, so far as is known, of the most casual kind. It is, however,
possible that he was well-known to the treasurer, Lord
Cromwell, whose fellow-commissioner he had been in the
previous year, and who had Nottinghamshire as well as
Lincolnshire and Derbyshire connexions. And through the
Rempston family, his neighbours in south Nottinghamshire,
he had links with William de la Pole, earl of Suffolk. For
a lawyer of evident ability there is singularly little evidence
that he had developed any other important and influential
ties. However this may be, there is little doubt that as speaker
he directed the commons' anti-Burgundian sentiments into
the right channels from the government's point of view, and
their grant of a subsidy of a tenth and fifteenth (admittedly
subject to a reduction of £4,000, as in 1433, and with its
collection spread over the next two years), the supplementary
grant of direct taxation in the form of a graduated income-tax
on freehold lands and offices, and the renewal of the customs
dues until November 1437 probably well exceeded the royal
council's hopes, especially so in view of the fact that the

---

[1] *ibid.*, 279, 425, 426.
[2] *Rot. Parl.*, IV. 482.

commons' grants since 1429 had averaged nearly one tenth and fifteenth a year. And a week before the session ended on 23 December, namely on 16 December, expressly as *pronunciator presentis parliamenti* Bowes was paid £13. 13s. 4d. *de regardo speciali pro labore et diligentia per ipsum habita in diversis materiis specialibus tunc temporis ibidem expediendis, per cuius labores multum domino Regi prevalebat.*[1]

One item of particular interest to Bowes himself which was recorded on the roll of this parliament was a petition made by the commons, probably at his own instance, on behalf of Sir Thomas Rempston, a Nottinghamshire neighbour of Bowes who had formerly been chamberlain to the duke of Bedford in France and who had been made a prisoner of war at the battle of Patay in June 1429. Rempston's captor, Sir Tanquy de Chastell, demanded the large ransom of 18,000 *écus d'or* (in English money, equivalent to about £3,000). Half of the ransom, the petition asserted, had had to be paid before Rempston was released ; for the remainder, De Chastell was to receive one of the hostages of Charles duke of Orléans, a French esquire who was now in the custody of the executors of the late Thomas Beaufort, duke of Exeter, as surety for Orleans's debts to Exeter and to the late dukes of Clarence and York as well. Rempston had been still ' in harde prisone ' in France in May 1433, when the royal council negotiated with Lord Fanhope for the release of the hostage to be exchanged for Rempston. The position remained unchanged over a year later (in July 1434), when the council took further steps to secure the exchange. Now, in 1435, the king was petitioned to allow (by authority of parliament) Thomas Beaufort's executors to deliver the hostage to the mother and friends of Rempston (Dame Margaret Rempston, Sir Thomas Chaworth, Sir William Plumpton, and others) to enable the transaction of the ransom and the exchange of prisoners to go through. The petition went on to state that William de la Pole, earl of Suffolk, *et autres des amyes de dit suppliant* had already entered into obligations with the executors of the duke of Exeter, guaranteeing (by recognisances made in the royal chancery) payment of the 9,000 *écus d'or* due

---

[1] Exchequer, Issue Rolls, P.R.O., E. 403/721, mem. 11. The payment is erroneously ascribed to *William* Bowes.

to them for the release of the French esquire. The lords
consented to the petition and the king agreed (provided that
the dowager duchess of Clarence did not object). Presumably
Rempston was liberated soon after this. The recognisance
referred to in the petition was almost certainly that made in
chancery some three years before (on 20 November 1432),
when the earl of Suffolk, Margaret widow of Sir Thomas
Rempston K.G. (the petitioner's mother), and others, men
mainly of Nottinghamshire and including John Bowes himself,
had been party to an agreement to pay 1,750 marks
(£1,166. 13s. 4d.) by instalments to the duke of Exeter's
executors.[1] Later, in 1437, Rempston went on to become
lieutenant of Calais and in 1440 seneschal of Guienne. Bowes's
connexions with the Rempstons were evidently of the closest,
and in 1441 he was to appear as one of Dame Margaret
Rempston's trustees in her manor of Arnold (Nottinghamshire).[2]

Shortly after his speakership, as an ex-knight of the shire
Bowes was made a commissioner in Nottinghamshire along
with Lord Cromwell (the treasurer), Chief Justice Babington,
and the other shire-knight, Richard Willoughby, for the
apportionment in the county of its share of the £4,000 general
reduction from the recently voted tenth and fifteenth, and
less than three weeks later he was almost certainly the *William*
Bowes who was appointed a commissioner of array in the
county.[3] In the course of his speakership he had been re-
commissioned as justice of the peace (on 29 November 1435)
and so he was again in May 1436. Nothing more is heard of
him, however, until 1439. Then, on 19 March, he was put on a
commission of five for the raising of crown loans in Nottinghamshire, and sometime in this year also he was appointed
as a commissioner for the oversight of weirs along the waters

---

[1]*Rot. Parl.*, IV. 488-9; *D.N.B.*, XVI. 896; *P.P.C.*, IV. 164-5,
278-9; J. H. Wylie, *The Reign of Henry V*, i. 23n; *C.C.R.*, *1429-35*,
228. (The names of the payees in the recognisance are identical with
those of Exeter's executors, cf. N. H. Nicholas, *Testamenta Vetusta*,
p. 210).

[2]*C.P.R.*, *1436-41*, 551.

[3]*C.F.R.*, *1430-37*, 289; *C.P.R.*, *1429-36*, 523. (From John Bowes's
will it is clear that he had a brother called William. But he himself
is occasionally called William, for example, in his exchequer payment
as speaker, and also in the first reference to him as recorder of London
in the Letter Books of the city, where he is afterwards referred to as
John Bowes).

of the North and South Idle, the Don, and ' Bekyrsdike ' in Yorkshire, Lincolnshire, and Nottinghamshire. In April and again in October 1439 he was confirmed in his justiceship of the peace and was once more elected at Nottingham as knight of the shire, for the fourth and last time, to the parliament which sat at Westminster from 12 November to 21 December 1439 and was then prorogued to reassemble at Reading after Christmas. On 20 April 1440, along with ex-Chief Justice Babington and his own recent fellow knight of the shire, Babington's son (William), he was again automatically appointed to make the appropriate adjustments in Nottinghamshire to the levies of the subsidy granted during the Reading session.[1]

It was during the following summer that John Bowes was appointed as its recorder by the city of London : he was sworn into office on 13 July 1440, and he was present in this capacity at the next election of the sheriffs in the gildhall on 21 September in this year. It was doubtless by reason of this civic office that he was included in a large commission of *oyer and terminer* appointed on 17 October 1441 to make inquests touching all treasons, rebellious acts, felonies, heresies and lollardries in London and the surrounding counties of Essex, Middlesex, Kent, and Surrey. And it was as recorder of London that he was next elected to parliament for the city early in 1442. The session lasted from 25 January to 27 March. On 14 July 1442 his successor in the recordership was elected and he himself was given a pension of 20 marks as being infirm ; he had held the office for precisely two years.[2]

That Bowes was by this time actually in failing health is suggested by his having already (on 20 June previous) drawn up his will. But he continued to be re-appointed as justice of the peace in Nottinghamshire in November 1443, in February following, and as late as 8 July 1444. Within a month of this last re-appointment, however, he died. His will was proved at York—his place at Costock was just inside the northern province—on 4 August 1444. In it he had desired to be buried wherever God should dispose. All his personalty,

---

[1]*C.P.R., 1436-41*, 250, 448 ; *C.F.R., 1437-45*, 140.

[2]R. R. Sharpe, *Letter Books of the City of London, Letter Book K*, 247, 250, 251, 261, 262, 273n ; *C.P.R., 1441-6*, 109.

except for a bequest of 40 marks to his servant (Thomas Neel), was to go to his wife, Margaret. All his lands were to go to her also for her life, and after her death—they evidently had had no issue—the property at Costock and Rempstone which had belonged to his father were to go to John's brother, William, and his heirs, with remainder to another brother, Henry, and his, with final remainder to the heirs general. Other property in these two adjacent south Nottinghamshire villages which had belonged to John Finderne was to go to this man's son and heir, Nicholas. Lands, again in Costock, which had once been John Croft's, were to go to Bowes's brother, Henry. Bowes appointed to act as his executors his wife, his fellow knight of the shire at the time of his speaker-ship, Richard Willoughby esquire of Wollaton, and the latter's step-mother's second husband, Richard Bingham of Carcolston, a serjeant-at-law and later a royal judge, who (like Bowes himself) had connexions with the Rempston family. It was to Willoughby that the letters of probate, granted by the court of Archbishop Kemp of York, were issued on 4 August 1444.[1] How long Bowes's widow survived him is not known.

John Bowes's will is of a piece with his career : remarkably colourless. Except for his speakership and his short term of office as recorder of London, what we know of Bowes's life is tedious to relate. But this is a fact remarkable in itself. The commons were not used to electing as speaker one who was so nearly a nonentity in the politics of his day.

---

[1] York, Register of Archbishop John Kemp, 19, fo. 208. I am indebted to Miss E. A. Ayres for this reference.

17

WILLIAM BURLEY OF BRONCROFT, SPEAKER FOR THE COMMONS IN 1437 AND 1445-6

The career of William Burley of Broncroft, who was Speaker in only the closing stages of the parliament of 1437 but for the whole duration of the parliament of 1445-6, supplies a useful illustration of the way in which a lawyer of that period could turn employment by the Crown and by magnates with territorial and other interests in his locality to the furtherance of his own career and the benefit of his family. It also shows how this employment might lead such a man into political courses where, provided he did not overreach himself, he stood to gain more than he was likely to lose. Although the most important judicial office Burley ever held was merely as one of a panel of Deputy-Justices in Cheshire and North Wales, his abilities as a lawyer and administrator not only took him into the service of Henry VI, but also gave him the *entrée* to the households of a fair number of peers, some of whom were mutual friends, some of whom were at least to become mutual enemies: Humphrey, Duke of Gloucester; Richard, Duke of York; William de la Pole, Duke of Suffolk; Thomas FitzAlan, Earl of Arundel; John Talbot, Earl of Shrewsbury; Hugh Lord Burnell; John Arundel, Lord Mautravers; and Richard Lord Strange (whose grandson married one of Burley's daughters). In the society of the local gentry of his shire Burley, it is hardly surprising, enjoyed considerable respect: it is true that he was sheriff of Shropshire only once and the King's escheator in the county no more than twice, but he was a J.P. for over forty years and, more positively suggestive still, during roughly the same period (1417-55) sat for the shire in three out of every four parliaments, quite consistently monopolising one of the two county seats in the ten parliaments which met between 1427 and 1446.

Born almost certainly in the second half of Richard II's reign, William Burley died in 1458. He was perhaps unfortunate in the time of his death. By then he was deeply committed to the support of Richard, Duke of York, the nearness of whose chief power-point, Ludlow, to Burley's place at Broncroft can only have strengthened this attachment. But on account of his age Burley might well have escaped being involved in the Yorkist rebellion of 1459 and the attainders which followed its failure, and, had he lived to see Edward IV's accession in 1461, this would surely have brought him profit. As it happened, it was his son-in-law, the celebrated Thomas Littleton who, rising to a royal judgeship in 1466, benefited from this course of events. But then Littleton would have given lustre to any legal bench. That relationship apart, Burley has a right to his place among Shropshire worthies: he is the only M.P. sitting for the county ever to have been Speaker.

*　　*　　*

Not to be confused with his kinsman, William Burley of Malehurst, M.P. for Shrewsbury in 1427 and 1437 and one of the yeomen of the Crown in 1450, William Burley, Esquire, of Broncroft in Corvedale (some eight miles north-east of Ludlow), which Leland knew a century later as "a very goodly place like a castle" built of red sandstone standing near Clee Hill, came of a family which had made its mark in the fourteenth century. His father's grandfather, great-uncle, and uncle had all been Knights of the Garter. The first of these, Sir John Burley, had been a witness to the will of Edward III; the second, Sir Simon Burley, governor and close friend of Richard II, was executed by the Lords Appellants of 1388; the third, Sir Richard Bùrley, was councillor to John of Gaunt whom he accompanied to Spain, whence in May 1387 he was brought back to England for burial in St. Paul's Cathedral. The family had first sprung into prominence in the person of Walter Burley, a fellow of Merton College, Oxford, tutor to Edward III (when Prince of Wales) and later to the Black Prince, to whose service he introduced his kinsman Sir Simon. In spite of these important political attachments, the family had not been represented in parliament until William Burley's father, John, was returned for Shropshire to the parliament which witnessed the deposition of Richard II and the accession of Henry IV (1399) and subsequently in 1401, twice in 1404, and again in 1410 and 1411. John Burley was concurrently standing counsel to Edmund, Earl of Stafford, who was killed at the battle of Shrewsbury in July, 1403, and to Thomas FitzAlan, Earl of Arundel. He was holding the position of steward in the FitzAlans' lordship of Oswestry in 1392-3, was one of the feoffees in their estates at Chirk and Chirklands in 1395, and was first witness to the charter granted by Earl Thomas to the burgesses of Oswestry in 1407.

Early in Henry IV's reign John Burley had successfully petitioned parliament to restore the forfeited estates of Sir Simon his great-uncle, and so William Burley's estates in Shropshire were considerable. Besides Broncroft, he held the manors of Thonglands (in Munslow), Felton Butler (in Great Ness), and Brocton (in Long Stanton), as mesne tenant of the Earls of Arundel, Aston Munslow (along with John Lord Talbot) as a Crown tenant, and towards the end of his life he was also occupying the manors of Aldon, Marshton, Clongonford, Whittingslow, Newton (in Westbury), Bromfield (formerly a FitzAlan estate), Alghampton, Affecott, and Norton-in-Hales. In Staffordshire, he held lands in Oakley (in Muckleston) and, purchased from the Duke of York, the manor of Arley. Another purchase from the Duke of York was the manor of Cressage in Shropshire.[2]

At the time of John Burley's death in the winter of 1415-16, William, his son and heir, was a rising young lawyer with ability and influential connexions, not the least factor in his career being his marriage with Alice, a daughter of Richard Lord Grey of Wilton. He soon filled his father's place on the commission of the peace in Shropshire and was a J.P. from February 1416 until his death in 1458, except for the latter half of 1453, when he was temporarily dropped, probably for political reasons. Before the end of Henry V's reign, he was one of the justices of the *quorum*.

Before his father's death, William Burley was already in close touch with Thomas, Earl of Arundel, whom Henry V on his accession had appointed Treasurer of England and to whom John Burley had long been a feoffee and counsellor. On 1 March, 1415, William Burley was given at the royal Exchequer £10 special reward, being appointed by royal commission to go to Calais with the Earl of Arundel to pay the garrison there. Royal letters patent of 29 May, 1415, licensed the settlement of a score of FitzAlan manors in Sussex and Surrey held in chief of the Crown, including the castles and lordships of Lewes and Reigate, on the Earl, his wife Beatrice (the illegitimate daughter of Joao I of Portugal), and their bodies' heirs; William Burley was one of the committee of feoffees, and he appeared in a similar capacity, respecting other FitzAlan estates in Wiltshire and Berkshire, in the Earl's *ultima voluntas* regulating their administration, drawn up on 10 August, 1415. Precisely two months afterwards, when the Earl had been invalided home from the siege of Harfleur, Burley was appointed one of his executors and, in the codicil of the *testamentum,* was authorised to take an annuity of £20. On 13 October, three days later, Arundel died. The executors and feoffees were still busy over the settlement of the late Earl's affairs when, towards the end of February 1416, four of them, including Burley, were associated with Gilbert Lord Talbot and William Troutbeck (the Chamberlain of Chester) in a royal com- mission to arrest those of the Earl's officers and tenants in his lordships of Bromfield, Yale, and Oswestry (in Denbighshire) who were refusing to pay debts and arrears of rents and so hindering the payment of the Earl's retinue in the recent expedition.[3] The Earl had left no issue, and the bulk of the FitzAlan estates was divided among his three surviving sisters. The lordship of Arundel itself passed, however, to his second cousin, John Arundel, Lord Mautravers, whose son was later summoned to parliament as Earl of Arundel. At the time of the latter's death in France in the summer of 1435, Burley was steward of his castle and lordship of Oswestry; it is probable that Burley had retained an administrative interest in the old FitzAlan estates in Shropshire uninterruptedly.

In November 1417 William Burley was for the first time returned as knight of the shire (M.P.) for Shropshire—he had been administering the office of royal escheator in the shire and its adjacent March since December 1416—and was successively re- elected to all but the last of Henry V's parliaments.[4] Much legal business continued to come his way in these years. On 12 April 1418 the then Lord-Lieutenant of Ireland, John Talbot, Lord Furnival, nominated him to act for a year as one of his four attorneys in England. Eight days later he was associated with Sir Roland Lenthall (as one of his feoffees) in a royal grant of the estates of the alien priory of Wootton in Warwickshire and Worcestershire and of three manors of the Norman monastery of Conches. At the time of the meeting of the important parliament of May 1421, Burley was doubtless immersed in business relating to the settlement of the estates (mainly in Shropshire) which had lately been held by Hugh Lord Burnell of Weoley (Herefordshire) and Holgate (Shropshire). This peer, of whose feoffees Burley was one, had died in November 1420 and been buried at Hales Abbey in Shropshire, leaving as his heirs his three granddaughters, one of whom had married a son of Lord Furnival, another, a son of the Steward of the King's Household, Sir Walter Hunger- ford. Royal patents licensing conveyances of their separate purparties passed the Great Seal on 10 May and 8 June, 1421.

One of the *quorum* of the commission of the peace in Shropshire, William Burley had been made a royal commissioner of array in the shire in May 1418, and on 15 July, 1421, following the parliamentary session of the spring, he was appointed to enquire into cases of concealment of feudal revenues due to the Crown in Shrop- shire.[5] He was not re-elected to parliament in the county court held at Shrewsbury on 20 November following, but was himself present there and attested the election of the new shire-knights, one of whom was Sir Richard Laken, his father's executor six years before. Burley was again returned, however, in November 1422, to the first parliament after Henry V's death. His colleague was Hugh Burgh (his own feoffee and a retainer of John Talbot, formerly Lord Furnival, now summoned to parliament as Lord Talbot), with whom he had sat eighteen months before, and with whom he was again to be elected to the parliament of April 1425. In the meantime, he had been present at the shire hustings on 23 September, 1423, and had been put by a royal patent of 23 November, 1424, on the commission controlling weirs in the rivers and meres of Shropshire and five days later included in an inquiry into escapes of felons from Shrewsbury castle. On 15 January, 1426, Burley was appointed sheriff of Shropshire and on 7 February, at Shrewsbury, in his official capacity held the shire-elections to the parliament of Leicester. In the following summer, in accordance with a royal writ of 23 July, he was a member of a commission in the county authorised to solicit individual loans to the Crown. A year later, on 20 July, 1427, he was authorised to serve, along with six other prominent lawyers domiciled in one or another of the counties of Gloucester, Hereford, Worcester, Shropshire, and Stafford (and with the sheriffs), in an inquiry into deficiencies in the administration of Crown estates, instances of failure to exact feudal dues, and official abuses, since the accession of Henry V.[6]

A month later, on 21 August, 1427, Burley was once again returned to parliament for Shropshire. He was now to be continuously re-elected to every one of the nine parliaments which sat between 1429 and 1446. Meanwhile, on 20 February, 1428, in the second session of the parliament of 1427-8, he was appointed Deputy-Justice in the county palatine of Chester, by letters patent of Humphrey, Duke of Gloucester, the Protector, issued by the Duke as Justice of Chester. (It was doubtless in this capacity that on 10 January, 1429, he was associated with William Troutbeck, Chamberlain of Chester, in a royal commission to arrest all those who, by arms or threats, sought to interfere with an election to the vacant abbacy at Vale Royal.) On 7 July, 1428, he was one of the *quorum* of a commission set up to inquire into a petition regarding the castle and manor of Mold, presented to the Council by the sole surviving feoffee of John Montague, Earl of Salisbury, by whose attainder in 1401 the estate had been forfeited to the Crown. Eight weeks earlier he had been associated with the Abbot of Shrewsbury and his own feoffee, Hugh Burgh, in a royal loan-raising commission in Shropshire. On 6 March, 1430, following the dissolution of the parliament of 1429-30, and again on 26 March, 1431, within a week of the end of the parliament of 1431, Burley served on similar commissions along with the Bishop of Coventry and Lichfield, the Abbot of Shrewsbury, and others. (On each occasion parliamentary sanction had been obtained for security being given to the creditors.) It is worth noting that Burley had acted in the parliaments of 1429-30 and 1431 as one of the parliamentary proxies of the Abbot of Shrewsbury.

After being re-elected to the parliament of May-July 1432, along with John Wynnesbury (his own feoffee), Burley was appointed royal escheator in Shropshire and the adjacent March on 5 November, 1432.[7] Early in his year of office, by patent of 24 February, 1433, he was made the key member of a commission of inquiry in his bailiwick into wastes committed in royal manors and other estates under the Crown's administration, and into attempts to conceal wardships, reliefs, escheats, and other feudal incidents due to the King. It was during his last four months as escheator that Burley again sat in the Commons, in the parliament which met in July 1433. When, two years later, he next sat in parliament, he again became escheator, his tenure of office dating from 7 November, 1435.

Between the two parliaments of 1433 and 1435 William Burley had been employed on numerous royal commissions in Shropshire. On 27th December 1433, following the dissolution of parliament, he and his fellow-knight of the shire, Sir Richard Laken, had been associated with the Abbot of Shrewsbury in a commission to apportion among the local units of taxation the county's share of the general remittance of £4,000 from the recently voted subsidy. Some three weeks later, he and Laken were together ordered to submit a schedule containing the names of Salopian gentry of sufficient status to take an oath not to "maintain" breakers of the King's peace, the oath which they themselves had sworn with the Lords and Commons during the recent session; and on 1 May, 1434, along with the Bishop of Lichfield and Lord Talbot, they were appointed commissioners to administer the oath. Meanwhile, on 26th February, 1434, Burley had been authorised to act with the Bishop, the Abbot of Shrewsbury, the Earl of Stafford, and the sheriffs of Shropshire, Staffordshire, and Derbyshire, as a commissioner for negotiating Crown loans in these counties. (In July 1435 Burley himself received security for a loan of 100 marks.) On 18 November of the same year he was put on the *quorum* of a royal commission of inquiry into the alleged misappropriation of murage-dues, during the last three years, by the Shrewsbury bailiffs; the commissioners were authorised to ascertain the facts from the Abbot of Shrewsbury, the overseer of the collection, and to audit the murage accounts. Five months later, on 20 April, 1435, the delivery of Shrewsbury gaol was entrusted to Burley and one or two other local lawyers. He was appointed to act as a justice in the same capacity four weeks after parliament met in the autumn of the same year.

Three months before the opening of parliament on 10 October, 1435, following the death of the Earl of Arundel in France and the seizure of his estates by the Crown for the duration of his son's minority, Burley had taken out royal letters patent to ensure his being allowed by the Exchequer to continue in the office (which he had held under the late Earl) of steward of the castle and lordship of Oswestry and the Earl's property in Shropshire. (How long he had held this post is not known.)[8] His appointment as escheator in Shropshire on 7 November, 1435 (in the course of the parliamentary session) doubtless facilitated the royal administration of the Arundel estates. Six days before this appointment, Burley had been put on the *quorum* of another commission set up to investigate, this time in Staffordshire, Shropshire, and Herefordshire, cases of feudal incidents due to the Crown being withheld. Obviously these commissions would have to wait until after the parliament. But along with a number of other apprentices-at-law, most of whom were occupying seats in the parliament— William Tresham (M.P. for Northants), John Hody (M.P., Somerset), Nicholas Metley (M.P., Warwicks.), Nicholas Ayssheton (M.P., Truro), Robert Rodes (M.P., Newcastle upon Tyne), John Vampage (the King's Attorney-General), and John Chamberlain—Burley was certainly engaged on important royal business during the session itself. And, even before its close, rewards began to be paid to him and his legal colleagues: for expediting divers necessary matters for the King's profit, he was paid at the Lower Exchequer on 2 December the sum of 5 marks (£3 6s. 8d.); and a fortnight later (16 December) he received a special reward of £3 *pro laboriosis scripturis et ingrosacione diversis concessis* (sic) *tam dominorum quam Communitatis regni Angliae in presenti parliamento Regi concessis pro commodo ipsius domini Regis per ipsos sic ingrossatis.*

In the year of his third tenure of the escheatorship in Shropshire (November 1435-6), Burley served on only one special royal commission, namely, the commission of array for the county issued on 6 August, 1436. In the previous February he had himself made a loan of £40 to the Crown, part of the country's answer to a vigorous drive by the government to meet the immediate costs of an expedition for the relief of Calais, which was then being threatened by the Duke of Burgundy. Burley was still a member of the *quorum* of the commission of the peace in Shropshire, Deputy-Justice in Cheshire and North Wales, and steward of the late Earl of Arundel's estates in Shropshire and the March, when, at the end of his year of office as escheator, he was for the sixth consecutive time re-elected to parliament. The session opened at Westminster on 21 January, 1437. On 19 March, following news of the illness of the then Speaker, Sir John Tyrell (Treasurer of the King's Household), the Commons elected William Burley instead.[9] The session lasted, however, only another eight days, until 27 March, when Burley declared the financial results of the session, that is, the renewal of the grants of the previous parliament, and an allowance of parliamentary authority for security to be given for Crown loans up to £100,000.

Over two and a half years passed before parliament was again summoned to meet. In the meantime, on 12 December, 1437, doubtless as Deputy-Justice in North Wales, William Burley was put on a royal commission, which also included the Chamberlain of North Wales and the Chamberlain of Chester, authorised to induce the communities and tenantry of the lordships of Anglesey, Flint, Chirk, Chirklands, Hawarden, and Mold, to grant the aids and subsidies now due by custom following the death of Henry V's Queen, Catherine of Valois, who had held those lordships in dower. Nine weeks afterwards, Burley was associated with Sir John Sutton of Dudley as attorney for the King in another Welsh commission, their duty being to receive the attornment of the tenants of the former FitzAlan lordship of Chirk and Chirklands, which had now been purchased by the Crown, and to demand the customary reliefs. A year later, by patent of 19 March, 1439, he was again commissioned to raise Crown loans in Shropshire, along with the Abbot of Shrewsbury and his late fellow knight of the shire.

On 12 November, 1439, parliament assembled at Westminster and sat until 21 December, when it was prorogued to meet at Reading on 14 January, 1440. Here it continued in session until 9 February. Roughly a fortnight after the dissolution (24 February), Burley received from the Exchequer a special reward of £5 "for his labour and diligence in the parliament at Reading in expediting certain matters specially touching the King's profit" (Issue Roll). This payment was made to him by the hands of Richard Blyke, one of the parliamentary burgesses for Bridgnorth in this parliament, who was himself given one mark (13s. 4d.) for his services there. On the previous day (23 February), Burley had been re-appointed as a Deputy-Justice of Chester, the office of Chief Justice itself being now held by William de la Pole, Earl of Suffolk. On 20 August following he was also included in a royal commission of oyer and terminer touching all offences committed since Henry V's accession in the counties of Carmarthen, Cardigan, and Pembroke. Some three months later he was put on a royal loan commission in Shropshire along with the Bishop of St. Asaph, the Abbot of Shrewsbury, the sheriff, and his own feoffee, John Wynnesbury. Three months later again, by patent of 18 February, 1441, he was appointed a member of another commission in Shropshire, one authorised to treat for the earlier payment of an instalment of the subsidy granted to the King in the parliament of the previous winter.[10]

An instructive illustration of the way in which local animosities could be created is furnished by a piece of business which came up before the royal Council in December 1441, and in which Burley was concerned. He made a declaration to the Duke of Gloucester, Cardinal Beaufort, and other lords of the Council, in which he drew their attention to the fact that no profit had accrued either to the present King or his predecessor from the lands which Thomas Foulesherst had held in chief of the Crown by knight-service in Cheshire, Shropshire and Herefordshire, at the time of his death in 1417-8. The daughter and heir's marriage had been disposed of by William Trout-beck, who still occupied her inheritance. Troutbeck, who had recently been superseded as Chancellor of the County Palatine of Lancaster (a Duchy of Lancaster office) and also as Chamberlain of Chester, was clearly no friend of Burley, who was now promised by the Council a reward of £100 if his information proved true.[11]

Nearly two years elapsed between the dissolution of the parliament of 1439-40 and the meeting of its successor in January 1442. Burley—it seems almost as a matter of course—was again returned for Shropshire. On the last day of the session, 27 March, 1442, he was granted for life a Crown annuity of £40, over half of which was charged on the fee-farm of the borough of Shrewsbury and the rest on three royal manors in Staffordshire. The date suggests that the grant may have been in the nature of a recognition of "diligence" in the recent parliament, such as he had been accorded two years before. In August following he was again a commissioner for raising a royal loan in Shropshire, and in May 1443 and October 1444 he himself advanced loans to the Exchequer, £20 in each case. Meanwhile, by 1442 (perhaps earlier) Burley was steward of Richard, Duke of York's lordship of Montgomery and a member of his council, with an annual fee of 20 marks (£13 6s. 8d.), a connexion of importance, especially because Burley was later to become very prominent as a Yorkist retainer and partisan.

In the next parliament, which met on 25 February, 1445, William Burley was again elected Speaker for the Commons, only this time he served for the whole of the parliament in the normal way. In the course of its long duration—it sat with several prorogations until April 1446—this parliament yielded grants amounting to as much as two tenths and fifteenths. It was during its first recess that, on 30 April, 1445, Henry VI's Queen, Margaret of Anjou, was crowned. On 4 June following, Suffolk, the contriver of the royal marriage, for whom Speaker Burley was Deputy-Justice in the palatinate of Chester, repeated in the Commons the account of his recent diplomatic missions which, two days before, he had given before the Lords. On 2 July, during the summer recess, Burley was appointed to serve on a royal commission of oyer and terminer in Cardiganshire and also to inquire about the activities of a rebel of Aberystwyth. Nearly a year later, following the dissolution of parliament, by patent of 1 June, 1446, he was again authorised to co-operate in raising Crown loans in Shropshire. By this time (but for how long before or after is not known)

Burley was steward of Denbigh. About the same time the borough of Shrewsbury recognised his "labour in parliament about the business of the town" by arranging for a London draper to provide him with a gift of cloth worth £4. It is quite probable that Burley was already standing counsel to the burgesses of the county town; he was certainly occupying that position at the end of his life with a fee of 11 shillings a year.[12] By September 1446 he was in receipt of a livery of cloth from the Keeper of the Great Wardrobe of the Royal Household, almost certainly as a lawyer retained by the King.

In 1447 William Burley, for the first time in twenty years, was not returned to parliament, although he was present in the shire-court when the elections were held at Shrewsbury on 12 January. He also missed the next parliament. In November 1449, however, he was again elected for Shropshire. During the last decade, in spite of the prestige which his various offices, his frequent service in parliament, and his two elections to the Speakership must have given him, Burley had not been in great demand as a party to private land settlements important enough to be registered in the royal archives. One exception had been his appointment in 1439 to membership of a committee of feoffees in the manor of Colham Green (near Uxbridge, Middlesex) for the Shropshire peer, Richard Lord Strange of Knockin, whose grandson, John Hopton, was married to Burley's daughter Elizabeth. A little later Burley was first witness to a series of charters disposing of the Shropshire estates of Lord Strange. In 1443 he had witnessed a charter of John Talbot, Earl of Shrewsbury, relating to his manors at Whitchurch (Shropshire). More important than all this, however, was his connexion with the Duke of York, which clearly was becoming stronger as time passed. Already the Duke's steward in Montgomery and a member of his council, Burley was included among York's feoffees when the Duke made a settlement of some of his estates, in a series of final concords arranged in the Court of Common Pleas, during the Trinity and Michaelmas terms of 1449 and in Hilary term 1450. In the course of the previous year Burley had been involved in purchasing from the Duke the manor of Cressage (Shropshire) and also the manor of Arley (Staffs.), over which the Duke had been recently engaged in a suit with the Crown grantee of the manor, John Harpour, a retainer of the Duke of Buckingham.[13] The way was certainly open for Burley to become a Yorkist.

When parliament met at Westminster early in November 1449, York was abroad as the King's Lieutenant in Ireland. But his interests did not go unrepresented in the Commons. Besides Burley, who sat for Shropshire with William Laken, a serjeant-at-law, two of the Duke's other feoffees were returned in the persons of the apprentices-at-law, William Tresham and Thomas Young, respectively elected for Northamptonshire and Bristol. (Thomas Young was at this time town-clerk of Shrewsbury, where Burley's interest was also strong.) On re-assembling after the Christmas recess, parliament witnessed the impeachment of Suffolk. The parliament's final session, which was held at Leicester from late in April to early in June, saw a general Act of Resumption passed, but Burley was able to procure the insertion of a clause providing that his own Crown grants should in no way be prejudiced. He and Laken were re-elected for Shropshire to the parliament which met at Westminster on 6 November following. A strongly Yorkist Lower House elected his co-feoffee, Sir William Oldhall, York's chamberlain, as its Speaker, and Thomas Young actually proposed the Duke's recognition as heir to the throne and was thrown into the Tower for his rashness. Before this parliament began, both Burley and Young had done their best to secure Speaker Oldhall's help for two former supporters of the recently murdered Duke of Suffolk, John Heydon and Sir Thomas Tuddenham, who were now in peril from the reaction against the court party. Although he was present at the Shropshire elections, Burley was not returned in March 1453 to the parliament summoned to Reading, a parliament where Lancastrian sympathies were strong, and on 7 April, 1453, he saw fit to procure royal letters of pardon. Official recognition of his close standing with York came in July following when he was omitted from the commission of the peace in Shropshire. In December, however, he was re-included.[14]

York's administration of the office of Protector from March 1454 (during Henry VI's mental illness) was met at the end of a year by the challenge of a resurgent court party, now under the leadership of the Duke of Somerset, and civil war was not long delayed. After the military victory of the Yorkist lords at St. Albans in May 1455, parliament was summoned to meet on 9 July following. Burley was again returned to what proved to be his last parliament—it was his nineteenth election as knight of the shire. After a short session of some three weeks, parliament was prorogued to meet on 12 November. By this date the King was again insane, and, on the second day of the second session, the Commons, as in the previous year, requested the nomination of a Protector. A broad hint of their sympathies was contained in their choice of Burley as head of the deputation to the Lords on this occasion, similarly two days later, on 15 November, and for a third time, on 17 November; on each occasion he used the situation in the West Country to bring the unwelcome issue to the fore. The Commons' pressure proved irresistible in the end, and on the day of the last deputation, the Chancellor announced the Duke of York's appointment. Three days later Burley took out a general pardon. Parliament continued to sit until 13 December; it met again on 14 January, 1456, and sat until the end of February, by which date the King's recovery had made the Protectorship no longer necessary.

Before parliament next met, at Coventry nearly three years later, Burley was dead. Apart from the commission of the peace, he had served on no more than a few local commissions in the meantime: a Shropshire commission of array in September 1457, a levy of archers nearly three months later, and, by patent of 20 June, 1458, on a royal commission of inquiry in Staffordshire, Shropshire and Worcestershire, into riots, forfeitures of the peace, cases of illicit granting of liveries, and other trespasses. On 9 April, 1458, he had mediated in a tithe dispute between the prior of Wenlock and the abbot of Haughmond. He died on 10 August, 1458, leaving a widow, Margaret (not his first wife), and two daughters, Elizabeth and Jane. Elizabeth married Sir Thomas Trussell of Billesly (Warwickshire). Jane had married, firstly, Philip Chetwynd of Ingestre; her second husband, to whom she was married sometime before 1445, was the great common lawyer, Thomas Littleton of Teddesley (Staffordshire), the author of the celebrated treatise on Tenures, a member of the Inner Temple, Recorder of Coventry at the time of Henry VI's visit to the city in 1450, serjeant-at-law from July 1453, king's serjeant-at-law from May 1455, and eleven years later appointed a Justice of Common Pleas. Littleton's rise may well have owed something to his father-in-law's influence in Yorkist circles.[15] The royal writs of *diem clausit extremum*, authorising inquiries by the King's escheators into Burley's lands in Shropshire and

Staffordshire were issued by the Chancery two months after his death (10 October, 1458). Burley died intestate, and it was to his son-in-law, Littleton, his daughter, Jane (Littleton's wife), William More, chaplain, and Humphrey Swynnerton (M.P. for Staffordshire in 1455-6), that, at Lambeth on 6 November, 1458, Archbishop Bourchier of Canterbury issued letters of administration, ordering an inventory of Burley's goods to be drawn up and exhibited before Candlemas following.

NOTES

The following abbreviations have been used in the footnotes: BM—British Museum; CCR—Calendar of Close Rolls; CFR—Calendar of Fine Rolls; CPR—Calendar of Patent Rolls; DKR—The Reports of the Deputy-Keeper of the Public Records; PRO—Public Record Office; Rot. Parl.—Rotuli Parliamentorum (Record Commission).

1. *Official Return of Members of Parliament*, i, 290-351.

2. *Trans. Shropshire Arch. and Nat. Hist. Soc.*, 4th Series, Vol. VI, 223 *et seq.*; *ibid.*, XI, 4; J. B. Blakeway, *The Sheriffs of Shropshire*, 60; *Feudal Aids*, IV, 249, 250, 252, 267-8; T. F. Dukes, *The Antiquities of Shropshire*, 229; *CCR*, 1447-54, 482; *ibid.*, 1468-78, 165.

3. *CPR*, 1413-16, 422, 336, 344; Exchequer, Issue Roll, *PRO*, E 403/619, mem. 15; *The Register of Henry Chichele*, ed. E. F. Jacob, ii, 71.

4. *CPR*, 1429-36, 464; *Catalogue of Ancient Deeds*, II, C 2398; *PRO List of Escheators*, 127.

5. *CPR*, 1416-22, 153, 331, 362, 371, 198, 390.

6. *PRO* C 219, bundle 12, no. 6; *ibid.*, bundle 13, nos. 2, 4; *CCR*, 1422-29, 207; *CPR*, 1422-29, 276, 354, 406.

7. *DKR*, XXXI (*Chester Plea Rolls*), App. 181; *BM*, Harleian MS. no. 139, fo. 237; *DKR* XXXVII (*Recognisance Rolls of Chester*), 109; *CPR*, 1422-29, 481, 496; *ibid.*, 1429-36, 50, 126; *CCR*, 1422-29, 207; 396; *PRO*, S.C. 10, nos. 2390, 2396; *PRO, List of Escheators*, 127.

8. *CPR*, 1429-36, 275, 354, 408, 467, 470, 474, 518, 464; *CFR*, 1430-37, 187, 282, 352; *CCR*, 1429-35, 271.

9. *PRO List of Escheators*, 127; *CPR*, 1429-36, 526, 524; *Proceedings and Ordinances of the Privy Council*, ed. N. H. Nicolas, IV, 323; *Rot. Parl.*, IV, 502.

10. *CPR*, 1436-41, 147-8, 249, 452, 505, 537; *DKR*, XXXVII (*Recog Rolls of Chester*) 673.

11. Privy Seal warrants for issue, *PRO*, E 404/53/158.

12. *CPR*, 1441-46, 73, 369; *Rot. Parl.*, V, 67; *Ancient Deeds*, VI, C 4190; *Trans. Shropshire A.* and *L. H. Soc.*, 4th Series, VI, 223; *ibid.*, XII, 167.

13. *PRO*, C 219, bundle 15, no. 4; *CCR*, 1435-41, 355, 362; *ibid.*, 1441-7, 155. *Dorset Fines*, 327-8, 368; *Somerset Fines*, 113, 201; I. H. Jeayes, *The Lyttelton Charters*, 89-92.

14. *Rot. Parl.*, V, 196; *Paston Letters* (Library Edition), ed. James Gardiner, ii, 175; *CPR*, 1452-61, 676.

15. *Rot. Parl.*, V, 284-6; *CPR*, 1452-61, 403, 407, 442; R. W. Eyton, *Antiquities of Shropshire*, V, 43; *The Genealogist*, vol. 37, pp. 23-4.

16. *CFR*, 1454-61, 211; *Registrum Thome Bourgchier*, ed. F. R. H. Du Boulay, 190.

18

SIR JOHN POPHAM, KNIGHT-BANNERET,
OF CHARFORD

IN 1415 Henry V went to war with France, and in the seven years before his death in August 1422 had been recognized by Charles VI of France (in the Treaty of Troyes) as his Regent and Heir, had married Katherine, Charles's daughter, by whom he had had a son (Henry of Windsor), and had conquered most of the French kingdom north of the Loire. On Charles VI's death in October 1422 Henry V's infant heir became King of France as well as of England. For a time all went well in France under the Regency of John, duke of Bedford, Henry's elder surviving brother. But the effort to make Henry VI's French title more of a reality eventually ceased to be effectual, and before Henry VI could be crowned in France (in December 1431) the supporters of his uncle and competitor, Charles VII, had already won considerable military success. The English struggled, increasingly however by diplomatic activity, to retain their diminishing hold on French territory. The defection of Burgundy from its English alliance at the Congress of Arras in 1435 and the untimely death of Bedford in the same year were hard blows. Much was expected of the accommodation which resulted in 1445 in the marriage between Henry VI and Margaret of Anjou, niece of Charles VII's Queen. But the losses by diplomacy—the surrender of Anjou and Maine in return for the marriage—surpassed even those which had been the product of military inefficiency and strain. The marriage resulted in an uneasy truce. But early in 1449 fighting broke out again and, when parliament met in November following, almost all that was left to the English in France was in process of being rapidly lost: Rouen was recently gone; Harfleur was soon to go ; before long only Calais would remain. The policy of peace through diplomacy, pursued by Cardinal Beaufort and by his kinsman through marriage and political heir, William de la Pole, duke of Suffolk, was utterly discredited. England was disturbed by a deep sense of national frustration and bitterness.

The Lancastrian government was politically bankrupt and perhaps seemed to be moribund. Before parliament met in November 1449, the Treasurer (Bishop Lumley) had resigned. He was quickly followed by the Keeper of the Privy Seal (Bishop Moleyns) and then by the Chancellor (Archbishop Stafford). In the first parliamentary session there was open hostility to the duke of Suffolk and, in the second, the Commons impeached him of treason, especially for surrendering Anjou and Maine. Suffolk, although not formally convicted, was banished by the King and then, when the parliament was beginning its third and last session in the spring at Leicester, was murdered at sea on his way to exile.

The domestic malaise was intensified by the prevalent uncertainty of the succession to the throne. The problem had been brought into sharper focus by the death in 1447 of Henry VI's only surviving uncle, Humphrey, duke of Gloucester, and by the continued failure of the royal couple to produce a direct heir. The claim of Richard, duke of York, as both heir-male and heir-general of Edward III, was not the only one in this circumstance for which a plausible case could be made out, but his keenest rival, Edmund Beaufort, duke of Somerset, grandson of John of Gaunt, had been associated not only with the policy of peace with France but also with the latest phases of the military débâcle in Normandy.   York was the natural leader of any opposition to the discredited party of the Court.   That a potential danger from this quarter had already been anticipated by the Lancastrian government is suggested by its earlier removal of York from military control in France in favour of Somerset, and by his appointment in 1447 as King's Lieutenant in Ireland.   This appointment was regarded at the time as equivalent to banishment.   York managed not to leave England for a year and a half, but when the parliament of November 1449 met he was in Ireland and was to stay there until the late summer of the following year.

Sir John Popham of South Charford, knight banneret, first elected to represent Hampshire in the parliament of 1439-40, was once more elected knight of the shire to the parliament which met in November 1449.[1]   On this occasion, he was promptly elected by the Commons to be their Speaker.   Just as promptly he declined to accept office.   Since 1381, when Sir Richard de Waldegrave had asked (but with no success) to be excused from the Speakership, it had been common form for the Speaker-elect to refer modestly to his own inadequacy and request to be passed over.   It had been equally common form for this excusation not to be admitted.   Popham's case is remarkable, therefore, because his request to be exonerated was granted.   And the Commons went on to elect in his place a lawyer, William Tresham, the Chancellor of the Duchy of Lancaster, who had already been Speaker in three out of the previous five parliaments.

In making his request to be discharged from the office of Speaker, Popham had pleaded age and also ill-health because of wounds received in the wars.   There may have been something in all this.   He was probably about sixty years old, and he certainly had seen much military service in France under Henry V and since, and after his 'active service' had ended he had been, on and off, quite strenuously engaged in diplomacy across the Channel.   On the other hand, although he now began to retire from public affairs, he survived this parliament of 1449-50 by nearly thirteen years, and he was at any rate hale enough at the time to attend it. It may very well be that the Lancastrian court party found Popham's Speakership a discomfiting prospect, in spite of his once (in 1437-9) having held the Treasurership of the royal Household, and that he preferred, in order to ensure the least embarrassment to himself and all concerned, to seek exoneration.   An examination of the known facts of Popham's career goes far to substantiate such a hypothesis.

It is almost sure that of all the Commons elected to this parliament of 1449-50, Popham alone was a veteran of Henry V's opening campaign of the attack on France in 1415. (He had been rewarded by Henry V for his prowess at Agincourt.)   And certainly none of the Commons knew at first-hand as much as he did about the French conquest and the hard struggle to maintain it, whether under Henry V, or under Bedford, to whom he had been chamberlain in France, or since Bedford's death.   In 1449, as a knight banneret and in age, he was senior among those of the Lower House who were knights by rank, and, in fact, he was one of the very few professional soldiers returned. (He had recently, in 1447, been nominated, if unsuccessfully, for election to the Order of the Garter.)   It is possible that the Commons had all this in mind when they chose Popham to be Speaker, and not improbable that it was also remembered that, under Bedford, he had held the office of Chancellor of Anjou and Maine, those very provinces which Suffolk had let go in his effort perhaps to

1.   *C.F.R.*, 1437-45, 139; *Official Return of Members of Parliament*, i, 342; *Rot. Parl.*, v, 171.

salvage Normandy and Guienne. But the foremost single reason behind Popham's election is almost certain to have been his long connection with the duke of York and earlier members of his family: a retainer of York's uncle and predecessor in the title, Edward of Norwich, who had been killed at Agincourt, Popham had eventually become a pensioner of York himself (after the duke came of age), and he had been a member of York's council when the duke held an over-all command in France as the King's Lieutenant-General in the late 'thirties and the early 'forties.

In this larger context of mid-fifteenth century English politics, Popham's biography should prove of use in testing the theory I have proposed to explain his peculiar exoneration from the Speakership in November 1449. But his career is also worth the attention of the local historian, if only because he is the sole parliamentary representative for the county of Hampshire to have been elected as Speaker, with the single exception of Charles Shaw-Lefevre, member for North Hampshire, who was Speaker between 1839 and 1857.

*   *   *   *   *   *   *   *   *

Sir John Popham's family, whose main stock resided at Popham (between Basingstoke and Winchester), had long been established in Hampshire, certainly from the reign of Henry I. Members of it had frequently represented the county (in over a score of parliaments) during the fourteenth century. Sir John's uncle, Henry Popham, who died in 1418, had sat as knight of the shire in seven parliaments between 1383 and 1404 and been sheriff in 1388-89; Sir Stephen Popham, Henry's son and Sir John's cousin, represented Hampshire in the parliaments of 1420, 1423, 1425, 1431, and 1442, and was sheriff of Hampshire in 1427-8 and 1440-1 and, in the meantime, of Wiltshire in 1434-5. Sir John's father, Sir John Popham, himself a younger son, had been knight of the shire in the parliaments of January 1397, 1402, January 1404, and 1407. He was sheriff of Hampshire for no more than a month early in 1404 and did not account, but in March 1404 he was made constable of Southampton castle and was confirmed in this office by Henry V ten years later (by patent of 9 March 1414)[2]. Sir John, the father, was evidently still alive in January 1418, when he was executor to his brother Henry, but was presumably dead by October 1418 when Sir John, the son, the subject of this biography, was granted the custody of Southampton castle. Nothing is known of Sir John's mother, except that her name was Matilda.[3]

What were the estates of this cadet branch of the Popham family to which Sir John belonged is not precisely known. But he certainly resided at Charford in the valley of the Avon in south-west Hampshire. And here in 1428 he held a quarter of a knight's fee and in South Charford a third of one. From 1445, by virtue of an entail, he was also in possession for life of his cousin Stephen's former manor of Binstead in north-east Hampshire, similarly the manors of West Dean (in West Tytherley) and East Grinstead (across the Wiltshire border near Salisbury), and the manors of Alvington and Fairlee (in the Isle of Wight), these two last places as tenant of the Yorkist honour of Carisbrooke. Apart from this related *bloc* of lands in Wessex, by 1433 he had come to have a possessory interest in the manor of Great Paxton (Huntingdonshire), in the manor of Rolleston (Leicestershire), and in a rent from the manor of Chesham Boys (Bucks). He probably had estates also in Berkshire and

2. *D.N.B.*, xvi, 146 ; *C.P.R.*, 1377-81, 110; *ibid.*, 1413-6, 168.

3. E. F. Jacob, *The Register of Archbishop Chichele*, ii, 138-9; *C.P.R.*, 1416-22, 64; *ibid.*, 1422-9, 111. Sir John Popham, the subject of this biography, had a cousin John, the son of Henry Popham and brother of Sir Stephen Popham, but he seems not to have been knighted.

Oxfordshire at his death in 1463.[4] By this time, certainly, he had a place in the parish of St. Sepulchre outside Newgate, London, and as early as 1436 he had a town house in English Street, Southampton.[5]

It is just possible that the John Popham who, as a commoner of Bishop Wykeham's new College of St Mary of Winchester, was pardoned by the founder in 1400 for 31 weeks' arrears of commons, was our John Popham and not a cousin of his of the same name.[6] Paying scholars, largely drawn from the gentry, were admitted, and normally between the ages of eight and twelve years. If the identification of the Wykehamist of 1400 with the Speaker-elect of half-a-century later could be presumed, we might conjecture that our John Popham had been born sometime between the years 1388-92. However this may be, nothing further is heard of him during the course of Henry IV's reign.

Sir John, the father, was from March 1404 constable of Southampton castle. He shared the commission of mustering the duke of Clarence's forces before they left Southampton for Aquitaine in July 1412, and it was he who, three years later, just before Henry V set sail on his first expedition to Normandy in 1415, had custody in Southampton castle of Richard of Conisborough, earl of Cambridge, Henry Lord Scrope of Masham, and others implicated in the Southampton Plot, pending their arraignment on charges of high treason.[7] At this time John Popham, the son, was a member of the household and immediate entourage of the earl of Cambridge's elder brother, Edward of Norwich, duke of York, whose reputation for fidelity was none of the best but who had been expressly exonerated by his brother of all complicity in this plot.

Both John and his cousin, Stephen Popham, were among the ' launces ' of the retinue which the duke of York now took overseas, and when on 17 August, 1415, during the siege of Harfleur, the duke made his will, he bequeathed to John Popham 'mes nouvelles brigandiers couvertez de rouge velvet queux Grove me fist, mon bassinet qe je port, et mon meilleur chival except ce dessuis '. Popham fought at Agincourt, where York was killed when commanding the English right wing, and presumably was knighted before or after the battle. On 28 January, 1416, the ducal feoffees granted to him for life a yearly rent of 20 marks from the Wiltshire manor of Vastern (in Wootton Bassett). This was done at the request of the late duke by his letters patent and for good service, and Sir John junior was put in possession by payment of half a noble; under York's will he was still enjoying the annuity in 1433 when the duke's young nephew and heir, Richard, duke of York, on entering his inheritance, undertook with the feoffees to continue it.[8] Popham's work in the field at Agincourt had meanwhile evidently commanded Henry V's attention. For, as he claimed nearly forty years later in a petition (against the Resumption Act of 1455), it was expressly in recognition of his services at Agincourt that Henry V on 12 February 1417 granted to him an annuity of 100 marks charged on the Lower Exchequer. The allowance was handsome enough. But it was not

4. *Feudal Aids*, ii, 349, 371; *V.C.H., Hampshire and the Isle of Wight*, IV, 562; II, 484; IV, 522, 562; V, 199, 228; *C.F.R.*, 1445-54, 94; Cambridge Antiq. Soc. Octavo publications, no. XXXVII, *Cal. of Feet of Fines, Huntingdonshire*, 1194-1603, ed. G. J. Turner, p. 104; *Cal. of Ancient Deeds*, i, B 910; ii, B 3127-8; John Nichols, *The History and Antiquities of the county of Leicester*, vol. ii, part ii, p. 442; *C.F.R.*, 1461-71, 94.

5. J. C. Wedgwood, *History of Parliament*, 1439-1509, *Biographies*, 693, n. 1; *C.C.R.*, 1435-41, 48.

6. *V.C.H., Hampshire and the Isle of Wight*, ii, 272.

7. *C.P.R.*, 1408-13, 431; *P.P.C.*, II, 33; *Rot. Parl.*, iv, 66 (*D.N.B.*, XVI, 147, is at fault in describing Sir John Popham junior as keeper of Southampton castle in 1415; John the father had been confirmed in office on 9 March, 1414 [*C.P.R.*, 1413-6, 168]).

8. Exchequer, Accounts Various, P.R.O., E 101/45/2; E. F. Jacob, *Chichele Register*, ii, 65; *C.C.R.*, 1413-9, 294; *ibid.*, 1429-35, 260. In the duke of York's will of 17 August, 1415, John Popham is not described as ' knight '; in the grant of 28 January, 1416, he is referred to as John Popham knight, junior.

until four years later that, on 17 February 1421, Popham was granted at the Receipt two assignments for payment of a mere part of only his first year's annuity, amounting to no more than £41 15*s.* 1*d.*[9]

At the time of the original grant of this annuity Popham was already committed to taking part in Henry V's resumption, on a larger scale than in 1415, of the war of conquest in France. And on 23 February, 1417, the Treasurer for the War was instructed by the Council to pay Popham his own wages and those of the 10 men-at-arms and 30 archers in his retinue for a first quarter's service; a second quarter's pay would be advanced on the day of their muster, which was to take place on 19 March at Southampton. From there Popham was to cross to Harfleur.[10] He was perhaps a member of this garrison until the King's own crossing late in July, soon after which he very probably joined the royal forces in their task of reducing first Lower and then Upper Normandy.

The Sir John Popham who was a commissioner for supervising musters at Southampton in November 1417 and April 1418 and then a commissioner of array in Hampshire is most likely to have been the father,[11] for on Christmas Eve 1417 Sir John the son had been appointed *bailli* of Caen, and in the spring of 1418 he was certainly in France. It was while Henry V was at Caen, superintending from this centre the piecemeal penetrations of his lieutenants and doubtless planning the siege of Rouen, that, on 5 May, 1418, Popham received a royal grant in tail male of the castles and lordships of Torigny-sur-Vire and Planquery and of a number of houses in Caen and Bayeux. Three months after the siege of Rouen began, namely, on 27 October, 1418, and by letters dated from before the Norman capital, Popham was appointed governor of Southampton castle, presumably after the death of his father (whom Henry V had confirmed in office in 1414).[12]

Through the next few years of extending conquest in northern France, Popham remained in control of the *bailliage* of Caen, certainly in 1419, 1420, 1421, and 1422, and presumably at least until Henry V's death,[13] having been appointed in the meantime, on 18 January, 1421, as captain of the castle and town of Bayeux, a score of miles to the west.[14] This was shortly before Henry V returned for his last brief visit to England. It is possible that Popham came back with him. Certainly, a week before the coronation of the new Queen (Katherine of Valois), he was given assignments at the Exchequer representing the first two terms' arrears of the annuity of 100 marks granted him early in 1417. A further payment, in cash, of the arrears of Easter term 1418 was made to him in July 1421, but as this was made by the hands of a Chancery clerk it would seem that Popham had returned to France (assuming that he had ever left it).[15]

Whether after Henry V's death in August 1422 Sir John Popham returned to England or stayed in France under the Regent, John, duke of Bedford, and, if he stayed in France, whether or not he retained the *bailliage* of Caen and the captaincy of Bayeux, is not clear.

9. Ancient Petitions, P.R.O., S.C. 8, file 28, no. 1364; *C.P.R.*, 1416-22, 64; Exchequer, Issue Roll, P.R.O., E 403/646, mem. 14.

10. *P.P.C.*, ii, 213; *C.P.R.*, 1416-22, 75.

11. *C.P.R.*, 1416-22, 145, 148, 197, 199.

12. *Rotuli Normanniae*, ed. T. D. Hardy, 231; *D.K.R.*, XLI, 681; 686; 702; *ibid.*, XLII, 367.

13. *D.K.R.*, XLI, 753, 759; XLII, 27; Exchequer, Accounts Various, E 101/187/14 (account-book of William Allington, Treasurer-General of Normandy and France, 30 April 1419-20); Exchequer, Enrolled Foreign Accounts, L.T.R., E 364/61, mem. C.

14. *D.K.R.*, XLII, 397; E 364/61.

15. Exchequer, Issue Rolls, E 403/646 (mem. 14), 649 (mem. 13).

But it seems more probable, the question of his formal retention of the Norman offices put on one side, that he was in England in the first years of Henry VI. It is likely that he was embarrassed by his financial relations with the government, as were others of Henry V's captains. On 12 May, 1423, by advice of the Council and by warrant of the privy seal, Popham was enabled to take out a letter patent confirming his annuity of 100 marks granted him in February 1417 and the custodianship of Southampton castle to which he had been appointed in October 1418. On 5 June, 1424, he was paid at the Lower Exchequer in cash £68 5s. 5d. and by assignments £340 5s. 11d. in settlement of the arrears of his annuity which had accrued since 1417. These payments represented as much as 86 per cent. of what had become due to him in the course of over seven years; but of these arrears he was now only receiving roughly a fifth in cash. Almost certainly Popham was in England at this time, the conjecture being strengthened by the fact of his appointment (for the first time) as a justice of the peace in Hampshire on 20 July, 1424.[16]

Early in 1425, however, Popham was preparing to resume military activities in France. Here the English cause had gained a renewed momentum from the duke of Bedford's victory at Verneuil in August 1424. But there was no prospect of the war being ended, and English relations with Burgundy were now distinctly uneasy. On 22 March, 1425, Popham was paid at the Lower Exchequer an advance of some £412 for the first quarter's wages of his considerable force of 30 men-at-arms (himself as captain included) and 90 archers. On 16 May following, a commission was issued for his and other companies to be mustered at Dover nine days later, an order which was countermanded on 20 May by writs ordering the muster to be at Calais instead. On 1 June, along with other captains, Popham was given a commission to take the whole force in charge and convey them to the duke of Bedford, the Regent in France, or where he should order.[17] On 26 June the Exchequer paid him his second quarter's wages, another £412 odd. Popham's contingent evidently joined the force with which the earl of Salisbury conducted a highly successful campaign in Upper Normandy, in Maine where he received the surrender of Le Mans, Mayenne, St Suzanne and other towns, and in Anjou. It was then that Popham was made captain of St Suzanne, and it is most likely then also that he was appointed to the more important office of Chancellor of Anjou and Maine. Probably sometime after this date, but before 1435 (when Bedford died), Popham was a member of the duke's household; William of Worcester refers to him as the duke's chamberlain (*camerarius ducis*).[18] Between 1425 and July 1429, when Popham was confirmed in his office of J.P. in Hampshire, there is no discovered English record-evidence bearing upon his activities, and the inference is that he was in France during that time. His re-appointment as J.P. in 1429 suggests his temporary presence in England, and this conjecture is confirmed by the fact that on 16 November, 1429, he was party to a recognisance, the condition of defeasance of which was that he should ensure the payment overseas of 250 gold marks to John Lord Talbot. Lord Talbot had recently been defeated and taken prisoner by the French in the skirmish at Patay, and this recognisance was probably a part of the negotiation for his ransom.[19]

Ten days before this recognisance was made, Henry VI had been crowned at Westminster. In France, Joan of Arc's star had already waned, but her success while it lasted had been phenomenal and had at least revealed the possibility of English defeat, and in the

16. *C.P.R.*, 1422-9, 111; 563; E 403/666, mem. 6.

17. E 403/669, mem. 18; *C.P.R.*, 1422-9, 299, 300, 302.

18. E 403/671, mem. 9; *The Wars of the English in France*, ed. J. Stevenson (R.S.), vol. ii, part ii, 412, 435; *Itinerarium Willelmi de Worcestre*, p. 89; *Edward Hall's Chronicle* (London, 1809), p. 127.

19. *C.C.R.*, 1429-35, 27.

autumn of 1429 the French had made important gains in the Seine valley: English military prospects were not hopeful. It was felt necessary to have Henry of Windsor crowned in France; hence his coronation in England first. Sir John Popham was commissioned on 6 March, 1430, to help raise Crown loans in Hampshire against the expense of the royal expedition, of which he became a member with a retinue of 11 men-at-arms and 36 archers.[20] It is possible that he now remained continuously in France, attached to Bedford's entourage, for the next three years. He was not re-appointed as a justice of the peace when the Hampshire commission was changed in April 1431. Bedford returned to England in June 1433, and probably Popham came back with him. Certainly, he was present at a Great Council held at Westminster between 24 April and 8 May 1434 when Bedford and Gloucester quarrelled over the criticism of Bedford's conduct of the French war implied in Gloucester's offer to take charge of it.[21] Both Popham and his cousin, Sir Stephen Popham, appeared on the list of Hampshire notables who were to be sworn to the peace, following the nation-wide issue of commissions for this purpose on 1 May, 1434. A year later, by patent of 22 May, 1435, they were both included in a commission of array for the county.[22]

The duke of Bedford had returned to France in July 1434. If Popham returned with him, evidently he did not stay on continuously. For he was certainly in England when he was appointed a proper member of the English embassy sent to the great diplomatic congress held at Arras in the summer of 1435. The English military situation in France had recently deteriorated still further, and the Anglo-Burgundian alliance, upon which so much depended, was in serious jeopardy. It was Burgundy, in fact, who was bent on making the English government realize the necessity of peace on the basis of an acceptance of the claim of Charles VII to the French throne, that is, on the basis of a repudiation of the Treaty of Troyes of 1420. The formal proceedings of the Congress of Arras lasted from 4 August to 6 September, 1435, when the English embassy withdrew after refusing to discuss the possibility of Henry VI's renouncing the French Crown. Burgundy's defection from the English alliance was the work of the Congress's later stages. Popham's mission was regarded by the Exchequer, which paid him a pound a day for his personal expenses, as having begun on 13 July, although an advance of £91 was not made to him until 19 July. His retinue comprised eight horsemen. After the English had left the Congress Popham returned to Calais on 10 September. From there he sailed with the earl of Suffolk, his fellow ambassador, round to Harfleur (a manoeuvre very significant of the military situation in Picardy), whence they proceeded overland to Rouen. Whether they arrived before Bedford's death there on 14 September, is doubtful.

Popham's diplomatic mission was officially (in the Exchequer) regarded as ending on 15 November, by which time he had presumably returned to England.[23] He immediately plunged into the maelstrom of useless activity which resulted from the strong emotional reaction of the English to Burgundy's perfidy. Parliament had already agreed to a greater effort against France and the extension of the war against Burgundy, who was immediately bent on attacking Calais. Less than a month after his return to England, Popham was ordered on 12 December to take musters of nearly a thousand men at Portsdown after

20. *C.P.R.*, 1429-36, 51; *D.K.R.*, XLVIII, 271; Privy Seal warrants for issue, P.R.O., E 404/46/208.

21. *P.P.C.*, IV, 212.

22. *C.P.R.*, 1429-36, 396, 473.

23. Exchequer, Accounts Various, Q.R.; P.R.O., E 101/322/nos. 38-9; *Wars of the English in France*, *op. cit.* vol. ii, part ii, p. 431; E 403/719, mem. 12 (Popham had evidently taken advantage of his *rapport* with the Exchequer to secure (on 16 July) assignments for the payment of instalments of his life annuity of 100 marks for the period Michs. 1433-35 [*ibid.* mem. 7]).

Christmas, and on 18 January, 1436, to act as a commissioner of array in Hampshire. A month later, when on 14 February writs were issued by the Council's order requesting loans for a new expeditionary force to Normandy, Popham was put down for a subscription of 100 marks.[24]

This new expedition was to be under the supreme command of Richard, duke of York, who had recently been chosen to fill the place in France vacated by the death of the Regent, Bedford. York was to be called Lieutenant-General and Governor of the kingdom of France and the duchy of Normandy. Now in his twenty-fifth year, Richard of York had inherited the entailed lands of his father, Richard of Conisborough, earl of Cambridge, who had died a traitor's death at Southampton in 1415, the estates of his paternal uncle, Edward of Norwich, duke of York, who had been killed at Agincourt, and the great Mortimer properties in England and Ireland which had been his since the death of his maternal uncle, Edmund, earl of March, in 1425. He had also inherited the Mortimer claim to the Crown which had been disregarded at the accession of Henry IV in 1399. In 1436 it was over twenty years since the death of Sir John Popham's lord, Edward of Norwich, and since then Popham had made his own successful way in the French wars, for the most part apparently in the household of the duke of Bedford. With Bedford dead, the circumstances were clearly propitious for a renewal of Popham's Yorkist affiliations. Some sort of connection between Popham and Richard of York was already there; it only needed cultivation and development. On 1 July, 1433, shortly before his coming of age, York had agreed with the feoffees of Edward of Norwich to make certain appropriations of revenue from the estates which he was about to possess, in order to fulfil his uncle's will, including the continued payment (for which Duke Edward had provided) of the annuities of a number of his retainers, of whom Sir John Popham was by this time the most important.[25] Already, therefore, as an ex-retainer of Edward of Norwich, Popham was a pensioner of Duke Richard. The link soon matured into a complete, and apparently exclusive, connection.

It was not until towards the end of May 1436 that York formally undertook to serve in France for one year. When he landed at Harfleur in the following month, Paris had been re-taken by the French and a great part of Normandy was already in their hands.

For some time before York left England, Popham had himself been negotiating with the royal Council the terms on which he would join the duke's expedition as a member of his council in France. It was on 5 May that the articles of his petition were formally considered. His requirements were largely financial, his desire being to secure a favourable balance between what he owed to the Crown and what was due to him, especially the arrears of his annuities. Firstly, he asked to be discharged of the prests for which he was still held responsible in the accounts of William Allington, a former Treasurer of Normandy, but all that he secured here was a surcease of process while he was overseas with York. His demand for the £38 odd still due to him for his mission to Arras and Rouen was granted. So was his request that he should be given fresh Exchequer tallies of assignment for arrears of his 100 marks annuity amounting to some £265, and that he should immediately be paid the instalments of this annuity of 100 marks for the last two previous terms. To his demand that the annuity should henceforward be taken from the revenues of the coinage of tin or from other income of the Duchy of Cornwall by the hands of the duchy receiver, it was merely answered that he should be preferred before other aspirants to such an appropriation. His demand that the tenure of his Norman lordships of Torigny, etc., should be converted from fee tail male to

24. *C.P.R.*, 1429-36, 525, 522; *P.P.C.*, IV, 326.
25. *C.C.R.*, 1429-35, 260.

fee simple seems to have been ignored; perhaps, in the military situation of the day, it struck the Council as rather irrelevant. Popham evidently was not over-satisfied with what he got, for on 11 May he indentured to serve in France for half a year with only a small retinue comprising no more than 3 men-at-arms and 12 archers (he himself taking 4 shillings a day); but he undertook to have this force ready for muster at Winchelsea on 14 May. He was clearly bent on extracting the best terms that he could get for himself, because, in addition to the demands he put to the Council on 4 May, he subsequently asked that his term of service as a member of York's council in Normandy should be limited to a year, that he and his retinue should be paid in advance for their first half-year of service, and that afterwards he should take what other members of this council for Normandy of his rank were receiving. These requests were conceded. Another demand that he should be given command of a force of 40 men-at-arms and 400 archers was committed to the discretion of the duke of York. An additional demand, that he should have a free home-coming (that is, expenses of enshipment) at the end of a year's foreign service, was not, however, there and then answered.[26]

The Exchequer did not entirely implement, in fact, the Council's concessions, such as they were. By 9 May Popham had been paid £136 odd, the wages of his company for half a year, but the promise to pay his 100 marks annuity for the previous year was redeemed by nothing more substantial than an Exchequer grant of assignment on 30 June.[27] By this time he was presumably in France with the duke of York. Certainly, on 15 May the muster of his retinue was due to take place, evidently after a postponement, at Winchelsea four days later. Here had been mustered the retinues of York himself and of the earls of Suffolk and Salisbury, amounting together to 800 men-at-arms and 3,760 archers ; Popham, along with the master of the royal ordnance in France, was commissioned on 22 May to muster this company on its arrival overseas.[28] The expedition had a limited success in Normandy. But York found the financial strain heavy and, against the wish of the royal Council, insisted on returning to England at the end of the agreed year of service. And soon after his successor, the old earl of Warwick, had gone out in August 1437, York came home.

Popham had seemingly been back in England at the beginning of the year, because on 23 January, 1437, he and his cousin, Sir Stephen, had both been made royal commissioners to inquire about the merchandise of certain Genoese and Hanseatic merchants which had been illegally seized at Southampton.[29] Certainly, he was in England when on 10 April, 1437, he was one of four men nominated by the Council in Henry VI's presence—the other three were Sir Henry Bromflete, Sir John Stourton, and Robert Whittingham—pending a final selection for the office of Treasurer of the royal Household. Popham's candidature was evidently favoured strongly, because he was sent for to come to the King with all haste, and a week later (on 17 April) he assumed office, there by succeeding to Sir John Tyrell. He was destined to hold the post for all but two years. It is important to notice that now, as Treasurer of the Household *alias* Keeper of the Wardrobe, Popham became *ex officio* Treasurer for the War as well.[30] It is not altogether improbable that his appointment was in some way connected with York's dissatisfaction at the financial difficulties which the duke's military service in France had brought him.

26. *P.P.C.*, IV, 337, 340, 342.
27. P.R.O., E 403/724.
28. *C.P.R.*, 1429-36, 536, 608.
29. *Ibid.*, 1436-41, 86.
30. *P.P.C.*, V, 8; Exchequer, Accounts Various, E 101/408/13; E 101/408/23.

It is at any rate clear that Popham's connection with York was now of the closest and gained strength during his occupation of this office in the royal Household. On 12 February, 1438, the day on which Popham secured exemplification of the letters patent (of 1417, 1418, and 1423) granting and then confirming his Exchequer annuity of 100 marks and the custody of Southampton castle (on the grounds that the originals had been lost), he acquired the concession that for his life he might have the annuity charged on the fee-farm which, as heir of the Mortimers, the duke of York paid to the Crown for his possession of the castle and cantred of Builth (on the border of Radnor and Brecknock). It is interesting to note that, on 30 April following, the rest of the fee farm—70 marks—was released to York, who was also then granted the reversion of Popham's annuity, should the latter die before him; in that event a total remission of York's fee-farm for Builth would occur.[31] The new arrangement, whereby Popham would draw his annuity from his lord instead of from the Exchequer, was obviously to his advantage. He had always had trouble at the Exchequer over its arrears, as well as over his Exchequer assignments on other counts. In fact, only six days after this change of source for his long-standing 100 marks annuity, namely on 18 February, 1438, he received fresh assignments at the Receipt of the Exchequer for as much as £254 odd in lieu of payment of some £287, for which he held as many as twelve tallies of assignment. These he now restored to the Exchequer as a fictitious loan; nine of them, together nominally valued at £218 odd, were between nearly five and nine years old.[32]

The Exchequer had incurred fresh liabilities to Popham in his capacity as Treasurer of the Household, and at this point was about to incur more. For, on 17 March, 1438, along with Lord Scales, the Abbot of Fécamp, and others, he was appointed as a member of an embassy to treat for peace with France. In January, in fact, Popham had already been appointed by the English Council to go first to the earl of Warwick and the Council of Normandy and then to the duke of Brittany, and on 22 January he had received a prest of £100 for this purpose. He and one of his companions had been also empowered since then to see to the state of the garrisons in France while they were about it, and to report back.[33] Not until after mid-March, however, did Popham begin his mission.

The whole of the spring, summer, and early autumn of 1438 passed before his share in this business ended for the time being. He sailed from Poole on 19 March, met the earl of Warwick and his council at Rouen, and then rode west into Brittany. His visit to this province was to see the duke of Brittany and to treat for peace there with the Bastard of Orleans and other representatives of the duke of Orleans, who was still a prisoner in England, and with an embassy from King Charles VII as well. Popham returned to Cherbourg on 23 June, when the intention was that he should cross to England to give an interim account of the negotiations to Henry VI. Here, however, he was ordered from England to await the arrival of certain members of the English Council who were to carry the negotiations further. And Popham remained at Cherbourg for over two months until, on 28 August, a new commission for him and his fellow-ambassadors was sent out. This authorized a negotiation on fresh terms with Charles VII's party, and so Popham went from Cherbourg to Rouen again to consult with Warwick and his council. By 30 September no answer had been received from Charles VII himself, but the Bastard of Orleans had written from Blois saying that Charles, before treating for a truce or peace, must first send an embassy to confer with the duke of Orleans in England and have his reply. These multi-cornered negotiations clearly had

31. *C.P.R.*, 1436-41, 134, 139, 168.
32. Exchequer, Issue Roll, E 403/729, mem. 12.
33. *D.K.R.*, XLVIII, 322; *P.P.C.*, V, 86, 88-9, 95.

broken down so far as Popham's commission was concerned, and he subsequently returned from Rouen, sailing in *The Swan of Sandwich* from Honfleur. He reached London on 20 October after a fruitless absence of just seven months.

Popham's own payment at the rate of £2 a day as a knight banneret and the costs of his retinue of fourteen men had entitled him to £346 over and above any advances or assignments he had received at the Exchequer. Not until 4 February, 1439, was a privy seal writ issued authorizing an audit of his account for the mission.[34]

Three weeks later, on 24 February, 1439, Popham was one of only five commoners who attended a Great Council of the lords held at Westminster.[35] But on 17 April following he surrendered his office as Treasurer of the Household to Sir Roger Fiennes. This was perhaps because his diplomatic usefulness was making him too much of an absentee, and perhaps also because the financial strain of his multiplied duties was proving over-strong—more than six years later he was still receiving assignments for debts owing to him from the time of his Treasurership.

Certainly, the government added to its already considerable indebtedness on Popham's account when it required him to go overseas again, on another embassy, not long afterwards. He was given a prest of £100 at the Exchequer on 13 May, 1439, but this was something of a nominal advance, because on the same day he was recorded as making a loan to the Exchequer of 100 marks, for which two days later (on 15 May) he merely received a tally of assignment.[36] It was on 23 May that he was made a member of an embassy to treat about commercial intercourse between England and Flanders and Brabant, and also a member of a bigger embassy to treat with a mission from Charles of Valois for a peace.[37] In 1438 the diplomatic plan of the French had been to waste time while the military situation continued to work in their favour. Now, in 1439, the English government was being compelled by the circumstances to consider the possibility of a renunciation of the French Crown, if a plan to partition France into two spheres of sovereign interest failed. A contraction of the English claims might pay dividends, provided it resulted in a renewal of the Anglo-Burgundian combination. The main body of the embassy did not cross to Calais, where the exchanges were to take place, until 26 June. Sir John Popham, however, had left London on 15 May in the company of Master Stephen Wilton, LL.D. These two inferior members of the embassy were engaged in preliminary discussions and arrangements for the formal meetings of the parties, and it was they who, on 30 June at St Omer, received oaths of security from the duchess of Burgundy in anticipation of the conference between her, the French embassy, and Cardinal Beaufort, the head of the English delegation. By 30 July the deliberations had reached a point where the English embassy was compelled to submit the French proposal, for Henry VI's renunciation of the French Crown in return for a long truce, to Henry VI himself; and a part of the embassy, including the archbishop of York, the earl of Stafford, Lord Hungerford and also Sir John Popham, returned to England on 5 August for this consultation. Popham returned to Calais on 30 August. The archbishop of York came on 9 September, his 'instruction', seemingly fabricated under pressure from Gloucester, being an utter refusal of the French terms. Nothing more could be done *vis-à-vis* France, although the English achieved the positive gain of a three years' truce with Burgundy, to the negotiation of which Popham was party. He was back at Westminster on 7 October. Allowed £2 a day as usual

34. Exchequer, Accounts Various, Q.R., E 101/323/5, 6.
35. *P.P.C.*, V, 108.
36. P.R.O., E 403/735, mem. 3.
37. T. Carte, *Catalogue Des Rolles Gascons, etc.* (French Rolls), ii, 295.

as a knight banneret, his own expenses amounted to £290, of which £190 was still owing to him.[38]

It was shortly after this that Sir John Popham was for the first time elected as knight of the shire for Hampshire to the parliament which met at Westminster on 12 November, 1439, and which, adjourned on 21 December following, sat at Reading from 14 January into the second half of February 1440. It was during the Christmas recess that at Windsor on 26 December he took out a patent exempting him for life from being put on juries of assize, or being made sheriff, escheator, collector of subsidies, etc. On 12 May, 1440, he mainperned William Lord Bardolf, an old companion-in-arms, formerly (in Henry V's time) Captain of Harfleur and Treasurer of the royal Household, when now he was given a 10 years' custody of Dunwich at an annual farm payable in the Exchequer.[39] The recent parliament had been stirred, by ' great murmur and clamour ' at the non-payment of the royal Household, to make a special appropriation of revenues from the two royal duchies of Lancaster and Cornwall and from the parliamentary subsidy. The concession to Bardolf may well have been a device for paying him off as a royal creditor, similar to that by which, on 27 July following, Popham himself was given a new and additional annuity of £40 for life charged on the petty custom in the port of London, expressly in consideration of his good service to Henry V and the present King in England and overseas, his readiness to serve the King in war and on embassy, and his management of the office of Treasurer of the Household, for all of which he had had no reward beyond his custody of Southampton castle (worth no more than £4 a year) and his old annuity of 100 marks (now charged on the fee-farm of Builth).[40]

This grant of a fresh annuity of £40, although retrospective in its formal justification, may well have been made to induce Popham to undertake further work in France or to reward him for having already agreed to do so. At the beginning of the month in which it was made, on 2 July, 1440, the duke of York had again been appointed the King's Lieutenant-General in France and Normandy, in succession to Cardinal Beaufort's nephew John, earl of Somerset. York had undertaken to serve for five years, until Michaelmas 1445, on certain conditions. His provisos included the royal Council's acceptance of at least one of three bishops, one of three temporal lords, and one of three knights, nominated by him, as members of his official council overseas. Sir John Popham was one of the three knights named by the duke.[41] Perhaps mainly owing to difficulties between Cardinal Beaufort and the duke of Gloucester, to whose party York inclined, almost a whole year went by before the latter went over to France in June 1441. Certainly, Popham did not yet go overseas again: on 28 November, 1440, he was made a commissioner for raising a royal loan in Hampshire with a view to subsidizing York's expedition.[42] Nor, when he went, was it as a regular member of York's council. On 13 November, 1441, he was chosen by the English Council to convey to York (at Rouen) instructions including warnings about the danger to Harfleur, Caen, and Honfleur, and he was to advise all captains of towns and fortresses on the French coast to keep strict watch and ward. The customs officials at Southampton on 24 November were ordered to requisition two large ships and a balinger to ensure a speedy passage for Popham and the members of an embassy to England, who were to accompany him to Normandy. Sometime before this, Popham had expressed his desire that his life-interest in the custody of the castle

38. Exchequer, Enrolled Foreign Accounts, E 364/73, mem. A^v; *P.P.C.*, V, 339, 377.
39. *C.P.R.*, 1436-41, 363; *C.F.R.*, 1437-45, 154.
40. *C.P.R.*, 1436-41, 432.
41. *Wars of the English in France, op. cit.*, vol. ii, part ii, 586.
42. *C.P.R.*, 1436-41, (502) 504.

of Southampton should be cancelled in favour of the earl of Huntingdon (an hitherto unsuspected attachment), and this was done on 25 November. On 1 December Popham left on his mission, taking £5,000 with him for the payment of York's forces. He was away almost exactly three months, returning on 28 February, 1442. Having given him an advance of £120 on 20 November, the Exchequer owed him another £60 on his return.[43]

This visit to Normandy in the winter of 1441-2 seems to have been Popham's last enterprise overseas, and he now begins to slip back out of the prominence which his long French experience had given him in the diplomacy of the last seven years. His activities by royal commission now take on a mainly local complexion. On 30 March and 28 August, 1442, he was again appointed to act as a commissioner for raising Crown loans in Hampshire.[44] On this latter date Popham was also ordered to take the musters of a force of 2,260 men-at-arms, archers, and seamen who were to man 28 ships and safe-keep the sea in 1442 and 1443 according to the provision of the financial grant made in the parliament of January-March 1442 ; the four captains of this force had all been knights of the shire in this recent parliament, one of them being Sir Stephen Popham, Sir John's cousin, who had been shire-knight for Hampshire.[45] In the following year Sir John was occasionally similarly engaged: on 12 March, 1443, when commissions of array were set up for the counties of the south and the west country, he was appointed for Hampshire, and on 7 June he was made one of a mustering commission at Portsmouth, prior to the departure of an expedition under the duke of Somerset. Three years passed before, on 1 June, 1446, he was included on another royal commission, this time a Crown loan-raising commission once more in Hampshire. In February 1448 he next served on an inquiry in Hampshire into cases of concealment of feudal and other forms of royal income.[46] What were his other activities at this time it is impossible to say. He himself had made a loan of £40 to the Exchequer on 25 August, 1444, the advance being met by an assignment in November on the customs of Southampton or, failing which, on the next parliamentary subsidy to be levied. The Exchequer was in the following summer (July 1445) still owing him moneys for the time when he was Treasurer of the Household, and in June 1448 he needed to secure a royal patent exemplifying a series of petitions and memoranda shown by him in Chancery in a suit brought against the administrators of the will of a former cofferer who had received moneys to pay Household expenses, part of which were still unpaid; these related to Popham's Treasurership.[47]

Although, for reasons of age, he was past active employment in the field in this period of French military recovery, Popham's reputation as a veteran was high, and this may have prompted both the duke of Buckingham and Lord Sudeley to nominate him for election to membership of the Order of the Garter, at a chapter held at Windsor on 22 April, 1447, to occupy the stall vacated by the recent death of Humphrey, duke of Gloucester. Popham was unsuccessful, the young King of Portugal, Alfonso V, being elected.[48]

Two and a half years later, after lately serving on a royal commission of array and on another for raising Crown loans in Hampshire,[49] Popham was elected a second time as knight

43. *P.P.C.*, V, 155, 158, 162, 168, 179; *C.P.R.*, 1441-6, 48; E 403/745, mem. 14; Exchequer, Accounts Various, Q.R., E 101/324/3.

44. *C.P.R.*, 1441-6, 62, 92.

45. *Ibid.*, 106-7, 407; *P.P.C.*, V, 204. The use of Sir John Popham's name among the first list of captains is clearly an error.

46. *Ibid.*, 200, 201, 430; *ibid.*, 1446-52, 139.

47. *Ibid.*, 1441-6, 312; E 403/753, mem. 12; E 403/757; *C.P.R.*, 1446-52, 134.

48. J. Anstis, *Register of the Order of the Garter*, 132-3.

49. *C.P.R.*, 1446-52, 316, 299.

of the shire for his county. This parliament sat for two sessions at Westminster, from 6 November to 17 December, 1449, and from 22 January to 30 March, 1450, and at Leicester for one which lasted from 29 April following to early in June. When the first session began, Rouen had just fallen; when it closed, Harfleur was about to fall. By the end of the parliament, the English in Normandy were vainly defending Caen, the chief hold in the duchy still in their control. It was at the beginning of a presumably very stormy first session that, on 7 November, 1449, Popham was elected by the Commons as their Speaker. Whether it was because of his Yorkist connection or on account of the wounds which (as Popham stated) he had received in the service of Henry V and Henry VI and his infirmities and age, when he asked to be exonerated his excuses were accepted, a suspiciously unique proceeding in the case of the medieval Speakers. And so the Commons elected a lawyer instead, William Tresham, the Chancellor of the Duchy of Lancaster, a member who had already been Speaker three times.[50] The Commons' first choice of Popham, in view of his long military and diplomatic career, clearly suggests their concern for the situation in France, and possibly the growth of a feeling of sympathy with Popham's lord, the duke of York. Before the first session even began, the dismissal of the Treasurer of the Exchequer had already taken place; before it ended, the Keeper of the Privy Seal had also resigned. The second session saw the impeachment for treason and the banishment of the duke of Suffolk himself; and also the great seal changed hands. All this recrimination came too late to affect events across the Channel: by mid-August 1450 the English rule in northern France was ended.

Sir John Popham did not sit in parliament again, and, although he lived on for another thirteen years, there is little to record of this last phase of his life. After the parliament of 1449-50 he was made, on 8 August, 1450, one of the Hampshire commissioners for the assessment of the recently granted subsidy on incomes from freehold land. On 15 October following he was also put on a commission set up to investigate a breach of the truce between England and Burgundy occasioned by the seizure of a hulk of Bruges homeward-bound from Portugal. In January 1453 he was a member of a royal commission appointed to raise loans in Hampshire for the relief of the necessities of the earl of Shrewsbury, then operating in Aquitaine. He himself contributed to the loan and received assignment at the Exchequer by way of repayment.[51] In this year, by patent of 16 May, he saw fit to renew the exemption for life from jury service and from appointment as sheriff, escheator, collector of subsidies, etc., that he had first obtained in 1439. On 19 August, 1453, he was authorized to act as a royal commissioner for the taking of musters at Portsmouth. Apart from a commission of array in Hampshire, to which he was appointed in September 1457, this was the last royal commission upon which Popham was directed to serve.[52] That he was no longer in close touch with affairs is suggested by the fact that in the parliament of 1455, summoned to meet after the Yorkist military victory at St. Albans, he was not able to secure a complete exemption from the Resumption Act passed in that parliament, regarding his annuity of 100 marks which, first of all charged on the Exchequer in 1417, had been charged since 1438 on the duke of York's fee-farm for the castle and cantred of Builth. Now, in 1455, the Lords scaled down this grant to 40 marks, unless Popham wished it to be re-charged at the old rate on the Exchequer, a much more uncertain source of income, as he had good reason to know.[53]

50. *Rot. Parl.*, V, 171-2.

51. *C.F.R.*, 1445-54, 173; *C.P.R.*, 1446-52, 432; *ibid.*, 1452-61, 52; E 403/791, mem. 9.

52. *C.P.R.*, 1452-61, 74, 125, 400.

53. *Rot. Parl.*, V, 312a; Ancient Petitions, P.R.O., S.C. 8, file 28, no. 1364.

It is very doubtful whether Popham played any part at all in the circumstances which brought the Yorkist dynasty to the throne in 1461. On 4 October, 1462, as ' late of South Charford (Hampshire), *alias* late of St. Sepulchre-outside-Newgate in the suburbs of London ', he took out a royal pardon, and he died on 14 April, 1463.[54] One of his executors was Maurice Berkley esquire of Beverstone (Glos.), who, in his place at Bisterne (Hants) in the valley of the Avon, was a neighbour of Popham's; Berkley was a firm Yorkist and by 1467 was an Esquire of the Body to Edward IV.[55] Writs ordering the royal escheators in the counties where Popham had landed interests to take inquisitions post mortem were issued from the Chancery on 1 May, 1463. There is no certain evidence that Sir John Popham ever married, and his heir was Alice, wife of one William Harteshorn. Ultimately, his estates in Hampshire and Wiltshire went to the four coheirs of his cousin, Sir Stephen Popham, who had died in 1444.[56]

Sir John Popham was buried in the London Charterhouse, the House of the Salutation of the Virgin Mary of the austere and spiritually progressive monastic order of the Carthusians, founded, in 1371, by one of the greatest of Edward III's captains of war, Walter Lord Mauny. Among the early donors of cells had figured another great soldier, Sir Robert Knolles, and also William of Ufford, earl of Suffolk. Sir John Popham had been one of this class of knightly benefactor to the London Carthusians, having (by 1453) endowed two chapels on the south side of the priory church; he gave his property at Rolleston (Leics.) to the Charter-house for this purpose. He was admitted on 1 July, 1460, to the confraternity of the priory and at his death was buried in one of the two chapels which he had established, the one dedicated to St Michael and St John the Baptist.[57]

54. J. C. Wedgwood, *History of Parliament, Biographies*, p. 693. The date of Sir John Popham's death is confirmed by a remnant of his commemorative brass (which went to form a palimpsest) which is now in the church of St Lawrence, Reading: it is inscribed, ' Hic jacet Johannes Popham miles quondam dominus de Gurney in Normandia et dominus de Chardeford, de Dene, ac de Alvyngton et Alibi in Anglia qui obiit xiiii° die mensis Aprilis Anno domini millesimo CCCCLXIII° cuius anime propicietur Deus ' (*V.C.H., Berkshire*, iii, 373). I am grateful to Lady Stenton for confirming the transcriptions.

55. *Catal. of Ancient Deeds*, vol. ii, B 2168; J. C. Wedgwood, *op. cit.*, p. 68.

56. *C.F.R.*, 1461-71, 94.

57. D. Knowles and W. F. Grimes, *Charterhouse: the medieval foundation in the light of recent discoveries* (1954), pp. 29-30, 58; J. Nichols, *op. cit.*, vol. ii, part ii, p. 442.

The following abbreviations have been used in the footnotes :

Rot. Parl.	-	*Rotuli Parliamentorum* (Records Commission).
P.P.C.	-	*The Proceedings and Ordinances of the Privy Council*, ed. N. H. Nicolas.
C.P.R.	-	*Calendar of Patent Rolls.*
C.C.R.	-	*Calendar of Close Rolls.*
C.F.R.	-	*Calendar of Fine Rolls.*
D.N.B.	-	*Dictionary of National Biography.*
V.C.H.	-	*Victoria County History.*
P.R.O.	-	Public Record Office.
R.S.	-	Rolls Series.

19

WILLIAM ALLINGTON OF BOTTISHAM,
SPEAKER IN THE PARLIAMENTS OF 1472-5 AND 1478

WILLIAM ALLINGTON, Speaker in the parliaments of 1472–5 and 1478,[1] was the younger son of William Allington and his wife Elizabeth, who was the elder grand-daughter and eventual sole heir of Sir William Argentine, and a grandson of William Allington, Speaker in 1429. His elder brother, John Allington of Horseheath, who came into the major part of the Allington estates in Cambridgeshire and the Argentine properties in Hertfordshire, Buckinghamshire and Suffolk, did not sit in parliament (so far as is known), but he was royal escheator in Cambridgeshire and Huntingdon-shire in 1447–8 (the year after his grandfather's death) and was Edward IV's first sheriff in these counties in 1461. Aged only thirty-one at his father's death in 1459, John had already shown Yorkist sympathies and, at the time of his receiving a royal pardon in 1455, was one of the Duke of York's retainers, enjoying an annuity of 10 marks from the honour of Clare.[2] He was well connected through his marriage with Mary, daughter of Laurence Cheyne of Fen Ditton and Long Stanton (Cambs): Mary's sister, Elizabeth, was first wife to Sir John Say of Broxbourne (Herts), Speaker for the Commons in the parliaments of February 1449, 1463, and 1467, Under-Treasurer of England in 1455–6, 1461–4, and 1475–8, and sometime Chancellor of the Duchy of Lancaster. John Allington was Say's feoffee in 1478.[3]

William Allington of Bottisham, John's younger brother, also married into a Cambridgeshire family, one of lesser social standing than the Cheynes but, neverthe-less, of some solidity and influence. His wedding with Joan, one of the three daughters of John Anstey senior of Stow-cum-Quy, his near neighbour and a lawyer like him-self, took place in the chapel of the manor of Holme Hall in that parish, presumably shortly after 9 January 1457, when William Grey, Bishop of Ely, issued a licence for the purpose.[4] John Anstey senior had been sheriff of Cambridgeshire and Hunting-donshire in 1430–1, escheator in 1433–4, and knight of the shire for Cambridgeshire in 1455–6, and was a J.P. of the *quorum* in Cambridgeshire from 1433 to within a

---

[1] *Official Return of Members of Parliament*, vol. I, pp. 357, 360, 363; *Rot. Parl.* vol. VI, pp. 4, 168.
[2] Catherine E. Parsons, 'Horseheath Hall and its Owners', *Proc. C.A.S.* n.s. vol. XLI, pp. 204 ff.
[3] J. E. Cussans, *op. cit.* vol. II, p. 51; *C.C.R. 1476–85*, p. 101.
[4] G. Lipscomb, *op. cit.* vol. IV, p. 105; *Notes and Queries*, 13th series, vol. VI, p. 26; *The Genealogist*, n.s. vol. XIX, p. 160; E. Hailstone, *op. cit.* pp. 108 ff.

year of his death in August 1460. His son and heir, Allington's wife's brother, John Anstey junior, another lawyer, already before his father's death had served twice as knight of the shire (in 1445–6 and 1450–1), and he sat twice more (in 1461–2 and 1467–8); in Cambridgeshire and Huntingdonshire he was sheriff in 1471–2 and escheator in 1473–4; and he was bailiff of the liberty of all the Bishop of Ely's lordships in these counties outside the Isle of Ely from 1453 to his death in 1477.[1] Joan Anstey also had two sisters: Mary, wife of one Henry Langley, and Elizabeth, wife of the William Tailard of Diddington (Huntingdonshire) who was a J.P. of the *quorum* in Huntingdonshire from 1461 to his death in 1505, knight of the shire for Huntingdonshire in 1467–8 and 1472–5, and sheriff of Cambridgeshire and Huntingdonshire in 1487–8.[2]

It was about the time of his marriage that William Allington the younger (as he then was) received his first royal commission, joining his father as a J.P. in Cambridgeshire on 1 July 1457. This was an appointment which he may have owed to his wife's family's and his own connection with William Grey, Bishop of Ely, the patron of scholars and a friend of the politically still neutral Archbishop Bourchier, whom Grey had followed in this fenland diocese in 1454. A week later Allington was also made a J.P. in the borough of Cambridge. Both he and his father, on 17 December 1457, were made commissioners for dividing out among the Cambridgeshire hundreds and vills the responsibility for mustering some 300 archers, the county's share of a force previously sanctioned for royal service in the Reading parliament of 1453. After another year the father ceased to be a J.P., but William junior continued to be reappointed until, in July 1459 (about the time of his father's death), he also was omitted.[3] Nothing of a special political significance need be read into this, because Allington junior was then escheator for Cambridgeshire and Huntingdonshire. (He acted from 7 November 1458 to 7 November 1459,[4] being in office when his father died.) And in February 1460, when the Lancastrians were seemingly in complete control, he was reappointed by them as a J.P. in the borough of Cambridge. That he was clearly not active as a Lancastrian partisan at this time of commotion is indicated, however, by the fact that it was the Yorkists who reappointed him to the commission of the peace for the county and even gave him a place on the *quorum* of the bench on 26 August 1460, that is, after the Yorkists' recent victory at Northampton had placed the administration of the country at their disposal. Allington was to be dropped from the commissions of the peace for county and borough alike during the temporary Lancastrian 'restoration' of 1470–1. Otherwise he served on both commissions, continuously, from 1460 until his death in 1479.[5]

It was in all probability the Lancastrians' military failures in the summer of 1460 which disposed William Allington to assume a less indifferent attitude to political

[1] J. C. Wedgwood, *History of Parliament, Biographies*, p. 13.
[2] *Ibid.* pp. 833–4.   [3] *C.P.R. 1452–61*, pp. 662; 407.
[4] P.R.O. *List of Escheators*, 14.
[5] *C.P.R. 1452–61*, p. 662; *ibid. 1461–7*, pp. 560–1; *ibid. 1467–77*, p. 609; *ibid. 1477–85*, p. 555.

affairs. The pronounced partiality of his elder brother John is also likely to have been an important factor. For that John was a Yorkist partisan, there can be little doubt: he was appointed by Edward IV on 6 March 1461 to be the first sheriff of his reign in Cambridgeshire and Huntingdonshire.[1] Certainly Edward IV's first regnal year saw William Allington placed on a number of local royal commissions, apart from his commissions of the peace in Cambridgeshire and the county town. On 18 June 1461 he was associated with the Chancellor of the University of Cambridge and others in a commission ordered to inquire into the narrowing and obstruction of the River Cam, as a result of which the great bridge in Cambridge was being damaged by the flow of water, and to see that the proper authorities undertook repairs.[2] At the end of the year, by patent of 1 December, he was put on a commission of oyer and terminer following a complaint by Barnwell Priory that its villeins at Chesterton were repudiating their bondage; and when, two months later, this commission was enlarged to include the Bishop of Ely and the Earl of Worcester, Allington continued to serve.[3] On 12 February 1462 he was also made a commissioner for sewers in south and south-east Essex.[4]

Early in March 1462 Edward IV himself was at Cambridge for a few days, part of his programme of watching the east coast in case of a Lancastrian landing. The opportunity was taken by some of the colleges to straighten out their business with the Crown. Corpus Christi got its royal charters confirmed, and the Master's accounts, which contain a note of a fee of 6s. 8d. already paid to Allington in 1459 for drawing an acquittance in a transaction with Barnwell Priory, again mention his employment, presumably as legal counsel, when the College now negotiated with the Chief Baron of the Exchequer and other members of the royal Council.[5] On 5 March, the Provost of King's College, Henry VI's new foundation which just now was precariously situated and uncomfortable about the consequences of Henry's deposition, appeared before a select committee which comprised Lord Hastings (the King's Chamberlain), Sir John Scot (Controller of the Royal Household), Master Richard Scrope (the Chancellor of the University), Dr Thomas Turney and William Allington. The purpose of this meeting was to acknowledge the Provost's quitclaim (made a week before) releasing to the Bridgettine nunnery of Syon (near Richmond) the priory of St Michael's Mount in Cornwall and other alien priory estates bestowed upon the College by the late King.[6]

There is some evidence to suggest that Allington had a connection with his Bishop, William Grey, who in 1469 was to become Treasurer of England for a short time. On 6 May 1462, for example, he stood surety for Grey when the latter superseded the Bishop of Carlisle in the right to farm for the next ten years the Cambridgeshire manor of Isleham, an entailed estate which had belonged to the posthumously attainted Lancastrian Earl of Northumberland and was now in the King's hands.[7]

---

[1] *List of Sheriffs* (P.R.O. *Lists and Indexes*, no. IX), p. 13.
[2] *C.P.R. 1461–7*, p. 133.
[3] *Ibid.* p. 68.
[4] *Ibid.* p. 35.
[5] *Proc. C.A.S.* n.s. vol. XVI, pp. 81 ff.
[6] *C.P.R. 1461–7*, p. 177; *C.C.R. 1461–8*, p. 132.
[7] *C.F.R. 1461–71*, p. 80.

Two months later, on 5 July, Allington was party with three local men, including his brother-in-law, John Anstey (the Bishop of Ely's bailiff), to a series of recognizances undertaking payment of £160 to one Thomas Bray, esquire of Colchester. At the end of August following, he and a London stockfishmonger received a grant of lands in Fingringhoe (Essex) belonging to a mariner of that place, along with all his personalty.[1] But most of these activities relate to private business, and little that has a bearing on public affairs is known of William Allington until after Edward IV's restoration in 1471, following the brief Lancastrian Readeption.

Allington continued to be a J.P. in the county and borough of Cambridge all through the first period of Edward IV's reign, and he was appointed in August 1463 to a general oyer and terminer in the shire.[2] On 11 November 1464 he was appointed a J.P. in Huntingdonshire as well, a commission which he held down to the Lancastrian Readeption.[3] It is possible that in the meantime he had been elected for Cambridgeshire to the 1461–2 parliament, when his brother was responsible as sheriff for the conduct of the local elections. But the Cambridgeshire returns have been lost for both that parliament and the next (the 1463–5 parliament), and, so far as is known for sure, William Allington's election to the parliament which sat in June and July 1467 and in May and June 1468 was his first. To this third of Edward IV's parliaments, his brother-in-law, John Anstey, went up as shire-knight from their own county of Cambridge (Allington himself being present at the hustings and attesting the indenture of return), and their brother-in-law, William Tailard, sat for Huntingdonshire. But Allington himself, along with a rising Lincolnshire lawyer and later Speaker, Thomas FitzWilliam of Louth, had to be content with being returned for the borough of Plympton in Devon.

Little is known of William Allington's doings during the period of rising hostility between the new Court party of the Wydevilles and Herberts and the house of Neville, preceding Henry VI's brief restoration in 1470–1. In March 1468 Allington and his brother were put on a royal inquiry into escapes of felons from gaols in Cambridgeshire.[4] In Easter term following, he and his wife were associated with her sisters and their husbands as plaintiffs in the Court of Common Bench against Sir Thomas Tyrell, an ex-Lancastrian, in a plea relating to the manor of Maudelyn (Bucks).[5] On 5 June 1470 (at a time when the great Earl of Warwick and his son-in-law George, Duke of Clarence, Edward IV's next younger brother, had already fled to France and were preparing to ally themselves with Margaret of Anjou in order to effect a Lancastrian restoration), Edmund Grey, Earl of Kent, made Allington one of his feoffees in the Norfolk manor of Saxthorp.[6] Grey's affiliations were with the new Court party, his eldest son having married into the family of Edward IV's Queen, the Wydevilles. The connection between the Earl of Kent and Allington might go some way to explain the latter's identification with the party of the King's

[1] C.C.R. 1461–8, pp. 138, 141. [2] C.P.R. 1461–7, p. 281.
[3] Ibid. p. 565. [4] Ibid. 1467–77, p. 101.
[5] The Genealogist, n.s. vol. XIX, p. 160.
[6] H.M.C. Report, MSS. of Marquess of Lothian at Blickling Hall, Norfolk, p. 55.

friends. On the other hand, Allington's connection with the Court party may well have resulted from his relations with Bishop Grey of Ely who was Treasurer of England from October 1469 until his dismissal by the Earl of Warwick in 1470. It is possible that Allington shared Edward IV's brief exile in Flanders during Henry VI's restoration in 1470–1 (and certainly he was dropped from his commissions of the peace in both Cambridgeshire and Huntingdonshire).[1] If this was so, it would in itself account for the rapidly accelerated growth of Allington's influence in Court circles in the few years of life that remained to him, after Edward IV had regained his throne.

Edward IV's military victories at Barnet on 14 April and at Tewkesbury on 4 May 1471 ended the Lancastrian Readeption, the sole effect of the Bastard of Fauconberge's attempt on London later in May being to seal the personal fate of Henry of Windsor. It was doubtless in anticipation of trouble in this direction, and probably also in the north where the Nevilles had been so formidably strong, that commissions of array had been issued by Edward IV on 11 May, a week after the battle of Tewkesbury; Allington was appointed to act on such commissions in both Cambridgeshire and Huntingdonshire.[2] On 15 July following, he was also included in a royal commission, set up under the new Treasurer (the Earl of Essex), to inquire into subsidiary rebel movements in Essex, to punish offenders themselves or hand them over to the Constable of England (Richard, Duke of Gloucester), and to sequester their land and other property to the King's use.[3] Allington was reintroduced to the commission of the peace in the borough of Cambridge on 4 November 1471.[4] And a week later he was appointed as Controller of the wool customs and of tunnage and poundage in the port of Bishop's Lynn,[5] a post which he continued to hold until his death. In March and May 1472, but now in anticipation of trouble from the French and from Hanseatic merchants, he was again made a commissioner of array, respectively in Cambridgeshire and Suffolk.[6]

In the summer of 1472, in spite of the gathering clouds of discontent between the King's brothers of Clarence and Gloucester, Edward IV and his Council regarded the domestic situation as safe enough to allow the meeting of parliament, the first Yorkist parliament for over four years. On 10 September Allington was elected at Cambridge as knight of the shire along with Sir Thomas Grey of Crawdon, a nephew and the overseer of the lands of Bishop Grey of Ely. The sheriff who held the county court was the bishop's bailiff, Allington's brother-in-law, John Anstey, who two days later also conducted the Huntingdonshire elections, when their brother-in-law, William Taylard of Waresley, was elected shire-knight.[7]

Parliament met on 6 October 1472. On the following day the Commons informed the acting-Chancellor that they had chosen William Allington as their Speaker. On 8 October he was presented to the King, who formally accepted his election, and he

[1] J. C. Wedgwood, *op. cit. Biographies*, p. 9.
[2] *C.P.R. 1467–77*, p. 285.
[3] *C.P.R. 1467–77*, p. 287.
[4] *Ibid.* p. 609.
[5] *Ibid.* p. 268.
[6] *Ibid.* pp. 349, 353.
[7] J. C. Wedgwood, *op. cit. Register*, pp. 410, 413.

then made the customary excuse and protestation.[1] Five days later, on the Feast of Edward the Confessor, Allington declared before the King and Lords some of the Commons' views, praising the Queen's firmness of demeanour during the King's exile when, in the Westminster sanctuary, she had given birth to her first son, Edward (an event which, said the Speaker, had afforded *grete joy and suerty to this . . . londe*), and also recommending the conduct of the King's brothers, of the Earl of Rivers (the Queen's brother) and Lord Hastings, of those who had gone into exile with the King, of those who had in any way suffered from the Lancastrian 'restoration', and also of the acting-Chancellor (John Alcock, Bishop of Rochester). He also saw fit to praise Louis de Bruges, Seigneur de la Gruthuyse, for the great humanity and kindness which this Flemish nobleman, who was now to be created Earl of Winchester, had lately shown to the King in Holland and Flanders. Now in England as Charles the Bold's envoy, Gruthuyse was to act as a sort of liaison-officer in the negotiations which were already going forward to complete an Anglo-Burgundian offensive alliance against France. Allington and the Commons were pressed to grant funds for an aggressive war and urged not to let slip the opportunity of lessening the danger at home from disbanded soldiers and of recovering, in such favourable circumstances overseas, the King's ancestral Duchies of Normandy and Guienne and the French Crown.[2] When the first session of this parliament ended on 30 November 1472 the Commons had made a preliminary grant of the service of 13,000 archers for a year at a daily rate of pay of 6*d*. each. For their provision, however, they had voted no more than a special tax of a tenth on all property and income (which the Lords confirmed), and even this was voted on condition that the tax should be repaid if no expedition had set out by Michaelmas 1474.

The business of this first session of the parliament had included a ratification by its authority of the royal heir-apparent's titles of Prince of Wales and Earl of Chester (already given him in June 1471) and also an Act confirming his endowment with the Duchy of Cornwall (as from Michaelmas 1472). One of the provisos inserted in the latter Act included one for the Speaker himself: it undertook that he should not be prejudiced regarding any grant or office held by him in the Duchy.[3] Clearly, Allington's interest was already engaged in this most important part of the infant Prince Edward's appanage. Equally clearly, he was being drawn into the orbit of the Queen's very influential family, the Wydevilles. For shortly after parliament came together again after the Christmas recess, namely on 20 February 1473, an imposing group of twenty-five, including the Queen, the King's two brothers, the Queen's brother (the Earl of Rivers), the Chancellor of England and three other bishops, the Earl of Shrewsbury, Lord Hastings (the King's Chamberlain), two royal judges, and other lords and notables, including members of the King's Council and the young Prince of Wales's own Chancellor and Chamberlain, to which list Speaker Allington

[1] *Rot. Parl.* vol. VI, p. 4.
[2] C. L. Kingsford, *English Historical Literature of the Fifteenth Century*, App. xv, p. 382; *The Letter Books of the Monastery of Christ Church, Canterbury* (R.S.), ed. J. B. Sheppard, vol. III, pp. 274–85.
[3] *Rot. Parl.* vol. VI, p. 16a.

himself must be added, were appointed to be the Prince's Tutors and Councillors until he reached the age of fourteen. They were to have authority to control his estates in Wales, the Duchy of Cornwall, Cheshire and Flintshire.[1] Four days later, along with other members of the Prince's Council, Allington was appointed to join the commissions of the peace in the Welsh border shires of Gloucestershire, Herefordshire, Worcestershire, and Shropshire.[2] These preparations were in anticipation of an attempt that was to be made in the early spring to quell the disturbed state of the Marches by the holding of a special Assize. This was meant to be an answer to a parliamentary petition in which had been expressed the fear that those who had committed felonies in the March would go unpunished, unless the King came in person or sent *grete myght and power*. The Prince of Wales himself was now to set up permanent household at Ludlow and represent the royal authority in the Marches. Meanwhile, the second session of the parliament had witnessed an important financial arrangement with the Calais Staplers (for the payment of their Crown debts out of the wool-dues) and also a replacement of the special income-tax of the first session by a subsidy of the usual kind, leviable by midsummer but on the same conditions as before.

When, after sitting for just two months, parliament was again prorogued on 8 April 1473, Allington stayed with Edward IV and accompanied him in his progresses in the Midlands between May and September. One object of these was to stifle unrest that was at least partly a result of the conflicting ambitions of the royal dukes (Clarence and Gloucester). On 5 December following, the Speaker was to be granted by the King 40 marks in ready money at the Lower Exchequer in view of the expenses he had borne *in attending upon us this somer season laste passed in the counties of Leicester, Notyngham, Derby, Stafford, Salop, Hereford, and the Marches of Wales*.[3] Already the special sessions of oyer and terminer in the Marches had begun, the jurors at Hereford emphasizing to the commissioners their fear of making indictments without *the especiall comfort of the Kynges goode grace and assistance of the Lordes there present*, and undertaking to proceed only when given assurances that those whom they indicted would not lightly be given their liberty. These promises were confirmed when Edward IV himself visited Hereford and, to prevent any covert acquittals, in the presence of the jurors himself ordered Allington (in his capacity as a J.P. in the county) to take the records of the indictments for delivery to the King's Bench. All this came out in a further parliamentary petition, presumably presented in the autumn (1473) session of parliament. This petition complained that, in spite of what had been formerly agreed, at *a prive cessions* held at Ross-on-Wye on 28 October before justices of gaol delivery, twenty-three persons indicted of felony had secretly

[1] *C.P.R. 1467–77*, p. 366.

[2] *Ibid.* pp. 615–16, 628, 636. Allington was to serve as J.P. in Gloucestershire from 24 February 1473 to 24 November 1474; in Herefordshire from 24 February to 5 December 1473 and from 12 May 1474 to 19 August 1475; in Worcestershire from 24 February to 16 November 1473 and from 12 May to 26 November 1474; in Shropshire from 24 February to 8 November 1473 and from 12 May to 5 August 1474.

[3] P.R.O. Privy Seal warrants for issue, E 404/75/3, no. 52.

been arraigned on bills remaining with the clerk of the peace and there and then acquitted; the petition successfully asked for these acquittals to be annulled by parliamentary authority and for process to be entered in the King's Bench.[1]

In the meantime, Speaker Allington, along with John Sulyard, a lawyer of Wetherden (Suffolk), parliamentary burgess for Hindon (Wilts) in the present parliament and one of the recently created members of the Council of the Prince of Wales, had been appointed on 5 July 1473 by their fellow-councillor, Anthony Wydeville, Earl of Rivers, the Queen's eldest brother and the Prince of Wales's Governor, acting in his capacity as Chief Butler of England, to serve as his deputies in the port of Ipswich.[2] And on 18 August, in patents issued at Lichfield, Allington and his brother John were put on a commission to inquire in Cambridgeshire into lapses of certain financial rights of the Crown; the commissioners here and elsewhere were to report to the King's Council a week after parliament was due to come together again.[3]

The third session of the parliament in which Allington occupied the Speakership began on 6 October 1473 and lasted for nearly ten weeks, until 13 December. No progress had been made with the projected expedition to France, and the main public business of the session was the passage of a Resumption Act and parliament's approval of a treaty with the merchants of the Hanseatic League that had recently been concluded at Utrecht.

In the course of this third session, Allington was involved in a private transaction arising out of a debt of £1000, contracted by Isabel, widow of John Neville, Marquis of Montagu, with William Parker, a London tailor, which resulted in a threefold indenture being drawn up on 1 November. Just over a year after the death of her husband at the battle of Barnet, the Marchioness married Sir William Norreys, a Knight of the Body to Edward IV. For the repayment of the debt and £20 court costs, it was now agreed that a party of feoffees, of which Chief Justice Billing, the Master of the Rolls, and William Allington were among the members, should recover (by legal process) certain manors and lands in Cambridgeshire and elsewhere and then lease them for life to the Marchioness's mother, a sister of the late Earl of Worcester; after the mother's death, the feoffees were to have possession to the use of the creditor, Parker, for a term of six-and-a-half years. This period, it was believed, would see the debt and costs repaid, and when this result had been achieved the feoffees were to entail the estates on the Marchioness and her body's heirs. If the Marchioness were to die before this entail could be created, then her second husband, Norreys, was to have a life interest with remainder to his wife's heirs under the entail.[4]

The parliamentary session was almost over when, on 10 December 1473, Allington was reappointed to the Cambridgeshire commission of the peace, an office which he was now to hold until his death, and then, on the very last day of the session, 13 December, he was for the first time made a J.P. in Suffolk, a commission which he retained until November 1475.[5]

---

[1] *Rot. Parl.* vol. VI, p. 160.   [2] *C.P.R. 1467–77*, p. 410.   [3] *Ibid.* p. 406.
[4] *C.C.R. 1468–76*, p. 329.   [5] *C.P.R. 1467–77*, pp. 609, 631.

The fourth session of the parliament in which Allington exercised his first Speakership began on 20 January 1474. Its proceedings were vitiated by uncertainty about Burgundy's attitude to the proposed English attack on France, and the session lasted less than a fortnight. On 9 May following, parliament began its fifth session. This lasted until Whitsuntide. Then, after a short break, parliament reassembled for its sixth session on 6 June and sat for six weeks, until 18 July. After it had been made clear to them that the invasion of France would have to be put off for another year, the Commons then made a grant of a tenth and fifteenth, instead of their previous grant of April 1473 (which had not yet been collected); plus a supplemental subsidy of £51,147 odd to meet the full costs of the force of 13,000 archers originally voted in November 1472, The tax was to be raised in 1475, half at midsummer, half at Martinmas; the proceeds were not to be turned over to the King until he was ready to cross to France, but the time by which he must so qualify for the grant was extended to midsummer 1476. The new Chancellor, Bishop Rotherham of Lincoln, then prorogued the parliament. But before he did so, he thanked the Commons, as well he might: 'the whole amount voted in the parliament was nearly equal to four subsidies to be raised in three years; more than Edward had received in all the previous years of his reign' (Ramsay). Thus supplied with the sinews of war, the King straightway (before the end of July 1474) committed himself with the Duke of Burgundy's embassy in London to an invasion of France in the following spring.

Edward IV clearly realized the Speaker's part in persuading the Commons to accept these financial burdens, and on 16 July 1474 (two days before the end of this sixth session) a privy seal warrant was issued authorizing the Lower Exchequer to pay Allington £100 *in redy money* on sight of it, on the ground that he *hath doon his true and due diligence in awaityng and attending upon our...parlement to his grete costis, charges, and expenses* without fees, wages, or other rewards; the warrant further provided that he should have *at thende of the said parlement an othir £100 withouten prest or eny othir charge to be sette upon him,...eny statute, act, ordenance, or restraint to the contrary notwithstanding.* Whether Allington was able to lay hands on all that was so made due to him is perhaps doubtful: his warrant of privy seal was endorsed by the Under-Treasurer (Sir John Say, himself a former Speaker) with only two notes of payment and they for no more than £20 and 20 marks respectively.[1]

Parliament came together again on 23 January 1475 for its seventh and what proved to be its last session. An indenture between Thomas Daniel, esquire, and William Hussey of Sleaford, the King's Attorney-General, drawn up on 12 March, two days before parliament was dissolved, illustrates, *inter alia*, the important measure of control over the promotion of private bills that the Speaker was able to exercise at this time. Formerly an Esquire of the Body to Henry VI, a follower of the Duke of Suffolk at the time of his fall in 1450, and a thoroughgoing Lancastrian who had also taken an active part at the Coventry parliament of 1459, Daniel had fought against Edward IV at Towton and accordingly had incurred forfeiture by Act of Attainder in the first Yorkist parliament of 1461–2. Sometime during the parliament

[1] Privy Seal warrants for issue, P.R.O. E 404/75/4, no. 29.

of 1472–5 but before the summer session of 1474, Daniel and Hussey agreed that if Hussey got Daniel's attainder annulled (and procured him a grant of certain manors in Ireland) he should within a month be given an annuity of 10 marks from Daniel's forfeited demesne manor of Burton Pedwardine (Lincs). On 6 June 1474 a petition by Daniel for the reversal of his attainder had been exhibited and granted. (Earlier sessions of this parliament had witnessed other reversals of Lancastrian attainders, and the political climate was favourable.) But Speaker Allington had had to be specially won round not to oppose the bill: the Attorney-General represented in the indenture that he had only performed his promise to have the attainder revoked after he had interceded with Allington, the latter being incensed with Daniel because his father had once been put in prison in London by Daniel's agency. Now, in March 1475, on the eve of parliament's dissolution, for £8 paid by Hussey and because of another bill endorsed by the King granting two more manors in Ireland to Daniel, the latter released to the Attorney-General all his title in Burton Pedwardine, binding himself in a bond for £500. The whole transaction, in all its brazen chicanery, was enrolled on the Close Roll of the royal Chancery.[1]

This last session of the 1472–5 parliament was very much occupied over the projected war with the French. Its financial business was mainly concerned with converting the supplemental subsidy of the previous session into a grant of a whole subsidy of a tenth and a fifteenth and three-quarters of another. The session closed with the dissolution of parliament on 14 March 1475. Its financial provisions represented a very solid achievement on the part of the Speaker. His mere tenure of the office for so long a period was in itself a substantial contribution to the work of the parliament: seven sessions, spread over two-and-a-half years and totalling over three hundred days, the longest parliament up to this time. If Cambridgeshire paid him his proper wages as knight of the shire, he received over £60 on that score alone.

Edward IV's long-intended invasion of France began with the shipment of his forces at the beginning of the summer of 1475, the King himself crossing from Dover to Calais on 4 July. A fortnight before, the infant Prince of Wales had been appointed Warden of England, and a Great Council of Regency had been set up to control affairs under his nominal headship. This Council inevitably included some of the Prince's own personal council, including its president, Bishop Alcock of Rochester (who was to act as Chancellor in England during Bishop Rotherham's absence with the King), Richard Fowler (Under-Treasurer of England and Chancellor of the Duchy of Lancaster) and Thomas Vaughan (the Prince's Chamberlain). William Allington was also a member.[2] Within three months the expeditionary force was back in England, the King having agreed with Louis XI, at Picquigny (near Amiens), to leave France in return for a life-pension of about £10,000 a year and a payment of £15,000 down, an act of *realpolitik* from both the English and French points of view. This also involved a welcome postscript to the acts of the 1472–5 parliament, the outstanding three-quarters of a subsidy, exigible at Martinmas, being now remitted by the King.

[1] *C.C.R. 1468–76*, p. 411.   [2] C. L. Scofield, *The Life and Reign of Edward IV*, vol. ii, p. 125.

At this time, except that in the presence of the Keeper of the Privy Seal on 1 November 1475 he attested the delivery of a release by the Earl of Rivers of all actions against Sir Geoffrey Gate,[1] nothing is known of William Allington's doings. This is also the case in 1476. Almost certainly, however, he remained a member of the Prince of Wales's Council, and possibly of the royal Council as well. In November 1476 his nephew, William Allington junior, became sheriff of Cambridgeshire and Huntingdonshire.[2] The ex-Speaker himself was made a commissioner for sewers in the valley of the Lea in Essex and Herts on 13 February 1477.[3] Later in the year two much more important appointments came Allington's way: on 24 July 1477 the Queen nominated him to be one of her Justices-in-Eyre in the forests granted her ten years before,[4] and on 1 September Bishop Grey of Ely gave to him for life the office of bailiff of the liberty of all his lordships in Cambridgeshire and Huntingdonshire, outside the Isle of Ely, an appointment in which he followed his brother-in-law, John Anstey, who had held the office for the past quarter of a century.[5]

In the course of this year, 1477, there came to a head all the disquiet that had long been centred in the person of the King's brother George, Duke of Clarence, and Edward IV decided to end it by getting rid of him. In this he certainly had the backing of the Wydevilles and doubtless of his other brother, the Duke of Gloucester. Parliament was summoned on 20 November to give colour to what was intended. A week later in Cambridgeshire, whose county court was haply the first to meet after the writs went out, both Allington and his fellow shire-knight in the previous parliament, Sir Thomas Grey, were re-elected. Parliament assembled on 16 January 1478. The Commons re-elected Allington as Speaker and on 19 January presented him for the King's acceptance.[6]

The main business of the session was the attainder of Clarence on the grounds of his incorrigible unfaithfulness and because he threatened, so it was alleged, the tranquillity of the kingdom. The Commons approved the bill, and on 7 February Clarence was condemned before the High Steward. After a delay the Commons demanded execution of the sentence of death, their Speaker coming before the Lords and asking that what was to be done should be done; but it was secretly and in the Tower that within a fortnight Clarence was, so to say, 'liquidated'. No taxation was demanded of the Commons, and a short session of six weeks ended with parliament's dissolution on 26 February. Three days later, in a privy seal warrant dated at Greenwich, Allington was granted £100 for *good and laudable service* as his reward for his Speakership. By the end of the current Exchequer term, however, he had been granted only half this amount, and even that by assignment and not in ready money.[7]

---

[1] *C.C.R. 1468–76*, pp. 432–3.

[2] J. C. Wedgwood (*op. cit. Biographies*, p. 9) is in error in stating that it was the Speaker who was sheriff.

[3] *C.P.R. 1477–85*, p. 22. On 14 February 1477 a letter from Sir John Paston to his brother John referred to Allington's interference with the younger Paston's efforts to marry Margery, daughter of Sir Thomas Brewes of Sturton Hall (Norfolk), a match that was being held up by disagreements over the lady's dowry. (*Paston Letters* (1910 ed.), vol. III, p. 173).

[4] *C.P.R. 1477–85*, p. 51.

[5] E. Hailstone, *loc. cit.*

[6] *Rot. Parl.* vol. VI, p. 168.

[7] P.S. warrants for issue, E 404/76/3, no. 37.

Meanwhile, the Clarence estates were mainly kept in the King's hands, being administered under the control of the royal Chamber, and by patents of 16 March and 4 May Allington was made one of the commissioners authorized to inquire into the late Duke's estates in Cambridgeshire.[1] Sometime between now and 4 July following, when he was ordered to make certain arrests in Suffolk on behalf of the Council, Allington was knighted.[2] Incidentally, within a few days he was further commissioned to investigate the liability for repairing the great bridge at Cambridge and to act as a commissioner for sewers in the marshland between Markham and Bishop's Lynn.[3] Possibly these were vacation 'recreations'.

That since June 1475 (when he had been one of the Council of Regency) Allington had himself been a continuing member of the King's Council seems likely, since on 11 August 1478 he was appointed as one of the King's councillors for life; he was then also given, expressly in consideration of his good service in this office before and since 8 July previous, the issues of a third of the Cambridgeshire manor of Bassingbourne and a third of the lands of the honour of Richmond, which Clarence had held by royal grant.[4] By this time he had also risen to be the Prince of Wales's Chancellor for the Duchy of Cornwall.[5] Clearly by now Allington had joined that company of fifteenth-century lawyers who attached themselves to the royal administration in one or another of its branches—the Treshams, the Says, the Fowlers, and, to look a little ahead, the Empsons, the Dudleys, and the Mores—and who managed so much of the royal business.

The effect of these additional signs of royal favour, Allington did not live long to enjoy. For he died on 16 May 1479, a writ of *diem clausit extremum*, authorizing an inquiry into his lands in Cambridgeshire, being issued by the royal Chancery to the local escheator on 16 June.[6] He died without issue, so leaving his elder brother John, then stated to be aged sixty, as his heir.[7] Already by March 1474 William had provided for there to be built at Bottisham a chantry-chapel which was to be served by a monk of the priory of Anglesea (Cambs) and where prayers were to be made for the good estate of Edward IV, Queen Elizabeth, Allington himself and his wife Joan, and for their souls after death.[8] It was here that Allington was buried.

Sir William Allington's wife outlived him and was still a widow in 1493–4.[9] His brother John, surviving him by only fifteen months, died on 25 August 1480. It was the latter's son, William Allington of Horseheath, who had been sheriff of Cambridgeshire and Huntingdonshire in 1476–7. At his father's death this man was stated to be thirty-one years of age,[10] but it was not until June 1483, immediately after

---

[1] *C.P.R. 1477–85*, pp. 109, 111.   [2] *Ibid.* p. 112.
[3] *Ibid.* pp. 112, 113.   [4] *C.P.R. 1477–85*, p. 142.
[5] R. and O. B. Peter, *History of Launceston and Dunheved*, p. 155.
[6] *C.F.R. 1471–85*, p. 173.   [7] J. C. Wedgwood, *op. cit. Biographies*, p. 9.
[8] *C.P.R. 1467–77*, p. 507.   [9] *Notes and Queries*, 13th series, vol. VI, p. 26.
[10] Catherine E. Parsons, 'Horseheath Hall and its Owners', *loc. cit.* Miss Parsons confuses the Speaker and his nephew when attributing to the latter the tutorship of the Prince of Wales and membership of the royal council. The problem of identification is simplified if it is remembered that the Speaker was knighted and that his nephew remained an esquire. The above article does not mention the Speakerships of the two William Allingtons in 1429 and in 1472–5 and 1478, respectively.

Richard III's accession, that he was appointed as a J.P. in Cambridgeshire.[1] He was killed at Bosworth Field, fighting for Richard III, having made his will a week before. Apparently, the family estates did not incur forfeiture, and this William Allington's son, Giles, the Speaker's great-nephew, a boy of twelve in 1485, was considered a good enough prospect for his wardship and the disposal of his marriage to be taken up by John, Earl of Oxford, for the sum of 800 marks payable in the Exchequer. The earl had already agreed to transfer these rights to Richard Gardiner, an alderman and mercer of London who had sat for London in Speaker Allington's last parliament and had been Mayor of the city in the year in which the Speaker died. This the earl did, and Giles was subsequently married to Gardiner's daughter and heir, Mary.[2] With the later history of the family which survived in the male line until 1723, we are not concerned. Suffice it to say that their representative was introduced into the Irish peerage on the eve of the Great Rebellion, and this Irish peer's brother and heir into the English peerage not long before the end of Charles II's reign.

An advance in the status and influence of a middle class land-owning family, such as the fifteenth-century Allingtons were, could be achieved in a variety of ways. Employment in war, if war there happened to be, was a chancy business, even if only financially considered. A quick, spectacular, and attractive way to an improvement of fortune was that of pursuit of favour and interest at Court. Given the talent and the opportunity, and the ability to be circumspect in political crises, service in the royal administration provided certainly one way to success. Neither of the two Allingtons who became Speaker had overmuch financial capital to start with. The first was not well-off initially, and the second was a younger son, also with his own way to make. They both, obviously, had no small measure of ability. But much else was needed: good fortune at the right time. With the fifteenth-century Allingtons, it is often a story of advance and set-back. In the case of the first Speaker Allington, early in Henry IV's reign he made a good recovery from the effects of personal associations which could have been very prejudicial; then, near the end of Henry V's reign, there came a great reverse with the adventitious death of the Duke of Clarence who had long been his lord, at a time when he was too far on in life to make a fresh start and build up credit in another quarter. In the case of the second Speaker Allington, death came when the tide of his promotion was running at its swiftest.

---

[1] *C.P.R. 1477–85*, p. 555.

[2] Somerset House, Register Milles, fo. 3; *Materials Illustrative of the Reign of Henry VII* (R.S.), ed. W. Campbell, vol. I, pp. 213–15, 412; *C.P.R. 1485–94*, p. 100; H.M.C. Report, Various Collections, vol. II, *MSS. of Lord Edmund Talbot*, p. 297; *Proc. Soc. Antiq.* 2nd series, vol. I, p. 357.

20

SIR JOHN WOOD OF MOLESEY
SPEAKER IN THE PARLIAMENT OF 1483

V ERY many of the Speakers for the Commons in the parliaments of the fifteenth century were men who had some
influence at Court as members of the King's Household or
belonged to some branch of the central administrative services of the
Crown. Sir John Wood of Molesey, who was Speaker in the last
parliament of Edward IV (1483), was one of this latter type. His
long career in the Exchequer under both Lancastrians and Yorkists,
to the headship of which main financial department of the Crown
he was to rise in the year of his Speakership, is of some general
interest. He had been knight of the shire for Sussex in 1449-50, for
Surrey in 1460-1, for Sussex once more in 1472-5, and for Surrey
again in 1478. It is very probable that he was representing Surrey
when he was Speaker, although we cannot be sure because the
electoral returns to this parliament from both Surrey and Sussex
have been lost.[1] If in fact he was knight of the shire for Surrey in

---

[1] *The Official Return of Members of Parliament*, i. 343, 355, 362, 365, XXV.
The identification of the John Wood who was Speaker in Edward IV's last
parliament is a nice problem, for he had a number of contemporaries of the
same name. He himself had a younger brother John, from whom he is frequently
but by no means invariably differentiated by being called "John Wood senior,"
the younger brother being sometimes designated as "John Wood junior."
The latter, a bencher of Lincoln's Inn, had houses in London, Midhurst and
Chichester, and it was probably he who represented Midhurst in the parliament
of 1467-8. John junior was escheator of Surrey and Sussex in 1460-1. He was
also in the service of Bishop John Arundell of Chichester (1458-77) and perhaps
attached to him as a friend, for he chose for his own tomb a place alongside the
bishop's tomb in the cathedral, and on the bishop's death he was given custody
of the temporalities of the see. (*The Genealogist*, N.S. vol. XXXVI, p. 57;
Notes and Queries, 12th series, vol. 8, p. 206; vol. 11, p. 408; *Ancient Deeds*, I
B1518-9; *C.F.R.*, *1471-85*, 143.) There were also a John Wody senior and
a John Wody junior, both of Ifield in Sussex, and both alive in 1478. (*C.P.R.*,
1477-85, 114.) In deciding what data relate to these men and to John Wood
grocer and merchant stapler of Calais (*ibid.*, *1461-7*, 487), to John Wood of
Keele (Staffs.), and to John Wood, collector of customs at Bristol (1469-70),
there is no great difficulty. The most serious problem is that of separating
information about the careers of the Speaker and his namesake John Wood
esquire, master of the King's ordnance in 1463-70 and 1471-7, keeper of the
royal mints at London and Canterbury in 1468-85, probably the same who had
been victualler of Calais in 1461-5. This latter John Wood, parliamentary
burgess in 1467-8 for Newcastle-on-Tyne, where he was constable of the castle
and deputy-butler and collector of customs dues, was of Bedstone (Shropshire).
The *Pardon Rolls* of Henry VI and Edward IV, in which this John Wood and
John Wood the Speaker both figure, afford quite invaluable aid in discriminating
between them and their proper offices, and the risk of confusion between these
two John Woods in the light of the evidence from this source becomes very
marginal (Wedgwood, *History of Parliament, Biographies*, pp. 965-7). The
chief difficulties over the Speaker are not with his offices in the central royal
administration but with some of his local royal commissions, where there is
occasionally danger of confusing him and his younger brother.

1483, Wood has an especial claim on the interest of local historians as the only member of parliament for the county ever to act as Speaker until the eighteenth century, when the Onslows filled the Chair, Sir Richard from 1708 to 1710, and Arthur Onslow from 1728 to 1761.

John Wood the Speaker was the son and heir of John Wood, who may very well have been he of that name who was clerk of the estreats in the Exchequer in Henry V's reign and who was still occupying that office in 1422-3.[1] The family appears to have originally belonged to West Wittering in the rape of Chichester, but also held lands in Midhurst and elsewhere in west Sussex. It was probably either the Speaker or his younger brother, John, who from Midhurst entered Wykeham's collegiate foundation at Winchester in 1426. Whichever it was, he left the same year.[2]

Although Wood came into the entailed lands of his family in Sussex, his official commitments in the Exchequer, whose staff he had joined by 1444, obviously required him to live near enough to Westminster. Possession of a handy country seat was equally desirable, and this came his way when some time between 1450 and 1452 he married, perhaps as his first wife, a presumably wealthy widow, Elizabeth, daughter and coheir of John Michell, grocer (later fishmonger) and alderman of London, who had been mayor of the City in 1424-5 and 1436-7 and who had died in 1445, and widow of Thomas Morstead, surgeon to each of the Lancastrian kings, who died in 1450. By this marriage, on the death (in 1455) of his wife's mother, Margaret, daughter and coheir of Hamelin de Matham, Wood came into possession of portions of the Michell manors of "Hauvills," "Botteles," and "Hooks" in Clothall (Herts.), and also into Margaret's manor of East Molesey, not far up-river from Kingston-on-Thames. Here he made his home, but towards the end of his life at any rate he also had a place nearby at Hampton Court. Through his marriage with Elizabeth Michell he also came into possession of Rivers Hall in Boxted in north Essex, a part of the manor of Great Oakley in Northants, and some lands in Cambridgeshire.[3] Wood's first wife died on 26 March 1464 without issue,[4] and he subsequently married Margery, daughter of Sir Roger Lewkenore of Trotton (Sussex), knight of the shire for Sussex in 1439-40 and 1453-4, and sister of Sir Thomas Lewkenore, sheriff of Surrey and Sussex in 1473-4, who, made knight of the Bath on the eve of Richard III's coronation, rose against the usurper in the following autumn in Buckingham's revolt, was attainted and temporarily incurred forfeiture.[5]

---

[1] Exchequer, Issue Roll, P.R.O., E403/612; Duchy of Lancaster, Accounts Various, P.R.O., 28/4/11.   [2] *Notes and Queries*, 12th series, vol. 8, p. 460.
[3] *C.C.R., 1454-61*, 92; *V.C.H., Herts*, iii. 223; J. E. Cussans, *History of Hertfordshire*, i. 64; *V.C.H. Surrey*, iii. 453; *The Genealogist* (N.S.), XXXVI. 57; P. Morant, *History and Antiquities of the County of Essex*, ii. 241; *C.F.R., 1454-61*, 152; J. Bridges, *History and Antiquities of Northamptonshire*, ii. 325.
[4] Cussans, *loc. cit.; C.F.R., 1461-71*, 126.
[5] *Notes and Queries, loc. cit.; The Genealogist, loc. cit.*

John Wood was to be connected with the Exchequer for the greater part at least of his working life. He had joined its staff by 1444, and it was doubtless as an Exchequer clerk that on 12 April 1448 he received an Exchequer tally for £57 odd owing to Sir Roger Fiennes, late Treasurer of the royal Household.[1] To the second parliament of 1449, which met in November and sat in three sessions until June 1450, Wood was for the first time elected knight of the shire for Sussex. This was the parliament in the course of which the Duke of Suffolk was impeached and later executed at sea, the late Keeper of the Privy Seal, Bishop Moleyns of Chichester, was murdered, and Cade's revolt broke out in Kent and spread into Surrey and Sussex. To the parliament, which met in the autumn of 1450 after the return of the Duke of York from Ireland and in which the Court party was further discredited, Wood was not re-elected. Few of the "Westminster crowd" were. From these events Wood himself experienced no personal difficulties at the Exchequer. The recently advanced loans for which he received Exchequer assignments, amounting to over £105 between 5 and 15 July 1452, were probably book-keeping "loans," that is to say, not genuine loans but wages due to him, immediate payment of which he undertook not to press for. He was certainly now better able than formerly to allow such a postponement of his claims, for by this date he had followed Thomas Rothwell as Under-Treasurer of the Exchequer, *alias* Clerk to the Treasurer. His promotion had taken place some time in the Easter term of 1452, probably concurrently with the appointment on 15 April of John Tiptoft, Earl of Worcester, to the Treasurership. Worcester's appointment was perhaps designed to please Richard of York, whose duchess was the earl's aunt by marriage; in any case, it followed upon something of an accommodation between the duke and Somerset's party at Court. It is difficult not to imagine that the Yorkists regarded Wood as sympathetic to their political views; he was, of course, especially through his wife, associated with the City, and the City was developing at this time a strong anti-Lancastrian bias. His wages as Under-Treasurer were 8d. a day and 5d. a day "pro dietis suis," plus the ancient fee of the office, £40 a year.[2] That his promotion was not simply a routine one is suggested by the fact that he followed Tiptoft out of office just before Easter 1455, one of the effects of the King's recovery of health and of the end of York's Protectorship and the liberation of Somerset. At roughly the same time as his appointment to the Under-Treasurership was made, he was moreover for the first time appointed a justice of the peace in Surrey (on 29 June 1452), a commission he continued to bear until January 1459. If he did house pro-Yorkist sentiments in 1452 he was, however, soon to disembarrass himself.[3]

---

[1] Exchequer Issue Roll, E403/771, mem. 1.

[2] *Ibid.*, E403/788, mems. 3–4.

[3] *C.P.R., 1446–52*, 596; *ibid., 1452–61*, 678–9. The John Wood who was appointed J.P. in Sussex on 23 July 1453 and who remained a member of this commission until September 1460 was probably the younger brother.

In the three years of this his first Under-Treasurership, Wood was involved in a variety of activities related to his Exchequer work. On 19 August 1453 he was one of a party, nominally headed by the Treasurer, instructed to muster the retinues of Lord Say and others at Barham Down in Kent in anticipation of their departure to relieve the Talbots in Aquitaine.[1] In the following month, along with the Treasurer and Thomas Thorpe, Baron of the Exchequer and the then Speaker, he was involved in negotiating the transference to a City monopoly syndicate of a large quantity of rock alum and black foil (worth £2,000) then in Crown possession at Southampton and London. This raw material was doubtless part of a large consignment of alum worth £8,000 belonging to Genoese merchants that had been requisitioned to the King's use at Southampton in 1451, for the purpose of creating a monopoly—the price to be restricted to a gain of 2s. in the £—from which the Exchequer was evidently designed to profit. (In the parliament of 1450-1 the Genoese merchants had been given freedom to by-pass the Calais staple and a lien on the customs generally at Southampton to secure repayment.[2]) He was also engaged in these three years of his Under-Treasurership in selling or exporting royal wool, and did very well out of it himself: on 17 April 1454 the Council approved a pardon granted to him, to two men of the King's Household and to a London draper who was also controller of customs in the port of London, of all the moneys received by them for the king's wool, waiving their accounts, and remitting the consequences of any trespasses they had committed in shipping or in customing the wool.[3] On 15 March 1455, the day when the Earl of Wiltshire superseded Tiptoft as Treasurer, but before Wood had himself relinquished his office as Clerk to the Treasurer (which he did about mid-April), he was licensed to ship some 214 sacks of wool at Southampton for the Mediterranean direct (an evasion of the Calais staple) and free of custom, on condition that he surrendered tallies worth £572, a sum he had himself spent on victuals for the King's Household.[4] These practices soon brought him under fire. In the parliament that began its sessions in July 1455, after the Yorkist victory at St. Albans, Wood was directly petitioned against by the Commons. The main object of the bill to the King was to protest against evasions of the Calais staple route, and it stated that upwards of 1,226 sacks of wool had been recently shipped at London in the King's name ("and markyd with the Crowne") to pass overseas elsewhere than to Calais, to the owners' great profit but of little advantage to the revenues. The reason alleged for this was that Wood had embezzled the greater part of the customs due on the wool—the whole calculated at £3,000—Thomas Osberne and others being appointed the King's factors by Wood's arrangement. This was evidently the business for which Wood and his friends had been pardoned in April 1454. Now,

---

[1] *Ibid.*, 124.
[3] *C.P.R., 1452–61*, 157.
[2] *Ibid.*, 155; *Rot. Parl.*, V. 214–5.
[4] *Ibid.*, 218.

it was requested that his appearance in the King's Bench early in the Michaelmas term following should be required by proclamation in the City, that his failure to answer to the charge be met with a penalty equivalent to the amount of his defalcation (£3,000), and that any attempt on his part to bar or delay process by pleading any royal pardon should involve him in a forfeiture of 10,000 marks. The petition was turned down.[1]

Wood's Under-Treasurership had been profitable in other ways. It is true that in July 1453 he had to be given a mere assignment for £600, which was due either for repayment of a loan or as arrears of government indebtedness to him, and that some three months later he was associated with the Treasurer and other colleagues in the administration in making an advance to the Lower Exchequer of 2,000 marks.[2] But, in addition to the profits of his wool speculations, he had received at times substantial rewards over and above his wages and fees: on 8 March 1454 he had received £66 13s. 4d. in cash at the Lower Exchequer for his work in expediting royal business in the parliament that was then in its third and last session, and £100 (again in cash) as a special guerdon for his attendances in London; and on 19 February 1455 a further £100 in ready money came his way "for all the great costs and expenses borne by him in the time of the Treasurer and for furthering special causes and matters committed to him by the Lords of the Council at different times for the utility and profit of the King."[3]

During the four years of uneasy peace between the two main factions before their enmity flared up once more into open war in the autumn of 1459, little is known of John Wood's activities. Early in October 1456, when the royalist party, now led by the Queen, felt itself strong enough to make important changes in the ministries of State and to exclude the friends and sympathizers of the Duke of York, and when as part of this policy the control of the Exchequer was entrusted to the Earl of Shrewsbury instead of Viscount Bourchier, there was a rumour current that John Wood would regain his office as Under-Treasurer: as one of John Paston's correspondents wrote to him from Southwark on 8 October, three days after Shrewsbury's appointment, "John Wode shalb Under-Tresorer. Thus thei say in the Chequer."[4] This intelligence proved unfounded. It suggests, however, where at this time Wood's political sympathies were considered to be. He certainly continued through these years of tension as J.P. in Surrey; on 17 December 1457 he was put on the commission authorized to assess in the county the incidence of responsibility for maintaining its contribution to the royal force of archers sanctioned in the Reading parliament of 1453; and on 5 September 1458 he was a commissioner of array in Surrey.[5] A year later

---

[1] *Rot. Parl.*, V. 335–6.
[2] Issue Rolls, E403/793, mem. 8; E403/796, mem. 15.
[3] *Ibid.*, E403/796, mem. 1; E403/800, mem. 10.
[4] *Paston Letters*, iii. 103.   [5] *C.P.R., 1452–61*, 408, 490.

both political parties resorted openly to arms but, after an initial success at Bloreheath, the Yorkists were unable to withstand the King and at the rout of Ludford Bridge their leaders dispersed. Their treason was registered in the parliament which met at Coventry, as soon as could be, in November and December. Although in the previous January he had been dropped from the Surrey commission of the peace, on 21 December 1459, the morrow of the parliamentary dissolution, Wood was included among the county's commissioners of array appointed to resist the supporters of the rebellious lords, and on 27 April 1460 he was also one of a commission set up to inquire into escapes of prisoners in the county.[1] Since at latest November 1458 he had been Keeper of the Great Wardrobe of the Household, and he was still holding this office on 22 May 1460 when, in aid of the expenses of his department, he was granted the wardship and marriage of the daughter and heir of John Michelgrove, a tenant of the Crown in Sussex and Kent.[2] He had lost the office by the end of October 1460, but he had clearly kept out of trouble in the summer of this year. The season saw the false dawn of Yorkist success when the rebel leaders at Calais returned to England, secured possession of the capital, defeated the King's army at Northampton, and summoned parliament in the name of Henry VI (who was their prisoner) to meet on 7 October at Westminster. John Wood was elected for Surrey as senior shire-knight. His fellow knight, Nicholas Gaynesford, was during the first session appointed sheriff by the new masters of the administration, and his younger brother, John Wood junior, escheator of Surrey and Sussex. On Christmas Eve, during the recess, Wood himself was reappointed J.P. in the county and joined the *quorum* of the commission.

The parliament witnessed the bestowal of the reversion of the Crown on the Duke of York. He met his death at Wakefield in Christmas week, but although the Lancastrians followed up this victory with another at St. Albans, Edward, York's heir, seized the capital, had his claim to the throne recognized, and sealed his royal title with his overwhelming victory at Towton in March 1461. Wood had already by this time come over to the winning side. A week before Towton Field, on 22 March, he had been included in a royal commission to arrest some servants of Thomas Lord Roos who made his escape from the battle,[3] and on 12 April, as King's servitor, he was granted the minor office of keeper of swans along the whole course of the Thames from Cirencester to Gravesend.[4] At the beginning of the reign he had been dropped from the commission of the peace in Surrey, but on 5 July following he was made once again a J.P. in Sussex and retained office until the Lancastrian Readeption in November 1470.[5] He was very probably the John Wood who, as

---

[1] *Ibid.*, 557, 607.
[2] *Ibid.*, 596; Issue Rolls, E403/817, 820.
[3] *C.P.R.*, *1461–7*, 31.
[4] *Ibid.*, 15.
[5] *Ibid.*, 574.

one of the yeomen of the King's Chamber, was employed in the first
half of 1462 in a variety of ways: on 22 February he was paid at the
Receipt £5 expenses for missions on unspecified royal business to
different parts of the kingdom; on 8 July he was given £1 11s. 4d.
for his expenses when sent from London to Leicester to show the
King divers matters at the order of the Treasurer; a week later
21s. for a like errand on the Treasurer's behalf; and a week later
again he was paid 25s. for a journey from London to Fotheringhay
with letters from the Council to the King and a further 30s. for his
conveyance of £600 released by the Exchequer to the King's
Chamber for Edward IV's private expenses.¹ He seems here to have
been mainly acting as a messenger between the Exchequer and the
King, a likely employment for an ex-Under-Treasurer and yeoman
of the Chamber, and it is very likely that he was the John Wood
esquire who in Easter term 1462 came to hold the office of one of the
two ushers of the Receipt of the Exchequer and held it until 1469.²
What makes the identification more feasible is that on 26 May 1463
he was associated with the Earl of Worcester (his old chief when
Under-Treasurer from 1452–5, and now once again Treasurer from
14 April 1462 to 27 June 1463) and John Say, the present Under-
Treasurer, in making a loan to the Exchequer of £200, for which they
received an assignment four weeks later.³ In the meantime, on
4 July 1462 he had been made a member of a special commission of
enquiry into the Surrey lands of the late John Busbrigge and, more
recently, by patent of 30 March 1463, of a commission set up to
investigate the illegal taking of swans and cygnets along the Thames
and its tributaries and to arrest offenders, a commission directly
connected with his own office of swan-keeper.⁴

Apart from the constant recurrence of his name as usher of the
Receipt of the Exchequer in the Issue Rolls of that department, not
a great deal else is known of John Wood in this first phase of
Edward IV's reign. On 8 April 1464 he was re-included as a
member of the Surrey commission of the peace, upon which he
was now to serve without a break until 1475.⁵ On 10 June 1465
he was made a commissioner of *oyer and terminer* regarding
offences against the peace in Surrey and Sussex, and on 22 July
following for the arrest and production in Chancery of one John
Lute.⁶ No further special royal commissions came his way for a
number of years, but a few notices of a private description appear
from time to time: on 18 October 1466 he was witness to a quitclaim
of lands in the parish of St. Olaf, in Southwark;⁷ he may be the John
Wood esquire who in November 1466 was one of the grantees of a
London mercer's goods and chattels and debts and in September 1467
of those of a London tailor,⁸ and he was most probably the John

---

¹ Issue Rolls, E403/824, mem. 8; *ibid.*, E403/825, mems. 4, 7, 8, 10.
² Issue Rolls, *passim.*   ³ *Ibid.*, E403/829, mem. 6.
⁴ *C.P.R., 1461–7*, 201, 278.   ⁵ *Ibid.*, 573; *ibid., 1467–77*, 632.
⁶ *Ibid., 1461–7*, 487, 489.   ⁷ *C.C.R., 1461–8*, 377–8.
⁸ *Ibid.*, 460, 445.

Wood who in May 1468 was one of the feoffees in the manors of Luton Hoo (Beds.) and Offley and Cockhernehoe (Herts.) on behalf of Thomas Hoo esquire of Roffey (Sussex), then parliamentary burgess for Horsham in Edward IV's third parliament of 1467-8, the parliament in which John Wood's younger brother sat for Midhurst.[1] In August 1469 he was the grantee of the personalty of another London mercer, and in the following November witnessed a grant of goods and chattels to the marshal of the College of Arms.[2]

John Wood evaded any serious consequences for himself of the commotions of 1469 which led up to the reinstatement of Warwick's political influence a year later, the restoration of Henry VI, and the temporary exile of Edward IV. Shortly after Edward returned to London in October 1469 (after being Warwick's prisoner in the north as a result of the battle of Edgecote), Wood was put on a royalist commission of array in Sussex, and again he served in this capacity in February 1470.[3] But he was so little of a partisan that after Warwick's landing in September 1470, (following his reconciliation with Queen Margaret in France and the agreement to restore the Lancastrian line), Wood was put on a commission of *oyer and terminer* set up in Surrey on 18 October in Henry VI's name, on 27 October was included on inquiries in Surrey and Sussex into cases of felony, and although dropped from the Sussex commission of the peace was reappointed J.P. in Surrey on 15 December.[4] On 14 March 1471 Edward IV returned from Flanders, landed in Yorkshire and four weeks later entered London. On 14 April Warwick was killed in Edward's great victory at Barnet, and at Tewkesbury on 4 May the Lancastrians were irretrievably defeated. In the short space between these two engagements, on 22 April, along with Richard Fowler (Chancellor of the Exchequer), William Essex (King's Remembrancer of the Exchequer) and John Roger (Under-Treasurer), Wood was bound by obligation to repay a group of London civic notables, including William Taylor (mayor in 1468-9) and Richard Gardiner (sheriff in 1469-70), a loan of £200 which they had advanced to the King some time before November 1469 when repayment had been due.[5] As J. H. Ramsay justly remarks of the attitude of the City to the political crisis, its "higher mercantile community were bound to Edward by the money he owed them and by their interest in Flemish trade." The obligation illustrates Wood's continued close connection with the Exchequer.

Not until August 1472 was the country settled enough to warrant the King summoning parliament once again. It met on 6 October and was to continue in being, through seven sessions, until 14 March 1475. Wood's family interest in Sussex and perhaps official pressure were sufficient to secure him election as senior knight of the shire

[1] *Ibid., 1468–76*, 327.
[2] *Ibid.*, 78, 96.
[3] *C.P.R., 1467–77*, 196, 199.
[4] *Ibid.*, 247–9; 632–3.
[5] Privy Seal Warrants for Issue, E404/74(2)/105; E404/75/1, no. 2.

for the first time for Sussex, his late first wife's nephew, William Druell, being returned as one of the Midhurst burgesses. Apart from the fact that on 18 August 1473, in the recess between the second and third sessions, Wood was put on the commission for investigating lapses of Exchequer rights by negligence on the part of sheriffs and other officials in both Surrey and Sussex, and that during the sixth parliamentary session, on 3 July 1474, he was made a commissioner for sewers along the south bank of the Thames between East Greenwich and Wandsworth, nothing is known of his doings through-out the course of this long parliament.[1] In the autumn after the dissolution of the parliament, however, on 5 November 1475, Wood was appointed as sheriff of Surrey and Sussex,[2] and four days later a privy seal warrant allowed him £40 at the Exchequer as a recom-pense for the great charges that his office would require him to sustain.[3] Three weeks before this appointment he was present at the dating of a deed in which on 15 October Robert Langton of Bramber undertook to be faithful to Bishop Waynflete of Winchester and to Waynflete's foundation at Oxford, Magdalen College, which was now in possession of the former alien priory of Sele near Bramber, and to assist it to recover the property of the priory, in return for the bishop's good lordship and other rewards, including a fee of 20s. a year from the college.[4] During his shrievalty, on 15 February 1476, he was a grantee, along with the marshal of the King's Marshalsea, of the goods and chattels of a tailor of Southwark, and on 1 April both he and his brother John attested the grant by a kinswoman, Alice Dautre, of some of her late husband's lands in Sussex.[5] His year of office as sheriff ended on 5 November 1476. A month later, by royal patent of 7 December, as John Wood of Hampton Court, he was made one of the justices and surveyors of the lower and middle Thames, a commission which included the oversight of all weirs. Dropped from the commission of the peace in Surrey because of his appointment as sheriff, he was re-included when the next commissions were issued on 15 January 1477, and on 13 February following was made a commissioner once more for inquiring into the taking of swans and cygnets in the Thames and its tributaries from Cirencester to its mouth.[6] On 16 December 1477 he was elected as knight of the shire for Surrey to the parliament that was to meet a month later on 16 January 1478, his fellow shire-knight being Sir George Browne, a former man of the Duke of Clarence, Edward IV's brother, whose condemnation for treason this parliament was mainly summoned to witness. The parliament ended, after a single session of six weeks, on 26 February, by which time Clarence had met his death in the

---

[1] *C.P.R.*, *1467–77*, 405, 462.

[2] *P.R.O.*, *Lists and Indexes*, IX (List of Sheriffs), p. 137.

[3] E404/76/1, no. 54.

[4] Edmund Cartwright, *The Parochial Topography of the Rape of Bramber of the West Division of Sussex* (London, 1830), vol. II, part ii, p. 233.

[5] *C.C.R.*, *1468–76*, 435; *ibid.*, *1476–85*, 44.

[6] *C.P.R.*, *1477–85*, 23–4.

Tower. In the course of the session, on 13 February, a privy seal writ had been issued warranting Wood's being paid 35 marks reward out of his account at the Exchequer as sheriff for 1475-6.[1] A number of commissions came his way in this year. On 16 March 1478, when inquiries were set going to permit the seizure of all Clarence's lands, Wood was put on the commissions appointed for Surrey and Middlesex; on 20 April he was included in another commission to find out what estates Clarence had held in Surrey by royal patents and what was their value. Two months later, on 20 June, his commission as surveyor for the Thames downstream from Oxfordshire and Berkshire was renewed.[2] On 25 June 1478 he was one of a group of feoffees for her lands in Southwark set up by Elizabeth, widow of the recently deceased Sir Thomas Cook, a City alderman who had made himself conspicuous by his support of the Lancastrian administration of the Readeption in 1470-1, after which he had fled to Flanders; among Wood's co-feoffees were Lords Hastings and Dacre and John Morton, then Master of the Rolls.[3] In the autumn of this year, on 5 November 1478, Wood was appointed sheriff of Essex and Hertfordshire.[4] Just as three years earlier when sheriff of Surrey and Sussex he had received a reward in advance, so now he was given a "grant in aid," only this time it was the substantial sum of £198 that he was allowed by privy seal warrant on 10th November. He held office until 5 November 1479.[5]

Dropped from the Sussex commission of the peace at the time of the Lancastrian Readeption, he was once again reappointed J.P. in this county—he was still J.P. in Surrey—on 12 July 1480. He continued to hold both commissions from now on until his death.[6] He still continued to act on more occasional commissions in these counties from time to time. For example, on 1 August 1480, along with his younger brother and namesake, he was put on the inquiry in Sussex into cases of smuggling of wool and evasion of the Calais Staple by exporters; the commissioners had authority to examine sheep-farmers about the disposal of their wool during the previous five years.[7] On 10 October following he was made a commissioner of array in Surrey, probably part of Edward IV's preparations for war against Scotland.[8] In the meantime, at Michaelmas 1480, Wood returned to his old office as Under-Treasurer of the Exchequer, to serve as clerk to the King's uncle, Henry Bourchier, Earl of Essex, who had held the Treasurership since 1471.[9] It was probably by his influence that his younger brother, John Wood junior, on 17 May

---

[1] E404/76/3, no. 32.
[2] *C.P.R., 1477–85*, 109, 111, 144.
[3] *C.C.R., 1476–85*, 136.
[4] *List of Sheriffs, op. cit.*, 45.
[5] E404/76/4, No. 84.
[6] *C.P.R., 1477–85*, 574–5.
[7] *Ibid.*, 216.
[8] *Ibid.*, 244.
[9] P.R.O., *Typescript List of Officials*, under *Treasurer's Clerks*.

1481 was appointed controller of customs and subsidies in the port of Chichester.[1] Three days later (20 May) Wood senior himself was appointed deputy to the Earl of Essex in his office of Chief Steward of the estates of the Duchy of Lancaster south of Trent for as long as Bourchier held it.[2] Wood's predecessor in the deputy-stewardship (since 1474), William Hussey, was now promoted Chief Justice of the King's Bench. Wood's duchy appointment forms a minor comment on the Yorkists' scheme for treating the Lancastrian inheritance as an important appendage to their generally available sources of revenue. By this time, as Under-Treasurer, he was busy supervising the collection of a clerical tenth recently granted by the southern province of Canterbury.[3] And not long after this, on 12 June 1481, the Under-Treasurer was included on a commission set up to survey Clarence's escheated lordship of Cheshunt and the land of the abbot of Waltham on the confines of Herts and Essex respectively, and to ascertain what their boundaries were, certifying the King in person.[4]

In the next year and a half, during which John Wood continued to occupy the Under-Treasurership, little is known of any of his extraneous pursuits. On 12 October 1481 he and his brother John, as feoffees of Robert Williamson of Isleworth, were party to a release which the latter made to Sir Thomas Frowyke and others of rights in estates in Isleworth abutting on lands of the abbess of Syon.[5] He was an assignee of the lands and shops in Thames Street, London, belonging to a London draper on 10 February 1482.[6] On 3 July following he and Sir Thomas Vaughan, Treasurer of the King's Chamber, conveyed to William Catesby esquire the office of steward of the manors of Burton Latimer and Corby (Northants)— it carried with it a fee of 2 marks a year—during the minority of Richard Neville, Lord Latimer, who was then in wardship to Cardinal Bourchier, his maternal great-uncle.[7] Three days later, by royal patent of 6 July, Wood as Under-Treasurer, and John Fitzherbert were granted the right to present to the church of High Ongar (in Essex, London diocese), at the living's next voidance.[8]

At this time Edward IV's policy towards Scotland was going well and, thanks to the Duke of Gloucester (Richard Crookback), Berwick was soon to be taken. The royal schemes regarding France were, however, anything but as successful. The prospect of marriage between Edward's daughter Elizabeth and the Dauphin had to be abandoned when the latter became engaged to Margaret, infant daughter of Maximilian of Austria, immediately after the death of

---

[1] *C.P.R., 1477–85*, 257.
[2] R. Somerville, *Duchy of Lancaster*, vol. 1, 431; P.R.O., D.L., 28/5/11.
[3] *C.F.R., 1471–85*, 229.
[4] *C.P.R., 1477–85*, 288.
[5] *Cat. of Ancient Deeds*, I, B1518–9.
[6] *C.C.R., 1476–85*, 244.
[7] *Ancient Deeds, op. cit.*, IV. A8428.
[8] *C.P.R., 1477–85*, 315.

Edward IV's niece, Mary Duchess of Burgundy, the match being arranged in Maximilian's despite by his Flemish subjects of Ghent. The treaty of Arras of 23 December 1482 also brought to an end the pension to England undertaken by Louis XI at Picquigny over seven years before. Edward IV summoned parliament, for the first time for nearly five years, to meet him at Westminster on 20 January 1483, almost certainly to consider the prospect of reopening the former policy of war with France, or of blackmail by preparation for war. It was in these not so happy circumstances that Wood was elected to the parliament (he was very probably re-elected for Surrey whose electoral returns are, however, lost), and then chosen by the Commons as their Speaker.[1] The single session saw a certain amount of desultory legislation, mainly of a social and economic character, some semi-public business of significance (including the sanctioning of the conferment on the Duke of Gloucester of extraordinary rights on the N.W. border as a reward for his work against the Scots, and arrangements for the King's second son, the Duke of York, to acquire the Mowbray estates and for the Queen's sons by her first marriage to be given provision out of the estates of the King's late sister, the Duchess of Exeter), and the voting of a subsidy and a tax on foreigners. After sitting for only thirty days, the parliament was dissolved on 18 February, the Speaker being knighted for his pains, along with Justice Catesby, on parliament's rising.[2]

Some seven weeks later, on 9 April 1483, Edward IV died, leaving a kingdom whose stability was still very uncertain. The divisions at Court, mainly the result of Edward IV's partiality for the Queen's kinsmen, the Greys and Wydevilles, became intensified in the circumstances of the minority of the new King, Edward V. Little more than a month passed before Richard of Gloucester established himself as Protector, having already arrested the Queen's brother, Earl Rivers, the young King's late Governor, and other members of his council. A new Chancellor was appointed in Bishop Russell of Lincoln. It was Sir John Wood, the ex-Speaker, who was called upon to fill the Treasurership already left vacant by the death of the Earl of Essex, who had died a few days before the late King. Wood's appointment (during pleasure) passed the great seal on 17 May 1483.[3] Two days later he undoubtedly exercised his official patronage in securing for his younger brother the post of the tronage and pesage of wool for the port and customs area of Southampton.[4]

On 26 June the Duke of Gloucester installed himself as King, mainly on the ground that his royal nephew was a bastard, Edward IV having been supposedly contracted in marriage before he wedded his

---

[1] *Rot. Parl.*, VI. 196.

[2] W. C. Metcalfe, *A Book of Knights Banneret, Knights of the Bath, and Knights Bachelor*, (1885), p. 6.

[3] *C.P.R., 1477–85*, 349.

[4] *Ibid.*, 352; Wood junior was confirmed in his Southampton office on 25 July (*ibid.*, 404).

Queen. On 2 July, four days before Richard III's coronation, Sir John Wood was reappointed Treasurer.[1] He is known to have attended the coronation.[2] Less than three weeks later Richard left London on tour. Early in his absence Edward IV's two young sons were murdered in the Tower. The royal progress was disturbed by the rising of Buckingham, Richard's late supporter, and of other malcontents (in the Queen's and the Lancastrians' interest), and when the revolt had been crushed and Richard had once again returned to London, it was the end of November. In the meantime, on 1 August, the Treasurer had been included on the commission set up for the assessment and the appointment of collectors in Sussex of the paltry subsidy from aliens granted during his late Speakership.[3] He was, of course, still a J.P. in the county and also in Surrey. And on 28 August he was appointed a commissioner of *oyer and terminer* in London and also in Oxon, Berks, Surrey, Sussex, Kent, Middlesex, Herts and Essex.[4] Nothing further is known of Wood, apart from details of his routine employment at the Exchequer, until on 8 April 1484, he and Brackenbury, the constable of the Tower, and three civil lawyers were appointed as the King's commissaries-general of the Admiralty with authority to execute all that belonged to the office and to engage a notary to register their acts; Wood and Brackenbury were to be the King's vice-admirals.[5] The Treasurer was evidently most sincerely trusted by his royal master, for this was a time when invasion in the interest of Henry Tudor, Earl of Richmond, was continually awaited. He was not, however, a member of the inner circle of Richard's closest advisers. Sir John Wood was also a commissioner of array in Surrey by patent of 1 May 1484, and his younger brother was another in Sussex.[6] Later in this same month, on 24 May, Sir John Wood's brother-in-law, Sir Thomas Lewkenore, who had been implicated in Buckingham's rising of the previous autumn and had been attainted in the four-weeks parliament held earlier in this year, undertook in a bond for 1,000 marks to be true to the King, to serve him in peace and war when commanded, and also to remain in the Treasurer's custody until the King's pleasure was known.[7]

No further activity on Wood's part is recorded. He was spared the final débâcle of Richard's régime; not that, had he survived it, it need have involved his own. He died on 20 August 1484, and the writs of *diem clausit extremum* authorizing inquiries into his estates in Surrey and Essex and the City of London issued from the royal Chancery on 15 September following. He left no issue by either of his two wives, so that the entailed estates of his family, which he had

---

[1] *Ibid.*, 361.
[2] British Museum, Harleian MS. No. 2115, fol. 124.
[3] *C.P.R., 1477–85*, 394.
[4] *Ibid.*, 465.
[5] *Ibid.*, 391.
[6] *Ibid.*, 400, 397.
[7] *C.C.R., 1476–85*, 365.

held, went to his younger brother, John, who survived him only until 4 October 1485, when he too died childless. Another brother's (Thomas's) daughters then came into the property. The Treasurer's second wife, Margery (born Lewkenore), survived him by over forty years. She remarried, her second husband being Thomas Garth, parliamentary burgess for Bletchingley in 1491–2. She survived him also—he died in 1505 when marshal of Berwick-on-Tweed— and held her first husband's estate at Rivers Hall in Essex until her death in 1526.[1]

---

[1] *Notes and Queries*, 12th series, vol. 8, p. 206; *C.F.R.*, *1471–85*, 289; Morant, *Essex*, II. 241.

Index (to Vol. III)